Christopher J. H. Wright

The
MISSION
of GOD

Unlocking the
Bible's grand narrative

Inter-Varsity Press

INTER-VARSITY PRESS
Norton Street, Nottingham NG7 3HR, England
Email: ivp@ivpbooks.com
Website: www.ivpbooks.com

First published 2006
Reprinted 2007, 2008, 2009, 2011

British Library Cataloguing in Publication Data
A catalogue record for this book is available from the British Library.

ISBN 978-1-84474-152-6

Typeset in the United States of America
Printed and bound in Great Britain by the MPG Books Group

Inter-Varsity Press publishes Christian books that are true to the Bible and that communicate the gospel, develop discipleship and strengthen the church for its mission in the world.

Inter-Varsity Press is closely linked with the Universities and Colleges Christian Fellowship, a student movement connecting Christian Unions in universities and colleges throughout Great Britain, and a member movement of the International Fellowship of Evangelical Students. Website: www.uccf.org.uk

FOR TIM AND BIANCA

Contents

CONTENTS

Outline of the Book

Preface
Introduction

PART I: THE BIBLE AND MISSION

1 SEARCHING FOR A MISSIONAL HERMENEUTIC

Beyond "Biblical Foundations for Mission"
Biblical Apologetic for Mission
The Danger of Inadequate Proof-texting

Beyond Multicultural Hermeneutical Perspectives
Global Church, Global Hermeneutics
Mission as a Focus of Hermeneutical Coherence

Beyond Contextual Theologies and Advocacy Readings
Contexts and Interests
Exploding the Missionary Stereotype
Missional Reading Embraces Liberation

Beyond Postmodern Hermeneutics
Plurality Yes; Relativism No
Christian Mission Has Long Experience of "Postmodern" Challenges

2 SHAPING A MISSIONAL HERMENEUTIC

The Bible as the Product of God's Mission
Biblical Authority and Mission
Authority as Command
Authority and Reality
Authority and Jesus

Biblical Indicatives and Imperatives in Mission
The Biblical Theocentric Worldview and the Mission of God
God with a Mission
Humanity with a Mission
Israel with a Mission

Preface

W hat are you working on at the moment?" It has been hard to give a straight answer to this common question during the past few years I have been working on this book. "A book on the Bible and mission," has been my usual reply, but I have never been sure which of the two words to put first. Am I seeking to understand Christian mission in the light of the Bible, or to understand the Bible in the light of God's mission? Or, in phrases that are explained in the introduction, is this book a biblical theology of mission, or a missional reading of the Bible? I think the final product is probably a bit of both, but with more emphasis on the second. Many others have produced fine and comprehensive works establishing a biblical foundation for Christian mission. My major concern has been to develop an approach to biblical hermeneutics that sees the mission of God (and the participation in it of God's people) as a framework within which we can read the whole Bible. Mission is, in my view, a major key that unlocks the whole grand narrative of the canon of Scripture. To that extent I offer this study not only as a biblical reflection on mission but also, I hope, as an exercise in biblical theology.

Books that offer a biblical theology of mission typically have an Old Testament section and then a (usually much larger) New Testament section. Then, in each section (and especially in the second), they tend to examine different parts of the canon or isolate the mission theology of particular authors, such as each Gospel writer, the apostle Paul and so on.

My approach has been rather different. I have tried to identify some of the underlying themes that are woven all through the Bible's grand narrative—themes that are the foundational pillars of the biblical worldview and therefore also of biblical theology: monotheism, creation, humanity, election, redemption, covenant, ethics, future hope. In each case I have then tried to pay full attention to their Old Testament roots before moving through to see the New Testament development, fulfillment or extension in each case. Most of the chapters therefore include reflections drawn from both Testaments, sometimes moving backward and forward between them.

Since my own field of special interest has been the Old Testament for more than thirty years, it is inevitable that much more space and much greater depth of discussion has been accorded to Old Testament texts and themes. There was a time I thought the book would be simply an Old Testament theology of mission (and there are few enough good models of that genre). However, I write as a Christian theologian, and while I endeavor to read and listen to the Old Testament with its own integrity and on its own terms, I cannot fail to read it also as a Christian. And, as I understand it, that means that I read it in submission to the One who claimed to be its ultimate focus and fulfillment—Jesus Christ, in the light of the New Testament Scriptures that bear witness to him and in relation to the mission he entrusted to his disciples. If, in the end, however, there is a lot more of the Old Testament than of the New in this book, I suppose I can at least claim that the same is true of the Bible, after all.

Since my main aim has been to argue for a missiological reading of biblical theology, I have not felt it necessary to devote acres of space to footnotes documenting all shades of scholarly exegesis or critical analysis of all the texts I have referred to. For certain key texts that are of pivotal importance in my argument, I have sought to present adequate exegesis and documentation. In many other cases, scholars or students who wish to pursue such issues in commentaries and journals will know where to look.

All authors know the debt they owe to others in the formation of their own thoughts and perspectives. So I offer my hearty thanks to a host of people who have walked this road with me for longer or shorter stretches. These include:

Two decades of students at the Union Biblical Seminary, Pune, India, and All Nations Christian College, England, who shared my developing efforts to relate Bible and mission through more classes than any of us care to remember, and many of whom are still wrestling with the issues in practical mission service all over the world.

Jonathan Bonk, director of the Overseas Ministries Study Center, New Haven, Connecticut, and Gerald Anderson before him, who, along with their marvelous staff and community, have given me repeated hospitality at OMSC for research and writing on his project.

John Stott, who has constantly encouraged and prayed for me in this project, and graciously allowed me the frequent benefit of his writing retreat cottage, the Hookses, on the west coast of Wales.

Langham Partnership International Council, for giving me not only a job that keeps me in touch with the realities of world mission but also specified time for study and writing each year.

Eckhard J. Schnabel, M. Daniel Carroll R., Dean Flemming and Dan Reid, who read the original manuscript and made dozens of constructively critical comments that have helped me to clarify and improve what I wanted to say in many places. Thanks also to Chris Jones for helping to prepare the indexes.

My wife and family, who have been as encouraging (and patient) in this as in all previous projects, and are represented in the dedication by the one who, as Israel was for God, is our firstborn son, Tim and his wife Bianca, with the joy and the prayer of 3 John 4.

Christopher J. H. Wright

Introduction

I remember them so vividly from my childhood—the great banner texts around the walls of the missionary conventions in Northern Ireland where I would help my father at the stall of the Unevangelized Fields Mission, of which he was Irish Secretary after twenty years in Brazil. "Go ye into all the world and preach the Gospel to every creature," they urged me, along with other similar imperatives in glowing gothic calligraphy. By the age of twelve, I could have quoted you all the key ones—"Go ye therefore and make disciples . . ." "How shall they hear . . . ?" "You shall be my witnesses . . . to the ends of the earth." "Whom shall we send? . . . Here am I, send me." I knew my missionary Bible verses. I had responded to many a rousing sermon on most of them.

By the age of twenty-one I had a degree in theology from Cambridge, in which the same texts had been curiously lacking. At least, it is curious to me now. At the time there seemed to be little connection at all between theology and mission in the mind of the lecturers, or of myself, or, for all I knew, in the mind of God either. *Theology* was all about God—what God was like, what God had said and done, and what mostly dead people had speculated on all three. *Mission* was about us, the living, and what we have been doing since William Carey (who of course was the first missionary, or so we erroneously thought).

"Mission is what *we* do." That was the assumption, supported of course by clear biblical commands. "Jesus sends me, this I know, for the Bible tells me so." Many years later, including years when I was teaching theology myself as a missionary in India, I found myself teaching a module called "The Biblical Basis of Mission" at All Nations Christian College—an international mission training and graduate school in southeast England. The module title itself embodies the same assumption. *Mission* is the noun, the given reality. It is something *we* do, and we basically know what it is; *biblical* is the adjective, which we use to justify what we already know we should be doing. The reason why we know we should be doing mission, the basis, foundation or grounds on which we justify it, must be found in the Bible. As Christians, we need a biblical basis for everything we do. What then is "the biblical basis for mission"? Roll out the texts. Add some that nobody else has thought of. Do some joined up theology. Add some motivational fervor. And the class is heartwarmingly appreciative. Now they have even more biblical support for what they already believed anyway, for these are All Nations students, after all. They only came to the college because they are committed to doing mission.

This mild caricature is not in the least derogatory in intent. I believe passionately that mission is what we should be doing, and I believe the Bible endorses and mandates it. However, the more I taught that course, the more I used to introduce it by telling the students that I would like to rename it: from "The Biblical Basis of Mission" to "The Missional Basis of the Bible." I wanted them to see not just that the Bible contains a number of texts which happen to provide a rationale for missionary endeavor but that *the whole Bible is itself a "missional" phenomenon*. The writings that now comprise our Bible are themselves the product of and witness to the ultimate mission of God. The Bible renders to us the story of God's mission through God's people in their engagement with God's world for the sake of the whole of God's creation. The Bible is the drama of this God of purpose engaged in the mission of achieving that purpose universally, embracing past, present and future, Israel and the nations, "life, the universe and everything," and with its center, focus, climax, and completion in Jesus Christ. Mission is not just one of a list of things that the Bible happens to talk about, only a bit more urgently than some. Mission is, in that much-abused phrase, "what it's all about."

Some Definitions

At this point it would be as well to offer some definitions of the way I am planning to use the term *mission*, and the related words: *missionary, missional* and *missiological*.

Mission. It will be immediately clear from my reminiscences above that I am dissatisfied with popular use of the word *mission* (or more commonly in the United States, *missions*) solely in relation to human endeavors of various kinds. I do not at all question the validity of Christian active engagement in mission, but I do want to argue throughout this book for the theological priority of *God's* mission. *Fundamentally, our mission (if it is biblically informed and validated) means our committed participation as God's people, at God's invitation and command, in God's own mission within the history of God's world for the redemption of God's creation.* That is how I usually answer when I am asked how I would define *mission*. Our mission flows from and participates in the mission of God.

Furthermore, I am dissatisfied with accounts of mission that stress only the "roots" of the word in the Latin verb *mitto*, "to send," and which then see its primary significance in the dynamic of sending or being sent. Again, this is not because I doubt the importance of this theme within the Bible, but because it seems to me that if we define *mission* only in "sending" terms we necessarily exclude from our inventory of relevant resources many other aspects of biblical teaching that directly or indirectly affect our understanding of God's mission and the practice of our own.

Generally speaking, I will use the term *mission* in its more general sense of a long-term purpose or goal that is to be achieved through proximate objectives and planned actions. Within such a broad mission (as applied to any group or enterprise), there is room for subordinate missions, in the sense of specific tasks assigned to a person or group that are to be accomplished as steps toward the wider mission. In the secular world "mission statements" seem to be much in vogue. Even restaurants (whose purpose in life one would have thought rather obvious), sometimes display them on their front windows, in an effort to link the task of feeding customers to some wider sense of mission. Companies, schools, charities—even some churches (whose purpose in life ought to be more obvious than it is, even to their own members)—feel it helps them to have a mission statement, which summarizes the purpose for which they exist and what they hope to accomplish. The Bible presents to us a portrait of God that is unquestionably purposeful. The God who walks the paths of history through the pages of the Bible pins a mission statement to every signpost on the way. It could be said that the mission of this book is to explore that divine mission and all that lies behind it and flows from it in relation to God himself, God's people and God's world, insofar as it is revealed to us in God's Word.

Missionary. The word is usually a noun, referring to people who engage in mission, usually in a culture other than their own. It has even more of a flavor of "being sent" than the word *mission* itself. Thus missionaries are typically those who are sent by churches or agencies to work in mission or on missions. The word is also used as an adjective, as in "the missionary mandate" or "a person of missionary zeal." Unfortunately, the word has also generated something of a caricature, the missionary stereotype, as a regrettable side effect of

the great nineteenth- and twentieth-century mission effort of the Western
churches. The term *missionary* still evokes images of white, Western expatri-
ates among "natives" in far off countries—and it still does so all the more re-
grettably in churches that ought to know better, and certainly ought to know
that already the majority of those engaged in crosscultural mission are not
Western at all but from the growing indigenous churches of the majority
world. As a result, many mission agencies that now build networks and part-
nerships with majority world churches and agencies prefer to avoid the term
missionary because of these unreconstructed mental images, and describe
their personnel as "mission partners" instead.

Because of the dominant association of the word *missionary* with the activity
of sending and with crosscultural communication of the gospel—that is, with a
broadly centrifugal dynamic of mission—I prefer not to use the term in connection with the Old Testament. In my view (which is not agreed on by all), Israel
was not mandated by God to send missionaries to the nations. So while it will
be abundantly clear that I certainly do read the Old Testament missiologically,
I would not choose to speak of "the missionary message of the Old Testament"
(the title of an early and excellent book by H. H. Rowley in 1944).[1] There are
many biblical resources (in the Old as well as the New Testament) that are profoundly enriching in our understanding of mission in its broadest sense (and especially the mission of God) that are not about sending missionaries. It is probably inappropriate therefore to refer to those texts and themes as "missionary."[2]
Unfortunately, until recently *missionary* seemed to be the only available English
adjective formed from *mission*. Another form, however, is being rightly welcomed into wider use.

Missional. Missional is simply an adjective denoting something that is related to or characterized by mission, or has the qualities, attributes or dynamics of mission. Missional is to the word *mission* what covenantal is to *covenant,* or fictional to *fiction.* Thus we might speak of a missional reading of the
exodus, meaning a reading that explores its dynamic significance in God's
mission for Israel and the world and its relevance to Christian mission today.
Or we might say that Israel had a missional role in the midst of the nations—
implying that they had an identity and role connected to God's ultimate inten-

---

[1] H. H. Rowley, *The Missionary Message of the Old Testament* (London: Carey Press, 1944).
[2] Interestingly, though, the term *missio Dei* (mission of God) in its earliest use referred to the
inner sending of God—that is the Father's sending of the Son into the world, and the sending
of the Holy Spirit by the Father and the Son. It is in this sense (among others) that John Stott
can speak of our "missionary God"; see, "Our God Is a Missionary God" in John Stott, *The
Contemporary Christian* (Downers Grove, Ill.: InterVarsity Press, 1992), pp. 321-36.

tion of blessing the nations. Thus I would argue that Israel had a missional reason for existence, without implying that they had had a *missionary* mandate to go to the nations (whereas we could certainly speak of the missionary role of the *church* among the nations).

Missiology and *missiological.* Missiology is the study of mission. It includes biblical, theological, historical, contemporary and practical reflection and research. Accordingly, I will normally use *missiological* when such a theological or reflective aspect is intended. In the two examples above, one might equally speak of a missiological reading of exodus, but it would be less appropriate to speak of Israel having a missiological role in the midst of the nations. In fact, in this latter case it is because neither "missionary role" nor "missiological role" seems quite right that the word *missional* is increasingly helpful.

The Journey Ahead

A word is also in order at this point regarding the structure of the book. Returning to my personal reminiscence: for years I continued to teach "The Biblical Basis of Mission." At one point I introduced an opening lecture raising the specific issue mentioned in my passing comments at the start of the course—the missional basis of the Bible itself. This arose partly from the ambient theological culture at All Nations Christian College, which was intentionally to approach every subject in the curriculum from a missiological angle. It happened that I also taught the module on the doctrine of Scripture and biblical hermeneutics, so it was natural to ask how a missiological perspective affected one's understanding of what Scripture is in itself, how it came to be as we now have it, and the hermeneutical assumptions and principles with which we approach it as readers. My thinking tended to oscillate between both courses in a cross-fertilizing way. Biblical mission and biblical hermeneutics seemed to morph into each other in unexpected but fascinating ways.

But the need to look more carefully at a missiological hermeneutic of the Bible also arose from the specific challenge of a colleague in another institution. In 1998 I was invited to give the Laing Lecture at London Bible College (now called the London School of Theology [LST]). I offered the title " 'Then they will know that I am the Lord': Missiological Reflections on the Ministry and Message of Ezekiel." At the time I was working on my exposition of Ezekiel in the Bible Speaks Today series, and this was a useful opportunity to expose these reflections to friendly criticism. And that is what they got.

In his response, Anthony Billington (lecturer in Hermeneutics at LST), while warmly appreciating the lecture's content, raised questions over the validity of using missiology as a framework for interpreting Ezekiel (or any other biblical text). There are of course many frameworks within which people read the text (feminist, psychological, dispensational, etc.). This is not intrinsically wrong since we all have to start somewhere. But, Billington said, the question is

> Does this or that particular framework *do justice* to the thrust of the text in its biblical-theological context? Or does it *distort* the text? In other words, it's not that the bringing of a framework to a text is necessarily wrong in and of itself, nor even that the text may not be illuminated in significant ways when we do— for it frequently is. The question is more what sort of *control* the framework exercises over the text, and whether the text is ever allowed to *critique* the framework at any point.[3]

The entirely appropriate challenge of Billington's words led me to reflect further on what a missiological hermeneutic of Scripture actually means and whether or not it is a framework that does justice to the text or seriously distorts it. This is the concern that I seek to address in part one, "The Bible and Mission." It is my objective in this book not only to demonstrate (as many others have done) that Christian mission is fully grounded in the Scripture (though I deliberately pay more attention to its Old Testament roots than most books on the subject do), but also to demonstrate that a strong theology of the mission of God provides a fruitful hermeneutical framework within which to read the whole Bible.

So in chapter one I survey some steps that have already been taken toward a missiological hermeneutic, but argue that a more thorough effort is needed to go beyond them. Chapter two is a sketch of some contours of what I think a missiological hermeneutic of the Bible entails. If all hermeneutical frameworks are like maps of the territory of Scripture, then the only test of a map is how faithfully it interprets the territory for the traveler in terms of what he or she wants or needs to know to make sense of the journey. The rest of the book tests whether the map provided by approaching the whole Bible from the perspective of the mission of God fulfills the subtitle of the book, enabling us to grasp the driving dynamic of the Bible's grand narrative.

The remaining three parts of the book take up in turn three major focal points of the worldview of Israel in the Old Testament, which are also foundational to a Christian worldview when understood in relation to Christ:

---

[3]From Anthony Billington's unpublished written response to my Laing Lecture at London Bible College, October 1998.

- The God of Mission (part 2)
- The People of Mission (part 3)
- The Arena of Mission (part 4)

In part two I examine the missiological implications of biblical monotheism. The identity, uniqueness and universality of YHWH, the God of Israel (chap. 3), and the directly related claims that the New Testament makes for Jesus (chap. 4) have enormous implications for mission. Indeed, Christian mission would have no foundation at all apart from these biblical affirmations about the one and only living God who wills to be known to the world through Israel and through Christ. But we cannot do full justice to biblical monotheism without seeing it in conflict with the gods and idols of human construction that consume so much biblical rhetoric and ink. The conflict with idolatry is a somewhat neglected biblical theme that we subject to some analysis and missiological reflection in chapter five.

In part three we move on to consider the primary agent of the mission of God, namely, the people of God. We will follow the order of the biblical narrative as we walk first with Old Testament Israel. They were chosen in Abraham, redeemed out of Egypt, brought into covenant relationship at Sinai and called to a life of ethical distinctiveness from the nations. Each of these great successive themes is rich in missional significance. Thus we will be reflecting on

- election and mission (in chaps. 6-7)
- redemption and mission (in chaps. 8-9)
- covenant and mission (in chap. 10)
- ethics and mission (in chap. 11)

In part four we move to the wider canvas of the world itself—the earth, humanity, cultures and the nations. So we will explore first the missional implications of the goodness of creation and the connections between creation care and Christian mission (chap. 12). The paradox of human dignity (because we are made in God's image) and human depravity (because we are mired in rebellion against God's authority) has profound implications for mission, to be explored in chapter 13, along with reflections on the comprehensive response that gospel mission must make to the comprehensive onslaught of evil. The Wisdom tradition in the Old Testament is the most international of all biblical literature and provides a rich source for reflecting on a biblical theology and missiology of human cultures. The biblical world is a world full of nations, by God's creative intention. How do they figure in God's redemptive intentions? The Old Testament's eschatological vision for the nations surely provides some of the most exciting of all its trajectories of missional rhetoric, to be explored in chapter 14, and then traced into the centrifugal horizons of New Testament mission theology and practice in chapter 15.

A diagrammatic outline of the book, then, might look something like this:

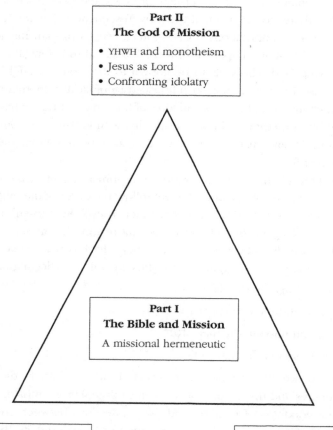

Part II
The God of Mission

• YHWH and monotheism
• Jesus as Lord
• Confronting idolatry

Part I
The Bible and Mission

A missional hermeneutic

Part III
The People of Mission

• Election
• Redemption
• Covenant
• Ethics

Part IV
The Arena of Mission

• The earth
• Humanity, sin and evil
• Wisdom and culture
• The nations and the future

Figure 0.1

PART I   THE BIBLE AND MISSION

M ission is what the Bible is all about; we could as meaningfully talk of the missional basis of the Bible as of the biblical basis of mission. Now this is a bold claim. One would not expect to be able to turn the other way any phrase that began "The biblical basis of . . . " There is, for example, a biblical basis for marriage, but there is not, obviously, a marital basis for the Bible. There is a biblical basis for work, but work is not what the Bible is all about. So isn't my assertion rather exaggerated or even conceited? Indeed, in view of the enormous variety of the contents of the Bible and the huge scholarly literature devoted to exploring every highway and byway of genre, authorship, context, ideology, date, editing, and history of all these documents, does it make sense to speak of the Bible being "all about" anything?

I take some encouragement in persisting with my claim from the words of the risen Jesus as recorded in Luke 24.[1] First to the two on the road to Emmaus and then later to the rest of the disciples, Jesus made himself as Messiah the focus of the whole canon of the Hebrew Scriptures that we now call the Old Testament (vv. 27, 44). So we are accustomed to speaking of the christological focus or center of the Bible. For Christians the whole Bible revolves around the person of Christ.

Jesus went on, however, beyond his *messianic* centering of the Old Testament Scriptures to their *missional* thrust as well.[2]

Then he opened their minds so they could understand the Scriptures. He told them,

---

[1] This text was also taken as a starting point for a biblical theology of mission in 1971 by Henry C. Goerner, *Thus It Is Written* (Nashville: Broadman, 1971).

[2] The use of *missional* rather than *missiological* here seems appropriate in the light of the definitions in the introduction (pp. 24-25), since Jesus was not only offering a fresh theological reflection on the Scriptures but also committing his disciples to the mission, such reflection must now mandate ". . . must be preached," "You are witnesses . . . ."

"This is what is written: The Christ will suffer and rise from the dead on the third day, and repentance and forgiveness of sins will be preached in his name to all nations, beginning at Jerusalem." (Lk 24:45-47)

Jesus' whole sentence comes under the rubric "this is what is written." Luke does not present Jesus as quoting any specific verse from the Old Testament, but he claims that the mission of preaching repentance and forgiveness to the nations in his name is "what is written." He seems to be saying that the whole of the Scripture (which we now know as the Old Testament) finds its focus and fulfillment *both* in the life and death and resurrection of Israel's Messiah, *and* in the mission to all nations, which flows out from that event.[3] Luke tells us that with these words Jesus "opened their minds so they could understand the Scriptures," or, as we might put it, he was setting their hermeneutical orientation and agenda. The proper way for disciples of the crucified and risen Jesus to read their Scriptures, is *messianically* and *missionally*.

Paul, though he was not present for the Old Testament hermeneutics lecture on the day of resurrection, clearly found that his encounter with the risen Jesus and his recognition of Jesus as Messiah and Lord radically transformed his (Paul's) own way of reading his Scriptures. His hermeneutic now had the same double focus. Testifying before Festus he declares, "I am saying nothing beyond what the prophets and Moses said would happen—that the Messiah would suffer and, as the first to rise from the dead, would proclaim light *to his own people and to the nations*" (Acts 26:22-23, modified NIV, emphasis added). This dual understanding of the Scriptures then shaped Paul's whole resumé as the apostle of the Messiah Jesus to the Gentiles.

Down through the centuries it would probably be fair to say that Christians have been good at their messianic reading of the Old Testament but inadequate (and sometimes utterly blind) at their missional reading of it. We read the Old Testament messianically or christologically in the light of Jesus; that is, we find in it a whole messianic theology and eschatology that we see as fulfilled in Jesus of Nazareth. In doing so we follow his own example, of course, and that of his first followers and the authors of the Gospels. But what we have so often failed to do is to go beyond the mere satisfaction of ticking off so-called messianic predictions that have "been fulfilled." And we have failed to go further because we have not grasped the *missional* significance of the *Messiah*.

---

[3]I use Messiah here as the conventional indicator of the wide diversity of Old Testament terms used to describe the one through whom YHWH would bring about his expected redemption and restoration of Israel, even though "messiah" as a term in Hebrew is not used in the Old Testament as a functional title of the coming redeemer (except probably in Dan 9:25).

The Messiah was the promised one who would embody in his own person the identity and mission of Israel, as their representative, King, Leader and Savior. Through the Messiah as his anointed agent, YHWH, the God of Israel, would bring about all that he intended for Israel. But what was that mission of Israel? Nothing less than to be "a light to the nations," the means of bringing the redemptive blessing of God to all the nations of the world, as originally promised in the title deeds of the covenant with Abraham. For the God of Israel is also the Creator God of all the world.

Through the Messiah, therefore, the God of Israel would also bring about all that he intended for the nations. The eschatological redemption and restoration of Israel would issue in the ingathering of the nations. The full meaning of recognizing Jesus as Messiah then lies in recognizing also his role in relation to God's mission for Israel for the blessing of the nations. Hence, a messianic reading of the Old Testament has to flow on to a missional reading—which is precisely the connection that Jesus makes in Luke 24.

We recognize that the *christological focus of the Bible* operates in many different ways—some direct and others much more indirect. To speak of the Bible being "all about Christ" does not (or should not) mean that we try to find Jesus of Nazareth in every verse by some feat of imagination. Rather we mean that the person and work of Jesus become the central hermeneutical key by which we, as Christians, articulate the overall significance of these texts in both Testaments. Christ provides the hermeneutical matrix for our reading of the whole Bible.

The same is true of *the missiological focus of the Bible*. To say that the Bible is "all about mission" does not mean that we try to find something relevant to evangelism in every verse. We are referring to something deeper and wider in relation to the Bible as a whole. In a missiological approach to the Bible we are thinking of

- the purpose for which the Bible exists
- the God the Bible renders to us
- the people whose identity and mission the Bible invites us to share
- the story the Bible tells about this God and this people and indeed about the whole world and its future

This is a story that encompasses past, present and future, "life, the universe and everything." There is the closest connection between the biblical grand narrative and what is meant here by biblical mission. To attempt a missional hermeneutic, then, is to ask: Is it possible, is it valid, is it profitable, for Christians to read the Bible as a whole from a missional perspective, and what happens when they do? Can we take mission as a hermeneutical matrix for our understanding of the Bible as a whole?

Before outlining in chapter two some contours of an approach that would answer those questions affirmatively, we will look first in chapter one at several ways in which the Bible is related to mission in contemporary writing on the matter—ways that have their own validity and significant contributions to make, but do not seem quite adequate to what I have in mind as a comprehensively missional approach to biblical hermeneutics. Chapter one, then, outlines some steps in the search for a missional hermeneutic—but in each case I believe we need to go further.

1

Searching for a
Missional Hermeneutic

There are more than enough books offering biblical foundations for Christian mission.[1] Not all of them are of the same quality, however. Some are tracts to the already converted, providing justification for the task to which writer and readers are already committed. Some pay no attention to critical scholarship; others, perhaps, too much.[2] Too many, more culpably, pay scant attention to the bulk of the Bible itself—the Old Testament. What they seek to do, however, is clear: to find appropriate biblical justification and authority for the mission of

---

[1]The substance of this chapter, along with chap. 2, first appeared as Christopher J. H. Wright, "Mission as a Matrix for Hermeneutics and Biblical Theology," in *Out of Egypt: Biblical Theology and Biblical Interpretation,* ed. Craig Bartholomew et al. (Carlisle, U.K.: Paternoster; Grand Rapids: Zondervan, 2004), pp. 102-43. This fine volume contains other papers from the Scripture and Hermeneutics Seminar which are relevant to the overall theme of this book.

Regarding books offering biblical foundations for Christian mission, see, for example, as a short selection, Johannes Blauw, *The Missionary Nature of the Church* (New York: McGraw Hill, 1962); David Burnett, *God's Mission, Healing the Nations,* rev. ed. (Carlisle, U.K.: Paternoster, 1996); Roger Hedlund, *The Mission of the Church in the World* (Grand Rapids: Baker, 1991); Andreas J. Koestenberger and Peter T. O'Brien, *Salvation to the Ends of the Earth: A Biblical Theology of Mission* (Leicester, U.K.: Apollos, 2001); Richard R. de Ridder, *Discipling the Nations* (Grand Rapids: Baker, 1975); Donald Senior and Carroll Stuhlmueller, *The Biblical Foundations for Mission* (London: SCM Press, 1983); Ken Gnanakan, *Kingdom Concerns: A Biblical Theology of Mission Today* (Bangalore: Theological Book Trust, 1989; Leicester, U.K.: Inter-Varsity Press, 1993).

[2]There is, of course, a proper place for the critical disciplines in our ground-laying work for biblical theology, but we also need to go beyond those foundations to the Bible's missiological thrust. See David J. Bosch, "Hermeneutical Principles in the Biblical Foundation for Mission," *Evangelical Review of Theology* 17 (1993): 437-51; and Charles Van Engen, "The Relation of Bible and Mission in Mission Theology," in *The Good News of the Kingdom,* ed. Charles Van Engen, Dean S. Gilliland and Paul Pierson (Maryknoll, N.Y.: Orbis, 1993), p. 34.

the Christian church to the nations. This may be in order to encourage those already engaged in such mission with the assurance that what they do is biblically grounded, or it may be to motivate those who are not yet engaged in it with the warning that they are living in disobedience to biblical imperatives.

Beyond "Biblical Foundations for Mission"

Biblical apologetic for mission. Such work, which might be called "biblical apologetic for mission," is of great importance. It would, after all, be a shattering thing if the church were suddenly seized by the conviction that all the missionary effort of two thousand years was grounded in no clear warrant of Scripture. From time to time, of course, there have been voices that argued exactly that. Indeed, it was against such voices, arguing theologically and biblically (as they thought), that mission to the nations was not required of good Christian citizens, that William Carey developed his biblical case for "the conversion of the heathens," becoming one of the first in the modern period to do so.[3]

The illustrious example of Carey, however, points to a shortcoming inherent in many "biblical foundations for mission" projects. Carey built the whole of the biblical section of his case on a single text, the so-called Great Commission of Matthew 28:18-20, arguing that it was as valid in his own day as in the days of the apostles, and that its imperative claim on the disciples of Christ had not lapsed with the first generation (as the opponents of foreign mission argued). While we would probably agree with his hermeneutical argument and that his choice of text was admirable, it leaves the biblical case vulnerably thin. We might defend Carey with the consideration that it was an achievement in his context to make a biblical case for mission at all, albeit from a single text. Less defensible has been the continuing practice in many missionary circles to go on and on building the massive edifice of Christian missionary agency on this one text, with varying degrees of exegetical ingenuity. If you put all your apologetic eggs in one textual basket, what happens if the handle breaks?

What happens, for example, if all the emphasis on the word *Go* in much mis-

---

[3]There were, of course (contrary to popular mythology), Protestant missionaries long before William Carey. However, Carey was among the first to include a clearly argued biblical case for establishing a missionary society—in his use of Matthew 28:18-20 as his key text in his justly famous *An Enquiry into the Obligations of Christians, to Use Means for the Conversion of the Heathens* (1792). David Bosch comments: "Protestants . . . have always prided themselves on the fact that they do what they do on the basis of what Scripture teaches. Still, in the case of the earliest Protestant missionaries, the Pietists and the Moravians, very little of a real biblical foundation for their missionary enterprises was in evidence. Wm. Carey was, in fact, one of the very first to have attempted to spell out such a foundation for the Church's missionary mandate" ("Hermeneutical Principles," p. 438).

sion rhetoric is undermined by the recognition that it is not an imperative at all in the text but a participle of attendant circumstances, an assumption—something taken for granted? Jesus did not primarily command his disciples to go; he commanded them to make disciples. But since he now commands them to make disciples of *the nations* (having previously restricted their mission to the borders of Israel during his earthly lifetime), they will have to go to the nations as a necessary condition of obeying the primary command.

What happens if one questions the common assumption that this text gives some kind of timetable for the return of Christ: he will come back just as soon as we have all the nations discipled? And is discipling a task that can ever be said to be completed (noting in passing that the text does say "disciple," not evangelize)? Doesn't every fresh generation of long-evangelized nations need fresh discipling? The Great Commission is an expanding and self-replicating task, not a ticking clock for the end times.

What happens if, even more controversially, one heeds the voices of critical scholars who question whether Jesus ever actually uttered (in Aramaic of course) the words recorded in Greek in Matthew 28:18-20?[4] In response to such a challenge one might make several defensive moves:

- seek to defend the authenticity of Matthew's text against the skeptics, and there are good grounds for doing so[5]

- argue that even if this text is not a transcripted recording of words from the mouth of Jesus, it does authentically express the inevitable implication of his identity and achievement as understood by the postresurrection church engaged in mission

- search for more texts to back up this one, to show that Matthew has indeed captured an essential element of the witness of Scripture and legitimately linked it with Jesus, who saw the mission of himself and his disciples as thoroughly grounded in the Scriptures

The last option is the most common. Most books offering a biblical basis of mission see their task as assembling as many texts as possible, texts that can be said to mandate or, in more indirect ways, support the missionary enterprise. Now this is important as far as it goes. Such biblical inducement to mission engagement is needed in churches that seem rather selective in their reading of the Bible.

---

[4]As, e.g., Alan Le Grys does in *Preaching to the Nations: The Origin of Mission in the Early Church* (London: SPCK, 1998).

[5]James LaGrand, *The Earliest Christian Mission to "All Nations" in the Light of Matthew's Gospel* (Grand Rapids: Eerdmans, 1995).

There are many ordinary and worthy Christians whose personal piety relishes those Scriptures that speak to them of their own salvation and security, that encourage them in times of distress, that guide them in their efforts to walk before the Lord in ways that please him. But it comes as a surprise for them to be confronted with such an array of texts that challenge them in relation to God's universal purpose for the world and the nations, the multicultural essence of the gospel and the missional essence of the church. But they need to get over that surprise and hear the burden of the Bible.

Equally, there are many theological scholars and students whose understanding of theology is bounded by the horizon of the classical shape of the curriculum, in which mission in any form (biblical, historical, theological, practical) seems remarkably absent. If it can be shown (as I believe it certainly can) that there is a surprisingly vast number of texts and themes in the Bible that relate to Christian mission, then missiology may regain respectability in the academy (of which there are encouraging signs already).

The danger of inadequate proof-texting. However, whether one text or many, the danger that attends all proof-texting is still present. We have already decided what we want to prove (that our missionary practice is biblical), and our collection of texts simply ratifies our preconception. The Bible is turned into a mine from which we extract our gems—"missionary texts." These texts may indeed sparkle, but simply laying out such gems on a string is not yet what one could call a missiological hermeneutic of the whole Bible itself. It does not even provide an adequate whole-Bible grounding for mission.

Commenting on this text-assembly approach, David Bosch observes:

> I am not saying that these procedures are illegitimate. They undoubtedly have their value. But their contribution towards establishing the validity of the missionary mandate is minimal. This validity should not be deduced from isolated texts and detached incidents but only from the thrust of the central message of both Old and New Testaments. What is decisive for the Church today is not the formal agreement between what she is doing and what some isolated biblical texts seem to be saying but rather her relationship with the essence of the message of Scripture.[6]

Now we may feel that Bosch makes a false contrast here between things that are actually both necessary. There ought indeed to be formal agreement between what the church does and what biblical texts say. And texts with mission relevance are far from isolated. To point out the inadequacy of proof-texting through shallow and hermeneutically spurious sprinkling of texts at a problem

---

[6]Bosch, "Hermeneutical Principles," pp. 439-40.

is not by any means to reject the painstaking effort to prove a case through patient study of texts. Returning to Bosch's quote, articulating what "the thrust of the central message" or "the essence of the message of Scripture" might be is of course precisely the issue we are wrestling with in these pages. To be able to say that the thrust or essence is "mission" requires a lot more than just a list of helpfully benevolent texts.

A final limitation of this list of texts approach is that it has a suspicion of circularity. The danger is that one comes to the Bible with a massive commitment to the task of mission already in place, with a heritage of hallowed history, with methods and models in the present, and with strategies and goals for the future. All this we have assumed to be biblically warranted. So in searching the Scriptures for a biblical foundation for mission, we are likely to find what we brought with us—our own conception of mission, now comfortably festooned with biblical luggage tags.

To establish a biblical grounding for *mission per se* is legitimate and essential. To claim to find biblical grounding for *all our missionary practice* is much more questionable. Some would say it is impossible—even dangerous. Rather than finding biblical legitimation for our activities, we should be submitting all our missionary strategy, plans and operations to biblical critique and evaluation. Marc Spindler articulates this point well:

> If "mission" is understood as the sum total of all actual missionary activities in the modern period or as everything undertaken under the banner of "missions," then an honest biblical scholar can only conclude that such a concept of mission does not occur in the Bible. . . . It is therefore anachronistic and hence meaningless to attempt to base all modern "missionary" activities on the Bible, that is, to seek biblical precedents or literal biblical mandates for all modern missionary activities. Mission today must, rather, be seen as arising from something fundamental, from the basic movement of God's people toward the world [i.e., with the good news of salvation through Jesus Christ]. . . . The genuineness of our biblical grounding of mission stands or falls with the orientation of modern missions to this central thought. All "missionary" activities that have grown up in history must be reassessed from this perspective. Once again, a biblical grounding of mission by no means seeks to legitimate missionary activities that are actually being carried out. Its goal is, rather, evaluation of those activities in the light of the Bible.[7]

But in order to do that evaluative task, we have to have a clearer understand-

---

[7]Marc R. Spindler, "The Biblical Grounding and Orientation of Mission," in *Missiology: An Ecumenical Introduction,* ed. A. Camps, L. A. Hoedemaker and M. R. Spindler (Grand Rapids: Eerdmans, 1995), pp. 124-25.

ing of that "something fundamental"—mission in its biblical sense or, more precisely, a missiological framework of biblical theology.

Beyond Multicultural Hermeneutical Perspectives

Global church, global hermeneutics. Slowly but inexorably the world of Western academic theology is becoming aware of the rest of the world. The impact of missiology has brought to the attention of the theological community in the West the wealth of theological and hermeneutical perspectives that are, in some cases at least, the product of the success of mission over the past centuries. Mission has transformed the map of global Christianity. From a situation at the beginning of the twentieth century when approximately 90 percent of all the world's Christians lived in the West or North (i.e., predominantly Europe and North America), the beginning of the twenty-first century finds at least 75 percent of the world's Christians in the continents of the South and East—Latin America, Africa and parts of Asia and the Pacific. The whole center of gravity of world Christianity has moved south—a phenomenon described, not entirely felicitously, as "the next Christendom."[8] Others prefer terms such as "The Global South" or "The Majority World."

We live in an age of a multinational church and multidirectional mission. And appropriately we now live with multicultural hermeneutics. People will insist on reading the Bible for themselves, you see. There is a great irony that the Western Protestant theological academy, which has its roots precisely in a hermeneutical revolution (the Reformation), led by people who claimed the right to read Scripture independently from the prevailing hegemony of medieval Catholic scholasticism, has been slow to give ear to those of other cultures who choose to read the Scriptures through their own eyes, though the situation is undoubtedly improving.[9]

The phenomenon of hermeneutical variety goes right back to the Bible itself, of course. The New Testament was born out of a hermeneutical revolution in

---

[8]Philip Jenkins, *The Next Christendom: The Coming of Global Christianity* (Oxford: Oxford University Press, 2002). Cf. Christopher Wright, "Future Trends in Mission," in *The Futures of Evangelicalism: Issues and Prospects,* ed. Craig Bartholomew, Robin Parry, and Andrew West (Leicester, U.K.: Inter-Varsity Press, 2003), pp. 149-63, and bibliography there cited.

[9]Ignorance (whether innocent or wilful) of major issues in non-Western Christianity that non-Western theology must grapple with was illustrated for me at a combined faculty meeting of several London theological colleges. A Ghanaian lecturer at All Nations Christian College said that in his pastoral work in Ghana about at least 50 percent of his time went in helping believers, pastorally and theologically, in the area of dreams and visions and the spiritual world. A British lecturer at another college commented with ill-concealed disdain to me over lunch, "I rather thought we'd grown out of that kind of thing."

reading those Scriptures we now call the Old Testament. And within the early church itself there were different ways of handling those same Scriptures, depending on the context and need being addressed. Jewish and Greek forms of Christian identity, the product of the church's mission, felt themselves addressed and claimed in different ways by the demands of the Scriptures. Paul wrestles with these differences in Romans 14—15 for example. He makes his own position clear (in identifying himself theologically with those who called themselves "strong"), but he insisted that those who differed strongly on matters of interpretation and application of scriptural injunctions must accept one another without condemnation from one side or contempt from the other because of the prior claims of Christ and the gospel.

So a missional hermeneutic must include at least this recognition—the multiplicity of perspectives and contexts from which and within which people read the biblical texts. Even when we affirm (as I certainly do) that the historical and salvation-historical context of biblical texts and their authors is of primary and objective importance in discerning their meaning and their significance, the plurality of perspectives from which readers read them is also a vital factor in the hermeneutical richness of the global church. What persons of one culture bring from that culture to their reading of a text may illuminate dimensions or implications of the text itself that persons of another culture may have not seen so clearly.[10]

Reflecting on such plurality, James Brownson argues that it is a *positive* thing with biblical roots and emerges out of the reality of missional engagement all over the world.

> I call the model I am developing a *missional* hermeneutic because it springs from a basic observation about the New Testament: namely, the early Christian movement that produced and canonized the New Testament was a movement with specifically *missionary* character. One of the most obvious phenomena of early Christianity is the way in which the movement crossed cultural boundaries and planted itself in new places. More than half of the New Testament was in fact written by people engaged in and celebrating this sort of missionary enterprise in the early church. This tendency of early Christianity to cross cultural boundaries is a

---

[10]Western translators of the book of Genesis into Chadian Arabic told me how Chadian believers, reading the stories of Joseph for the first time in their own language, discerned in the narrative, and especially its climax in chap. 50, aspects of the relationship between Joseph and his brothers and the protracted process of reconciliation and the removal of shame (which was not completed till after Jacob's death), which made profound sense to them in their own culture. They found, e.g., as much power in Joseph's personal commitment in Gen 50:21 as in his theological insight in Gen 50:20.

fertile starting point for developing a model of biblical interpretation. It is fertile, especially for our purposes, because it places the question of the relationship between Christianity and diverse cultures at the very top of the interpretative agenda. This focus may be of great help to us in grappling with plurality in interpretation today. . . . The missional hermeneutic I am advocating begins by affirming the reality and inevitability of plurality in interpretation.[11]

Mission as a focus of hermeneutical coherence. However, it would be inadequate to think that a missional hermeneutic of the Bible amounted only to aggregating all the possible ways of reading its texts, from all the multicolored church and mission contexts around the globe. That is, of course, a fascinating and enriching thing to do. It is the common witness of those, including myself, who have lived and worked in cultures other than their own that reading and studying the Bible through the eyes of others is a challenging, mind-blowing and immensely instructive privilege. But are we left only with plurality? And if so, are we consigned to a relativism that declines any evaluation? Are there any boundaries as to readings of biblical texts that are right or wrong—or even just better or worse? And how are those boundaries or criteria to be defined?

It is important to point out here that "plurality in interpretation" is not pluralism as a hermeneutical ideology, nor is it a relativist charter. The starting point for understanding the meaning of biblical texts, in my view, remains a careful application of grammatico-historical tools in seeking to determine as far as is possible their authors' and editors' intended meaning in the contexts they were spoken or written. But as we apply those tools and then move to appropriate the significance and implications of these texts in our own context, cultural diversity plays its part in the hearing and receiving of them. But it is a diversity with methodological and theological limits.

Brownson goes on from his discussion of a missional hermeneutic of *diversity,* to argue for "a hermeneutic of *coherence.*" The plurality of interpretative stances requires that we speak and listen to one another with respect and love, affirming our common humanity and our common commitment to the same biblical texts. "Once we have affirmed plurality, however, we need also to grapple with how the Bible may provide a center, an orienting point in the midst of such

---

[11]James V. Brownson, "Speaking the Truth in Love: Elements of a Missional Hermeneutic," in *The Church Between Gospel and Culture,* ed. George R. Hunsberger and Craig Van Gelder (Grand Rapids: Eerdmans, 1996), pp. 232-33. See also Christopher J. H. Wright, "Christ and the Mosaic of Pluralisms: Challenges to Evangelical Missiology in the 21st Century," in *Global Missiology for the 21st Century: The Iguassu Dialogue,* ed. William Taylor (Grand Rapids: Baker, 2000), reprinted in *Evangelical Review of Theology* 24 (2000): 207-39.

diversity. What does it mean to speak *the truth* in love?"[12] The answer Brownson offers is the shape, the content and the claim of the biblical gospel itself. He agrees with scholars who have found a core of nonnegotiable affirmations in the varied New Testament presentations of the gospel and insists that this must provide the hermeneutical framework or matrix for assessing all claimed readings of the texts.

> An understanding of the hermeneutical function of the gospel is critical to a healthy approach to plurality and coherence in biblical interpretation. Interpretation will always emerge out of different contexts. There will always be different traditions brought to bear by various interpreters. . . . In the midst of all this diversity, however, the gospel functions as a framework that lends a sense of coherence and commonality.[13]

While agreeing wholeheartedly with this, I would go further and point out that the gospel (which Brownson discusses in exclusively New Testament terms) actually begins in Genesis (according to Paul in Gal 3:8). I would thus want to bring a whole-Bible perspective to the question of what Brownson calls "a hermeneutic of coherence."

This surely is also implied in Luke's messianic and missional hermeneutic of the Hebrew canon in Luke 24. Luke, who had lived and worked with Paul and who wrote the turbulent story of the earliest theological controversies in the church in Acts, knew perfectly well the diversity of interpretation of Old Testament texts even within the first generation of those who followed the Way of Jesus. Nevertheless, the words of Jesus "opened their minds so they could understand the Scriptures" (Lk 24:45). In other words, *Jesus himself* provided the hermeneutical coherence within which all disciples must read these texts, that is, in the light of the story that leads *up to* Christ (messianic reading) and the story that leads *on from* Christ (missional reading). That is the story that flows from the mind and purpose of God in all the Scriptures for all the nations. That is a missional hermeneutic of the whole Bible.

Beyond Contextual Theologies and Advocacy Readings

Contexts and interests. The diversity of contextual approaches to reading the biblical texts includes those that are explicit in their interested stance—that is, readings done in the midst of and on behalf of or in the interests of particular groups of people. As against the rather blinkered view of theology that devel-

---

oped in the West since the Enlightenment, which liked to claim that it was scientific, objective, rational and free from either confessional presuppositions or
ideological interests, theologies have emerged that declare such disinterested
objectivity to be a myth—and a dangerous one in that it concealed hegemonic
claims. These theologies argue that contexts do matter, that in the act of reading
and interpreting the Bible, the questions of who you are, where you are, and
whom you live among as a reader make a difference. The Bible is to be read
precisely in and for the context in which its message must be heard and appropriated.

So these approaches to the Bible and theology came to be called "contextual
theologies" within the Western academy. This term in itself betrayed the arrogant ethnocentricity of the West, for the assumption was that other places are
contexts and they do their theology for those contexts; we, of course, have the
real thing, the objective, contextless theology. This assumption is being rightly
challenged, and the West is seen for what it is—a particular context of human
culture, not necessarily any better or any worse than any other context for reading the Bible and doing theology.[14] But it does happen to be the context within
which a certain mode of being Christian emerged and sustained itself for centuries, and then came to have a dominant position in the world, largely through
missionary activity and its sequel. It is the cultural context that culminated in the
great tower of Babel that we call Enlightenment modernity, which is now in the
process of fragmenting, like its Genesis prototype, into the scattered diversity of
postmodernity.

What many of these newer theologies have in common is their advocacy
stance. That is, they arise from the conviction that it is fundamental to biblical
faith to take a stand alongside the victims of injustice in any form. Thus the Bible
is to be read with a liberationist hermeneutic—that is, with a concern to liberate
people from oppression and exploitation. The earliest to make its impact on
theological thinking in the West in the twentieth century was Liberation Theology from Latin America.[15] Theology was not to be done in the study and then

---

[14]I put it like this because there is no point, it seems to me, in swinging the pendulum from
Western hermeneutical hegemony and ignorance of majority world biblical scholarship to the
fashionable adulation of anything and everything that comes from the rest of the world and
the rejection of established methods of grammatico-historical exegesis as somehow intrinsically Western, colonial or imperialistic.

[15]The contemporary time frame is deliberate since earlier centuries have seen their own theological developments with liberationist orientation. The Anabaptist movements of the Radical
Reformation, for example, developed a range of hermeneutical strategies in their struggle
against the intense persecution they encountered from both Roman Catholic and mainline
Protestant churches and states.

applied in the world. Rather, action for and on behalf of the poor and oppressed was to be undertaken as a first priority, and then out of that commitment and praxis, theological reflection would follow. This presented a radical paradigm challenge to the standard Western way of doing theology. Other examples include Dalit Theology from India, Minjung Theology in Korea, and Black Theology in Africa and among African Americans. Feminist movements have also generated a broad and influential hermeneutic and theology, which has probably been more influential in the West than any of the others. All these approaches to the text offer a hermeneutic that is intentionally "interested." That is, they read in the interests of those they speak on behalf of—the poor, the outcastes, Blacks, women and so forth.

Exploding the missionary stereotype. So could a missional hermeneutic be presented as a liberation theology for missionaries? Or missiologists? The idea is mooted only half in jest. Given that missionaries in popular mythology are seen as the compromised adjuncts of colonialism and almost synonymous with Western arrogance and cultural totalitarianism, it might be more natural to propose a liberation theology *from* missionaries (which is what some radical forms of non-Western theology have in fact advocated).

However, the multinational nature of the global church has generated a new reality that is hardly yet acknowledged in the churches of the West, let alone in the popular culture and media there. And that is the fact that much more than half of all the Christian missionaries serving in the world today are not white and Western. It is the churches of the majority world that are now sending the majority of people into all kinds of crosscultural mission work. So one is as likely to meet an African missionary in Britain as a British one in Africa; the same is true for Brazilians in North Africa; Nigerians in parts of West Africa, where few white people now venture; and Koreans almost anywhere in the world. While it remains true that the United States still sends the highest number of missionaries to other parts of the world, the country that has the *second* highest number of crosscultural missionaries is India.[16] There are at least thirty times more Indian national missionaries than there are Westerners serving as missionaries within India.

What simply cannot be said of this new phenomenon of world mission is that all these Christian missionaries are agents of oppressive colonial powers or that they operate as a religious veneer to political or economic imperialism. On the

---

[16]And there are recent estimates that suggest that the number of Protestant crosscultural missionaries within India may already have surpassed the total number sent around the world from the United States.

contrary, for the most part Christian mission as carried out by the churches of the majority world operates out of powerlessness and relative poverty, and often in situations of considerable opposition and persecution. Such missionaries may not qualify as an oppressed class on the scale of, say, the poor in Latin America or the Dalits in India (though many Indian missionaries are also Dalits). But they could do with some liberation from the oppressive stereotypes and unjust caricatures that still surround their calling as well as from the marginalization that mission experiences in many churches and that missiology still battles with in the strongholds of theological academia.

So, yes, a missional hermeneutic is "interested." It reads the Bible and develops a biblical hermeneutic in the interests of those who have committed their own personal life story into the biblical story of God's purpose for the nations. But it does so with the even stronger conviction that such commitment should be the normal stance for the whole church, for, on this reading of Scripture, a church that is governed by the Bible cannot evade the missional thrust of the God and the gospel revealed there.

Missional reading embraces liberation. However, a missional hermeneutic goes further. It is not content to take its place as just one of several liberationist, advocacy or "interested" theologies on offer—though even as such, I contend, it has a right to exist, a right to advance and defend its own validity.[17] Rather, a broadly missional reading of the whole Bible, such as I hope to outline in these pages, actually subsumes liberationist readings into itself. Where else does the passion for justice and liberation that breathes in these various theologies come from if not from the biblical revelation of the God who battles with injustice, oppression and bondage throughout history right to the eschaton? Where else but from the God who triumphed climactically over all such wickedness and evil (human, historical and cosmic) in the cross and resurrection of his Son, Jesus Christ? Where else, in other words, but from the mission of God?

Biblically, all true liberation, all truly human best interests flow from God—not just *any* god but the God revealed as YHWH in the Old Testament and incarnate in Jesus of Nazareth. So inasmuch as the Bible narrates the passion and action (the mission) of *this* God for the liberation not only of humanity but of

---

[17]For a penetrating reflection on the plurality of readings of the biblical texts in the postmodern academy and the impact that this has had on the traditional hegemony of Western theology, particularly in the field of Old Testament studies, see Walter Brueggemann, *Theology of the Old Testament: Testimony, Dispute, Advocacy* (Minneapolis: Fortress Press, 1997), pp. 61-114. It seems to me that a missiological reading has as much right to set out its stall in the marketplace of contemporary hermeneutics as any other. See also my own comments in Wright, "Mosaic of Pluralisms."

the whole creation, a missional hermeneutic of Scripture must have a liberationist dimension. Once again we are driven back to see how important it is to ground our theology of mission (and our practice of it) in the mission of God and in our worshiping response to all that God is and does. From that perspective, we are advocates for *God* before we are advocates for *others*.

> This trinitarian grounding of mission should make clear that God and not the church is the primary subject and source of mission. Advocacy is what the church is about, being God's advocate in the world. The church must therefore begin its mission with doxology, otherwise everything peters out into social activism and aimless programs.[18]

Beyond Postmodern Hermeneutics

Plurality yes, relativism no. The rise of contextual theologies and then the recognition that all theology is in fact contextual, including the Western "standard" variety, has coincided with the arrival of postmodernism and its massive impact on hermeneutics (as on all the academic disciplines). The contemporary Western theological academy was largely built on an Enlightenment modernity worldview, which privileged objectivity and sought a singular all-embracing theological construct. Naturally, then, it had difficulty with theologies that seemed so situated in local and historical contexts. But the postmodern shift, in deliberate contrast, welcomes and elevates precisely such locality and plurality.

Postmodernism, however, not only celebrates the local, the contextual and the particular, it goes on to affirm that this is all we've got. There is no grand narrative (or metanarrative) that explains everything, and any claims that there is some truth for all that embraces the totality of life and meaning are rejected as oppressive power plays. Thus radically postmodern hermeneutics delights in a multiplicity of readings and perspectives but rejects the possibility of any single truth or unitive coherence.[19]

On the other hand, for two thousand years Christian mission, ever since the

---

[18]Carl E. Braaten, "The Mission of the Gospel to the Nations," *Dialog* 30 (1991): 127. See also the still relevant reminder of the trinitarian, God-centered priorities of mission from Lesslie Newbigin, *Trinitarian Doctrine for Today's Mission* (Edinburgh: Edinburgh House Press, 1963; Carlisle, U.K.: Paternoster, 1998).

[19]A major element in the challenge of postmodernity has come at the level of epistemology—how we know what we claim to know. This in turn has a significant impact on how we view mission, since Christian mission, if it is anything, is founded on what Christians claim to know about God and the world, about history and the future. Some of these epistemological problems for mission were tackled in a symposium recorded in J. Andrew Kirk and Kevin J. Vanhoozer, eds., *To Stake a Claim: Mission and the Western Crisis of Knowledge* (Maryknoll, N.Y.: Orbis, 1999).

New Testament church, has wrestled with the problems of multiple cultural contexts. And yet in the midst of them all it has sustained the conviction that there is an objective truth for all in the gospel that addresses and claims people in any context. I would go further and argue that Israel in the Old Testament wrestled with a similar dynamic, namely, the need to relate the faith of YHWH to changing cultural and religious contexts through the millennium and more of Israel's history. Cultural plurality is nothing new for Christian mission. It is rather the very stuff of missional engagement and missiological reflection. We may be challenged by swimming in the postmodern pool, but we need not feel out of our depth there.[20]

In an interesting and complex article Martha Franks explores the way Christian theology of mission within the span of the twentieth century has moved from a fairly flat presentation of a single biblical message through a more historically nuanced understanding (as in the theology of von Rad) to a recognition of the plurality within the Bible and within the contexts of mission (as in Senior and Stuhlmueller). She observes how Lesslie Newbigin, for example, sensitively balances the particularity of election with the plurality of the Bible's vision for all nations and cultures, and sees the fullness of the gospel brought into ever more visible glory through the two-way task of crosscultural mission. She then goes on to link this to the concerns of postmodernism and claims that Christian mission has long preceded postmodernism in recognizing the validity of multiple contexts as "home" for the gospel.

Christian mission has long experience of "postmodern" challenges. Mission, Franks points out, has never been merely a matter of transferring an object from one subject to another. Rather, the living dynamic of the gospel has been such that, while it has an unchanging core because of its historical rootedness in the Scriptures and the Christ event, it has been received, understood, articulated, and lived out in myriad ways, both vertically through history and horizontally in all the cultures in which Christian faith has taken root.

> Newbigin . . . argues that mission work in the world's plurality is "two-way." Hearing the new understandings of the gospel that arise when the message of Christ is brought to a new context is an important part of understanding the whole meaning of the Lordship of Jesus. This insight from mission work is sympathetic to the similar suggestion of postmodernism with regard to the meaning of texts—that com-

---

[20]Andrew Walls provides richly stimulating surveys of the way the Christian church throughout history has developed ever-growing pluriformity, taking root in culture after culture, while preserving the essential nonnegotiable and transcultural objective core of the gospel. See Andrew F. Walls, *The Missionary Movement in Christian History: Studies in the Transmission of Faith* (Maryknoll, N.Y.: Orbis; Edinburgh: T & T Clark, 1996).

munication between people, even when it is by book, is always "two-way." . . . Moreover, Newbigin's understanding of mission points to the fact that Christian missiology has long preceded the postmodern world in recognizing the possible problem of the fact that transplanting language and concepts from one context to another leads to wholly new ways of understanding them. Having centuries of experience with the very problem on which the postmoderns have tumbled, it is appropriate to respond to the challenge of postmodernism not with revulsion, but with counsel. We know about these questions. We have something to offer.[21]

What we have to offer, I contend, is a missional hermeneutic of the Bible. The Bible got there before postmodernity was dreamed of—the Bible which glories in *diversity* and celebrates multiple human *cultures,* the Bible which builds its most elevated theological claims on utterly *particular* and sometimes very *local* events, the Bible which sees everything in *relational,* not abstract, terms, and the Bible which does the bulk of its work through the medium of *stories*.

All of these features of the Bible—cultural, local, relational, narrative—are welcome to the postmodern mind. Where the missional hermeneutic will part company with radical postmodernity, is in its insistence that through all this variety, locality, particularity and diversity, the Bible is nevertheless actually *the* story. This is the way it is. This is the grand narrative that constitutes truth for all. And within *this* story, as narrated or anticipated by the Bible, there is at work the God whose mission is evident from creation to new creation. This is the story of God's mission. It is a coherent story with a universal claim. But it is also a story that affirms humanity in all its particular cultural variety. This is the universal story that gives a place in the sun to all the little stories.[22]

---

[21]Martha Franks, "Election, Pluralism, and the Missiology of Scripture in a Postmodern Age," *Missiology* 26 (1998): 342.

[22]Richard Bauckham explores the constant biblical oscillation between the particular and the universal, and its implications for a missiological hermeneutic, with special attention to its relevance to postmodernity, in *The Bible and Mission: Christian Mission in a Postmodern World* (Carlisle, U.K.: Paternoster, 2003).

2

Shaping a Missional Hermeneutic

In chapter one I noted some of the steps that have been taken already toward a missiological reading of the Bible, but argued that none of them quite meets the challenge. Some responsibility inevitably then rests on the person who points out the deficiencies of others to come up with something more adequate. With some diffidence, since I am sure the task of establishing missiology as a viable framework for biblical hermeneutics is still very much in the construction stage, I offer the reflections of this chapter as at least some scaffolding for the project.

The Bible as the Product of God's Mission

A missional hermeneutic of the Bible begins with the Bible's very existence. For those who affirm some relationship (however articulated) between these texts and the self-revelation of our Creator God, the whole canon of Scripture is a missional phenomenon in the sense that it witnesses to the self-giving movement of this God toward his creation and us, human beings in God's own image, but wayward and wanton. The writings that now comprise our Bible are themselves the product of and witness to the ultimate mission of God.

> The very existence of the Bible is incontrovertible evidence of the God who refused to forsake his rebellious creation, who refused to give up, who was and is determined to redeem and restore fallen creation to his original design for it. . . .
> The very existence of such a collection of writings testifies to a God who breaks through to human beings, who disclosed himself to them, who will not leave them unilluminated in their darkness, . . . who takes the initiative in re-establishing broken relationships with us.[1]

---

[1]Charles R. Taber, "Missiology and the Bible," *Missiology* 11 (1983): 232.

Furthermore, the processes by which these texts came to be written were often profoundly missional in nature. Many of them emerged out of events or struggles or crises or conflicts in which the people of God engaged with the constantly changing and challenging task of articulating and living out their understanding of God's revelation and redemptive action in the world. Sometimes these were struggles internal to the people of God themselves; sometimes they were highly polemical struggles with competing religious claims and worldviews that surrounded them. So a missional reading of such texts is very definitely not a matter of (1) finding the "real" meaning by objective exegesis, and only then (2) cranking up some "missiological implications" as a homiletic supplement to the text itself. Rather, it is to see how a text often has its *origin* in some issue, need, controversy or threat that the people of God needed to address in the context of their mission. The text in itself is a product of mission in action.

This is easily demonstrated in the case of the New Testament.[2] Most of Paul's letters were written in the heat of his missionary efforts: wrestling with the theological basis of the inclusion of the Gentiles, affirming the need for Jew and Gentile to accept one another in Christ and in the church, tackling the baffling range of new problems that assailed young churches as the gospel took root in the world of Greek polytheism, confronting incipient heresies with clear affirmations of the supremacy and sufficiency of Jesus Christ, and so on.

And why were the Gospels so called? Because they were written to explain the significance of the *evangel*—the good news about Jesus of Nazareth, especially his death and resurrection. Confidence in these things was essential to the missionary task of the expanding church. And the person to whom we owe the largest quantity of the New Testament, Luke, shapes his two-volume work in such a way that the missionary mandate to the disciples to be Christ's witnesses to the nations comes as the climax to volume one and the introduction to volume two.

---

[2]Marion Soards surveys four current issues in New Testament studies (first-century Judaism, the life of Jesus, Pauline theology, and the character of the early church) and shows how they are relevant to mission studies also. But he concludes with a converse comment in line with the point being made here: "Mission studies should remind biblical scholars that many of the writings that we study (often in painstaking and even painful detail) came to be because of the reality of mission. An awareness of, and a concern with, the key issues of mission studies may well help biblical studies find foci that will bring deeper appreciation of the meaning of the Bible." Marion L. Soards, "Key Issues in Biblical Studies and Their Bearing on Mission Studies," *Missiology* 24 (1996): 107. With this I fully agree. See also Andreas J. Koestenberger, "The Place of Mission in New Testament Theology: An Attempt to Determine the Significance of Mission Within the Scope of the New Testament's Message as a Whole," *Missiology* 27 (1999), and the works referred to there.

Thus Howard Marshall sees this as the focal point of New Testament theology. Obviously all the New Testament documents hang together around their recognition of Jesus of Nazareth as Savior and Lord.

> It may, however, be more helpful to recognize them more specifically as the documents of a mission. The subject matter is not, as it were, Jesus in himself or God in himself but Jesus in his role as Savior and Lord. *New Testament theology is essentially missionary theology.* By this I mean that the documents came into being as the result of a two-part mission, first the mission of Jesus sent by God to inaugurate his kingdom with the blessings it brings to people and to call people to respond to it, and then the mission of his followers called to continue his work by proclaiming him as Lord and Savior and calling people to faith and ongoing commitment to him, as a result of which his church grows. The theology springs out of this movement and is shaped by it, and in turn the theology shapes the continuing mission of the church. . . . The New Testament thus tells the story of the mission and lays especial emphasis on expounding the message proclaimed by the missionaries.[3]

But also in the case of the Old Testament we can see that many of these texts emerged out of the engagement of Israel with the surrounding world, in the light of the God they knew in their history and in covenantal relationship. People produced texts in relation to what they believed God had done, was doing or would do in their world. The Torah records the exodus as an act of YHWH that comprehensively confronted and defeated the power of Pharaoh and all his rival claims to deity and allegiance. It presents a theology of creation that stands in sharp contrast to the polytheistic creation myths of Mesopotamia. The historical narratives portray the long and sorry story of Israel's struggle with the culture and religion of Canaan, a struggle reflected also in the preexilic prophets. Exilic and postexilic texts emerge out of the task that the small remnant community of Israel faced to define their continuing identity as a community of faith in successive empires of varying hostility or tolerance. Wisdom texts interact with international wisdom traditions in the surrounding cultures, but do so with staunch monotheistic disinfectant. And in worship and prophecy, Israelites reflect on the relationship between their God, YHWH, and the rest of the nations—sometimes negatively, sometimes positively—and on the nature of their own role as YHWH's elect priesthood in their midst.

All of the items referred to in the last paragraph deserve chapters of their own, and some of them will get one. The point being made here is simply that the Bible is in so many ways a *missional phenomenon* in itself. The individual

---

[3]I. Howard Marshall, *New Testament Theology: Many Witnesses, One Gospel* (Downers Grove, Ill.: InterVarsity Press, 2004), pp. 34-35, emphasis added.

texts within it often reflect the struggles of being a people with a mission in a world of competing cultural and religious claims. And the canon eventually consolidates the recognition that it is through these texts that the people whom God has called to be his own (in both Testaments) has been shaped as a community of memory and hope, a community of mission, failure, and striving. Indeed, as David Filbeck has observed, this missiological thrust provides theological coherence to the Bible, including the relationship of the Testaments.

> Indeed, it is this missionary dimension, so often neglected in modern theological interpretation, that unifies both Old and New Testaments and coordinates their various themes into a single motif. It is the logical connection between the Testaments that many modern theologians unfortunately seem to despair of ever finding. . . .
> In short, the dimension of missions in the interpretation of the Scriptures gives structure to the whole Bible. Any theological study of the Scriptures, therefore, must be formulated with the view of maintaining this structure. The missionary dimension to the interpretation of the Old Testament as displayed in the New Testament, I believe, accomplishes this in a way that no other theological theme can hope to match.[4]

In short, a missional hermeneutic proceeds from the assumption that *the whole Bible renders to us the story of God's mission through God's people in their engagement with God's world for the sake of the whole of God's creation.*[5]

Biblical Authority and Mission

The Great Commission implies an imperative, a mandate. So it also presupposes an authority behind that imperative. We find this and other similar missionary imperatives in the Bible. So our involvement in mission is, at one level, a matter of obedience to the authority of Scripture, regarded as the Word of God. This offers an immediate illustration of one of the distinctions I referred to in chapter one.

A *biblical basis of mission* seeks out those biblical texts that express or describe the missionary imperative, on the assumption that the Bible is authoritative.

A *missional hermeneutic of the Bible,* however, explores the nature of biblical authority itself in relation to mission. Does a missional approach to the Bible help us in articulating what we mean by biblical authority?

---

[4]David Filbeck, *Yes, God of the Gentiles Too: The Missionary Message of the Old Testament* (Wheaton, Ill.: Billy Graham Center, 1994), p. 10.

[5]On the need to take the Bible as a whole in constructing a theology of mission, see also, Charles Van Engen, "The Relation of Bible and Mission in Mission Theology," in *The Good News of the Kingdom,* ed. Charles Van Engen, Dean S. Gilliland, and Paul Pierson (Maryknoll, N.Y.: Orbis, 1993), pp. 27-36.

Authority as command. This is not the place for a full account of the Christian doctrine of the authority of the Bible. One aspect, however, is important for our purpose here. For many people the concept of authority that they subconsciously bring to their understanding of the authority of the Bible is a military one. Authority is what gives the officer the right to issue commands. Commands are to be obeyed. The Bible is our authority. It issues the commands and tells us what to do or not to do. Authority, then, is simply a matter of orders on the one hand and obedience on the other.

In missionary circles the Great Commission is frequently surrounded with military metaphors of this sort. This text is said to provide the church's marching orders, for example, not to mention the whole range of other military metaphors that follow—warfare, mobilization, recruits, strategies, targets, campaigns, crusades, frontlines, strongholds, the missionary "force" (i.e., personnel) and the like. The language of authority seems easily converted into the language of mission, with the military metaphor functioning as the dynamic connector.

However, even if we strongly affirm our acceptance of biblical authority, the association of authority primarily with military-style command does not sit comfortably with much of the actual material in the Bible. There are of course many commands in the Bible, and indeed the psalmists celebrate this as a mark of God's goodness and grace (e.g., Ps 19; 119). Those commands that we do have from God are to be cherished for the light, guidance, security, joy and freedom they bring (to mention a few of the benefits praised by the psalmists). But the bulk of the Bible is not command—in the sense of issuing direct commands either to its first readers or to future generations of readers, including ourselves.

Much more of the Bible is narrative, poetry, prophecy, song, lament, visions, letters and so on. What is the authority latent in those forms of utterance? How does a poem or a story or somebody's letter to somebody else tell *me* what *I* must do or not do? Is that even what it was intended to do? And more importantly in relation to our task here, how do such nonimperative sections of the Bible connect to mission, if mission is seen primarily as obedience to a command? I would suggest that it is partly because we have so tightly bound our understanding of mission to a single (and undeniably crucial) imperative of Jesus that we have difficulty making connections between mission and the rest of the Scriptures, where those other Scriptures are not obviously or grammatically imperative. We do not perceive any missional *authority* in such nonimperative texts because we conceive authority only in terms of *commands*.

Authority and reality. We need to widen considerably our understanding of the word *authority*. In his majestic apologia for evangelical biblical ethics, *Resurrection and Moral Order,* Oliver O'Donovan argues that authority is a dimension of reality that constitutes sufficient and meaningful grounds for action. The created order itself, by its objective reality, provides an authority structure within which we have freedom to act (both in the sense of permission to act and a wide range of options).[6] Authority is not just a list of positive commands; authority includes legitimating permission. Authority authorizes; it grants freedom to act within boundaries. Thus the authority of my driver's license and my bishop's license as an ordained presbyter in the Church of England is not to order me every day where I must drive or what sacred service I must render. Rather these licenses *authorize me* to make those choices, give me freedom and authority to drive where I wish or to take services, preach, baptize and so forth. In those contexts I am an *authorized* person, liberated by, while still subject to, the authority of the realities that stand behind those documents (the laws of the road; the canons of the church).

Authority then is the predicate of reality, the source and boundary of freedom. Now, as O'Donovan argues, the created order itself as the fundamental reality structure of our existence is also a structure of authority. A physical brick wall, for example, by its simple real existence constitutes an authority. You have freedom on this side of it or on that side of it. But your freedom ends when you attempt to run through it at high speed. It exerts its authority rather abruptly. Gravity as a force in the physical universe is an authority built into the way the universe exists. For us humans it authorizes an immense freedom of action on and above the surface of the planet provided we work with it. But it also sets limits to that freedom. You may freely choose to step off a cliff, but the authority of gravity will decree it to be the last free choice you make. Reality kicks in. The authority of the laws of nature lies in the fact that nature itself is real. The universe is simply there, and we are not at liberty to behave as though it weren't.

Now, how do these considerations help our understanding of the authority of the Bible? The authority of the Bible is that it brings us into contact with reality—primarily the reality of God himself whose authority stands behind even that of creation. In fact, the Bible renders to us several connected realities, each of which has its own intrinsic, predicated authority. Reading and knowing the Scriptures causes us to *engage with reality*. That in turn functions to authorize

---

[6]Oliver O'Donovan, *Resurrection and Moral Order: An Outline for Evangelical Ethics* (Leicester, U.K.: Inter-Varsity Press, 1986). I have discussed O'Donovan's insight further in relation to the authority of Scripture in an age of historical and cultural relativism in Christopher J. H. Wright, *Walking in the Ways of the Lord: The Ethical Authority of the Old Testament* (Downers Grove, Ill.: InterVarsity Press, 1995), chap. 2. The topic is developed further in relation to Old Testament ethics in Christopher J. H Wright, *Old Testament Ethics for the People of God* (Downers Grove, Ill.: InterVarsity Press, 2004).

and to set boundaries around our freedom to act in the world. And more specifically for our purpose here, these realities authorize our action in mission. They make our mission appropriate, legitimate and indeed necessary and inevitable. The authority for our mission flows from the Bible because the Bible reveals the reality on which our mission is based.

I have three realities in mind, which are rendered to us first by the Old Testament Scriptures and then confirmed in the New. In these biblical texts we encounter the reality of *this God,* the reality of *this story* and the reality of *this people.*

The reality of this God. It is becoming increasingly important in any talk of God to be clear who we are talking about. *God* is merely an Anglo-Saxon monosyllable that in its origins would more commonly have been plural, *the gods*—the generic term for the deities of the early tribes and settlers of northern Europe. The Bible introduces us to the very specific, named and biographied God known as YHWH, the Holy One of Israel (and other titles). This is the God whom Jesus called Abba. This is the God worshiped as the Lord by Israelites and as Father, Son and Holy Spirit by Christians. This is not a generic god at all.

While the Bible does insist that there is much that has been disclosed about this God through the natural world around us (which is in fact this God's creation), it is fundamentally the texts of the canon of Scripture in both testaments that bring us knowledge of this God. Not only is YHWH the God "enthroned as the Holy One" and "the praise of Israel" (Ps 22:3), he is the God rendered to us by the lips and pens of Israel.[7] YHWH is the reality to which the Old Testament Scriptures testify. His, therefore, is the authority that those Scriptures mediate, because we have no other access to YHWH's reality than through these Scriptures.

This "rendering of God" in the Old Testament includes both God's identity and God's character. The point here is simply this: if the God YHWH, who is rendered to us in these texts, is really God, then that reality (or rather *his reality)* authorizes a range of responses as appropriate, legitimate and indeed imperative. These include not only the response of worship but also of ethical living in accordance with this God's own character and will, and a missional orientation that commits my own life story into the grand story of God's purpose for the nations and for creation. Mission flows from the reality of this God—the biblical God. Or to put it another way: mission is authorized by the reality of this God.

The reality of this story. That the Old Testament tells a story needs no defense.

---

[7]It will be evident that I am indebted here to the fascinating study of Dale Patrick, *The Rendering of God in the Old Testament,* Overtures to Biblical Theology (Philadelphia: Fortress Press, 1981).

My point is much greater, however. The Old Testament tells its story as *the* story or, rather, as a part of that ultimate and universal story that will ultimately embrace the whole of creation, time, and humanity within its scope. In other words, in reading these texts we are invited to embrace a metanarrative, a grand narrative. And on this overarching story is based a worldview that, like all worldviews and metanarratives, claims to explain the way things are, how they have come to be so, and what they ultimately will be.[8]

The story that engages us in the Old Testament answers the four fundamental worldview questions that all religions and philosophies answer in one way or another:[9]

- *Where are we?* (What is the nature of the world around us?)
  Answer: We inhabit the earth, which is part of the good creation of the one living, personal God, YHWH.

- *Who are we?* (What is the essential nature of humanity?)
  Answer: We are human persons made by this God in God's own image, one of God's creatures but unique among them in spiritual and moral relationships and responsibility.

- *What's gone wrong?* (Why is the world in such a mess?)
  Answer: Through rebellion and disobedience against our Creator God, we have generated the mess that we now see around us at every level of our lives, relationships and environment.

- *What is the solution?* (What can we do about it?)
  Answer: Nothing in and of ourselves. But the solution has been initiated by God through his choice and creation of a people, Israel, through whom God intends eventually to bring blessing to all nations of the earth and ultimately to renew the whole creation.

Now the reality of this story is such that it includes us in its scope, for it points to a universal future that embraces all the nations. It is the story that is taken up without question (though not without surprise) in the New Testament. It is the story that stretches from Genesis to Revelation, not merely as a good yarn or

---

[8]On the recent emphasis on the importance of story in biblical hermeneutics, its relevance to missiology, and a defense of treating the biblical story as metanarrative, see Craig Bartholomew and Michael W. Goheen, "Story and Biblical Theology," in *Out of Egypt: Biblical Theology and Biblical Interpretation,* ed. Craig Bartholomew et al. (Carlisle, U.K.: Paternoster; Grand Rapids: Zondervan, 2004), pp. 144-71.

[9]It will be evident here that I am indebted to the helpful analysis of worldviews in J. Richard Middleton and Brian J. Walsh, *Truth Is Stranger Than It Used to Be: Biblical Faith in a Postmodern Age* (Downers Grove, Ill.: InterVarsity Press, 1995).

even as a classic of epic literature, but fundamentally as a *rendering of reality*—an account of the universe we inhabit and of the new creation we are destined for. We live in a storied universe.

And once again, such a rendering of reality carries its intrinsic authority. For if this is truly the way things are, how they have become so and where they are going, then there are all kinds of implications for how we ought to respond personally and collectively. Again, worship, ethics and mission all spring to mind. These responses, including mission, are authorized by the reality of this story.

The reality of this people. The third reality, which the Old Testament Scriptures render to us, is that of the people of Israel. Ancient Israel, with their distinctive view of their own election, history and relationship to their God, YHWH, is a historical reality of enormous significance to the history of the rest of humanity.[10] Christian mission to the nations is deeply rooted in the calling of this people and in the way they saw themselves and their story. In Old Testament terms the story had a past and a future, and both are important in shaping ethical and missional response, for, like Israel, the church is also a community of memory and hope.

Israel's *celebration of its past* is legendary. It was the very stuff of their existence, for it rendered to them not only their own identity and mission, but also that of YHWH, their God.

> Sing to the LORD, praise his *name;*
>> proclaim his *salvation* day after day.
> Declare his *glory* among the nations,
>> his *marvelous deeds* among all peoples. (Ps 96:2-3 emphasis added)

The name, salvation and glory of YHWH were all bound up with "his marvelous deeds." YHWH was known through what he had done, and Israel knew that to preserve YHWH's identity they must tell this story—whether to themselves or (in some way that remained a mystery in Old Testament times) to the nations. For in the telling of the story stood the rendering of the God who was its prime character. So Israel told the story as a bulwark against idolatry (Deut 4:9-40). They told the story as an explanation and motivation for the law (Deut 6:20-25). They told the story as a rebuke to themselves (Ps 105—106; Mic 6:1-8; Amos 2:9-11) or to YHWH himself (Ps 44; 89). They told the story as a comfort and anchor for hope (Jer 32:17-25). Israel's whole theology depended on its memory,

---

[10]Among Old Testament scholars there is, of course, considerable debate over their historical reconstruction of the events by which Israel emerged in the land of Canaan and into the annals of history. But that historical debate need not concern us here since, by whatever process, Israel certainly did emerge and produce a society and a body of traditions and texts that have had an unquestionably profound impact on subsequent human history.

and Israel's memory was constitutive of their peoplehood. The same identity as the people of God with this storied memory constitutes also for us the authority for our mission.

But the story Israel told had an *anticipated future* right at its beginning. They were a people with a future in the purposes of God. The call of Abraham included the promise that through his descendants God intended to bring blessing to all the nations of the earth. That vision shone with greatly varying degrees of clarity or obscurity at different eras of Israel's life, but there is in many places an awareness of the nations as spectators both of what God did in and for Israel, and of how Israel responded positively or negatively (Deut 4:5-8; 29:22-28; Ezek 36:16-23). Ultimately, Israel existed *for the sake of* the nations. We will explore these themes in depth, of course, in the chapters to follow.

So there is a teleological (purposeful) thrust to Israel's existence as a people and the story they narrated and projected. Here is a God with a mission and a people with a mission. Israel's mission was to be a light to the nations so that ultimately "all flesh will see the glory of the LORD" (Is 40:5). Such a vision undoubtedly generated a range of responses within Israel itself. For if this is the future guaranteed by the faithfulness of God, what should be the impact on the way Israel should live now? The question remains authoritative for us too. For we share the same vision of the future, one which to the eyes of faith is a reality, "the substance of things hoped for" (Heb 11:1 KJV), and thereby an ethic-generating and mission-mandating authority for those who live in its light.

So the reality of this people, rendered to us through the texts of the Old Testament, carries authority for an ethic of gratitude in view of God's actions for Israel in the past and carries authority also for our missional intentionality in view of God's purposes for humanity in the future.

Authority and Jesus. These three features of the Old Testament—God, story, and people—are affirmed as realities also for Christian believers in the New Testament. They are all, in fact, focused on Jesus in such a way that their authority and missional relevance is not only sustained but enhanced and transformed for those who are in Christ. At this point we are approaching the missiological significance of a truly *biblical* (i.e., cross-testamental) theology.

In Jesus we meet *this God.* The New Testament unquestionably affirms (as we will see in chap. 4) that Jesus of Nazareth shares the identity and character of YHWH and ultimately accomplishes what only YHWH could.[11] So to know Jesus

---

[11] See especially, N. T. Wright, *Jesus and the Victory of God* (London: SPCK, 1996), and Richard Bauckham, *God Crucified* (Carlisle, U.K.: Paternoster; Grand Rapids: Eerdmans, 1999), my discussion in chap. 4.

as Savior and Lord is to know the reality of the living God. It is to know the way, the truth and the life, the Word, the Creator, Sustainer and heir of the universe. As it was for Israel in knowing YHWH, so for us knowing the reality of Jesus carries its own authority for how we are to live and act in God's world.

In Jesus we have the climax of *this story* and the guarantee of its final ending. This story is also our story, for if we are in Christ then, according to Paul, we are also in Abraham and heirs according to the promise. Our future is the future promised by God to Abraham, achieved by Jesus and to be enjoyed by the whole of redeemed humanity from every nation, tribe, people and language (Rev 7:9-10). Our lives also then are to be shaped by the gratitude that looks back to what God has promised and the mission that looks forward to what God will accomplish.[12]

In Jesus we have become part of *this people,* sharing the comprehensive range of identity and responsibility that was theirs. For through the cross and the gospel of the Messiah Jesus, we have become citizens of God's people, members of God's household, the place of God's dwelling (Eph 2:11—3:13). Such an identity and belonging generate an ethical and a missional responsibility in the church and the world, which the New Testament spells out in some detail.

So then our mission certainly flows from the authority of the Bible. But that authority is far richer and deeper than one big biblical command we must obey. Rather, our obedience to the Great Commission, and even the Great Commission itself, is set within the context of these realities. The Great Commission is not something extra or exotic. Rather, the authority of the Great Commission itself is embedded

- in the reality of the *God* whose universal authority has been given to Jesus

- in the reality of the *story* that the Great Commission both presupposes and envisages

- in the reality of the *people* who are now to become a self-replicating community of disciples among all nations

This is the God we worship, this is the story we are part of, this is the people we belong to. How should we then live? What then is our mission?

Biblical Indicatives and Imperatives in Mission

Another way of looking at this issue is to focus on the point often observed in

---

[12]A fine popular-level portrayal of the whole biblical story as the story of God's commitment to his mission, with its challenge to our participation in it, is provided by Philip Greenslade, *A Passion for God's Story* (Carlisle, U.K.: Paternoster, 2002).

biblical theology, namely, that biblical *imperatives* are characteristically founded on biblical *indicatives*. An indicative is simply a statement of reality (or it claims to be). It is an affirmation or declaration or proposition: This is so; this is how things are. By situating its imperatives in the indicative contexts we have just considered, the Bible effectively grounds their authority in those realities.

A familiar example of this dynamic is the way the Old Testament law is set within a narrative context. The narrative expresses the indicative: Here is what has happened in your history, and these are the things that YHWH your God has done. Then the law expresses the responsive imperative: Now then, this is how you must behave in the light of such facts.

Exodus 19:3-6 classically articulates this order:

> You have seen what I did . . . (the indicative)
> Now, if you will obey me fully and keep my covenant, then . . . (the imperative)

Similarly, the Decalogue begins not with the first imperative commandment but with the indicative statement of God's identity and Israel's story (so far): "I am the LORD your God who brought you out of Egypt, out of the land of slavery" (Ex 20:2). In other words, the indicative of God's grace comes before and is the foundation and authority for the imperative of the law and responsive obedience.

This fundamental priority of grace over law is even more explicit in the answer the father is instructed to give his son when he asks (as countless Christians have done ever since, and might have saved themselves much theological blood, sweat and ink by attending to the father's answer), "What is [the meaning of] all this law?" The father responds not simply with a reinforced imperative ("Just do it") but with a story, the exodus story, the old, old story of YHWH and his love—that is, with the indicative of redemption. The very meaning of the law is grounded in the gospel of God's saving grace in history (Deut 6:20-25).

Now when we think of the Great Commission, it is sometimes pointed out that whereas the text is never actually given that title in the Gospels themselves, Jesus did emphatically endorse the Great *Commandment,* in so many words. Asked about the greatest commandment in the law (a familiar debating point in his day), he pointed to the magnificent *šĕmaʿ* of Deuteronomy 6:4-5, which is about loving God with all our heart and soul and strength, complementing it with Leviticus 19:18, the command to love our neighbors as ourselves. But what we must not miss is that both these commandments are founded on indicatives about the identity, uniqueness, singularity and holiness of YHWH as God.

> Hear, O Israel: The LORD our God, the LORD is one. (Deut 6:4)

> Be holy because I, the LORD your God, am holy. (Lev 19:2)

It is *the reality of* YHWH that constitutes the authority for these greatest commandments, on which, Jesus declared, hang all the rest of the law and the prophets.

Here, then, we have a very clear imperative—to love God with the totality of our being and to love our neighbor as ourselves. This could easily be described, with even more textual justification, as "the great commission," for it governs the whole of life whatever our specific calling. This fundamental twin commandment certainly precedes, underlies and governs the so-called Great Commission itself, for we cannot make disciples of the nations without love for God and love for them.

So it is no surprise, therefore, to find that when we come to the Great Commission, it too follows the same formula: indicative followed by imperative. Jesus begins with the monumental cosmic claim, words that echo the affirmation of Moses about YHWH himself (Deut 4:35, 39), that "all authority in heaven and on earth has been given to me" (Mt 28:18). This is the reality behind the command, the indicative behind the imperative. The identity and the authority of Jesus of Nazareth, crucified and risen, is the cosmic indicative on which the mission imperative stands authorized.

But in order to understand all that such an indicative claim for Jesus implies and includes, we need the whole of the Scriptures—as he himself affirmed when, in Luke's version, he draws both the significance of his own messianic identity and the anticipation of the church's missional future from the bold indicative "this is what is written" (Lk 24:46). We need, then, both a missional hermeneutic of the *whole* Bible and its great indicatives as well as committed obedience to a major imperative text like the Great Commission.[13]

A missional hermeneutic, then, is not content simply to call for obedience to the Great *Commission* (though it will assuredly include that as a matter of nonnegotiable importance), nor even to reflect on the missional implications of the Great *Commandment*. For behind both it will find the Great *Communication*—the revelation of the identity of God, of God's action in the world and God's saving purpose for all creation. And for the fullness of this communication we need the whole Bible in all its parts and genres, for God has given

---

[13]This point is made, somewhat differently but with a similar desire to avoid "the abuse of the imperative," by Graeme Goldsworthy. He also notes that the apparent absence of a missionary mandate in the Old Testament (i.e., that Israelites should actually go to the nations) is balanced by the assumption of what Israel was simply meant to be in the world: "The function of Israel in the purposes of God to bring salvation to the nations is in the indicative, not the imperative." Graeme L. Goldsworthy, "The Great Indicative: An Aspect of a Biblical Theology of Mission," *Reformed Theological Review* 55 (1996): 7.

us no less. A missional hermeneutic takes the indicative and the imperative of the biblical revelation with equal seriousness, and interprets each in the light of the other.

Such mutual interpretation of indicative and imperative in the light of each other means that, on the one hand, biblical missiology (like biblical and systematic theology) revels in exploring the great indicative themes and traditions of the biblical faith in all their complexity and remarkable coherence. But biblical missiology recognizes, on the other hand, that if all this indicative theology is indicative of *reality,* then that carries a massive missional imperative for those who claim this worldview as their own. If this is how it really is with God, humanity and the world, then what claim does that make on the life of the church and individual believers?

Conversely, a missional hermeneutic of the whole Bible will not become obsessed with only the great mission imperatives, such as the Great Commission, or be tempted to impose on them one assumed priority or another (e.g., evangelism or social justice or liberation or ecclesiastical order as the only "real" mission). Rather we will set those great imperatives within the context of their foundational indicatives, namely, all that the Bible affirms about God, creation, human life in its paradox of dignity and depravity, redemption in all its comprehensive glory, and the new creation in which God will dwell with his people.

A missional hermeneutic, then, cannot read biblical indicatives without their implied imperatives. Nor can it isolate biblical imperatives from the totality of the biblical indicative. It seeks a holistic understanding of mission from a holistic reading of the biblical texts.

The Biblical Theocentric Worldview and the Mission of God

However, even if we accept, returning to the introduction, that Jesus offers us a Messiah-focused and mission-generating hermeneutic of the Scriptures, we may still query the claim that somehow there is a missional hermeneutic of the whole Bible such that "mission is what it's all about." This uneasiness stems from the persistent, almost subconscious, paradigm that mission is fundamentally and primarily something *we* do—a human task of the church. This is especially so if we fall into the reductionist habit of using the word *mission* (or *missions*) as more or less synonymous with evangelism. Quite clearly the whole Bible is not just about evangelism, and I am certainly not trying to claim that it is—even though evangelism is certainly a fundamental part of biblical mission as entrusted to us. To be sure, evangelism *is* something we do and it *is* validated by clear biblical imperatives. But it will not bear the weight of the case for saying that the whole Bible can be hermeneutically approached from a missional perspective.

The appropriateness of speaking of "a missional basis of the Bible" becomes apparent only when we shift our paradigm of mission from

- our human agency to the ultimate purposes of God himself

- mission as "missions" that we undertake, to mission as that which God has been purposing and accomplishing from eternity to eternity

- an anthropocentric (or ecclesiocentric) conception to a radically theocentric worldview

In shifting our perspective in this way and trying to come to a biblical definition of what we mean by mission, we are in effect asking the question, *Whose mission is it anyway?* The answer, it seems to me, could be expressed as a paraphrase of the song of the redeemed in the new creation. "Salvation belongs to our God, / who sits on the throne, / and to the Lamb" (Rev 7:10). Since the whole Bible is the story of how this God, "our God," has brought about his salvation for the whole cosmos (represented in concentric circles around God's throne in the magnificent neck-craning vision of Revelation 4—7), we can affirm with equal validity, "Mission belongs to our God." *Mission is not ours; mission is God's.* Certainly, the mission of God is the prior reality out of which flows any mission that we get involved in. Or, as has been nicely put, it is not so much the case that God has a mission for his church in the world but that God has a church for his mission in the world. Mission was not made for the church; the church was made for mission—God's mission.[14]

A missional hermeneutic of the Bible, then, begins there—with the mission of God—and traces the flow of all other dimensions of mission as they affect human history from that center and starting point.

God with a mission. The term *missio Dei,* "the mission of God," has a long history.[15] It seems to go back to a German missiologist Karl Hartenstein. He coined it as a way of summarizing the teaching of Karl Barth, "who, in a lecture on mission in 1928, had connected mission with the doctrine of the trinity. Barth and Hartenstein want to make clear that mission is grounded in an intratrinitarian movement of God himself and that it expresses the power of God over his-

---

[14]See chap. 2, "God's Mission and the Church's Response," of J. Andrew Kirk, *What Is Mission? Theological Explorations* (London: Darton, Longman & Todd; Minneapolis: Fortress Press, 1999), pp. 23-37.

[15]For a brief survey of the history, see David J. Bosch, *Transforming Mission: Paradigm Shifts in Theology of Mission* (Maryknoll, N.Y.: Orbis, 1991), pp. 389-93.

tory, to which the only appropriate response is obedience."[16] So the phrase originally meant "the sending of God"—in the sense of the Father's sending of the Son and their sending of the Holy Spirit. All human mission, in this perspective, is seen as a participation in and extension of this divine sending.

The phrase became popular in ecumenical circles after the Willingen world mission conference of 1952, through the work of Georg Vicedom.[17] It had the strength of connecting mission to the theology of the Trinity—an important theological gain. Mission flows from the inner dynamic movement of God in personal relationship. But in some circles the concept of *missio Dei* then became seriously weakened by the idea that it referred simply to God's involvement with the whole historical process, not to any specific work of the church. The affirmation that mission was God's came to mean that it was not ours! Such distorted theology virtually excluded evangelism, and quite rightly therefore came under sustained criticism.

In spite of such misuse, however, the expression can be retained as expressing a major and vital biblical truth (as the title *The Mission of God* is intended to reaffirm). The God revealed in the Scriptures is personal, purposeful and goal-orientated. The opening account of creation portrays God working toward a goal, completing it with satisfaction and resting, content with the result. And from the great promise of God to Abraham in Genesis 12:1-3 we know this God to be totally, covenantally and eternally committed to the mission of blessing the nations through the agency of the people of Abraham. In the wake of Genesis 3—11 this is good news indeed for humanity—such that Paul can describe this text as "the gospel in advance" (Gal 3:8). From that point on, the mission of God could be summed up in the words "God is working his purpose out / as year succeeds to year," and as generations come and go.[18]

The Bible presents itself to us fundamentally as a narrative, a historical narrative at one level, but a grand metanarrative at another.

- It begins with the God of purpose in creation
- moves on to the conflict and problem generated by human rebellion against that purpose
- spends most of its narrative journey in the story of God's redemptive pur-

---

[16]L. A. Hoedemaker, "The People of God and the Ends of the Earth," in *Missiology: An Ecumenical Introduction,* ed. A Camps, L. A. Hoedemaker and M. R. Spindler (Grand Rapids: Eerdmans, 1995), p. 163. Hoedemaker provides an interesting and critical survey of the history of *missio Dei,* and its weaknesses.

[17]Georg F. Vicedom, *The Mission of God: An Introduction to a Theology of Mission,* ed. Gilbert A. Thiele and Dennis Hilgendorf (1958; reprint, St. Louis: Concordia Press, 1965).

[18]Arthur Campbell Aigner, "God Is Working His Purpose Out" (1894).

poses being worked out on the stage of human history

- finishes beyond the horizon of its own history with the eschatological hope of a new creation

This has often been presented as a four-point narrative: *creation, fall, redemption,* and *future hope.* This whole worldview is predicated on teleological monotheism: that is, the affirmation that there is one God at work in the universe and in human history, and that this God has a goal, a purpose, a mission that will ultimately be accomplished by the power of God's Word and for the glory of God's name. This is the mission of the biblical God.

It is of course not just a single narrative, like a river with only one channel. It is rather a complex mixture of all kinds of smaller narratives, many of them rather self-contained, with all kinds of other material embedded within them— more like a great delta. But there is clearly a direction, a flow, that can be described in the terms I have layed out. Richard Bauckham says it is important that "the Bible does not have a carefully plotted single story-line, like, for example, a conventional novel. It is a sprawling collection of narratives." It is not an aggressively totalizing story that suppresses all others—the accusation that postmodernism makes against all metanarratives. Rather,

> these inescapable features of the actual narrative form of Scripture surely have a message in themselves: that the particular has its own integrity that should not be suppressed for the sake of a too readily comprehensible universal. The Bible does, in some sense, tell an overall story that encompasses all its other contents, but this story is not a sort of straitjacket that reduces all else to a narrowly defined uniformity. It is a story that is hospitable to considerable diversity and to tensions, challenges and even seeming contradictions of its own claims. [19]

To read the whole Bible in the light of this great overarching perspective of the mission of God, then, is to read with the grain of this whole collection of texts that constitute our canon of Scripture. In my view this is the key assumption of a missional hermeneutic of the Bible. It is nothing more than to accept that the biblical worldview locates us in the midst of a narrative of the universe behind which stands the mission of the living God.

> Glory be to the Father, and to the Son, and to the Holy Ghost,
> As it was in the beginning, is now, and ever shall be,
> World without end, Amen.

---

[19]Richard Bauckham, *The Bible and Mission: Christian Mission in a Postmodern World* (Carlisle, U.K.: Paternoster, 2003), pp. 92-94.

This is not just a liturgically conventional way to end prayers and canticles. It is a missional perspective on history past, present and future, and one day it will be the song of the whole creation.

Humanity with a mission. From this theocentric starting point, *God with a mission,* we can in summary see the other major dimensions of mission flowing through the Bible, which we will explore further in the rest of this book. In its opening chapters we meet *humanity with a mission* on the planet that had been purposefully prepared for their arrival—the mandate to fill the earth, subdue it and to rule over the rest of creation (Gen 1:28). This delegated authority within the created order is moderated by the parallel commands in the complementary account, "to work . . . and to take care of" the Garden (Gen 2:15). The care and keeping of creation is our human mission. The human race exists on the planet with a purpose that flows from the creative purpose of God himself. Out of this understanding of our humanity (which is also teleological, like our doctrine of God) flows our ecological responsibility, our economic activity involving work, productivity, exchange and trade, and the whole cultural mandate. To be human is to have a purposeful role in God's creation. We will return to these themes in chapters twelve and thirteen.

Israel with a mission. Then, against the background of human sin and rebellion in Genesis 3—11, we encounter *Israel with a mission,* beginning with the call of Abraham in Genesis 12. Israel came into existence as a people with a mission entrusted to them from God for the sake of God's wider purpose of blessing the nations. Israel's election was not a rejection of other nations but was explicitly for the sake of all nations. This universality of God's purpose, that nevertheless embraces the particularity of God's chosen means, is a recurrent theme and a constant theological challenge (to Israel as much as to contemporary theologians). With Israel, of course, we embark on the longest part of the biblical journey, and the great themes of election, redemption, covenant, worship, ethics, and eschatology all await our missiological reflection. They will fill part three of this book.

Jesus with a mission. Into the midst of this people—saturated with Scriptures, sustained by memory and hope, waiting for God—steps *Jesus with a mission.* Jesus did not just arrive. He had a very clear conviction that he was sent. The voice of his Father at his baptism combined the identity of the Servant figure in Isaiah (echoing the phraseology of Is 42:1), and that of the Davidic messianic king (echoing the affirmation of Ps 2:7). Both of these dimensions of his identity and role were energized with a sense of mission. The mission of the Servant was both to restore Israel to YHWH and also to be the agent of God's salvation reaching to the ends of the earth (Is 49:6). The mission of the Davidic messianic king was both to rule over a redeemed Israel, according to the agenda of many prophetic texts, and also to receive the nations and the ends of the earth as his heritage (Ps 2:8).

Jesus' sense of mission—the aims, motivation and self-understanding behind his recorded words and actions—has been a matter of intense scholarly discussion. What seems very clear is that Jesus built his own agenda on what he perceived to be the agenda of his Father. Jesus' will was to do his Father's will, so he said. God's mission determined his mission. In Jesus the radically theocentric nature of biblical mission is most clearly focused and modeled. In the obedience of Jesus, even to death, the mission of God reached its climax. For "God was reconciling the world to himself in Christ" (2 Cor 5:19).

The church with a mission. Finally, the biblical narrative introduces us to ourselves as *the church with a mission*. As Luke 24:45-47 indicates, Jesus entrusted to the church a mission that is directly rooted in his own identity, passion and victory as the crucified and risen Messiah. Jesus immediately followed this text with the words, "You are witnesses"—a mandate repeated in Acts 1:8, "You will be my witnesses." It is almost certain that Luke intends us to hear in this an echo of the same words spoken by YHWH to Israel in Isaiah 43:10-12.

> "You are my witnesses," declares the LORD,
>   "and my servant whom I have chosen,
> so that you may know and believe me,
>   and understand that I am he.
> Before me no god was formed,
>   nor will there be one after me.
> I, even I, am the LORD,
>   and apart from me there is no savior.
> I have revealed and saved and proclaimed—
>   I, and not some foreign god among you.
> You are my witnesses," declares the LORD, "that I am God."

Israel knew the identity of the true and living God, YHWH; therefore they were entrusted with bearing witness to that in a world of nations and their gods. The disciples now know the true identity of the crucified and risen Jesus; therefore they are entrusted with bearing witness to that to the ends of the earth.[20] The church's mission flows from the identity of God and his Christ. When you

---

[20]It is probable that in its immediate context (Lk 24 and Acts 1), the language of "witness" refers primarily to the role of the apostles as direct eyewitnesses of the Lord Jesus Christ, and especially of his resurrection. However, since that specific and unique apostolic witness forms the basis of the continuing witness by all believers to the gospel of Christ, it is not inappropriate to discern the wider and long-term missional implications of the term here.

know who God is, when you know who Jesus is, witnessing mission is the un-avoidable outcome.

Paul goes further and identifies his own mission with the international mission of the Servant of the Lord. Quoting Isaiah 49:6 in Acts 13:47 he declares quite bluntly:

> This is what the Lord has commanded *us:*
> "I have made you a light for the Gentiles,
>   that you may bring salvation to the ends of the earth." (emphasis added)

This is a missiological hermeneutic of the Old Testament if ever there was one. As the NIV footnote shows, Paul has no problem applying the singular "you" (which was spoken to the Servant) to the plural "us" (himself and his small band of church planters). So again, the mission of the church flows from the mission of God and the fulfillment of God's mandate.

Mission, then, in biblical terms, while it inescapably involves us in planning and action, is not *primarily* a matter of our activity or our initiative. Mission, from the point of view of our human endeavor, means the committed *participation* of God's people in the purposes of God for the redemption of the whole creation. The mission is God's. The marvel is that God invites us to join in.

> Mission arises from the heart of God himself and is communicated from his heart to ours. Mission is the global outreach of the global people of a global God.[21]

Putting these perspectives together, a missional hermeneutic means that we seek to read any part of the Bible in the light of

- God's purpose for his whole creation, including the redemption of humanity and the creation of the new heavens and new earth

- God's purpose for human life in general on the planet and of all the Bible teaches about human culture, relationships, ethics and behavior

- God's historical election of Israel, their identity and role in relation to the nations, and the demands he made on their worship, social ethics, and total value system

- the centrality of Jesus of Nazareth, his messianic identity and mission in relation to Israel and the nations, his cross and resurrection

- God's calling of the church, the community of believing Jews and Gentiles who constitute the extended people of the Abraham covenant, to be the

---

[21]John Stott, *The Contemporary Christian: An Urgent Plea for Double Listening* (Downers Grove, Ill.: InterVarsity Press, 1992), p. 335.

agent of God's blessing to the nations in the name and for the glory of the
Lord Jesus Christ

A Hermeneutical Map

The validity of any framework for hermeneutics or for biblical theology must
always be open to critique, and the one who offers it must be humble enough
to recognize that ultimately it is the text that must govern the framework, and
not the other way round. This is the challenge of Anthony Billington's question:
"Does this or that particular framework *do justice* to the thrust of the text in its
biblical-theological context? Or does it *distort* the text?"[22] I repeat my agreement
with Billington's concern. All I would ask is that the missional framework I propose in this volume be evaluated for its heuristic fruitfulness. Does it in fact do
justice to the overall thrust of the biblical canon? Does it illuminate and clarify?
Does it offer a way of articulating the coherence of the Bible's overarching message? Only the reader can answer, if he or she can stay with me through the
long biblical journey ahead.

There is, however, a sense in which *any* framework necessarily distorts the
text to some degree. The only way not to distort the biblical text is simply to
reproduce it as it is. Any attempt to summarize or provide some system or pattern for grasping it, or some structure to organize its content, cannot but distort
the givenness of the original reality—the text itself.

In this respect, a hermeneutical framework for reading the Bible (like any
scheme of biblical theology) functions rather like a map. As cartographers will
agree, every existing map and any possible map is a distortion to some degree
of the reality it portrays. Maps of the world are the clearest examples of this.
There is simply no way of producing on a two-dimensional plane the reality of
the three-dimensional globe without distortion. So all world maps ("projec-
tions") compromise on where the unavoidable distortion occurs—the shape of
the continents, their relative area, the lines of latitude and longitude, distortion
at the poles or compass orientation, and so forth. The choice will depend on
who the map is for and what it is intended primarily to show.

With larger scale maps of smaller areas (e.g., for walking in the countryside
or finding one's way in a city), the question becomes one of what is included
or excluded from the symbolic representation that all maps are. Not every feature of the real landscape can be on a map, so the question again is, What purpose is the map intended to serve? What are the most significant features that

---

[22]Anthony Billington, unpublished written response to my Laing Lecture at London Bible College, October 1998.

the person using this map will need to see clearly? What can then be omitted—not because they don't exist in the geographical reality but because they are not of primary relevance to this particular way of viewing that reality? Somewhere there must be maps of the sewers of London. They are doubtless of crucial importance to local city engineers, but they are of limited value to tourists. It is more than they need to know. The map of the London Underground is a classic and brilliant representation of that transport system, invaluable to tourists while underground but of very limited value on the streets above. It distorts and omits in order to simplify and clarify. And indeed that iconic diagram provides a much more comprehensible framework for understanding London by Tube (subway) than any map would do that showed all the Underground lines in their actual twists and turns, distances and directions. Furthermore, we all know that the Underground map is a distortion of reality for the purpose for which it was designed—to enable us to navigate the actual reality of the Tubes simply and safely. The degree of distortion is justified and accepted for what it is, and we do not accuse it of falsehood or of misleading the public. Distortion, in this context, is not at all the same thing as inaccuracy. In its own terms the London Underground map is a comprehensively accurate document.

I think there is some value in this analogy of comparing hermeneutical frameworks to maps. The given reality is the whole text of the Bible itself. No framework can give account of every detail, just as no map can represent every tiny feature of a landscape. But like a map, a hermeneutical framework can provide a way of seeing the whole terrain, a way of navigating one's way through it, a way of observing what is most significant, a way of approaching the task of actually encountering the reality itself (just as a map tells you what to expect when you are actually in the terrain it portrays).

A missional hermeneutic such as I have sketched seems to me to fulfill some of these mapping requirements. It does not claim to explain every feature of the vast terrain of the Bible, nor to foreclose in advance the exegesis of any specific text. But when you encounter on your hike some feature of the landscape that is not marked on your map, you do not deny its existence because it has no place on your map. Nor do you necessarily blame the map for choosing not to include it. Rather, the map enables you to set that feature in its proper geographical location and relationship with the other features around you.

The more I have attempted to use (or stimulate others to use) a missional map of the Bible, orientated fundamentally to the mission of God, the more it seems that not only do the major features of the landscape stand out clearly but also other less well-trodden paths and less scenic scholarly tourist attractions turn out to have surprising and fruitful connections with the main panorama.

PART II THE GOD OF MISSION

To the LORD your God belong the heavens, even the highest heavens, the earth and everything in it. (Deut 10:14)

O LORD, God of Israel, . . . you alone are God over all the kingdoms of the earth. You have made heaven and earth. (2 Kings 19:15)

I am the LORD, the God of all mankind. Is anything too hard for me? (Jer 32:27)

The Holy One of Israel is your Redeemer;
he is called the God of all the earth. (Is 54:5)

Will not the Judge of all the earth do right? (Gen 18:25)

For God is the King of all the earth. (Ps 47:7)

Wherever you look in the canon of the Old Testament, there are texts to be found that declare that YHWH, the Lord God of Israel, is the one and only universal God of all the earth or of all the nations or of all humanity. YHWH made all, owns all, rules all. The sample texts above are drawn from the Torah, narratives, Prophets and Psalms. The uniqueness and universality of YHWH are foundational axioms of Old Testament faith, which in turn are foundational to New Testament Christian faith, worship and mission. In the three chapters of part two we will survey some dimensions of that axiomatic monotheistic worldview as they affect our understanding of biblical mission.

If YHWH alone is the one true living God who made himself known in Israel and who wills to be known to the ends of the earth, then our mission can contemplate no lesser goal (chap. 3).

If Jesus of Nazareth is the one who embodies the identity and mission of YHWH, the one to whom the Lord God has given all authority in heaven and earth, the one to whom every knee will bow and every tongue confess that he is Lord, then the Christ-centered heartbeat and witness of all our mission is non-negotiable (chap. 4).

If the conflict between the living God and his Christ, on the one hand, and all that human and satanic effort erects in the form of other gods and idols, on the other, constitutes the great cosmic drama of the biblical narrative, then our mission must involve us in that conflict with idolatry, assured of the ultimate victory of God over all that opposes his universal reign (chap. 5).

Before we embark on these tasks, however, two further introductory points need to be made.

First, questions surrounding the *historical origins* of monotheism in ancient Israel are not our concern here. This has been the focus of very extensive scholarly and critical inquiry for many years, and it is beyond the scope of this work to survey it in depth. What we have in our hands as the Hebrew Scriptures, our Old Testament as Christian readers, is of course just that—the Scriptures as preserved and handed down within the canonical tradition by those who represented the "official" faith of Israel, as it were, but it is difficult to have access to the religious minds of average Israelites at any given point in Israel's Old Testament history, except to say that much confusion seems to have resided there. Even within the pages of Israel's Scriptures we are explicitly informed of the long struggle through many generations of Israel between popular religion and advocates of the monotheistic covenant faith portrayed in the documents. There were those who understood this covenant faith to demand the worship of YHWH alone and there were those who saw fit, for many reasons, to worship other gods instead of (or more probably often as well as) YHWH. Such archaeological evidence as we have appears to confirm the impression we get from prophets like Hosea, Jeremiah and Ezekiel that there was a confusion of popular polytheistic cults being practiced on the soil of Israel (including cults of female deities, such as Asherah).[1]

Historians of the religion of Israel offer us various reconstructions of the stages by which it is assumed Israel became truly monotheistic. It seems clear that from a very early stage Israel had a conviction that to be Israelite required an exclusive attachment to YHWH as their God. This is sometimes called "mono-Yahwism." Whether this commitment to YHWH originally included the conviction that YHWH was the *only* deity in reality (as distinct from the only deity Israel was to worship), and if not, by what stages and by what date such

---

[1]The most recent survey of this archaeological material and its bearing on Israelite religion and Old Testament monotheism is provided by William Dever, *Did God Have a Wife? Archaeology and Folk Religion in Ancient Israel* (Grand Rapids: Eerdmans, 2005).

a conviction eventually took hold, is a matter of continued and inconclusive debate. [2]

However, it seems to me that the extent to which affirmations of *YHWH's uniqueness and universality* penetrated all the genres of Israel's texts allows room for believing that there was a radically monotheistic core to Israel's faith from a very early period, however much it was obscured and compromised in popular religious practice.[3]

Second, however, we have to ask, What does *monotheism* mean in this context? If we bring to our investigation a predefined assumption about monotheism in abstract philosophical terms and then measure Israel against our definition, we will get a rather reduced perspective on Israel's monotheism. In fact, as Nathan MacDonald and Richard Bauckham have shown, the captivity of the Western theological academy in general to Enlightenment categories as the framework for defining monotheism has led on the one hand to serious misunderstanding of the core claims of Israel regarding YHWH and, on the other hand, to speculative reconstructions of the evolution of monotheism in Israel which are intrinsically unverifiable and incompatible with the witness of the biblical text itself.[4]

If, instead, we ask what the people of *Israel* meant when they said such things as "YHWH is God and there is no other," then we may come to an understanding of monotheism more in line with Israel's own dynamic faith. That is, we should seek to understand Israel's religious and theological world from within, rather than squeezing it through the sieve of our categories.

---

[2]There is an enormous quantity of scholarly study of the question of monotheism in the religion of Israel and the theology of the Old Testament, which we cannot engage with here. A recent study that provides a comprehensive survey and bibliography of the range of scholarship on the matter is, Robert Karl Gnuse, *No Other Gods: Emergent Monotheism in Israel,* JSOT Supplement Series 241 (Sheffield, U.K.: Sheffield Academic Press, 1997). A shorter but very perceptive assessment of the topic (including a critique of Gnuse) is provided by Richard Bauckham, "Biblical Theology and the Problems of Monotheism," in *Out of Egypt: Biblical Theology and Biblical Interpretation,* ed. Craig Bartholomew et al. (Carlisle, U.K.: Paternoster; Grand Rapids: Zondervan, 2004), pp. 187-232.

[3]Peter Machinist surveyed some 433 texts affirming different elements of the distinctiveness of Israel's faith—particularly those affirming the uniqueness of Israel's God—and comments on the striking fact that they are found in all the genres and at every stage of the Old Testament literature: "The Question of Distinctiveness in Ancient Israel," in *Essential Papers on Israel and the Ancient Near East,* ed. F. E. Greenspan (New York: New York University Press, 1991), pp. 420-42. A similar point is made by Ronald E. Clements, "Monotheism and the Canonical Process," *Theology* 87 (1984): 336-44.

[4]Nathan MacDonald, *Deuteronomy and the Meaning of "Monotheism"* (Tübingen: Mohr Siebeck, 2003). See also, Nathan MacDonald, "Whose Monotheism? Which Rationality?" in *The Old Testament in Its World,* ed. Robert P. Gordon and Johannes C. de Moor (Leiden: Brill, 2005), pp. 45-67. Richard Bauckham, "Biblical Theology and the Problems of Monotheism."

Or if we ask, What did Israel mean by "*knowing* the LORD," we will open up a rich vein of biblical monotheistic teaching. This wonderfully flexible term has several significant dimensions. YHWH presents himself as the God who wills to be known. This self-communicating drive is involved in everything God does in creation, revelation, salvation and judgment. Human beings therefore are summoned to know YHWH as God, on the clear assumption that they *can* know him and that God wills that they *should* know him. Those who stand in elect and covenant relationship with God are entrusted with this knowledge and must live accordingly, but ultimately all humanity will know YHWH to be the true God one way or another. Accordingly, making God known is part of the mission of those who are called to participate in the mission of the God who wills to be known. *"Knowing YHWH,"* then, is among those dynamic Old Testament expressions by which an Israelite might have expressed what we would call monotheism. So it is that voyage of discovery on which we now embark. How did Israel come to know YHWH as God alone? How did they envisage others coming to the same knowledge?

Our pathway through these three chapters then, will be as follows. In chapter three we will note how Israel came to know the uniqueness of YHWH through their experience of God's redemptive grace, especially in the key events of the exodus and the return from exile. But then we will also note the converse—how Israel and other nations came to know YHWH through exposure to God's judgment. Then in chapter four, moving on from the Old Testament, we will see how the New Testament fills out the knowledge of God by recognizing his identity in the person of Jesus of Nazareth as Lord and Christ. After that, we will draw the threads of those two chapters together and ask why biblical monotheism is missional, or to put it another way in line with the purpose of this book, how a missional hermeneutic illumines our reading of these great biblical monotheistic affirmations regarding YHWH and Jesus Christ. We cannot leave our survey of monotheism and mission, however, without attention to its dark side—the conflict with gods and idols. So in chapter five we will analyze what the Old Testament has to say about this phenomenon, tackling in the process what seem to me to be some rather superficial and patronizing misunderstandings of its polemic. Finally we will reflect on how Christian mission should address the continuing reality of idolatry, drawing on the nuanced tactics that we find in the mission practice and writings of the apostle Paul.

3

The Living God
Makes Himself Known in Israel

I t is something of a truism that in the Bible God is known through what God does and says. So the combination of the mighty acts of God and the words through which those acts were anticipated, explained and celebrated form the twin core of so much of the Old Testament literature. Two mighty acts in particular, at either end of Israel Old Testament history, are recorded as occasions par excellence when Israel came to know their God—the exodus and the return from exile. In both cases we will consider some of the key truths that Israel associated with these events and how they relate to the uniqueness and universality of YHWH. This in turn shapes and informs our understanding of this dimension of God's mission—his will to be known for who he is.

Knowing God Through the Experience of God's Grace

The exodus. The exodus stands in the Hebrew Scriptures as the great defining demonstration of YHWH's power, love, faithfulness and liberating intervention on behalf of his people. It was thus a major act of self-revelation by God, and also a massive learning experience for Israel. Indeed, even before it happened, the prophetic word of God through Moses in anticipation of it emphasizes this as part of its purpose.

YHWH wills to be known. Exodus 5:22—6:8 is a pivotal text in the developing story. Since Moses' arrival in Egypt and his demands on Pharaoh to grant freedom to the Hebrew slaves, things have gone from bad to worse (Ex 5:1-14). As the oppression becomes more severe, the leaders complain to Moses, and Moses in turn complains to God. He accuses God of failing to deliver on his rhetoric of salvation at the burning bush (Ex 5:15-23). In response God offers a renewed clarification of his identity (Ex 6:2-3) and a concise but comprehensive summary of his redemptive intentions (Ex 6:6-8). Exodus 6:6-8 is God's mission statement in relation to this whole narrative.

On the warranty of his own name and character ("I am the LORD" is repeated at the beginning and end, vv. 6, 8), God promises to do three things for Israel:

- to liberate them from the Egyptian yoke

- to enter into a mutual covenant relationship with them

- to bring them into the land promised to their forefathers

The only thing that Israel will do in the whole scenario is that they will come to *know YHWH* conclusively as God through these events: "Then you will know that I am the LORD your God, who brought you out from under the yoke of the Egyptians" (Ex 6:7). The following months and years would see Israel on a steep learning curve, but by the end of it their worldview would be changed forever. They would know who was truly God in Egypt (and everywhere else).

So the anticipated outcome of the exodus was that Israel should know YHWH as God and should also know some fundamental truths about his character and power. This indeed is how Deuteronomy looks back on the great events of that generation. Those events constituted an unprecedented and unparalleled revelation of the identity and uniqueness of the Lord, the God of Israel. And they had been planned for exactly that purpose.

> Ask now about the former days, long before your time, from the day God created man on the earth; ask from one end of the heavens to the other. Has anything so great as this ever happened, or has anything like it ever been heard of? Has any other people heard the voice of God speaking out of fire, as you have, and lived? Has any other god ever tried to take for himself one nation out of another nation, by testings, by miraculous signs and wonders, by war, by a mighty hand and an outstretched arm, or by great and awesome deeds, like all the things the LORD your God did for you in Egypt before your very eyes?
>
> *You were shown these things so that you might know that the LORD is God; beside him there is no other.* (Deut 4:32-35 [repeated in 36-39], emphasis added)

What then did Israel come to know about YHWH through the exodus? Three lessons stand out for attention, two drawn from Exodus 15: (1) that YHWH is *incomparable* and (2) that he is *sovereign;* and one drawn from Deuteronomy 4: that YHWH is *unique.*

The Song of Moses (Ex 15:1-18), which is acknowledged by most scholars to be among the earliest of the poetic texts in the Old Testament, celebrates two ringing conclusions that could be drawn from what God had done for Israel in bringing them out of Egypt and safely across the sea to freedom.

YHWH is incomparable. This is the thrust of the rhetorical question, "Who is like you?" which surfaces here and echoes in other texts.

Who among the gods is like you, O LORD?
Who is like you—
majestic in holiness,
awesome in glory,
working wonders? (Ex 15:11)

YHWH had proved himself superior to "all the gods of Egypt" (Ex 12:12) in the massive demonstration of power that occupies the previous eight chapters of Exodus. Whatever may or may not have been believed about YHWH in relation to what we call monotheism—that is, whether this is a claim for YHWH's sole deity—is not the concern here. All that matters is that Israel's God is clearly the most powerful God around. YHWH is beyond comparison when it comes to a conflict of wills and power. Whoever or whatever the gods of Egypt may be (and the narrator does not even trouble to name them, any more than he names the Pharaoh who claimed to be one of them), the God of Israel is more than a match for all of them.

Similar rhetoric is used elsewhere in the Old Testament to express wonder and admiration for YHWH as the God without equal. The affirmation that there is no god like YHWH ("none like him" or "none like you") declares him to be beyond comparison:

- in keeping promises and fulfilling his word (2 Sam 7:22)

- in power and wisdom, especially as seen in creation (Jer 10:6-7, 11-12)

- in the heavenly assembly (Ps 89:6-8)

- in ruling over the nations (Jer 49:19; 50:44)

- in pardoning sin and forgiving transgression (Mic 7:18)

- in saving power on behalf of his people (Is 64:4)

And because there is none like YHWH, all nations will eventually come and worship *him* as the only true God (Ps 86:8-9). This is the missional dimension of this great truth, which we will pick up and expand in chapters fourteen and fifteen.

So an important truth that Israel came to know about YHWH through the exodus is that he is incomparably greater than other gods. This is affirmed with such superlative intensity that it is tantamount to the more truly monotheistic claim. That is to say, the simple reason why YHWH is incomparable is that there is nothing in reality to compare him with. YHWH stands in a class of his own.

YHWH is King. The climax of the Song of Moses is the triumphant acclamation: "The LORD will reign for ever and ever" (Ex 15:18). The form of the Hebrew verb is imperfect; it has the flexibility of meaning "he has now demonstrated that he is king, he is now reigning, and he will go on reigning forever."[1] This is the first significant time the kingdom of God is mentioned in the Bible, and it comes in the specific context of YHWH's victory over those who have oppressed his people and refused to know him (Ex 5:2). So there is a confrontational, polemical dimension to this affirmation of YHWH as king. Because YHWH is king, *other* kings (Egyptian or Canaanite) tremble.

In this Exodus text the kingship of YHWH is set in the context of the historical crossing of the sea and defeat of Pharaoh's army. But the Hebrew poetic imagery draws on mythic traditions of the ancient Near East and particularly from Canaanite epics of El and Baal. At Ugarit, Baal was praised as "our king" and "Lord of Earth." He achieved this position after great victories over the primordial chaos represented by the great god Yamm (Sea). Then, having defeated Sea, Baal sits enthroned above it, on the sacred mountain from where he exercises his "eternal kingdom." Such motifs as the defeat of the sea, command of the winds, crushing of the sea dragon (Rahab), being enthroned over the deep (or the flood) and reigning from the holy mountain are drawn from the world of Canaanite mythology.[2] But they are also found within the Old Testament (as here in Ex 15), as a way of expressing and celebrating the reign of YHWH as king. Clear echoes of this Canaanite mythology are to be found, for example, in Psalm 29:10; 74:12-14; 89:9-10; 93:3-4; 104:3-9; Habakkuk 3:3-15; and Isaiah 51:9-16. The use of this Canaanite imagery does not mean, of course, that the Old Testament *endorsed* the myths of El and Baal. On the contrary, the faith of Israel subordinated any affirmations about these gods to the reign of YHWH. The Old Testament took over the language of Baal's kingship for the purpose of countering it by ascribing all rule in heaven and on earth to YHWH alone.

And furthermore, while using such mythic imagery, the Old Testament earthed the reign of YHWH fully in actual history. Using such imagery was a way of affirming that events which had taken place on the plane of human history bore a significance that was cosmic and revelatory. In this historical sequence of events, Israel must now recognize truth about their God, YHWH. And that truth is that the enemies of YHWH (whether human or claimed deities) are no match

---

[1]John Durham translates the line, "Yahweh reigns forever and without interruption," in *Exodus,* Word Biblical Commentary (Waco, Tex.: Word, 1987), pp. 201-2.

[2]See, e.g., John Day, "Asherah," "Baal (Deity)," and "Canaan, Religion of," in *Anchor Bible Dictionary,* ed. David Noel Freedman (New York: Doubleday, 1992), 1:483-87, 545-49, 831-37; and N. Wyatt, *Religious Texts from Ugarit* (Sheffield, U.K.: Sheffield Academic Press, 1998).

for his victorious kingship. "*The LORD* is king," sings Moses, with the unspoken but clear implication, "*and not Pharaoh*, or any other of the claimed gods of Egypt or of Canaan."[3]

The nature of YHWH's kingship, however—that is, the way YHWH actually functions as king— is unexpected. He exercises his kingship on behalf of the weak and oppressed. This is implied already in the Song of Moses at the Sea; what is being celebrated is precisely the liberation of an ethnic minority community who had been undergoing economic exploitation, political oppression and eventually a state-sponsored campaign of terrorizing genocide. But into the empire of Pharaoh steps the reign of YHWH, the God who hears the cry of the oppressed, the God who hears, sees, remembers and is concerned (Ex 2:23-25).

Yet again Deuteronomy provides commentary on the events we are considering. Deuteronomy 10:14-19 paradoxically puts YHWH's universal *reign* right beside YHWH's highly localized *compassion*. The passage is structured like a hymn and takes the form of two main panels with three verses in each. The first verse of each panel (vv. 14, 17) is a *doxology*. The second (vv. 15, 18) is a contrasting *surprise*. And the third (vv. 16, 19) is the practical and ethical *response* required of Israel to the affirmations just made (see table 3.1).

Table 3.1. Deuteronomy 10:14-19

14 To the LORD your God belong the heavens, even the highest heavens, the earth and everything in it.	Hymn/Doxology	**17** For the LORD your God is God of gods and Lord of lords, the great God, mighty and awesome, who shows no partiality and accepts no bribes.
15 Yet the LORD set his affection on your forefathers and loved them, and he chose you, their descendants, above all the nations, as it is today.	Surprise	**18** He defends the cause of the fatherless and the widow, and loves the alien, giving him food and clothing.
16 Circumcise your hearts, therefore, and do not be stiff-necked any longer.	Response	**19** And you are to love those who are aliens, for you yourselves were aliens in Egypt.

---

[3]The idea of YHWH's world dominion over all nations and gods will be discussed further in chap. 14.

The two opening doxologies make a remarkable double claim: YHWH is the God who *owns* the universe (for it belongs to him in its entirety, v. 14), and YHWH is the God who *rules* the universe (for all other powers and authorities are subject to him, v. 17). Elsewhere God's claim of universal *ownership* is based on the right of creation (e.g., Ps 24:1-2; 89:11-12; 95:3-5). Similarly, his claim to universal *sovereignty* is grounded in his power as Creator (Ps 33:6-11; 95:3; Is 40:21-26). But the startling claim in Deuteronomy 10 is, first, that this God who rules over the entire universe has chosen Israel of all people as his covenant partner (v. 15), and second, that the power of this God over all other forms of power and authority, human or cosmic ("gods and lords") is exercised on behalf of the weakest and most marginalized in society—widow, orphan and alien (v. 18). Indeed, the balance between verses 15 and 18 implies that when God saved *Israel* from their suffering as aliens in Egypt, when he fed *them* and clothed *them* in the wilderness, God was simply acting in character—doing for Israel what he typically does for others. That is what YHWH does for aliens generically. That is the kind of God he is. YHWH is the God who loves to love, and especially to love the needy and the alien. Since the Israelites were in that needy condition in Egypt, they became the objects of his compassionate justice. YHWH, whom Israel now knows to be *king,* is the King who reigns in compassion and justice. For indeed: "Righteousness and justice are the foundation of your throne / love and faithfulness go before you" (Ps 89:14).[4]

YHWH is unique. Turning again to our Deuteronomic commentary on the exodus and Sinai events in Deuteronomy 4:32-39, what was Israel expected to deduce from their experience of God's grace in redemption (the exodus, vv. 34, 37) and in revelation (Sinai, vv. 33, 36)? The bottom line of Moses' argument is that "the LORD is God . . . in heaven above and on the earth below. *There is no other*" (vv. 35, 39, emphasis added).

The language of there being "no other" god than YHWH is found in a number of other texts that should be brought alongside this one.

There is no one holy like the LORD;
    there is no one besides you;
    there is no Rock like our God. (1 Sam 2:2)

So that all the peoples of the earth may know that the LORD is God and that there is no other. (1 Kings 8:60)

---

[4]On the widespread expectation throughout the ancient Near East that gods and kings should be agents of justice, see the comprehensive study of Moshe Weinfeld, *Social Justice in Ancient Israel and in the Ancient near East* (Minneapolis: Fortress Press, 1995).

> Then you will know that I am in Israel,
>> that I am the LORD your God,
>> and that there is no other. (Joel 2:27)

> I am the LORD, and there is no other;
>> apart from me there is no God. (Is 45:5; cf. 6, 18)

There are scholars who question whether (with the exception of the Isaiah text) a fully monotheistic claim is being made in such passages. Some argue that such language still falls in the category of mono-Yahwism—that is, all these texts imply is that YHWH and "no other" is to be the only God worshiped *by Israel*. Whether or not the other gods of other nations have any real existence is not at issue and is not being denied in such texts, it is claimed. Indeed the assumption in such texts (according to these scholars) is that other gods *do* exist, but none of them has any claim on Israel's worship or allegiance.

However, this seems to me a very a priori assumption, which is virtually impossible to refute. For it seems that whatever an Israelite were to claim about the uniqueness of YHWH, it could be understood by the determined reader in that reductionist way. But suppose an Israelite truly wanted to make the ontological claim that YHWH was indeed the sole universal deity, what more could he or she say than Deuteronomy 4:39? Nathan MacDonald is right to say that Deuteronomy is not dealing with Enlightenment categories or definitions of deity in the abstract. But Deuteronomy does put the whole universe before our eyes ("in heaven above and on earth below") and then affirms that wherever you look, YHWH is God and "there is no other." Where else was there to be god? The implication, which the Isaiah text makes explicit ("apart from me there is no god"), seems virtually built in to the other affirmations. Even if not expressed in so many words, it is a conclusion not far from the surface.

Having made that point, however, we do need to acknowledge that the Old Testament often speaks of other gods in a way that seems to imply some kind of existence—even if it is not be compared to the categorically distinct reality of YHWH as "the God." We will return to this tension in chapter five on YHWH and the gods and idols of the nations. But for the moment I would agree with the carefully articulated argument of Richard Bauckham, who uses the phrase "YHWH's transcendent uniqueness," and defines it as follows:

> The essential element in what I have called Jewish monotheism, the element that makes it a kind of monotheism, is not the denial of the existence of other "gods," but an understanding of the uniqueness of YHWH that puts him in a class of his own, a wholly different class from any other heavenly or supernatural beings, even if these are called "gods." I call this YHWH's transcendent uniqueness (Mere

"uniqueness" can be what distinguishes one member of a class from other members of it. By "transcendent uniqueness" I mean a form of uniqueness that puts YHWH in a class of his own). Especially important for identifying this transcendent uniqueness are statements that distinguish YHWH by means of a unique relationship to the whole of reality: YHWH alone is Creator of all things, whereas all other things are created by him; and YHWH alone is the sovereign Lord of all things, whereas all other things serve or are subject to his universal lordship.[5]

This way of understanding the uniqueness of YHWH converges with the above point on his incomparability. The reason why there is no other god *like* YHWH is because there is no other god, period. YHWH is "*the* God"—*hā ʾĕlōhîm*. As Bauckham points out, the use of the definitive article in this way effectively puts YHWH into a class of his own.

> What Israel is able to recognize about YHWH, from his acts for Israel, that distinguishes YHWH from the gods of the nations is that he is "the God" or "the god of gods." This means primarily that he has unrivaled power throughout the cosmos. The earth, the heavens and the heaven of heavens belong to him (Deut. 10:14). By contrast, the gods of the nations are impotent nonentities, who cannot protect and deliver even their own peoples . . . (see especially Deut. 32:37-39).[6]

This reinforces the view that those texts which speak of YHWH as being incomparable imply more than just mono-Yahwism (that YHWH is the only God for Israel). To see that they mean more than just limited or relative mono-Yahwism, we should notice that some of them significantly combine the phraseology of *incomparability* (none *like* him) with that of transcendent *uniqueness* (no *other* god). Examples of this combination include:

> There is no one like you, and there is no God but you. (2 Sam 7:22)

> Among the gods there is none like you. / . . . You alone are God. (Ps 86:8, 10)

> I am God, and there is no other;
> I am God, and there is none like me. (Is 46:9)

> O LORD, God of Israel, there is no God like you in heaven above or on earth below. . . .

> So that all the peoples of the earth may know that the LORD is God and that there is no other. (1 Kings 8:23, 60).

---

[5]Richard Bauckham, "Biblical Theology and the Problems of Monotheism," in *Out of Egypt: Biblical Theology and Biblical Interpretation,* ed. Craig Bartholomew et al. (Carlisle, U.K.: Paternoster; Grand Rapids: Zondervan, 2004), p. 211.
[6]Ibid., p. 196.

On this last text, Bauckham comments:

> [It] can surely not mean that all the peoples of the earth will know that YHWH is the only god *for Israel*. What they will recognize is that YHWH alone is "the God." They need not deny that there are other *gods,* but they will recognize the uniqueness of YHWH as the only one who can be called "*the God.*" It is in this category that "there is no other."[7]

The return from exile. We will think later about the lessons Israel learned about God from the experience of being *sent* into exile, when we consider how they shared with other nations in knowing God through exposure to his judgment. At the point, however, when the prophetic word assured them of God's gracious intention to bring an end to the exile and *restore* them to their own land and to renewed covenant relationship with himself, there was another huge burst of learning to be done. And at each point, something more is being affirmed about the uniqueness and universality of YHWH. Here again, then, we have a section of Israel's history and Scripture that speaks directly to our theme. For if God has the mission of bringing salvation to the nations and re-creation to the whole earth, then he needs to be capable of accomplishing such a mammoth agenda. The confidence of the great exilic prophets is that he will not be found wanting in any aspect of his promises. The following great affirmations flow mainly from the book of Isaiah, along with some of the visions of Jeremiah and Ezekiel.

YHWH is sovereign over history. The older idea within Old Testament scholarship that Israel was unique among all the nations of the ancient Near East in an unparalleled belief that YHWH their God was active in history has been shown to be false. Other nations did make similar claims for their gods, albeit not with the sustained intensity and scope of the claim made in Israel for YHWH.[8] Getting involved in the affairs of their own nations, especially through prospering their military efforts, is what gods were for. The question however is not which nation believed their god had some control over historical events? But rather, which nation was right? Or rather, of which god was the claim (to be in control of history) vindicated and valid?

What is remarkable about the repeated claim made in Israel's prophetic texts

---

[7]Ibid., p. 195.

[8]The classic work on this topic is still Bertil Albrektson, *History and the Gods: An Essay on the Idea of Historical Events as Divine Manifestations in the Ancient near East and in Israel* (Lund: Gleerup, 1967). More recently, see also Daniel I. Block, *The Gods of the Nations: Studies in Ancient near Eastern National Theology,* 2nd ed. (Grand Rapids: Baker; Leicester, U.K.: Apollos, 2000).

at the time of the exile is not just the vehemence and insistence with which it is made. (Israel's rhetoric about the sovereignty of YHWH over events far outstrips any of the extant texts we possess about the claims made on behalf of the gods of other nations at the time.) What is remarkable is, first, the fact that such claims were made at all, given the circumstances. For a great imperial power to claim that its gods were in control of events would seem natural enough. For one of the defeated little nations—scarcely a nation at all any longer—to claim the same for its own deity would seem absurdly arrogant. Surely these people are living in delusion, in pathetic denial of the reality that has dashed them down and will soon delete them and their little god from the annals of history altogether.

Yet the prophetic texts that spoke into the captivity of the Judean exiles dared to call the other nations and their gods into court, to challenge them to a grand contest to see which of their gods really was in control of history—and which one could therefore legitimately claim to be the true God.

> Bring in your idols to tell us
>   what is going to happen.
> Tell us what the former things were,
>   So that we may consider them
>   and know their final outcome.
> Or declare to us the things to come,
>   tell us what the future holds,
>   so that we may know you are gods. (Is 41:22-23)

> I am God, and there is no other;
>   I am God, and there is none like me.
> I make known the end from the beginning,
>   From ancient times, what is still to come.
> I say: My purpose will stand,
>   And I will do all that I please. (Is 46:9-10)

A second remarkable feature of the claims made on behalf of Israel's God, however, is that YHWH controls the whole history of *all* nations, not just the affairs of *his own* covenant people. On the whole, other nations in the ancient Near East were content to affirm their gods' involvement in events that either extended their own power or that defended the national territory or city. It is rare to find any reference to other ancient Near Eastern gods claiming to get involved in the history, politics or fortunes of third parties, and when they do, it is usually through the agency of their own nation. Yet precisely this is claimed for YHWH. Not only does he intervene in the fortunes of nations who do not worship him, he is perfectly able to do so with or without the direct agency of his own covenant people and independently of their particular interests. In exilic prophecies he can use Babylon as the agent of his judgment on Israel, but he can also use Cyrus as his agent against Babylon—and in the same breath claim that all Cyrus's victories over other nations are attributable to YHWH's sovereignty also (Is 41:2-4, 25; 44:28—45:6). These are astonishing claims.

They are also unprecedented and unparalleled claims. Simon Sherwin studies this feature of the Old Testament's claim for YHWH in detailed comparison with the kinds of claim made by contemporary nations for their gods and finds it quite distinctive. He surveys material from a wide range of ancient Near Eastern cultures over a wide span of history. Significantly, he argues that this feature of Israelite polemic is most likely linked to Israel's monotheistic worldview. Sherwin points out that most of the claims of ancient Near Eastern gods were concerned with territorial gains or losses. It was common enough for other nations to claim that it was their own national god who had obtained territory for them, in the distant or recent past. The actions of these national gods was entirely focused on the fortunes of the nation that worshiped them.

> However, the claims of Yahweh go beyond this. He claims to be able to appoint kings in other countries; he can use nations not his own to punish others; he is even able to take the real superpowers of the day, use them for his own purposes and then dispose of them. On a positive note he is also able to bring deliverance to nations that are not his. This is remarkable given the size of the kingdoms of Israel and Judah and their insignificant position on the political world stage and the fact that even the superpowers of Assyria and Babylon stop short of such claims. The explanation may well lie in the monotheistic outlook of the final form of the Hebrew Bible. If Yahweh is the only God, the creator of the ends of the earth, the "Most High" who "rules the kingdom of men and gives it to whom he will" (Dan. 4:17, 32) or, to quote Jehoshaphat, "You rule over all the kingdoms of the nations" (2 Chr. 20:6), then it is well within his jurisdiction to use whom he pleases to accomplish his purposes.[9]

YHWH exercises sovereignty through his word. The power of the word of God was already an established part of Israel's faith. Not only in Genesis 1 but also in the worship of Israel the link was made between the word of the Lord and the creation of the cosmos.

> By the word of the LORD were the heavens made,
> Their starry host by the breath of his mouth. . . .

---

[9]Simon Sherwin, " 'I Am Against You': Yahweh's Judgment on the Nations and Its Ancient Near Eastern Context," *Tyndale Bulletin* 54 (2003): 160.

For he spoke, and it came to be;
    he commanded, and it stood firm. (Ps 33:6, 9)

The same psalm moves from the sovereignty of the word of God in creation to its governing role in history.

The LORD foils the plans of the nations;
    he thwarts the purposes of the peoples.
But the plans of the LORD stand firm for ever,
    the purposes of his heart through all generations. (Ps 33:10-11)

This article of faith is raised to new prominence, however, by the exile. And in that context the potency of God's word is highlighted all the more vividly by the impotence of God's people. If there ever had been any idea that YHWH accomplished his purpose and thus demonstrated his incomparable sovereignty through the agency of Israel's military victories (which in some situations had been true, as, e.g., the song of Deborah celebrated in Judg 5), that option was manifestly not available for the God of a struggling community of war captives. In any case, Israel was in exile not because YHWH was incapable of defeating his enemies but because he had used Babylon as the agent of his judgment on Israel. His sovereignty had been exercised through military victory, paradoxically achieved against his own people. Would he now prove his sovereignty (and deity) by reversing the polarity and raising up the Israelites again to military victory over Babylon? Precisely not. YHWH's superiority over the nations and their gods would be demonstrated not on the battlefield but in the law court, not by weapons but by his word.

At this point we need to be careful about the implications we might draw from this. The shift from coercive force was not an admission of YHWH's impotence—as though he had no other option. It was not as if YHWH had now been militarily defeated and so had to resort to other means of imposing his will. Westermann's comment at this point is dangerously open to such misunderstanding: "Since Israel had ceased to be an independent state, her God could not now prove his superiority to the gods of Babylon by means of victory over her foes. So Deutero-Isaiah shifts the arena of decision from the battlefield to the law court."[10]

Israel had not been an independent state at the time of the exodus either, yet God decisively proved his superiority to the gods of Egypt by a victory routinely described as having been achieved by "his mighty hand and outstretched arm." God could exercise coercive power without human agency if he chose to. So Westermann's immediately following comment is more acceptable.

---

[10]Claus Westermann, *Isaiah 40—66*, trans. D. M. H. Stalker (London: SCM Press, 1969), p. 15.

It [the shift from battlefield to law court] does not, however, in any way imply a severance of the link between God's action and history; it only means that the hitherto accepted proof of a god's divinity, his power to win military victory for his own people, was replaced by another, the dependable and unremitting continuity between what a god says and what he does.[11]

It was the word of God that counted. Even the great display of God's power in the exodus had been accompanied by the predictive and interpretative word of God through Moses, and was quickly followed by the massive "word event" of God's revelation at Sinai. And, more sharply pertinent to the exiles, even the military victory of Nebuchadnezzar and destruction of Jerusalem was proof of the truth and power of the word of God spoken through the prophets beforehand. Millard Lind comments:

Deutero-Isaiah is saying that the politics which tries to control by coercion is ineffective in terms of the continuity of community and that the "gods" of such communities are therefore not really divine. The only effective politics of the continuity of community is based not on military might but rather upon the continuity of the creative word and deed of Yahweh, *who therefore is alone God.*[12]

So through the great demonstrations of God's redemptive grace, the exodus and the return from exile, Israel learned that part of the uniqueness of YHWH their God was that he exercised his sovereignty over the ebb and flow of international history *through his word*. The claim of Isaiah 40—55 is that this capacity established not just his superiority over all other claimed gods but in fact his sole deity.

YHWH acts for the sake of his name. Two questions introduce our point in this section. First, what motivated YHWH to bring his people back from exile in a second great act of redemption? Second, why did it matter that he should, in the process, demonstrate his claim to deity by his sovereign control of history through his word? The answer to both questions lies in God's concern for his own name.

To the first question—the motivation for God's action: YHWH would deliver his people from their captivity because the only alternative (to allow the status quo to continue) threatened permanent damage to his own reputation as God. There was an ancient principle at work here, first articulated in Moses' intercession with God on behalf of sinful Israel at the time of the golden calf apostasy and again in the midst of the rebellion at Kadesh Barnea. On both of those oc-

---

[11]Ibid.

[12]Millar C. Lind, "Monotheism, Power and Justice: A Study in Isaiah 40-55," *Catholic Biblical Quarterly* 46 (1984): 435, emphasis added.

casions Moses appealed against God's declared intention to destroy the people
of Israel. And he based his appeal (among other things) on the grounds that
God had a reputation to think of. What would the nations (especially the Egyptians in that context) think of YHWH as God if he first delivered Israel from Egypt
and then destroyed them in the wilderness (Ex 32:12; Num 14:13-16; Deut 9:28)?
They would think YHWH was either incompetent or malicious. Is that the kind
of reputation YHWH wanted? The name (reputation) of YHWH among the nations
was at stake in what God did *against* his own people, just as it was involved in
all that he did *for* them.

It was Ezekiel, however, who took this principle to its most radically theocentric extreme. In Ezekiel 36:16-38, Ezekiel argues, first, that the exile had been
a moral necessity as an act of God's punishment on a nation that had proved
incorrigibly and unrepentantly wicked for generations. The result of the exile,
however, had been that the name of YHWH was being "profaned" among the nations. That means, the name "YHWH" was being treated as the common or ordinary name of just another defeated god among the long list of gods whose nations had been conquered and exiled by Babylon. This was a situation YHWH
could not tolerate as a permanent state of affairs. Indeed, in Ezekiel's graphic
phrase, YHWH "had pity for [his] holy name"—such was the disgrace it was suffering (Ezek 36:21 KJV). So, yes, YHWH would act again to deliver his people, but
the primary motivation, in Ezekiel's uncompromising theocentricity, would be
to salvage YHWH's own name from the gutter of profanity among the nations—
not (in the first place) for Israel's own sake.

> It is not for your sake, O house of Israel, that I am going to do these things, but
> for the sake of my holy name, which you have profaned among the nations where
> you have gone. I will show the holiness of my great name, which has been pro-
> faned among the nations, the name you have profaned among them. Then the na-
> tions will know that I am the LORD, declares the Sovereign LORD, when I show
> myself holy through you before their eyes. (Ezek 36:22-23)

Isaiah also captures the fact that YHWH will act in forgiveness and restoration
primarily for his own sake (cf. Is 43:25), but he lays greater emphasis on the
final part of Ezekiel's concern, namely, that YHWH wills to be known among the
nations for who he truly is. This brings us to the second of our two questions:
Why did it matter that God's sovereignty through his word should be clearly—
even forensically—demonstrated? Repeatedly, Isaiah declares that the purpose
of this demonstration is that the name of the true and living God should be universally known. The prophecies in relation to Cyrus are explicit on this point,
and gloriously ironic. To prove the power of his word YHWH, through his

prophet, names Cyrus in advance and predicts his initial rise to power, his eventual defeat of Babylon, and his instrumentality in the release of the exiles and the rebuilding of Jerusalem. The irony lies in the fact that although *Cyrus* is named (Is 44:28; 45:1), his name will not be known to the ends of the earth. That honor will go to YHWH, whom Cyrus does not even acknowledge.

> I am the LORD, and there is no other;
> > apart from me there is no God.
> I will strengthen *you* [Cyrus],
> > though you have not acknowledged me,
> so that from the rising of the sun
> > to the place of its setting
> men may know that there is none besides *me*. (Is 45:5-6, emphasis added)

So from the prophet's perspective, the historical events that were being set in motion through the word of God would demonstrate the transcendent uniqueness of YHWH as God, and would eventually result in the universal acknowledgement of that fact. The proof of his words is confirmed by the fact that today not many people other than ancient historians know the name of sixth-century B.C. Cyrus whereas there are millions who worship the Lord God of Israel through his Son Jesus Christ.

YHWH's sovereignty extends over all creation. A theme that had not been lacking in Israel's preexilic faith and worship comes to particular prominence around the time of the exile and return, namely, YHWH's sovereignty over all of creation as the only living God. Psalm 33 directly links this affirmation to YHWH's governance of international history. Jeremiah explicitly contrasts YHWH's power as Creator with the impotence and transience of other gods.

> The LORD is the true God;
> > he is the living God, the eternal King. . . .

> "These gods, who did not make the heavens and the earth, will perish from the earth and from under the heavens."

> But God made the earth by his power. (Jer 10:10-12)

But it is the prophecies in the book of Isaiah, given to renew the faith of the exiles, that make the most of this sovereignty of YHWH as Creator—precisely because the exiles needed to regain their confidence in the universality of YHWH. Far from being defeated, far from being confined to either his own people or his own land, he was still Lord of the whole cosmos as much as he had ever been.

This truth had a double edge, however. On the one hand it meant that Israel could believe, against all the appearances of their present circumstances, that when YHWH would act to bring about their return from exile, nothing could stand in his way, for everything was under his sovereign control—the earth, the heavens, the great deep, even the stars (and their alleged astral divinity). This was Israel's ancient creation faith, so let them be reminded of it: "Do you not know? / Have you not heard?" (Is 40:21-26).

On the other hand, it meant that if Israel should be inclined to protest at the means by which God would bring about their deliverance (i.e., through a pagan king who did not even know YHWH, yet is provocatively described as YHWH's "shepherd" and "anointed"), they would do well to remember who it was they presumed to argue with—the Creator of the universe.

> Concerning things to come, do you question me . . . ?
>   It is I who made the earth
>   and created mankind upon it.
>   My own hands stretched out the heavens;
>   I marshaled their starry hosts.
>   I will raise up Cyrus in my righteousness: . . .
>   He will rebuild my city
>   and set my exiles free. (Is 45:11-13)

So, the reason why God's planned action for Israel's deliverance will be spectacularly successful is that it is grounded in his universal sovereignty as Creator. And the effect of that saving action will be to demonstrate the unique identity and status of YHWH to the rest of the world. Israel would do well not to protest, for they have a role to play in that divine agenda. If Israel's ultimate mission was to be a blessing and a light to the nations, they need to cooperate with God's means of executing that purpose, whether they approved of it or not.

YHWH entrusts his uniqueness and universality to the witness of his people. How will the rest of the world come to know these great truths about YHWH? This essentially missiological question receives the remarkable answer that YHWH entrusts his intention for the nations to the *witness* of his own people. Returning to the metaphor of the law court again, we are to envisage the other nations being brought in to present whatever they can in support of the claimed reality and power of their gods. There are criteria, however, for what constitutes admissible evidence. It will not be a case of which of the gods claims the greatest military victories but which of them had the ability to predict and interpret history, in the way that YHWH had done through his prophets. Can the nations bear witness to anything like that for their gods? Israel has abundant witness to bear on precisely those points on behalf of YHWH. So it will be through Israel's witness that YHWH's powers of revelation and salvation, and ultimately YHWH's identity as sole God, will be posted in the public arena of world history.

> All the nations gather together
>> and the peoples assemble.
> Which of them foretold this
>> and proclaimed to us the former things?
> Let them bring in their witnesses to prove they were right,
>> so that others may hear and say, "It is true."
> "You are my witnesses," declares the LORD,
>> "and my servant whom I have chosen,
> so that you may know and believe me
>> and understand that I am he.
> Before me no god was formed,
>> nor will there be one after me.
> I, even I, am the LORD,
>> and apart from me there is no savior.
> I have revealed and saved and proclaimed—
>> I, and not some foreign god among you.
> You are my witnesses," declares the LORD, "that I am God." (Is 43:9-12)

Now the primary responsibility of a witness is to tell what they *know*. Herein, then, lies the huge responsibility of knowing *God*. This is what gives such powerful significance to the words of Moses to Israel in Deuteronomy 4:35. Pointing to all that the Israelites had witnessed of the words and works of the Lord, he draws the conclusion: "*You* were shown these things so that *you* might *know* that the LORD is God; beside him there is no other" (emphasis added).

The "You" is in an emphatic position in the sentence. An expanded paraphrase of the text might render it: "*You,* Israel, know that YHWH is '*the* God.'[13] Other nations do not yet share the privilege of this knowledge, precisely because they have not experienced what you have just done, through the exodus and Sinai encounters. So this unique knowledge of this unique God is now your unique stewardship."

Israel then, alone among the nations, is the people who *do know* YHWH. Other nations as yet do not. Idolatry is, among other things, a form of ignorance (Is 44:18). The nations do not know YHWH's laws, which he had given only to Israel (Ps 147:19-20). Israel, therefore, as the people who do know the true identity of the living God, through his acts of self-revelation and redemption, must

---

[13]The precise phrase is literally "YHWH, he is the God." This is exactly the same formula as the acclamation of the people after Elijah's fiery demonstration that YHWH, not Baal, was the God who could answer by fire (1 Kings 18:39).

bear witness to that knowledge among the nations. It is not necessary to read a missionary mandate into this role within the Old Testament itself, in the sense of Israelites being physically sent out to travel to the nations to bear witness to this knowledge. But the concept is clearly there: this knowledge *is to be* proclaimed to the nations, just as much as the good news of its liberation was to be proclaimed to Jerusalem. Or to be more precise, the good news of what God had done for Jerusalem would constitute part of the good news that would go also to the nations, when "all the ends of the earth will see the salvation of our God" (Is 52:10; cf. Jer 31:10). *How* this would happen is never clearly articulated in the Old Testament, but *that* it would happen is unequivocal.[14] It is celebrated in advance in worship and prophecy.

> Sing to the LORD a new song;
> > sing to the LORD all the earth.
> Sing to the LORD, praise his name;
> > proclaim his salvation day after day.
> Declare his glory among the nations,
> > his marvelous deeds among all peoples. (Ps 96:1-3)

> Give thanks to the LORD, call on his name;
> > make known among the nations what he has done,
> > and proclaim that his name is exalted.
> Sing to the LORD, for he has done glorious things;
> > let this be known to all the world. (Is 12:4-5)

It is clear then, in concluding this section, that through their major historical experiences of YHWH's grace in redemption and deliverance, Israel believed that they had come to know him as the one and only true and living God. In his transcendent uniqueness there was no other god like YHWH. Furthermore, they had a sense of stewardship of this knowledge since it was God's purpose that ultimately all nations would come to know the name, the glory, the salvation and the mighty acts of YHWH and worship him alone as God.

Knowing God Through Exposure to His Judgment

We have seen, then, that Israel's primary source of knowing YHWH to be the one true and living God *(the God)* was their experience of his grace in historical acts of deliverance. But those acts of deliverance for *Israel* meant judgment on their

---

[14]The single exception to the lack of "how" is Is 66:19, which does predict a sending out to the nations to proclaim the glory of YHWH among them. The whole context shows this to be an eschatological expectation. Fuller discussion of the nations in Old Testament theology is found in chap. 14.

oppressors. These enemies too would come to know God, but they would know him as the God of justice who could not be resisted with impunity. And when Israel themselves by persistent rebellion put themselves into the company of the enemies of YHWH, they too would know him in that way. So we turn again to the exodus and the exile, but this time from the perspective of Egypt and Israel respectively as the objects of God's judgment and as the subjects of some sharp learning. After that, we will look further forward, with Ezekiel, to the final judgment of the enemies of God and God's people, and summarize what will then and thereby be known about God.

Egypt. The exodus narrative has as its major plot, of course, the deliverance of Israel from their oppression under the Pharaoh. It also has as its major subplot, however, the massive power encounter between YHWH, God of Israel, and Pharaoh, king (and god) of Egypt—and all the other gods of the Egyptians. The trigger for this subplot is the fateful refusal of Pharaoh to recognize YHWH as having any jurisdiction in his territory. To Moses' request that Israel should be released in order to worship their God, YHWH, Pharaoh answers: "Who is the LORD, that I should obey him and let Israel go? I do not know the LORD and I will not let Israel go" (Ex 5:2).[15]

This challenge introduces the vivid narrative of the plagues on Egypt, during which we hear the recurring motif, "Then you will know . . . ," throughout Exodus 7—14. YHWH, the God who would make himself known to the Israelites by delivering them, would simultaneously make himself known to Pharaoh by overthrowing his oppression.

What then did Pharaoh come to know about YHWH? If we run through the sequence of relevant passages in Exodus we discover numerous items on the curriculum of Pharaoh's education, arranged, probably in an ascending order in table 3.2. It was a steep learning curve, which eventually ended in destruction. More happily, though this was God's final word for that particular Pharaoh and the forces he ranged against YHWH and his people, it was not God's final word for Egypt. The great empire of the Nile does come in for even more words of judgment as Israel's history unfolded,[16] but Isaiah 19:19-25, in one of the most remarkable pieces of prophetic vision in the Old Testament, puts Egypt on to

---

[15]An interesting implication of Pharaoh's words, which is not particularly taken up in this narrative but is certainly a major point with Deuteronomy and the prophets, is the link between knowing YHWH as God and obeying him. Pharaoh feels no obligation to obey because he claims not to know. Conversely, to know YHWH is to be committed to obeying him (cf. Deut 4:39-40). Jeremiah actually defines the knowledge of God in that way, using Josiah as his example (Jer 22:16), and Hosea can sum up Israel's disobedience to so many of God's commandments in the stark verdict, "There is no . . . knowledge of God in the land" (Hos 4:1 KJV).

[16]See, e.g., Is 19:1-15; Jer 46; Ezek 29—32.

Table 3.2. The Curriculum of Pharaoh's Education

Scripture	Comment
The Egyptians will know that I am the LORD. (Ex 7:5, 17)	YHWH, the God whom Pharaoh had refused to acknowledge, truly is God. The Egyptians will be forced to recognize at the very least that there is such a god as this one who declares, "I am YHWH."
So that you may know there is no one like the LORD our God. (Ex 8:10)	YHWH, the God of the despised Hebrew slaves, has no rivals. There is none like him. The incomparability of YHWH was something Israel would learn also.
So that you will know that I, the LORD, am in this land. (Ex 8:22)	YHWH is God in Egypt—regardless of Pharaoh's own claim to be god—and whatever the status of all the other gods of Egypt, YHWH was not subject to Egypt's visa controls or confined to the territory where the Israelites lived.
So that you may know that there is no one like me in all the earth. (Ex 9:14)	YHWH is without peer, not just in Egypt but throughout the earth.[a]
I have raised you up for this very purpose, that I might show you my power and that my name might be proclaimed in all the earth. (Ex 9:16)	YHWH, far from being subject to Pharaoh's whim and favor, is the one who is using Pharaoh for his own universal purpose—the extension of his name in all the earth.[b]
I will bring judgment on all the gods of Egypt. I am the LORD. (Ex 12:12)	YHWH is the judge of all the supposed gods of Egypt, though they are gods of its great imperial power and glory.
The Egyptians will know that I am the LORD when I gain glory through Pharaoh, his chariots and his horsemen. (Ex 14:18; cf. Ex 14:4, 25)	YHWH is the God who has the power to protect his people by defeating his enemies, even without human agency.

[a]Assuming that *kōl hāʾāreṣ* here probably means "all the earth," not just "all the land" (of Egypt).
[b]There is an irony here similar to the one we observed above in relation to Cyrus. God had raised up Cyrus, and even called him by name (Is 45:4), but the name that would be universally known as a result, would be the name of YHWH. Even more ironic in the exodus context is the fact that we do not for certain know the name of this Pharaoh ("Pharaoh," of course, is a title, not a personal name). Whatever conclusion we may arrive at as to the historical dating and identity of the Pharaoh of the exodus, the text itself pointedly declines to name him. The name that will be known to the world will be the name of YHWH, the name of the God this anonymous Pharaoh had refused to know. The Pharaoh whose name we can't be sure of will forever be linked with the God whose name we know for certain—the Lord, the mighty one of Israel.

the same learning curve as Israel. That is, the prophet looks forward to the day when Egypt too will come to know YHWH as Savior, defender and healer.[17]

What is unmistakeably clear is that whether we look at what Israel learned through the experience of God's grace or at what Egypt learned through exposure to God's judgment, the same *monotheizing dynamic* is evident. More than anything else this great epic of YHWH God in action demonstrated his uniqueness and universality, and was intended to do so. The statements of purpose in the exodus narrative are frequent and unmistakeable: "then you will know," "so that you will know." Clearly, the motivation from God's point of view was not only the liberation of his enslaved people but this driving divine will to be known to all nations for who and what he truly is. The mission of God to be known is what drives this whole narrative.

Israel in exile. The exile raised huge questions about God in the mind of Israel and the prophets of that era. Israel was defeated, God's city destroyed and God's people driven out of their land. Did this mean that YHWH had met his match in the gods of Nebuchadnezzar's Babylon? Was YHWH himself also defeated? In the macro-cultural worldview of the ancient Near East, the assumption (shared by Israel) was that events on earth mirrored events in the heavenly realm. The fate of human armies reflected the cosmic battles of the gods. Hitherto, Israel believed, YHWH, the God of Israel, was without serious rival. Even if gods of the other nations had any reality at all (and in some sense they must have, inasmuch as the affairs of nations were bound up with their gods), those gods had never succeeded in challenging the power of YHWH and his covenant commitment to Israel and their land.

So how then was the shattering defeat of Israel and destruction of Jerusalem at the hands of Nebuchadnezzar to be interpreted? Was it a delayed vindication of the arrogant claims of the Assyrian commander who, at the time of Sennacherib's siege of Jerusalem in Hezekiah's and Isaiah's time, had boasted that YHWH would prove no more powerful than any of the other petty national gods swallowed up by mighty Assyria?

> Do not listen to Hezekiah, for he is misleading you when he says, "The LORD will deliver us." Has the god of any nation ever delivered his land from the hand of the king of Assyria? Where are the gods of Hamath and Arpad? Where are the gods of Sepharvaim, Hena and Ivvah? Have they rescued Samaria from my hand? Who of all the gods of these countries has been able to save his land from me? *How then can the LORD deliver Jerusalem from my hand?* (2 Kings 18:32-35, emphasis added)

---

[17]We will study this passage and many others with similar implications if not quite so dramatic language in chap. 14.

In spite of the Assyrian officer's boast, the Lord had summarily seen off the Assyrians. But now, just over a century later, the Babylonians had trampled Jerusalem to dust, captured the king, torched the temple and carried off the surviving population into exile. Had the enemies of YHWH triumphed at last?

Paradoxically, the prophets gave to their people (before, during and after the event itself), the explanation they were most reluctant to hear: It was not that YHWH was defeated; on the contrary, he was as much in control as ever. YHWH was still in the business of dealing with his enemies. The question now was, Who is YHWH's real enemy? Or more pointed still, *who was Israel's real enemy?* Israel by its persistent rebellion against their covenant Lord had turned YHWH into their own enemy. *"I myself am against you"!* These ominous words, words that had been spoken by God against many other nations through many a prophet, were now turned against the covenant people themselves (Ezek 5:8). So the victory of Nebuchadnezzar was not a victory *over* YHWH (though Nebuchadnezzar doubtless interpreted it thus) but a victory *of* YHWH. Nebuchadnezzar had become merely God's agent in his covenant conflict with his own people. With the Lord on their side, Jerusalem could not be destroyed. With the Lord against them, Jerusalem could not be defended. The paradoxical sovereignty of YHWH as God is affirmed throughout.

So Israel went into exile and found themselves, like the Egyptians, the Canaanites, and even more recently the Assyrians, exposed to God's judgment. Pursuing our inquiry throughout this chapter, how did this experience lead to a greater knowing of God? What did Israel learn when God treated them as an enemy? Particularly, what did their learning include in relation to the uniqueness and universality of YHWH as God? From a number of texts we may assemble the following points.

YHWH has no favorites. Israel learned that to have YHWH as their covenant partner did not mean that he was their national god who could be always counted on to be on their side, no matter what. To know that YHWH was the God of all the earth, sovereign over all the nations, meant that they must recognize that Israel's election into covenant partnership was not a matter of favoritism at all but a huge responsibility. Indeed, as Amos had pointed out more than a century before the exile, their status as God's uniquely chosen people, far from granting them any kind of immunity from God's judgment, only served to expose them all the more fully to his punishment when they failed to live out the ethical implications of that status.

> You only have I chosen
>> of all the families of the earth;

> Therefore I will punish you
> > for all your sins. (Amos 3:2)

Amos had further challenged the idea that even the exodus, considered simply as the historical act of God bringing them up out of Egypt to settle in the land of Canaan, conferred some kind of unique or favorite position for them. And again, Amos did so on the basis of YHWH's universal sovereignty over the histories of other peoples.

> "Are not you Israelites
> > the same to me as the Cushites?" declares the LORD.
> "Did I not bring Israel up from Egypt,
> > the Philistines from Caphtor
> and the Arameans from Kir?" (Amos 9:7)[18]

Like so many other aspects of Israel's faith, this understanding was already articulated in Deuteronomy. Deuteronomy 2:10-12, 20-23 are short parenthetical sections describing YHWH's prior involvement with surrounding nations before Israel even came on the scene. Though they are almost incidental to the main narrative, they imply the same theological affirmation: YHWH, though the covenant God of Israel as his elect and redeemed people, is the universal God who has already been active in the history and movements of other nations.[19] So it is not surprising that even in a prime text in which God's particular election of Israel is highlighted, it is balanced (as if to avoid precisely any suspicion of favoritism), with the strong defining affirmation of YHWH's universality and therefore of his impartiality: "The LORD your God is God of gods and Lord of lords, the great God, mighty and awesome, *who shows no partiality*" (Deut 10:17, emphasis added).

God's impartiality in dealing with the nations, with its correlative truth that there was no favorite status for Israel, is upheld by those prophets closest to the exile. Jeremiah affirmed through the imagery of the potter that God would respond to *any* nation (including Israel) on the basis of its response to his word to them (Jer 18:1-10). Ezekiel set Jerusalem "in the midst of the nations," but only so as to show not some kind of elevation beyond punishment but rather the horrific deformity of the fact that they were behaving even worse than the nations that did not know YHWH. God was now as much against Israel as he had ever been against their enemies (Ezek 5:5-17). Knowing God through this whole

---

[18]See chap. 14 for more detailed discussion of this key text.

[19]Patrick Miller reflects further on the theological significance of these geographical parentheses in "God's Other Stories: On the Margins of Deuteronomic Theology," in *Realia Dei*, ed. P. H. Williams and T. Hiebert (Atlanta: Scholars Press, 1999), pp. 185-94.

era, then, meant learning that his universality stood above and beyond all petty national favoritism.

YHWH can use any nation as his agent of judgment. There was nothing new about this idea insofar as it related to *Israel* as the agent of God's judgment. The conquest of Canaan had been portrayed in those terms quite explicitly. When the Lord drove out the nations before Israel, Israel functioned as the agent of God's judgment on the wickedness of the Canaanites (cf. Lev 18:24-28; 20:23; Deut 9:1-6). Nor was it entirely new to interpret the oppression of Israel by her enemies as indicative of God's anger against Israel's unfaithfulness—as the whole pattern of the book of Judges shows. The prophets, however, expressed this side of the matter very forcefully. Isaiah could describe Assyria as simply a stick in the hand of YHWH, with which he would chastise Israel (Is 10:5-6). Jeremiah went further and invaded an international diplomatic conference in Jerusalem to inform the gathered ambassadors that YHWH, the God of Israel, had given all their countries into the hand of "my servant Nebuchadnezzar." This startling interpretation of contemporary international politics was founded on the equally uncompromising claim that YHWH the God of Israel had every right and authority to do this, since he was the Creator and disposer of the whole earth and its inhabitants.

> This is what the LORD Almighty, the God of Israel, says: "Tell this to your masters: With my great power and outstretched arm, I made the earth and its people and the animals that are on it, and I give it to anyone I please. Now I will hand all your countries over to my servant Nebuchadnezzar, King of Babylon: I will make even the wild animals subject to him. All nations will serve him and his son and his grandson until the time for his land comes; then many nations and great kings will subjugate him. (Jer 27:4-6)

Here then, the uniqueness and universality of YHWH—as Creator of the earth and Lord of history—is combined with his sovereign freedom to use any nation as agent of his purposes.[20]

YHWH's judgment is righteous and justified. It is one thing to make such affirmations. It is another to defend them before a shocked and smarting people, for whom the fall of Jerusalem proved only that YHWH was either incompetent or unfair. Ezekiel faced the first generation of exiles, fresh from the trauma of the event itself. It was their bitter complaint that if indeed these events were to be viewed as the work of YHWH, then "the way of the Lord is not just" (Ezek 18:25). God was treating them unfairly. On the contrary, argued Ezekiel, in his combination of evangelistic and pastoral rhetoric, what YHWH had done was ut-

---

[20]We will return to this theme also in more depth in chap. 14.

terly justified by the persistent and incorrigible rebellion of the house of Israel. Israel's flagrant sin had left God with no moral alternative but to punish them. Not only must *Israel* be made to know that YHWH had done nothing against Jerusalem "without cause" (Ezek 14:23), *the nations too* will come to know it, in order that the justice of God's ways may be known on earth (Ezek 38:23). For this was one of the essential aspects of affirming the universal rule of YHWH as sole God: namely that *justice* is the very essence of his rule and that *this applied as much to Israel as to all the nations.*

God's people, even under judgment, remain God's people for God's mission. Jeremiah's letter to the exiles in Jeremiah 29:1-14 began by offering them a fresh, prophetic perspective on what had happened to them. There is a significant contrast between the way the narrative, quite correctly, refers to the exiles as "the people Nebuchadnezzar had carried into exile" (v. 1), and the way the letter addresses them as "all those *I [YHWH]* carried into exile" (vv. 4, 7). On the plane of human history, it was perfectly true that the exiles of Judah were the victims of Nebuchadnezzar's imperial conquest. From the perspective of God's sovereignty, however, they were still a people in the hands of their God. The sword of Nebuchadnezzar was being wielded by the God of Israel. With this perspective Jeremiah urged the exiles to settle down and accept the reality of their circumstances. God had exiled them to Babylon; they had better treat it as home for the time being (vv. 5-6). They would not be home in two years (as false prophets were saying); they would be in Babylon for two generations. Babylon was not their permanent home, but it was their present home.

This, however, was far from a despairing resignation to their fate. Jeremiah goes on: "Increase in number there; do not decrease" (Jer 29:6). The echo of the Abrahamic covenant is surely not accidental. The great fear of this people, decimated by siege, famine, disease, the sword and captivity, was that they would die out altogether. What then would become of the promise of God to Abraham, so foundational to their very existence as a nation, that they would be as numerous as the sand or the stars (Gen 15:5; 22:17)? They need not fear, for God would not abandon that promise. Israel would not die out but prosper—as other prophets likewise affirmed (Is 44:1-5; 49:19-21; Ezek 36:8-12).

But if this advice to Israel (to increase in numbers) is a clear echo of the Abrahamic covenant, then so is the very next piece of instruction—which must have been startlingly unwelcome to the victims of Babylon's aggression: "And seek the shalom of the city to which I have exiled you, and pray on its behalf to YHWH, for in its shalom there will be shalom for you" (Jer 29:7, my translation).

The exiles had a task—a mission no less— even in the midst of the city of their enemies. And that task was to seek the welfare of that city and to pray for the blessing of YHWH upon it. So they were not only to be the *beneficiaries* of God's promise to Abraham (in that they would not die out but increase), they were also to be the *agents* of God's promise to Abraham that through his descendants the nations would be blessed. The promise had said "all nations"—enemy nations not excluded. So let Israel assume the Abrahamic position in Babylon. They now found themselves right in the midst of one of those nations. Let them be a blessing there to those they live among by seeking and praying for their welfare.

There is something deeply ironic about this since of course the whole story of Israel had begun with Abraham being called *out of* the land of Babylon-Babel. It might seem that history is going into reverse, with Israel being exiled "from Jerusalem to Babylon" (Jer 29:1, 4)—the opposite direction from the whole narrative of Israel thus far. But in the mysterious purpose of God, the descendants of the one called out of Babylon in order to be the fount of blessing to the nations now return to Babylon in captivity and are instructed to fulfill that promise right there. There is a typically divine irony, possibly noticed by Jesus, in this challenge to Israel to be a *blessing* to the nations by first of all *praying* for their enemies (cf. the combination of blessing and prayer in Mt 5:11, 44).

Such teaching, conveyed by Jeremiah's letter, turned victims into visionaries. Israel not only had a hope for the future (in the famous words of vv. 11-14), they also had a mission in the present. Even in Babylon they could be a community of prayer and *shalom*. As Ezekiel saw, YHWH was just as much alive and present in Babylon as in Jerusalem. His universal power and glory would be felt in judgment, but would also protect and preserve his people through judgment for the sake of God's own name, and for the fulfillment of his wider purposes among the nations.

The nations under judgment. Several of the prophets in their eschatological vision clearly anticipate some among the nations eventually turning to YHWH for salvation, coming to share in the blessing of Israel, even being included among and identified with Israel. Whether Ezekiel shared this hope is impossible to say, since he never explicitly gives voice to it. In Ezekiel's recorded sayings about the nations there is nothing to compare with the redemptive universality that we find in the book of Isaiah, for example.[21] There is, however, a tremendous universality

---

[21] I have discussed more fully the issue of Ezekiel's view of the future knowledge of God among the nations and what is implied by it in Christopher J. H. Wright, *The Message of Ezekiel: A New Heart and a New Spirit*, The Bible Speaks Today (Leicester, U.K.: Inter-Varsity Press; Downers Grove, Ill.: InterVarsity Press, 2001), pp. 268-72, relying significantly on the fine survey of the matter in David A. Williams, " 'Then They Will Know That I Am the Lord': The Missiological Significance of Ezekiel's Concern for the Nations as Evident in the Use of the Recognition Formula" (master's diss. All Nations Christian College, 1998).

about Ezekiel's passion for the *knowledge of God*. The one thing that burns throughout his whole book is the certainty that YHWH will be known as God—by Israel *and* by the nations. The phrase "Then you [or they] will know that I am YHWH" is virtually Ezekiel's signature—occurring some eighty times in his prophetic memoir. In relation to our earlier discussion about YHWH's transcendent uniqueness, this cannot mean merely that the nations will acknowledge that there happens to be a god named YHWH among all the rest of the gods in their catalog. It means that the nations will come to the decisive and irrevocable knowledge that YHWH alone is the true and living God, unique in his identity, universal in his rule, and unchallenged in his power.

There are many examples of this affirmation throughout Ezekiel, but they come to a cacophonous climax in the grim and grizzly portrayal of the fate of Gog of Magog, in chapters 38-39. This is an apocalyptic vision, using much symbolic language and imagery, of the ultimate defeat of the enemies of God's people. It is the necessary prelude to the climactic vision of the whole book, in chapters 40-48, of God dwelling in the midst of his renewed and sanctified people. Before such unchallenged cohabitation of God and his people can happen, God's enemies must be dealt with.[22]

The two chapters, Ezekiel 38—39, tell a basic story twice over, with lurid, cartoonlike imagery that draws from various other Old Testament sources (such as the flood and Sodom and Gomorrah). A fierce enemy from the north forms a coalition of enemies; there is a massive attack on a peaceful, unsuspecting and unarmed Israel; these enemies are comprehensively defeated and destroyed by God (alone—not by human armies); the defeat of these vicious enemies will be sealed by their burial (a mammoth task in itself), and will be total, climactic, final, and forever. So the major point of these chapters is the ultimate victory of God, on behalf of his people, over all the forces that will ever oppose and seek to destroy them. As such, the vision of the defeat of Gog has had multiple proximate fulfillments in the course of history, and it is pointless to expend too much hermeneutical sweat and tears trying to make definitive identifications of the mysterious names of persons and places. In the end, says Ezekiel, God wins. In the end, God's people are kept safe. And in the end, the enemies of God and God's people will be comprehensively and conclusively defeated and destroyed.[23]

---

[22]The same eschatological order of events is found in Revelation: first the enemies of God and God's people must be destroyed and only then can God dwell in the midst of his redeemed people forever.

[23]For a fuller account of my interpretation of Ezekiel 38—39, see Wright, *Message of Ezekiel,* pp. 315-26.

But what we must not miss (though sadly this is often missed by those who are so obsessed with identifying Gog or predicting end-times timetables) is the repeated refrain: "then you [or they] will know." Once again we find that the result of a great demonstration of the *power* of God is a great extension of the *knowledge* of God—by Israel, by their enemies and by all nations. The phrase occurs as the preface to the whole scenario in the final verse of the preceding chapter (Ezek 37:28). It then punctuates the narration in Ezekiel 38:16, 23; 39:6-7, 21-23, and finally draws the whole section to a close in Ezekiel 39:27-28. It is well worth reading this sequence of verses together to feel the theocentric force of what Ezekiel most wants to convey through this bizarre vision. The world must know, beyond all contradiction or confusion, the identity of the living God.

> Then the nations will know that I the LORD make Israel holy, when my sanctuary is among them for ever. (Ezek 37:28)

> In days to come, O Gog, I will bring you against my land, so that the nations may know me when I show myself holy through you before their eyes. (Ezek 38:16)[24]

> And so I will show my greatness and my holiness, and I will make myself known in the sight of many nations. Then they will know that I am the LORD. (Ezek 38:23)

> I will send fire on Magog and on those who live in safety in the coastlands, and they will know that I am the LORD.
> I will make known my holy name among my people Israel. I will no longer let my holy name be profaned, and the nations will know that I the LORD am the Holy One in Israel. (Ezek 39:6-7)

> I will display my glory among the nations, and all the nations will see the punishment I inflict and the hand I lay upon them. From that day forward the house of Israel will know that I am the LORD their God. And the nations will know that the people of Israel went into exile for their sin, because they were unfaithful to me. (Ezek 39:21-23)

> I will show myself holy through them in the sight of many nations. Then they will know that I am the LORD their God, for though I sent them into exile among the nations, I will gather them to their own land, not leaving any behind. (Ezek 39:27-28)

So, then, what will Gog and all the nations come to know through this ulti-

---

[24]Note the same divine irony as we observed in God's address to Pharaoh and Cyrus: "I will bring you . . . so that the nations may know me." This makes it doubly regrettable that people spend so much effort trying to know who Gog might be, when the whole point is to know who God is.

mate exposure to the judgment of God? Three words dominate the curriculum: (1) the holiness, (2) the greatness and (3) the glory of YHWH.

First, the world will come to know that YHWH, far from being the name profaned as just another common deity and not a terribly important one at that, is the "Holy One in Israel," utterly distinct, transcendently unique. Second, the world will know that YHWH, far from being just one of the minor defeated deities of a region ravaged by imperial armies, is incomparably great. And third, the world will come to know the glory of YHWH—that is, that he alone is real, the God of substance and weight. Beside the holiness, greatness and glory of YHWH, all the gods and idolatries of the nations will be exposed as unholy, pathetic and empty.

The missional relevance of this great vision is surely apparent when we consider its express purpose in these terms. Like Israel in the Old Testament, the people of God throughout history have often felt mocked and attacked by the gods of the surrounding dominant cultures. There are the idols of the rich and powerful, the symbols of arrogance and greed. There are the blatant, boasting battalions of economic and military power. There is the threat and rivalry of competing faiths and ideologies. Sometimes there are the all-out assaults of social and physical persecution and attempted extermination. The language of Gog and Magog seems appropriate in such times, when God's people can feel weak, marginal, vulnerable, defenseless and exposed. But precisely for such times this vision brings the assurance of the ultimate victory of the living God, when all other gods and powers will be exposed for the empty sham they really are—though not without massive struggle. Such a vision, inasmuch as it also involves the final judgment of the wicked, brings us no pleasure, for the same prophet reminds us emphatically that God himself takes no pleasure in the death of the wicked (Ezek 18:32; 33:11). But it does set all the struggles of the present within the certainty of the ultimate exposure and destruction of God's enemies, and the universal acknowledgement of the one, transcendently unique God.

Summary

Drawing together the threads of our discussion in this chapter, I have been seeking to define what monotheism means in the faith of Israel. It is the affirmation of the transcendent uniqueness and universality of the Lord, the Holy One of Israel. Whatever may be said about other gods (which will be explored further in chap. 5), the Lord alone is "*the* God." The Lord stands in a class of his own: there is none like him; there is no other anywhere in the cosmos. Summarizing the knowledge of the Lord gained through his acts of revelation, redemption and judgment, the affirmations in table 3.3, while not exhaustive, capture the broad outline of Old Testament monotheism.

Table 3.3. Broad Outline of Old Testament Monotheism

The Lord alone is	In relation to the heavens, the earth and all the nations:	
Creator	The Lord made them.	Ps 33:6-9; Jer 10:10-12
Owner	The Lord owns them.	Ps 24:1; 89:11; Deut 10:14
Ruler	The Lord governs them.	Ps 33:10-11; Is 40:22-24
Judge	The Lord calls all to account.	Ps 33:13-15
Revealer	The Lord speaks the truth.	Ps 33:4; 119:160; Is 45:19
Lover	The Lord loves all he has made.	Ps 145:9, 13, 17
Savior	The Lord saves all who turn to him.	Ps 36:6; Is 45:22
Leader	The Lord guides the nations.	Ps 67:4
Reconciler	The Lord will bring peace.	Ps 46:8-10

And these, as Job might have whispered, are but the edges of his ways (Job 26:14).

4

The Living God Makes
Himself Known in Jesus Christ

Jesus was born among a people who believed all of the affirmations concluded in the last chapter. Jesus himself learned and loved these Scriptures and fed his soul on their truth. This was the theocentric, monotheistic worldview of first-century Jews, the assumptive bedrock of Jesus and all his first followers. It was their foundational certainty that there was one and only one living God. This God, known only by "the Name that is above every name,"[1] was acknowledged now by Israel, his covenant people. But the God of Israel was also the universal God to whom all nations, kings, and even emperors must finally submit. And yet, within the pages of the New Testament and within what would have been the normal life span of Jesus himself (but for his crucifixion), we find the name of Jesus set alongside "the Name"—the name of Israel's God. And this is so, not just in one or two marginal or late texts but in a systematic and clearly intentional way that seems to have originated among the followers of Jesus before the earliest New Testament documents were even penned.

The New Testament, it is sometimes said, never states in just so many words "Jesus is God." We may perhaps be grateful for this, since the word *god* in English, like the word *theos* in Greek, is really far too vague and ambiguous to give such a sentence any kind of clarity or specificity. Many ancient Greeks or Romans, like many contemporary Hindus, would not balk at such a sentence, provided the word *god* is left undefined and anarthrous (i.e., without the exclusive definite article). What is so startling, and what we unquestionably do find in the

---

[1] It is not known exactly when the divine name YHWH was no longer pronounced aloud in reading. As well as the oral substitution of *'ădōnay* (Lord) for the Tetragrammaton, the expression "the Name" was also used as a circumlocution.

New Testament, is that people who knew YHWH, the Holy One of Israel, to be *the* God and that YHWH was transcendently unique in all the rich dimensions of his scriptural identity, character and actions, constructed a careful, persistent, point-by-point identification of Jesus of Nazareth with this same YHWH.

In this chapter, then, we will examine first this startling development that presented Jesus as sharing the identity of YHWH, the God of Israel and Israel's Scriptures. Second, we will observe how certain major functions of YHWH are linked to Jesus in the New Testament. Third, we will explore the missional significance of this combination of identity and function between YHWH and Jesus. The Old Testament presented YHWH as the God who wills to be known to the ends of the earth; where does the New Testament fit Jesus into that divine mission? Or to put it in our more formal categories, what is the missiological significance of full, biblical, Christocentric monotheism?

Jesus Shares the Identity of YHWH

Prayer and confession are two of the clearest indications of any person's or any community's understanding of the content and object of their faith. And the New Testament provides us with concise examples of both reaching back to the very earliest worship of the Christian communities, back to the time before Paul wrote his letters or the traditions took written shape in the canonical Gospels. One is the ancient prayer *maranatha!* ("O Lord, come"). The other is the primal confession *Kyrios Iēsous* ("Jesus is Lord").

Maranatha. At the end of his first letter to Corinth Paul concludes with an Aramaic expression, *maranatha,* that, since he leaves it untranslated, must have been familiar even to Greek speaking Christians. The phrase must therefore have been a significant and well-established part of the worship of the original Aramaic speaking followers of Jesus long before the missionary journeys of Paul into the Gentile world of Asia Minor and Europe. It must then have traveled with him and the other early missionaries as a regular part of Christian worship even when the language was Greek.

Maranatha! Paul exclaims, writing it with his own hand and expecting his readers to understand it and echo it themselves (1 Cor 16:22).[2] It is clear that the "Lord" Paul is referring to by the Aramaic *mar* is Jesus, since the immediately following verse speaks of "the grace of the Lord Jesus." And equally clearly, the

---

[2]Although the phrase in Aramaic could be taken as either a confessional declaration ("the Lord has come!") or as a prayer ("Our Lord, come!"), it is widely agreed that the latter is most likely. In the immediate context (preceded by a curse and followed by a salutation), a prayer is more fitting. In its translated Greek form in Rev 22:20, it is clearly a prayer.

Aramaic expression was used by early Christian communities referred to Jesus. But it is also the case that the Aramaic *mar (marah, maran)* was used among Aramaic speaking Jews as a term for God—that is, for YHWH, God of Israel. It could also be used (and indeed still is in the Orthodox tradition) for human beings in positions of authority (just like the Greek *kyrios*), but there are plenty of occasions in Aramaic texts of the period (including the Qumran scrolls) where the term is used of God.[3] So, by directing their appeal to *mar* Jesus, the earliest Aramaic-speaking believers addressed their prayer to the only one who can legitimately be invoked in prayer—the Lord God.

The *Maranatha* invocation of 1 Corinthians 16:22, therefore, represents an old Palestinian formula of prayer, directed to the Lord Jesus. It is a plea for him to come in power and glory. Had these first believers only considered Jesus *maran,* as their rabbi, prayer would not have been directed to him. Rather, it demonstrates decisively that the early Aramaic believers . . . placed this Coming One at the center of their worship and adoration. Paul adopted this Aramaic phrase and used it, without explanation, to include in his closing remarks to the Corinthian church.[4]

Kyrios Iēsous. The second piece of early evidence for the content of the faith of the first believers is the simple affirmation, *kyrios Iēsous,* "Jesus is Lord."[5] While Paul uses the term *kyrios* 275 times, almost always with reference to Jesus, he was by no means the first to do so. As with the primitive expression *maranatha,* he inherited this designation from those who were followers of Jesus before him. Indeed he probably knew the expression and hated it in the days when he was persecuting those who dared to claim that the crucified carpenter from Nazareth was (God forbid, he thought) the Messiah and (even worse) Lord. It was Paul's encounter with the risen Jesus on the road to Damascus that made him blindingly aware that the phrase was not a heinous blasphemy but the simple truth.[6] When he uses the two-word phrase in his own writings, it is clearly already a christological formula. It needed no explanation, because it was already universally accepted as the standard and defining confession of Christian identity. It occurs in this formulaic way in Romans 10:9, 1 Corinthians 12:3 and with slight expansion (to Jesus Christ) in Philippians 2:11.

---

[3]See David B. Capes, *Old Testament Yahweh Texts in Paul's Christology* (Tübingen: Mohr, 1992), pp. 43-45, and bibliography there cited.

[4]Ibid, pp. 46-47.

[5]When the two words occur alone in this order, *Jesus* is the subject and *Lord* is the predicate.

[6]Cf. Seyoon Kim, *The Origin of Paul's Gospel* (Grand Rapids: Eerdmans, 1982), pp. 104-5, who sees a connection between the Damascus road encounter and Paul's acknowledgement of Jesus as *kyrios* in 1 Cor 9:1-2; 2 Cor 4:5. Luke also, who doubtless owed his account to Paul's own memoirs, emphasizes this factor in Acts 9:5, 17.

We saw that the evidence that Aramaic *mar* was used for God is clear and convincing. In the case of *kyrios,* it is overwhelming. The word could, of course, be used as an honorific title for human beings (just as *lord* can be in English). But by far the most significant use of the term, in relation to its application to Jesus in the New Testament, is its use by those who had translated the Hebrew Scriptures into Greek long before Christ. In the collection of those translations we now know as the Septuagint, the word *kyrios* is used virtually as the standard technical term to translate the Tetragrammaton, YHWH. They did not attempt to transliterate the Hebrew form but chose to replicate in Greek the already-established Hebrew oral tradition of reading in the word *'ădōnay* (Lord) when YHWH occurred in the text. This latter word they rendered *ho kyrios,* "the Lord." It is used as the Greek rendering for the name of the God of Israel more than 1,600 times in the Septuagint.

Any Greek-speaking Jew of the first century would have been entirely familiar with this usage. So to the extent that he or she would have read the Scriptures in Greek, it was second nature to read *ho kyrios* and think "the Name," YHWH. It is altogether remarkable then that even before Paul's letters (i.e., within the first two decades after the resurrection) the term was being applied to Jesus. And applied not merely as a term of honor for a respected human being (as it might understandably have been), but with the fully freighted theological significance of its application to YHWH in Old Testament Scriptures. We know this from Philippians 2:6-11, which many scholars think may have been a pre-Pauline Christian hymn quoted here by Paul for its support of the point he is making in context. Not only does this passage celebrate the "super-exaltation" of Jesus (language that refers to his resurrection and ascension, elsewhere closely linked as proof of his lordship [cf. Acts 2:32-36; Rom 14:9]), not only does it say that God has given to Jesus "the name above every name" (which can mean only one name—YHWH), it clinches its argument by applying to Jesus one of the most monotheistic texts in the Old Testament about YHWH:

> that at the name of Jesus every knee should bow,
>   in heaven and on earth and under the earth,
> and every tongue confess that Jesus Christ is Lord,
>   to the glory of God the Father. (Phil 2:10-11)

This is a partial quotation from Isaiah 45:22-23 of words that were originally spoken by YHWH about himself. And in that context the point of the words was to underline YHWH's uniqueness as God and his unique ability to save.

There is no God apart from me
a righteous God and a Savior;
>   there is none but me.
Turn to me and be saved,
>   all you ends of the earth;
>   for I am God, and there is no other.
By myself I have sworn,
>   my mouth has uttered in all integrity
>   a word that will not be revoked:
Before me every knee will bow;
>   by me every tongue will swear.
They will say of me, "In the LORD alone
>   are righteousness [salvation] and strength. (Is 45:21-24)

The magnificent prophecies of Isaiah 40—55 assert again and again that YHWH is utterly unique as the only living God in his sovereign power over all nations and all history, and in his ability to save. Therefore Paul, or the composers of the early Christian hymn which he may be quoting in Philippians 2, by deliberately selecting a Scripture from such a context and applying it to Jesus, was affirming that Jesus shares the identity and uniqueness of YHWH in those same respects. So sure was this identification that he (they) did not hesitate to insert the name of Jesus where the name YHWH had occurred in the sacred text. By doing this they

- gave to Jesus a God title
- applied to Jesus a God text
- anticipated for Jesus God worship[7]

The missional implications of this opening point about Jesus should be clear. If the mission of the biblical God includes his will to make himself known in his true identity as YHWH, the living God of Israel's faith, then by identifying Jesus with YHWH, the New Testament sees Jesus as central to that self-revelatory dimension of God's mission. But there is far more to this than formal identity, as we now explore.

Jesus Performs the Functions of YHWH

Paul's application of an Old Testament text about YHWH to Jesus in Philippians 2:10-11 is the most notable but far from the only example of its kind. There are

---

[7]I owe this triplet to John R. W. Stott and quote it from memory after many enjoyable hearings of his lecture "Jesus Is Lord: A Call to Radical Discipleship."

a considerable number of other places where Paul quotes Old Testament Scriptures in which YHWH/*ho kyrios* stood, when he (Paul) is referring to Jesus.[8] Nor is Paul the only New Testament writer to do so. The author of Hebrews, for example, launches his epistle with a whole salvo of God texts applied to Jesus. Many of these applied Scriptures are functional—that is, they speak of things that YHWH does or provides or accomplishes. By such scriptural quotation those functions are then attributed to, or closely associated with, Jesus. As with the simple expressions of identity *(maranatha, Kyrios Iēsous),* Paul did not originate this practice. Nor did the early church. It goes right back to Jesus himself. For the Gospels preserve numerous ways that Jesus in word, deed and implicit claim linked himself with the unique functions of the God of Israel.

The material we could consider under this heading is abundant, so I will attempt to organize it around certain key functions of YHWH (similar to the list that concluded the last chapter), and in each case draw exemplifying texts from the Epistles and Gospels. We will look at four key ways that the activity of YHWH is described in the Old Testament: as Creator, Ruler, Judge and Savior. And in each case we will see how Jesus is described in the same way.

The point to note carefully, in view of our overall purpose in this chapter, is that all of these are functions that belonged uniquely and exclusively to YHWH in our definition of Old Testament monotheism. These are the things that defined what it meant to say that "the LORD is (the) God and there is no other." These are the attributes, accomplishments and prerogatives that put YHWH in a class of his own, that constituted his transcendent uniqueness. This is what makes it so astonishing and so profoundly significant for Christian identity and mission that the New Testament portrays Jesus and his earliest followers calmly demanding that Jesus must be viewed within the same frame of reference and with the same exclusive suite of functions and claims as YHWH himself.

From a missiological angle, if these are the prerogatives and functions that YHWH exercises in fulfillment of his mission, then it will be of critical importance to any concept of Christian mission to understand how the mission of God in Christ is exercised in these terms.

Creator. Paul had the knack of bringing the most massive theological affirmations to bear upon the most mundane practical issues. Mundane, but not minor. In Corinth the issue of whether or not Christians could eat meat that had been previously sacrificed to idols occupies Paul's pastoral and theological at-

---

[8]E.g., Rom 10:13 (Joel 2:32); 14:11 (= Is 45:23-24); 1 Cor 1:31; 2 Cor 10:17 (= Jer 9:24); 1 Cor 2:16 (= Is 40:13); 2 Tim 2:19 (= Num 16:5).

tention for three whole chapters (1 Cor 8—10). Two issues are intertwined: the status of idols (are they in any sense real?), and the state of the meat (is it somehow contaminated by having been sacrificed to an idol?). Paul tackles the first head on at the beginning of his argument (1 Cor 8:4-6), and the second toward the end (1 Cor 10:25-26, though he refers to it also in 1 Cor 8:7-8). And significantly he applies a strong creation theology to both questions.

In 1 Corinthians 8:4-6 Paul throws the full weight of the *Shema*—the great Jewish monotheistic confession—at the problem. Whatever these so-called gods and lords may be, we know that there is in reality only one God and one Lord. But rather than merely quoting Deuteronomy 6:4 in its stark Old Testament form, Paul quotes it in what was possibly already a christologically expanded form within the Christian communities. It is a remarkable battery of twenty-seven words in Greek without a single main verb, which goes literally as follows:

> For us, one God, the Father,
> from whom all things
> and we for him;
> and one Lord, Jesus Christ,
> through whom all things
> and we through him. (1 Cor 8:6, my translation)

As the NIV translation makes clear, necessarily providing some connecting verbs, this not only inserts Jesus into the "one God, one Lord" of the *Shema,* it also connects Jesus with the creating work of God the Father.

> For us there is but one God, the Father, from whom all things came and for whom we live; and there is but one Lord, Jesus Christ, through whom all things came and through whom we live. (1 Cor 8:6)

All things came from one God, the Father, and all things came through one Lord, Jesus Christ. So if Jesus is Lord of all creation, these other so-called gods and idols have no real divine existence in the universe. The christological implications for biblical monotheism of what Paul does here are well brought out by Richard Bauckham.

> The only possible way to understand Paul as maintaining monotheism is to understand him to be including Jesus in the unique identity of the one God affirmed in the Shema'. But this is in any case clear from the fact that the term "Lord," applied here to Jesus as the "one Lord," is taken from the Shema' itself. Paul is not adding to the one God of the Shema' a "Lord" the Shema' does not mention. He is identifying Jesus as the "Lord" whom the Shema' affirms to be one. In this unprecedented reformulation of the Shema', the unique identity of the one God consists of the one

God, the Father, and the one Lord, his Messiah (who is implicitly regarded as the Son of the Father).[9]

Moving to the other end of his argument, what about the meat? Should it be shunned as contaminated by its contact with idolatry? Matching the negative point that "an idol is nothing at all in the world" (1 Cor 8:4) comes the positive point that all created things belong to the Lord anyway. So Paul quotes another great creation text, Psalm 24:1, as authority for the basic principle of freedom to eat anything (1 Cor 10:25-26—subject, of course, to the situational qualifications that follow): "The earth is the LORD's, and everything in it."

The Hebrew text, of course, made this bold affirmation about YHWH. But it is most probable that Paul applies it here to Jesus, as the Lord to whom the whole earth belongs. This is partly because of the way he has already linked Jesus to God in the expanded *Shema* in 1 Corinthians 8:6, partly because "the Lord" in the preceding context is clearly Jesus ("the cup of the Lord; . . . the Lord's table," 1 Cor 10:20-21) and partly because Psalm 24 had already gained messianic significance with its summons to make way for the "King of glory" (vv. 7, 9, 10)— a phrase possibly echoed by Paul when he referred to Jesus as "the Lord of glory" in 1 Corinthians 2:8.

So the whole earth belongs to Jesus as Lord. The missiological, ethical and (here) practical implications of such a worldview are staggering—just as staggering as the exalted vistas of Deuteronomy 10:14, 17, that we explored in chapter three. For if the whole earth belongs to Jesus, there is no corner of the earth to which we can go in mission that does not already belong to him. There is not an inch of the planet that belongs to any other god, whatever the appearances. A Christ-centered theology of divine ownership of the whole world is a major foundation for missional theology, practice and ultimate confidence.

The summit of Paul's creational christology comes in Colossians 1:15-20—a passage of unmatched exaltation. The verses relevant at this point run:

> He is the image of the invisible God, the firstborn over all creation. For by him all things were created: things in heaven and on earth, visible and invisible, whether thrones or powers or rulers or authorities; all things were created by him and for him. He is before all things and in him all things hold together. (Col 1:15-17)

---

[9]Richard Bauckham, "Biblical Theology and the Problems of Monotheism," in *Out of Egypt: Biblical Theology and Biblical Interpretation,* ed. Craig Bartholomew et al. (Carlisle, U.K.: Paternoster; Grand Rapids: Zondervan, 2004), p. 224. The passage is also thoroughly discussed in relation to Old Testament monotheism and its christological expansion by N. T. Wright, "Monotheism, Christology and Ethics: 1 Corinthians 8," in *The Climax of the Covenant: Christ and the Law in Pauline Theology,* ed. N. T. Wright (Edinburgh: T & T Clark, 1991), pp. 120-36.

The repeated term *ta panta,* "all things," and the way it is expanded to include all possible realms of reality makes it unmistakeably clear: Jesus Christ stands in the same relationship to creation as anything that is said of YHWH in the Old Testament. He is behind it and before it. He is the agent of its creation and the beneficiary of its existence. It belongs to him as owner by right of creation and inheritance. He is the Source and Sustainer of all that exists.

Essentially the same claims are made in Hebrews 1:2 and John 1:3.

In the other Gospels Jesus' power over the natural order compelled the disciples to ask astonished questions about his identity. "Who is this?" they gasped, "He commands even the wind and the water, and they obey him" (Lk 8:25, par.). There could really be only one answer to that question, and the Psalms had already given it (cf. Ps 65:7; 89:9; 93:3-4; 104:4, 6-9, and esp. relevant for the amazed disciples, Ps 107:23-32). But it was not only in the implied answer to such questions that Jesus' identity as being one with the Creator lay. "Heaven and earth will pass away," he said, "but my words will never pass away" (Mk 13:31, par.). To claim that his word had a status and durability greater than the whole creation was to equate it with the creative word of God himself, in what was probably a deliberate echo of the great creational affirmations of Isaiah 40 (esp. v. 8).

The New Testament, then, unequivocally puts Jesus alongside YHWH in the primary biblical activity of God—the creation of the universe. The implications are correspondingly universal.

> Of the Jewish ways of characterizing the divine uniqueness, the most unequivocal was by reference to creation. In the uniquely divine role of creating all things it was for Jewish monotheism unthinkable that any being other than God could even assist God (Is 44:24; 4 Ezra 3:4 . . .). But to Paul's unparalleled inclusion of Jesus in the Shema' he adds the equally unparalleled inclusion of Jesus in the creative activity of God. No more unequivocal way of including Jesus in the unique divine identity is conceivable, within the framework of Second Temple Jewish monotheism.[10]

Jesus then is associated with all that the Old Testament Scriptures affirm about God as Creator. Since creation forms the platform of all God's mission in history, as well as being the final eschatological beneficiary of all God's redemptive intention, the centrality of Christ in that great mission of God within and for creation is clearly focused.

Ruler. We have seen that in the Old Testament the transcendent uniqueness of YHWH is expressed, first through the affirmation that he alone is the sole cre-

---

[10]Bauckham, "Biblical Theology and the Problems of Monotheism," p. 224.

ator of all that exists, and second through the equally robust affirmation that he alone is the sovereign ruler of all that happens. YHWH reigns, both as the source of all reality and as the governor of all history. As Psalm 33 expresses it, the Lord calls the world into existence through his word (vv. 6-9), rules the world according to his plans (vv. 10-11) and calls the world to account before his watching eye (vv. 13-15). And as Isaiah 40—55 proclaims, he does all these things utterly unaided and unrivalled. YHWH alone is ruler of all. Where, then, could Jesus the carpenter from Nazareth possibly fit in such a view of things?

The answer came from Jesus himself. In a bold stoke he applied to himself the words of a psalm that then went on to become the most quoted christological text in the New Testament, namely Psalm 110.

> The LORD says to my Lord:
>   "Sit at my right hand
>   until I make your enemies
>   a footstool for your feet." (Ps 110:1)

The synoptic Gospels all record Jesus using this text twice: first as a teasing question about the identity of the Messiah (how could he be just a son of David, if David himself called him "Lord" [Mk 12:35-37, par.]), and second, at his trial in answer to the high priest's question, "Are you the Christ?" (Mk 14:61-64, par.). In the latter case, Jesus' expanded his answer with a double scriptural allusion: "You will see the Son of Man sitting at the right hand of the Mighty One and coming on the clouds of heaven."

The language of the Son of Man coming on the clouds of heaven echoes Daniel's great vision in Daniel 7:13-14 and thereby associates Jesus with the universal power and authority of the Ancient of Days. The other phrase, "sitting at the right hand of the Mighty One," clearly echoes Psalm 110 and equally clearly associates Jesus with the governing authority of YHWH. For "the right hand of God" was a powerful symbol in the faith and worship of Israel for YHWH's power in action. By his right hand YHWH:

- accomplished the work of creation (Is 48:13)
- defeated his enemies in his great act of redemption (Ex 15:6, 12)
- saves those who take refuge in him (Ps 17:7; 20:7; 60:5; 118:15-16)
- will exercise final judgment, as in the parable of the sheep and the goats (Mt 25:31-46).

Taking their cue from Jesus' own teaching, then, the earliest Christians used the imagery of Psalm 110:1 to describe the present "location" of the risen and ascended Jesus. Jesus was not just "absent." Jesus was now already "seated at the right hand of God." That is to say, Jesus was already now sharing in the exercise of universal governance that belonged uniquely to YHWH. This exalted claim is found in the preaching of Peter on the day of Pentecost, when he links Psalm 110 to the historically witnessed fact of the resurrection of Jesus and then draws the cosmic conclusion about the lordship of Jesus (Acts 2:32-36).

For Paul, the double imagery of Psalm 110:1 (the right hand of God, enemies beneath the feet) provided the most powerful way that he could express not only the authority of the risen Christ but the ultimate source of that authority, namely, the fact that Jesus shared the identity of YHWH himself, and therefore shared in his universal rule. Paul uses this imagery a lot; for example:

- in reassuring believers with the guarantee that no other power in the universe can separate us from the love of God (Rom 8:34-35)

- in seeing all God's enemies, including eventually death itself, under the feet of the reigning Christ (1 Cor 15:24-28)

- in urging Christians to live their lives under the perspective of Christ's risen and ascended position at the right hand of God (Col 3:1)

- in ringing affirmation of Christ's universal lordship (Eph 1:20-23)

All of these affirmations, of course, underlie Paul's own theology and practice of mission, for it was only out of the conviction that these claims were the sober truth about the one whom he had met on the road to Damascus that he obeyed Christ's mandate to be the apostle to the nations.

The identification of Jesus with YHWH as ruler of the universe comes to its climax (like so much else) in the Revelation. The letters from Jesus to the seven churches imply, and sometimes state, the cosmic authority of Jesus. To do this they use language and imagery to describe him that the Old Testament used for God—particularly as drawn from Daniel's vision of the Ancient of Days and Ezekiel's vision of the glory of YHWH. Dispensing with such imagery, however, the letter to the church in Laodicea simply speaks directly and unequivocally of Jesus as "the ruler of God's creation" (Rev 3:14), echoing the complementary claim of Revelation 1:5 that he is "the ruler of the kings of the earth." In terms of Old Testament monotheism, both of these bald statements (ruler of creation, ruler of the nations) could only ever be made about YHWH. Yet here both statements are explicitly made about Jesus. In the later visions the Lamb that was slain stands in the center of the throne, along with the One who sits on it, such that the combined worship of the vast choir of the whole creation can sing praise simultaneously

> To him who sits on the throne and to the Lamb
> Be praise and honor and glory and power, for ever and ever! (Rev 5:13)

From then on the identification of Jesus the Lamb with the sovereign God on the throne, in various aspects and functions, cascades through the book (Rev 7:10, 17; 11:15; 12:10; 15:3-4; 17:14; 21:1, 3, 13).

The New Testament, then, joins together the lordship of Jesus Christ with the sovereign government of the living God of the faith of Israel. And that was precisely the connection that Jesus makes in the premise of the Great Commission.

The psalmist's shout, "The LORD is king," is echoed and equated with the believer's confession, "Jesus is Lord."

Judge. One of the core functions of YHWH in the Old Testament, which was a dimension of his sovereign rule, was that he judges the whole earth. This conviction is found in the mouth of Abraham (Gen 18:25) and echoes through the narratives, psalms and prophets as a basic datum of Israel's faith. It is a matter of cosmic rejoicing, for the whole of creation can be summoned to

> Sing before the LORD for he comes,
>   he comes to judge the earth.
> He will judge the world in righteousness
>   and the peoples in his truth. (Ps 96:13)

If Jesus shares in the rule of God, being exalted to his right hand, then this must also include sharing in the delivery of God's judgment. And this indeed is what the New Testament affirms unambiguously. Paul sees it as a datum of what he called "my gospel." He takes the language of the "Day of the LORD"—which certainly included judgment as well as salvation in its broad Old Testament usage—and habitually links it with Christ. It can now be called "the day of Christ," "the day when God will judge men's secrets through Jesus Christ, as my gospel declares" (Phil 2:16; Rom 2:16; cf. 2 Thess 1:5-10). Just as the Old Testament envisioned all nations being summoned before YHWH as their ultimate judge, so, says Paul, "we must all appear before the judgment seat of Christ" (2 Cor 5:10). By that expression he doubtless meant exactly the same as "we will all stand before the God's judgment seat" (Rom 14:10).

Characteristically, the future judgment of God is affirmed in Scripture in order to effect changed behavior in the present. Paul uses this dynamic as one of the foundations for his appeal to Gentile and Jewish background believers in Rome to accept one another.[11] In Romans 14:9-12 Paul urges the two groups to refrain from judging one another precisely because we all alike face God's judgment. But he makes this point by combining the resurrection with an Old Testament

---

[11]It seems to me the most likely explanation of Paul's language of "the strong" and "the weak" in Romans 14—15, that he is addressing the mutual differences of the Gentile and Jewish Christians respectively.

text anticipating the universal acceptance of the lordship of YHWH. It is Isaiah 45:23 again—the same text as quoted in Philippians 2:10-11, where we saw that the name of YHWH in the original Hebrew text has been replaced by the name of Jesus in the Christian hymn. Here, Paul leaves the original term "the Lord," but the context (including the repetition of "the Lord" in vv. 6-8) leaves no doubt that Jesus is intended as the subject of the sentence, and the object of worship and submission.

> For this very reason, Christ died and lived again so that he might be Lord both of the dead and of the living. You, then, why do you judge your brother? Or why do you look down on your brother? For we will all stand before God's judgment seat. It is written:
>
> "'As surely as I live,' says the Lord,
> 'every knee will bow before me;
>   every tongue will confess to God.' "
>
> So then, each of us will give an account of himself to God. (Rom 14:9-12)

The attribution to Jesus of the authority to act as judge, hitherto the sole prerogative of YHWH, is also not something Paul invented. This too goes back to Jesus himself. The language of the Son of Man, in those contexts where it reflected the imagery of Daniel 7, certainly had overtones of judgment, since it is linked with the sovereign throne of the Ancient of Days. Jesus' parable of the sheep and the goats significantly begins with the Son of Man occupying that divine seat of judgment (Mt 25:32).

John's portrayal of Jesus stakes the claim to ultimate judgment on Jesus' repeatedly taking upon himself the divine name "I am." Salvation or judgment hangs on acknowledgement or refusal of that claim. "I told you that you will die in your sins; if you do not believe that I am, you will indeed die in your sins (Jn 8:24, my translation).

And of course the Revelation from beginning to end portrays Christ as the Lamb of God exalted on the throne of God's judgment. And the songs of the redeemed proclaim that his position there is utterly worthy, willed by God and vindicated by his divine role in creation, redemption, and control of history.

The New Testament, then, reaffirms the final judgment of the living God of the Old Testament but sees it now embodied in the one God has appointed to that seat of final authority—Jesus Christ his Son.

The psalmist's song of joy "He comes to judge the earth" (Ps 96:13; 98:9) is echoed by Christ's own promise, "Behold, I am coming soon" (Rev 22:12).

Savior. Among the songs of the redeemed in Revelation is this great affirmation:

Salvation belongs to our God,
who sits on the throne,
and to the Lamb! (Rev 7:10)

That salvation belonged to God was a core assertion of Israel's Old Testament faith. That it could be celebrated as belonging now also to Jesus Christ is typical of what we have already seen—the identification of Jesus with the great defining functions of Israel's God.

Saving is one of the most dominant activities and characteristics of YHWH in the Old Testament. Indeed it is hardly going too far to say that salvation defines this God's identity. "Our God is a God who saves" (Ps 68:20). One of the earliest celebrations of salvation coming immediately in the wake of the crossing of the sea at the exodus sings, "the LORD is my strength and my song; / he has become my salvation" (Ex 15:2). Among the oldest poetic metaphors for YHWH in early Hebrew poetry is one that describes him as "the Rock" of Israel's salvation (Deut 32:15). In the psalms YHWH is above all else the God who saves, simply because that is who he is and what he does consistently, often and best. The 136 occurrences of the root *yāša‘* in the Psalms account for 40 percent of all the uses of the root in the Old Testament. The Lord is the God of my salvation (Ps 88:1), the horn of my salvation (Ps 18:2), the rock of my salvation (Ps 95:1), my salvation and my honor (Ps 62:6-7), my Savior and my God (Ps 42:5-6). And not just mine, and not even just of humans, for this God saves "both man and beast" (Ps 36:6). Robert Hubbard is right: "theologically, Israelite worship and instruction supremely associated Yahweh with salvation."[12] No wonder that the prophet who sought to restore Israel's faith in their great God at the time of their lowest ebb in exile reminded them of this great heritage of worship by presenting God in the terms "I am the LORD, your God, / the Holy One of Israel, your Savior" (Is 43:3).

The name Jehoshua (Joshua, Jeshua, Jesus) means "Yahweh is salvation." Through the arrival of Jesus of Nazareth, God was bringing in the promised new era of salvation for Israel and for the world, because through Jesus God would deal with sin. In preparation for his coming John the Baptist preached a message of repentance and forgiveness of sin (Mt 3:6), while pointing to Jesus as the one who "takes away the sin of the world" (Jn 1:29). Matthew records the angel's explanation of the name Jesus: "he will save his people from their sins" (Mt 1:21). Luke, however, goes the furthest in festooning the language of salvation around the arrival of Jesus. Luke uses salvation terms seven times in his first three chapters (Lk 1:47, 69, 71, 77; 2:11, 30; 3:6). There is a particular resonance

---

[12]Robert L. Hubbard, *"yāša‘,"* in *New International Dictionary of Old Testament Theology and Exegesis,* ed. Willem A. VanGemeren (Grand Rapids: Zondervan, 1997), 2:559.

when the aged Simeon, knowing he would not die before he had seen "the Lord's Christ," held the infant Jesus in his arms (probably having asked his name from his parents) and thanked God that now "my eyes have seen your salvation"—your Jehoshua (Lk 2:30).

Salvation, in its fullest biblical sense, involves more than the forgiveness of sin—though that lies at the deepest core of it since sin is the deepest root of all the other dimensions of need and danger from which God alone can save us. But it was the claim to forgive sin that most quickly and clearly raised the question of Jesus' identity in the Gospel narrative. Combining his healing of the paralytic with a declaration that his sins were forgiven, Jesus faced the indignant question, "Why does this fellow talk like that? He's blaspheming! Who can forgive sins but God alone?" (Mk 2:7). Quite so. What then is to be deduced about Jesus?

Actions speak louder than words, as all the prophets knew when they engaged in prophetic sign acts. So when Jesus decided that he needed to ride into Jerusalem on a donkey (Mt 21), it was certainly not because he needed the rest. Having walked all the way from Galilee he could have managed the last half mile on foot. For all who had eyes to see and who knew their Scriptures, the action was a graphic acting out of the prophecy of Zechariah 9:9.

> Rejoice greatly, O Daughter of Zion!
>   Shout, Daughter of Jerusalem!
> See, your king comes to you,
>   righteous and having salvation,
>   gentle and riding on a donkey.

The language of salvation, expressed in the familiar text, was picked up by the crowds that accompanied him. "Hosanna," they shouted, which is an urgent cry meaning, "Save us, now." And they cried it to the one they hailed as "coming in the name of the Lord." "Who is this?" asked the residents of Jerusalem. "Jesus, the prophet from Nazareth in Galilee" (Mt 21:10-11), came the reply of the crowds, which was certainly true, but inadequate. For the full expectation of the Old Testament text, being acted out by this prophet on a donkey, was that the Lord himself would come to Zion, to his temple. And in the temple on the very next day, Jesus acknowledged the praise of the children in the lines of Psalm 8:2, praise that was directed to God now being directed to this one who had come in God's name.

In the rest of the New Testament the language of salvation as applied to Jesus is commonplace and well-known, but we should not fail to register the surprising nature of this, in view of the deep Old Testament roots that confined true salvation to the God of Israel alone. It is worth noting that the word *savior* in the New Testament is applied to God eight times, to Jesus sixteen times and to nobody else at all, ever. And yet the Greek word *sōtēr* (savior) was a fairly common term in the classical world. It was applied as an honorific title both to human kings and military conquerors, and also to the great gods and heroes of mythology. But not in New Testament Christianity. "Salvation belongs to our God . . . and to the Lamb" (Rev 7:10). Nobody else merits even the vocabulary.

The earliest Jewish followers of Jesus, as devout scriptural believers, knew that YHWH alone is God and there is no other source of salvation among the gods or on the earth. This they knew because their Bible told them so, not least Deuteronomy and Isaiah. Yet now they were so utterly convinced that Jesus of Nazareth, their contemporary, shared the very identity of YHWH their God that they could use the same exclusive salvation language of Jesus. Peter declares that salvation is now to be found exclusively in Jesus and in no other name under heaven (Acts 4:12). This is consistent with all the preaching recorded in that book (cf. Acts 2:38; 5:31; 13:38), and it was the settled resolution of the first council of the church: "We believe it is through the grace of our Lord Jesus Christ that we [Jews] are saved, just as they [Gentiles] are" (Acts 15:11). Later, another Jewish believer describes Jesus as the author or pioneer of salvation (Heb 2:10), the source of our eternal salvation (Heb 5:9), and the mediator of complete salvation for all who come to God through him (Heb 7:25). New Testament salvation is as utterly Christ-shaped as Old Testament salvation is YHWH-shaped.

Paul echoes the theme when he piles up the phrases "God our Savior" or "Christ our Savior" seven times in the tiny letter to Titus alone (or both together: "our great God and Savior, Jesus Christ" [Tit 2:13]). In one other text, however, he makes crystal clear his scriptural and theological foundation for this by quoting an Old Testament text concerning YHWH's salvation and applying it deliberately to Jesus.

> If you confess with your mouth, "Jesus is Lord," and believe in your heart that God raised him from the dead, you will be saved. . . . For there is no difference between Jew and Gentile—the same Lord is Lord of all and richly blesses all who call on him, for, "Everyone who calls on the name of the Lord will be saved." (Rom 10:9, 12-13)

The Old Testament text is Joel 2:32, which promised God's deliverance to those of Israel who would turn back to their God before the great day of his judgment (quoted also by Peter in Acts 2:21). Paul not only expands the scope of the appeal to Gentiles as well as to Israel (a missiological point we will return to later) but also sees the promise as now available to all who call on the name of Jesus as Lord. In view of the immediately preceding context with its great christological affirmation "Jesus is Lord," it is unquestionable that Paul here intends that the "Lord" in his text (which was YHWH / *kyrios*) be understood now as signifying Jesus. It was this fundamental conviction about the saving identification of Jesus with YHWH that could inspire him in a moment of instinctive evangelism to urge the Philippian jailer to "believe in the Lord Jesus, and you will be saved" (Acts 16:31).

Calling on the name of the Lord is an action and a theme that also has deep Old Testament roots. It was the great heritage of Israel's worship, part of the privilege of knowing YHWH as God. By contrast, other nations could be described as "nations that do not know you, / kingdoms that do not call on your name" (Ps 79:6, my translation). So again, it is significant that Paul's use of the expression here with reference to Jesus is only one example of a usage that we find in several other places in the New Testament where believers "call on the name" of Jesus—an action from which Jews would certainly have recoiled in horror as blasphemy, if they had not been convinced that in doing so they were in effect calling on the name of the Lord himself (Acts 9:14, 21; 22:16; 1 Cor 1:2; 2 Tim 2:22).

The New Testament, then, building on the massive foundations of Israel's faith in YHWH, their saving God, sees the climactic work of God's salvation in the person and work of Jesus. And since the mission of God could be summed up in that one comprehensive concept that so dominates YHWH's character and intentions in the Old Testament—salvation—the identification of Jesus with YHWH puts him right at the center of that saving mission.

The psalmist's confident trust in YHWH, "God of our salvation," is echoed and equated with Paul's joyful longing for the appearing of "our great God and Savior, Jesus Christ" (Tit 2:13).[13]

Jesus Fulfills the Mission of YHWH

Jesus then, according to the consistent witness of many strands in the New Testament documents, shares the identity of YHWH, the Lord God of Israel, and per-

---

[13]There is now a wealth of excellent books exploring the nature and substance of the New Testament's claims regarding the deity of Jesus Christ. As a selection see Richard Bauckham, *God Crucified: Monotheism and Christology in the New Testament* (Carlisle, U.K.: Paternoster, 1998); Murray J. Harris, *Jesus as God: The New Testament Use of Theos in Reference to Jesus* (Grand Rapids: Baker, 1992); Larry W. Hurtado, *One God, One Lord: Early Christian Devotion and Ancient Jewish Monotheism* (Edinburgh: T & T Clark, 1998); Larry W. Hurtado, *Lord Jesus Christ: Devotion to Jesus in Earliest Christianity* (Grand Rapids: Eerdmans, 2003); Leander E. Keck, *Who Is Jesus? History in Perfect Tense* (Columbia: University of South Carolina Press, 2000); Ben Witherington III, *The Christolology of Jesus* (Minneapolis: Fortress Press, 1990); N. T. Wright, *Jesus and the Victory of God* (London: SPCK, 1996).

forms functions that were uniquely and exclusively the prerogative of YHWH in the Old Testament. These include especially God's role as Creator and owner of the universe, Ruler of history, Judge of all nations and Savior of all who turn to him. In all of these dimensions of God's identity and activity, New Testament believers saw the face of Jesus, spoke of him in exactly the same terms and worshiped him accordingly.

But so what?

Why should it matter that the monotheistic faith of Old Testament Israel is expanded and redefined in this christocentric way? If, as James sharply pointed out, monotheism per se ("you believe that there is one God") gets you no further than the trembling belief of the demons (Jas 2:19), how much further does it get you merely to add Jesus to your monotheism? Supposing the New Testament had simply stated "Jesus is God." Might James perhaps have commented on mere intellectual assent to such a proposition: "You believe that Jesus is God? Good! even the demons believe that—and shudder"? My point is that if Old Testament monotheism and the New Testament's affirmation of the deity of Christ are left as merely creedal confessions, they remain, while possibly interesting for historians of religions, as dead as faith without works, as James would say.

This is where we need once again to underline the missional thrust of our investigation, which I have recalled at various points along the way in this chapter. What is the mission of this God, about whom the Old Testament affirms such transcendent uniqueness? And in what way is the New Testament confession of Jesus connected not just to the identity and functions of the God of Israel but also to his mission?

God wills to be known through Jesus. To answer these questions, we return to the overarching theme of chapter three—namely, YHWH's driving will to be known as God by all nations to the ends of the earth. Now there are, of course, many other ways that we might express the mission of God as articulated throughout the Old Testament, and the remainder of this book will explore some of the key ones. But this is one that we have seen clearly already. Whether through the experience of God's saving grace or through exposure to God's righteous judgment, Israel came to know who the true and living God is. And by the same means, ultimately, the nations too will come to know his identity, either in repentance, salvation and worship, or in defiant wickedness and destruction. "The earth will be filled with the knowledge of the glory of the LORD, as the waters cover the sea" (Hab 2:14). Such is God's will and purpose. Such is the mission of God.

In the New Testament this divine will to be universally known is now focused on Jesus. It will be through Jesus that God will be known to the nations.

And in knowing Jesus, they will know the living God. Jesus, in other words, fulfills the mission of the God of Israel. Or to put it the other way round: the God of Israel, whose declared mission was to make himself known to the nations through Israel, now wills to be known to the nations through the Messiah, the one who embodies Israel in his own person and fulfills the mission of Israel to the nations. Thus, the fact that the New Testament so carefully details all the ways that Jesus shares the identity and functions of YHWH now comes into even sharper significance in this missional perspective. For it will be precisely in knowing Jesus as Creator, Ruler, Judge and Savior that the nations will know YHWH. Jesus is not merely the agent through whom the knowledge of God is communicated (as any messenger might be). He is himself the very content of the communication. Where Jesus is preached, the very glory of God shines through.

> Unbelievers . . . cannot see the light of the gospel of the glory of Christ, who is the image of God. For we do not preach ourselves, but Jesus Christ as Lord *[Kyrios]*, and ourselves as your servants for Jesus' sake. For God, who said, "Let light shine out of darkness," made his light shine in our hearts to give us the light of the knowledge of the glory of God in the face of Christ. (2 Cor 4:4-6)[14]

The gospel carries the knowledge of God among the nations. Paul understood himself to be God's apostle to the nations, entrusted with the task of taking this gospel of the knowledge of the living God to the nations that knew him not. But he clearly saw this personal mission of his as entirely dependent on the prior mission of God, that is, of God's own will to be known. It was not the case that Paul chose to have a mission to the nations on behalf of Israel's God. It was that the God of Israel chose Paul for his mission to the nations. This is how Luke records Paul's own interpretation of his commissioning in Damascus.

> Then [Ananias] said, "The God of our fathers has chosen you to know his will and to see the Righteous One and to hear words from his mouth. You will be his witness to all men of what you have seen and heard." (Acts 22:14-15)

> I am sending you to [the Gentiles] to open their eyes and turn them from darkness to light, and from the power of Satan to God, so that they may receive forgiveness of sins and a place among those who are sanctified by faith in me. (Acts 26:17-18)

From then on Paul felt that the gospel had a power all of its own, which

---

[14]It seems very possible that Paul is alluding to Ezekiel's great vision of the glory of God (Ezek 1) here, and that he may have interpreted his own encounter with the glory of the risen Christ in such terms. If so, it is even more significant that he oscillates between "glory of Christ" and "glory of God"—another example of his identification of Jesus with YHWH.

swept him along in its universal scope and spread. God willed to be known and nothing could stand in his way. Paul was only a servant of the process.

> I have become its servant by the commission God gave me to present to you the word of God in its fullness. . . . God has chosen to make known among the nations the glorious riches of this mystery, which is the Messiah among you, the hope of glory. (Col 1:25, 27, my translation).[15]

Such was the unstoppable power of the spread of the gospel, because of God's will to be known, that Paul uses some geographical hyperbole, anticipating its universal proclamation.

> All over the world this gospel is bearing fruit and growing. (Col 1:6)

> This is the gospel that you heard and that has been proclaimed to every creature under heaven. (Col 1:23)

Regarding this Bauckham says:

> These Pauline hyperboles are not just "rhetorical" but express the urgent dynamic of the gospel towards its universal goal and Paul's overwhelming sense of his personal vocation within that dynamic.[16]

Later in life, Paul reflected on his calling to mission, seeing it as the priestly task of making God known. It was one of the functions of the priests in Israel to be stewards of the knowledge of God (cf. Hos 4:1-6; Mal 2:7; 2 Chron 15:3). Paul by analogy sees his evangelism as a priestly duty to the nations, significantly adding that he specially made it his ambition to exercise his gospel ministry "where Christ was not known" (Rom 15:16-22; notice his quotation of the Servant passage from Is 52:15, which speaks of the knowledge of the Servant among the nations). And later still, he again links his whole ministry

---

[15]In Paul's brief mention of "the mystery" in the parallel section of Ephesians, it is clear that the mystery is precisely that Jesus, as the crucified Messiah, has brought Gentiles and Jews together (Eph 3:2-13). It seems to me, therefore, that the phrase *Christos en hymin* refers not so much to the indwelling Christ of personal experience ("Christ within you") as to the reality that Christ is now "among you"—i.e., you Gentiles, in the same sense as the preceding *"en tois ethnesin,"* "among the nations."

[16]Richard Bauckham, *The Bible and Mission: Christian Mission in a Postmodern World* (Carlisle, U.K.: Paternoster, 2003), p. 22. Bauckham points to other examples of this geographical hyperbole and its eschatological significance for mission (Rom 1:8; 1 Thess 1:8; 2 Cor 2:14). On the other hand, Eckhard Schnabel suggests that these phrases may actually reflect missionary reality if there were early mission ventures going on in the regions that were popularly called "the ends of the earth" by the time Paul wrote Colossians; see *Early Christian Mission,* vol 1, *Jesus and the Twelve* (Downers Grove, Ill.: InterVarsity Press, 2004), pp. 436-554, which provides a superbly detailed account of the perceptions of geographical reality in Jewish and Greco-Roman culture of the first century, within which the early Christian mission took place.

to God's own will to be known and longing to save.

> God our Savior, who wants all people to be saved and to come to a knowledge of
> the truth. . . . And for this purpose I was appointed a herald and an apostle . . .
> and a teacher of the nations in faith and truth. (1 Tim 2:3-4, 7, my translation)

In between God's will to save and Paul's role in implementing it, Paul puts
yet another echo of the *Shema:* "For there is one God and one mediator between God and men, the man Christ Jesus, who gave himself as a ransom for
all" (1 Tim 2:5-6). Thus the God Paul proclaims is the one true living and only
God of Israel, but the means by which this God is now to be savingly known
to all humanity is through the unique humanity and self-offering of Jesus the
Messiah.

What we have here, then, is biblical monotheism and mission, combined in
the person of Jesus and the proclamation of the apostle.

For John, the universal revelatory function of Jesus' identity and mission is
highlighted from the very beginning, repeated at intervals through the Gospel,
and climaxes in the great prayer of Jesus in John 17. "No one has ever seen
God," John writes as he draws his prologue to a conclusion, "but the unique
God, the one in the bosom of the Father, that one has made him known" (Jn
1:18, my translation). God makes visible God's own self through the incarnation
of God the Son. So, then, to know Jesus is to know the Father (Jn 8:19; 10:38;
12:45; 14:6-11), and in knowing both stands eternal life (Jn 17:3).[17] But this
knowing God through knowing Jesus is not to be confined to those who saw
him in the flesh. On the contrary, that privilege was accorded to them for the
purpose of making him known to the world, "to let the world know that you
sent me" (Jn 17:23). So, in truly priestly fashion, Jesus dispenses the knowledge
of God, first to his immediate disciples and then through them to the world.

> My prayer is not for them alone. I pray also for those who will believe in me
> through their message, . . . that the world may believe that you have sent me. . . .
> Righteous Father, though the world does not know you, I know you, and they
> know that you have sent me. I have made you known to them, and will continue
> to make you known in order that the love you have for me may be in them and
> that I myself may be in them. (Jn 17:20-21, 25-26).

God's mission to be known to the world dominates the thinking of the Son
even as he engages in prayer with his Father. And the mission of the disciples,
implicit in Jesus' prayer before his crucifixion (Jn 17:18), becomes explicit in

---

[17]The same dynamic combination of the knowledge of God through the knowledge of Jesus
threads its way through 1 John as well (cf. 1 Jn 2:3-6, 23; 4:13-15; 5:20-21).

Jesus' commissioning after his resurrection: "As the Father sent me, I am sending you" (Jn 20:21).

And so John reaches his climax with Thomas's confession of faith, "My Lord and my God" (Jn 20:28), in which Thomas addressed to Jesus words that would only ever have dared to cross his lips in the worship of YHWH. On that basis alone, John's concluding statement of the missional purpose of his Gospel can be founded. "These things are written that you may believe that Jesus is the Christ, the Son of God, and that by believing you may have life in his name" (Jn 20:31).

Here then we have biblical monotheism and mission from the lips of the disciple and the pen of the evangelist.

Biblical Monotheism and Mission

In the course of chapters three and four we have surveyed vast tracts of biblical monotheism. I resisted at the outset the temptation to predefine monotheism in the Enlightenment categories by which religions are classified or to engage in speculative reconstructions of the alleged evolutionary process by which Israel is deemed to have reached that predefined monotheistic conceptualization. I chose rather to ask what Israel meant when they declared that "YHWH is God and there is no other." We particularly explored the dynamic experience of "knowing God." Israel claimed this for themselves on the basis of their historical experience, and they anticipated others eventually coming to such knowledge universally. Then we observed the amazing turn by which the YHWH-centered monotheism of the Old Testament became the Jesus-centered monotheism of the New Testament. This was accomplished not only without compromising the essential marks of Israel's faith but by actually affirming and amplifying them.

The question we need to ask as we summarize and conclude these two chapters is, In what way does a missional hermeneutical perspective shed light on what we call biblical monotheism, enabling us to articulate its inner dynamic and ultimate significance? Or, perhaps in simpler terms, Why is biblical monotheism missional? Three reflections may be offered in response: first, because of God's will to be known as God; second, because of the constant struggle in which biblical monotheism has always engaged and continues to be engaged today; and third, because biblical monotheism issues supremely in worship and praise, which are profoundly missional activities, in this world at least.

Biblical mission is driven by God's will to be known as God. The theme of "knowing God" was deliberately chosen as a thread for chapters three and four because nothing seems more appropriate to this driving force of biblical monotheism. The one living God wills to be known throughout his whole creation. The world must know its Creator. The nations must know their Ruler, Judge and Savior. This is a major subplot of the exodus narrative in the book of Exodus, but later recollections of that great event repeatedly highlight its prime purpose as making a great name for YHWH among the nations (e.g., Josh 2:10-11; 2 Sam 7:23; Ps 106:8; Is 63:12; Jer 32:20; Dan 9:15; Neh 9:10). "The exodus, then, establishes a paradigmatic link between God's particular identity as the God of Israel and God's purpose of universal self-revelation to the nations."[18] Later great acts of YHWH are recorded with the same intention: the crossing of the Jordan (Josh 4:24), David's victory over Goliath (1 Sam 17:46), God's covenant with David (2 Sam 7:26), God answering prayer in Solomon's temple (1 Kings 8:41-43, 60), God delivering Jerusalem from the Assyrians (2 Kings 19:19; Is 37:20), God bringing Israel back from exile (Is 45:6; Jer 33:9; Ezek 36:23). The whole history of Israel, we might say, is intended to be the shop window for the knowledge of God in all the earth. This is the reason the story is to be told from generation to generation.

> All the ends of the earth
> > will remember and turn to the LORD,
> and all the families of the nations
> > will bow down before him, . . .
> [because] . . .
> > future generations will be told about the Lord.
> They will proclaim his righteousness
> > to a people yet unborn—
> > for he has done it. (Ps 22:27, 30-31).

Richard Bauckham sees this as one of the major missional trajectories of the biblical revelation. "This trajectory is fundamentally about the knowledge of who God is, YHWH's demonstration of his deity to the nations." Aware of possible contemporary objections to such a view of God, Bauckham continues:

> We may have difficulty with this picture of God desiring and achieving fame for himself, something we would regard as self-seeking vanity and ambition if it were said of a human being. But this is surely one of those human analogies which is actually appropriate uniquely to God. The good of God's human creatures requires that he be known to them as God. There is no vanity, only revelation of truth, in God's demonstrating of his deity to the nations.[19]

---

[18]Bauckham, *Bible and Mission,* p. 37.
[19]Ibid.

This leads us to the first of three missiological conclusions from this point.

The good of creation depends on humanity knowing God. First, to repeat Bauckham's words: "the good of God's human creatures requires that he be known to them as God." We might add that the good of the whole creation requires that God be known and praised as its Creator. The frustration of creation in this primary role and task, on account of human sin, is one of the reasons why the whole creation looks forward eagerly to the redemption of humanity (Rom 8:19-21). But confining ourselves to the human dimension: it is crucial to emphasize the point that knowing God to be God is the supreme good and blessing for human beings made in God's image. Refusing or suppressing that knowledge lies at the root of all other kinds of sin, argues Paul in Romans 1:18-32. Conversely, knowing God in love and obedience is the source of all human well-being and good (Deut 4:39-40). Life itself, in all its fullness and eternity, lies in knowing and loving God (cf. Deut 30:19-20; Jn 17:3). For this we were created, and anything less falls short of the glory of God. "The chief end of man," as the Westminster Confession so succinctly and biblically expressed it, "is to glorify God and enjoy him forever"—which encapsulates the supreme task and blessing of what it means to know God, and thereby to be fully human. Accordingly, insofar as our missional engagement is a matter of making God known, it is by that very fact also a matter of bringing blessing and good to people, for "the LORD is good." Mission is not the imposition of yet another religious bondage upon an already overburdened humanity. It is the sharing of the liberating knowledge of the one true living God, "in knowledge of whom standeth our eternal life."[20]

The good of creation comes from humanity knowing the biblical God. Second, this good comes only from the knowledge of this God—the living and personal God of biblical monotheism. Biblical mission necessarily requires biblical monotheism. It means making known the biblical revelation of the living God in all the fullness of his identity, character, functions and saving acts. It means sharing, as it were, the biography of the God of the whole Bible. The personal and ethical quality of biblical monotheism is distinctive and definitive. As we observed, merely believing in the singularity of deity—abstract monotheism—is no great achievement. Nor was such belief the limit of what Israel was to learn from, say, the experiences of exodus and Sinai. The point of these events was not so that Israel would know the arithmetic of heaven but that they would know the identity and character of the One who alone

---

[20]From the second collect, for peace, in "The Order for Morning Prayer," *Book of Common Prayer.*

was "the God"—YHWH (Deut 4:32-40). He is the God whom they were to know as the God of justice, compassion, holiness, truth, integrity, love, faithfulness and sovereign power. These qualities of the one God would be the stuff of their narratives, the sanction for their laws, the platform for all the moods of their worship, the burden of their prophets and the foundation for their wisdom. And this is the God who promised to make himself known to the nations, in the most monotheistic tract in the Old Testament, as the Servant whose commitment to justice, compassion, liberation and enlightenment would lead him to vicarious suffering and death (Is 42-53).[21] And in fulfillment of that, this is the God whose transcendent uniqueness took flesh and dwelled among us in the humanity of Jesus, full of grace and truth. The only kind of monotheism that is "good" for people is the knowledge of this God. That is why God wills to be known for the God he truly is.

God's will to be known is the mainspring of our mission to make him known. Third, this great biblical dynamic that God wills to be known precedes and undergirds all of the efforts of God's people in their mission of making him known. Here again we find the priority of God's mission as the source of our own. In the Old Testament we find God's own clear intention that the knowledge of YHWH as the living God should go to the nations, who indeed are portrayed as waiting eagerly for it. In the New Testament we find the mechanism of that process revealed—the apostolic witness to the gospel of Messiah Jesus and the sending of the disciples of Jesus to make disciples of the nations. So Paul could describe himself as a "teacher of the true faith to the nations" (1 Tim 2:7; 2 Tim 1:11, my translation). "The mission to the nations in the New Testament also is directed to their acknowledgement and worship of the true God (1 Thessalonians 1:9; Acts 17:23-29; Revelation 14:7; 15:4) even before it is directed to the salvation that accompanies this."[22]

So all our missional efforts to make God known must be set within the prior framework of God's own will to be known. We are seeking to accomplish what God himself wills to happen. This is both humbling and reassuring. It is humbling inasmuch as it reminds us that all our efforts would be in vain but for God's determination to be known. We are neither the initiators of the mission of making God known to the nations nor does it lie in our power to decide how the task will be fully accomplished or when it may be deemed to be complete. But it is also reassuring. For we know that behind all our fumbling efforts and inadequate

---

[21]On this point, see especially Millar C. Lind, "Monotheism, Power and Justice: A Study in Isaiah 40-55," *Catholic Biblical Quarterly* 46 (1984): 432-46.

[22]Bauckham, *Bible and Mission,* p. 40.

communication stands the supreme will of the living God, reaching out in loving self-revelation, incredibly willing to open blind eyes and reveal his glory through the treasures of the gospel delivered in the clay pots of his witnesses (2 Cor 4:1-7).

Biblical monotheism involves constant christological struggle. One of the more facile a priori assertions of the evolutionary theory of human religious development is that although it might take a long time for a culture to reach the heights of monotheism, monotheism itself had such a self-evident power of conviction that people would never set off in the opposite direction by reverting to polytheistic forms of religion. Monotheism was a plateau from which no thinking person or culture could wish to descend. The alleged evolutionary process of religious maturation was not considered reversible.

But as Bauckham convincingly argues, the reason for the much more untidy account of Israel's religious history that the canonical books actually present is that biblical monotheism was not at all a self-evident vista, which, once glimpsed, could never be surrendered. It was, rather, as the Old Testament repeatedly portrays, a constant battlefield.[23]

Moving from the Old to the New Testament, we can see immediately that the same struggle surrounds the claims made for Jesus Christ. Christ-centered monotheism is no more self-evidently beyond challenge or dissent than YHWH-centered monotheism was in Israel. Nor is it any more immediately obvious to the world that Jesus alone is Lord, God and Savior, than it was to the nations around Israel that YHWH alone is the God of heaven and earth, Creator of the world and Ruler of all its nations. And yet these are precisely the truths to which Israel was called to bear witness, and which Christian mission declares to the world.

So one of the reasons why biblical monotheism is missional lies here: it is a truth to which we are constantly called to bear witness. It is a conviction that constantly engages us in the apologetic task of articulating and defending what we mean by our confession of faith in the living God of the Bible in both Testaments. As the New Testament records, from the very earliest days of the Christian faith, believers had to contend with challenges to the lordship of Christ from outside the church, and with denials or confusions concerning aspects of the person and achievement of Christ from within it. Today, as much as ever, to affirm that Jesus of Nazareth is uniquely God, Lord and Savior, is to find oneself immediately engaged in missional conflict on every side.

But what does it mean to say that Jesus Christ is unique? There are those who

---

[23]To remind ourselves yet again, by "biblical monotheism" I mean the actual assertion in Israel of the transcendent uniqueness of YHWH, not the abstract construct of Enlightenment categories.

would argue that the language is too imprecise and open to wilfull misunderstanding or distortion. Of course Jesus is "unique," the religious pluralist may congenially agree. Every religion and every great religious leader is unique. They all provide unique insights and unique opportunities for "saving contact with the Ultimate Divine Reality" (to use pluralist language). But used in this way, to say that Jesus is unique is no more than to say that he is a unique specimen of a particular species—the species being "religious leader" or "agent of salvific contact with the divine." He is one (unique, i.e., distinctive) way among many possible ways to find whatever one means by "God." And so, as has been said, the language of the uniqueness of Jesus can be the "trojan horse of pluralism." By using it, you may be allowing a lot of unsuspected and unwelcome theological assumptions into the vocabulary by those who are happy to use the phrase, but in that relativized pluralist way.

Accordingly, it seems all the more important to have worked through in these two chapters exactly what we mean by biblical monotheism. And especially we are grateful for Bauckham's clarification of what we mean by the uniqueness of YHWH. For the Old Testament texts clearly did not mean that YHWH was one unique god among many within the species "gods." Rather, in what Bauckham called "transcendent uniqueness," YHWH stood *sui generis,* entirely in a class of his own as *the* God, the sole Creator of the universe, and Ruler, Judge and Savior of the nations. And the New Testament repeatedly makes exactly the same affirmations about Jesus of Nazareth, putting him in the same exclusively singular, transcendent framework and frequently quoting the same texts to do so.

So when we speak missiologically of the uniqueness of Christ, we are not engaged in some kind of horizontal comparison of Jesus with other great founders of religions. It is not that we line them up together and at the end of such a comparative process we come to the conclusion that, somehow, Jesus is better than all the rest, or, less competitively, that "Jesus is the one for me." Rather we are engaged vertically in tracing the scriptural roots of the identity, mission and accomplishments of Jesus deeply into the uniqueness of YHWH, the Holy One of Israel. Christocentric biblical monotheism is profoundly missional, inasmuch as it says with equal strength (because both statements ultimately amount to the same univocal claim) that YHWH is God in heaven above and the earth beneath, and there is no other; and that Jesus is Lord, and there is no other name under heaven given to humanity by which we must be saved.[24]

---

[24]I have surveyed these dimensions of the uniqueness of Jesus in the context of religious pluralism more fully in Christopher J. H. Wright, *The Uniqueness of Jesus* (London and Grand Rapids: Monarch, 1997).

Biblical monotheism generates praise. I ought to conclude this chapter at the same destination as that to which biblical monotheism itself leads, doxology: the worship and praise of this great God, in and through the name of Christ.

The title of the book of Psalms in Hebrew is *těhillîm,* "Praises." This is so even though the largest single category of psalms are the psalms of lament. Praise in the Old Testament was not just about being happy and thankful but about acknowledging the reality of the one living God in the whole of life—including the tough times. So even in those psalms which are mostly in a troubled mode, there is a movement toward praise. Even the whole book of Psalms moves from the predominance of lament and petitionary psalms in the early sections to the almost complete dominance of praise in the final section. As Patrick Millar puts it in a warm and instructive article:

> To go through the Book of Psalms is to be led increasingly toward the praise of God as the final word. . . . That is so theologically, because in praise more than any other human act God is seen and declared to be God in all fullness and glory. That is so eschatologically, because the last word of all is the confession and praise of God by the whole creation.[25]

So there is a close link between the monotheistic dynamic of Israel's faith, and the glorious richness of Israel's worship. Since Israelites know YHWH to be "the God"— the God of such resplendent character, such robust redemptive action and such reliable faithfulness—the only right response is the outpouring of praise. And since they know YHWH to be the only God, there is a broad surge of universality coursing through Israel's worship. And this universality, in turn, inevitably implies that all nations, indeed all creation, must come to worship the living God of Israel and can be summoned to do so. And this, in a nutshell, is a missional perspective, even though there is no centrifugal missionary mandate. Miller makes the point by showing how Israel's worship combines theology and testimony, declaration and conversional anticipation.

> The praise of God in the Old Testament is always devotion that tells about God, that is theology, and proclamation that seeks to draw others into the circle of those who worship this God, that is testimony for conversion. . . . Perhaps less clear in the minds of many readers of the Old Testament is the fact that the praise of God is the most prominent and extended formulation of the universal and conversionary dimension of the theology of the Old Testament. One might even speak of a missionary aim if that did not risk distorting the material by suggesting a program

---

[25]Patrick D. Miller Jr., " 'Enthroned on the Praises of Israel': The Praise of God in Old Testament Theology," *Interpretation* 39 (1985): 8.

of proselytising to bring individuals into the visible community of Israel. That is not the case. But what blossoms and flourishes in the New Testament proclamation of the Gospel to convert all persons to discipleship to Jesus Christ is anticipated in the Old Testament's proclamation of the goodness and grace of God.[26]

Ultimately, the power of this declarative praise reaches not only to the fullest horizontal extent throughout the nations but also to the fullest vertical extent to future generations. Again, without creating or conceiving a missionary mechanism to accomplish what is being declared, the extent of this vision in Israel's worship is certainly missional by implication.

> [In Israel's worship] the Lord is praised and testimony is borne, a testimony that is meant to summon all humankind to the praise of God and thus to an acknowledgement and worship of the Lord of Israel. Here one sees the political and eschatological thrust of Israel's praise in its insistence that the lordship of this God is universal in scope and should bring forth the conversion of every being to the worship of Israel's God. This call to the nations and peoples to praise the Lord is no incidental or exceptional matter. It is pervasive in the Psalms, where "all the earth" (33:8; 66:21; 96:1; 98:1; 100:1), "the earth" (97:1), "the coastlands" (97:1), "all the inhabitants of the earth (33:8), "all flesh" (145:21), "peoples" (47:2; 66:8; 67:4,5,6; 148:11; Deut. 32:43) are called to praise and bless the Lord again and again. In Deutero-Isaiah the conversionary character of these songs of praise is explicit (Is 45:22-25). [But in Psalm 22:22-31] the power of this testimony does not stop there. Beyond Israel "all the families of the nations shall worship before you" (v. 27). Yet even that does not exhaust the circle of praise, for those who have died shall praise the Lord (v. 29), as well as generations yet unborn (vs. 30-31).[27]

I hardly need add that the New Testament shares the same vision of all humanity and all creation praising God, through Jesus Christ. It would not be an exaggeration to say that the church in Europe was born through the conversionary power of praise, if one thinks of the hymn-singing Paul and Silas in the Philippian jail (Acts 16:25; cf. 1 Pet 2:9).

In his superb opening to his book *Let the Nations Be Glad,* John Piper arrestingly writes, "Missions is not the ultimate goal of the church. Worship is. Missions exist because worship doesn't."[28]

This is well said and fundamentally true, of course. Praise will be the dominant reality of the new creation, whereas, since God's mission to redeem his

---

[26]Ibid., p. 9.

[27]Ibid., p. 13.

[28]John Piper, *Let the Nations Be Glad! The Supremacy of God in Missions,* 2nd ed. (Grand Rapids: Baker Academic, 1993), p. 17.

whole creation will be complete, our derivative mission within history will be at an end (though who knows what mission God may have for redeemed humanity in the new creation!). So, yes, mission exists because praise does not, for mission means bringing those who do not yet praise the living God to do so.

But in another equally biblical sense we could say that mission exists because praise does. The praise of the church is what energizes and characterizes it for mission, and also serves as the constant reminder we so much need, that all our mission flows as obedient response to and participation in the prior mission of God—just as all our praise is in response to the prior reality and action of God. Praise is the proper and primary stance or mode of existence of the created order to its Creator. So inasmuch as our mission is a part of our creaturely response to our God, praise must be its primary mode also.

We will return in chapter fourteen to the universality and missional significance of many of the psalms. But for now, it is sufficient to bring our survey in this and the previous chapter to a close with the observation that among the many models for mission that we find in the Bible (in addition to the much overused military one) is the concept of singing a new song among the nations. Mission means inviting all the peoples of the earth to hear the music of God's future and dance to it today. As Psalm 96 would remind us

- This is a new song that remixes the old words, for it celebrates the old story of what God has done for his people (Ps 96:1-3).

- It is a new song that radically displaces the old gods whose former worshipers must now bring all their worship into the courts of the Lord (Ps 96:4-9).

- It is a new song that transforms the old world into the anticipated righteousness and rejoicing of the reign of the Lord (Ps 96:10-13).

Monotheism is missional because it generates praise and also because it globalizes praise—the praise of the one true living God, known through his grace, his judgment, and above all his Messiah.

So then the missionary nature of Christian monotheism does not flow from an endemic religious imperialism or military-style triumphalism (however much it may have been infected with that virus in different eras), but from the roots of our faith in Old Testament Israel and their belief in the God, the only true and living God, whose mission of love for the world had led to the election of Israel and the sending of the church. It is this God, and no other, who so determined to bless the nations that he chose Abraham. It is only this God who so loved the world that he sent his only Son. Only this God was in Christ reconciling the world to himself. And it is this God who has entrusted the mission and ministry of reconciliation to the people to whom Jesus said "you will be my witnesses... to the ends of the earth." That is the *missionary* nature of biblical monotheism.

5

The Living God
Confronts Idolatry

If biblical monotheism is necessarily missional (because the one living God wills to be known and worshiped throughout his whole creation), and if biblical mission is necessarily monotheistic (because we are to call all people to and to join all creation in the praise of this one living God), then what about all the other gods that populate the pages of the Bible and surround us still today in many forms? In this chapter we will examine how the Bible handles the phenomenon of human beings worshiping many alleged deities other than the God of Israel. What exactly are they? And in chapter six we will consider a missional response to this phenomenon. What should we be doing in relation to idols and gods? It has long seemed to me that the biblical category of *idolatry* is in danger of shallow understanding and simplistic responses. Yet surely it is a fundamental, if negative, aspect of a fully biblical and missional account of biblical monotheism. And a greater understanding of it is therefore a vital part of authentic and sensitive Christian mission.

Paradoxes of the Gods

Something or nothing? A statue is real enough. A carved or molten image has three-dimensional existence in the real world. But what about the god or gods it supposedly represents? Are they real? Do they exist? Are they something or nothing? What did Israel believe about the gods in relation to their own God, YHWH? This last question has vexed the minds of Old Testament theologians for many decades. Having defined monotheism within the generic categories of human religion as the belief that only one divine entity exists, along with the consequent denial of the existence of any other deities whatsoever, the search was on for the process by which and the time when Israel could be said to have achieved monotheism in that sense. Clearly Israelites expressed their commitment to YHWH in some very exclusive terms. But did that mean that Israelites categorically denied the *existence* of the other gods whom they were forbidden to worship?

The classic answer given within the guild of Old Testament scholarship has been the evolutionary or developmental one recently summarized, repackaged and reissued by Robert Gnuse.[1] With variations as to the precise dating of the transitions, this view reconstructs the religious history of Israel as proceeding from polytheism (as conceded in Josh 24:14) through henotheism (the demand for exclusive worship of YHWH *by Israel*, while accepting the existence of the gods of other nations) to true monotheism (the explicit denial of the existence of any other gods than YHWH) as a final and fairly late conclusion of the process.

According to some scholars the first and second stages span most of the Old Testament history of Israel. That is, originally Israelite religion was virtually indistinguishable from Canaanite religion. Then, for centuries, the major drive within Israel was merely to get Israel to be loyal to their national covenant with YHWH and not "go after other gods." The other gods that they might be tempted to go after were clearly presumed to exist. Yair Hoffman, for example, argues that even in the Deuteronomic traditions, the characteristic phrase *ʾĕlōhîm ʾăḥērîm*, "other gods," presumes rather than denies their existence as gods. "The phrase, . . . although reflecting some idea of otherness, does not certify that these deities were considered an utterly different essence from the God of Israel. . . . They are *other* gods since they are not *ours*."[2] Finally, only in the late exile (to which Isaiah 40—55 are assigned) did anyone in Israel say in so many words that no other god than YHWH even existed.[3] Only at that final stage was it envisaged that the category of deity was a house with one sole and exclusive occupant—YHWH.

On this view the answer to our question about whether or not, in the religion

---

[1] Robert Karl Gnuse, *No Other Gods: Emergent Monotheism in Israel,* JSOT Supplement Series 241 (Sheffield, U.K.: Sheffield Academic Press, 1997). Gnuse's study, of course, is only one of a very large number of scholarly explorations of the origins and history of monotheism in Israelite religion, and its bibliography is a useful guide to that literature. As explained in the introduction to part two, however, it is beyond our scope to engage that issue here.

[2] Yair Hoffman, "The Concept of 'Other Gods' in the Deuteronomistic Literature," in *Politics and Theopolitics,* ed. Henning Graf Reventlow, Yair Hoffman, and Benjamin Uffenheimer (Sheffield: JSOT Press, 1994), pp. 70-71.

[3] For a general critique of this evolutionary view of Israel's religion and the historical reconstruction on which it is based, see Richard Bauckham, "Biblical Theology and the Problems of Monotheism," in *Out of Egypt: Biblical Theology and Biblical Interpretation,* ed. Craig Bartholomew et al. (Carlisle, U.K.: Paternoster; Grand Rapids: Zondervan, 2004), pp. 187-232.

of Israel, other gods existed depends on the point in the chronological development of Israel at which the question is asked. Supposing we could have approached an Israelite and asked, Do you believe that there are other gods as well as YHWH? For a long period, the answer we would have received (according to the critical consensus) would have been, "Of course. There are many gods. YHWH is one of the gods, and a very powerful one, so we're rather glad he's our god." Then, when the more exclusive ideas of a national covenant were introduced and emphasized by the prophets and the reforming Deuteronomistic party, the answer would have been, "Yes, other nations have their own gods, but YHWH is the only God that *Israel* must worship, or we will face the consequences of his anger." That view clashed with a more liberal, popular polytheism for a long time. Finally, however, with the triumph of the "official" Yahwistic party in the late exile and postexilic period, the answer eventually would have been a firm, "No, YHWH alone is 'the God,' and other gods have no real existence at all. All so-called gods are actually nonentities."

Such a neat linear view, however, is almost certainly just that—too neat. It is far too simple to put the question (or its answer) in a simple binary form: Do other gods exist, or do they not exist? Are they something or nothing? The issue is more complex and depends on the predicate of such questions. What needs to be added to the question is: Do other gods have existence of the same order as YHWH does? Are they the same "thing" as he is [the same divine "something"]? Or are they not what he is ["nothing", i.e., no divine thing]?

The essence of Israelite monotheism lies in what it affirms dynamically about YHWH, not primarily in what it denies about other gods. Nevertheless, what it affirms about YHWH has unavoidable consequences for whatever may be claimed about other gods. Commenting particularly on Deuteronomy, and disputing Nathan MacDonald's argument that the book does not deny the existence of other gods (and is therefore not formally monotheistic, in terms of the Enlightenment categories that MacDonald rightly rejects as irrelevant and damaging in Old Testament study), Richard Bauckham makes the following carefully nuanced point:

> What Israel is able to recognize about YHWH, from his acts for Israel, that distinguishes YHWH from the gods of the nations is that he is "the God" or "the god of gods." This means primarily that he has unrivalled power throughout the cosmos. The earth, the heavens and the heaven of heavens belong to him (10:14). By contrast, the gods of the nations are impotent nonentities, who cannot protect and deliver even their own peoples. This is the message of the song of Moses (see especially 32:37-39). The need to distinguish among "the gods" between the one who is supreme (YHWH) and the others who are not just subordinate but powerless,

creates, on the one hand, the usages "the God" and "the god of gods," and, on the other hand, the contemptuous "non-god" (32:17: *lo' 'eloah;* 32:21: *lo' 'el*), and "their mere puffs of air" (32:21: *hab^elehem*). Though called gods, the other gods do not really deserve the term, because they are not *effective* divinities acting with power in the world. YHWH alone is the God with supreme power. . . (32:39). . . . It is not enough to observe that Deuteronomy does not deny the *existence* of other gods. We should also recognize that, once we do attend to the ontological implications that MacDonald admits Deuteronomy's "doctrine of God" must have, this theology is driving an ontological division through the midst of the old category "gods" such that YHWH appears in a class of his own.[4]

So, coming back to the question, are the gods something or nothing? If asked *in relation to YHWH,* the answer has to be *nothing.* Nothing whatsoever compares with YHWH, or stands in the same category as he does. YHWH is not one of a generic category—"the gods." YHWH alone is "the God," in what Bauckham calls "transcendent uniqueness."[5] With reference to Yair Hoffman's point above, while it may be true to say that the phrase "other gods" does not by itself imply that "these deities were considered an utterly different essence from the God of Israel," nevertheless what is said about YHWH makes it categorically clear that *he* is of an utterly different essence from *them.* "YHWH, he is the God; there is no other beside him" (Deut 4:35, my translation).

But if the question is asked *in relation to those who worship* the other gods—whether the nations who claim them as their own national deities or even in relation to the temptation that Israel faced to "go after" them—then the answer can certainly be *something.* The gods of the nations, with their names, statues, myths and cults, clearly do have an existence in the life, culture and history of those who treat them as their gods. It is not nonsense to form sentences like, Marduk was a god worshiped by the people of Babylon. Only excessive pedantry would complain that since Marduk did not have any real divine existence it is meaningless to say that anybody worshiped him. In the context of such a sentence (and all similar descriptions of human religions), it makes understandable sense to talk about other gods as "something"—something that exists in the world of human experience. In other words, it is not impossible, theologically or in ordinary discourse, to answer the question, Are other gods something or nothing? with the paradox, both. They are *nothing in relation to YHWH;* they are *something in relation to their worshipers.*

This is precisely the paradox that Paul carefully articulates in his response to

---

[4]Ibid., p. 196.
[5]Ibid., p. 211.

the problem of meat sacrificed to idols in Corinth. Paul agrees with the creedal affirmation of those who based their freedom in the matter on the Jewish *Shema*. There is only one God and Lord, and so "an idol is nothing at all in the world" (1 Cor 8:4). Yet in the next sentence Paul says, "For even if there are so-called gods, whether in heaven or on earth (as indeed there are many 'gods' and many 'lords') . . ." There is *something* there, even if it is not in any sense equivalent to the one God, the Father and the one Lord, Jesus Christ. What that something actually is, Paul (and we) will return to. But his double assertion is clear enough: gods and idols do exist; but they do not have the *divine* existence that the one living God alone possesses.

If Paul, a first-century Jew, basing his whole theological worldview on the Scriptures we call the Old Testament, could sustain this dual perspective, there seems no reason why it would have been impossible for those who shared his faith in preceding centuries to have held a similar paradox quite comfortably. It is clearly the perspective of the great polemical chapters Isaiah 40—48, for example. From YHWH's point of view, expressed in the soaring poetry of the prophet, the gods are simply "less than nothing" and "utterly worthless" (Is 41:24). Yet from the point of view of the exiles with their cowering inferiority complex, the gods of Babylon can be challenged to come into court and be exposed there as powerless (Is 41:21-24), can be mocked as human artifacts (Is 44:9-20), can be caricatured as stooping down from heaven in a futile attempt to save, not their worshipers to whom they are now a useless burden but their own idols (Is 46:1-2). All of this rhetoric is expended on the gods because they are "something"—something that Israel must see for what it is and be freed from, something that must be debunked and dismissed, so that it no longer stands in the way of Israel's restoration to the worship of their living Redeemer God.

What was possible for the prophet was surely no less possible for the author of a book of such theological depth and subtlety as Deuteronomy. And indeed we find the same paradoxical duality. On the one hand, other gods are nothing when the point of reference or comparison is YHWH. I can find no other way to understand the following affirmations than that they simply mean what they say: YHWH alone is transcendently God, the sole owner and ruler of the universe.

> The LORD is God in heaven above and on the earth below. There is no other. (Deut 4:39).

> To the LORD your God belong the heavens, even the highest heavens, the earth and everything in it. (Deut 10:14)

> The LORD your God is God of gods and Lord of lords, the great God. (Deut 10:17)

See now that I myself am He!
> There is no god besides me.
I put to death and I bring to life,
>> I have wounded and I will heal,
>> and no one can deliver out of my hand. (Deut 32:39)

In the context of such affirmations the question as to what other gods may be receives its verdict: They are "not God (Deut 32:17), "what is no god" (Deut 32:21). In short, *nothing*—nothing in comparison to YHWH.

Yet on the other hand the same book, contemplating the enticing attractiveness and seductive power of the religious culture that lay ahead of Israel when they crossed the Jordan (the gods and idols, sacred places, the male and female fertility symbols, the apparent success of a whole civilization based on serving these gods) knew that in warning Israel repeatedly to avoid such idolatry, they were warning them against *something*—something very real and very dangerous. Furthermore, to the extent that other nations worshiped heavenly bodies, the objects of their worship were certainly something with real existence—"the sun, the moon and the stars—all the heavenly array" (Deut 4:19). Israel was not to worship them because they are part of the created order, and as such YHWH had assigned them "to all the nations under heaven"—not intending them to be worshiped but to be enjoyed for their created purpose as light givers.[6]

So, then, it seems a futile exercise to attempt to unravel the Old Testament documents and lay them out along a line of progressive religious development on the flawed assumption that people who speak about "other gods" as if they existed in some sense cannot at the same time have believed that YHWH alone is God. The logical conclusion of such an argument would be that once you become convinced of monotheism you should never again even speak about "other gods," lest you be thought to be granting them real existence as divine. Yet that would be an absurd restriction on theological discourse. How then could Paul have even discussed the relationship between the living God and the gods and idols of the world in which his mission took place? Are we to say that because Paul refers to these things, in order to critique them, he must have believed in their existence in some sense comparable to the divine reality of the living God of Israel revealed in Christ? We have Paul's own word for it that he assuredly did not mean that. And yet Old Testament scholars repeatedly allege

---

[6]In my view it is significant that Deut 4:19 does not explicitly say that God apportioned the heavenly bodies to be worshiped. He simply gave these gifts of creation to all nations—which included Israel. The fact that other nations do in fact worship them is not to be imitated by Israel.

that simply by referring to the gods of the nations around them the Israelites must have believed in their real existence on a par with YHWH.

What was true for Paul is equally true for us as contemporary Christians. Missiological discourse and missional practice necessarily have to take account of the existence (in some sense) of other gods and the phenomenon of idolatry. They are unquestionably "something." And yet we are able to engage in such discourse without compromising our fundamental biblical monotheism that there is one and only one living God, known to us in the fullness of his trinitarian revelation. If this were not so, then we would be guilty of implicit polytheism in singing such words as these from a missionary hymn:

Where other lords beside Thee
Hold their unhindered sway,
Where forces that defied Thee
Defy Thee still today . . . [7]

We can sing such words, of course, in full assurance of Paul's affirmation (which, we remember, was based on Deuteronomy and, apart from its christological claim, expressed a paradox that Deuteronomy would have understood and accepted) that although there are many gods and lords in the world, there is in reality only one Lord and one God, from whom and for whom all things exist. If *we* can sing such words and engage in the kind of theological discourse that underlies them without thereby placing ourselves at some inferior stage of religious evolution that falls short of true monotheism, I can see no reason why it is necessary to place an ancient Israelite in some such artificial location when he or she also sang, prophesied or legislated making reference to "other gods" that held sway over the nations or defied YHWH, the one living God.

So, if the gods are not God and yet exist as "something," what are they? If they do not exist within the realm of true divinity (the realm in which YHWH is the sole and exclusive incumbent), then they must exist within the only other realm of being—the created order. And if they are created entities, they must exist either within the world of the *physical* creation (which subdivides into the natural order created by God and the products of human manufacture) or in the *invisible* world of the nonhuman spirits also created by God. The Bible offers us all three as ways of categorizing the "something" of idolatry. Idols and gods may be (1) objects within the visible creation, (2) demons, or (3) the product of human hands.

Idols and gods as objects within creation. In the physical creation it was

---

[7]Frank Houghton, "Facing a Task Unfinished," 1930 by © Overseas Missionary Fellowship.

well observed in Israel that some people regarded the heavenly bodies as gods and worshiped them, while others did the same to creatures on the earth— whether nonhuman animals or even fellow human beings. All of these, of course, since they are created by the living God should not in themselves be objects of worship. The warning given against such deification of the created order in Deuteronomy 4:15-21 interestingly (and almost certainly deliberately) lists the objects thus worshiped in directly opposite order to the order of their creation in Genesis 1: humans, male and female; land animals; birds of the air; fish in the waters; sun, moon and stars. The rhetorical effect matches the theological implication: When people worship creation instead of the Creator, everything is turned upside down. Idolatry produces disorder in all our fundamental relationships.

Worship of the heavenly bodies was as ancient as it was widespread, but it was inconsistent with Israel's faith in YHWH as Creator. Thus even in the mouth of Job (who is not described as an Israelite but is commended by the narrator and by YHWH himself as a devout worshiper of God), it is rejected as sin and unfaithfulness.

> If I have regarded the sun in its radiance
>> or the moon moving in splendor,
> so that my heart was secretly enticed
>> and my hand offered them a kiss of homage,
> then these also would be sins to be judged,
>> for I would have been unfaithful to God on high. (Job 31:26-28)

Nevertheless, astral worship clearly infected Israel badly at times. Amos 5:26 is evidence for it as early as the eighth century B.C.[8] It is included in the list of idolatries for which the northern kingdom of Israel was judged and destroyed (2 Kings 17:16). Manasseh of Judah added worship of the starry host to all the other accumulated evils of his reign (2 Kings 21:3-5). Even in the wake of Josiah's great purging reformation, Ezekiel in his temple vision was horrified to see people in the very courts of the temple bowing down to the sun in the east, with their backsides (literally) raised to the temple of the Lord himself (Ezek 8:16). Star gods were of course the most powerful deities of the Mesopotamian cultures, so such actions were probably intended to placate the gods of their most powerful contemporary enemy—Babylon. A very different approach to such astral deities was taken in Isaiah 40:26. Inviting the exiles, who were probably dazzled by the apparent power of these gods of their conquerors, to look

---

[8]The text is somewhat difficult (see NIV footnote), but it certainly refers to the worship of star gods.

up to the heavens, the prophet simply asks the question, Who created all these? The very question unmasks them. The stars are not all-powerful gods controlling the destinies of nations. They are not even gods at all. They are merely creatures of the living God, summoned and controlled by his authority.

Worship of the nonhuman animal creation is also common, and in ancient Israel's context was particularly associated with Egypt, where a variety of animals and reptiles were deified. There is less evidence that animal worship ever seriously infected Israel's own worship, but again Ezekiel was shocked to be shown seventy elders of Israel (the phrase itself recalls the role that such a group had played in the covenantal communion with YHWH at Sinai [Ex 24:9-11]), in a darkened, smoke-filled inner room of the temple, worshiping "all kinds of crawling things and detestable animals" (Ezek 8:9-12). Some commentators suggest that this may also have been a political action aimed at securing the help of Egyptian forces against Babylon by supplicating their theriomorphic (animal-shaped) gods. If so, it would indicate the advanced degradation of the temple cult in the late monarchy, with some leaders appealing to the gods of Babylon and others just a few rooms away appealing to the gods of Egypt.

Idols and gods as demons. Turning to the nonphysical created order, Israel was well aware of the hosts of heaven, the spiritual beings that surround the seat of God's supreme government, that serve God's purposes and do God's bidding. Mostly. For Israel was also aware (though they gave the matter less theological reflection) of agencies within that exalted company that *questioned* God (as did "the satan," or the accuser, in Job 1) or *challenged* God's truthfulness and benevolence (as did the serpent, whatever it represents, in Gen 3) or *accused* God's servants (as the satan does to Joshua, the postexilic high priest, in Zech 3:1-2). Such spirits, however they were envisioned, remain entirely subject to YHWH's authority, so that even a "lying spirit" can be dispatched to serve the purpose of YHWH's intended judgment on Ahab (1 Kings 22:19-23).

Only rarely do Old Testament texts connect the worship of other gods with demons, but the rarity should not lead us to overlook the fact that the connection was made, for it was certainly picked up and amplified theologically in the New Testament. Thus, for example, it is an assumption made by Paul, doubtless with what he regarded as scriptural legitimacy, that flirting with idols could lead to participation with demons (1 Cor 10:18-21).

Although the Old Testament itself contains no theological reflection on this understanding of idolatry (that is, as the worship of demons), it was the natural development of Israel's realization that the "mute" gods of the pagans did in fact have supernatural powers. Since there was only one God, such power could not be attributed to a god; hence the belief arose that idols represented demonic spirits.[9]

The connection seems to have been made at an early stage since the first text specifically to speak of other gods as demons is the Song of Moses in Deuteronomy 32, which is acknowledged by many scholars to be very early Israelite poetry.[10]

> They made him jealous with their foreign gods
> > and angered him with their idols.
> They sacrificed to demons, which are not God. (Deut 32:16-17; cf. 21)[11]

Psalm 106 has a similar purpose to Deuteronomy 32: it recounts the history of Israel's unfaithfulness in contrast to all that God had done for them as a way of vindicating the judgment that had overwhelmed Israel and from which they now prayed to be saved. As in Deuteronomy 32 also, the primary focus is on the sin of idolatry. First, the idolatry of the golden bull calf at Mount Sinai is mentioned (Ps 106:19-20—in a wonderfully sarcastic contrast between YHWH as the "Glory" of Israel and "an image of a bull, which eats grass"!). Second, the terrible apostasy at Baal Peor is recalled, where the gods are described as "lifeless gods" (Ps 106:28, lit. "they ate sacrifices of dead ones/things"). Finally, in the land itself, Israel, against all instructions, followed the cultic practices of the Canaanites (lit. "learned their doings").

> They mingled with the nations
> > and adopted their customs.
> They worshiped their idols,
> > which became a snare to them.
> They sacrificed their sons

---

[9]Gordon D. Fee, *The First Epistle to the Corinthians,* New International Commentary on the New Testament (Grand Rapids: Eerdmans, 1987), p. 472

[10]Leviticus 17:7 prohibits the Israelites from sacrificing animals to "goat idols" *(śĕʿîrim).* This may refer to demons that were thought to assume goatlike forms, as "satyrs," in the wilds of the desert. Though they are not described as gods, the prohibition clearly shows that any sacrifice to such things (whatever they were) was incompatible with covenantally exclusive worship of YHWH alone. They may have been included in the idolatry of Jeroboam (2 Chron 11:15). Some scholars also think that the mysterious "Azazel," to which one of the goats was driven in the Day of Atonement ritual (Lev 16:8, 10, 26), may have been a desert demon. But this is disputed since the meaning of the word (occurring only in this context) is otherwise unknown. Again, no explicit connection with any other god is implied (and would in any case be inconceivable as part of the ritual of Israel's most holy day). Cf. John E. Hartley, *Leviticus,* Word Biblical Commentary 4 (Dallas: Word, 1992), pp. 236-38, 272-73.

[11]"Demons" in v. 17 is the Heb *šēdîm.* This rare word is found only here and in Ps 106:37. It is cognate with the Akkadian word *sedu,* which in ancient Mesopotamian religion referred to protective spirits associated with the dead. The association with human sacrifice, mentioned in Psalm 106, is also attested in Mesopotamian religion.

and their daughters to demons.
They shed innocent blood,
> the blood of their sons and daughters,
whom they sacrificed to the idols of Canaan,
> and the land was desecrated by their blood. (Ps 106:35-38)

The close connection here between idolatry as demonic and the perpetration of innocent bloodshed is one that we will revisit later.

These (Deut 32; Ps 106) are the only two Old Testament passages that clearly and explicitly equate gods and idols with demons, though there are hints elsewhere. Psalm 96:5, for example, speaks of the worship of the non-Israelite peoples and dismisses their gods as ʾĕlîlîm. On this occasion the Septuagint translated that term with *daimonia*—demons, but elsewhere the word ʾĕlîlîm does not necessarily mean demons but refers rather to something worthless, weak, powerless, useless, of no value (e.g., Is 2:8, 20; 19:1; 31:7; Hab 2:18). It is also possible that Isaiah 65:11, which describes cultic practices for "Fortune" and "Destiny," may consider these to have been regarded by their devotees as some kind of spiritual forces that needed to be placated or importuned. And we might also ponder Hosea's use of the phrase "a spirit of prostitution"; was he implying more than a human psychological disorder, intending a greater-than-human power at work in such a *rûaḥ*, "spirit," which "leads them astray" because it "is in their heart" (Hos 4:12; 5:4)? Similarly, Zechariah parallels "the names of the idols" with "the spirit of impurity" or uncleanness in a suggestive anticipation of the regular reference in the Gospels to "unclean spirits" (Zech 13:2). The demonic dimension is at least a possibility in texts like these. But, to repeat, Deuteronomy 32:16-17 and Psalm 106:19-20 seem to be the only texts to make the connection explicit.

However, they provided scriptural foundation for Paul's blunt assertion that "the sacrifices of pagans are offered to demons, not to God" (1 Cor 10:20). This conviction is of a piece with his theological assessment of idolatry elsewhere. In what was probably his earliest letter Paul recalls how the Thessalonians "turned to God from idols to serve the living and true God" (1 Thess 1:9)—"the clear implication being that their former worship of idols had been the worship of dead and false gods."[12] In Luke's record of Paul's description before Agrippa of his encounter with the risen Jesus, Paul deems this turning from idols as tantamount to being released from the power of Satan (Acts 26:18). Conversely, the book of Revelation portrays the finally impenitent and rebellious as those who,

---

[12]Brian Wintle, "A Biblical Perspective on Idolatry," in *The Indian Church in Context: Her Emergence, Growth and Mission,* ed. Mark T. B. Laing (Delhi: CMS/ISPCK, 2003), p. 60.

even after the initial manifestations of God's judgment, refuse to turn from their idolatry: They "did not repent of the work of their hands; they did not stop worshiping demons, and idols of gold, silver, bronze, stone and wood—idols that cannot see or hear or walk" (Rev 9:20).

I might add that even Jesus, when tempted by Satan to bow down in worship to him, recognized the idolatrous nature of such a temptation by resisting it with a text drawn from Deuteronomy: "Fear the LORD your God, serve him only"—a text immediately followed by the words, "Do not follow other gods, the gods of the peoples around you" (Deut 6:13-14; Mt 4:10). Satan is not more than one of God's creatures, whatever his angelic origin and spiritual power. So, given that Jesus has already been identified in the Gospel narrative as God's Son (Mt 3:17), the absurd insolence of Satan's suggestion is exposed, to imagine that God himself could be tempted to bow down to one of his own creatures. Nevertheless, given also that Matthew sees Jesus the man and the Messiah standing in the identity and place of Israel, and being tested like them in the wilderness, it was a serious question whether, like them, he could also be sucked into the idolatry of the nations by worshiping the Satan who stood behind the gods of the nations. The reversible nexus is clear: to worship other gods is to worship satanic demons; to bow down to Satan is to treat him as divine, which he is not, and thereby to be unfaithful to the living God of Israel.

Idols and gods as the work of human hands. Returning to the Old Testament, if the description of gods and idols as *demons* is rare, the description that Revelation 9:20 pairs with it—"the work of their hands"—is pervasive and typical. Indeed, second only to the fact that idolatry is fundamentally rebellion against the living God, this is probably the major basis of the critique of idolatry in the Old Testament. An idol is not even a *living* creature in its own right, but merely the *manufacture* of a creature. What possible claim can it have to be divine?

We need to take this biblical perception seriously and to sample the strength of this charge in some representative Old Testament texts. The expression "the work of a man's hands" *(ma'ăśēh yĕdê-'ādām)* is disparagingly applied to other gods a number of times. Hezekiah, for example, is not surprised that the Assyrians had been able to defeat other nations and at the same time destroy their gods. This was the point that the Assyrian general Rabshakeh had hoped would persuade Hezekiah that his own little god YHWH would fare no differently. Hezekiah knew better. So he prayed for deliverance so that the rest of the world might know better too (an interesting missional perspective that we considered on pp. 95-96). Thus Hezekiah comments, in his prayer:

It is true, O LORD, that the Assyrian kings have laid waste these nations and their lands. They have thrown their gods into the fire and destroyed them, *for they were not gods [or not God],* but only wood and stone, fashioned by men's hands. Now, O LORD our God, deliver us from his hand, so that all kingdoms on earth may know that you alone, O LORD, are God. (2 Kings 19:17-19, emphasis added)[13]

Psalmists also joined the contempt.

> Their idols are silver and gold,
>> made by the hands of men.
> They have mouths, but cannot speak,
>> eyes, but they cannot see;
> they have ears, but cannot hear,
>> noses, but they cannot smell;
> they have hands but cannot feel,
>> feet, but they cannot walk;
>> nor can they utter a sound with their throats.
> Those who make them will be like them,
>> and so will all who trust in them. (Ps 115:4-8; cf. Ps 135:15-18)

Prophets, as one would expect, adopt the same rhetorical polemic.

> With their silver and gold
>> they make idols for themselves
>> to their own destruction. . . .
> This calf—a craftsman made it;
>> it is not God. (Hos 8:4, 6)

> They make idols for themselves from their silver,
> cleverly fashioned images,
>> all of them the work of craftsmen (Hos 13:2)

> Of what value is an idol, since a man has carved it?
>> Or an image that teaches lies?
> For he who makes it trusts in his own creation;
>> he makes idols that cannot speak.
> Woe to him who says to wood, "Come to life!"
>> Or to lifeless stone, "Wake up!"
> Can it give guidance?
>> It is covered with gold and silver;
>> there is no breath in it. (Hab 2:18-19)

These sharp challenges are surpassed in rhetorical and descriptive force only

---

[13]The Deuteronomic historian's point here, in the mouth of Hezekiah, echoes the same assessment of idols that is made in Deuteronomy 4:28.

by the other two great prophetic texts that highlight the human origins of idols: Jeremiah 10:3-5, 9, 14 and Isaiah 40:18-20; 44:9-20. These two texts are too long to reproduce, but they need to be read to feel the full force of Israel's attack on man-made, hand-made idolatry.

This is the point at which ancient Israel is frequently accused by contemporary scholars of religious ignorance and naiveté. It is alleged that Israelites regarded all pagan worship as nothing more than fetishism. Israelites mistakenly (we are told) thought that pagan worshipers regarded physical idols as having life and power in themselves. And since they obviously didn't, the whole charade was laughable to the Israelites. They (the Israelites) failed to observe the distinction between the idols as images on the one hand, and the gods or heavenly powers that such images represented in the minds and devotions of their worshipers on the other hand. Committed to aniconic worship themselves (that is, worship of YHWH without images), Israel could not understand or appreciate the subtlety of iconic worship that they saw around them. The real spiritual and psychological dynamic of the use of idols in worship was not grasped by the Israelites, so they simply mocked what they did not understand.

An example of this assumption is found in an otherwise excellent article by John Barton. He argues that from the time of Isaiah

> there develops the tradition of seeing "idols" not as warped representations of the true deity but as images of false gods, and then of identifying the other gods with their images, as if the image were all there was. It has often been noticed that this is in a sense unfair to those who use images in worship. The iconoclast sees only the image and thinks that the worshipper who uses it is bowing down before a mere physical object. But this is the iconoclast's interpretation of what the worshipper is doing. For the worshipper the image is a representation of a divine power, which is not exhausted by the image but somehow symbolized by or encapsulated in it. Nevertheless this "unfair" interpretation of idols established itself as the main line of thinking about images in the pages of the Old Testament.[14]

So runs the argument, usually with the moral that we should avoid falling into the same ignorant condemnation of those whose objects or forms of worship differ from our own. It is a way of neutralizing the Old Testament's condemnation of idolatry that is particularly attractive to the advocates of religious pluralism.[15] It is also a way of indulging our own feeling of religious (and moral)

---

[14]John Barton, " 'The Work of Human Hands' (Ps 115:4): Idolatry in the Old Testament," *Ex Auditu* 15 (1999): 67.

[15]See, e.g., the pluralist perspective in W. Cantwell Smith, "Idolatry in Comparative Perspective," in *The Myth of Christian Uniqueness,* ed. John Hick and Paul F. Knitter (Maryknoll, N.Y.: Orbis; London: SCM Press, 1987), pp. 53-68.

superiority to the Old Testament. Since, as a result of modern anthropological research into human religion, we now understand the true spiritual dynamic of what Israel so lamentably ridiculed (we are encouraged to believe), we need not be bound by the narrow and ignorant exclusivism of these polemical texts in the Old Testament.

This widely held assumption, however, seems to me to be even more of a patronizing and unfair misunderstanding of the Israelites than that which it charges against them. For it seems very clear to me that the author of the great polemic against the gods of Babylon understood precisely the distinction that was supposed to exist between the physical idols themselves and the gods they represented. So well did he understand the pagan theology on this point that he could utilize it in cartoon form to critique idols, gods and worshipers together. So in Isaiah 46:1-2 he portrays the great Babylonian gods up in heaven—Bel and Nebo. But they are stooping down to earth. Why? Because their idols are in danger of falling off the oxcarts that they have been loaded on. The prophet understands perfectly well that the statues were not, in Babylonian thinking, the gods themselves. The gods were invisibly somewhere else "up there." Their statues were visibly "down here." His point is, however, that wherever and whatever those gods may be thought to be in a Babylonian worldview, when the crunch comes they are totally unable to save even their own statues, let alone save their worshipers. On the contrary, the gods become a burden to their worshipers who feel obliged to try to save their statues by whatever undignified means is available. The gods in the Babylonian heaven must abandon their statues to the ludicrous insecurity of staggering oxcarts on Babylonian streets.

The prophet's satire is not based on naive ignorance but on penetrating insight. In fact the whole power of his cartoon *presupposes and depends on* his understanding of the Babylonian distinction between images and the gods they stood for. He knew perfectly well that Babylonians distinguished between their idol statues and the gods they visibly depicted. His point is that the manifest failure of alleged gods even to save their own idols was laughably unimpressive.

There is evidence also in earlier narrative texts that Israelites were not so obtuse as the pluralist superiority complex wishes to paint them. They perceived that a statue or altar was not in itself the same as the god it was supposed to represent. It did not stop them mocking the impotence of the alleged god, however. Gideon's father Joash takes on a hostile crowd after his son had toppled the village altar to Baal and its Asherah pole. His words brilliantly capture the nonsense of a god who needs defending, when one had thought that the whole point of having a god was that *he* or *she* should defend *you*. At the very least a god should be able to defend its own turf and totem.

"Are you going to plead Baal's cause? Are you trying to save him? . . . If Baal really is a god, he can defend himself when someone breaks down his altar" (Judg 6:31).

Baal's tendency to go AWOL when most needed by his worshipers drew even sharper sarcasm from Elijah. Ahab had built him an altar and an Asherah pole. Jezebel had four hundred prophets to serve Baal. But wherever he was in spiritual reality, he was not around at the altar of his demented devotees on Mount Carmel. Elijah's mockery is an ad hominem argument addressed to their assumption that he *is* a god, after all, so he must be "somewhere else," if not here. "'Shout louder!' he said. 'Surely he is a god! Perhaps he is deep in thought, or busy, or traveling. Maybe he is sleeping and must be awakened'" (1 Kings 18:27).

Another superbly comic narrative could even be viewed as deliberately contradicting the idea that physical objects are to be merely identified with the gods they represent. The Israelites imagined that by taking the ark of the covenant into battle, they could compel the presence and support of YHWH. The Philistines initially thought the same and trembled. But events proved both sides wrong in their assumptions (1 Sam 4:1-11). YHWH was not to be identified with any physical object in Israel's manipulative possession—not even an object commanded by himself and built to his own specification. Then, as the ark does its unwelcome circuit round the cities of the Philistines, the Philistines clearly learn to distinguish it from the God of Israel that it represents. The ark is the physical object present, but it is the hand of YHWH, the God of Israel, that smites them (1 Sam 5:6-12). If the Philistines themselves could perceive this of Israel's God, how much more did the Israelite narrator and readers make the same assumption about the Philistines' god, Dagon, and his idol? The fact that the idol falls over twice (losing his head and his hands the second time) clearly means that Dagon's alleged divine power was unable to keep his own statue vertical before the symbol of the God of Israel (1 Sam 5:2-4). The comic motif and the theological presupposition are the same as are used by Isaiah 46:1-2 against the mighty gods of Babylon.

This brings us back to our main point. The Israelites, fully aware of what *idols* were supposed to signify among those who bowed down before them, nevertheless castigated them as "the work of human hands." What then did this signify for the *gods* that the idols represented? The radical conclusion has to be that the psalmists and prophets make no distinction between the images and the gods they represented—*not because they did not know that such a distinction was there in the minds of pagan worshipers but because ultimately there was no such distinction in reality.*

The visible idols were obviously made by humans. And whatever the gods might be thought to be (by their own worshipers or by Israelites tempted to join them), they too were nothing more than human constructs. The alleged gods that the idols represented had no *divine* reality or *divine* power, for such reality and power belonged to YHWH alone. The fact that the gods, in the myths and cult of their worshipers, were thought to inhabit some other sphere generally invisible to humans made no difference to their actual status as the product of human imagination. Mere invisibility was no proof of divinity. So, in declaring the idols, which anyone could see had been manufactured by human effort and skill, to be "the work of human hands," the Israelites were doing much more than merely stating the obvious. After all, the pagan worshipers would have agreed on that point! Idol statues were indeed the work of human hands in pagan minds. Not only did everybody know that, they actually prided themselves on the skill and expense that their hands put into making those great images (as is still true in countries, such as India, where idols are an important part of popular religion). Rather, the Israelite theologians were *including* in that assessment all that the idols were believed by their worshipers to stand for—the alleged gods as well. The gods too were just as much human constructs as their statues.

John Barton sees Isaiah as the one to whom Israel owed this breakthrough realization about the gods—that they were not in reality alternative sources of *divine* power but merely human "products."[16]

> [Isaiah] departs from the idea that other gods are an alternative source of divine power, distinct from YHWH, and presents them instead as products of human devising. Whereas for Hosea it is wrong to seek alliances with other nations because this involves getting entangled with their gods, who are threatening alternative sources of divine power forbidden to the Israelites, Isaiah regards trust in foreign nations as trust in merely human sources of strength. "The Egyptians are human, and not God; their horses are flesh, and not spirit" (Isa 31:3). The gods of other nations are similarly not gods at all, but human fictions: they are manmade and can be described as "the work of their hands" (2:8). To rely on a foreign god is not to rely on another [divine] source of strength, not even one which is forbidden, but to rely on something which human beings have devised and which is therefore no stronger than they are. Thus there is no talk of cultic *apostasy* in Isaiah in the sense of abandoning Yahweh for other gods who are real, but more of cultic *stupidity*, worshiping as a divine source of strength something that is no more powerful than the worshippers themselves.[17]

---

[16]Barton, "Work of Human Hands," pp. 63-72.
[17]Ibid., p. 66.

In my view Barton is absolutely right here.[18] He has perceived something quite radical and profound in Israel's assessment of idolatry, and something which has far-reaching missiological significance. Those gods that people worship, other than the one living God, are something within the created order, with no objective divine reality. When they are not objects within the physical creation (such as the sun and stars or living creatures), when they are not demons or spirits of some kind, then they must be (and are most commonly described as) "the work of human hands." *The alleged gods are in fact no different from the idols that represent them; they are both human constructs.* In worshiping them, we give allegiance, we attribute power and authority, we submit ourselves to something that we ourselves have created. In the final analysis the satire of Isaiah 44:9-20 is not off the mark. There is *in principle* no difference between the domestic fetishist and the sophisticated iconic worshiper of the great gods of Babylon. Whether addressing the piece of wood he has carved for himself as if it were actually a god (Is 44:17) or calling out to the invisible state gods supposedly represented in the gilded statues (Is 46:7), the worshiper is engaged in an exercise in futility. The one is as much the product of collective human imagination as the other is the work of individual human hands. There is no salvation in either.

It seems significant that most of the references to gods and idols being the work of human hands occur in contexts where it is particularly national or state gods that are in view. For this is where the power of the gods seems strongest and where Israel's radical assertion is correspondingly most countercultural and polemical. Surely these great national gods are mighty and powerful divinities! Not so, reply the prophets; they are no more powerful than the people who make them. And in making them, of course, the rulers of the nations have embodied their own pride, greed and aggression. National gods are the ultimate deification of human pride, but they remain human constructs, nevertheless.

For what did it actually mean to say that the great gods of Assyria had defeated the lesser gods of the smaller nations around Judah, for example? Only that the Assyrian king and his armies had rampaged through those countries with vicious cruelty and greed (Is 10:12-14). Indeed that was the identification made by the Assyrian king and his spokesman themselves (2 Kings 18:33-35).

---

[18]Except that I would not view the difference between Hosea and Isaiah in the terms Barton expresses it. I doubt if Hosea imagined that the other gods of the nations with whom Israel were getting politically entangled had objective divine reality alternative to YHWH any more than Isaiah did (particularly in view of the way he also dismisses them as human products in Hos 8:4, 6; 13:2; 14:3). So while I believe Barton rightly understands Isaiah's meaning, I am not convinced it was such a "breakthrough" as he makes out.

Within their worldview, what happened in the sphere of kings and armies reflected what was going on in the sphere of the gods. So there was no difficulty
for a king to claim to have defeated gods. Kings and gods could be interchange-
able in grammar or on the ground. The Israelite prophets accepted this worldview at one level but decisively rejected it at another. The international arena
was indeed the sphere of divine action (that was the part they agreed on). But
far from it being an arena packed with clashing gods (that was the part they
rejected), only one divine being was active within it—YHWH, the God of Israel,
to whom Hezekiah could say, "You alone are God over all the kingdoms of the
earth. You have made the heavens and the earth" (2 Kings 19:15). The gods to
which the Assyrians attributed their victory, just as much as the gods of the nations they had pillaged, were "not gods" or "not God"—that is they had no share
in the sovereign divine reality that belonged to YHWH alone—but were "fashioned by mens hands" (v. 18).

Habakkuk makes the same assertion. Having described in graphic detail the
arrogance, the violence, the human and ecological destructiveness of Assyria's
imperial expansion (Hab 2:3-17), he scoffs at the idea that their gods could provide any defense against the doom that is coming to them from the hand of the
Lord. That is the context of the following verses and the point of their scorn,
which is followed by the customary mockery of wood and stone, decked out in
silver and gold but devoid of life and breath:

> Of what value is an idol, since a man has carved it?
>   Or an image that teaches lies?
> For he who makes it trusts in his own creation;
>   he makes idols that cannot speak. (Hab 2:18)

There could hardly be a clearer articulation of exactly what Israel's prophets
believed about the great state gods of their imperial enemies than that single
line: "he who makes it trusts in his own creation" (lit. "the maker of the thing
he has made trusts in it"). There is no divine power in or behind or above the
idols. They are not representations of deity but fictions of humanity. By contrast,
Habakkuk goes on:

> But the LORD is in his holy temple;
>   let all the earth [not just Israel] be silent before him. (Hab 2:20)

If this was true for the Assyrian idol-worshipers themselves (that their gods
were the work of human hands), then the same shattering exposure could be
aimed at those *Israelites* who opted to worship the gods of Assyria (or any other
nation) as a means of cementing an alliance or gaining some benefit (or at least

a stay of execution). Thus, when Hosea writes a liturgy of repentance (sadly never used) for the people of Israel, he tells them that they needed to recognize the impotence of the Assyrian military machine to save them *precisely because* their trust in it was nothing more than trusting in gods *their own hands* had made. In other words, the power that Assyria's gods seemed to exercise over Israel was as much the product of *Israel's* imagination as of the Assyrians. To worship them was to connive in the attribution of divinity to what was a human construct. So to repent of trusting in Assyria's armed forces (and thereby trusting in Assyrian gods) was to repent of having *made gods for themselves*—not (as Barton suggests, mistakenly in my view) of trusting an alternative source of power that was assumed to be genuinely divine. The tight synonymous parallelism between "Assyria," "horses," "our gods" and "the work of our hands" makes this unmistakeable.

> Take words with you
> and return to the LORD.
> Say to him:
> "Forgive all our sins
> and receive us graciously,
> that we may offer the fruit of our lips.
> *Assyria* cannot save us;
> we will not mount *war-horses.*
> We will never again say '*Our gods*'
> to *what our own hands have made*." (Hos 14:2-3, emphasis added)

Hosea preached to the northern kingdom of Israel. There is some irony in telling them that in going after the gods of *Assyria* they were trusting in gods of their own manufacture, since the founding king of Israel had effectively done the same thing to YHWH himself and for the same reason—to bolster the security of his new and vulnerable state. "Jeroboam the son of Nebat who made Israel to sin" (e.g., 1 Kings 15:34; 16:19) is the name on the epitaph of the one who led the northern tribes in their secession from Judah. His sin, as reenacted in so many of his successors, was idolatry. But the description of its original emergence in 1 Kings 12:26-33 shows both its motivation and its subtlety. Jeroboam's intention was to prevent his population reverting to political allegiance to Jerusalem through religious pilgrimage to YHWH's temple there. So he provided calf images at opposite ends of his kingdom as places for the northern tribes to worship the God who had brought them up out of Egypt. Clearly he did not want to be seen to be suggesting the worship of any other god but YHWH, and indeed the text hints that Jeroboam may have been claiming the mantle of Moses in having delivered the tribes from the oppression of Solomon and son. Nevertheless, he reconstructed the whole religious apparatus of his state so that the cult of YHWH was clearly under his patronage.[19] So the narrative subtly implies that while the name at the top of the page still said "YHWH," the table of contents was very much of Jeroboam's own making. YHWH had been fashioned like a god made by human hands. The living God was being commandeered and crafted through state propaganda to serve the needs of national security—a form of idolatry that did not perish with Jeroboam.

Moving back from the prophets to the psalm that most sharply declares the human origin of idols, Psalm 115, it is noticeable again that the polemical context is between Israel and the nations. The familiar opening verse of the psalm also takes on greater significance in the light of our discussion thus far. If the gods of a nation are in fact the collective human construct of that nation's pride, then the glory of a god is identical to the glory of its nation and vice versa. To glorify the nation's god usually meant praising their combined military might. The Israelite psalmist denies that this can be any part of the motivation for praising YHWH, the God of Israel. On the contrary, he says, with double emphasis:

> Not to us, O LORD, not to us
>> but to your name be the glory,
>> because of your love and faithfulness. (Ps 115:1)

That is to say, to give glory to YHWH must never be construed as just another way of giving glory to his people *Israel*. On the contrary, YHWH must be praised for his own distinct identity and character, not just as a symbol or cipher for the people's own self-congratulation (a confusion that is as seductive as it is rampant among modern nations who claim to honor "God" or who ask God to "bless" them).

From this unusual beginning, the psalm continues with an imaginary exchange between the other nations and Israel.

> Why do the nations say,
>> "Where is their God?"
> Our God is in heaven;
>> he does whatever pleases him.
> But their idols are silver and gold,
>> made by the hands of men. (Ps 115:2-4)

---

[19]This state of affairs is exposed in the revealing indignation of the priest of Bethel against what he regarded as the seditious prophecies of Amos: "this is the king's sanctuary and the temple of the kingdom" (Amos 7:13).

"Where is your God?" the nations taunt Israel in mockery of Israel's lack of visible images of YHWH.

"In heaven, where are yours?" retorts Israel.

And in answering his own implied question—"Where are the gods of the nations?" the psalmist declares, "they are on earth like those who make them." YHWH's invisible name badge reads "Sole Ruler of heaven." The all-too-visible generic trademark of the other gods reads "Made on earth." The later part of the psalm then combines this contrast between heaven and earth (both of which have been made by YHWH, but as distinct realms for his own and human habitation) with the contrast between life and death. The implication is that the gods and idols critiqued in the first part of the psalm are not only *not* gods in heaven, they are of the earth, lifeless and incapable of giving blessing in the way that only YHWH can.

> May you be blessed by the LORD,
> the Maker of heaven and earth.
>
> The highest heavens belong to the LORD,
> but the earth he has given to man.
> It is not the dead who praise the LORD,
> those who go down to silence;
> it is we who extol the LORD,
> both now and for evermore. (Ps 115:15-18)[20]

The contrast between Yahweh and purported gods is thus underscored through a contrast between the higher realm in which Yahweh lives and the inhabited world below, as if to suggest that correspondingly the idols belong to the human world, not the divine one. This is Isaiah's point all over again. Second, there is a contrast between the living and the dead. . . . The fact that this point is made here, at the end of a Psalm about the superiority of Yahweh to other "gods" seems to me significant. For idols belong essentially to the world of the dead in OT thought: they are as lifeless as their worshippers, whereas Yahweh "is the true God; he is the living God and the everlasting King" (Jer 10:10). Thus this Psalm forms a carefully thought out unity, based on the contrast between the God of Israel and the "idols" of the nations and drawing in other significant contrasts: between heaven and earth, between the living and the dead, and between human and divine power.[21]

The pinnacle (or nadir) of gods as the work of human hands is when humans claim to be their own gods or to be the divine source of their own power. The

---

[20]Verse 16 literally reads, "to the sons of adam"—which provides connecting similarity to the description of the idols as "the work of the hands of adam" in v. 4.

[21]Barton, "Work of Human Hands," p. 70.

quip about the self-made man who worships his creator is recognized in the Old Testament and even comes in for the same kind of grim humor in the process of unmasking the absurdity and deception of such arrogance. Yet again, it is usually the vice of kings and emperors.

Ezekiel exposes the self-divination of the king of Tyre and the inevitable judgment it brings on him and his empire:

> In the pride of your heart
>   you say, "I am a god;
> I sit on the throne of a god
>   in the heart of the seas."
> But you are a man and not a god,
>   though you think you are as wise as a god. . . .
> Will you then say, "I am a god,"
>   in the presence of those who kill you?
> You will be but a man, not a god,
>   in the hands of those who slay you. (Ezek 28:2, 9)

Similarly, Ezekiel pointedly expresses the arrogance of the Pharaoh of Egypt who imagines himself to be the source of his own prosperity, claiming the divine power of creation over the Nile itself that provides the wealth of Egypt.

> I am against you, Pharaoh king of Egypt,
>   you great monster lying among your streams.
> You say, "The Nile is mine;
>   I made it for myself." (Ezek 29:3)

What insane arrogance and self-deception fuel such an absurd claim! Yet it is echoed in the idolatrous worship of mammon that characterizes contemporary global capitalism. Long before Ezekiel, Israel was warned against such economic arrogance and urged to remember the true source of their wealth in Deuteronomy 8:17-18.

Not surprisingly, Babylon is accused of similar divine pretensions, uttering words that should only ever come from the mouth of the living God.

> Now then, listen, you wanton creature,
>   lounging in your security
> and saying to yourself,
>   "I am, and there is none beside me.
> I will never be a widow
>   or suffer the loss of children."
> Both of these will overtake you
>   in a moment, on a single day. . . .

Your wisdom and knowledge mislead you
>   when you say to yourself,
>   "I am, and there is none besides me." (Is 47:8-10)

Nebuchadnezzar suffered from such pretensions of deity, it seems, but was humbled into seeing the insanity of them and then restored simultaneously to sanity and submission to the living God (Dan 4).

When we review the material we have surveyed in this section, it is enormously challenging to the whole world of gods and idols, and was clearly intended to be so. For we have observed this stance across the wide range of Old Testament literature from many different historical periods.

It is not unusual for any people to make great claims for their own deity. In this principle and practice, Israel was no different from its neighbors.[22] But to claim transcendent uniqueness and universality for that deity, to the exclusion of all others, and defend the claim by reference to his extraordinary and unparalleled "jealousy," as Israel did for YHWH, was something not found in anything like the same degree elsewhere. Referring to the uniqueness of the first commandment, in comparison to the more pluralistic tolerance of most ancient Near Eastern religion, Werner Schmidt comments:

> There is no real model for it, and it cannot be derived from the neighboring religions, but is opposed to their essential nature. History looks for analogies for all phenomena, but so far as we know at present it is impossible to show that the first and second commandments were borrowed from elsewhere. Exclusiveness of creed is unique to Israel.[23]

But then to go further still and declare again and again as a pervasive matter of theological worldview that the gods of the nations, like the idols that visibly represent them, are "the work of human hands"—a human construct with no divine substance—is something else and quite unparalleled. Yet there seems no other way to account for the extensiveness of this theme in the Old Testament. Israel did *not* misunderstand the nature of idolatry or the assumptions that were made by other worshipers about their own gods. On the contrary, understanding those assumptions and claims very well, they simply refused to accept them. The categorical assertion of Psalm 96:5 is devastating. "All the gods of the na-

---

[22]See, e.g., the survey provided by Morton Smith, "The Common Theology of the Ancient Near East," in *Essential Papers on Israel and the Ancient near East,* ed. F. E. Greenspan (New York: New York University Press, 1991), pp. 49-65. Smith, however, goes on to minimize any specific distinctiveness in the faith of Israel.

[23]Werner H. Schmidt, *The Faith of the Old Testament* (Philadelphia: Westminster; Oxford: Blackwell, 1983), p. 70.

tions are idols *['elilim]*"—that is, the gods themselves share the same insubstan-
tial transience as the idols, for they too are man-made.

To say that the gods are work of human hands is to prick human *hubris* and
to invite fierce repudiation. Paul saying it in Ephesus was enough to start a riot
(Acts 19:23-41). For if it is indeed true that the gods we exalt so highly are resplendent products of our own creativity, then it is not surprising that we defend
them so belligerently. And in our own jealous protectiveness of the gods we created for ourselves, we display a parody of the true jealousy that is the prerogative of the only true God whom we did not create. We invest so much of ourselves in our gods, spend so much on them and blend our identity and
significance with theirs that it simply will not do for us to have them unmasked,
mocked or toppled. And yet, of course, topple they must before the living God.
For that is the destiny of all human effort that is not for the glory of God or offered to be redeemed by him.

> Pride of man and earthly glory,
> Sword and crown betray his trust;
> What with care and toil he buildeth,
> Tower and temple fall to dust.
> But God's power,
> Hour by hour,
> Is my temple and my tower.[24]

In the end, the gods of human creation for all their arrogant claims and masquerade are no greater than gilded statues that have to be nailed down to keep
them vertical. Even then it's a precarious posture. Philistine god Dagon was as
flattened by the living God and Philistine giant Goliath was by David's sling—
and for the same didactic purpose: "And the whole world will know that there
is a God in Israel" (1 Sam 17:46).

Babylonian Bel and Nebo would exit the stage of history with no greater dignity (Is 46:1-2). Against all such pretensions of men and the products of men,
Isaiah affirms that

> The LORD Almighty has a day in store
>   for all the proud and lofty,
>   for all that is exalted
>   (and they will be humbled) . . .
> The arrogance of man will be brought low
>   and the pride of men will be humbled;

---

[24]Joachim Neander (1650-1680), "All My Hope on God Is Founded," adapted by Robert S.
Bridges in 1899.

the LORD alone will be exalted in that day,
> and the idols will totally disappear. (Is 2:12, 17-18)

And when the Lord's judgment falls it will include in its universal scope both the arrogant human rulers on earth and the gods they have located in heaven.

In that day the LORD will punish
> the powers in the heavens above
> and the kings on the earth below. (Is 24:21)[25]

Drawing on such scriptural roots, Paul affirms both the created nature of the powers and associated ideologies that hold sway over human lives and minds, and the decisive judgment of all these powers at the cross of Christ:

See to it that no one takes you captive through hollow and deceptive philosophy, which depends on human tradition and the basic principles of this world rather than on Christ. . . . Having disarmed the powers and authorities, [Christ] made a public spectacle of them, triumphing over them by the cross. (Col 2:8, 15)

Critique and hope. What then are the paradoxes of the gods in the Bible? We have discussed two.

The first is that they are *nothing* in terms of the divine reality that is claimed for them. There is only one rightful occupant of the category of deity, and that is the Lord God of the biblical revelation, Creator and Ruler of the universe. Beside him there is no other legitimate claim to deity. In that sense, as Paul affirmed as an item of the clear Old Testament monotheism that he took as axiomatic: a god is nothing in this world, and neither is an idol. And yet idols clearly do exist in our observable world, and the gods they represent also exist within history as part of human discourse, experience and activity. They are *something*—something whose existence is assumed in the command not to worship them. But as I have argued, the belief that gods exist in this sense is not incompatible with the fundamental bedrock of biblical monotheism—the

---

[25]The second line literally says, "the host of the height in the height." While this does not specifically describe these celestial armies as "gods," they are certainly powers such as are called gods elsewhere. Either, as elsewhere in Isaiah, they are regarded as human figments—the alleged divine sponsors of the rule of the kings or they may be actual spiritual powers, the angelic hosts that link themselves to human government in some way. In either case, "the gods" refers to something within the created order—either of human manufacture or angelic—not to anything that shares in the unique divinity of YHWH who is exercising judgment. Motyer suggests that the expression "alludes to guilty spiritual forces who will be dealt with in a comprehensive settlement over the whole field of divine creation. Isaiah's assertion of the punishment of every power wherever located is the more impressive by its calm assumption of total divine sovereignty." J. A. Motyer, *The Prophecy of Isaiah* (Downers Grove, Ill.: InterVarsity Press; Leicester, U.K.: Inter-Varsity Press, 1993), p. 206.

Lord our God is God in heaven above and the earth below; there is no other. The gods exist as something, but not as God does, with divine identity, status, power and eternity. They may be located in heaven by those who worship them, but in reality they are of the earth, as much part of the created order as their worshipers.

The second paradox is that gods may represent and manifest the demonic order. The Old Testament (occasionally) and the New Testament (more clearly) recognize the presence and power of spiritual forces behind the gods and idols. Equally clearly they both affirm the sovereignty of the living God over all such powers, and their conclusive defeat by Christ on the cross. But the Old Testament much more frequently and unambiguously describes both idols and the gods they are presumed to represent as the work of human hands. We are the makers of our own gods—which, of course, is part of the absurdity of worshiping them.

So if the question is asked, Are other gods demons or human constructions? the answer is that they can be either or both. However, the latter is the more significant theological truth and the more dangerous deception. Human beings did not need the devil to teach us idolatry. Once we chose to reject the authority of the living God, we have ended up creating gods for ourselves, either within the created order or within the imaginations of our hearts. We are experts in doing so and the devil fosters and thrives on our expertise.

The relative scarcity of texts connecting gods and idols to *demons* and the abundance of texts describing them as *human* constructs is surely theologically significant. The contrast ensures that we keep the balance of responsibility for the sin of idolatry where it truly belongs—with us human beings. Not that we owe the devil any exoneration, but neither should we shift the blame on to him for what is our own responsibility (another trick we learned as early as the Garden of Eden). If gods are primarily human constructs, then they are our own responsibility. We pay their debts, clear up their mess, suffer their consequences. Certainly we must acknowledge the extent and effect of satanic infiltration and spiritual blindness inflicted by the evil one. But gods and idols are fundamentally what we have made. The secularist accusation against the dire consequences of human religions has some point: the gods we make are as destructive as we are ourselves—for they are the work of our own hands, and our hands are full of blood.

But there is also an element of hope in this awareness. If gods are mainly human constructs, then they are not only destructive but also *destructible*—as destructible as anything else we make on earth. *The gods too are subject to decay and death*. They are no more durable than the men or empires that make them.

The scorn of the Assyrian on the defunct gods of the nations he had conquered rebounds on himself in the light of history. For where now are the gods of Assyria, Babylon, Persia, Greece or Rome? History is the graveyard of the gods.

Missiologically, these reflections clearly bear on the pressing question of the contemporary plurality of religions. What should be our biblically grounded response to the gods of the nations in our world today? At the very least it is clear that we cannot adopt simplistic categorizations, such as the view that all non-Christian religion is entirely demonic or that it is all purely cultural. The Bible's own subtle analysis of "other gods" makes such binary opposites completely unsatisfactory.

Mission and the Gods

Why is idolatry a missional issue? Why must mission "engage the gods," expose and unmask them? Why must we identify and condemn idolatry (as the prophets and apostles did), not only as it presents itself among those who do not yet acknowledge the living God but also (and even more so) as it works its insidious poison among those who *do* claim to know and worship the God of the Bible and who name the name of Christ (recalling that the prophets condemn idolatry in Israel far more often than in other nations)? What, in any case, is so wrong with people worshiping their own gods if they want to? And how are we to recognize the presence of other gods in human cultures? And even when we have identified them, how should we deal with them in the many different social, cultural, evangelistic and pastoral contexts in which we are called to minister? These are some of the questions to which we turn in the remainder of this chapter.

Recognizing the most crucial distinction. Arguably the most fundamental distinction in all reality is presented to us in the opening verses of the Bible. It is the distinction between the Creator God and everything else that exists anywhere. God alone is uncreated, self-existent, noncontingent. God's being depends on nothing else outside God's own self. All other reality, by contrast, is created by God and therefore is dependent on God for existence and sustenance. The creation is contingent on God. It cannot and would not exist without God. God did and could exist without it. This essential ontological duality between two orders of being (the created order and the uncreated God) is foundational to the biblical worldview.

Flowing from this, there are many other distinctions that the creation narrative alerts us to: the distinctions between day and night, between different environments on earth, between species, between humans in God's image and the rest of the animals, between men and women. But undoubtedly the primary and most crucial distinction is that between the Creator and the creation itself. Not surprisingly, therefore, it is that distinction which comes under attack when the mysterious power of evil makes its appearance in that profoundly simple, yet simply profound, narrative of Genesis 3.

"You will be like God, knowing good and evil," promises the serpent—if only humans would disregard God's boundary markers (Gen 3:5). What could be more plausible or natural for a creature made in the image of God than to want to be like God? The key to the temptation seems to be in the second phrase, "knowing good and evil," which I take to imply "having moral autonomy." That is, what was being offered by the serpent and then claimed by the human pair through their disobedient act was not just the ability to *recognize* the difference between good and evil (which is surely foundational to any genuine moral freedom or moral capacity, and is commended in the Bible elsewhere) but the right to *define for oneself* good and evil. It is the prerogative of God in the supreme goodness of his own being to decide and define what constitutes goodness and therefore conversely what constitutes evil. Humans however, in choosing to decide for ourselves what *we* will deem good or evil usurp the prerogative of God in rebellious moral autonomy. And at the same time, of course, by making our own definitions in a state of rebellion and disobedience, we end up in the moral perversions and chaos that pervade fallen human life. This interpretation of the phrase is supported by the way God recognizes the nature of what has happened: "The man has now become like one of us, knowing good and evil" (Gen 3:22). God accepts that humans have indeed breached the Creator-creature distinction. Not that humans have now *become* gods but that they have chosen to *act as though they were*—defining and deciding for themselves what they will regard as good and evil. Therein lies the root of all other forms of idolatry: we deify our own capacities, and thereby make gods of ourselves and our choices and all their implications. God then shrinks in horror from the prospect of human immortality and eternal life in such a fallen state and prevents access to the "tree of life." God has a better way to bring humanity, redeemed and cleansed, to eternal life.

At the root, then, of all idolatry is human rejection of the Godness of God and the finality of God's moral authority. The fruit of that basic rebellion is to be seen in many other ways in which idolatry blurs the distinction between God and creation, to the detriment of both.

Idolatry dethrones God and enthrones creation. Idolatry is the attempt to limit, reduce and control God by refusing his authority, constraining or manipulating his power to act, having him available to serve our interests. At the same time, paradoxically, idolatry exalts things within the created order (whether natural objects in the heavens or on earth, or created spirits, or the products of our own hands or imaginations). Creation is then credited with a potency that belongs only to God; it is sacralized, worshiped and treated as that from which ultimate meaning can be derived. A great reversal happens: God, who should be worshiped, becomes an object to be used; creation, which is for our use and blessing, becomes the object of our worship.

Once this fundamental distinction is blurred, once this reversal takes place, then devastating personal and social consequences follow. Creation, which derives its own meaning from God, cannot give us in itself the ultimate meaning we crave, so idolatry is doomed to disappointment (to put it at its mildest). Worship of the self eventually implodes in narcissism, nihilism or sheer amoral selfishness. If nature itself is treated as divine, then all other distinctions begin to be dissolved. There is no difference between human life and all other forms of life. There is no difference between good and evil since all is ultimately one. So any objective reference point for moral discrimination becomes impossible.

In the light of such confusion the mission of God is ultimately to restore his whole creation to what it was intended to be—*God's* creation, ruled over by redeemed *humanity,* giving glory and praise to its Creator. Our mission, in participation with that divine mission, and in anticipation of its final accomplishment, is to work with God in exposing the idols that continue to blur the distinction, and to liberate men and women from the destructive delusions they foster.

Discerning the gods. Much helpful work has been done in identifying and analyzing the gods that may be said to dominate modern cultures—especially in Western societies. Some of these studies make extensive use of combined biblical and sociological tools, others less so. Such analyses have powerful missiological relevance since they apply this distinctive biblical category (idolatry) to contemporary cultural phenomena, enabling us to see below the surface and recognize idolatrous or demonic forces at work. Some of them also are specifically addressed to the missiological question of how we are to expose and confront these cultural idols and address the liberating message of the biblical gospel to those who are captivated by them. A small sampling of such studies must suffice, since the following works range very widely.

Jacques Ellul was one of the earliest to connect biblical categories of idolatry with contemporary Western cultural trends, especially secularism.[26] He analyzes the sacred and symbolic aspects of technique, sex, the nation-state, revolution

---

[26]Jacques Ellul, *The New Demons* (London: Mowbrays, 1976).

and the mythology of history and science. J. A. Walter applied the same methodology to a range of social phenomena, many of which appear good in themselves, but easily become elevated to idolatrous status, such as: work, the family, suburbia, individualism, ecology, race, and the media.[27] Bob Goudzwaard extended the analysis to the whole realm of ideology, focusing especially on the ideologies of revolution, the nation, material prosperity and guaranteed security.[28] Walter Wink's trilogy is one of the most extensive studies of the "powers" in biblical (and especially New Testament) thought, but Wink is criticized for not giving sufficient weight to the biblical assertions about the objective demonic aspects of their infiltration of human structures.[29] Clinton Arnold is more balanced in that respect.[30] Vinoth Ramachandra presses the analysis of modernity and its sequel further in observing the violence of the new idolatries, the dogmatism of those who idolize science and the continuing idolatry of "reason and unreason."[31] Peter Moore tackles the various idolatries of Western culture in a more apologetic mode, addressing those who may be dazzled by them—including New Age-ism, relativism, narcissism and hedonism.[32] Craig Bartholomew and Thorsten Moritz edit a volume in which a number of biblical scholars examine consumerism as a form of contemporary idolatry.[33]

Returning, however, to the Bible itself, we find that there are different kinds of gods. That is to say, gods that humans worship other than the living God may be constituted by different things, or may exercise their grip over human lives in different ways. If we are in large measure responsible ourselves as human beings for the gods we create, then it is worth looking at the way the Bible portrays that process. What are the things that we tend to manufacture our gods from?

Things that entice us. "Do not be enticed" warns Deuteronomy 4:19; do not be enticed into worshiping heavenly bodies. The language suggests that there

---

[27]J. A. Walter, *A Long Way from Home: A Sociological Exploration of Contemporary Idolatry* (Carlisle, U.K.: Paternoster, 1979).

[28]Bob Goudzwaard, *Idols of Our Time* (Downers Grove, Ill.: InterVarsity Press, 1984).

[29]Walter Wink, *Naming the Powers: The Language of Power in the New Testament* (Philadelphia: Fortress Press, 1984); *Unmasking the Powers: The Invisible Forces That Determine Human Existence* (Philadelphia: Fortress Press, 1986); *Engaging the Powers: Discernment and Resistance in a World of Domination* (Minneapolis: Fortress Press, 1992).

[30]Clinton Arnold, *Powers of Darkness: A Thoughtful, Biblical Look at an Urgent Challenge Facing the Church* (Leicester, U.K.: Inter-Varsity Press; Downers Grove, Ill.: InterVarsity Press, 1992).

[31]Vinoth Ramachandra, *Gods That Fail: Modern Idolatry and Christian Mission* (Carlisle, U.K.: Paternoster; Downers Grove, Ill.: InterVarsity Press 1996).

[32]Peter C. Moore, *Disarming the Secular Gods* (Downers Grove, Ill.: InterVarsity Press; Leicester, U.K.: Inter-Varsity Press, 1989).

[33]Craig Bartholomew and Thorsten Moritz, ed., *Christ and Consumerism: A Critical Analysis of the Spirit of the Age* (Carlisle, U.K.: Paternoster, 2000).

are things in creation that are so awe-inspiring, so much beyond our reach, our control or our understanding that they exercise an enticing attraction to us. This is certainly the flavor of the sin that Job claims to have resisted.

> If I have regarded the sun in its radiance
>   or the moon moving in splendor,
> so that my heart was secretly enticed
>   and my hand offered them a kiss of homage,
> then these also would be sins to be judged,
>   for I would have been unfaithful to God on high. (Job 31:26-28)

Psalm 96 recognizes the same temptation.

> For all the gods of the nations are idols,
>   but the LORD made the heavens.
> *Splendor and majesty* are before him;
>   *strength and glory* are in his sanctuary. (Ps 96:5-6, emphasis added)

The parallelism and flow of thought between these verses implies that the gods worshiped by the nations are personifications of all that impresses us—splendor and majesty, strength and glory. We look for such magnificence and power, and worship these things wherever they inspire awe and trembling admiration: in the stadiums of great sporting triumph or in the lives of pampered sporting heroes; in massed battalions of soldiers, parades of military hardware or on the decks of aircraft carriers; on the stage of rock concerts or the glare of TV and movie celebrity;[34] on the pinnacles of the thrusting towers of corporate power and greed in great cities. All of these can be enticing and idolatrous. But such places, says our psalm, are not where we will find genuine deity. If we are looking for true *splendor, majesty, strength and glory,* they are to be found in the presence of the living Creator God alone. Some commentators see these four words as personifications, as if they were the great angelic companions of YHWH's throne, in stark contrast to the false gods that claimed such magnificence but lacked even real existence.

> I have read v 6 as expressing the great qualities of Yahweh's kingship as personi-
> fications, who attend him in the temple (cf. Ps 85:14; 89:15). The entourage of Yah-
> weh is not made up of a company of lesser gods, who are in reality no gods, but
> those "agents" of his own which are manifest in his saving work and wondrous
> deeds.[35]

---

[34]The language of idolatry is commonly and cheerfully used in that context, in Western culture, when the media pour adulation on celebrities as pop and fashion "idols" and "sex goddesses."

[35]Marvin E. Tate, *Psalms 51-100,* Word Biblical Commentary 20 (Dallas: Word, 1990), p. 514.

Things we fear. The converse is also true. We turn things that we fear into gods in order to placate them or ward them off by our worship. The psalmist affirms that the Lord "is to be feared above all gods" (Ps 96:4), which suggests that gods other than YHWH are indeed things that are objects of fear ("something," in the paradoxical sense discussed on pp. 136-42). So in the Canaanite pantheon Death (Mot) is a god; the Sea (Yamm), another object of awe and fear, is a god. And in other world religions the same phenomenon can be observed— some of the most fearsome faces of evil, anger, vengeance, blood lust, cruelty and so forth are divinized. And many routine ritual practices, such as avoiding "the evil eye," the wearing of protective charms, the use of apotropaic magic and mantras and the like, are manifestations of the deified power of fear. Since there are a great many things in this world for puny human beings to be afraid of, here surely lies one of the roots of polytheistic worldviews.

It is significant, therefore, that the fear of the Lord plays such a central role in the biblical worldview. It is a potent dimension of radical monotheism that if there is truly only one God, then he alone should be the object of our true fear. Then those who live in the fear of the Lord need live in fear of nothing else. Other objects of fear lose their divine power and their idolatrous grip. This is the testimony of the author of Psalm 34.

> I sought the LORD and he answered me;
>   he delivered me from all my fears. . . .
> The angel of the LORD encamps around those who fear him,
>   and he delivers them.
> Taste and see that the LORD is good;
>   blessed is the man who takes refuge in him.
> Fear the LORD, you his saints,
>   for those who fear him lack nothing. (Ps 34:4, 7-9)

Or as Nahum Tate put it, "Fear him, ye saints, and you will then / have nothing else to fear."[36]

The idolatrous power of fear is enormous and seems to bear no direct relation to the scale of what is feared. It has been pointed out that although in contemporary Western society we live lives that are immeasurably more safe, healthy and free from risk than any previous generation, yet we are consumed by anxieties, fears and neuroses. Fed by garish media hype, we swoon at the latest rogue virus and seem willing to spend exorbitant amounts on security measures that can never actually prevent the terror we struggle to fend off.

---

[36]Nahum Tate, "Through All the Changing Scenes of Life" (1696).

Things that we trust. Following naturally from the previous point, we tend to idolize the things (or people or systems) that we place our trust in to deliver us from the things we fear. The idolatrous dimension emerges when we place ultimate faith in such things, when we believe all the promises that are made or implied in them, and when we make all the sacrifices that they demand in exchange for what they speciously offer. So whether we aim at financial security to insure against all future threats, or pour vast quantities of the wealth of the planet and its nations into the gaping maw of military security, or just become personally obsessive about every latest fad that promises immunity from ill health or the wear and tear of physical ageing, these tend to be very costly gods indeed. And since we spend so much on them, we naturally feel cheated when they do not deliver what we demand in return for our investment. A country can spend billions on star-wars protective systems and then be psychologically devastated by a few knife-wielding men who hijack airplanes. We load blame and anger on health professionals who have not delivered our "entitlement" to disease-free virtual immortality. Ultimately, we pay the cost of putting ultimate trust in what can never deliver ultimate security. Ultimately, it seems, we never learn that false gods never fail to fail. That is the only thing about a false god you can depend on.

By contrast, after magnificent reflections on the sovereign power of the Lord and his word in redemption, creation, providence and history, the author of Psalm 33 warns us against investing our hope for salvation anywhere else.

> No king is saved by the size of his army;
>> no warrior escapes by his great strength.
> A horse is a vain hope for deliverance;
>> despite all its great strength it cannot save. (Ps 33:16-17)

Those whose blessing it is to know the Lord know that the only secure place to deposit one's investment of trust is in the Lord himself, and then to wait in hope, joy and patience for the outcome of his *unfailing* love.

> We wait in hope for the LORD;
>> he is our help and shield.
> In him our hearts rejoice,
>> for we trust in his holy name.
> May your unfailing love rest upon us, O LORD,
>> even as we put our hope in you. (Ps 33:20-22)

Things we need. "Do not worry, saying, 'What shall we eat?' or 'What shall we drink?' or 'What shall we wear?' For the pagans run after all these things, and your heavenly Father knows that you need them" (Mt 6:31-32).

The words of Jesus not only acknowledge the reality of basic human needs but also the way that "pagans run after" them. We are, of course, creatures with the same fundamental needs as the rest of the animals. Like other mammals, we humans need food, air, water, shelter, sleep and all the general necessities of survival and welfare. There is, therefore, a natural tendency to deify the sources from which these necessities are deemed to come. Having turned our back on the sole living Creator of all that provides for our needs, we invent surrogate deities to fill the vacuum. So we attribute the varied good gifts of our one Creator to the varied gods of the rain, the sun, the soil, sex and fertility, dreams, and so on. Much religious effort is then directed at persuading these gods to bestow their largesse in a way that meets human basic needs, or to reverse their apparent decision to withhold their favor. The behavior of the prophets of Baal that fell under Elijah's mockery, in their desperate attempts to persuade Baal to demonstrate his deity, was probably not untypical in such emergencies.

This was part of the burden of Hosea's accusation against Israel—that they were attributing to Baal and the Canaanite cults all the natural processes and products that were the gift of YHWH alone (Hos 2:5-8). But this feature of idolatry also gives a sharper polemical edge to the emphatic insistence in Israel's worship on acknowledging YHWH alone as the source of all that we need. No other god is to be asked for what we need or thanked when we receive it.

> You care for the land and water it;
>   you enrich it abundantly.
> The streams of God are filled with water
>   to provide the people with grain,
>   for so you have ordained it. (Ps 65:9)

> He makes grass grow for the cattle,
>   and plants for man to cultivate—
> bringing forth food from the earth:
>   wine that gladdens the heart of man,
>   oil to make his face shine,
>   and bread that sustains his heart. (Ps 104:14-15)

Deuteronomy 8 exposes another subtle form of this idolatry. Failure to acknowledge the living God as the source of all that provides for our needs and contributes to our flourishing can lead to the arrogance that attributes it all to one's own strength and effort. This is also a form of idolatry—the worship of oneself as the source of all that meets one's own need. Whether the Israelite farmer (or modern capitalist) who boasts, "My power and the strength of my hands have produced this wealth for me" (Deut 8:17), or the Egyptian Pharaoh (or modern economic superpower) who boasts, "The Nile is mine; I made it for myself" (Ezek 29:3), both must recognize the idolatrous nature (and insane arrogance) of such claims and acknowledge the true source of the blessings they enjoy.

A missiological perspective on idolatry, then, must include some analysis of the roots of the gods we make for ourselves. My reflections above suggest some of the ways the Bible itself recognizes what lies behind the things we idolize. Having alienated ourselves from the living God our Creator, we have a tendency to worship whatever makes us tremble with awe as we feel our tiny insignificance in comparison with the great magnitudes that surround us. We seek to placate and ward off whatever makes us vulnerable and afraid. We then counter our fears by investing inordinate and idolatrous trust in whatever we think will give us the ultimate security we crave. And we struggle to manipulate and persuade whatever we believe will provide all our basic needs and enable us to prosper on the planet. Doubtless there are other sources and motivations for endemic human idolatry, but these seem to be some of the primary ones, both observed in the Bible and evident to any observer of contemporary human cultures (whether predominantly religious or secular). And all of them stem from our basic rejection of the living Creator God, before whom all such considerations either evaporate or find their subordinate level of legitimacy.

The only antidote to such idolatries, and therefore the task of biblical mission, is to lead people back to acknowledge the only true and living God in all of these domains. Reviewing our list of the sources of idolatry once more, by way of contrast, the one who has set his glory above the heavens is the only one before whom we should tremble in awe and worship. To live in covenantal fear of the Lord as sovereign Creator and gracious Redeemer is to be delivered from the fear of anything else in all creation—material or spiritual. As the Rock, he is the utterly secure place to invest all our trust in all the circumstances of life and death, for the present and the future. And as the Provider of all that is needful for all life on earth, the God of the covenant with Noah and our heavenly Father, there is no other to whom we need turn, to plead, placate or persuade, for the needs he already knows we have.

Exposing the gods. We have already reflected more than once on the impotence of the gods of human manufacture. False gods fail. That is their only truth. Since the task of mission involves the exposure of false gods, it is worth exploring in more detail some dimensions of this failure. For although false gods never fail to fail, it seems humans never fail to forget that this is indeed the case. Some of the accusations that the Bible lays against idolatry include the following:

Idols deprive God of his proper glory. When human beings attribute to other gods gifts, powers or functions that belong to the one living God, then God is deprived of the honor that is due to his name alone. The whole creation exists for the glory of the Creator, and in rendering praise to God alone creation (including humanity) experiences its own true blessing and good. This is the meaning of the jealousy of YHWH in the Old Testament. It is God's proper protection of God's own identity and transcendent uniqueness.

> I am the LORD; that is my name!
>   I will not give my glory to another
>   or my praise to idols. (Is 42:8)

Accordingly the psalmist, having denounced all the gods of the nations as "nothings" (v. 5), issues the universal summons:

> Ascribe to the LORD, O families of nations,
>   ascribe to the LORD glory and strength.
> Ascribe to the *LORD* the glory due to *his* name;
>   bring an offering and come into *his* courts.
> Worship the *LORD* in the splendor of *his* holiness;
>   tremble before *him,* all the earth. (Ps 96:7-9, emphasis added)

This is not an invitation to the nations to make room for YHWH among the pantheon of their own gods and give him some shared respect. The psalmist is not inviting the nations to move their gods along the shelf a little to make room for YHWH among their number. No, this is a call for the radical displacement of all other gods before the sole, unique, transcendent Godness of YHWH, such that all honor, glory, worship and praise goes to him, as it rightfully should. As long as other gods are worshiped, the living God is to that extent denied what is rightfully his—the total worship of his total creation. This is what makes the struggle with idolatry a major dimension of the mission of God in which he commands our cooperation.

Idols distort the image of God in us. Since idolatry diminishes the glory of God, and since humans are made in the image of God, it follows that idolatry is also detrimental to the very essence of our humanity. As the Westminster Confession reminds us, "The chief end of man is to glorify God and enjoy him forever." To refuse to glorify God, and even worse, to exchange "the glory of the immortal God for images made to look like mortal man and birds and animals and reptiles" (Rom 1:23) is to frustrate the purpose of our very existence. Idolatry is radical self-harm.

It is also radically, terribly ironic. In trying to be as God (in the original temptation and rebellion), we have ended up less human. The principle affirmed in several places in the Bible that you become like the object of your worship (e.g., Ps 115:8; Is 41:24; 44:9) is very apparent. If you worship that which is not *God*, you reduce the image of God in yourself. If you worship that which is not even *human,* you reduce your humanity still further.

So Isaiah 44 holds before us very starkly the irony (or parody) of the one creature that was made in the image of the living God worshiping something that is merely a lifeless image of himself.

> The blacksmith takes a tool
> > and works with it in the coals;
> he shapes an idol with hammers,
> > he forges it with the might of his arm.
> He gets hungry and loses his strength;
> > he drinks no water and grows faint.
> The carpenter measures with a line
> > and makes an outline with a marker;
> he roughs it out with chisels
> > and marks it with compasses.
> He shapes it *in the form of a man,*
> > of man in all his glory,
> > that it may dwell in a shrine. (Is 44:12-13, emphasis added)

The words in italics are surely the focal point of the prophet's satire. "Man in all his glory" speaks of the human privilege of being made in the image of God. Yet here is a man worshiping as a god something that is nothing but an image of himself, the product of human skill and effort. The lifeless image of the living man languishes inside a little hut, while the living image of the living God is walking around outside, oblivious to the irony of his actions.

There is comparable (though perhaps more polite) irony also in Paul's argument with the Greek intelligentsia in Athens. Few cultures have equalled ancient Greece in exalting the human spirit, human art, literature, philosophy—even the human physical form. Yet in the process they had lost the very God in whose image all these wonderful dimensions of humanity have their source. Was it not absurd, Paul challenges them, to imagine that the One who is the *origin* of all this human glory needed to be housed and fed by human hands?

> The God who made the world and everything in it is the Lord of heaven and earth and does not live in temples built by hands. And he is not served by human hands, as if he needed anything, because he himself gives all men life and breath and everything else. . . . Therefore since we are God's offspring, we should not think that the divine being is like gold or silver or stone—an image made by man's design and skill. (Acts 17:24-25, 29)

The psalms similarly play on the contrast between the work of God's hands and the work of human hands. Human beings, like all the rest of creation, are the work of God's hands (Ps 138:8; 139:13-15). Yet we, unique among God's creatures, have been made "ruler over the works of [God's] hands" (Ps 8:6-8). And when we think about that in the light of contemplating the vastness of the heavens, which are also "the work of [God's] fingers" (Ps 8:3), it is astonishing. So, what a travesty it is when humans, who themselves are the work of God's hands and were made to rule the rest of the works of God's hands, choose instead to worship the work of their *own* hands (Ps 115:4). Without doubt, idolatry distorts, demeans and diminishes our humanity.

Idols are profoundly disappointing. In a polytheistic universe, we cannot expect all the gods to please all the people all the time. So disappointment with the gods is part of the lottery of life. Spread your bets among the gods, then, for you win some, you lose some. The assumption that some of the gods will disappoint you some of the time is actually built into such a worldview, and becomes inevitable when the conflicts of the nations are seen as mirroring the conflicts of the gods. Defeated nations have defeated gods. Threatened nations should face the likelihood of their gods failing them too. Best not to trust them too long. Switch to the gods of the winning side and avoid disappointment.

This is precisely the assumption that seemed gloatingly self-evident to the Assyrian commander swaggering below the walls of besieged Jerusalem.

> Do not listen to Hezekiah, for he is misleading you when he says, "The LORD will deliver us." Has the god of any nation ever delivered his land from the hand of the king of Assyria? Where are the gods of Hamath and Arpad? Where are the gods of Sepharvim, Hena and Ivvah? Have they rescued Samaria from my hand? Who of all the gods of these countries has been able to save his land from me? How then can the LORD deliver Jerusalem from my hand? (2 Kings 18:32-35)

In other words, reasoned the Assyrian, YHWH would turn out to be as big a disappointment to the people of Judah as the gods of the other nations had been to them. From where he stood, that seemed a solid, predictable bet. You just can't trust these lesser gods, you see.

Hezekiah and Isaiah, however, had a rather different perspective on events. On the one hand, Hezekiah knew that the reason why the other gods had disappointed the nations that trusted in them was that "they were not gods [or not God], but only wood and stone, fashioned by men's hands" (2 Kings 19:18). And on the other hand, Isaiah knew that Assyria's victories, far from proving the superiority of Assyrian gods, were actually planned and controlled by YHWH all along, and would very soon be reversed in the fires of his judgment (2 Kings 19:25-28).

No wonder then that the same prophet ridiculed Judah for turning away from the only source of protection that would *not* disappoint them to the armies, horses and gods of the Egyptians, who were notoriously untrustworthy and undoubtedly *would* disappoint them.

> Woe to the obstinate children . . .
> who go down to Egypt
> > without consulting me;
> who look for help to Pharaoh's protection,
> > to Egypt's shade for refuge.
> But Pharaoh's protection will be your shame,
> > Egypt's shade will bring you disgrace. (Is 30:1-3)

> But the Egyptians are men and not God;
> > their horses are flesh and not spirit. (Is 31:3; cf. Jer 2:36-37)

Given, then, that the gods of the nations were a disappointing failure even to the nations who worshiped them, and given that YHWH alone was the living God who could be trusted not to fail, it was doubly tragic that Israel should even think of exchanging the one for the other. There was something grossly unnatural about it, as Jeremiah observed in shocked disbelief.

> Has a nation ever changed its gods?
> > (Yet they are not gods at all.)
> But my people have exchanged their Glory
> > for worthless idols.
> Be appalled at this, O heavens,
> > and shudder with great horror. (Jer 2:11-12)

How could anyone abandon a guaranteed source of life for a guaranteed source of disappointment? Yet that is what Israel had done, in forsaking the living spring for a leaking cistern. "Broken cisterns that can hold no water" (Jer 2:13) is a powerful image of disappointment, futility and wasted effort.

The Lord himself then chides Israel for the ungrateful futility of their folly. Drawing from the ancient tradition of Deuteronomy 32:37-38, Jeremiah depicts the perversity of Israel in turning away from YHWH to worship despicable gods, but then brazenly expecting YHWH to save them when the multiple gods of their own manufacture utterly fail to deliver.

> They say to wood, "You are my father,"
> > and to stone, "You gave me birth."

They have turned their backs to me
>   and not their faces;
> yet when they are in trouble, they say,
>   "Come and save us!"
> Where then are the gods you made for yourselves?
>   Let them come if they can save you
>   when you are in trouble!
> For you have as many gods
>   as you have towns, O Judah. (Jer 2:27-28)[37]

Kings, armies, horses, treaties, riches, natural resources—all these things are *not* really gods and are unable to bear the weight of trust we put in them. However, what makes them into gods is that we insist on believing the spurious promises they make (or that we implicitly attribute to them). We keep on paying the enormous sacrifices they demand for our loyalty. And we keep on hoping against hope that they will not let us down. But of course, they always do in the end. Idolatry is wasted effort and dashed hopes. The worship of false gods is the fellowship of futility, the grand delusion whose only destiny is disappointment.

So when the editorial in a British national newspaper once ended its sad analysis of a society in which two children could callously murder a toddler with the words "All our gods have failed," it doubtless intended the words only as a figure of speech.[38] Sadly, such a metaphorical cry of despair also precisely captures the spiritual truth. Those things that we thought could deliver us from evil and in which we invested great amounts of intellectual, financial and emotional capital in the hope that they would deliver us, have instead spectacularly disappointed us. When will we ever learn?

Remembering that the battle is the Lord's. Johannes Verkuyl writes:

> The whole Old Testament (and the New Testament as well) is filled with descriptions of how YHWH-Adonai, the covenant God of Israel, is waging war against those forces that try to thwart and subvert his plans for his creation. He battles against those false gods that human beings have fashioned from the created world, idolized and used for their own purpose. Think, for example, of the Baals and the Ashteroth, whose worshipers elevated nature, the tribe, the state and the nation to a divine status. God fights against magic and astrology that, according to Deuteronomy, bend the line between God and his creation. He contends against every form

---

[37]In v. 27 Jeremiah scornfully reverses the "gender" of the idolatry here: the wooden pole was the female maternity symbol, while the standing stone was the male phallic symbol.

[38]From the editorial "It Must Be Someone's Fault—It Might Be Our Own," *The Independent,* February 28, 1993, in the wake of the murder of two-year-old James Bulger by two ten-year-old children.

of social injustice and pulls off every cloak under which it seeks to hide.[39]

The Bible clearly portrays the struggle with idolatry as a battle between YHWH, the living God, and all those forces that oppose him. Verkuyl mentions the gods of the Canaanite cults, but we could equally think of the great battle with the unnamed gods of Egypt in the exodus narrative (cf. Ex 12:12) that preceded Israel's life in Canaan, or of the sustained rhetorical polemic against the gods of Babylon in the context of Israel's exile, in the book of Isaiah.[40]

Now that we have surveyed the dismal devastation that idolatry wreaks in human life, we can see this conflict between God and the gods in a fresh light. Three points of missional relevance may be made.

The missional love of God repels idolatry. On the one hand, it is true that God battles with idolatry because it diminishes the glory that is rightfully God's own. God's jealousy for God's own self is a powerful dynamic throughout Scripture. But, on the other hand, God's battle against the gods of human hands (and all they represent) can be seen as a function of his *loving benevolence toward us* and indeed toward his whole creation. Divine jealousy is in fact an essential function of divine love. It is precisely because God wills our good that he hates the self-inflicted harm that our idolatry generates. God's conflict with the gods is ultimately for our own good as well as for God's glory. This further highlights why idolatry is such a primary sin in the Bible—identified as such by the primacy of the first two commandments of the Decalogue. It is not merely that idolatry steals God's glory but it also thwarts God's love—the love that seeks the highest good of all God's creation. Idolatry therefore contradicts the very essence, the Godness, of God, for "God is love."

Once again, it is important to take note of a strongly missional hermeneutic in our discussion. We are not approaching this matter from the perspective of an attempted reconstruction of the evolution of Israel's religion, nor merely from the perspective of the religious psychology of those who worshiped other gods. We remind ourselves constantly that the primary driving force of the biblical grand narrative is the priority of God's own mission. Israel's religion at the em-

---

[39]Johannes Verkuyl, *Contemporary Missiology* (Grand Rapids: Eerdmans, 1978), p. 95. See also, as a serious treatment of conflict as an essential element of mission in biblical thought, Marc R. Spindler, *La Mission: Combat Pour Le Salut Du Monde* (Neuchatel, Switzerland: Delachaux & Niestle, 1967).

[40]Robert B. Chisholm also observes these three broadly significant eras in the conflict between Yahweh and the gods, and then concentrates on the latter two. See, " 'To Whom Shall You Compare Me?' Yahweh's Polemic Against Baal and the Babylonian Idol-Gods in Prophetic Literature," in *Christianity and the Religions: A Biblical Theology of World Religions,* ed. E. Rommen and H. A. Netland (Pasadena, Calif.: William Carey Library, 1995), pp. 56-71.

pirical level of popular practice seems to have ebbed and flowed in terms of its commitment to the monotheistic dynamic within it, and more often than not succumbed to ambient polytheism. But the canon as a whole bears witness to the constant determination of the living God, in transcendent uniqueness and universality, to defeat and destroy all that seduces human beings away from the love they receive from God and the love they should give to God.

God's battle with the gods is an essential part of God's mission. God's mission is the blessing of the nations. And the blessing of the nations must ultimately include ridding them of gods that masquerade as protectors and saviors, but are actually devouring, destroying, disappointing deceptions. The battle to do so is a battle of divine love.

The battle and the victory belong to God. Second, by putting our emphasis again on the mission of God, not on human mission, we preserve the right biblical perspective on this matter. For we need to be clear that in the Bible *the conflict with the gods is a conflict waged by God for us, not a conflict waged by us for God.* To be sure, the people of God are involved in spiritual warfare, as countless texts in both testaments testify. However, it is assuredly *not* the case that God is waiting anxiously for the day when we finally win the battle for him and the heavens can applaud our great victory. Such blasphemous nonsense, however, is not far removed from the rhetoric and practice of some forms of alleged mission that place great store on all kinds of methods and techniques of warfare by which we are urged to identify and defeat our spiritual enemies. No, the overwhelming emphasis of the Bible is that *we* are the ones who wait in hope for the day when God defeats all the enemies of God and his people, and then we will celebrate *God's* victory along with angels, archangels and all the company of heaven. Indeed, in the company of heaven we already celebrate the victory of the cross and resurrection of Christ, the Easter victory that anticipates the final destruction of all God's enemies.

God fights for us, not we for him. We are called to witness, to struggle, to resist, to suffer. But the battle is the Lord's, as is the final victory.

Our battle is fought with love, not triumphalism. Third, insofar as our mission assuredly also includes the dimension of spiritual warfare, we need to recognize that our primary aim is not to "win" but to serve. That is to say, the idols, gods, demons and spiritual powers against which we declare war in the name of the gospel of Christ and his cross are things that oppress and ravage human existence. False gods destroy and devour lives, health and resources; they distort and diminish our humanity; they preside over injustice, greed, perversion, cruelty, lust and violence. It is possibly the most satanic dimension of their deceptive power that, in spite of all this, they still persuade people that they are the beneficent protectors of their worshipers' identity, dignity and prosperity, and must therefore be defended at all costs. Only the gospel can unmask these claims. Only the gospel exposes the cancer of idolatry. Only the gospel is good for people.

Our missional motivation, therefore, needs to be carefully examined. Spiritual warfare is not a matter of triumphalism pervaded by a horrid spirit of gloating superiority, in which we become obsessed with "winning a victory." Rather it is a matter of deep compassion for those oppressed by the forces of evil and idolatry—with all their attendant social, economic, political, spiritual and personal effects. We battle with idolatry because, like the God whose mission we thereby share, we know that in doing so we seek the best interests of those we are called to serve in his name. We combat idolatry not only to glorify God but also to bless humanity. Spiritual warfare, like all forms of biblical mission, is to be motivated by and exercised with profound love, humility and compassion—as modeled in Jesus himself.

Confronting Idolatry

Combating idolatry can take many forms. The Bible itself prepares us to recognize that different approaches may be relevant in different contexts. Wisdom in mission calls us to be discerning and to recognize that what may be appropriate in one situation may not be so helpful in another. Within the ministry of the apostle Paul, for example, we may observe the different approach adopted when, for example, (1) he tackles idolatry in the context of dense theological argument of an epistle and (2) he is confronting it in evangelistic engagement with the worshipers of other gods, and again (3) he is wrestling pastorally with questions raised within the church about surrounding idolatry. And to these we may add the prophetic conflict with idolatry, which exposes its futility but does so primarily for the ears of the people of God.

Theological argument. Writing to Christians, and speaking of idolatry objectively as a phenomenon, Paul pulls no punches. In his sharp analysis of human rebellion against God in Romans 1:18-32, he sets idolatry firmly within the realm of that which incurs the wrath of God. It is the result of deliberate suppression of the truth about God that is known and available to all humans. It involves the inversion of the creation order, exchanging the worship of the living God for the worship of images of creation. It claims wisdom but is rank folly. It issues in a catalog of vice and viciousness, polluting every aspect of human life—sexual, social, familial and personal. Idolatry is alienating, darkening, degrading, divisive and deadly. We must not separate any part of this analysis from the whole. Paul's attack on idolatry is theological, intellectual, spiritual, ethical and social. It is a powerful piece of theological argument, preparatory to his exposition of the fullness of the gospel.

Mission requires that we engage in such discourse when appropriate, for we have no liberty to dilute the lurid colors of Paul's exposure of idolatry here. This is the truth of the matter, the distillation of so many other biblical texts on the subject. The good news of the gospel has to be seen (as it very soon is in Romans) against the horrendously bad news of what human addiction to idolatry actually is. However, to repeat: the context here is tight theological argument, the prelude to Paul's full exposition of the gospel as "the power of God for the salvation of everyone who believes: first for the Jew and then for the Gentile" (Rom 1:16). These words are written by Paul *to Christians,* as words of teaching and warning.

Evangelistic engagement. The book of Acts gives us three glimpses of Paul in direct contact with pagan worshipers of the gods of the Greek culture:

- Lystra (Acts 14:8-20)
- Athens (Acts 17:16-34)
- Ephesus (Acts 19:23-41)

The circumstances were very different in each location, but there are some interesting common features.

In *Lystra,* the healing of a cripple led to Barnabas and Paul being hailed as the Greek gods Zeus and Hermes in human form, and a sacrifice being prepared in their honor. Paul countered with strong protestations of their own mere humanity and followed this with an appeal that the crowd should turn from "these worthless things" (v. 15) to the one living God, creator of heaven and earth, who had been giving them all the good things of life.

In *Athens,* discussions with some philosophers about Jesus and the resurrection led to a summons before the city authorities, the Areopagus, to submit his teaching to their inspection. This hearing was probably not merely a matter of polite curiosity but a public inquiry. Introducing new gods into Athens (as they thought Paul was trying to do) was not a problem religiously, but it had to be controlled by the civic authorities, to ensure that (1) claimed deities actually had some track record to their name and (2) the sponsor could afford to set up a temple, provide the sacrifices, pay the priests and so on.[41] Paul's speech stands this civic protocol on its head. The God he represented was not subject to human accreditation by the Athenian authorities but rather sat in judgment on

---

[41]For this reading of the situation in Acts 17 see Bruce Winter, "On Introducing Gods to Athens: An Alternative Reading of Acts 17:18-20," *Tyndale Bulletin* 47 (1996): 71-90.

them. Far from needing the services of human attendants for housing and feeding, it was this God who provided these things and much more for the whole human race.

In *Ephesus,* two years of systematic public lecturing (Acts 19:9-10) accompanied by remarkable healing miracles (Acts 19:11-12) led to a growth of truly converted believers (Acts 19:17-20). So many people were turning to the living God through faith in Christ that the bottom began to drop out of the market for the idol industry in the city (Acts 19:23-27). We have no direct record of Paul's teaching, but Luke summarizes it in the mouth of Demetrius: "He [Paul] says that man-made gods are no gods at all" (Acts 19:26).

The monotheistic message of the gospel thus challenged popular superstition in Lystra, intellectual and civic pride in Athens and economic interests in Ephesus. The thrust of Paul's evangelistic tactics in such circumstances—that is, when engaging directly with idol-worshiping pagans as distinct from offering theological teaching to established believers—is forthright and uncompromising but markedly softer and more polite than the language we observed in Romans 1.

In the two recorded speeches (in Lystra and Athens), Paul emphasises God as the one living Creator of heaven and earth (Acts 13:15; 17:24). In both he stresses the providence of God in giving humans all the necessities of life, even life and breath itself (Acts 13:17; 17:25). In Lystra he offers this as evidence of the kindness of God, bringing joy even to pagans; in Athens he offers it as proof that God longs for people to seek him, though he is in fact not far from any of us (supporting this from pagan poetry [Acts 17:27-28]). In both places, he allows that God has been patient and tolerant of pagan ignorance in the past (Acts 13:16; 17:30). But in both he also calls for a decisive turning away from the worship of "worthless things" (Acts 13:15), which are hopelessly inadequate for the divine being (Acts 17:29). This is consistent with his own testimony regarding the burden of his preaching in Thessalonica. He recalls how pagans there had "turned to God from idols to serve the living and true God" (1 Thess 1:9). In Athens, he goes on to speak of judgment and to link it to the resurrection of Christ (Acts 17:31).

What we learn from the lips of the pagans themselves in Ephesus is that Paul had argued that "man-made gods" are not gods at all (Acts 19:26—a thoroughly Old Testament perspective). But what we also learn most interestingly is that Paul had *not* engaged in specific defamation of Artemis/Diana—the patron goddess of Ephesus. This is not even a claim Paul makes for himself but is stated in his defense by the city clerk to pacify the riot fomented against Paul and his friends: "They have neither robbed temples nor blasphemed our goddess" (Acts 19:37). Clearly Paul's evangelism was uncompromisingly effective but it was not calculatingly offensive.

Comparing Paul's *theological* argument to Christians in Romans 1 with his *evangelistic* preaching to pagans recorded in Acts, there is a marked difference of tone, even though there is certainly no clash of fundamental conviction.

Romans, written to Christians, highlights the wrath of God. Acts, referring to speeches made to pagans, highlights God's kindness, providence and patience. Both, however, insist on God's judgment.

- Romans portrays idolatry as fundamentally rebellion and suppression of the truth. Acts portrays it as ignorance.

- Romans portrays the wickedness that idolatry spawns. Acts portrays idolatry as "worthless."

- Romans points out how perverted the idolater's thinking has to be. Acts points out how absurd it is when you stop and think about it.

- Paul could excoriate idolatry as "a lie" before Christian readers, but did not blaspheme Artemis before her pagan worshipers.

So there is a difference in tone and tactic in Paul's confrontation with idolatry, depending on the context of his argument. However, we should be clear that in both cases, he is building all he has to say on very solid scriptural foundations, for every one of the points mentioned above, even though they have differing and balancing emphases, can be related to the Old Testament's rhetoric against idolatry. It is particularly noteworthy that although Paul nowhere quotes Old Testament texts in his evangelistic preaching among Gentiles (as he so profusely does when speaking among Jews in synagogues), the content of his message is thoroughly grounded in and plainly proclaims the monotheistic creational faith of Israel.

Pastoral guidance. Those who came to faith in Christ out of a background of Greco-Roman polytheism embraced the biblical monotheistic worldview. But they still lived surrounded by all the idolatrous reality of the culture within which they were now called to live out their Christian identity. This posed daily dilemmas for them. The thoroughness of Paul's mission practice is that he was not content merely with evangelism and church planting but was concerned to build mature communities of believers who could think biblically through the ethical issues they faced in the ambient religious culture. His pastoral and ethical guidance to his churches was thus as much part of his missional task as his evangelistic zeal, and just as theologically grounded too.

First Corinthians 8—10 is the prime text on this matter. How were Christians to act in relation to meat that had been sacrificed to idols? The nub of the issue for the Corinthians was not primarily *theological* clarification: it seems the Corinthians knew their theology since Paul assumes it by way of reminder in 1 Corinthians 8:4-6. Nor was it primarily *evangelistic:* the Corinthians had already come to faith in Jesus Christ (1 Cor 1:1-9). But it was certainly *pastoral and ethical,* since there were divisions within the church on the matter and some members were being hurt and offended while others were being arrogant and reckless.

We have already discussed the passage in some depth around the question "are gods and idols something or nothing?" so we need not go over that ground again. However, it is worth recalling that there were two aspects to the problem, and Paul gives distinct answers to each of them. Both have a bearing on how Christians deal with the practical problems of ambient idolatry.

On the one hand, there was *the ordinary meat market.* Animals were slaughtered in sacrificial rituals to various gods and then the meat would end up on the butcher's slab in the market. Could Christians buy such meat in the market and serve it up without endorsing the prior idolatry involved in its production? Paul's answer is, in general terms, "Yes, you may. The gods and idols have no real existence; meat is a good gift of God the Creator and can be enjoyed in thankfulness to him." The only exception to this freedom is if it causes offense to someone else at the table—in which case you should refrain out of respect for that other person's more tender conscience. The rule of love takes precedence over the freedom one legitimately has. Apart from that restriction, "eat anything sold in the meat market" is Paul's down to earth advice (1 Cor 10:25).

But on the other hand, there were the meals that were hosted actually within the precincts of *the temples of the gods,* often as civic functions or as social events put on by wealthier citizens. These were opportunities for securing patronage, making advantageous deals and fitting in with the social expectations of the Corinthian elite. Since these involved actual participation in the sacrifices in the temples of the gods (as distinct from simply going to the butcher's stall and buying the meat that was a byproduct of the sacrifice), Paul would not endorse Christians attending such events.

Paul knew full well the negative social consequences for Christians of such self-exclusion from gatherings at the temples. They would not merely be seen to be negligent or offensive to the city's gods, they would also miss out on opportunities for social networking and very likely endanger their relationship with patrons and employers. But Paul was adamant. Stay away. First of all, attendance at such feasts in the temples, even done with full theological knowledge of their "emptiness," poses a far greater threat to the conscience of the weaker brother who sees you doing it, and is therefore sinning against Christ who died for him (1 Cor 8:10-13). But second, even though the idols and sacrifices are "nothing" in any divine sense, they can certainly be doorways to the demonic. Christians cannot mix participation in the body and blood of Christ with participation in the feasts of demons (1 Cor 10:14-22). For that reason Paul's advice on *this* part of the question is simple: "flee from idolatry"—that is, do not allow any suspicion that you are participating in it, even if you have your internal theological defenses up. Stay away.

The subtlety and sensitivity with which Paul constructs the pastoral and ethical application of his theology (i.e., the missiological implications of radical monotheism in the context of a powerful cultural polytheism) is very illuminating. It surely has much to offer to Christians in many different religious and cultural contexts, caught in the pressure between theological conviction and social conventions.

In contexts where other named gods are explicitly worshiped, Christians may have to distinguish between the byproducts of rituals associated with those gods and actual participation in the worship of them. Some Christians in India, for example, feel free to accept *prasad*—the gifts of sweets or fruits from those who have celebrated a birthday or other event by offering something first to the gods in their home or place of work, but they are not willing to join in actual rituals or to participate in multifaith worship, or anything that explicitly affirmed the reality of other gods. Other Indian Christians would exclude both for fear of misleading "the weaker brother."

In the West, gods and idols take more subtle forms, but similar issues may arise. Gambling, for example, could certainly be conceived as a form of idolatry to the god of mammon, with all the tendency to addiction that most idolatries feed. For that reason most Christians refuse to engage in it or intentionally to set out to profit from it either by participating in gambling (e.g., state lotteries) or by requesting money from the organizers of such lotteries. On the other hand, if someone who wins the lottery chooses, unasked, to give some of the money to the church or a Christian charity, there are those who would argue that such money can be accepted without raising questions of conscience, since all wealth belongs to the Lord in the first place. You are not participating in the evil of gambling by accepting such a gift, even though it was the product of gambling, any more than a Corinthian was participating in idolatry by buying meat at the butcher's shop, even though it was produced in an idolatrous ritual. Disagreement on this among Western Christians is as likely as that over *prasad* among Indian Christians.

Doubtless many other examples of the outworking of Paul's pastoral and ethical guidelines could be discussed. My point is that his handling of the matter in a pastoral context among new Christian believers has a different feel to either his evangelistic engagement with unbelievers or his theological invective in a strongly didactic context for mature Christians. Perhaps we have something to learn from Paul in the way we confront idolatry in our own multiple contexts.

Prophetic warning. The pastoral approach that we have just been considering involves helping God's people to cope with the dilemmas of living in a culture in which idolatry is endemic. The prophetic approach, however, involves identifying, exposing and denouncing the idolatry itself. But it is noteworthy that where this happens in the Bible it is normally for the ears of God's people. In evangelistic contexts in the New Testament, there is unambiguous repudiation of the polytheistic worldview, but we do not find public denunciation of specific gods or offensive mockery of their worshipers. And in the Old Testament, in the few places where an Israelite addresses pagan nations, the condemnation is typically targeted at their moral and social wickedness, not at their worship of the wrong gods (even though the two are connected). Examples of this might include Amos's catalog of the sins of the nations surrounding Israel (Amos 1:1—2:3, noticeably Amos only specifies worship of false gods when he gets round to Judah in Amos 2:4), and Jonah's condemnation of Nineveh, which is explicitly aimed at "its wickedness" and "their violence," not their gods (Jonah 1:2; 3:8). Elijah's mockery of the prophets of Baal should not be seen as the mockery of ignorant pagans, for many of them were actually apostates from Yahwism. Their main offense was in leading the people into their own idolatrous confusion.

However, no rhetorical device is redundant when prophetic voices address their denunciation of idolatry *to the people of God themselves*. We need only recall the penetrating polemic of Isaiah 40—48, the similar arguments of Jeremiah 10, or the warnings of Deuteronomy 4. What is the reason for this heavy imbalance? Of course it was true that idolatry was to be avoided for fear of incurring the jealous wrath of the living God. (Paul was no stranger to that argument either [1 Cor 10:22].) But prophets also exposed the futility of idolatry in order *to release God's people from undue fear of the gods of nations* that seemed more powerful. This is obvious in Isaiah 40—48. It is also Jeremiah's motivation:

> Do not learn the ways of the nations
>   or be terrified by signs in the sky,
>   though the nations are terrified by them. . . .
> Like a scarecrow in a melon patch
>   their idols cannot speak;
> they must be carried
>   because they cannot walk.
> Do not fear them;
>   they can do no harm
>   nor can they do any good. (Jer 10:2, 5)

Prophets also denounce the gods of the nations because they know that ultimately Israel will only be disappointed and humiliated if they go after them. Warning God's people against idolatry is for their own protection. The cost is too high—as Israel in exile discovered, through the retrospective explanations of Ezekiel.

It would not be out of place to include Romans 1:18-32 in this company, for Paul's searing exposure of the perverse roots and bitter fruit of idolatry stands in the same prophetic tradition. Like the prophets of old, Paul summons the redeemed to see idolatry from God's point of view and to recognize the appalling truth about what they have been redeemed from.

Ephesus again provides an interesting case study. Acts reveals that Paul preached the gospel in Ephesus, and many people there turned from idolatry and sorcery to the living God. In the course of that church-planting program, Paul did not indulge in public defamation of Artemis (according to the secular authorities). Yet in writing later to those new believers in Ephesus who had chosen to turn away from their worship of Artemis and trust in Christ, Paul did not hesitate to remind them of their perilous spiritual state *before* they came to faith in Christ. They had been alienated from Israel, from Israel's Messiah, Israel's covenant hope and Israel's God. In fact, in an ironic turn of phrase, Paul says that these Ephesians, with all their many gods, had in fact been *atheoi*—"without God," inasmuch as they had no knowledge of or relationship with the true and living God (Eph 2:12). Later, he again reminds them of the kind of life they had been rescued from—a life characterized by those things Paul elsewhere so closely linked with idolatry in Romans 1 (futility, darkness, hardness, sensual indulgence, etc. [Eph 4:17-19]). Part of Paul's purpose in writing thus is to remind believers of the moral and spiritual darkness of idolatry, to warn them against ever going back to it and to encourage them to live the distinctive holy life of the redeemed. It seems that Paul attacked idolatry much more fiercely in discipling those who had been delivered from it than he did in his public evangelistic ministry among those still involved in it.

In what way is this prophetic warning to the people of God against idolatry in both Testaments missiologically significant? The answer again lies in appreciating the mission of God in and through God's people. God's goal of blessing the nations requires not only that the nations eventually come to abandon their gods and bring their worship before the living God alone (as envisioned, e.g., in Ps 96 and many prophetic visions). God's mission also requires that God's own people in the meantime should preserve the purity and exclusiveness of their worship of the living God, and resist the adulterating syncretisms that surround them. An obedient and covenantally loyal Israel would be seen by the nations and the result would be praise and glory to YHWH the living God (Deut 4:6-8; 28:9-10). A disobedient and idolatrous Israel would bring disgrace on YHWH and drag his name through the gutters of profanity among the nations (Deut 29:24-28; Ezek 36:16-21). In other words, more is at stake in keeping God's people away from idols than their own spiritual health. God's own mission for the sake of the nations is also on the line.

Jeremiah, with his customary graphic imagery, captured both sides of this perception of the mission of Israel in a single piece of prophetic acted symbolism (Jer 13:1-11). As a beautiful piece of clothing brings honor and praise to the one who wears it, so God had bound Israel to himself "to be my people for my renown and praise and honor."[42] This triplet of words is the same as that which God had promised Israel would have among the nations (Deut 26:19). Whatever renown may accrue to God's people through their loyalty and obedience to him is ultimately for the honor and glory of God himself. That is the missiological dynamic. But the effect of Israel's idolatry (specified in Jer 13:10) is to make them like a beautiful piece of cloth that has been buried in wet soil for a long time—"ruined and completely useless" (vv. 7, 10). God cannot "wear" people who are sodden and soiled with the rotting rags of idolatry. How can God draw the nations away from the worship of false gods if the people he has chosen to be a blessing to the nations are themselves riddled with those gods? The scorching severity of the warnings against idolatry, then, are not just for the benefit of God's own people but ultimately, through them, for the benefit of the nations. That is their missional relevance.

Conclusion

What have we seen in this chapter concerning the missiological dimension of the Bible's polemic against idolatry?

We have seen the paradox that although gods and idols are *something* in the world, they are *nothing* in comparison to the living God.

We have seen that while gods and idols may be implements of or gateways to the world of the demonic, the overwhelming verdict of Scripture is that they are the work of human hands, constructs of our own fallen and rebellious imagination.

We have also seen that the primal problem with idolatry is that it blurs the distinction between the Creator God and the creation. This both damages creation (including ourselves) and diminishes the glory of the Creator.

---

[42]This is an unusual but richly meaningful metaphor for the covenant relationship. In its intimacy and mutuality, it is like the bond between a person and a favorite piece of clothing that is bound affectionately to one's body. The covenant is God wearing his people.

Since God's mission is to restore creation to its full original purpose of bringing all glory to God himself and thereby to enable all creation to enjoy the fullness of blessing that he desires for it, God battles against all forms of idolatry
and calls us to join him in that conflict.

A biblically informed missional approach to idolatry, however, seeks to understand the great variety of ways that human beings make gods for themselves,
the variety of forms those gods take and the variety of motivations behind our
worship of them.

Then we need to understand the whole breadth of the Bible's exposure of
the deleterious effects of idolatry in order to appreciate its seriousness and the
reason for the Bible's passionate rhetoric about it.

Finally, in confronting idolatry, we need to be discerning about what responses are appropriate in different contexts, learning from the apostles and
prophets as we do so.

All of these tasks need to be carried on not only in the light of the wide range
of biblical texts, such as those we have touched on in this and the previous
chapter, but also in relation to specific cultural and religious contexts and their
particular manifestations of the human addiction to idolatry. The prophets and
apostles set us the clear example of both claiming universality and transcen-
dence for YHWH and Christ, while at the same time engaging with cutting relevance in the particular and local contexts into which they were sent. Our mission demands no less.

PART III THE PEOPLE OF MISSION

Having completed our study of the themes at the apex of our structural diagram (see p. 28) under the heading of the "The God of Mission" and the dynamic interpenetration of biblical monotheism and biblical mission, we now move round to the next corner of the triangle—"The People of Mission."

Popular understanding of Christian mission would tend to locate its origin more or less simultaneously with the origin of the Christian church. Didn't Jesus say that his disciples should wait for the empowering of the Holy Spirit before setting off to preach repentance and forgiveness to the ends of the earth? And didn't the coming of the Holy Spirit also launch the church at Pentecost? The two things are joined by verbal Velcro in the way Luke ends his Gospel and begins the Acts of the Apostles.

This instinctive conjunction of ecclesiology and missiology is valid, of course, but any reader who has not just joined our journey at this point will not be surprised to hear that the link must be traced much further back than Pentecost but right back into the Old Testament. The New Testament church may have been birthed that day, but the people of God in history go back to Abraham. And as Paul was fond of pointing out to all and sundry, any person of any nation who is in Christ is thereby also in Abraham.

So as we turn to think of the people whom God has called and created to be the agent of his mission, that is where we must begin too. Arguably God's covenant with Abraham is the single most important biblical tradition within a biblical theology of mission and a missional hermeneutic of the Bible. We are going to see that it generates a vast, arching, trajectory that carries us from Genesis 12 to Revelation 22. So it well deserves the two chapters afforded to it here. First we explore in chapter six the meaning of God's election of Abraham and his descendants as the vehicle of blessing to the nations, and what is entailed in that original great commission. Then in chapter seven we trace the paradoxical duality of the covenant's universality (it is for the blessing of all nations) and particularity (it is by means of one nation). Both poles of the paradox have important missional implications.

Moving along the pathway of the Bible's grand narrative we come to the exodus. Theologically we move from election to redemption. Missiologically we move from the man for all nations (Abraham) to the people redeemed to be God's priesthood in the midst of the nations (Israel). The exodus stands as the primary model of God's redemption in history, and chapter eight explores its rich multidimensional relevance. But even a redeemed people still live on this planet and are susceptible to the social and economic effects of human fallenness. God's law takes this into account, and the jubilee year provides an example of God's comprehensive concern for human well-being through restorative mechanisms. Chapter nine explores its rationale and missiological implications, and takes it as a case study for reflection on holistic mission.

The people of God are constituted within a covenant relationship with him. This too is an overarching biblical theme that provides a skeletal framework for the Bible's grand narrative. Chapter ten surveys the span of the great covenant articulations from Noah to Christ and asks how they affect our understanding of the mission of God.

Having been chosen, redeemed and called into covenant relationship, the people of God have a life to live—a distinctive, holy, ethical life that is to be lived before God and in the sight of the nations. This too has crucial missional relevance, for as we will see in chapter eleven there is no biblical mission without biblical ethics.

This then is the unifying theme of the six chapters in this part of our book—the people of God, created and commissioned for the mission of God.

6

God's Elect People

Chosen for Blessing

If only all the theological disputes in Christian history had been caused by successful mission and rapid church growth. Undoubtedly the first dispute was. The first major council of the church (Acts 15) was convened to consider a knot of problems caused by the success of crosscultural church planting efforts. These had been initiated by the church of Antioch and carried out among the predominantly Gentile and ethnically diverse peoples of the Roman provinces that made up what we now call Turkey. Paul and Barnabas, who had been entrusted with this initiative, were not the first to cross the barrier from Jew to Gentile with the good news of Jesus Christ. Philip (Acts 8) and Peter (Acts 10) had already done that. They were, however, the first to establish whole communities of believers, from mixed Jewish and Gentile backgrounds—that is, to plant multiethnic churches. And furthermore, they had clearly been teaching these new believers that they now belonged fully to the people of God otherwise known as Israel—but without going through the process of becoming Jewish proselytes.

What exactly was Paul preaching? And why did it cause such consternation to some and even violent opposition from others?

Paul's Gospel

Paul's preaching was in essence the message we have been exploring in part two. From Luke's record of Paul's evangelistic preaching in Acts, and from the references in his own letters to the message he had brought to the churches he had planted, it is clear that Paul taught that

- There is only one supreme God, who has made himself known through creation and in the story of Israel.

- All other gods are false human constructs that do not provide for human needs and cannot achieve human salvation.
- The one living God has sent his own Son, Jesus of Nazareth, in fulfillment of his promise to Israel.
- Through the death and resurrection of Jesus, God has opened the way for people of all nations to find salvation, forgiveness and eternal life.
- Through faith in Jesus, God's appointed Savior and King, people of any nation can now belong to the redeemed people of God, and be found among the righteous when God would intervene again through Jesus in the approaching day of final judgment.
- This conversion through repentance and faith in Jesus was all that was needed to belong to God's covenant people.

This powerful message that brought hope and joy to diverse Gentile communities brought shock and anger to some of Paul's fellow Jews. Surely, they argued, it is clear from the Scriptures that the one living God has chosen Israel for salvation. Only those who belong to the elect and covenant people of Israel can be among the righteous and can expect to be safe in the day of God's wrath. Belonging to Israel necessarily involves being circumcised and observing the Torah of Moses, particularly those laws that most visibly demonstrate the distinctiveness of Jews from the rest of the world—the laws governing clean and unclean areas of life (especially food), and observance of the sabbath. If these Gentiles want to join the camp of the righteous and be assured of salvation, then they must effectively become Jews, through circumcision and careful keeping of the law of Moses. If they want the benefits of the covenant, they must join the people of the covenant and obey the rules of the covenant. They must follow the established path of becoming a proselyte Jew.

Not all of those who opposed Paul in this way were Jews who had *rejected* Jesus as Messiah (as Paul had done before his Damascus road experience) and who were consequently fired with violent hostility to all things Christian (as Paul had been also). There were Christian believers also from staunch Jewish backgrounds—some of them Pharisees like Paul—who had the same problem with Gentile conversions. Faith in Jesus was all very well, they argued, but it did not remove the fundamental scriptural criteria for covenant membership.

So Luke records the basic clash as it developed in the early church in response to the success of the Gentile mission. On the one hand, the church in Antioch rejoiced when Paul and Barnabas returned from their first missionary journey "and reported all that God had done through them and how he had opened the door of faith to the Gentiles" (Acts 14:27). But on the other hand: "Some men came down from Judea to Antioch and were teaching the brothers: 'Unless you are circumcised, according to the custom taught by Moses, you cannot be saved.' "[1] When the council to resolve the dispute was convened in Jerusalem, we read, "Then some of the believers who belonged to the party of the Pharisees stood up and said, 'The Gentiles must be circumcised and required to obey the law of Moses' " (Acts 15:1, 5).

Luke's account in Acts records Peter's, Paul's and Barnabas's involvement in that council, and finally the decisive, Scripture-based ruling of James. Paul's own theological answer to the issue is given in more colorful terms in his letter to the Galatian church, which had clearly been troubled by people persuasively peddling the same message.[2] This group challenged Paul's assurance that faith in the Messiah Jesus was sufficient for saving membership in God's people.

"But what about Moses?" they cried.

"Never mind Moses; what about Abraham?" Paul answered.

They thought they had clinching scriptural backing for their case. Paul trumped their appeal by taking them even further back and showing the priority of God's promise to Abraham. For both Paul and his opponents, the matter was one of scriptural authority. They both agreed that whatever mission strategy was adopted by the church must be compatible with the Scriptures (for them, what we call the Old Testament).[3] Paul offered a fresh hermeneutic that observed the priority of Abraham—chronologically and theologically—in the texts.

So in a classic passage, Paul combines four things:

- the promise of God

- the faith of Abraham

- the universal mission of God to bless all nations through the seed of Abraham

- the saving implications for all who have faith like Abraham

And *this,* says Paul—this dynamic narrative of God's saving purpose for all nations through Abraham—is the heart of *the gospel* as announced by the Scriptures.

---

[1]So presumably these people were bona fide Christian "brothers" themselves, though Paul had a more negative view of some of them, at least (Gal 2:4).

[2]The historical relationship between the Council of Jerusalem in Acts 15 and Paul's letter to the Galatians is a matter of continued scholarly dispute, which can be explored in the major New Testament introductions and commentaries.

[3]It is ironic how far we have moved from this early difficulty. For many contemporary Christians the problem lies with the Old Testament. For these early Christians the Old Testament was the given Word of God; the problem lay with the church. Our question so often is, Is the Old Testament really Christian? Their question was, Is the church scriptural (i.e., consistent with the Old Testament)?

Consider Abraham: "He believed God and it was credited to him as righteousness."
Understand, then, that those who believe are children of Abraham. The Scripture
foresaw that God would justify the Gentiles by faith, and announced the gospel in
advance to Abraham: "All nations will be blessed through you." So those who have
faith are blessed along with Abraham, the man of faith. (Gal 3:6-9)

So the Gentile mission, Paul argued, far from being a betrayal of the Scriptures, was rather the fulfillment of them. The ingathering of the nations was the
very thing Israel existed for in the purpose of God; it was the fulfillment of the
bottom line of God's promise to Abraham. Since Jesus was the Messiah of Israel
and since the Messiah embodied in his own person the identity and mission of
Israel, then to belong to the Messiah through faith was to belong to Israel. And
to belong to Israel was to be a true child of Abraham, no matter what a person's
ethnicity is, for "If you belong to Christ [the Messiah], then you are Abraham's
seed and heirs according to the promise" (Gal 3:29).

We will come back later to the wider missional implications of Paul's understanding of the gospel, but for the moment, we will respond more fully to his
invitation to "consider Abraham."

Consider Abraham

Genesis 12:1-3—A pivotal text. The word Paul describes as "the gospel in advance" ("all nations will be blessed through you") is first heard in Genesis 12:3. It
is the climax of God's promise to Abraham. It is also a pivotal text not only in the
book of Genesis but indeed in the whole Bible. So important is it in Genesis that it
occurs five times altogether, with minor variations of phraseology (Gen 12:3; 18:18;
22:18; 26:4-5; 28:14).[4] Clearly, therefore, it is not just an afterthought tacked on to
the end of God's promise to Abraham but a key element of it. *Blessing for the nations is the bottom line, textually and theologically, of God's promise to Abraham.*

Genesis 12:1-3 is pivotal in the book of Genesis: it moves the story forward
from the preceding eleven chapters, which record God's dealings with all nations (sometimes called "the primeval history"), into the patriarchal narratives
that lead to the emergence of Israel as a distinct nation. And it is pivotal in the
whole Bible because it does exactly what Paul says—it "announces the gospel
in advance." That is, it declares the good news that, in spite of all that we have
read in Genesis 1—11, it is God's ultimate purpose to bless humanity (which is
very good news indeed by the time you reach Gen 11). And the story of how
that blessing for all nations has come about occupies the rest of the Bible, with

---

[4]Gen 35:11 is similar, though it does not use the precise language of all nations being blessed.
It promises rather that a "community of nations" will come from Jacob.

Christ as the central focus. Indeed the closing vision of the canon, with people of every tribe and nation and language worshiping the living God (Rev 7:9-10), clearly echoes the promise of Genesis 12:3 and binds the whole story together.

The whole Bible could be portrayed as a very long answer to a very simple question: What can God do about the sin and rebellion of the human race? Genesis 12 through to Revelation 22 is God's answer to the question posed by the bleak narratives of Genesis 3—11. Or in terms of the overall argument of this book, Genesis 3—11 sets the problem that the mission of God addresses from Genesis 12 to Revelation 22.

The story so far. Genesis 12 comes after Genesis 1—11. This innocent observation not only relates to the point just made about the pivotal nature of the opening verses of Genesis 12, it also reminds us of the importance (here as everywhere in the Bible) of paying attention to the context of any text.

The primeval narrative introduces us first to the great work of God's creation of the universe. Then it portrays men and women, made in God's image, that are entrusted with the task of caring for the earth and enjoying God's blessing in that task. The story goes awry, however, when God's human creatures choose to rebel against their Creator, distrusting his benevolence, disobeying his authority and disregarding the boundaries he had set for their freedom in his world. The result of this human seizure of moral autonomy is radical fracture in all the relationships established in creation. Human beings hide from God in guilty fear. Men and women can no longer face one another without shame and blame. The soil comes under the curse of God and the earth no longer responds to human touch as it should.

These early narratives then combine an escalating crescendo of human sin alongside repeated marks of God's grace. The serpent's head will be crushed. Adam and Eve are clothed. Cain is protected. Noah and his family are saved. Life goes on, and creation is preserved under covenant. Things are very badly flawed, but the whole project is still moving forward.

> At the end of this story [of Genesis 1—11], God's world exists in a state that partially guarantees that the aim of creation will be achieved. God underwrites the rhythm of the day and the rhythm of the season. The process of filling the earth is under way. The structures of marriage, the relationships of parents and children, and the broader network of the extended family are firmly established. The patterns of agricultural life, shepherding, arts and crafts are in place. Nations have come into being.[5]

---

[5]John Goldingay, *Old Testament Theology*, vol. 1, *Israel's Gospel* (Downers Grove, Ill.: InterVarsity Press, 2003), p. 190.

In the aftermath of the flood God renews his promise to creation, and human beings are again sent forth under God's blessing to multiply and fill the earth (Gen 9:1). The two following chapters (Gen 10—11) need to be seen as complementary accounts of what happened next. On the one hand, chapter ten portrays the natural spreading of nations descended from the sons of Noah across the world known to the narrator. Three times this is described as "scattering" or "spreading" (Gen 9:19; 10:18, 32) in a way that suggests that such scattering of the nations was natural, unproblematic and indeed the expected outcome of the promise and command given in Genesis 9:1. How could they fill the earth unless they scattered over the face of it?

On the other hand, chapter eleven sees the matter from a very different angle.[6] The spreading stops as people settle in the plain of Shinar (in Mesopotamia). Their decision to settle and to build a city with a tower there seems to combine arrogance (in wanting to make a name for themselves) and insecurity (in wanting not to be scattered over the whole earth as God intended). I say "seems to" because the narrator is less explicit than we might wish in informing us exactly why the builders of the city and tower so alarmed God and provoked his response. Commentators differ on the weight they put on the two main elements of the reason the builders give for their project. Calvin sees in the desire to "make a name" "nothing other than man's proud contempt for God. . . . To erect a citadel was not in itself so great a crime. But to raise an eternal monument to themselves that might endure throughout all ages showed head-strong pride as well as contempt for God."[7] Gerhard von Rad, with more restraint, comments, "The city arises as a sign of valiant self-reliance, the tower as a sign of their will to fame."[8] Jewish commentators, however, focus on the second phrase ("and not be scattered"): "The intention of the builders was to gather the people into a centralized location, thereby resisting God's purpose that they should multiply, fill the earth, and subdue it."[9]

Whatever nuance is intended, the reader may certainly detect, with a sinking feeling, echoes of the arrogant attempt of Adam and Eve to seize control of their

---

[6]It is clear from Gen 11:1 that the accounts need to be read as theologically complementary, not as chronologically sequential. It must have been as obvious to the author/editor as it is to us that the opening words of chap. 11 ("the whole world had one language") stand oddly in relation to the reference in Gen 10:31 to "clans and languages . . . territories and nations," if the accounts are read merely in sequence.

[7]John Calvin, *Genesis,* Crossway Classic Commentaries, ed. Alister McGrath and J. I. Packer (Wheaton, Ill.: Crossway Books, 2001), p. 103.

[8]Gerhard von Rad, *Genesis,* 2nd ed. (London: SCM Press, 1963), p. 148.

[9]Bernard W. Anderson, "Unity and Diversity in God's Creation: A Study of the Babel Story," *Currents in Theology and Mission* 5 (1978): 74—quoting several Jewish scholars.

own destiny, and of the insecurity of the first person who built a city—Cain—as he wandered restlessly from the presence of God.[10] There may even be a reverse echo of the story of the angelic beings that breached the line that divides heaven and earth and aroused God's anger (Gen 6:1-4). "God insists that this line be recognized. That is not to say that there is no possibility of movement between earth and heaven. It is to say that such movement lies in God's gift. . . . God will not be invaded."[11] The Babel story presents us with people who seem intent on reaching the heavens even while resisting God's will for them on earth.

Even before God intervenes with his act of compulsory scattering, the pathetic futility of their efforts is mocked in a few graphic touches. The city they build is inferior even by human standards (baked bricks instead of solid stone; tar for cement), and though they claim that their tower reaches to the heavens, from the perspective of heaven itself and the God who lives there, it is so miniscule that he has to come down just to see it.

God's considered response is both preventative (he stops them achieving the unified and centralized closure that they desire) and compulsory (he forces them to scatter across the earth, as originally intended, but now in a state of dividedness and confusion). God's action is not explicitly described as punitive, but it is certainly doubly ironic. It is ironic because, on the one hand, their attempt to avoid being scattered has resulted in a scattering in worse conditions than before.

> Men had already been spread abroad before this [chap. 10], and that should not be thought of as a punishment, seeing that it flowed from the grace of God [chap. 9]. But now those whom the Lord had previously distributed with honor in various places, he ignominiously scattered, driving them here and there. This scattering, therefore, was not a simple dispersion in order to replenish. It was a violent rout because the principal bond between these men and God had been cut asunder.[12]

And it is ironic, on the other hand, because they had wanted to make a name for themselves and they got one, but it was not one they would have chosen. They will indeed be remembered forever, but by a name—Babel—that speaks of babbling confusion.

We can now see how chapters ten and eleven of Genesis complement each

---

[10]Claus Westermann observes the parallel with Genesis 3:5, and the further echo in the condemnation of the grasping arrogance of the king of Babylon in Isaiah 14:13-14. See his *Genesis 12—36*, trans. John J. Scullion (Minneapolis: Augsburg; London: SPCK, 1985), p. 554.

[11]Goldingay, *Old Testament Theology,* 1:190.

[12]Calvin, *Genesis,* p. 106.

other with their different perspectives on the observable reality that human beings live in great plurality and diversity.

> If we picture these two stories as two panels of a diptych, then Genesis 10 em-
> phasizes the world's unity: it has a positive ring to it as the divine command of
> Genesis 9:1 is fulfilled gradually. Panel 2, Genesis 11, has a negative ring: here the
> unity of the human race is shattered as people become unable to communicate
> with each other; their search for security, unity and technological mastery
> founders in disarray, dispersal, and divine disapproval. The human race has stum-
> bled from *mabbul* [flood, 10:32] to *babel*. Far from Babylon being the gate of the
> gods, as the Babylonians conceived it, the verdict of this story is babble, jabber-
> wocky, gabble, confusion![13]

All the previous stories in Genesis 3—11 have had some element of God's
grace. However, in this final narrative of the city and tower called Babel, no such
word of grace is found. It seems that the sad story of humanity has run into the
quicksand of chaotic dividedness. At one level, all the basic infrastructure of God's
great creation project is still there. The heavens and the earth follow their allotted
rounds and seasons. Crucial boundaries are being preserved between the day and
the night, the sea and the dry land, the earth and the great deep, human and divine realms. Vegetation and animals are proliferating as intended. Human beings
are multiplying in families and nations, and spreading to fill the earth.

But at another level everything is tragically adrift from the original goodness
of God's purpose. The earth lies under the sentence of God's curse because of
human sin. Human beings are adding to their catalog of evil as the generations
roll past—jealousy, anger, murder, vengeance, violence, corruption, drunken-
ness, sexual disorder, arrogance. With God's permission but hardly with their
Creator's best pleasure, animals are being killed for food. Women enjoy the gift
of childbirth along with suffering and pain. Men find fulfillment in subduing the
earth, but with sweat and frustration. Both enjoy sexual complementarity and
intimacy, but along with lust and domination. Every inclination of human hearts
is perduringly evil. Technology and culture are advancing, but the skill that can
craft instruments for music and agriculture can also forge weapons of violent
death. Nations experience the richness of their ethnic, linguistic and geographical diversity along with confusion, scattering, and strife.

> The whole primeval history, therefore, seems to break off in shrill dissonance, and
> we now ask the question even more urgently: Is God's relationship to the nations
> now finally broken; is God's gracious forbearance now exhausted; has God re-

---

[13]Howard Peskett and Vinoth Ramachandra, *The Message of Mission*, The Bible Speaks Today
(Downers Grove, Ill.: InterVarsity Press; Leicester, U.K.: Inter-Varsity Press, 2003), pp. 95-96.

jected the nations in wrath forever? That is the burdensome question that no thoughtful reader of chapter eleven can avoid; indeed we can say that our narrator intended by means of the whole plan of his primeval history to raise precisely this question and to pose it in all its severity. Only then is the reader properly prepared to take up the strangely new thing that now follows the comfortless story about the building of the tower: the election and blessing of Abraham. We stand here, therefore, at the point where primeval history and sacred history dovetail, and thus at one of the most important places in the entire Old Testament.[14]

We must also immediately add, *we stand here at one of the most important places in a missiological reading of the Bible*. I have stressed that the Bible's primary concept of mission is the mission of God. But in Genesis 1—11 we see the great creative mission of God being constantly thwarted and spoiled in ways that affect not just human well-being but the whole cosmos. Where can the mission of God go from here? What can God do next?

Whatever it may be, it will have to tackle a very broad redemptive agenda. Genesis 1—11 poses a cosmic question to which God must provide a cosmic answer. The problems so graphically spread before the reader in Genesis 1—11 will not be solved just by finding a way to get human beings to heaven when they die. Death itself must be destroyed if the curse is to be removed and the way opened to the tree of life. The love and power of God must address not only the sin of individuals but also the strife and strivings of nations; not only the need of human beings but also the suffering of animals and the curse on the ground. The longing of Noah's father, Lamech, for God's comfort to relieve the earth of its curse (Gen 5:29) remains to be fulfilled.

What can God do next? Something that only God could have thought of. He sees an elderly, childless couple in the land of Babel and decides to make them the fountainhead, the launch pad of his whole mission of cosmic redemption. We can almost hear the sharp intake of breath among the heavenly hosts when the astonishing plan was revealed. They knew, as the reader of Genesis 1—11 now knows, the sheer scale of devastation that serpentine evil and human recalcitrance have wrought in God's creation. What sort of an answer can be provided through Abram and Sarai? Yet that is precisely the scale of what now follows. The call of Abram is the beginning of God's answer to the evil of human hearts, the strife of nations and the groaning brokenness of his whole creation.

Genesis 12:1-3—A Closer Look

A new world, ultimately a new creation, begins in this text. But it is a new world

---

[14]Von Rad, *Genesis*, p. 152.

that bursts out of the womb of the old—the old world portrayed in Genesis 1—11. And yet that womb is barren. Not only has the story run into the sands of abandoned Babel but even the line of Shem, in whom hope seems fixed for the future, has run almost to a dead end in the barrenness of Sarah and the death of Terah in Haran (Gen 11:30, 32). History, like creation itself prior to the transforming word of God, seems shut up to futility and shrouded in darkness (Gen 1:2). But just as in Genesis 1:3, where we read "And God said," so here we read "And YHWH said." The word of God that spoke into darkness now speaks into barrenness with good news of astonishing reversal, holding before our imagination vistas of a future that is (almost) beyond belief. God's mission of world redemption begins.

Translation and structure.

> And YHWH said to Abram,
> Get yourself up and go[15]
>> from your land, and from your kindred, and from your father's house,
>> to the land that I will show you.
>>> And I will make you into a great nation;
>>> and I will bless you;
>>> and I will make your name great.
>> And be a blessing.
>>> And I will bless those who bless you;
>>> whereas the one who belittles you, I will curse;[16]
>>> and in you will be blessed all kinship groups[17] on the earth.
> And Abram went just as YHWH said to him. (Gen 12:1-4, author's translation)

---

[15]The opening verb has a reflexive pronoun after the imperative, which suggests this decisive action: *lek-lĕkā.*

[16]The syntax of this clause gives it the flavor of dealing with an exception, rather than being part of the list of promises. It is singular ("the one who belittles, or despises, or slanders you"), whereas the previous line is plural. And the inversion of object and verb means that the verb does not follow in the list of consecutive imperfects through which God states his composite divine purpose. "The word about curse is clearly not set here as a part of the divine intention. . . . God commands Abraham to go out in order to receive blessing and bring about a stream of blessing in the world. But YHWH does not command Abraham to go out in order to bring about curse, although that may happen in the process. . . . The curse of God is not the purpose of the divine command. It is a part of the blessing of Abraham in that it promises protection" (Patrick D. Miller Jr., "Syntax and Theology in Genesis Xii 3a," *Vetus Testamentum* 34 [1984]: 474). Miller accordingly translates verse 3: "and that I may bless the ones blessing you—and should there be one who regards you with contempt I will curse him. So, then, all the families of the earth can gain a blessing in you."

[17]The word is *mišpāḥâ.* It is sometimes translated "families," but that is too narrow in its common English meaning. *Mišpāḥâ* is a wider kinship grouping. In Israelite tribal structure it was the clan, the subgroup within the tribe. It can sometimes imply whole peoples, considered as related by kinship (as in Amos 3:1-2).

Laying out the text in this form makes clear what seems to me the best way of discerning its structure. Enveloped in between the narrative record of YHWH's address to Abram and Abram's obedience, God's actual speech falls into two halves, each launched by an imperative ("Go," and, "Be a blessing"). After each imperative follow three subordinate clauses that elucidate the implications of fulfilling the commands.

The second half is introduced by "and be a blessing." In the Masoretic Text the verb is clearly imperative, though some scholars emend it to another imperfect ("and you will be a blessing" [cf. NIV]). However, it is a feature of Hebrew (as indeed it is in English) that when two imperatives occur together the second imperative may sometimes express either the expected result or the intended purpose of carrying out the first imperative.[18] Thus the flow of thought in our passage is either "Abraham, you go . . . and I will do the following . . . and *in that way* you will be a blessing (as a result)."[19] Or, "Abraham, you go . . . and I will do the following . . . *so that* you may be a blessing, (which is my intention)." Either way, the message of the combined halves of the text clearly is that if Abraham does what he is told, and if God does what he says he will do, the result will be blessing all round. Good news indeed, as Paul remarked.

Verse 4 begins equally positively with *Abraham* in fact doing exactly what YHWH told him, so we read on with anticipation to see how *God* will keep his word also, and (though we will have to keep reading for a long time) how that mysterious concluding word of universal blessing will be accomplished. The mission is launched. Abraham obeys God's command; God's promise is thereby released into the history of the nations.

Leaving and blessing. Another interesting feature of Genesis 12:1-3 is the balancing way the three narrowing dimensions of Abraham's leaving (the first imperative) are set against the three broadening expressions of how and for whom he is to be a blessing (the second imperative). On the one hand, he is to leave his land (the widest sphere of his identity), his wider kindred and then his immediate extended family. On the other hand, he is to be a blessing. The object of this blessing is at first unspecified (except that it will include the fact that he himself individually will be blessed), then it progresses to those who bless him, and finally issues in blessing for all the kinship groups on earth.

---

[18]For example, in double commands like: "Go outside and get some fresh air" or "Come home with us and stay the night." The second imperative can only be realized if and when the first is fulfilled. The second is the purpose or result of the first. The first is a condition of enjoying the second. This is the relationship of the two imperatives in God's word to Abraham.

[19]Reverting for convenience here to the emended name (Abraham) of Gen 17:5 by which he is more commonly known.

Pursuing the same point by setting the opening and closing lines of God's address to Abraham alongside one another, we read (reverting to the NIV):

Leave *your* country, *your* people and *your* father's household . . .
and *all peoples on earth* / will be blessed through you. (Gen 12:1, 3)

Only Abraham's leaving releases the nations' blessing. In spite of all that we have witnessed of the fallen world in the primeval history, there can yet be blessing for that world. But it will not come from within that world itself. Abraham must relinquish all that ties him to the land of Babylon before he can be the vehicle of blessing to the whole earth. Babel, the climax of the problem portrayed in Genesis 1—11, cannot be the source of the solution. In this way even the great Mesopotamian empires are relativized and negated. The greatest human achievements cannot solve the deepest human problems. God's mission of blessing the nations is a radical new start. It requires a break, a radical departure from the story so far, not merely an evolutionary development from it.

> When Abraham first appears in Genesis 12, it is in the context of a society already marked by the story of the tower of Babel in chapter 11. Indeed, it is the land of Babel out of which Abraham was called. As the story indicates, it was a culture of immense self-confidence and pride. At the very least Abraham's God-required departure relativized it. Human salvation was not to be found in the state per se. The ultimate redemptive purpose of God lay elsewhere, invested in the tenuous human vessel of the ageing husband of a barren wife. The calling of Abraham out of his country and his people (Gen 12:1) was "the first Exodus by which the imperial civilizations of the Near East in general receive their stigma as environments of lesser meaning."[20]

Countering Babel. The comparison and contrast with Babel can be seen in two other textual hints. First, the builders of the city and tower wanted to "make a name" for themselves—that is, achieve their own renown and establish a permanent memorial to their cleverness or a citadel for their power. God put a stop to that ambition. To Abraham, however, God says, "I will make *your* name great" (v. 2). The echo is undoubtedly deliberate. What human beings try to achieve in their centralizing arrogance is doomed ultimately to frustration and failure.

> Pride of man and earthly glory,
> Sword and crown betray his trust.

---

[20]Christopher J. H. Wright, *Old Testament Ethics for the People of God* (Leicester, U.K.: InterVarsity Press; Downers Grove, Ill.: InterVarsity Press, 2004), p. 222. The quote at the end is from E. Voegelin, *Israel and Revelation* (Baton Rouge: Louisiana State University, 1956), p. 140.

What with care and toil he buildeth
Tower and temple fall to dust.[21]

True renown comes only from God's gift and in relation to God's blessing on those who trust and obey him, as Abraham did.

Second, the narrative of Babel five times uses the expression "the whole earth" (Gen 11:1, 4, 8, 9 [x2]). It is a tale with a truly global perspective. And it ends in global confusion and scattering. God's word to Abraham, by contrast, ends with the promise of global blessing for all nations on earth.[22] God's mission is "to make His blessings flow / far as the curse is found."[23]

Clearly, then, we are meant to see this new initiative as God's response to the world portrayed in the preceding chapters, especially the dual perspective on the world of nations that we found in the table of nations in Genesis 10 and the Babel episode in Genesis 11. The mission of God will be to preserve and maximize the blessing that is inherent in the multiplication and spread of the nations while removing the blight of human sin and arrogance represented by Babel. And Abraham will be the trigger for that process, a process that will ultimately include all nations in the scope of its blessing.

Whereas the other stories of Genesis 3—11 have their elements of divine saving grace, only the story of Babel has none. But in fact this new thing bursting on the scene in Genesis 12 is exactly that—though it significantly does not come *within* the story of Babel. It has to come from outside.

> The merciful grace of YHWH, which persists through all the narratives of the prologue save the last, now overcomes the final treason of the nations in their zealous efforts to build civilization without God, their insatiate lust for renown and power, and the final scattering over all the face of the earth. Abram becomes the embodiment of divine grace, and it is a grace qualitatively other than the deeds of grace in the primeval history. At Babel's tower and the nations' scattering, the gates to the future seemed closed once for all, but now YHWH opens them again and in a unique way, by summoning them [the nations] to him through the selection of the man Abram and the people Israel.[24]

---

[21]Joachim Neander (1650-1680), "All My Hope on God Is Founded," adapted by Robert S. Bridges in 1899.

[22]The phrase is slightly different, though the universal reference is clear. In Genesis 11 it is *kōl hāʾāreṣ*. In Genesis 12:3 it is *kōl mišpĕḥōt hāʾădāmâ*. However, *ʾereṣ* and *ʾădāmâ* are often used interchangeably, with the latter referring more particularly to the surface (soil) of the earth—the place of human habitation. Later versions of the promise to Abraham use *ʾereṣ* also. Genesis 18:18, e.g., speaks of *kōl gōyê hāʾāreṣ* (all nations of the earth).

[23]Isaac Watts, "Joy to the World" (1719).

[24]James Muilenburg, "Abraham and the Nations: Blessing and World History," *Interpretation* 19 (1965): 393.

The promise develops. Genesis 12:1-3 is the first in a series of promissory statements that God makes to Abraham and then reaffirms to Isaac and Jacob after the deaths of their respective fathers. We need to look at these additional texts to feel the full force of the Abahamic covenant.

In Genesis 15 (where the language of covenant is first used [v. 18]), the focus is on the gift of the land to Abraham's descendants (which had first been promised when Abraham arrived in it [Gen 12:7]). But this is preceded by a renewal of the promise of an heir, not just an adopted one as Abraham suggested (Gen 15:2-3) but a son of Abraham himself. From this son and heir would come a progeny as numerous as the stars—"a great nation" (Gen 12:2) indeed. It is to this promise that Abraham responds with that counterintuitive faith which YHWH credits as righteousness (Gen 15:6).

In Genesis 17 the focal point is the requirement of circumcision. Appropriately, in view of the moral commitment that circumcision was later understood to entail, the chapter begins with God telling Abraham, "Walk about in front of my face and be whole" (Gen 17:1, author's translation). This is followed by a summary repetition of God's earlier promises: "and I will establish my covenant between me and you, and I will multiply your numbers very greatly indeed" (Gen 17:2). The dynamic of the syntax is the same as in Genesis 12:1-3—a double command followed by statements of divine intention. The opening verb is the same, *hālak*—walk. But in Genesis 12:1 it is in the form of an abrupt command to set out on a journey from one place to another, whereas in Genesis 17:1 it is in the more general form, "walk about," that is, live your daily life. The inner logic is also similar: the two commands are related as purpose or result. It will be as Abraham lives his life in open transparency before God that he will be characterized by wholeness and integrity. Obedience to the first command enables the fulfillment of the second. Meanwhile, surrounding both commands are the covenant affirmations and intentions of God.[25]

In Genesis 17 the covenant with Abraham is called "an eternal covenant." And here also the language more familiar in the Sinai covenant is found, as God promises to be the God of Abraham's descendants (Gen 17:7-8). But the universal perspective of blessing for other nations is not lost. Rather it is amplified by the change of Abram's name to Abraham, with the repeated explanation that he

---

[25]The ethical focus sharpens even further in Gen 18. In Gen 18:19 God affirms in a pregnant and programmatic soliloquy that his whole intention in choosing Abraham was "so that he would teach his household after him to keep the way of YHWH by doing righteousness and justice" (author's translation). We will return for more extended reflection on the ethical dimensions of God's missional agenda through Abraham in chap. 11, "The Life of God's Missional People."

will be "the father of many nations" (Gen 17:4-5). Sarai, renamed Sarah, likewise is to be "the mother of nations," and kings will come from both of them (Gen 17:6, 16)—making it clear that the promise will be fulfilled through a child of Abraham and Sarah. Ishmael, as the child of Abraham and Hagar, will also be blessed in the same terms as Abraham himself, except that the everlasting covenant through which blessing will come to all nations is to be channeled through (the promised but as yet unborn) Isaac.

Genesis 22, "the aesthetic and theological summit of the whole story of Abraham,"[26] portrays the ultimate test of Abraham's trust and obedience in his willingness to sacrifice the child of promise at God's command to God himself. We will return in more depth to this chapter when we look at "Ethics and Mission" in chapter eleven. What matters for our purpose here is the way the episode ends with a climactic and intensified confirmation of God's covenant with Abraham and his descendants, specifically endorsed on the basis of Abraham's obedience.

> And he said,
> By myself I have sworn, oracle of YHWH,
> it is *because of the fact that you have done this thing*
> and have not kept back your son, your only one,
> that I will most surely bless you,
> and I will most surely multiply your offspring [seed],
> like the stars in the heavens and like the sand on the seashore,
> and your offspring will possess the gate of your enemies.
> And in your offspring all the nations of the world will find blessing,
> *on account of the fact that you obeyed me.* (Gen 22:16-18, author's translation, emphasis added)

Covenantal obedience and mission. Not only is Genesis 22:16-18 the strongest of all the accounts of God's promise to Abraham, confirmed with the highest possible form of oath (God swearing by God's own self), it also makes quite explicit the relationship between God's promised intentions on the one hand and Abraham's faith and obedience on the other. This had been quietly implicit from the moment the initial command was issued in Genesis 12:1, but it has become increasingly clear through the call to walk before God and be blameless in Genesis 17 and the requirement of righteousness and justice in Genesis 18.

In the light of the subtle but clear theology of these texts, the old dispute over whether the covenant with Abraham was conditional or unconditional

---

[26]Gordon J. Wenham, *Genesis 16—50*, Word Biblical Commentary 2 (Dallas: Word, 1994), p. 99.

seems far too simplistic in its neat binary alternatives. The reality incorporates both dimensions.

On the one hand, God's initial choice, address, command and promise to Abraham were all *unconditional* in the sense that they did not depend on any *prior* condition that Abraham had fulfilled. They emerge out of the unexpected and unmerited grace of God and out of God's undaunted determination to bless this human race of divided nations in spite of all that has thwarted his good will so far.

And yet on the other hand there is an *implied conditionality* in the very form of the foundational address in Genesis 12:1-3. Everything hinges on the opening command "Get yourself up and go from [here] to the land I will show you." The subsequent statements about God blessing Abraham, magnifying his name and multiplying his progeny are all predicated on Abraham actually getting up and going forth. Likewise, the second command "And be a blessing," with its anticipated universal scope, is dependent on Abraham's obedience to the first command, combined with God keeping his word. Though the form of the speech is a double command with attendant promises, the implied thrust of it is "*If* you will go (as I command), *then* I will do these things (as I promise) . . . and all nations will be blessed." No leaving, no blessing. Bluntly put, if Abraham had not got up and left for Canaan, the story would have ended right there, or with an endless recycling of the fate of Babel. The Bible would be a very thin book indeed.

Nevertheless, it is certainly true that the emphasis in the first address of God to Abraham in Genesis 12:1-3 is on God's own gracious initiative and astonishing unprompted promises. However, by Genesis 22 the faith and obedience of Abraham, which have been developing (not without setbacks) in the intervening chapters, are fully incorporated into the covenant to such an extent that they can even be cited as a validating justification for it. God's speech in Genesis 22:16-18 emphatically begins and ends by making Abraham's obedience the reason for God now binding himself irrevocably on oath to do what he has promised.

It should hardly need to be said that this does not in any way mean that Abraham has *merited* God's covenant promises. We are not slipping into some caricature of works righteousness by making these observations on the biblical text itself. God had addressed Abraham out of the blue and prior to any action on Abraham's part. But Abraham's response of faith and obedience not only moves God to count him as righteous but also enables God's promise to move forward toward its universal horizon.

> Abraham by his obedience has not qualified to be the recipient of blessing, be-
> cause the promise of blessing had been given to him already. Rather, the existing

promise is reaffirmed but its terms of reference are altered. A promise that previously was grounded solely in the will and purpose of YHWH is transformed so that it is now grounded *both* in the will of YHWH *and* in the obedience of Abraham. It is not that the divine promise has become contingent on Abraham's obedience, but that Abraham's obedience has been incorporated into the divine promise. Henceforth Israel owes its existence not just to YHWH but also to Abraham. Theologically this constitutes a profound understanding of the value of human obedience—it can be taken up by God and become a motivating factor in his purposes towards humanity.[27]

Paul and James between them capture both poles of Abraham's response to God. Paul focuses on the faith that led Abraham to *believe in the promises of God*, however impossible they seemed, and that was thereby counted as righteousness. Paul can draw from that the message that righteousness comes by trusting God's gracious promise, not through any work of the law, such as circumcision, which comes later in the narrative (Rom 4; Gal 3:6-29). James focuses on the faith that led Abraham to *obey the command of God*, thus demonstrating in practice the genuineness of his faith (Jas 2:20-24).[28] Hebrews captures both by headlining Abraham's faith while substantiating it through his obedience, from his initial departure from his homeland to the classic account of his obedience in Genesis 22 (Heb 11:8-19).

For ourselves, with our concern for a missiological reading of these texts, the important point to notice is the way God's intention to bless the nations is combined with human commitment to a quality of obedience that enables us to be the agent of that blessing. The glorious gospel of the Abrahamic covenant is that God's mission is ultimately to bless all the nations. The enduring challenge is that he planned to do that "through you and your descendants." The faith and obedience of Abraham therefore are not merely models for personal piety and ethics. They are also the essential credentials for effective participation in the limitless mission encapsulated in the two Hebrew words translated as "Be a blessing." There is no blessing for ourselves or for others without faith and obedience. Those whom God calls to participate in his redemptive mission for the

---

[27]R.W. L. Moberly, "Christ as the Key to Scripture: Genesis 22 Reconsidered," in *He Swore an Oath: Biblical Themes from Genesis 12-50,* ed. R. S. Hess et al. (Carlisle, U.K.: Paternoster; Grand Rapids: Baker, 1994), p. 161.

[28]John Goldingay points out that the Hebrew text does not particularly distinguish between "promise" and "command" in its record of God's address to Abraham. Often it simply has "and God said." So faith and obedience are actually complementary responses to the word of God. Neither can truly exist without the other. You cannot obey God's word unless you believe it. But you cannot truly claim to believe God's word unless you obey it. Goldingay, *Old Testament Theology,* 1:198.

nations are those who exercise saving faith like Abraham *and* demonstrate
costly obedience like Abraham. So, *the things God said to Abraham* become the
ultimate agenda for God's own mission (blessing the nations), and *the things
Abraham did in response* become the proximate model for our mission (faith
and obedience).

"Go . . . and be a blessing"

There can be no mistaking what the central theme of Genesis 12:1-3 is. The
words *bless* and *blessing* gleam like jewels in an ornamental goblet. The Hebrew
root, *brk,* as verb or noun, occurs five times in these three verses. God declares
that he will *bless* Abraham, that Abraham is to be a *blessing*, that God will *bless*
those who *bless* Abraham and that all families on earth will count themselves
blessed through him.[29] In the wake of the stories that have battered the reader
for the past nine chapters of Genesis, this is a most surprising and exhilarating
chorus. The God whose blessing first bathed creation is on the move to bless
yet again with repetitive intensity and startling extent. But what exactly, we are
bound to ask, do the words mean? What might an attentive reader of Scripture
understand by *blessing* here?

To answer that question we must properly begin in the immediate environment of our text—the book of Genesis. But the word obviously gathers a wide
range of rich content in the faith and literature of Israel. So for the sake of our
missiological hermeneutic we need to scan this inventory of blessing, however
briefly. Furthermore we have seen that the last line of our text, "through you all
nations on earth will be blessed," generated a canonical trajectory of expectation
that ultimately comes to earth in the missional theology and eschatology of Paul
in the New Testament.

Blessing is creational and relational. The first creatures to be blessed by
God were fish and birds. In the majestic account of creation in Genesis 1, God's
blessing is pronounced three times: on day five, he blessed the creatures of the
sea and air; on day six, he blessed human beings; and on day seven he blessed
the sabbath. The first two blessings are immediately followed by the instruction
to multiply and fill the seas and the earth. The third is followed by the words of
sanctification and rest that define the sabbath. Blessing then, in this foundational
creation account, is constituted by fruitfulness, abundance and fullness on the
one hand, and by enjoying rest within creation in holy and harmonious relationship with the Creator on the other. Blessing is off to a good start.

---

[29]We will examine the disputed meaning of the final verb on pp. 217-19.

The next time we hear of God's blessing, it is launching the new world after the flood, and the language is almost the same as in the first creation account (Gen 9). God blesses Noah and his family, and instructs them to be fruitful, multiply, and fill the earth. At the same time he enters into a relationship with them that includes respect for life—whether animal or human blood—and the preservation of life. That blessing and command are then worked out in the spreading of the nations in Genesis 10.

So when we come to Genesis 12:1-3, the word of blessing must include at least the concept of multiplication, spreading, filling and abundance. But Abraham's wife, we are told, is barren and both of them are elderly. So the word in such a context is surprising to say the least. It is clear to any reader of Genesis so far what blessing *ought* to mean, but the means by which blessing might be enjoyed by this old couple is decidedly unclear. The fruitfulness of creation has surely passed them by. The window of blessing that had never opened because of Sarah's barrenness is now finally shuttered by her advancing years.

As we read on in Genesis, the creational content of blessing predominates. In fact, the root *brk,* as verb or noun, occurs eighty-eight times in Genesis, which is just over a fifth of all its occurrences in the whole Old Testament. When God blesses someone, it normally includes increase of family, flocks, wealth or all three. God's blessing means enjoying the good gifts of God's creation in abundance.

God's blessing is manifested most obviously in human prosperity and well-being; long life, wealth, peace, good harvests and children are the items that figure most frequently in lists of blessings such as Genesis 24:35-36, Leviticus 26:4-13, and Deuteronomy 28:3-15. What modern secular man calls "luck" or "success" the Old Testament calls "blessing," for it insists that God alone is the source of all good fortune. Indeed, the presence of God walking among his people is the highest of his blessings (Lev 26:11-12). Material blessings are in themselves tangible expressions of divine benevolence. Blessing not only connects the patriarchal narratives with each other (cf. Gen 24:1; 26:3; 35:9; 39:5), it also links them with the primeval history (cf. Gen 1:28; 5:2; 9:1). The promises of blessing to the patriarchs are thus a reassertion of God's original intentions for humans.[30]

However, there is nothing mechanical about this. The *relational* element is seen both vertically and horizontally.

Vertically, those who are blessed know who it is that is blessing them and seek to live in faithful relationship with their God. We do not know as much as

---

[30]Gordon J. Wenham, *Genesis 1—15,* Word Biblical Commentary 1 (Dallas: Word, 1987), p. 275.

we might like about the personal religious faith and practice of the ancestral families of Israel (and some of what we do know is puzzling). But it clearly did include sincere worship, building of altars, prayer, trust and (in the case of Abraham at least) a deepening personal intimacy with God.

Even outsiders like Abimelech knew that it was YHWH who was blessing their strange neighbors (Gen 26:29). Indeed, the patriarchs normally do not hesitate to witness concerning the God who has blessed them.

> Theirs is not a mute faith. The patriarchs verbalize to others the reality of Yahweh that they have experienced in their lives: they tell of his provision of wealth (30:30; 31:5-13; 33:10-11; cf. 24:35), his protection and guidance (31:42; 50:20; cf. 24:40-49, 56); his giving of children (33:5); . . . and their commitment to his moral standards (39:9).[31]

That relationship with God is never easy. For Abraham the final sworn confirmation of blessing comes only after the most severe testing imaginable (Gen 22). And the mysterious account of Jacob wrestling with God ends with him eliciting a blessing through a bruising face-to-face encounter (Gen 32:26-29). When blind and aged Jacob blesses the two sons of Joseph, he acknowledges that the blessing he now passes on is one that has attended his own life like a shepherd protecting a wandering and vulnerable sheep, and one that had marked the life of his father and grandfather as they walked before God.

> May the God before whom my fathers
>   Abraham and Isaac walked,
> the God who has been my shepherd
>   all my life to this day,
> the Angel who has delivered me from all harm—
>   may he bless these boys. (Gen 48:15-16)

Horizontally, the relational element of blessing reaches out to those around. Genesis has several instances of people being blessed through contact with those whom God has blessed. Unselfconsciously (usually—Jacob is perhaps an exception), those who inherit the Abrahamic family blessing fulfill the intention that they should be a blessing to others. Laban is enriched by God's blessing on Jacob (Gen 30:27-30). Potiphar is blessed through the presence of Joseph (Gen 39:5). Pharaoh is blessed by Jacob (Gen 47:7, 10). The one remarkable reversal of this (to which Hebrews gives considerable theological significance) is the moment when Abraham himself is blessed by Melchizedek (Gen 14:18-20; cf. Heb 7).

---

[31]M. Daniel Carroll R., "Blessing the Nations: Toward a Biblical Theology of Mission from Genesis," *Bulletin for Biblical Research* 10 (2000): 29.

The most beautiful combination of the creational and relational dimensions of blessing is found in Jacob's blessing on Joseph. It holds together three dimensions: first, the source of all blessing—God; second, the personal and possessive relationship within which that blessing is enjoyed (he is "your father's God," "the Rock of Israel," etc); and third, the creational abundance that the blessing envisions.

> Because of the hand of the Mighty One of Jacob,
>> because of the Shepherd, the Rock of Israel,
> because of your father's God, who helps you,
>> because of the Almighty, who blesses you
> with blessings of the heavens above,
>> blessings of the deep that lies below,
>> blessings of the breast and the womb.
> Your father's blessings are greater
>> than the blessings of the ancient mountains,
>> than the bounty of the age-old hills.
> Let all these rest on the head of Joseph. (Gen 49:24-26)

Blessing is missional and historical. "Go . . . and be a blessing." The words that launch both halves of God's address to Abraham are both imperatives. Both therefore have the nature of a charge or a mission laid on Abraham. The first mission was geographical and limited. He was to leave home and go to the land God would show him. That mission is completed in a relatively short time in the next three verses—though of course the mission of taking possession of the land as promised in Genesis 12:7 would take many more generations. But the second mission is unbounded—"be a blessing." And its scope is unlimited in time and geography. Abraham must leave his own land so that blessing will come to peoples of all lands. *Blessing* here as a command, as a task, as a role is something that goes beyond the sense of creational abundance that we have seen so far in Genesis. "Be a blessing" thus entails a purpose and goal that stretches into the future. It is, in short, missional.

In fact, this is the opening command of the mission of God to restore what humanity seemed intent on wrecking, and to save humanity itself from the consequences of their own wicked folly. It is the third great missional command from God to human beings. The first two are *creational* and virtually identical. In Genesis 1—2 God charges human beings with the great task of ruling over the rest of the creation through keeping and serving the earth in which he has placed them (Gen 1:28; 2:15). And in Genesis 9, after the flood, God renewed his original creation mandate to Noah and his sons. Blessed by God, and living in a stable environment guaranteed by God's covenant with all life on earth, they were to go forth, be fruitful and fill the earth.

Here in Genesis 12:2, however, we have the launch of God's *redemptive* mission. The word *blessing* links it with the creation narratives that precede it. The work of redemptive and restorative blessing will take place within and for the created order, not in some other heavenly or mythological realm beyond it or to which we can escape. It is creation that is broken by human sin, so it is creation and humanity together that God intends to mend. "Mission is the address of God's blessing to the deficit brought about by human failure and pride."[32]

And since it was by human hands that sin and evil have invaded life on earth, it would be by human means that God would act to redress it. The declaration of *blessing* on Abraham and the anticipation of the *inclusion* of all kindreds and nations in the blessing of Abraham answer the language of *curse* and *exclusion* in Genesis 3. "Mission is God's address to humanity's forfeit."[33] God had promised that it would be the seed of Eve (i.e., a human being) that would crush the head of the serpent and thereby destroy his deleterious handiwork (Gen 3:15). Attentive readers will have been wondering who this serpent crusher will be. From Genesis 12:1-3 onward we know it will be one of the seed of Abraham. A son of Abraham will be a blessing for the sons of Adam. "For just as through the disobedience of the one man the many were made sinners, so also through the obedience of the one man the many will be made righteous" (Rom 5:19).

Paul was of course thinking of Christ in the whole argument in which this statement comes. But it could have been said with relative theological validity about Abraham, for we have seen that the obedience of Abraham is a key element in the confirmation of God's covenant with him for the blessing of all nations (Gen 22:16-18). And indeed it *was* said about Abraham in Jewish tradition long before Paul. Abraham, it was said, was God's "second Adam"—the one through whom God made a fresh start for humanity in such a way that Israel could be seen as the core of a new, redeemed, human race.[34] Building on this understanding of the relationship between Abraham and Adam, Paul affirms that *Jesus,* the seed of Abraham, is the one through whom that promise has become a reality.

With the same dynamic understanding of the place of Jesus within the nar-

---

[32]Christopher Seitz, "Election and Blessing: Mission and the Old Testament," lecture given at the Divinity School, Cambridge University in October 2000.

[33]Ibid.

[34]"Israel's covenantal vocation caused her to think of herself as the creator's true humanity. If Abraham and his family are understood as the creator's means of dealing with the sin of Adam, and hence with the evil in the world, Israel herself becomes the true Adamic humanity." N. T. Wright, *The New Testament and the People of God* (London: SPCK, 1992), p. 262. Wright substantiates this widely from rabbinic sources and Old Testament texts.

rative of "the gospel announced in advance to Abraham," Matthew begins his gospel affirming Jesus the Messiah as the son of Abraham and ends it with the mission mandate that would encompass all nations. He thus sets the church also under the authority of the Abrahamic mission. The words of Jesus to his disciples in Matthew 28:18-20, the so-called Great Commission, could be seen as a christological mutation of the original Abrahamic commission—"Go . . . and be a blessing . . . and all nations on earth will be blessed through you."

And since the mission to "be a blessing" is given to a human being and his seed after him, it necessarily takes on a *historical* dimension. Blessing in and of itself need not be a historical thing. Hitherto in Genesis it has been simply a relatively static, inbuilt feature of the created order, the enjoyment of fruitfulness and abundance. However, by making blessing a *promise* for the future ("I will bless you") and by including blessing in a *command* to be carried on into the future ("Be a blessing"), our text transforms it into a historical dynamic.[35] Genesis 12:1-3 injects blessing into history. It launches a mission that holds hope for the future.

The unfolding biblical story of all the generations yet to come will doubtless give plenty more evidence of *human fallenness*. All the marks of the prototypical narratives of the primeval history will replay themselves again and again. We have not seen the last of the disobedience of Adam and Eve, the jealousy and violence of Cain, the vengeance of Lamech, the corruption and violence of the generation of Noah or the arrogant insecurity of Babel. But what we now know we must look for as well are the footprints of *divine blessing* on the road of history—blessing received from God and blessing passed on to others. We will look for the "great nation" that God here promises. We will discern the dividing line that people will create by their reaction to what God will do through this blessed people. And we will look for the growing evidence that the blessing of God through the people of Abraham will eventually spread throughout the whole earth. *We will, in short, be watching the mission of God in the midst of human history, the key that unlocks the Bible's grand narrative, and it all starts here.*

Genesis 12:1-3, then, launches redemptive history within the continuum of

---

[35]This point is emphasized by Claus Westermann: "Blessing is not of its nature a historical thing. It can be given to anyone, as in Gen. 27. However, it need not, as originally understood, have in view some future point in time; that is, it need not be a promise. In 12:1-3 J links blessing and history, and thereby links the story of the patriarchs with the history of the people. . . . The effect of the blessing is that Abraham becomes a great people. This sentence expresses in the clearest possible way that J is looking beyond the history of the patriarchs Abraham, Isaac and Jacob into the future." Westermann, *Genesis 12—26,* p. 149.

wider human history—all of which is also, of course, under the sovereign plan of God. And it launches that history as the history of mission—the mission that God takes on himself in his categorical commitments to Abraham and his offspring, and the mission that God lays on Abraham in consequence—"Be a blessing." It would be entirely appropriate, and no bad thing, if we took *this* text as "the Great Commission." Certainly it is the biblical foundation on which the text in Matthew is based that is usually elevated to that role. We may know a great deal more than Abraham did of "the whole counsel of God," of the mystery hidden for ages but now revealed in the Messiah Jesus through the gospel. But even with all that greater knowledge and fuller revelation, it would not be an inappropriate slogan with which to grace all the church's concept and practice of mission. There could be worse ways of summing up what mission is supposed to be all about than "Go . . . and be a blessing."

Blessing is covenantal and ethical. The blessings of creation continue and are showered on all. Genesis shows God blessing many others besides Abraham and his descendants. The growth and diversity of nations reflect his purpose after the flood. So God's blessing is not confined to the sphere of the covenant or redemptive history. The covenant includes God's blessing, but God's blessing is not limited to the covenant. Even those who are not included within that specific sphere may enjoy the blessing of numerical growth along with all the nations. Thus, although much ink is spilled telling the story of how Esau was irreversibly cheated of his father's blessing by Jacob (Gen 27), it did not stop Esau going on to become a numerous nation, the Edomites, or producing kings among his offspring before Israel had any (Gen 36, cf. v. 31). Clearly the blessing that he lost and Jacob obtained included more than nationhood alone.

The distinction between the general blessing of God and the specifically covenantal blessing that is enjoyed by the descendants of Abraham and Sarah through the line of promise is most clearly seen in the case of Ishmael. It is noteworthy that both God and Abraham speak warmly of Ishmael (only Sarah responds negatively to his perceived threat to her Isaac [Gen 21:8-10]). In response to Abraham's plea "If only Ishmael might live under your blessing," God responds that indeed he will: "I will surely bless him; I will make him fruitful and will greatly increase his numbers. . . . And I will make him into a great nation" (Gen 17:18-20)—words that unmistakably echo the promise made to Abraham himself. Later this promise regarding Ishmael is repeated, and even after his expulsion from Abraham's household it is recorded that "God was with the boy as he grew up" (Gen 21:13, 20). Nevertheless, it is with *Isaac* (named but as yet unborn in chap. 17), that God intends to make his *covenant* (Gen 17:19, 21). This indicates something unique about the nature of the blessing that will reside within the covenant relationship. It does not deny that God can and will bless others outside the Abrahamic covenant in all kinds of ways, but it does point to a form of blessing that goes beyond creational abundance and natural fertility.[36]

As the Old Testament story proceeds, the nature of the blessing that Israel enjoys within the covenant becomes increasingly specific. It includes the experience of God's faithfulness, on account of Abraham, and God's rescue of them from slavery in Egypt in the exodus. It goes on to encompass his protective care of them in the wilderness, providing for their needs and forgiving their offenses. The revelation of God's name, the giving of the law at Sinai and the means of continued fellowship through the tabernacle and sacrificial system are all marks of God's covenantal blessing. The gift of land is in direct fulfillment of the promise to Abraham and is seen as the most tangible of all the blessings that flowed from it.

In all these things, Israel is called on to respond in the same way as the paradigm Abraham has set—in faith and obedience. Blessing within the covenant thus includes knowledge of who the only true and living God is (through the revelation of his name, YHWH), and commitment to love and obey him in such a way that the blessing may continue to be enjoyed (Deut 4:32-40). The whole book of Deuteronomy climaxes in the powerful appeal to Israel to "choose life," that is, to sustain the blessing in which they stood through the covenant promises of God by living in loving, trusting and obedient relationship with their God (Deut 30).

This ethical dimension of blessing within the covenant relationship protects the creational element from degenerating into any kind of "prosperity gospel." While it is certainly true to say that material abundance can be a tangible sign of God's blessing, the link between the two is neither automatic nor reversible.

---

[36]On this point, therefore, I differ from John Goldingay, who draws from this passage that Ishmael, through the blessings promised to him and through receiving circumcision (the sign of the covenant in Gen 17), is included within the Abrahamic covenant along with all his descendants (Goldingay, *Old Testament Theology*, 1:201, 203). It seems to me that the text distinguishes between Isaac, who explicitly inherits the covenant promise, and Ishmael, who, though circumcised and blessed, does not. However, as Goldingay well shows (pp. 224-31), there are areas of ambiguity in these stories as to "who counts" as belonging within the sphere of covenant blessing. What about Moab and Ammon, descendants of Lot, or Edom, descendants of Esau? The later Old Testament has similar ambiguity as to their status. In any case, one might point out, even if the line of covenant blessing moves exclusively from Abraham through Isaac to Jacob and the people of Israel, we have been told from the start that the whole point of it is so that others will be blessed, or bless themselves, through Abraham. So while Ishmael may not be included in the covenantal family line, his descendants will certainly be among the "all nations" that will be blessed through Abraham.

That is to say, God calls for faith, obedience and ethical loyalty to the demands of the covenant in bad as well as good times. Not all material loss or physical suffering is the result of disobedience (as the books of Job and Jeremiah illustrate). And not all wealth is obtained under God's blessing (as Amos and other prophets made clear). The realities of injustice and oppression, which reduce some people to poverty and make other people very rich, undercut any simplistic correlation between wealth (or lack of) and God's blessing (or absence of). We will look further at the ethical dimension of the covenant as it relates to mission in chapter eleven.

Blessing is multinational and christological. The bottom line of God's address to Abraham in Genesis 12:1-3 is universal. The outcome of God's blessing of Abraham and commanding Abraham himself to be a blessing would be blessing for "all the kinship groups of the earth." This universal scope of the Abrahamic promise is the clinching argument for recognizing the missiological centrality of this text—which is already quite explicit anyway in the command "Be a blessing." It is time to look at the final phrase more closely. For although its universal reach is clear, precise exegesis of its meaning is less so.

Variants of the phrase occur in the following five texts.[37]

1. "In you will be blessed all kinship groups of the earth *[mišpĕḥōt hā'ădāmâ]*" (Gen 12:3). This is the original promise to Abraham.

2. "In him will be blessed all nations of the earth *[gôyê hā'āreṣ]*" (Gen 18:18). God reminds himself of the future significance of Abraham.

3. "In your seed all nations of the earth *[gôyê hā'āreṣ]* will bless themselves" (Gen 22:18). In the wake of Abraham's obedient willingness to sacrifice Isaac, the promise is repeated to Abraham with strong emphasis.

4. "In your seed all nations of the earth *[gôyê hā'āreṣ]* will bless themselves" (Gen 26:4). Here the promise is reaffirmed to Isaac in identical words, but again with an immediately following emphasis on Abraham's moral obedience.

5. "In you will be blessed all kinship groups of the earth *[mišpĕḥōt hā'ădāmâ]*, and in your seed" (Gen 28:14). This time God is reaffirming the promise to Jacob at Bethel.

The key verb is of course, *bārak,* "to bless." It occurs in two verbal forms in these verses, and there has been much dispute over the precise nuance of translation. In the first, second and fifth texts, it is in the niphal form, and in third

---

[37]All are my own translations.

and fourth, it is in hithpael. The niphal form of the Hebrew verb can be passive or reflexive or "middle," but the hithpael is more naturally reflexive. The three possible ways of reading the words, then, are passive, reflexive or middle, which I will explain.

A *passive* rendering is simply "will be blessed," with the assumption "by God" or "by me." Most ancient versions rendered it this way, and so does the New Testament (e.g., by Paul in Gal 3:8). There were simpler forms of the Hebrew verb that would express the passive, however (the pual), and the niphal has a flavor just beyond a merely passive sense.

A *reflexive* rendering "will bless themselves" means that people would use the name of Abraham in blessing one another. That is, either praying for themselves to be blessed as Abraham was or invoking the name of Abraham in praying a blessing for others ("may God bless you like Abraham"). This would fit with the known practice of invoking the names of particularly blessed individuals in praying for oneself or others (e.g., Gen 48:20; Ruth 4:11-12). It also better fits the sense in Psalm 72:17.

A *middle* sense (at least for the three niphal texts) is argued for by Gordon Wenham, who translates, "they will find blessing." Another way of expressing this sense is "they will count themselves blessed."[38]

Since it would seem natural to assume that the variations in the five texts are so minor that the main verbs should all be taken in the same way,[39] the debate has been whether all should be taken as passive (*be blessed,* closer to the natural niphal)[40] or as reflexive (*bless themselves,* closer to the natural hithpael).[41]

However, it is increasingly being realized that in the end a reflexive sense carries a passive inference anyway. This is because of the rest of the things God promises. If someone uses the name of Abraham as a blessing—that is to say, they pray to be blessed as Abraham was—it presupposes that they know about the God who blessed Abraham so much that he became a showcase of the power of that God to bless. Such people thereby acknowledge both Abraham and Abraham's God. But God has just said he will bless those who "bless Abraham"—that is, those who regard Abraham as blessed in this way. So those who

---

[38]Wenham, *Genesis 1—15,* pp. 277-78.

[39]Though Carroll R. suggests there may be specific reasons why the hithpael is used in the two cases where it occurs. Carroll R., "Blessing the Nations," pp. 23-24.

[40]As in early translations of the Hebrew Scriptures, the NIV and cf. O. T. Allis, "The Blessing of Abraham," *Princeton Theological Review* 25 (1927): 263-98.

[41]As in many critical scholars and cf. RSV and NEB. A recent defender of the passive reading, however, is Keith N. Grueneberg, *Abraham, Blessing and the Nation: A Philological and Exegetical Study of Genesis 12:3 in Its Narrative Context,* Beihfte zur Zeitschrift für die alttestamentliche Wissenschaft (New York: Walter de Gruyter, 2003).

bless themselves by Abraham (if we give the hithpael its full force) will end up being blessed by God because he promises to do so. The reflexive implies the passive as an outcome. Claus Westermann comes to this conclusion.

> In fact, the reflexive translation is saying no less than the passive. . . . When "the families of the earth bless" themselves "in Abraham," i.e., call a blessing on themselves under the invocation of his name . . . then the obvious presupposition is that they receive the blessing. Where one blesses oneself with the name of Abraham, blessing is actually bestowed and received. Where the name of Abraham is spoken in a prayer for blessing, the blessing of Abraham streams forth; it knows no bound and reaches all the families of the earth. There is then no opposition in content between the passive and reflexive translation. . . . [Verse 3] includes the concrete fact of being blessed. . . . God's action proclaimed in the promise to Abraham is not limited to him and his posterity, but reaches its goal only when it includes all the families of the earth.[42]

A further missiological consideration strengthens this point. As mentioned above, if a simple passive had been intended, Hebrew has such a form (the pual, as in 2 Sam 7:29 and Ps 112:2, or the qal passive participle, as in Is 19:24). But niphal and hithpael forms have been deliberately used, which, while they do include a passive sense, have the reflexive, self-involving nuance as well. Why should this matter? I think it does for the following reason. The act of blessing oneself, or counting oneself blessed, by (the name of) Abraham indicates that one knows the source of the blessing. To know Abraham as a model of blessing and to seek to be blessed as he was must surely include knowing the God of Abraham and seeking blessing from that God and not other gods.

Now actually, a person may "be blessed" (in the passive sense) without necessarily knowing or acknowledging the source of the blessing. Tragically, many (including within Old Testament Israel) attribute the blessings they have in fact received from the living Creator God to other gods. Such experience of general blessing simply by living in God's blessed creation (along with what is often called "common grace") is not in itself redemptive, for it does not include "knowing God."[43] But a person cannot intentionally and specifically invoke *blessing in the name of Abraham* without acknowledging the source of Abraham's blessing, namely, Abraham's God. There is thus what we might call a con-

---

[42]Westermann, *Genesis 12—26*, p. 152.

[43]Paul corrected the false views of the citizens of Lystra on this score when he pointed them to the true source of the everyday blessings they enjoyed (Acts 14:15-18). His address was an emergency response and quickly cut short, but we can presume that with more time and less volatile circumstances he would have moved on from the story of creation to the rest of the biblical story that climaxed in the resurrection of Jesus.

fessional dimension to the anticipated blessing of the nations. They will be blessed as they come to acknowledge the God of Abraham and "bless themselves" in and through him.

In chapter seven we will consider the further vital importance of the qualifier *in you* or *through you,* which points to this particularity. But at this point we simply observe that the intention of God at this climax of his promise to Abraham is not merely that all nations should be blessed (purely passive) in some unspecified way, regardless of their relationship with Abraham. Or that they would be blessed in some independent way unrelated to what God has just declared he will do for and through Abraham. No, the combined force of the crucial word "in you," along with the *self-involving* form of the verb, shows that God's intention is that nations will self-consciously share in the blessing of Abraham through deliberate appropriation of it for themselves. This is not just randomly sprinkled blessing. It is a deliberate act that will activate God's promise of blessing for them. The nations will indeed be blessed as Abraham was, but only because they will have turned to the only source of blessing, Abraham's God, and identified themselves with the story of Abraham's people. They will know the God of Abraham.

I referred to this as a missiological perspective because it certainly connects with a major emphasis that we explored in chapter four, namely, the biblical God's will to be known for who he is. The creation must know its Creator. The nations must know their Judge and Savior. And this is the God who, as Hebrews tells us, "is not ashamed to be called *their* God"—that is the God of Abraham, Isaac and Jacob (Heb 11:16). And the story of Abraham looks both backward to the great narrative of creation and forward to the even greater narrative of redemption. And the vocabulary of blessing is the umbilical cord between both traditions. It is the blessing of God that links creation and redemption, for redemption is the restoration of the original blessing inherent in creation.

So the fulfillment of God's promise to Abraham comes about not merely as nations are blessed in some general sense but only as they specifically come to know the whole biblical grand story, of which Abraham is a key pivot. This is profoundly important for mission. One of the reasons for the appalling shallowness and vulnerability of much that passes for the growth of the church around the world is that people are coming to some kind of instrumental faith in a God they see as powerful, with some connection to Jesus, but a Jesus disconnected from his scriptural roots. They have not been challenged at the level of their deeper worldview by coming to know God *in and through the story that is launched by Abraham.* Paul had not left his converts vulnerable at this level but had taught them clearly and reminds them in Galatians that their faith in *Christ* had embedded them in the faith and lineage of *Abraham*. The living God they had turned to from their dead idols had indeed announced the gospel in advance through Abraham, and they could count themselves blessed in Abraham, through his seed, the Messiah Jesus.

And following Paul, of course, we who read this text as Christian believers know that its fulfillment is rooted in that same Jesus. Its multinational vista is possible only through Christ. So, to widely diverse representatives of the nations, the Gentile believers in the churches around the Mediterranean, Paul could say what he said to the Galatians: "You are all sons of God through faith in Christ Jesus. . . . If you belong to Christ, then you are Abraham's seed, and heirs according to the promise" (Gal 3:26, 29).

Calvin used this christological hermeneutic as an interesting way of deciding the exegetical problem over the precise rendering of the main verb in Genesis 12:3, for he was clearly aware of the different grammatical options. In the end he argues that since we know that it is in and through Christ that the nations are in fact being blessed, and since Christ was "in the loins" of Abraham, we can understand God's promise to Abraham in the fuller sense implied by the passive "be blessed." Commenting on that final phrase of Genesis 12:3, Calvin writes:

> Should anyone choose to understand this passage in a restricted sense, as a proverbial way of speaking (those who will bless their children or their friends will be called after the name of Abram), let him enjoy his opinion; for the Hebrew phrase will bear the interpretation that Abram will be called a signal example of happiness.
>
> But I extend the meaning further because I suppose the same thing to be promised in this place that God later repeats more clearly (see Genesis 22:18). And the authority of Paul brings me to this point as well [Gal. 3:17]. . . . We must understand that the blessing was promised to Abram in Christ, when he was coming into the land of Canaan. Therefore, God (in my judgment) pronounces that all nations should be blessed in his servant Abram because Christ was included in his body. In this manner, he not only intimates that Abram would be an *example,* but a *cause* of blessing. . . . [Paul] concludes that the covenant of salvation that God made with Abram is neither stable nor firm except in Christ. I therefore thus interpret the present place as saying that God promises to his servant Abram that blessing that will afterwards flow to all people.[44]

Conclusion

How then are we to answer the question posed at the start of this section: What is the meaning of "blessing"? It is obvious that Genesis 12:1-3 (as indeed Genesis

---

[44]Calvin, *Genesis,* pp. 112-13.

itself as a book) is saturated with concern for blessing. But what do the rich and resonant phrases mean and where do they lead (for the horizon of the text is very distant indeed)?

We have seen that blessing is initially and strongly connected with creation and all the good gifts that God longs for people to enjoy in his world—abundance, fruitfulness and fertility, long life, peace, and rest. Yet at the same time, these things are to be enjoyed within the context of healthy relationships with God and with others. Yet such relationships have been radically fractured by the events described in Genesis 3—11. How then can such blessing be enjoyed apart from the redemptive intervention of God?

Then we observed that the combination of command and promise in the text gave it a strongly missional dynamic, while its orientation toward the future made it a programmatic address to history. In a creation spoiled by sin and the curse, history will be a hope-filled story of how God will bring about for Abraham what he has promised him (Gen 18:18). If that is the mission of God, however, we quickly observed that it also demands the faith and obedience of Abraham, and the subsequent commitment of his people to the ethical demands of the covenant. So the Abrahamic covenant is a moral agenda for God's people as well as a mission statement by God.

Finally, we stand amazed at the universal thrust (repeated five times) of the Abrahamic promise—that ultimately people of all nations will find blessing through Abraham. And we confess, with Paul, that it is of the essence of the biblical gospel, first announced to Abraham, that God has indeed made such blessing for all nations available through the Messiah, Jesus of Nazareth, the seed of Abraham. In Christ alone, through the gospel of his death and resurrection, stands the hope of blessing for all nations.

7

God's Particular People
Chosen for All

Our initial survey of the election of Abraham in chapter six focused mainly on blessing—that he was chosen to be blessed and to be a blessing. We move on now to unpack more fully the implications of both parts of that famous bottom line of the Abrahamic covenant, immortalized by Paul as "the gospel in advance," that "through you all nations on earth will be blessed."

The tension between the universality of the goal *(all nations)* and the particularity of the means *(through you)* is right there from the very beginning of Israel's journey through the pages of the Old Testament. It is a tension that is fundamental to our biblical theology of mission, so we need to explore both poles of it further now. It is also a tension that has generated many unsatisfactory attempts to resolve it in either direction—by drawing from it a kind of universalism that loses touch with the particularity of God's redemptive work through Israel and Christ, or by accusing Israel of a chauvinistic exclusivism that neglected God's wider concern for other nations. We can only respond to such distortions by turning to the biblical text in all its breadth and depth—and that is the rationale underlying the nature of this chapter as a wide-ranging biblical journey. As we embark on it, we recall that our purpose throughout is to discern how thoroughly the mission of God is woven into the whole tapestry of Scripture. That mission of God unquestionably has a universal horizon and an equally unquestionably particular historical method. Both are crucial in unlocking the Bible's grand narrative.

Universality—Old Testament Echoes of Abraham
Once we move beyond the narratives of the ancestors of Israel in Genesis to the

narratives of their national history from the exodus onward, the narrator focuses the attention of the reader on God's specific dealings with the nation of Israel itself. Those elements of the Abrahamic promise that were most important within the history of Old Testament Israel are given prominence: the growth of the "great nation" in spite of threats and opposition, the establishment of a covenant relationship of blessing between YHWH and Israel, the acquisition of the Promised Land. In all of these things (posterity, covenant and land), the faith of Israel (particularly as expressed in Deuteronomy) looked back to Abraham and praised God for his faithfulness in keeping these dimensions of his promise to their fathers.

But what about "all nations on earth"? Outside Genesis, with its fivefold reference to God's mission of blessing all nations through Abraham and his seed, there is much less frequent mention of this final clause of the promise. Nevertheless, it is certainly not lost altogether, and we need now to survey those places in the rest of the Old Testament that directly or indirectly refer to this universal aspect of God's intention for the world beyond the boundaries of Israel itself. We will be looking for texts in which either phrases such as "all nations" or "all the earth" are used in connection with God's saving purposes, or where the theme of blessing occurs with a wider-than-Israel perspective. Later, in chapter fourteen, we will explore more widely and in greater depth the theme of "the nations" in general in the Old Testament. Our focus here is not on all texts that refer in any way to YHWH and the nations but on those that articulate some element of universality, either directly or implicitly echoing the Abraham promise. After we have followed the trajectory of Abrahamic universality through the Old Testament, we will then observe its impact when it lands in the New Testament among those who saw in Jesus Christ the final key to its fulfillment.

The Pentateuch. *Exodus 9:13-16.* "This is what the LORD, the God of the Hebrews, says: Let my people go, so that they may worship me, or this time I will send the full force of my plagues against you and against your officials and your people, so you may know that there is no one like me in all the earth. For by now I could have stretched out my hand and struck you and your people with a plague that would have wiped you off the earth. But I have raised you up for this very purpose, that I might show you my power and that my name might be proclaimed in all the earth."

This statement to Pharaoh comes within the narrative of the plagues. As we saw in chapter three (p. 76), a major subplot of that narrative is that Pharaoh should come to know who God is. He will ultimately know that YHWH (whom he refused to acknowledge) is God, just as much in Egypt as anywhere else on earth. But here a wider knowing than Pharaoh's alone is envisioned. Not only must Pharaoh realize that there is no God like YHWH "in all the earth" but also all the earth must hear about the power and name of YHWH. Whether they would do so as an experience of YHWH's blessing or of his judgment would depend on whether they followed Pharaoh's example or learned enough from it to choose a better way. Pharaoh thus becomes here a classic illustration of the protective line in the Abrahamic covenant—"the one who treats you with contempt, I will curse" (Gen 12:3, author's translation).

The missiological significance of this text is observed (though not with this terminology) by Terence Fretheim in his perceptive comment:

> Here God's ultimate goal of the creation comes into view. In three "knowing" texts (8:22; 9:14, 30) the relationship of God to the entire earth is emphasized. Yahweh is no local god, seeking to best another local deity. The issue for God *finally* is that God's name be declared *(sapar)* to the entire earth. This verb is used elsewhere for the proclamation of God's good news (e.g. Ps. 78:3-4; Isa. 43:21). This is no perfunctory understanding of the relationship of non-Israelites to Yahweh. To say that God is God of all the earth means that all its people are God's people; they should know the name of this God. Hence God's purposes in these events are not focussed simply on the redemption of Israel. *God's purposes span the world.* God is acting in such a public way so that God's good news can be proclaimed to everyone (see Rom. 9:17).[1]

Exodus 19:5-6. "Now if you obey me fully and keep my covenant, then out of all nations you will be my treasured possession. [For (or indeed)] the whole earth is mine, and you will be for me a kingdom of priests and a holy nation."[2]

This is a key missiological text to which we will return more than once as we work our way through this book. It is as pivotal in the book of Exodus as Genesis 12:1-3 is in Genesis. It is the hinge between chapters 1-18, describing God's gracious initiative of redemption (the exodus), and chapters 20-40, which describe the making of the covenant, the giving of the law, and the building of the tabernacle. Like Genesis 12:1-3 it also has a combination of imperative (how Israel must behave) and promise (what Israel will be among the rest of the nations).

The universal perspective, for which we enlist it here, is explicit in the double phrase *all nations* and *the whole earth*. Although the action is taking place be-

---

[1] Terence E. Fretheim, *Exodus,* Interpretation (Louisville: John Knox Press, 1991), p. 125.
[2] I have changed the NIV text at the beginning of the second sentence. This is a much more natural rendering of the Hebrew conjunction *kî* here—rather than "although" (NIV). The point is not "in spite of" but rather "because of" the fact that the whole earth belongs to God, Israel will have a priestly and holy function, and is called to exercise the positive role of mediating God to the nations.

tween YHWH and Israel alone at Mount Sinai, God has not forgotten his wider mission of blessing the rest of the nations of the earth through this particular people whom he has redeemed. Furthermore, since the exodus itself had been explicitly motivated by God's faithfulness to his promises to Abraham (Ex 2:24; 6:6-8), the full weight of that great theme in Genesis is echoed here. The universality of God's ultimate purpose for all the earth is not lost sight of. Indeed, this verse sets the rest of the Pentateuch in its light, just as Genesis 12:1-3 did for the rest of Genesis.

The whole Sinai experience—including the giving of the law, the making of the covenant, the building of the tabernacle and even including the renewal of the covenant with the following generation on the plains of Moab in Deuteronomy—is prefaced by this text.

The significance of this great covenant event for Israel's future, the privileges and the obligations, are contained with the introductory speech of YHWH, Exodus 19:3-6. In this nutshell we find a summary of the purpose of the covenant, presented from the mouth of YHWH himself. Here is the given goal of Israel's future.[3]

And that "given goal" is explicitly universal in outlook. Once again, the missiological significance is noticed by Fretheim: "the phrases relate to a mission that encompasses God's purposes for the entire world. *Israel is commissioned to be God's people on behalf of the earth which is God's.*"[4]

Numbers 23:8-10.

> How can I curse
> those whom God has not cursed?
> How can I denounce
> those whom the LORD has not denounced?
> From the rocky peaks I see them,
> from the heights I view them.
> I see people who live apart
> and do not consider themselves one of the nations.
> Who can count the dust of Jacob
> or number the fourth part of Israel?
> Let me die the death of the righteous,
> and may my end be like theirs!

---

[3]Jo Bailey Wells, *God's Holy People: A Theme in Biblical Theology*, JSOT Supplement Series 305 (Sheffield, U.K.: Sheffield Academic Press, 2000), p. 35.

[4]Fretheim, *Exodus*, p. 212. Likewise, John Durham recognizes the universal implications of the role given here to Israel: "Israel as a 'kingdom of priests' is Israel committed to the extension throughout the world of the ministry of Yahweh's Presence." John I. Durham, *Exodus*, Word Biblical Commentary 3 (Waco, Tex.: Word, 1987), p. 263.

Balaam's oracle does not quite express the universality of the climax of the Abrahamic covenant, but it certainly is an echo of that text. His refusal to curse Israel may have been under divine constraint, but there was an element of self-preservation in it too. The distinctiveness of Israel's role among the nations is also referred to, as is the expectation of their numerical growth like "dust"—a clear echo of part of God's promise to Abraham (Gen 13:16). And finally, Balaam probably echoes the final line of Genesis 12:3 by wishing to be like Israel. "In this wish he may be invoking upon himself the kind of blessing found in Gen. 12:3, that through Abraham and his offspring, all nations of the earth will bless themselves."[5]

> YHWH had promised that Abraham's family would become as numerous as the grains of sandy soil in the land (Gen 13:16; 28:14); Balaam testifies that this has come about (Num 23:10). YHWH had promised that people would pray for blessing like Abraham's (Gen 12:3); Balaam does so (Num 23:10).[6]

Balaam's next oracle is even more emphatic in affirming the blessing of God on Israel, which no human sorcery can reverse (Num 23:18-24), and his third oracle virtually quotes God's original words to Abraham (Num 24:9).

Tragically, what Balak failed to achieve in three chapters (Num 22—24) by hiring Balaam to bring God's curse on Israel, the Israelites managed to achieve in one (Num 25) by their own ill-disciplined surrender to the temptations of immorality and idolatry. Numbers 31:16 suggests that Balaam had a hand in this, in spite of his Spirit-inspired oracles, so that his hope that his death might be among the righteous and blessed like Israel was doomed by his actions (Num 31:8).

Deuteronomy 28:9-10. "The LORD will establish you as his holy people, as he promised you on oath, if you keep the commands of the LORD your God and walk in his ways. Then all the peoples on earth will see that you are called by the name of the LORD, and they will fear you."

The rest of the nations do not feature very much in Deuteronomy, though when they do, it is of considerable missiological interest. For example, one of the early motivations for obeying the law is that Israel would then become a

---

[5]Timothy Ashley, *The Book of Numbers,* New International Commentary on the Old Testament (Grand Rapids: Eerdmans, 1993), p. 472, (and similarly most commentators).

[6]John Goldingay, *Old Testament Theology,* vol. 1, *Israel's Gospel* (Downers Grove, Ill.: InterVarsity Press, 2003), p. 471. Goldingay further points to the universal dimension of the episode in the way it reverts to the creational theme of blessing, after the immediately preceding narratives of redemption: "The reappearance of the theme also advertizes that the story needs to make the transition back from deliverance talk to blessing talk. Israel's story (the world's story) is not ultimately about deliverance but about blessing" (ibid.).

visible example to the nations of the nearness of God and of wise and just social structures (Deut 4:6-8). This text comes within the great chapter of blessings and curses by which the covenant was sanctioned. The blessings listed in Deuteronomy 28:1-14, as elsewhere in the book, follow the pattern of blessing already seen clearly in Genesis. Alongside those standard marks of blessing, however, this text points to a wider effect. There will be universal recognition of YHWH's blessing on Israel and thereby universal recognition of YHWH's own name. This can only happen on the assumption of Israel's obedience to the covenant, by living as God's "holy people" (which echoes Ex 19:5-6). "The thought belongs to the Deuteronomic theme of Israel as a witness to the nations by reason of Yahweh's blessing and their keeping his commands (cf. 4:6-8; 26:19)."[7]

The historical books. The Deuteronomistic History follows the general ethos of the book of Deuteronomy by being primarily taken up with the story of Israel itself and God's dealings with them within the terms of his covenant promises and threats. However, the wider significance of Israel within God's purposes for the rest of the world does shine through from time to time—often either in editorial comments or in the mouths of key characters at critical moments in the story.[8] Most of the related passages speak of all the earth *coming to know YHWH* rather than explicitly referring to them *being blessed.* This is parallel to the way Israel itself had been granted its great historical experiences of YHWH in action: "So that you might know that the LORD is God; beside him there is no other" (Deut 4:35). All nations on earth will eventually come to know what Israel knows. But since the Abrahamic promise of being blessed, or blessing oneself, through Abraham presupposes knowing Abraham's God, and since knowing YHWH as God is unquestionably one of the greatest blessings enjoyed by Israel, there is a theological affinity between these "knowing" texts and the Abrahamic "blessing" promise, even if it is not so explicit as elsewhere.

Joshua 4:23-24. "The LORD your God did to the Jordan just what he had done to the Red Sea when he dried it up before us until we had crossed over. He did this so that all the peoples of the earth might know that the hand of the LORD is powerful and so that you might always fear the LORD your God."

Joshua here puts the crossing of the Jordan on the same paradigmatic level

---

[7]J. G. McConville, *Deuteronomy,* Apollos Old Testament Commentary (Leicester, U.K.: Apollos; Downers Grove, Ill.: InterVarsity Press, 2002), pp. 404-5.

[8]Jonathan Rowe provides a fascinating study of the language of universality and its common linkage with the condemnation of idolatry in the Deuteronomistic History, and offers a missiological perspective on the relevant material. Jonathan Y Rowe, "Holy to the Lord: Universality in the Deuteronomic History and Its Relationship to the Authors' Theology of History" (M.A. diss., All Nations Christian College, 1997).

as the Exodus crossing of the Sea of Reeds. Not only did it accomplish a major step forward in the saving history of Israel, it would also, and for that reason, form part of the education of the nations by which they too would know something of the power of YHWH.

1 Samuel 17:46. "This day the LORD will hand you over to me. . . . And the whole world will know that there is a God in Israel."

David puts his imminent defeat of Goliath in the same universal frame of reference. Youthful hyperbole? Perhaps, but the narrator doubtless meant it to be taken as sober theological comment.

> The purpose of David's victory is not simply to save Israel or to defeat the Philistines. The purpose is the glorification of Yahweh in the eyes of the world. . . . This is an extraordinary speech by David, with a disciplined and eloquent theological substance. David is the one who bears witness to the rule of Yahweh. In so doing he calls Israel away from its imitation of the nations and calls the nations away from their foolish defiance of Yahweh. In a quite general sense this is a "missionary speech," summoning Israel and the nations to fresh faith in Yahweh.[9]

It is worth noting that in his eschatological vision, a later prophet envisioned "a remnant" of Goliath's people, the Philistines, being so absorbed into the future people of God that they would even become leaders in the city and state that David went on to establish (Zech 9:7).

2 Samuel 7:25-26, 29. "And now, LORD God, keep for ever the promise you have made concerning your servant and his house. Do as you promised, so that your name will be great for ever. Then men will say, 'The LORD Almighty is God over Israel!' . . . Now be pleased to bless the house of your servant, that it may continue for ever in your sight; for you, O Sovereign LORD, have spoken, and with your blessing the house of your servant will be blessed for ever."

David's response to God's promise to him regarding the establishing of his "house" seems to draw on the Abrahamic language. There are other parallels between David and Abraham in the biblical narrative (e.g., the secure possession of the land promised to Abraham, the promise of a great name [2 Sam 7:9], the promise of a son). Here David reflects God's promise of a great name back to God himself in the prayer that God's name will be widely honored, and uses the double language of blessing.

1 Kings 8:41-43, 60-61. "As for the foreigner who does not belong to your people Israel but has come from a distant land because of your name—for men will hear of your great name and your mighty hand and your outstretched arm—

---

[9]Walter Brueggemann, *First and Second Samuel,* Interpretation (Louisville: John Knox Press, 1990), p. 132.

when he comes and prays towards his temple, then hear from heaven, your dwelling place, and do whatever the foreigner asks of you, so that all the peoples of the earth may know your name and fear you as do your own people Israel.

". . . so that all the peoples of the earth may know that the LORD is God and that there is no other. But your hearts [Israel] must be fully committed to the LORD our God, to live by his decrees and obey his commands, as at this time."

This is the most remarkable of all the passages with a universal vision in the historical books, "possibly the most marvelously universalistic passage in the Old Testament."[10] It is all the more noteworthy since it occurs in the context of what might be regarded as the most particular focus of the faith of Israel—the temple. Yet here, at its dedication, Solomon's prayer envisions the blessing of foreigners and the spreading fame of YHWH.

The *assumptions* Solomon makes in pressing his request are revealing. It is *assumed* that people will hear of the reputation of YHWH. It is *assumed* that people from afar will be attracted to come and worship Israel's God for themselves. It is *assumed* that Israel's God can and will hear the prayers of foreigners. All these assumptions are important theological foundations in any summary of the missiological significance of the faith and history of Old Testament Israel. And it is a missiological reading of a text like this which highlights the theological significance of its assumptions.

The *content* of his request is no less surprising. Though Israelite worshipers rejoiced in the wonderful way their God answered their prayers (or protested vigorously when he apparently failed to), and even recognized it as a mark of their own distinctiveness among the nations (Deut 4:7), at no time did God ever promise in so many words to do for Israel *whatever they might ask of him* in prayer (hence the newness of the promise Jesus made to his disciples to this effect). Yet here Solomon asks exactly that for the "foreigner who does not belong to your people Israel." Solomon asks God to do for foreigners what God had not even guaranteed to do for Israel. And the consideration with which Solomon seeks to persuade God to do that is equally impressive: so that the knowledge and fear of the Lord should spread to *all the peoples of the earth*. Though Abraham is not mentioned, we can picture him nodding in agreement.

In the second text (1 Kings 8:60-61), Solomon is addressing the people, not God. But his concern is the same. This time, however, we notice the strong connection between mission and ethics—the mission of God to be known to all peoples and the ethical condition that Israel must live in obedience to God, just

---

[10]Simon J. DeVries, *1 Kings,* Word Biblical Commentary 12 (Waco, Tex.: Word, 1985), p. 126.

as Abraham did. The dynamic connection here is the same as in Genesis 18:18-
19; 22:16-18; 26:4-5.

2 Kings 19:19. "Now, O LORD our God, deliver us from his hand, so that all
kingdoms on earth may know that you alone, O LORD, are God."

This is Hezekiah's prayer, seeking to motivate God to deliver Israel from the
Assyrians by reminding him of the universal acknowledgement of YHWH's sole
deity that will result. It is basically the same, only on a greater scale, as the confidence of young David facing Goliath.

The psalms. In Israel's worship we find the richest expressions of their faith
and theology, their hopes, fears, and visions of the future. There are many
psalms that refer to the nations in one way or another, and we will look at some
of them more systematically in chapter fourteen. Here our attention is only on
those that include phrases which express the universality of Israel's expectation,
phrases which deliberately or unselfconsciously echo the language of God's
promise to Abraham.

Psalm 22:27-28.

> All the ends of the earth
>   will remember and turn to the LORD,
> and all the families of the nations
>   will bow down before him,
> for dominion belongs to the LORD
>   and he rules over the nations.

This universal affirmation stands out in a psalm in which the first half expresses the most intense suffering of the worshiper. But out of that experience,
he comes to praise God for his expected deliverance (vv. 22-24). Then, as so
often in the psalms, the individual concerns of the worshiper suddenly broaden
out on to a much wider horizon. From the depth of personal suffering he moves
to a breadth of faith that encompasses polar opposites: the poor (v. 26) and the
rich (v. 29), those who have already died (v. 29) and those not yet even born
(vv. 30-31). The saving work of God will thus embrace all classes in society and
all generations in history. In the midst of this comes the echo of Abrahamic universality in verse 27, using both of the terms found in the Genesis texts: "all the
families *[mišpĕḥōt]* of the nations *[gôyim]*."

When we remember that Jesus died with the first and last lines of this psalm
on his lips (from "My God, my God, why have you forsaken me" to "It is finished" = "He [God] has done it"), we can see the christological connection between the two halves of the psalm. Otherwise they are so jarringly different in
tone that many commentators have had difficulty believing the psalm is a unity

and have exercised some critical surgery on it. But Jesus found in the first half of the psalm the words and metaphors that so vividly described his own actual sufferings, and found in the second half the assurance that his death would not be in vain. For as the rest of the New Testament makes clear, it would be through his death and resurrection that God would open the way for the universal worship of all the nations to become a reality. For this reason, a christological reading of the psalm connects it both backward to the Abrahamic promise it embodies and forward to the missional universality it anticipates.

Psalm 47:9.

> The nobles of the nations assemble
> as the people of the God of Abraham,
> for the kings of the earth belong to God;
> he is greatly exalted.

This psalm begins on a universal note, inviting "all the nations" *(kōl hāʿammîm)* to clap in praise of YHWH (Ps 47:2). The original context of the psalm may perhaps have been an occasion of celebration after military victory, in which representatives of the conquered nations are required to join in the worship of YHWH, the victorious God. This might give a straightforward historical meaning to verse 9—the leaders of the conquered nations on some unspecified occasion have been assembled with the victorious Israelites to do their homage to Israel's God.[11] However, its inclusion in the Psalter gives it significance beyond such a limited hypothetical occasion and endows it with an eschatological perspective.

The second line of verse 9 is remarkable, if we can take the Masoretic Text as it stands. It simply reads "The leaders of the nations gather, the people of the God of Abraham." This implies an identification of the leaders of the nations with Israel. Because YHWH is king over all the earth, so that all the kings of the earth belong ultimately to him, the psalmist can take a huge leap and envision the nations actually becoming one with the people of Abraham's God. So they gather together as that people to worship that God. Critical emendation has suggested inserting "with" before "the people,"[12] slightly weakening the effect and preserving the distinction: "the leaders of the peoples gather *with* the people of the God of Abraham." But even if this were the correct reading, it is still making

---

[11]This is suggested by Peter C. Craigie, *Psalms 1—50,* Word Biblical Commentary 19 (Waco, Tex.: Word, 1983), pp. 348-50.

[12]I.e., insertingʿim beforeʿam, and assuming that it may have dropped out by haplography. The LXX has read the word as if pointed ʿim anyway, rendering the phrase "with the God of Abraham."

a noteworthy statement about the faith of Israel that ultimately the reign of God over all the earth will be a cause for applauding praise among all the nations. "Israel doesn't rejoice in its unique status but, rather, that her God has become king over all the earth and that the representatives of the peoples gather together as the people of Israel's God. The world becomes one in the oneness of Israel's God."[13]

Psalm 67:1-2.

> May God be gracious to us and bless us
> and make his face shine upon us,
>
> *Selah*
>
> that your ways may be known on earth,
> your salvation among all nations.

Some Israelite worshiper, doubtless having heard the Aaronic blessing many times from the lips of priests (Num 6:22-27), decided to turn it into a prayer. The opening two lines unmistakeably recall Numbers 6:25. But he was not content to leave it as a prayer for himself or for Israel. He turns the blessing inside out and directs it outward to the nations, praying that the blessings of the knowledge and salvation of God, hitherto enjoyed uniquely by Israel, should be showered on "all nations" and "all peoples" so that they too would joyfully praise God. Several key things are combined in this psalm:

- experiencing blessing so that others should be blessed
- the just rule of God and the nations' ready submission to his guidance
- spiritual blessing and material harvest of the land
- the particular (God will bless us) and the universal (all the ends of the earth will fear him)

All of these point to a strongly Abrahamic undercurrent in the theology of the psalmist.[14]

Psalm 72:17.

> May his name endure for ever,
> may it continue as long as the sun.

---

[13]James Muilenburg, "Abraham and the Nations: Blessing and World History," *Interpretation* 19 (1965): 393.

[14]"This psalm seems to involve two major subjects: blessing and the spread of life-giving knowledge of Yahweh to the people of the earth." Marvin E. Tate, *Psalms 51—100,* Word Biblical Commentary 20 (Dallas: Word, 1990), p. 158. Though Tate does not observe the Abrahamic bass line beneath this melodic duet.

> All nations will be blessed through him,
>   and they will call him blessed.

The allusion to the Abrahamic covenant is unmistakeable here. I mentioned in relation to 2 Samuel 7 that there are thematic connections between Abraham and David. Here they are extended to the king in the line of David, the object of this prayer. The prayer combines the *creational* blessings of fruitfulness and abundance with the *covenantal* blessings of justice and righteousness (both of which we have seen to be included in the Abrahamic tradition). As a result, the kingly figure is not only the object of universal submission ("All kings will bow down to him / and all nations will serve him" [Ps 72:11]) but also the object of prayers for blessing ("May people ever pray for him / and bless him all day long" [Ps 72:15]). The prayer that "his name may endure for ever" echoes God's promise regarding Abraham's name. And the affirmation of universal and mutual blessing in verse 17 ("be blessed" and "call him blessed") is equally clearly Abrahamic. The final verse of the psalm celebrates the ultimate universality of God's mission within creation that "the whole earth be filled with his glory" (Ps 72:19).

Setting this psalm alongside 2 Samuel 7, we can see that the purpose of God's covenant with David and his house fits within the wider framework of the purpose of God's covenant with Abraham. God's mission is that all the nations of the earth should count themselves blessed through Abraham and his seed, Israel. At a historical level the monarchy within Israel must fit within that broader mission of Israel itself, in the same way as the Mosaic covenant did (as we will see in chap. 11). But in a more eschatological sense it will be the reign of God himself that will bring about the full restoration of all that God intends for humanity within creation. And of that reign, the Davidic king in Zion becomes the model and messianic prototype. The universal blessing of the nations (as promised to Abraham) will come about through the universal reign of God and his anointed (as promised to David [cf. Ps 2]), whom the New Testament identifies as Jesus of Nazareth.

The opening words of the New Testament take on even richer significance, then, as we embark there on the story of "the genesis of Jesus the Messiah, the son of David, the son of Abraham" (Mt 1:1, author's translation). Here, in every possible way, we are being introduced to a person and a story of *universal* significance, the story of one who inherits and embodies both Abrahamic and Davidic promise. He then is also the one who, at the end of Matthew's Gospel, passes on the missional task to Abraham's spiritual heirs, the Messiah's disciples.

Psalm 86:9.

> All the nations you have made
>> will come and worship before you, O Lord;
>> they will bring glory to your name.

Although the point being made here is similar to those above, the context in which it stands contrasts considerably with the previous text. Whereas Psalm 72 is a deliberate and extensive piece of acclamatory theologizing around the Davidic monarchy, Psalm 86 (like Ps 22) is a cry of personal struggle in a time of opposition and danger. In a bid to motivate God to hear and answer him, the psalmist appeals to the knowledge of God he has from the exodus traditions (vv. 6 and 15 allude to Ex 34:6, while v. 8 echoes Ex 15:11) and here also to the Genesis tradition of "all nations." The precise language of blessing is not used, but it was clearly understood in Israel that worship was a *response* to God's blessing (not a means of manipulating it for one's own benefit). So the assumption of our text is that the nations will come to worship and glorify YHWH *because they will have already experienced his saving blessing.*

The subtext, then, of the implied logic in the psalmist's appeal is that if all the nations are going to have something to praise God for, it should not be too difficult for God to sort out the psalmist's personal problems and give him a more immediate cause for praise (Ps 86:12). The psalmists were not opposed to a spot of realized eschatology. Their challenge to God was "if this is what you intend ultimately to do for the whole earth, an advance deposit in relation to this particular crisis would not come amiss. Now would be good."

The Abrahamic promise thus becomes not just a majestic vista of the ultimate mission of God but a very potent engine of personal hopefulness in the immediate saving power of God. The combination of appeal to the exodus (looking back) and the promise to Abraham (looking forward) produced a powerful appeal for help in the present. "God if you did that in the past, and are going to do that in the future, then why not repeat the past and anticipate the future here and now in the present?"

Psalm 145:8-12.

> The LORD is gracious and compassionate,
>> slow to anger and rich in love.
> The LORD is good to all;
>> he has compassion on all he has made.
>
> All you have made will praise you, O LORD;
>> your saints will extol you.

They will tell of the glory of your kingdom
  and speak of your might,
so that all men may know of your mighty acts
  and the glorious splendor of your kingdom.

Universality breathes through this wonderful psalm. The word *all* or *every* in Hebrew *(kōl)* occurs seventeen times like a chiming bell, from "every day" in verse 2, to "every creature" in verse 21. It is worth reading the psalm to count each occurrence and marvel at the incredible range of all these affirmations.

Once again we find an Israelite psalmist drawing on the great traditional language of Israel's faith, and then universalizing it.[15] This is clearest in the transition from verse 8 to verse 9. Verse 8 virtually quotes YHWH's self-description at Mount Sinai (Ex 34:6). In that context it was Israel who had just experienced the truth of these words (and had most needed to), and it was to Israel (through Moses) that they were spoken. But verse 9 immediately universalizes it: "The LORD is good *to all;* / he has compassion *on all* he has made." This is then repeated with variations at verses 13 and 17, with many other aspects of the great affirmation being touched on in the surrounding verses, as applied to needy humans and hungry animals.

The drama of Exodus (God's saving, faithful, generous, providing love) is being played out in the amphitheater of Genesis (the whole breadth of the created order, from all humanity to "every living thing"). The only exception in this litany to the universality of God's love are the wicked who choose, in their wickedness, to refuse it. Their destiny is destruction (Ps 145:20b). The half-verse acceptance of this sad truth matches the recognition within the Abrahamic promise that even against the background of a fivefold repetition of God's desire to bless, there would still be "the one who disdains you" (Gen 12:3) whom God would curse. The curse and final destruction of the enemies of God's people, of those who choose to remain wicked in the face of the profligate outpouring of his love, is of course a sad but necessary dimension of God's own protection of the love that longs to bring blessing to all. It is the implication of one part of the Abrahamic covenant.

The prophets.
Isaiah 19:24-25. "In that day Israel will be the third, along with Egypt and Assyria, a blessing on the earth. The LORD Almighty will bless them, saying, 'Blessed be Egypt my people, Assyria my handiwork, and Israel my inheritance.' "

---

[15]The same universalizing dynamic happens in Psalm 33. Note the transition between vv. 4-5a and v. 5b, and between v. 12 and vv. 13-14.

Personally, I find this one of the most breathtaking pronouncements of any prophet, and certainly one of the missiologically most significant texts in the Old Testament. Detailed exegesis of the chapter can wait until chapter fourteen. But for our immediate purpose here, we take note of the Abrahamic allusions. The identity of Israel will be merged with that of Egypt and Assyria, such that the Abahamic promise is not only fulfilled *in* them but *through* them.

The two verbal references to the text of Genesis 12:1-3 are (1) the use of the piel of *brk* in verse 25 ("The LORD Almighty will bless them," matching the same form as "I will bless you" in Gen 12:2b), and (2) the phrase "will be a blessing" (*hyh* with *bĕrākâ* [v. 24]). In Genesis 12:2d this combination is in the form of an imperative with intention ("be a blessing" or "so that you will be a blessing"). In Isaiah 19:24 it is a prophetic affirmation about Israel, Egypt and Assyria combined (they will together "be a blessing in the midst of the earth").

So these foreign nations come not only to *experience* blessing but to *be* "a blessing on the earth." In other words, both dynamic movements in God's word to Abraham are at work here. The recipients of the Abrahamic blessing become the agents of it. The principle that those who are blessed are to be the means of blessing others is not confined to Israel alone, as if Israel would forever be the exclusive transmitters of a blessing that could only be passively received by the rest from their hand. No, the Abrahamic promise is a self-replicating gene. Those who receive it are immediately transformed into those whose privilege and mission it is to pass it on to others.

The identity of Israel is already being redefined and extended in the direction that the New Testament will bring to climactic clarity in Christ. The multinational nature of that community of people through whom God plans to bless all nations of the earth is here already prefigured. So also is the similarly self-replicating nature of Christ's mandate to his disciples to go and reproduce their own discipleship among the nations, "teaching them to observe all that I have commanded you." Or, as we might add, "blessing them as the Lord has blessed you." Yet again, the Abrahamic promise can stake its claim to be not only the "gospel in advance" but even more so, the Great Commission in advance.

Once again we find that a missiological reading of a text like this points us first backward to the Abrahamic promise and the inherent universality that it programmed into the genes of Israel, then forward to the messianic fulfillment in Jesus Christ, and then forward yet again to its missional implications for those who are disciples from all nations to be agents of blessing to all nations, "a blessing on the earth."

Isaiah 25:6-8.

> On this mountain the LORD Almighty will prepare
>   a feast of rich food for all peoples,
> a banquet of aged wine—
>   the best of meats and finest of wines.
> On this mountain he will destroy
>   the shroud that enfolds all peoples,
> the sheet that covers all nations;
>   he will swallow up death for ever.
> The Sovereign LORD will wipe away the tears
>   from all faces;
> he will remove the disgrace of his people
>   from all the earth.

Although the connection with the Abrahamic promise is much weaker here than in the previous text, consisting only of the universalizing phrases "all peoples" and "all the earth," it does have another dimension that links it to the Genesis tradition—the promise of the final destruction of death itself. Genesis 3—11 certainly portrays death as the primary result of sin, even if there is a mystery over the precise link between God's warning that it would be and the actual way it entered human experience. The paired expressions "curse and death" and "blessing and life" are familiar (e.g., the strong use of them in Deut 11; 30). The longing for God to lift the curse is a longing for human life to be released from the sweat and toil on a cursed earth that ends finally in death, as is shown by Lamech's (sadly futile) hope at the naming of his son, Noah, after the long line of death in Genesis 5. So the reader of Genesis 12:1-3 would certainly know that if God's blessing is ultimately to remove God's curse, then it must deal with the problem of death. This word in Isaiah, then, assures us that this will ultimately be the case. And although the closing line turns this into a promise for "his people" (the ending of their disgrace throughout the world), the body of the vision applies to humanity as a whole in the double use of "all peoples" and "all nations" in v. 7.

Though this text may not have been in his mind, Paul certainly connects the promise of God through Abraham with the triumph of resurrection life over the reign of death in the world, a triumph that (as his gospel so resolutely insisted) is available to people of all nations (see Rom 4:16-17; 5:12-21).

Isaiah 45:22-23.

> Turn to me and be saved,
>   all you ends of the earth;

for I am God, and there is no other.
By myself I have sworn,
　　my mouth has uttered in all integrity
　　a word that will not be revoked:
Before me every knee will bow;
　　by me every tongue will swear.
They will say of me, "In the LORD alone
　　are righteousness and strength."

This classic text expressing God's appeal to the nations comes in the midst of those pulsating chapters of Isaiah in which the same nations and their gods are comprehensively defeated "in court" and in the arena of the control and interpretation of history (Is 40—48). Yet God's ultimate purpose is not the destruction of the nations but their salvation. That, however, can only come about when they turn to him, for he, YHWH, is the only saving God available to them, by virtue of the simple fact that he is the only God, period.

So the invitation here stands in line with the great Abrahamic anticipation of the blessing of the nations, but the connection is somewhat stronger than that. "By myself I have sworn" (v. 23) is a precise verbal repetition of the words that opened the final and most definitive announcement by God of his covenant with Abraham, in Genesis 22:16. That great oath on God's own self is here uttered afresh, in a way that explains further how it can be that "all nations on earth will be blessed." It will happen only as people turn in submission to YHWH, acknowledging him to be sole deity and the exclusive source of righteousness (probably equivalent here to salvation) and strength. We need hardly add that it was this same universality and uniqueness that is unhesitatingly attributed to Jesus by Paul in Philippians 2:10-11 (see p. 108).

Isaiah 48:18-19.

If only you had paid attention to my commands,
　　your peace would have been like a river,
　　your righteousness like the waves of the sea.
Your descendants would have been like the sand,
　　your children like its numberless grains;
their name would never be cut off
　　nor destroyed from before me.

The echo of Abraham is unmistakable here in the mention of the numberless grains of sand, the promised extent of his progeny. It is also notable that the blessing Israel could have been enjoying by this time is not merely numerical growth but the qualitative and relational blessings of peace and righteousness.

In its immediate context the longing probably refers to the growth of national Israel. The fear of the exiles that they might diminish and die out would remain unfounded. But, in the wider context, the very reason why God would not let Israel perish but, on the contrary, would revive and refertilize them (cf. Is 44:1-5) is that God intended them to be the means of a wider multiplication—the multinational growth of God's people among all nations. The Abahamic promise of a "great nation" and of "all nations" lies under the surface.

The tone of this passage is divine wistfulness. God is indulging in the very human emotion of "If only . . . then imagine what could be." The reality sadly belied the dream. Or rather, the dream was not yet a reality, because of Israel's continuing rebellion and disobedience. That is how the chapter begins (48:1-4). This highlights again the moral dimension of the Abrahamic covenant. Just as God's promise came to include within itself Abraham's faith and obedience, so for Israel, its fulfillment required the same covenantal response from them. But it had not been forthcoming.

So the link between ethics and mission is here found in an unusual key—the divine "if only." The effect is to show how close that link lies to the heart of God. God longs for innumerable offspring for Abraham (missional growth), but he also longs for the existing offspring of Abraham to walk ethically in the way Abraham modeled (missional obedience). We might reflect on what divine frustration there must be with a church that sometimes lacks both, or with a church that even in its missional enthusiasm for Abrahamic growth in numbers ignores God's demand for Abrahamic growth in ethical commitment to righteousness and justice.

Isaiah 60:12. "For the nation or kingdom that will not serve you will perish; / it will be utterly ruined."

This verse comes in the wider context of God's promises to Zion in Isaiah 60—62. The prophet envisions the nations of the world coming over to Israel (personified in Zion) and bringing their riches as tribute. At the same time, Israel is portrayed as priest for the nations, receiving their gifts on YHWH's behalf, as it were, and dispensing the blessing of God in return. This is the role that Exodus 19:5-6 had first articulated for Israel among the nations.

Here, however, in the midst of the concentric poem of Isaiah 60, it is possible that one element from the Abrahamic covenant makes an impact. God had declared that he would bless those who bless Abraham and his seed, but he would curse any who despised Abraham. Those nations, therefore, that bless Zion and Zion's God will find themselves blessed by him. Those who refuse to do so, by contrast, will suffer the curse of God in perishing ruin. It appears that the prophet puts Zion itself in the Abrahamic position. Zion of course, even in these

texts, has become more than the physical city of Jerusalem. It has become a term
for the wider people of God and indeed for the very presence and salvation of
God himself. So again we find the Abrahamic principle of discrimination oper-
ative: Those who willingly surrender to all that God has done in and for Zion
will find blessing. Those who resist and refuse, exclude themselves from the
sphere of blessing and are left with no alternative but destruction.

Verse 12, then is

> the pivotal statement that the nation which does not serve Zion will perish. . . .
> Thus, the poem centres on the Abrahamic theme that those who bless him will be
> blessed and those who curse him will be cursed (Gen. 12:3; 27:29). The coming of
> glorious Zion is the consummation of the world-wide purposes of God. . . . This
> verse is the dark pivot of the whole poem. Zion really is the key to international
> destiny, the final form of the Abrahamic system.[16]

Jeremiah 4:1-2.

> "If you will return, O Israel, return to me,"
> > declares the LORD.
> "If you put your detestable idols out of my sight
> > and no longer go astray;
> and if in a truthful, just and righteous way
> > you swear, 'As surely as the LORD lives,'
> then the nations will be blessed by him
> > and in him they will glory."

Jeremiah was appointed a "prophet to the nations" (Jer 1:5), and he has many
things to say concerning them, including God's utter fairness in dealing with
them, whether in judgment or mercy (Jer 12:14-17; 18:7-10), which we will look
at in chapter fourteen. Here, however, he links the destiny of *nations* directly to
the response of *Israel* to God. The appeal for Israel genuinely to repent is familiar enough from the surrounding chapters of Jeremiah's early ministry, when
he seems to have passionately believed that they could be induced to do so.
The emphasis on the truly spiritual and ethical nature of such repentance is also
familiar: it must involve the radical rejection of all other gods and idols, and it
must combine genuine worship of YHWH with social integrity and justice. So far,

---

[16]J. A. Motyer, *The Prophecy of Isaiah* (Leicester, U.K.: Inter-Varsity Press; Downers Grove, Ill.:
InterVarsity Press, 1993), pp. 493, 496. Eliya Mohol studied the Abrahamic nature of the Zion
theme in the whole of Isaiah 56—66 and also affirms the pivotal nature of this verse in the
way the possible destinies of the nations are described in these texts. Eliya Mohol, *The Covenantal Rationale for Membership in the Zion Community Envisaged in Isaiah 56—66* (Ph.D.
diss., All Nations Christian College, 1998).

we might say, we have heard this before in all the law and the prophets.

Previously, however, we might have expected the conditional phrases of verses 1-2a to be followed by an assurance that God would withdraw his threat of judgment against Israel. If only *Israel* will truly repent, then God will not have to punish *them*. In what Jeremiah actually does say, however, it feels as if he almost impatiently brushes that aside as self-evident ("Yes of course, if *Israel* repents, *Israel* will be blessed") and jumps ahead to a much wider perspective altogether. If Israel will return to their proper place of covenant loyalty and obedience, then God can get on with the job of blessing the *nations,* which is what Israel was called into existence for in the first place. "It becomes clear that true repentance on Israel's part would have far-reaching consequences not merely for Israel but also for mankind in general."[17]

The Abrahamic echo in the final two lines is very clear, but the logic of the whole sentence is remarkable.[18] God's mission to the nations is being hindered because of Israel's continuing spiritual and ethical failure. Let Israel return to *their* mission (to be the people of YHWH, worshiping him exclusively and living according to his moral demands), and God can return to *his* mission—blessing the nations.

This interesting perspective sheds fresh light on the full scale and depth of God's problem with Israel. Rebellious Israel were not just an affront to God; they were also a hindrance to the nations. Ezekiel will make the same point even more sharply to Israel in exile. Not surprisingly, then (and for both prophets), the restoration of Israel to covenant obedience and thereby to covenant blessing (peace, fruitfulness, abundance) will make a corresponding impact on the nations also (cf. Jer 33:6-9; Ezek 36:16-36).

> The turning of Israel, the dominant motif of the whole liturgy, will mean that the nations will bless themselves (*hithpa'el*) in Yahweh. That will be the people's highest reward; they could not ask for more. The turning of Israel to their true self is inextricably bound with the confessions and praises of the nations.[19]

Zechariah 8:13. "As you have been an object of cursing among the nations, O Judah and Israel, so will I save you, and you will be a blessing."

---

[17] J. A. Thompson, *The Book of Jeremiah,* New International Commentary on the Old Testament (Grand Rapids: Eerdmans, 1980), p. 213.

[18] "The consequence of repentance and reorientation of life is the implementation of God's promise to Abraham. . . . The restoration of covenant thus will benefit not only Judah but the other nations that derive new life from that covenant." Walter Brueggemann, *To Pluck up, to Tear Down: A Commentary on the Book of Jeremiah 1—25,* International Theological Commentary (Grand Rapids: Eerdmans; Edinburgh: Handsel, 1988), pp. 46-47.

[19] Muilenburg, "Abraham and the Nations," p. 396.

The NIV here interprets the literal balance of the phrases "as you were a curse among the nations, . . . so . . . you will be a blessing." The exile had resulted in Israel being regarded (and indeed described by their prophets) as cursed by their God. Thus they became the subject (not so much the object) of the nations cursing, that is, the comparison one would make in order to declare curse on someone else ("May you be cursed like Israel"). The reversal of this is that God will so save and restore them, and bless them so abundantly (Zech 8:12) that they will be seen to be blessed and therefore the subject of blessing ("May you be blessed like Israel").[20]

It seems very probable that the Abrahamic duality of blessing and curse is at work in this saying, since it is oriented toward the nations and their destiny. In the surrounding context Zechariah has several very hopeful words for the ultimate ingathering and salvation of the nations (e.g., Zech 2:10-11; 8:20-22; 14:9, 16).

What we have found, then, in this survey of Old Testament texts, is that the thrust toward universality is more of a feature of the faith, worship and expectations of Israel than we may have thought. Abraham himself may not figure greatly in the rest of the major Old Testament texts, but like Abel, "he being dead yet speaketh" (Heb 11:4 KJV). The legacy of God's words to him lived on—not only in Israel's prime worldview certainties (their own election, the gift of the land, the covenantal bond between them and YHWH) but also in that haunting bottom line—"through you all nations will find blessing." Somehow, sometime, there would be universal effects from these very particular realities. For YHWH, the God of Israel, is also the God of all creation, to whom belong the whole earth and all its nations. Nothing less could adequately define the scope of God's mission of blessing. No smaller framework can adequately encompass a biblical theology of mission either.

We will have much more to consider when we return to the theme of the nations in chapter fourteen. At this point, however, we must press on to see how the New Testament takes up specifically this theme of the universality of God's saving purpose through Abraham and his seed. We are not, on this occasion,

---

[20]Gordon Wenham uses this text as support for arguing that the expression in Gen 12:2, "be a blessing," means that Israel is to become such a subject of blessing. *Blessing* is taken as simply a form of words, as in the expression, "say a blessing before the meal." This would imply that the phrase means much the same as the reflexive understanding of "in you the nations will bless themselves," i.e., "May you be like Israel" would be what it means to "be a blessing." However, this seems to me unnecessarily to weaken the intention of the imperative in the Genesis text. While agreeing that this is the most probable sense of "you will be a blessing" in Zech 8:13, it does not seem to fit so well in Is 19:24, where Israel, Egypt and Assyria are said to "be a blessing in the midst of the earth." See *Genesis 1-15,* Word Biblical Commentary 1 (Waco, Tex.: Word, 1987), p. 276.

examining all the New Testament has to say about the Jews and Gentiles in general. We will take that up in chapter fifteen. Our focus here is on texts where there is either a direct or indirect use of the Abraham tradition in the direction of the universality of God mission.

Universality—New Testament Echoes of Abraham

The Synoptic Gospels and Acts. *Matthew.* We have noted already how Matthew introduces Jesus as "the son of David, the son of Abraham" (Mt 1:1).[21] By combining the Abrahamic and Davidic covenant reminders in this way, Matthew highlights the universal significance of the one who would, as son of Abraham, fulfill what was promised for Abraham's seed (blessing for all nations), and as son of David, would exercise the prophesied messianic reign over all the earth. By inverting the historical order "Matthew 1:1 moves from Jesus to Abraham, and 1:2-16 moves from Abraham to Jesus, with the result that the name Abraham appears juxtaposed to itself (vv. 1-2). This literary pivot on Abraham turns the spotlight on him."[22] Verse 17 then summarizes the genealogy to make the point even clearer. Jesus is the goal of the story that flows through Abraham and David and includes God's promises to both.

Matthew 8:11 is the foremost among several places in his Gospel where Matthew indicates the wider significance for the nations of the work of Jesus. Astonished by the faith of the Gentile Roman centurion, a quality of faith that he has not found matched in Israel (cf. the same language in Mk 6:6), Jesus declares, "Many will come from the east and the west, and will take their places at the feast with Abraham, Isaac and Jacob in the kingdom of heaven." Jesus here makes several very significant moves.

First, he anticipates Paul in making *faith* (which in the story clearly means faith in Jesus) rather than *ethnicity* (physical descent from Abraham) the defin-

---

[21]I have not included John's Gospel in this survey because, although its universality is self-evident in the prominent use of "the world" as the object of God's love, as the scope of Christ's redemptive action and as the destination of God's sending of Christ and Christ's sending of his disciples, it is does not seem to be explicitly linked to the Abrahamic promise (though doubtless this was as fundamental to the theology of the author of the Fourth Gospel as to any other Jew of his day). The word *nations* (plural) does not occur in John (though Jn 11:52 does speak of ingathering of others beyond Israel). And the one chapter where Abraham occurs (Jn 8) focuses on Abraham as a contrast to the attitude and behavior of Jesus' opponents and as a means of affirming the divine claims of Jesus. So the missiological significance of the chapter lies in its christology rather than by reference to the universality of God's promise to Abraham.

[22]Robert L. Brawley, "Reverberations of Abrahamic Covenant Traditions in the Ethics of Matthew," in *Realia Dei*, ed. Prescott H. Williams and Theodore Hiebert (Atlanta: Scholars Press, 1999), p. 32.

ing criterion for membership in the kingdom of God.

Second, he restores the theme of the great messianic banquet to its properly universal extent. The idea of an eschatological banquet goes back to Isaiah 25:6, which is being prepared by God "for all peoples." But Jewish apocalyptic tradition by the time of Jesus had narrowed the guest list to Israelites and appointed the patriarchs as hosts. Jesus endorses the latter but says that if Abraham, Isaac and Jacob are the hosts, then the invitations will go as widely as God's original promise to them, that is, to all nations.

Third, he rather shockingly uses texts that originally spoke of God gathering in Israelites from exile, "from the east and the west" (Ps 107:3; Is 43:5-6; 49:12), and implies that they will be fulfilled when Gentiles like this centurion arrive at the banquet, whereas some of the original guest list will find themselves excluded for their lack of believing response to him.

Fourth, he implicitly abolishes the food laws that had symbolized the distinction between Israel and the nations. Those laws meant that Jews would not sit at table with Gentiles. Yet Jesus here pictures Gentiles sitting down with the patriarchs themselves, and not an eyebrow is raised. Again, by implication, Jesus antipicates the universalizing, barrier-breaking thrust of the gospel of the kingdom, based on faith, which Peter came to realize through his encounter with Cornelius and which Paul spent his life explaining and defending.

Finally, Matthew closes his Gospel by making quite explicit what the opening of his Gospel had implied—the universality of Jesus Christ and the worldwide extent of the demand for discipleship. The language of the Great Commission is drawn more from Deuteronomy than from Genesis, but it is here in the words of the risen Jesus that we are given the means by which the original Abrahamic commission can be fulfilled, to "Go . . . and be a blessing . . . and all the nations on earth will find blessing through you" (Gen 12:1-3).

Luke-Acts. Possibly it was because Luke knew that he, as a Gentile himself, was personally a recipient of the blessing of Abraham through Christ that he seems to have had a soft spot for Abraham.

He opens his Gospel with a series of songs that are saturated in Old Testament allusion. The songs of Mary and of Zechariah both thank God for the renewal of his mercy on his people Israel, and both see this as faithfulness to his promise to Abraham (Lk 1:55, 73). Whereas the focus in those songs is very much on the salvation and restoration of *Israel,* Luke quickly moves on to a universal understanding of the saving significance for *the nations* of what is taking place in the birth of Jesus. Simeon takes the infant Jesus in his arms and sees in him exactly what his name meant: "the Lord is salvation." But he recognizes that this is a salvation prepared for "all people," and so Simeon beautifully summarizes the double significance of Christ for Israel and for the nations (Lk 2:29-32) in anticipation of the risen Jesus doing exactly the same at the end of the Gospel (Lk 24:46-47). Then Luke provides his own theological interpretation of the preparatory mission of John the Baptist by quoting the familiar words of Isaiah 40:3-5, ending in the universal expectation: "all mankind will see God's salvation" (Lk 3:4-6).

Following that, Luke portrays Satan attempting to subvert the universal mission of Jesus by deceptively pulling it over into his own domain. Jesus is offered "all the kingdoms of the world" and "all their authority and splendor" in exchange for worshiping Satan (Lk 4:5-7). "The devil's temptation to give Jesus all the kingdoms of the world parades as the fulfillment of God's promise to give Abraham and his descendants the whole world."[23] But as we know, this universal reign was already promised to the messianic Son (e.g., Ps 2:8-9) and in another sense already belonged to him anyway. The temptation seems to be that Jesus should capitalize on what was rightfully his by enjoying all that international power, wealth and glory *for himself*, whereas the whole point of the Abrahamic promise was that it should be for the *blessing of others*. Thus Luke not only shows Jesus resisting the temptation decisively and in the spirit of Deuteronomic exclusive loyalty to God, but also gives us the true significance of Abrahamic universality in Acts 3:25-26.

> The devil's temptations in Luke are all set up as tests of whether or not God will bless Jesus for his own benefit or not. That is, the devil's Christology . . . embraces an expectation that God will act for Jesus' particular interest. But God's promise to Abraham is to bless all the families of the earth—not Jesus for his own sake, even as a beloved son, but all the families of the earth.[24]

In four of his narratives Luke makes an explicit connection with Abraham. All of them illustrate the healing, transforming or restoring power of God and seem designed to affirm that this is part of what receiving the blessing of Abraham entails. All of them relate to characters who were in some way excluded from normal life in the community of Israel by demonic bondage, poverty, social contempt or illness. These four narratives are

- Luke 13:10-16. The healing on the sabbath of a crippled woman. Jesus describes her as in bondage to Satan but nevertheless "a daughter of Abraham" and therefore a proper candidate for healing on the sabbath.
- Luke 16:19-31. The story of the poor beggar Lazarus, who on death is carried

---

[23]Robert L. Brawley, "For Blessing All Families of the Earth: Covenant Traditions in Luke-Acts," *Currents in Theology and Mission* 22 (1995): 21.
[24]Ibid., p. 22.

to Abraham's side, where his sufferings are over. In this story Jesus employs Abraham as a character, whose climactic words point to the significance of the Law and the Prophets as the God-given and unmistakeably clear instructions on how people should exercise justice and mercy. Abraham here testifies to what he himself (according to Genesis) had observed in his own obedient walk with God. The irony in the story is that the rich man might have been thought by his contemporaries to be manifestly enjoying the blessing of Abraham. But not so. He is not walking as Abraham did, nor keeping "the way of the LORD by doing what is right and just" (Gen 18:19). So his destiny is to see Abraham but only far away across an unbridgeable gulf.

- Luke 19:1-10. The story of Zacchaeus, the tax collector whose profession (and his extortionate exploitation of it) would have made him unwelcome in any crowd following Jesus. But in his encounter with Jesus, he comes to personal repentance, demonstrated in both adherence to the standards of the law and an even greater act of generosity. In response, Jesus declares him "a son of Abraham" (v. 9). Unlike the rich man in the parable, this real man has now turned to righteousness and to the place of Abrahamic blessing.

- Acts 3:1-25. The healing of the lame man at the temple, through Peter and John, in the name of Jesus. In his message following this healing, Peter not only connects what the people have just witnessed to the story of Jesus but to Abraham. He does this at the beginning of his word ("The God of Abraham, Isaac and Jacob, the God of our fathers, has glorified his servant Jesus" [v. 13]), and then again at the end ("You are heirs of the prophets and of the covenant God made with your fathers. He said to Abraham, 'Through your offspring all peoples on earth will be blessed.' When God raised up his servant, he sent him first to you to bless you by turning each of you from your wicked ways" [Acts 3:25-26]).

"The healing of the lame man is a concrete case of God's blessing of all the families of the earth. . . . [It is] a blessing that is potentially available to Peter's audience."[25] Yes, these Israelite spectators were nationally children and heirs of Abraham. Yet the only way for them to enter into the blessing of Abraham is the same way as for all—including the Gentiles—repentance and faith in the name of Jesus. So, in his even longer defense the following day, Peter draws the conclusion that is as universal as it is uncompromising, "Salvation is found in no one else, for there is no other name under heaven given to men by which we must be saved" (Acts 4:12).

---

[25]Ibid., pp. 25-26.

Finally, Luke ends his Gospel on the same universal note as Matthew ended his, but with even more explicit reference back to the Scriptures of the Old Testament.

> Then he opened their minds so they could understand the Scriptures. He told them, "This is what is written: The Christ will suffer and rise from the dead on the third day, and repentance and forgiveness of sins will be preached in his name to all nations, beginning at Jerusalem. (Lk 24:45-47)

This text provides the hermeneutical compass for the way disciples of Jesus must read the Old Testament Scriptures, that is, both messianically and missiologically. But in the light of all we have now surveyed of the great theme of universality drawn from the Abrahamic tradition, and in the light of Luke's own manifest interest in Abraham, we can undoubtedly feel the pulse of that promise in these great phrases. For how else will the blessing of Abraham come to all nations than by the message of repentance and forgiveness in the name of Jesus the Christ, crucified and risen?

Paul. We began chapter six observing the challenge that Paul's understanding of the universal availability of the gospel posed to his fellow Jews. We have now surveyed in this chapter some of the Scriptures on which doubtless Paul himself meditated deeply as he forged his missionary theology and practice. Let's now sample some of the places where Paul articulates the universality of God's mission in terms that recall Abraham, explicitly or simply as part of his "narrative thought world, which was so totally founded on the story of God and Israel in the Old Testament."[26]

Romans 1:5. "Through him [Jesus Christ our Lord] and for his name's sake, we received grace and apostleship to call people from among all the Gentiles to the obedience that comes from faith."

Repeated at the end of the letter to Rome (Rom 16:26), this is one of Paul's defining statements of his apostolic mission. Having already claimed (as he also does in chap. 16) that his gospel was promised through the Scriptures, it is not surprising that the Abrahamic echoes are strong here. First, the phrase "all the Gentiles" is the same phrase (lit. "all the nations," *panta ta ethnē*) that Paul uses in his quotation of Genesis 12:3 in Galatians 3:8. Second, "the obedience of faith" is exactly what Abraham demonstrated in response to God's command and promise. Faith and obedience are the two words that are most definitive of Abraham's walk with God.

---

[26]The phrase "narrative thought world" is borrowed from the title of Ben Witherington's excellent book that fully supports the kind of narrative missiology of both Testaments that I seek to develop in this work, *Paul's Narrative Thought World: The Tapestry of Tragedy and Triumph* (Louisville: Westminster/John Knox, 1994).

So Paul sees Abraham not only (as all Jews did) as the model for what should have been *Israel's* covenantal response to God but also as the model for *all the nations* who would be blessed through him. We can summarize this double message thus: The good news of Jesus is the means by which the nations will be blessed through Paul's missionary apostleship; the faith and obedience of the nations will be the means by which they will enter into that blessing, or indeed in Abrahamic terms, "bless themselves."

Romans 3:29—4:25. Abraham is the central figure in Paul's argument in this section of his letter. Paul's point is to demonstrate that Jews and Gentiles stand on equal footing before God in their access to God's saving righteousness (just as they stand on an equal footing as sinners in chapters 1-2). The dimensions of universality in this passage stem both from the fact that there is only one God, so therefore he must be God of Gentiles as well as of Jews (Rom 3:29-30), and from the designation of Abraham as "father of many nations." He thus becomes "father of all who believe," as he had done prior to his circumcision (Rom 4:11), and "father of us all" (Rom 4:16).

Romans 10:12-13. "For there is no difference between Jew and Gentile—the same Lord is Lord of all and richly blesses all who call on him, for, 'Everyone who calls on the name of the Lord will be saved.'"[27]

If there is only one God, as Paul has affirmed with all his Jewish monotheistic conviction, then there is only one Lord also. The word *Lord* here, of course does double duty, since on the one hand it clearly reflects the LORD, that is, YHWH of Old Testament Israel's covenant. And the text quoted from Joel certainly meant YHWH. But a few verses earlier Paul has said, "If you confess with your mouth, 'Jesus is Lord' . . ." (Rom 10:9), so undoubtedly he is attributing to Jesus here the same universal Lordship as that exercised by YHWH. And by virtue of that, Jesus dispenses what God had promised to Abraham (rich blessing for all), and Jesus saves all who call on his name. The universal "all" and "everyone" to whom the Abrahamic promise now applies draws its validity from the universal Lordship of Christ.

Galatians 3:26-29. "You are all sons of God through faith in Christ Jesus, for all of you who were baptized into Christ have clothed yourselves with Christ. There is neither Jew nor Greek, slave nor free, male nor female, for you are all one in Christ Jesus. If you belong to Christ, then you are Abraham's seed, and heirs according to the promise."

It is clear from the whole body of Paul's writing that he preached and taught

---

[27]I have postponed further reflection on the major chapters Romans 9—11 until chapter fifteen, on the nations in the New Testament.

a message with universal claims: one universal God, one universal Savior, one universal climax to history for the entire creation. Yet it is equally clear that this never evaporated into an abstract or philosophical universality. It was always rooted in the story of Israel and especially in the promise to Abraham. So in the case of the Galatians, it is interesting to see Paul correcting a misunderstanding of the universal Gospel he had been preaching.

Paul had told them that faith in Jesus Christ alone was the universal criterion for acceptance into the people of the one living God. His opponents had misled the Galatians into thinking that that was not enough. They needed to belong to the covenant people of Abraham as well, and the only way to do that was through circumcision and keeping the law of Moses. Paul's answer is emphatically *not to deny* that they need to belong to Abraham but to *assure* them that they already do! The universality of the Abrahamic promise is already theirs if they are in Christ. And for that reason all the old barriers and distinguishing marks of race, social status or gender are no longer valid or relevant. This is truly biblical universality; that is, it is founded on the great story the Bible tells from Abraham to Christ.[28]

> There is clear evidence that while [Paul's] gospel could be expressed in universal terms [—Christ a universal savior who died and rose for all—], this universal message was proclaimed and received within an explicitly Israel-centred framework. The evidence suggests further that Paul led his converts to believe that by receiving this message they were being incorporated into the community to whom the scriptures were addressed, that is, "Israel."[29]

Revelation. The only way to end such a biblical survey is in the final book of the Bible itself. Revelation 4—7 is a comprehensive single vision—a neck-stretching, mind-boggling vision—in which John "sees" the whole universe from the vantage point of God's throne at its center. The meaning of the history of the world is symbolized in a scroll in God's right hand, which none is found worthy to open, except Christ, pictured as the Lamb who was slain. In other words, the cross of Christ is the key to the unfolding purpose of history; or, in terms of our argument here, the unfolding mission of God. Why is Christ worthy to govern history? Because he was slain. And what difference has that made? The song of the living creatures and twenty-four elders explain it for John, and for us.

---

[28]Cf. N. T. Wright, "Gospel and Theology in Galatians," in *Gospel in Paul,* ed. L. Ann Jervis and Peter Richardson (Sheffield, U.K.: Sheffield Academic, 1994).

[29]Terence L. Donaldson, " 'The Gospel That I Proclaim Among the Gentiles' (Gal. 2.2): Universalistic or Israel-Centred?" in *Gospel in Paul,* ed. L. Ann Jervis and Peter Richardson (Sheffield, U.K.: Sheffield Academic Press, 1994), p. 190.

You are worthy to take the scroll
    and to open its seals,
because you were slain,
    and with your blood you purchased men for God
    from every tribe and language and people and nation.
You have made them to be a kingdom and priests to serve our God,
    and they will reign on the earth. (Rev 5:9-10)

This song gives three reasons why *the cross is the key to history.*

- First, it is *redemptive.* People who were lost, defeated, or enslaved in sin have been "purchased" for God. Humanity will not go down the drainpipe of history into the abyss.

- Second, it is *universal.* Those who have been so redeemed will come from "every tribe and language and people and nation."

- Third, it is *victorious.* The Lamb wins! He and his redeemed people will reign on the earth.

The echoes of Old Testament Scripture are clear. The universality of the Abrahamic promise is captured in the list of tribe, language, people and nation. And the specific calling on Israel in Exodus 19:5-6, to be God's kingdom of priests in the midst of all the nations of the whole earth, has now itself been internationalized and projected into an eternal future of serving God (as priests) and reigning on earth (as kings). The rightful place of redeemed humanity is that they are restored to their original status and role within creation: under God and over creation, serving and ruling. This is the wonderful combination of priesthood and kingship that redeemed humanity will exercise in the redeemed creation.

The climax of this vision, with the sixth seal, brings together the 144,000 crowd, representative of the historic twelve tribes of Israel, with the immediately following panorama of that innumerable multinational host of the redeemed, the final fulfillment of what God promised Abraham:

After this I looked and there before me was a great multitude that no one could count, from every nation, tribe, people and language, standing before the throne and in front of the Lamb. They were wearing white robes and were holding palm branches in their hands. And they cried out in a loud voice:

"Salvation belongs to our God,
who sits on the throne,
and to the Lamb." (Rev 7:9-10)

If, when God first called Abraham and designated him and his barren wife in their old age to be the fountainhead of his whole mission to rescue creation and humanity from the woes of Genesis 3—11, we imagined the sharp intake of breath among the astonished heavenly hosts, then in John's vision we are not left merely to our own imagination. For he goes on to tell us:

> All the angels were standing round the throne and around the elders and the four living creatures. They fell down on their faces before the throne and worshiped God, saying:
>
> "Amen! Praise and glory
> and wisdom and thanks and honor
> and power and strength
> be to our God for ever and ever.
> Amen!" (Rev 7:11-12)

And God, in the midst of the resounding praises, will turn to Abraham and say, "There you are. I kept my promise. Mission accomplished."

All the nations in all the Scriptures. Beyond doubt, then, there was a universal purpose in God's election of Abraham, and therefore also a universal dimension to the very existence of Israel. Israel as a people was called into existence because of God's mission to bless the nations and restore his creation.

> Thus, the sense of election to which the texts of the Old Testament bear witness is joined with a universalism potentially capable of embracing all that is human. The God of the historical election of Israel is also the God of cosmic benedictions. The people of Israel, who know themselves to be chosen of God, also see themselves placed amidst nations and a world that are submitted to the governance of that same God. . . . Election does not cut Israel off from the nations. It situates that people in relationship with them.[30]

The sheer breadth of texts surveyed shows that this was not just an afterthought or even just an evolving historical consciousness. It is a mistake, in my view, to speak of the universal dimension in the Old Testament as a late-developing awareness that emerged out of centuries of more narrowminded nationalism.[31] On the contrary, it is found in texts of different historical eras and various canonical genres.

Still less is this universal perspective merely a New Testament imposition on the Old Testament that provides *ex post facto* justification for the innovating early church's missionary outreach. Rather, it is exactly the other way round. It

---

[30]Lucien Legrand, *Unity and Plurality: Mission in the Bible* (Maryknoll, N.Y.: Orbis, 1990), p. 14.

[31]Such an evolutionary view is common in critical scholarship, but it occasionally surfaces elsewhere within a different framework of assumptions, as, e.g., David Filbeck, *Yes, God of the Gentiles Too: The Missionary Message of the Old Testament* (Wheaton, Ill.: Billy Graham Center, 1994), p. 75.

was their awakening to the powerful universalizing thrust of their own Scriptures, in the light of Jesus the Messiah and under the effect of his own teaching, that propelled his first followers (and generations since) in that direction. It was Old Testament universality that drove the New Testament's concept and practice of mission.

The Bible as a whole presents the universal God with a universal mission

- announced to Abraham
- accomplished in anticipation by Christ
- to be completed in the new creation.

Whatever mission God calls us to must be a participation in this.

Particularity—"Through You And Your Seed"

We must now turn to the other side of God's declaration of blessing. We have explored its universal implications and traced their trajectory through the rest of the Bible. But God did not merely say to Abraham, after promising to bless him and his descendants, "Oh, and by the way, just to encourage you, I am going to bless all the other nations as well." No, the text expresses God's plan for the nations with considerable care and precision. It does not put it in the form of an independent repetition of the active verb "I will bless [the nations]" in the same absolute sense in which God says to Abraham himself, "and I will bless you." Nor does it use a simple unconnected passive verb: "the nations will [also] be blessed." Rather, it puts the more subtle, self-involving forms of the verb (niphal and hithpael) alongside a crucial personal pronoun—*bĕkā,* "through you," with the added phrase, in some of the texts, "and through your seed." The nations will not be blessed without some form of self-involvement in the process (the forms of the verb). And they will not be blessed without reference to what God now promises and plans for Abraham (the accompanying pronoun).

Thus, whatever God planned to do for the nations *universally* is connected in some way with Abraham and his descendants. And whatever God planned to do for Abraham in *particular* is bound up with his ultimate goal for all nations. This is the intriguing balance and tension between the universality and particularity of the "bottom line" of God's word to Abraham.

"Through you": The particular means of God's blessing. What is the meaning of the Hebrew preposition *bĕ* in "through you"? In its normal usage it is most frequently translated by "in" or "through." What does it mean in connection with Abraham here?

It cannot mean that Abraham will be the *agent* of blessing—that is, the one who does the blessing—for that is clearly only God, the source of all blessing. It is of course possible for one person to bless others (by invoking *God's* blessing on them) and in that sense for the others to be "blessed by him" (as, e.g., Pharaoh was blessed by Jacob, or Abraham by Melchizedek), but it is not conceivable that our text envisioned Abraham in person blessing all the peoples on earth even in that secondary sense. So the translation "all peoples on earth will be blessed *by* you" would not be correct here.

Nor is it *comparative,* "like Abraham," as if God promises that other peoples will be blessed in the same way as Abraham, but not necessarily in connection with him. Nor is it simply *associative,* "along with Abraham." This would be closer, but it is still not quite what the word implies. Hebrew has prepositions that mean "like" *(kĕ)* and "with" *('im)*, but neither is used here.

The most probable nuance is that it is *instrumental*—"through you." God's blessing of all peoples on earth will come about *through* Abraham and his offspring. They will neither be the *agent by whom* nor the *source from which* blessing will come, but they will be the *means through which* God (the true agent and source) will extend his blessing to the universal scope of his promise.

The preposition could also bear the meaning "in you." In this case, the promise could have the more metaphorical sense that all peoples would ultimate come to experience blessing through *incorporation* into Abraham and his seed. This certainly fits with the way some of the later texts we have considered looked to the future and saw the nations eventually being included within Israel as God's blessed people. That is an important theological and eschatological truth in both Testaments. However, it seems more straightforward to me, at least in the initial exegesis of the text as it stands in Genesis, to read it in a broadly instrumental sense. God chooses not only to make Abraham and his offspring the *object* of his blessing but also to make them the *instrument* of his blessing to the world. This particular person, family and nation who are to be blessed by God will be the means of others coming into the same blessing.

Another clue to this interpretation is found in the discrimination that God declares he will exercise in relation to how people respond to Abraham and his offspring (Gen 12:3). People (plural) will be blessed through choosing to bless Abraham. That is, there will be positive hope for those who recognize the God of Abraham and acknowledge with thankful blessing what God has done through him and his descendants, including of course, through the One whom Paul sees individually as *the* Seed of Abraham, Jesus the Christ. Conversely, the way for someone (singular) to remain outside the sphere of God's blessing and within the realm of the curse that God has already pronounced on the earth and its inhabitants is by refusing to recognize what God has done in the story that leads from Abraham to Christ, by treating the whole thing with contempt and rejection. Either way, Abraham (and all he represents in the whole biblical narrative of salvation) becomes the criterion of blessing or curse, the pivot on which turns the destiny of individuals and peoples.

This double clause in Genesis 12:3a makes it clear that the concluding reference to "all kinship groups/all nations" (3b) does not imply that *every individual human being* will ultimately be blessed through Abraham. It is not that kind of universalism that this text expresses. Rather, it encourages us in the sure hope that the saving mission of God extends to his whole world, to all peoples, to all ethnic groups. God's blessing will encompass all kinds and conditions of people from all over the world, as Revelation 7:9 envisions.

So we find in these six pregnant Hebrew words of Genesis 12:3b *a universal ultimate goal* (all peoples on earth will find blessing) to be accomplished through *a particular historical means* ("through you," and later, "and your seed"). Each of these poles is inseparable from the other, and both must be held together as utterly essential to a biblical theology of mission.

The uniqueness of Israel's election. We surveyed above the *trajectory of universality* that soars through the biblical canon in a great parabola launched by God's promise to Abraham, landing finally among the redeemed humanity in a redeemed creation in Revelation. A less prominent *trajectory of particularity* can be discerned as well, from the same launch pad. Israel, the people of Abraham, was conscious of a unique role and status among the nations given to them by God in his act of choosing and calling Abraham. Certain things were true of them that were not true of other peoples. God did certain things in relation to them that he did not do to others. Much was demanded of them that was not, in quite the same way, demanded of others. Great was their privilege. Greater still their responsibility.

The number of texts we can assemble along this trajectory is fewer than along the trajectory of universality. This is not because Israel's awareness of their uniquely elect status was any less than their awareness of God's ultimate purpose for the nations. On the contrary, the balance of awareness was undoubtedly the other way round. Israel was no different from the rest the human race in being more inclined to think about themselves than about others, even when thinking about the purposes of God. Israel's self-understanding as a people uniquely chosen by the God YHWH for himself was part of the very core of Israel's world view and national identity. To assemble texts expressing that conviction alone would generate a very large portfolio indeed, into which some whole books, such as Deuteronomy, would need to be inserted.[32]

My point here, however, is not merely with Israel's sense of unique election alone but with *those texts where this distinctive conception of themselves is related in some way (directly or by implication in the context) to the universal purpose of God for the nations or God's universal sovereignty over creation.* That is to say, I am concerned to see the missional dimension of Israel's particular election, corresponding to the missional dimension of God's world-embracing promise to Abraham.

Exodus 19:5-6.

> Now then, if you really obey my voice and keep my covenant,
>> you will be for me a special personal possession
>>> among all the peoples;
>>>> for indeed to me belongs the whole earth
>>> but you, you will be for me a priestly kingdom and a holy nation.
>> (author's translation)[33]

We have already noted this text in the section on universality (see p. 224-25) The background scenery of the text is YHWH's universal rule over "all nations" and "the whole earth," but the foreground action is certainly YHWH's particular intentions for Israel. It is the latter that focuses our attention here (and we will return to the text yet again when we consider the ethical dimensions of biblical mission in chap. 11). "Exodus 19:3-6 is a crucial speech for introducing the central chapters of the Pentateuch; it presents the rest of the Pentateuch from a new perspective, namely *the unique identity of the people of God.*"[34]

Laying out the text as I have shows precisely the balance between universality and particularity that I am seeking to elucidate in this chapter. After the initial conditional clause (the first line), there is a chiastic structure of four phrases, in which the two central lines portray God's universal ownership of the world and its nations, while the two outer lines express his particular role for Israel. This structure also makes clear that the double phrase "priestly king-

---

[32]Peter Machinist assembles a list of "433 distinctiveness passages in the Hebrew Bible" and classifies their thematic variety. He links this aspect of Israel's self-identity more to the sociological needs of their historical origins in marginality as a "recent" arrival on the international scene than to the theological significance of these beliefs. There is room for both perspectives on the material. Peter Machinist, "The Question of Distinctiveness in Ancient Israel," in *Essential Papers on Israel and the Ancient Near East,* ed. F. E. Greenspan (New York: New York University Press, 1991), pp. 420-42.

[33]My translation; cf. Wells, *God's Holy People,* p. 44.

[34]Wells, *God's Holy People,* pp. 33-34, emphasis added.

dom and holy nation" stands in apposition to "personal possession." In other words, the final line defines more fully what the single metaphorical word *sĕgullâ* is meant to imply.

Sĕgullâ, translated by the NIV as "treasured possession," is a word that comes from royal contexts. It was used (in Hebrew and Akkadian) to describe the personal treasure of the monarch and his family (cf. 1 Chron 29:3; Eccles 2:8). The whole country and people might be thought of as the wider property of a king, but he also had his own personal treasure, in which he took particular delight. This is the metaphor God uses to describe the identity of Israel. YHWH is the God who owns and rules the whole earth and all nations (a remarkable affirmation in itself). But YHWH has chosen to place Israel in a special personal relationship to his worldwide kingship. What that special position entails is then explained in verse 6. They have a role that matches their status. The *status* is to be a special treasured possession. The *role* is to be a priestly and holy community in the midst of the nations.

Inasmuch as a king chooses his personal treasure for himself, this text clearly expresses the concept of Israel's unique election by YHWH for a special relationship with himself within the worldwide community of nations. This is the case even though the vocabulary of "choosing" is not present here.

Although the specific Hebrew term for election, *bāḥar,* does not occur in this passage (nor anywhere, used of God's choice of his people, prior to the book of Deuteronomy), subsequent texts which make reference to these words at Sinai do include the term (see, e.g., Deut 7:6; 14:2). Clearly we have the concept if not the term here in Exodus: Israel as "God's own" is discussed from a universal perspective and the notion of covenant is made explicit (Ex 19:5). Thus the idea of choice is presupposed.[35]

But this divine choice is presupposed within a framework that emphatically prevents it from being narrow or exclusive. Just as the call of Abraham is explicitly for the benefit of the nations, so the choice of Israel for a special relationship with God is likewise made with the rest of the world clearly in view.

In fact, the emphasis in the word *sĕgullâ* must be on the treasured and personal nature of the relationship rather than on the concept of "possession" by itself. It is not the case that *Israel* alone belongs to God and other nations do *not,* or that Israel was more "possessed" by God than they were. For the text expresses God's possession of the world (and by implication its nations)[36] in ex-

---

[35]Ibid., p. 27.

[36]Cf. the same affirmation made in a very similar grammatical structure in Ps 24:1. If the whole earth belongs to YHWH, then so do all who dwell on it (i.e., all nations).

actly the same terms as God's anticipated possession of Israel.[37] All nations belong to God, but Israel will belong to God in a unique way that will, on the one hand, demand covenantal obedience, and, on the other hand, be exercised through a priestly and holy identity and role in the world. What the latter will mean is not defined further here, but some of the texts below do amplify the idea. The important point to note for the moment is the balance between the exalted titles given to *Israel* and the substratum of God's claim on the *whole earth*. "What the reader is given is not a description of Israel in isolation, but in relation to the whole of God's earth."[38] Or in other words, *the particularity of Israel here is intended to serve the universality of God's interest in the world. Israel's election serves God's mission.* This is an utterly crucial point to grasp.

The trajectory of this text (Ex 19:3-6) within Scripture is intriguing. There are several very clear echoes within Deuteronomy, which then in turn generate further ones in Jeremiah.

Deuteronomy 7:6. "For you are a people holy to the LORD your God. The LORD your God has chosen you out of all the peoples on the face of the earth to be his people, his treasured possession."

All of Deuteronomy 7 is concerned with the distinctiveness of Israel from the Canaanites, in order to prevent them going down the road of Canaanite idolatry and corrupt religious and social practice.[39] The point of Israel's separation was not *ethnic exclusiveness* (there were all kinds of ways that foreigners could be incorporated into the worshiping community of Israel) but *religious protection.* The same rationale governs another use of the Exodus 19 text in Deuteronomy 14:2—at the head of a chapter dealing with Israel's clean and unclean food regulations. That distinction was meant to symbolize the distinctiveness of Israel from among the nations. As YHWH had made his choice among the nations of the one nation that would be separate—holy to himself, for his own purpose—so of all the animals, Israel must make a distinction that would reflect that more fundamental distinction and be a constant reminder of it in everyday life.

Two further references, however, link the (implicitly) election language of Exodus 19 (especially *sĕgullâ* and "a holy people") more significantly to God's longer term mission among the nations.

---

[37]Lit. "to me *[lî]* you will be a *sĕgullâ* among all the peoples; for to me *[lî]* is the whole earth."
[38]Wells, *God's Holy People,* p. 49.
[39]On the question of the destruction of the Canaanites and their places of worship in Deuteronomy 7, and how that can be fitted into a missiological understanding of Israel's calling to be a blessing to the nations, see, Christoher J. H. Wright, *Deuteronomy,* New International Biblical Commentary (Peabody, Mass.: Hendrikson; Carlisle, U.K.: Paternoster, 1996), pp. 108-20.

Deuteronomy 26:18-19; Deut 28:9-10.

> The LORD has declared this day that you are his people, his treasured possession
> as he promised, and that you are to keep all his commands. He has declared that
> he will set you in praise, fame and honor high above all the nations he has made
> and that you will be a people holy to the LORD your God, as he promised. (Deut
> 26:18-19)
>
>   The LORD will establish you as his holy people, as he promised you on oath, if
> you keep the commands of the LORD your God and walk in his ways. Then all the
> peoples on earth will see that you are called by the name of the LORD, and they
> will fear you. (Deut 28:9-10)

The final section of Deuteronomy 26 is probably one of the most succinct
and balanced statements of the covenant relationship between YHWH and Israel
in the Old Testament. It records two balancing affirmations: by Israel on the one
hand (declaring who their God is, and what their will is), and by YHWH on the
other (declaring that Israel belongs to him in a uniquely treasured way—clearly
echoing Ex 19:6).

God, then, declares the purpose of Israel's election in relation to the rest of
the nations. It is that there should be *"praise, fame and honor."* To whom do
these belong? On the surface of the text in Deuteronomy 26:19 they are for Israel. But the closely linked Deuteronomy 28:9-10 shows that the nations will not
merely show high regard for Israel but will do so because they recognize the
God to whom Israel belongs: "all the peoples on earth will see that you are
called by the name of the LORD." So the reputation of Israel and of YHWH are
bound up together. Such is the inescapable nature of the covenant. This is what
is at stake in Israel's covenantal obedience (or lack of).

Such also is the necessary implication of election. If YHWH chooses to attach
Israel to himself, he chooses in consequence to attach himself to Israel. What
the nations think of Israel will translate into what they think of YHWH—a high
risk mission strategy. The so-called "scandal of particularity" was scandalous to
the Almighty before it was ever a problem for the rest of us. Yet it was a risk, a
scandal and a potentially massive embarrassment that God was prepared to endure for the sake of his ultimate mission for the whole of humanity. With that
wider purpose in view, "God is not ashamed to be called their God" (i.e., the
God of the patriarchs, and by implication, their descendants [Heb 11:16]).

Jeremiah draws on the election-linked language of Deuteronomy to highlight
both the ideal purpose of God in choosing to have such a people identified with
himself, and to point out the contemporary failure of Israel to live up to their
calling.

Jeremiah 13:11; 33:8-9.

"For as a belt is bound round a man's waist, so I bound the whole house of Israel and the whole house of Judah to me," declares the LORD, "to be my people for my renown and praise and honor. But they have not listened." (Jer 13:11).

I will cleanse them from all the sin they have committed against me and will forgive all their sins of rebellion against me. Then this city will bring me renown, joy, praise and honor before all nations on earth that hear of all the good things I do for it; and they will be in awe and will tremble at the abundant prosperity and peace I provide for it. (Jer 33:8-9)

Both of these verses use the same triplet of words "*renown* (or fame; Heb *šēm,* "name"), *praise* and *honor,*" as in Deuteronomy 26:19 (Jer 33:9 adds *joy* to the list). But it is clear in both cases that the beneficiary is God himself. Whatever levels of renown, praise and honor may come Israel's way among the nations is actually for YHWH, the God who chose them as his covenant people. The imagery of Jeremiah's acted parable in chapter 13 expresses this well. A bright, new piece of clothing (probably a sash, not just a belt) would be selected, bought and then worn with pride as something that was beautiful in itself. But the point of wearing it was to bring pleasure and praise to the wearer. That was how God regarded Israel. He wanted to "wear them." Election here is expressed under the figure of choosing a piece of clothing to put on. It may indeed be "an honor" for the tie that gets chosen instead of the others, but that is not the point of the exercise. The intention is to enhance the wearer. Similarly, it was doubtless an incredible privilege and honor for Israel to be chosen as YHWH's covenant partner, but that in itself was not the reason for YHWH making the choice. God had a wider agenda, namely, the exaltation of his own name among the nations through what he would ultimately accomplish "dressed with" Israel.

And it is that wider purpose of God that his people, Israel, were frustrating by their disobedience. They had become as corrupt as a new sash that has lain in wet soil for many months—to return to Jeremiah's graphic acted parable. God simply could not wear them anymore. Far from bringing him praise and honor, they brought him disgrace and contempt.[40] For that reason, if God's purpose for the nations is to proceed, God will have to deal with Israel first. Hence the promises in Jeremiah 33 and the surrounding context. The restoration of the elect is not for their sole benefit but so that the mission of God, for which they had been elect in the first place, can be accomplished among the nations. This

---

[40]This is what Ezekiel means in Ezek 36 when he says that "Israel profaned [YHWH's holy name] among the nations," i.e., they brought YHWH into disrepute.

is why, in broader canonical terms, the restoration of Israel had to happen before the ingathering of the nations—a sequence that Paul profoundly understood in his own mission theology.

We can see, then, that Exodus 19:4-6 has exercised a strong influence on subsequent thinking about Israel's role and responsibilities. One further observation may be made about the missional significance of this fact before moving on to some final texts on the particularity of Israel's election. It is impossible to observe these connections with Exodus 19:4-6 without calling to mind the additional phrase in the text that Israel was to be God's "priesthood" in the midst of the nations, a term implying a representative, mediatorial role. Israel would bring the knowledge of Yahweh to the nations (just as the priests taught the law of Yahweh to his people) and would ultimately bring the nations into covenant fellowship with Yahweh (just as the priests enabled sinners to find atonement and restored fellowship through the sacrifices). Israel's very existence in the earth was for the sake of the nations, and it had been since God's promise to Abraham. This is a theme to which we need to return.

Deuteronomy 4:32-35; 10:14-15.

> Ask now about the former days, long before your time, from the day God created man on the earth; ask from one end of the heavens to the other. Has anything so great as this ever happened, or has anything like it ever been heard of? Has any other people heard the voice of God speaking out of the fire, as you have, and lived? Has any god ever tried to take for himself one nation out of another nation, by testings, by miraculous sings and wonders, by war, by a mighty hand and an outstretched arm, or by great and awesome deeds, like all the things the LORD your God did for you in Egypt before your very eyes?
>
> You were shown these things so that you might know that the LORD is God; beside him there is no other. (Deut 4:32-35)
>
> To the LORD your God belong the heavens, even the highest heavens, the earth and everything in it. Yet the LORD set his affection on your forefathers and loved them, and he chose you, their descendants, above all nations, as it is today. (Deut 10:14-15)

These two texts express the uniqueness of Israel in very clear terms by setting it within the universality of YHWH's power in creation and the rule of history. In the first (Deut 4), Moses challenges Israel to search through all of human history and all of geographical space. The rhetorical questions, of course, expect the answer "No." They are in fact emphatic affirmations that Israel's experience of God has been unique—unique in the double sense that it was without precedent (God had never done anything like it before) and without parallel (God had not done it anywhere else). This text goes on to specify the two events in

Israel's recent history: the Sinai experience of God's revelation, and the exodus experience of God's redemption. Both, says Moses, are unique to Israel.

The second text (Deut 10) specifies the earlier foundation of Israel's uniqueness—the election of the patriarchs. And it sets that event within the even wider arena of God's cosmic ownership and governance of the whole of creation. Just as Exodus 19:5-6 speaks of Israel belonging to YHWH as a unique personal treasure and in the same breath says that the *whole world of nations* belongs to God, so here, Deuteronomy speaks of God's choice of the patriarchs and in the same breath says that the *whole universe of heaven and earth* belongs to God. Whatever else we may say about the election of Israel, it cannot be construed as a narrow and exclusive favoritism that paid no attention to the wider world. In the light of these texts, it can only be considered within that wider context.

So the particularity of Israel's election is set in a universal framework, looking back. But is there any hint that it serves a wider purpose, looking forward, related to God's mission of blessing the nations? Such a connection is present in Deuteronomy 4, through the ethical agenda and demand that is laid on Israel as a result of their election. And since the same ethical challenge is strongly present in Deuteronomy 10, we may feel that the wider relevance is implicit there also. In Deuteronomy 4 the rhetorical questions in verses 32-34 about *the uniqueness of Israel's experience of YHWH's action* on their behalf are balanced earlier in the chapter by another short series of rhetorical questions about *the uniqueness of Israel's possession of YHWH's law*. But significantly this is set in full view of *the nations* as spectators of how Israel responds to God's law.

> Observe them [God's laws] carefully, for this will show your wisdom and understanding to the nations, who will hear about all these decrees and say, "Surely this great nation is a wise and understanding people." What other nation is so great as to have their gods near them the way the LORD our God is near us whenever we pray to him? And what other nation is so great as to have such righteous decrees and laws as this body of laws I am setting before you today? (Deut 4:6-8)

One of the most characteristic features of Deuteronomy is its motivational rhetoric. It gives multiple reasons why Israel should obey God's law and frame their community life according to his standards. Here, in an emphatic position in the opening section of the book, a primary motivation for Israel's obedience is given, namely, the watching nations. Israel has been called to be a special possession of God in the midst of all the peoples. That calling includes the demand of ethical holiness. By fulfilling that demand, Israel becomes a kind of model to the nations, or, to borrow the language of Isaiah, "a light to the nations" (Is 51:4). Thus, when we find the same strong ethical language coursing through the rhetoric of Deuteronomy 10:12-19, it is likely that this wider significance of Israel's obedience is only just below the surface.[41]

One further clue to the wider missional significance of Israel's unique experience of God that flowed from the particularity of their election is in the explicit reason given for it in Deuteronomy 4:35: "You were shown these things so that you might know that the LORD is God; besides him there is no other."

The great actions of God in the history of Israel were not merely cosmic theater. They constituted an education. Because of what they had experienced, Israel now *knew* the identity of the living God. In a world full of nations that did not yet know YHWH as God, Israel was now in the privileged position of being the nation who did. But with that privilege came huge responsibility. Israel was the steward of the knowledge of God. But God's will to be known to all people is one of the driving forces of biblical mission. Through doing what he had done for Israel, in revelation and redemption, God had initiated that mission by creating one people on earth who enjoyed the inestimable privilege of knowing him. This was something the psalmists could marvel at with thanksgiving (Ps 33:12; 147:19-20). But it was not something God ever intended to be restricted to Israel. *Israel knew God in order that through them all nations would come to know God.* Once again, therefore, we find a strongly missional pulse beating in texts that affirm Israel's election and uniqueness.

Conclusion: Biblical election and mission. Having traced the biblical trajectory of the key texts that speak of the unique particularity of Israel, especially of their election by YHWH, we need to draw the threads together. The concept of divine election has always been, of course, one of the more controversial of all the biblical doctrines. We shudder at the long and sometimes violent history of controversy within the church between advocates of Augustinian Calvinism and Arminianism. Or we feel the force of the accusation that God somehow sullied his saving plans through the selective favoritism shown to the Jews. On the former, it has to be said that much of the debate over the meaning of election, predestination, reprobation and associated concepts has been carried on at a level of systematic abstraction and binary logic that seems oblivious to the way the Old Testament speaks of God's choice of Israel. Between election in the Hebrew Scriptures of Jesus and election in the formulations of theological systems there sometimes seems to be a great gulf fixed. Few and narrow are the bridges from one to the other.

On the latter, the accusation that election is intrinsically partial, unfair and

---

[41]I will give more extended attention to the missiological significance of Old Testament ethics in chap. 11.

incompatible with the alleged love of God for the whole world, there are several considerations that need to be recalled. From the range of texts that we have now considered, the following affirmations can be made about election in the Old Testament.

The election of Israel is set in the context of God's universality. Far from being a doctrine of narrow national exclusivism, it affirms the opposite. YHWH, the God who chose Israel, is the God who owns and rules the whole universe, and whatever purpose he has for Israel is inextricably linked to that universal sovereignty and providence.

The election of Israel does not imply the rejection of other nations. On the contrary, from the very beginning it is portrayed as for their benefit. God did not call Abraham from among the nations to accomplish their rejection but to initiate the process of their redemption.

The election of Israel is not warranted by any special feature of Israel itself. When the people of Israel were tempted to think that they were chosen by God on the grounds of numerical or moral superiority to other nations, Deuteronomy very quickly removed such arrogant illusions.

The election of Israel is founded only on God's inexplicable love. There was no other motive than God's own love, and the promises he made to Israel's forefathers (which included, of course, his promise in relation to the nations). We might paraphrase John 3:16, in a way that John would doubtless accept, "God so loved *the world* that he chose Abraham and called Israel."

The election of Israel is instrumental, not an end in itself. God did not choose Israel that they alone should be saved, as if the purpose of election terminated with them. They were chosen rather as the means by which salvation could be extended to others throughout the earth.[42]

The election of Israel is part of the logic of God's commitment to history. The salvation that the Bible describes is woven into the fabric of history. God deals with the realities of human life, lived on the earth, in nations and cultures. His decision to choose one nation in history as the means by which he would bring blessing to all nations within history is neither favoritism nor unfairness.

The election of Israel is fundamentally missional, not just soteriological. If we allow our doctrine of election to become merely a secret calculus that deter-

---

[42]Craig Broyles makes this point in relation to Psalm 67. "Psalm 67 shows us that election does not mean that God has his favorites but simply that he has a chosen channel of blessing for all. Election has to do not with God's goal for humanity, that his blessing is restricted to some and denied to others. It has to do with his means of extending that blessing to all." Craig C. Broyles, *Psalms,* New International Biblical Commentary (Peabody, Mass.: Hendrikson; Carlisle, U.K.: Paternoster, 1999), p. 280.

mines who gets saved and who does not, we have lost touch with its original biblical intention. God's calling and election of Abraham was not merely so that he should be saved and become the spiritual father of those who will finally be among the redeemed in the new creation (the elect, in another sense). It was rather, and more explicitly, that he and his people should be the instrument through whom God would gather that multinational multitude that no man or woman can number. Election is of course, in the light of the whole Bible, election unto salvation. But it is first of all election into mission.

8

God's Model of Redemption
The Exodus

How big is our gospel? If our gospel is the good news about God's redemption, then the question moves on to, How big is our understanding of redemption? Mission clearly has to do with the redemptive work of God and our participation in making it known and leading people into the experience of it. If, as I am seeking to argue throughout this book, mission is fundamentally God's before it is ours, what is God's idea of redemption? The scope of our mission must reflect the scope of God's mission, which in turn will match the scale of God's redemptive work. Where do we turn in the Bible for our understanding of redemption? Already it will be clear enough that in my view it will simply not do to turn first to the New Testament. If you had asked a devout Israelite in the Old Testament period "Are you redeemed?" the answer would have been a most definite yes. And if you had asked "How do you know?" you would be taken aside to sit down somewhere while your friend recounted a long and exciting story—the story of the exodus.

For indeed it is the exodus that provided the primary model of God's idea of redemption, not just in the Old Testament but even in the New, where it is used as one of the keys to understanding the meaning of the cross of Christ.

"The People You Have Redeemed"

In your unfailing love you will lead
the people you have redeemed.
In your strength you will guide them
to your holy dwelling. (Ex 15:13)

Moses and the Israelites are celebrating the great deliverance from the army of Pharaoh at the crossing of the Red Sea. Among the rich poetic imagery used to describe the event and its historic and cosmic significance is this metaphor of *redemption*. In bringing Israel out of Egypt, YHWH has *redeemed* them. A little later in the same song, the same thought is expressed with a different word: "the people you bought" (Ex 15:16). The people thus celebrate in this song the fulfillment of what God had promised to do for them (to their great initial skepticism) while they were still in Egypt. God's great declaration of intent, given to Moses when he needed some serious encouragement, majors on the same theme: redemption.

> Therefore, say to the Israelites: "I am the LORD, and I will bring you out from under the yoke of the Egyptians. I will free you from being slaves to them, and I will redeem you with an outstretched arm and with mighty acts of judgment." (Ex 6:6)

With the single exception of Jacob's blessing in Genesis 48:16,[1] these two references (Ex 6:6; 15:13) are the first occasions that the Bible uses the language of redemption. The Hebrew verb in both cases is *gāʾal*. When a person is the subject of this verb (whether God or a human being), he is described as a *gōʾēl*—a redeemer. The historical event of the exodus of the Israelites from Egypt is thus being interpreted through the use of a metaphor drawn from the social and economic life of Israel, which we need to understand. The English word "to redeem," with its Latin roots, suggests a financial transaction in which one "buys back" something that one had previously forfeited, or in which one party pays a price to another in order to obtain freedom for a third party. A *goʾel* in Israel certainly sometimes had to make some financial outlay for the object of his efforts, and indeed the verb in Exodus 15:16 *(qānâ)* can include acquisition by purchase. But there were much wider social dimensions to the role of a *gōʾēl* in ancient Israel, associated particularly with the demands of kinship.

A *gōʾēl* was any member within a wider family group upon whom fell the duty of acting to protect the interests of the family or another member in it who was in particular need. The term might be translated "kinsman protector" or "family champion." Three situations illustrate the scope of the role.

- *Avenging shed blood.* If someone was murdered, a member of the victim's family took on the responsibility of pursuing the guilty one and bringing him

---

[1] Jacob speaks of "the angel, the one redeeming me from all harm" (author's translation)—i.e., the one who has stood up for me and defended me against all my enemies and tough circumstances.

or her to justice. This quasi-official role was called the *gōʾēl* in Numbers 35:12 (where the NIV translates "the avenger" or "avenger of blood" in Num 35:19).

- *Redeeming land or slaves.* If a kinsman fell into debt and was forced to sell some land in the hope of staying economically afloat, any better-off kinsman had the responsibility of preempting or redeeming the land in order to keep it in the wider family. If the kinsman fell into such economic destitution that he had no choice but to offer himself or his family into bonded labor for his debts, it was again the duty of a wealthier kinsman to act as *gōʾēl* and rescue them from servitude (these regulations are interwoven through Lev 25).

- *Providing an heir.* If a man died without a son to inherit his name and property, a kinsman was under moral (if not legal) duty to take the dead man's widow and seek to raise an heir for the deceased. The law on this practice in Deuteronomy 25:5-10 does not use the *gāʾal* root, but the most likely illustration of the practice in the story of Ruth and Boaz repeatedly does (Ruth 4).

The *gōʾēl,* then, was a near kinsman who acted as protector, defender, avenger or rescuer for other members of the family, especially in situations of threat, loss, poverty, or injustice. Such action would always involve effort, often incurred cost, and sometimes demanded a degree of self-sacrifice. Deuteronomy 25:7-10 recognizes that some men might be reluctant to exercise such duty in relation to a deceased kinsman's wife, even in the face of public shame, while Ruth 4 strongly commends Boaz for his willingness to do so.

So, in portraying YHWH as the one who promises to *gāʾal* his people (Ex 6), and as the one who can be praised for having done so (Ex 15), Israel uses a rich and powerful metaphor. Three things are at the heart of the matter:

- family relationship
- powerful intervention
- effective restoration

As Israel's *gōʾēl,* YHWH affirms a bond between himself and Israel that is as close and as committed as any bond of human kinship, and with it YHWH accepts the obligation that comes from taking Israel as his own family. As *gōʾēl,* therefore, YHWH will exert himself to whatever extent is necessary on their behalf for their protection or rescue. The language of YHWH's "mighty hand and outstretched arm" colorfully captures the *gōʾēl* in action. And as *gōʾēl* he will restore Israel to a right and proper situation, freed from the shackles of slavery and oppression.

We have focused here on the single word *gāʾal* as the commonest verb used to express the exodus as an act of redemption, but it is far from the only verb in

Israel's rich vocabulary connected with the exodus. Walter Brueggemann lists six dynamic verbs that occur frequently in the narrative and poetic celebrations of it.[2]

God's Comprehensive Redemption

Here then we have the first and foundational account in which the God of the Bible is presented as Redeemer. What does it tell us? When God decided to act in the world and in human history in a way that could be pictured as a *gōʾēl* in action, what did he do? If we are to develop a biblical understanding of the meaning of redemption (which is essential to developing a biblical understanding of the meaning of mission), we must start here and explore all that these narratives have to tell us about the situation from which God redeemed Israel, the reasons for which he did so, and the changed reality into which their redemption led them.

Political. The Israelites in Egypt were an immigrant, ethnic minority people. They had originally come to the host country as famine refugees and had been welcomed and given the asylum they sought.[3] However, with a change of dynasty had come a change of policy toward them, and Exodus 1:8-10 portrays how vulnerable they were to being made the target of irrational fear, political cunning and unjust discrimination. They had no political freedom or voice within the Egyptian state, even though they had grown in numbers. In fact their numerical growth is cited as one of the major reasons for the Egyptian hostility. This is a story with modern echoes.

In the narrative of the exodus and its longer term outcome, God acted to liberate the Israelites from the political injustice of their situation, and in the course of time to establish them as a nation in their own right. Provisional survival through Egyptian hospitality was one thing. Permanent servitude under Egyptian oppression was quite another. The former served the purpose of God for the seed of Abraham, but only temporarily. The latter frustrated it and was therefore intolerable.

Economic. The Israelites were being exploited as slave labor (Ex 1:11-14).

---

[2]They are *yāṣāʾ* (in Hiphil, "to bring out"), *nāṣal* ("to deliver" or "to rescue"), *gāʾal* ("to redeem"), *yāṣaʿ* ("to save"), *pādâ* ("to redeem, purchase"), *ʿālâ* (in Hiphil, "to cause to go up, bring up"). "What is important . . . is that Yahweh is the subject of all of these verbs. This cluster of verbs becomes a poignant and elemental way in which Yahweh is characterized in the testimony of Israel. . . . Thus the Exodus grammar saturates the imagination of Israel." Walter Brueggemann, *Theology of the Old Testament: Testimony, Dispute, Advocacy* (Minneapolis: Fortress Press, 1997), pp. 174-78.

[3]A fact which was not forgotten. Even though the predominant memory of Egypt in the Old Testament is of the oppression, one law at least skips over that and recalls the fact that Egypt had given succour to the family of Jacob as aliens in need (Deut 23:7-8).

They did not own the land they lived on (mind you, neither did the Egyptians, ironically because of the actions of Joseph generations earlier, but that's another story). But rather than being able to use that land for their own benefit (for which it had originally been given), their labor is now being syphoned off to the benefit of the host nation for its own economic advantage. Israelite labor is being exploited for Egyptian agriculture and construction projects. An ethnic minority does the dirty and heavy work for the king of Egypt. The modern echoes continue.

Among the explicit promises of God in advance of the exodus was that he would give to the Israelites a land of their own (Ex 6:8). The economic dimension of their liberation is thus built into it, both in historical reality and in the metaphoric use of the *gōʾēl* institution to describe it. For as we have seen, it was particularly in circumstances of economic threat and loss that the *gōʾēl* was expected to act in order to restore economic viability to the needy. Rescuing the Israelites from slave labor was the very heart of the exodus redemption.

Social. The rest of Exodus 1 goes on to describe the escalating state violence against the Israelites by a government that piles brutality on stupidity. Failing to subvert the community from within, because of the midwives respect for life and their courageous combination of wit and disobedience, the Pharaoh embarks on state-sponsored genocide—inciting "all his people" to a murderous campaign against Israelite male babies. So the people suffer intolerable violation of fundamental human rights and aggressive interference in their family lives. Israelite families are made to live in constant fear—nine months of fear as every pregnant mother waited for the news that should normally have brought great joy ("it's a boy!"), but would now bring terror and grief (Ex 2:1-2).

In the ensuing narrative, the plagues strike back with increasing violence at a regime that has sunk to such depravity. The climactic death of Egypt's own firstborn sons mirrors their destruction of Israel's (Ex 4:23). The Passover forever reminds Israel of the social and family nature of God's redemption and the precious delivery out of such demented evil. And when Israel is established as a new kind of society in covenant relationship with YHWH, the sanctity of human life and the preservation of social justice are among the key elements in their social and legal structures.

Spiritual. While the narrator highlights the political, economic and social dimensions of Israel's plight in Exodus 1—2, once YHWH appears as a character in the drama, we become aware of a further dimension. The Israelites' slavery to Pharaoh is a massive hindrance to their worship and service of the living God, YHWH.

One way that the story makes this point is a simple play on a single Hebrew verb and noun. ʿ*ābad* means to serve—that is to work for another; ʿ*ăbōdâ* means service or slavery. Thus the Israelites cried out to God "because of their slavery" (Ex 2:23). But the same words can be used for worship, the service of God. And of course, Israel's destiny was to serve and worship YHWH. How could they, however, as long as they were chained in slavery to Pharaoh? The point is made most sharply in Exodus 4:22, where Moses is told to tell Pharaoh on behalf of YHWH, "Israel is my firstborn son. . . . Let my son go, so he may worship me [ʿ*ābad*]." English translations vary between "so he may worship me" and "so he may serve me." The truth is, YHWH was asking for both, and Pharaoh was preventing both.

The spiritual nature of the conflict is made in two other ways. One is the repeated request by Moses to Pharaoh that Israel should be allowed to make a journey into the wilderness to worship their God YHWH and offer him sacrifices—a request that is repeatedly rejected, then grudgingly granted with conditions, then withdrawn, granted again, only to be regretted, and finally sending Pharaoh's army to a watery grave in futile pursuit. Whatever our opinion on the truthfulness of Moses and Aaron's requests and undertakings (and is truth owed to a mass murderer?), the emphasis of the story as the suspense builds up is that YHWH is not merely intent on liberating slaves but on reclaiming worshipers. The stakes are high in the spiritual realm, not just on the floor of political history.

The second indication of the spiritual nature of Israel's bondage and their redemption, is the presentation of the conflict as a power encounter between the true divine power of YHWH and the usurped divine claims of Pharaoh and "all the gods of Egypt" (Ex 12:12). The sequence of plagues was not just a series of natural phenomena, though of course the natural order was catastrophically affected. All of them were directed at aspects of what Egyptians regarded as divine power—especially the first (the attack on the Nile) and the last but one (darkness, blotting out the sun). The Nile and the sun were among the foremost of all Egypt's deities. YHWH proves his devastating sovereignty over both.[4]

The exodus demonstrates who is truly God. YHWH stands alone and incomparable. And as a result of his decisive victory over all that opposed him and resisted his will, Israel is to know that YHWH is God and there is no other (Deut 4:35, 39), and to celebrate that "the LORD will reign / for ever and ever (Ex 15:18). The permament memorial to the exodus is not some stone statue sunk in the sands of Sinai to commemorate the victory of Israel over Egypt. No, it is the song of Moses celebrating the victory of YHWH over the human and divine

---

[4]Cf. M. Louise Holert, "Extrinsic Evil Powers in the Old Testament" (Master's thesis, Fuller Theological Seminary, 1985), pp. 55-72.

forces of oppression and injustice and proclaiming his universal reign into the unlimited future. Truly, the Lord is enthroned not on pillars of stone but on the praises of Israel (Ps 22:3).

The spiritual dimension of the exodus, then, is that God makes it clear that his purpose in the whole process is that it should lead to the *knowledge, service* and *worship* of the living God. The implication is that all three of these were difficult if not impossible as long as they were in the depths of bondage to Pharaoh.

The Bible's first account of God in action as Redeemer then is broad and deep and dynamic. As indeed God had said it would be. His word to Moses in advance of the events cover the whole spectrum. Notice how the piled up phrases of Exodus 6:6-8 speak of God's intention to rescue Israel from political and economic slavery (which included the social abuse and injustice), to give them a land of their own to live in, and to bring them into covenant relationship with himself as the God they would truly know to be YHWH. And these words are only in reconfirmation of what God had initially said to Moses at Mount Sinai in Exodus 3:7-10.

> I am the LORD, and I will bring you out from under the yoke of the Egyptians. I will free you from being slaves to them, and I will redeem you with an outstretched arm and with mighty acts of judgment. I will take you as my own people, and I will be your God. Then you will know that I am the LORD your God, who brought you out from under the yoke of the Egyptians. And I will bring you to the land I swore with uplifted hand to give to Abraham, to Isaac and to Jacob. I will give it to you as a possession. I am the LORD. (Ex 6:6-8) [5]

In the exodus God responded to *all* the dimensions of Israel's need. God's momentous act of redemption did not merely rescue Israel from political, economic and social oppression and then leave them to their own devices to worship whom they pleased. Nor did God merely offer them spiritual comfort of hope for some brighter future in a home beyond the sky while leaving their historical condition unchanged. No, the exodus effected real change in the people's real historical situation and at the same time called them into a real new relationship with the living God. This was God's total response to Israel's total need. The whole narrative repeatedly reminds us that this was *God's* doing. Moses and Aaron, of course, play their instrumental part, but the people are told to stand back and watch. So here we have the prime, opening, definitive case

---

[5] Elmer Martens identifies four key commitments in this passage and argues that they are like central wires that are intertwined in the whole cable of Old Testament (and indeed biblical) theology: redemption, covenant, knowledge of God, and land. He uses this quartet of themes as a framework for his account of the faith of Israel. Elmer A. Martens, *God's Design: A Focus on Old Testament Theology*, 2nd ed. (Grand Rapids: Baker; Leicester, U.K.: Apollos, 1994).

study of the Redeemer God acting in history out of his own motivation, achieving comprehensive objectives, and pinning his own identity and character to the narrative as a permanent definition of the meaning of his name, YHWH.

God's Motivated Redemption

What was it that motivated God to act thus? The narrative leaves us in no doubt about two primary triggers for God's redeeming initiative: his concern for Israel's suffering, and his consideration of the covenant he had made with their ancestors.

God's knowledge of the oppressed. Exodus 1 has presented the scene of Israel's oppression under a Pharaoh that "did not know about Joseph," that is, Pharaoh acknowledged no sense of duty toward Joseph's family and their descendants. As a result, we are shocked to read of the fearful suffering of the Israelites. In Exodus 2 we read that that particular king died. The change in government brought no change in the state's policy of genocidal oppression, however, and for the first time we read that "the Israelites groaned in their slavery and cried out" (Ex 2:23).[6] We are not actually told to whom they cried out. They may have cried out to the new king for relief, but if they did it was obviously in vain. But whoever they thought they were crying to (if anybody), we know who *heard* their cry—the same God who heard the outcry from Sodom and Gomorrah in Genesis 18:20-21 (where again we are not told that the outcry was particularly directed to YHWH, but simply that it was YHWH who heard it).[7]

Not only does God *hear,* God also *sees.* And out of hearing and seeing, God *knows* the suffering of the people. These three words are repeated: first the narrator uses them in Exodus 2:24-25, and then God affirms them of himself in Exodus 3:7. "I have indeed [surely] *seen* the affliction of my people in Egypt. I have *heard* their outcry because of their slave-masters, and I *know* their sufferings" (author's translation). The NIV translates *know,* as "concerned about"—which is probably an attempt to strengthen the meaning, but rather weakens it. It is not merely an emotional *concern* that moves God but a profound knowledge, or better, an acknowledgement, of the intolerable circumstances that the Israelites were enduring.

---

[6]There are strong echoes of this story in the narrative of the division of the kingdom after the death of Solomon. A new king meant an opportunity for relief from the yoke of oppression, and the people cried out for that. Rehoboam's harsh answer led to the split of the kingdom. The textual echoes in 1 Kings 13 seem to portray Rehoboam in the role of Pharaoh and Jeroboam in the role of Moses (though the comparison is sadly short-lived).

[7]The same word is used in both texts: ṣĕʿāqâ—the technical term for the cry of protest or pain out of a situation of injustice, cruelty or violence.

Looking means God now bears the burden of knowledge. That, too, has to be more than merely cognitive. Knowledge, recognition or acknowledgement is a key theme in the story of Israel's deliverance, for integral to this story is Israel and Egypt's coming to acknowledge YHWH. But the background to that is two other acts of acknowledgement. The first is the king's not acknowledging Joseph (Ex 1:8). The second is YHWH's acknowledging Israel and its situation, and specifically Israel's suffering. God is not such a transcendent being as to be exalted above engagement with people. . . . God gets involved with their suffering. Insofar as knowing is more than an intellectual matter, it is more directly a matter of the will than the feelings. Acknowledging the reality of Israel's affliction is a start to taking action to change things.[8]

God's covenant memory. God's covenant memory is mentioned twice—by the narrator and then repeatedly in the mouth of YHWH who identifies himself as the God of Abraham, Isaac and Jacob. "God remembered *[zākar]* his covenant." The word *zākar* does not mean a sudden recollection after a period of amnesia. It denotes thoughtful consideration of something one has deliberately called to mind with a view to taking action on it. So here, Exodus connects itself to Genesis as God recalls his connection with the ancestors of the people whose cry he hears, whose affliction he sees and whose slavery he knows.

In later stories Moses will deliberately jog YHWH's memory on this point and appeal to the same covenant commitment as he intercedes for Israel in their sin (Ex 32—34). Here we are not told exactly that Israel appealed to God's covenant commitment to their ancestors. But God feels the force of an unspoken appeal. He had "sworn by himself" to the father of this nation. That oath, ritually enacted in Genesis 15 and confirmed with great intensity at the end of Genesis 22, generates divine self-compulsion. God, we might say, subjects himself to himself and puts his own identity and integrity on the line in the action that follows.

And so the reader is made constantly aware that this new story that will portray God in a new role (as *gō'ēl,* redeemer) is in fact the next phase of the story that unfolded in Genesis, the same story that had been launched by God's "great commission" to Abraham and its accompanying words of promise. If there were missional implications to that great Abrahamic tradition, then we can be sure there will be missional implications to this one also.

For this is the same God, and he is still on the same mission.

God's model redemption. The exodus narrative, then, makes it clear that two things in combination motivated divine action in redemption: the sight

---

[8]John Goldingay, *Old Testament Theology,* vol 1, *Israel's Gospel* (Downers Grove, Ill.: InterVarsity Press, 2003), p. 302.

and sound of human misery under oppression, and the thought of God's own promise and purpose. There is a kind of push and pull effect motivating God's action. On the one hand, he is pulled down by human cries to investigate and rectify injustice on earth. On the other hand, he is driven forward by his own declared intention to bless the nations and fulfill his covenant to Abraham. Both of these continue to be prominent themes in the way the Old Testament subsequently uses the exodus story as a model for understanding the character and action of God.[9]

In the later history of Israel, of course, the injustice that God was drawn to in judgment was more often injustice *within* Israel than oppression from external enemies. So the exodus is frequently used negatively as a foil to critique Israel's own toleration of injustice within her borders against her own people. In spite of the example of YHWH's action on their behalf, an outpouring of redemptive power that they celebrated every Passover, Israel could allow the same kind of Egyptian exploitation, oppression, slavery and violence to flourish against their own poor people. The prophets poured shame on such scandal (e.g., Jer 2:6; 7:22-26; Hos 11:1; 12:9; Amos 2:10; 3:1; Mic 6:4).

However, when Israel did experience again the oppression of external enemies, or indeed when individual Israelites felt the pain of persecution, unjust accusation, or life-threatening violence, they appealed to the God of exodus to do again what he had done before—to act as *gō'ēl*. In worship, psalmists appealed to the exodus deliverance as the basis for fresh deliverance, individual or national (e.g., Ps 44; 77; 80). Prophets used the exodus as template for speaking of God's future deliverance for his people, in the same comprehensive terms as the original. That is, it would be a deliverance that would encompass a reign of justice without oppression, the blessings of economic fruitfulness without exploitation, freedom from violence and fear, and perfect obedience to YHWH based on total forgiveness. Indeed the promised new exodus would replace the old as a cause for marveling recollection (e.g., Is 40; 43:14-21; Jer 23:7-8).

All of this widespread use of the exodus tradition and vocabulary is based on the conviction that God (meaning God as Israel knows him to be through his revealed name YHWH) is characteristically and perpetually motivated by the same impulses that triggered the exodus. Indeed, according to the text, God himself insists that he is to be known in this way. What he is about to do in the

---

[9]The exodus permeates the rest of the Old Testament at many levels. Richard Patterson and Michael Travers, in their survey of this theme, classify the many allusions to the exodus according to its use: as historical witness against Israel; as a source of instruction, warning and admonition; as testimony of praise and prayer; as a source of hope. See "Contours of the Exodus Motif in Jesus' Earthly Ministry," *Westminster Theological Journal* 66 (2004): 25-47.

great redemption of Israel from oppression will forever be linked to the revelation of his personal divine name, YHWH, and will also forever define the flavor of that name. YHWH is the exodus God. YHWH is the God who sees, hears and knows about the suffering of the oppressed. YHWH is the God who hates what he sees and acts decisively to bring down the oppressor and release the oppressed so that both come to *know* him, either in the heat of his judgment or in glad worship and service. YHWH is the faithful God, who calls to mind the things he has promised, the purposes he has declared, the mission to which he is committed. YHWH is the God who will not stand by to watch these great goals snuffed out by the stubborn recalcitrance of genocidal tyrants.

All these affirmations about God, made at the time of the exodus, are repeated elsewhere in universalizing contexts. So although the exodus stands as a unique and unrepeatable event in the history of Old Testament Israel, it also stands as a paradigmatic and highly repeatable model for the way God wishes to act in the world, and ultimately will act for the whole creation. The exodus is a prime lens through which we see the biblical mission of God.

Exodus and Mission

What are we to take from our survey of the exodus narrative and its subsequent use in the rest of the Bible for our theology and practice of mission? We have seen that the exodus must be taken as a whole in all its dimensions. In this great event, as rendered to us through the biblical narrative, God *redeemed* Israel. The Bible tells us so. We have no liberty to extract some part of the whole and define redemption more narrowly or even exclusively in those terms. Exodus 15:13 celebrates the *whole* event under the metaphor of YHWH as Redeemer.

The exodus, of course, was not God's *only* redeeming act or even (in a full biblical perspective) his greatest. But it is the *first* that is described as such in the Bible, and the rest of the Bible clearly takes it as paradigmatic. That is, the exodus models for us the contours of what God himself means by redemption, even if of course it was not yet all he planned to do in his redemptive purpose for humanity and creation.

If then, redemption is biblically defined in the first instance by the exodus, and if God's redeeming purpose is at the heart of God's mission, what does this tell us about mission as we are called to participate in it? The inevitable outcome surely is that *exodus-shaped redemption demands exodus-shaped mission*. And that means that our commitment to mission must demonstrate the same broad totality of concern for human need that God demonstrated in what he did for Israel. And it should also mean that our overall motivation and objective in mission be consistent with the motivation and purpose of God as declared in the exodus narrative. I have argued from the start of this book that *our* mission must be derived from *God's* mission. And the mission of God is expressed with exceptional clarity and repeated emphasis throughout the whole exodus narrative. The whole story is shaped and driven by God's agenda.

Two interpretative options fall short of a holistic missional hermeneutic of the exodus. One is to concentrate on its spiritual significance and marginalize the political, economic and social dimensions of the narrative. The other is to concentrate so much on its political, economic and social dimensions that the spiritual dimension is lost from sight. My critique in what follows is not meant to take sides by affirming that one is right and the other wrong. For both do have strong biblical support for the positive aspects of what they advocate. My point rather is that either approach, if its one-sided reductionism is driven too far, ends up in an unbalanced, less than fully biblical, missiological position. Both approaches may be accused of putting asunder what God has joined together, when what we need to do is to hold together the integrated totality of the narrative's impact.

Spiritualizing interpretation. The spiritualizing approach pays close attention to the way the New Testament uses the exodus as one model for explaining the significance of the death of Christ for the believer. Those who take this approach are fully right and justified in doing so, for this is clearly part of the New Testament's rich catalog of explanatory models for the cross. Indeed, well before the cross, the exodus is used by all Gospel writers in their portrayal of the life, teaching and ministry of Jesus.[10]

The problem is that, having rightly affirmed this spiritual and christocentric interpretation of the exodus in the New Testament, popular preaching of the exodus then tends to dismiss or ignore the historical reality that constituted the original event for Israel, namely, the actual deliverance out of real, earthy, injustice, oppression and violence.

The thought process goes something like this (I remember it well, for it was how I was taught in Sunday school, with that close attention to biblical foundations and connections for which I am very grateful):

---

[10]The use of the exodus (and new exodus) theme in the New Testament is well documented by many scholars, e.g., F. F. Bruce, *This Is That: The New Testament Development of Some Old Testament Themes* (Exeter, U.K.: Paternoster; Grand Rapids: Eerdmans, 1968); Rikki Watts, *Isaiah's New Exodus in Mark* (Grand Rapids: Baker, 1997); David Pao, *Acts and the Isaianic New Exodus* (Grand Rapids: Baker, 2000); Richard D. Patterson and Michael Travers, "Contours of the Exodus Motif in Jesus' Earthly Ministry," *Westminster Theological Journal* 66 (2004): 25-47. This last is an excellent compact summary of all relevant biblical material and a helpful survey of scholarship on the theme.

- In the exodus, God delivered the Israelites from slavery to Egypt.
- And through the cross of Christ, God delivered us from slavery to sin.

The wonderful spiritual truth of the second line is thus affirmed to be "the real meaning" of the original Old Testament story. The exodus was all about deliverance. But we know what "real" deliverance means, and it is spiritual. We know what we really need to be delivered from: our slavery to sin. We also know the only place real spiritual deliverance can be found: at the cross. *This,* then (the cross), is *that* (the exodus). Within a typological framework of interpretation, the exodus stands as a type of the cross. The exodus was a foreshadowing of the greater redemptive work of God.

The implication for mission follows. If the exodus narrative has anything to contribute to mission, it lies in the imperative to evangelize. For only through evangelism can we bring people deliverance from their slavery to sin, which is their deepest problem and is basically spiritual. This can be linked to the wonderful narrative of Moses' missionary call; for just as God sent Moses with the good news that God was going to save the Israelites from slavery to Pharaoh, so God sends us with the good news of how people can be saved from sin.

I am not for one moment denying the wonderful truth contained in this line of interpretation. I gladly affirm the typological relationship between key Old Testament events such as the exodus and their New Testament fulfillment in Christ. There is no doubt at all that the New Testament connects the cross with the exodus and the events that preceded it (especially the Passover). I also affirm (and will show that the Old Testament itself does too) that the deepest need of human beings is the sin within themselves, such that all other forms of deliverance are ultimately inadequate if that fundamental need is not decisively addressed. And of course I agree with all my heart that the cross of Christ is God's only and final solution to the problem of sin at its deepest roots, and that it is our evangelistic responsibility to tell people that good news. All these things I gladly affirm.

My difficulty with this position and its missiological outcome is not in what it *affirms* (for I recognize its valid biblical foundations) but in what it simultaneously *omits*. I am not suggesting that it is *not* biblical but that it is not biblical *enough*. Several reasons may be given for this.

Whose sin? First, the parallel between exodus and cross, at least in the popular form of expressing it, does not quite fit. Being delivered from slavery to our own sin is not quite parallel to the deliverance the Israelites experienced. For the exodus was decidedly not deliverance *from their own sin*. The Old Testament does know what it means to be delivered from the results of God's wrath on one's own sin. That is what the return from exile is all about. Nothing could be clearer than that Israel ended up in exile in Babylon because of the anger of God against their persistent wickedness over many generations. And equally the prophets interpret the return from exile not merely as deliverance from Babylon but as the blotting out of the sin that put them there. But there is no hint whatsoever that Israel's suffering in *Egypt* was God's judgment on their sin. The exodus, then, was indeed deliverance from slavery to sin—not Israel's own sin, but *the sin of those who oppressed them*.

The exodus was a climactic victory for YHWH against the *external* powers of injustice, violence and death. In the exodus God brought his people up and out from under the enslaving power to which they were in bondage.

> This is not for a moment to imply that the Israelites were not themselves sinners, as much in need of God's mercy and grace as the rest of the human race. The subsequent story of their behavior in the wilderness proved that beyond a doubt. Just as it also proved God's infinite patience and forgiving grace toward their sinful and rebellious ways. The sacrificial system indeed was designed precisely to cope with the reality of sin on the part of the people of God and to provide a means of atoning for it. The point here is that atonement and forgiveness for one's own sin is not what the exodus redemption was about. It was rather a deliverance from an external evil and the suffering and injustice it caused by means of a shattering defeat of the evil power and an irrevocable breaking of its hold over Israel, in all the dimensions—political, economic, social and spiritual.[11]

When we grasp this, it would seem more appropriate to link the exodus to the cross not so much in terms of release from slavery to our own sin (which of course is gloriously also part of its reality) but in terms of release from slavery to all that oppresses human life and well-being and opposes God. The cross, like the exodus, was the victory of God over his enemies, and through the cross God has rescued us from slavery to them. There is plenty of New Testament support for this reading of the cross as cosmic victory and of our salvation as rescue from bondage. Paul probably makes an exodus allusion as he thanks God the Father "for he has rescued us from the dominion of darkness and brought us into the kingdom of the Son he loves, in whom we have redemption, the forgiveness of sins" (Col 1:13-14). Later he speaks of Christ's triumph on the cross over all powers and authorities (Col 2:15). Hebrews rejoices that the death of Christ is the means by which he has been able to "free those who all their lives were held in slavery by their fear of death" (Heb 2:15).

---

[11]Christopher J. H. Wright, *Knowing Jesus Through the Old Testament* (London: Marshall Pickering; Downers Grove, Ill.: InterVarsity Press, 1992), p. 32.

Which reality? Second, those who press a spiritualized application of the exodus, which airbrushes the *socioeconomic* and political dimensions of the original historical event, are misusing the typological method of relating the Old to the New Testament. They treat the Old Testament merely as "foreshadowing" the New, in such a way that the Old Testament story loses all intrinsic significance in its own right. By a misuse of the "shadows" comparison in Hebrews (Heb 8:5), this is given a twist of Platonic dualism, such that the material and historical realm is deemed inferior and transient, whereas only the spiritual and timeless is considered "really real." So the historical elements of the exodus story, which are so prominent within the biblical text, are discarded as a material husk once the spiritual kernel has been extracted. So, now we know what the story "really" means (you can be released from slavery to sin by Christ), we can relegate the rest of its content to the zone of dispensable local color.

But this is not the way the Bible itself deals with the organic continuity between Old and New Testament. Undoubtedly of course, there are aspects of Old Testament *religious practice* that we rightly dispense with because of their fulfillment in Christ. But that is not how the *whole narrative of God's action* in Old Testament times is handled. It is not discarded and replaced by Christ. Rather it is absorbed and fulfilled in him. In the New Testament we reach the completion of all that God has accomplished in redemption.

That does not mean a crude contrast in which we say, "Previously God's redemption involved political liberation and social justice; but now we know it really means spiritual forgiveness." Rather we see the totality of God's redemption in a way that now *includes* all that God has done—from the exodus to the cross. It is not that the New Testament *exchanges* a social message for a spiritual one but that it *extends* the Old Testament teaching to the deepest understanding of and the most radical and final answer to the spiritual dimension of our human predicament, which is already there in embryo in the exodus narrative.

To change the metaphor yet again, the great historical account of God's redemption in the Old Testament is not like a booster rocket that, once the space capsule is launched, drops off and falls away into redundant oblivion. Rather, to adapt Paul's own metaphor, the biblical narrative is like a tree. We now enjoy the spreading branches and abundant fruit in its New Testament fulfillment. But the Old Testament is like the inner rings of the trunk—still there, the evidence of a history long past, but still the supporting structure on which the branches and fruit have grown. The relationship is one of organic continuity, not ruptured discontinuity and abandonment.

What kind of God? Third, a simplistic spiritualized interpretation of the exodus seems to me to presuppose a quite remarkable change in the character and concerns of God. Now of course, the prophets are not afraid to speak of God changing his plans in response to Israel's (or any nation's) response to him. There is progression and development also in the biblical grand narrative. But this is much more radical than that.

This spiritualizing way of interpreting the Bible, and the missiological implications that go with it, requires us to imagine that for generation after generation, century after century, the God of the Bible was passionately concerned about social issues—political arrogance and abuse, economic exploitation, judicial corruption, the suffering of the poor and oppressed, the evils of brutality and bloodshed. So passionate, indeed, that the laws he gave and the prophets he sent give more space to these matters than any other issue except idolatry, while the psalmists cry out in protest to the God they know cares deeply about such things.

Somewhere, however, between Malachi and Matthew, all that changed. Such matters no longer claim God's attention or spark his anger. Or if they do, it is no longer our business. The root cause of all such things is spiritual sin, and that is now all that God is interested in, and that is all that the cross dealt with. A subtle form of Marcionism underlies this approach. The alleged God of the New Testament is almost unrecognizable as the Lord God, the Holy One of Israel. This alleged God has shed all the passionate priorities of the Mosaic law and has jettisoned all the burdens for justice that he laid on his prophets at such cost to them. The implications for mission are equally dramatic. For if the pressing problems of human society are no longer of concern to God, they have no place in Christian mission—or at most a decidedly secondary one. God's mission is getting souls to heaven, not addressing society on earth. Ours should follow suit. There may be an element of caricature in the way I have sketched this view, but it is not unrepresentative of a certain brand of popular mission rhetoric.

It will be clear that I find such a view of God and of mission to be unbiblical and frankly unbelievable, if one takes the *whole Bible* as the trustworthy revelation of the identity, character and mission of the living God. But to repeat, I do *not* reject or reduce the terribly serious spiritual realities of sin and evil that the New Testament exposes, or the glories of the spiritual dimension of God's redemptive accomplishment in the cross and resurrection of Jesus of Nazareth. I simply deny that these truths of the New Testament *nullify* all that the Old Testament has already revealed about God's comprehensive commitment to every dimension of human life, about his relentless opposition to all that oppresses, spoils and diminishes human well-being, and about his ultimate mission of blessing the nations and redeeming his whole creation. Deriving our own missional mandate from this deep source precludes the kind of spiritualized reductionism that can read the exodus narrative, discern one vital dimension of its truth and yet bypass the message that cries out from its pages as loudly as the Israelites cried out in their bondage.

Politicizing interpretation. At the other end of the hermeneutical spectrum are those who are drawn to the exodus narrative precisely *because* of its robust affirmation of YHWH's passionate concern for justice, and his execution of that justice on a rogue state that first exploited the weak and then turned against them with murderous ferocity. They see this as the prime meaning of the exodus story: YHWH is the God who hates oppression and acts decisively against it. The political, economic and social dimensions of Israel's plight, and the matching dimensions of God's deliverance, are thus explored to the full and built into a theology, an ethic and a missiology of committed advocacy for the weak and marginalized of the world.

The most well-known protagonists of such a hermeneutic in the modern era, of course, have been the different brands of liberation theology that emerged in Latin America and then spread to other parts of the world.[12] In some (though by no means all) of these, the position is taken that God is at work redemptively wherever there is struggle against injustice and oppression. The biblical God declares himself, through the exodus story, to be on the side of all who are oppressed, so any action to throw off that oppression and to bring liberty and justice is, by its very nature, redemptive, saving—whether or not anybody comes to faith in Jesus Christ as Lord and Savior, whether or not churches are planted. So we have the opposite of the first error, which was to emphasize the spiritual interpretation of the exodus in the New Testament and overlook its societal dimensions; in this case it is to emphasize the social justice dimension of the exodus while overlooking both its own inbuilt spiritual purpose as well as its explicit New Testament connection to the saving work of Christ. An exclusively political interpretation of the exodus, however, is as biblically deficient as an exclusively spiritual one. As before, my objection is not to the main case that such interpretations build (namely, that the God of the Bible is committed to social justice and so should we be) but rather when the whole exodus tradition is reduced to that dimension alone or severed from its

---

[12]I say, "in the modern era," in recognition of the fact that both Jews and Christians through the centuries have found in the exodus story powerful dynamics for political, social and economic struggle against the forces of oppression in many previous generations. See, e.g., Michael Walzer, *Exodus and Revolution* (New York: Basic Books, 1985). See also (but with a more subverting perspective on the normal liberationist reading of exodus) J. David Pleins, *The Social Visions of the Hebrew Bible: A Theological Introduction* (Louisville: Westminster John Knox, 2001), chap. 4.

spiritual and evangelistic implications. Again, several points need to be made.

An unfair objection. One major objection that has been made to the use of the exodus by liberation theologies is that it takes an illegitimate hermeneutical step in moving from the fact that God undoubtedly did rescue Israel from political and economic oppression to the assumption that this is what God wants or intends to do for all other people in similar circumstances. Such a move, it is objected, overlooks the uniqueness of Israel in the plan of God and the fact that the narrative itself makes it clear that the exodus was motivated by God's faithfulness to Abraham. We cannot say that all nations stand before God as Israel did in their covenant relationship to YHWH, and we cannot say that God is motivated by his promise to Abraham in relation to any other nation than Israel. So we are not at liberty to extrapolate from what God uniquely did for Israel out of faithfulness to Abraham to what he wishes to do, or what we should endeavor to do, for the oppressed anywhere in the world.

This was the argument put forward by John Stott in his rejection of the way some liberation theologians politicized the whole concept of salvation in a manner that he rightly regarded as a serious confusion of categories. Writing against those in the World Council of Churches who wished to turn the exodus into "the type of liberation which God intends for all the downtrodden," Stott does not deny that "oppression in every form is hateful to God," but points to

> the special relationship which God had established between himself and his people Israel [e.g., Amos 3:2]. . . . It was this same special relationship which lay behind the Exodus. God rescued his people from Egypt in fulfillment of his covenant with Abraham, Isaac and Jacob and in anticipation of its renewal at Mount Sinai (Ex. 2:24; 19:4-6). He made no covenant with the Syrians or the Philistines, nor did his providential activity in their national life make them his covenant people.[13]

There is a lot of force in this objection, and it is of course correct to point out the uniqueness of Israel and the emphasis on God's promise to Abraham. I have stressed the same things repeatedly. However it is not the whole truth. For while I agree with John Stott's point, I do not think it goes far enough in recognizing the paradigmatic nature of the exodus, on the basis of the paradigmatic significance of Israel itself for the rest of humanity. Consider two further points.

On the one hand, we must remember that God's promise to Abraham was never intended for Israel's exclusive benefit. It always had that universalizing dynamic of the bottom line. So, there is always something paradigmatic about what God does in and for Israel. Certainly, there is a uniqueness and a particu-

---

[13]John R. W. Stott, *Christian Mission in the Modern World* (London: Falcon, 1975), p. 96.

larity about Israel's redemptive history, but it was a uniqueness and particularity that *defined and demonstrated the character of God*—the God who was not the God of Israel only but of *all the earth and of all nations.*

So while we accept the historical fact that God did not deliver all the oppressed in all the empires of the ancient Near East, we cannot deduce that he was ignorant or unconcerned about them or that his anger did not also rest on the perpetrators of injustice elsewhere. Rather, we recognize again the importance of a missiological perspective on this part of the biblical story.

> By virtue of being the recipients of Abraham's promise, Israel stands as a model of the way YHWH works in the world as a whole, in deliverance, in obligation, in blessing and in danger. There is something distinctive about YHWH's involvement with Israel, but this distinctiveness does not lie in Israel's being the only people YHWH is involved with. YHWH is ultimately no more concerned for Israel's freedom and blessing than for other people. . . . YHWH's distinctive involvement with Israel lay in what YHWH was set on achieving through this people. It is through this people that God has wanted to bless the world.[14]

And on the other hand, the Old Testament itself actually does draw universal conclusions on the basis of exodus about the character of God and his response to all who cry out under oppression. Psalm 33, for example, moves from celebrating the "exodus" character of God (right, true, faithful, lover of righteousness and justice [Ps 33:4-5a]) to the universal claim that "the earth is full of his unfailing love" (v. 5b) and that all human life on the planet is under is gaze (Ps 33:13-15). Psalm 145, similarly, moves from celebrating the mighty acts of God in Israel's history to the affirmation that he has "compassion on all he has made," and especially that he hears the cry of all who cry out to him—which is exodus imagery extended. And most impressive of all, even Egypt itself is scheduled for redemptive blessing when they cry out to the Lord in the remarkable reversal of the plagues portrayed in Isaiah 19.

So it seems legitimate to me to draw the same conclusion that Israelite worshipers seem to have drawn, which is that the loving concern and redemptive action that God had demonstrated in the social arena of Israel's history, while they were unique within the framework of his covenantal relationship with them, were not exceptional and exclusive. Rather they were, in the proper sense, *typical.* That is simply how it is with YHWH God. Such concern and action are definitive of his character.

> The LORD your God is God of gods and Lord of lords, the great God, mighty and

---

[14]Goldingay, *Old Testament Theology,* 1:294-95.

awesome, who shows no partiality and accepts no bribes. He defends the cause of the fatherless and widow, and loves the alien, giving him food and clothing. And you are to love those who are aliens, for you yourselves were aliens in Egypt. (Deut 10:17-19)

This key text binds together the sole sovereignty of the sole God—YHWH—with his generic moral integrity, justice and compassion, and then goes seamlessly on to the ethical and missional implication for those who have experienced this God's exodus love: they are to go and do likewise.

Not far enough. So my objection to the politicized interpretation of the exodus is not that it is hermeneutically wrong to use the exodus as evidence for God's passionate concern for justice and for human rights and dignity in wider society or the international arena (any more than the spiritual interpretation is wrong to use the exodus as a picture of the victory of the cross). The problem is not with what it says but where it stops. An interpretation that limits the relevance of the exodus to the political, social and economic realm, or prioritizes such issues at the expense or even to the exclusion of the spiritual question of whether or not people come to know the one living God and to worship and serve him in covenant commitment and obedience is simply not handling the text as a whole and is therefore seriously distorting it.

The goal of the exodus in the biblical story was clearly *not* confined to political liberation. Indeed, "liberation" (with its modern sense of achieving freedom or independence) is not even the best word to describe the whole narrative. In various texts in Exodus, God or Moses speak of YHWH's intention to "bring out," "rescue," "redeem" or "save" Israel from the Egyptians (e.g., Ex 6:6; 14:13, 30). They do not talk merely of finding freedom in the modern sense of independence or self-determination. Rather, the purpose of the exodus was to bring Israel out of slavery (*'ăbōdâ*) to Pharaoh so that they could properly enter the service/worship (*'ăbōdâ*) of YHWH. Israel's problem was not just that they were slaves and ought to be free. It was that they were *slaves to the wrong master and needed to be reclaimed and restored to their proper Lord.*

> The exodus does not take Israel from serfdom to the freedom of independence but from service of one lord to service of another. . . . Freedom in Scripture is the freedom to serve YHWH. This dynamic suggests another direction in which we might need to reframe the emphases of liberation theology.[15]

So to work for political reform, the replacement of tyranny with democratic freedoms, to devise programs of economic uplift and community development,

---

[15]Ibid., p. 323.

to campaign for redistribution of resources, social justice, the restraint of state-sponsored violence or genocide and so forth are all positive things in themselves and Christians who engage in them can assuredly motivate their efforts by reference to the character and will of God as revealed prominently throughout Scripture. But to *confine* oneself to such an agenda without also seeking to lead people to know God through repentance and faith in Christ, to worship and serve him in covenant love, faithfulness and obedience (in other words without effective evangelism and discipling) simply cannot be considered an adequate expression of exodus-shaped redemption and is certainly not holistic, exodus-shaped mission.

Sin and exile. Furthermore, to focus exclusively on the exodus as the biblical foundation for a theology and mission of sociopolitical engagement is unbalanced in that it ignores the rest of the biblical history of Israel. The people who enjoyed the great benefit of YHWH's redeeming intervention, who were delivered from political discrimination, economic exploitation and social violence, went on to allow all these things to poison their own life as a society in the centuries that followed. And the wrath of God's judgment bore in upon rebellious Israel just as severely as it had on the Egyptians—even more so. So the story that began with the exodus ended with the exile. And this is a story that proved, as the prophets and psalmists perceived, that Israel's deepest problem was the same as that which afflicts all the rest of humanity—their own sinful rebellion, their hardness of heart, their blindness to God's acts, their deafness to God's word, their congenital unwillingness to do the one thing he asked—to fear the Lord, walk in his ways, love him, serve him and obey him (Deut 10:12).

And so, from the death and despair of exile, comes the voice that tells Israel that although, yet again, God will indeed intervene in their national history with another exodus (this time out of Babylon), their real need is not just *restoration to Jerusalem* but *restoration to God*. What Israel needed was not just the ending of their exile but also the forgiveness of their sin. Both are contained in the prophets' vocabulary of salvation (e.g., Is 43:25; Jer 31:34; Ezek 36:24-32). Cyrus as God's agent could take care of the first, but only the suffering Servant of the Lord would accomplish the second.[16] So the spiritual dimension of Israel's (and humanity's) need, and the spiritual dimension of God's ultimate redemptive goal, are both recognized within the Old Testament itself. The New

---

[16]"One does not want to make a false distinction between the material and the spiritual, but in some sense the man of war can effect the former kind of restoration, but only the suffering servant the latter. A military victor can bring the Jews back to Jerusalem; but their history has exposed the depth of the problem of their sin, and it will take a suffering servant to bring them back to God." John Goldingay, "The Man of War and the Suffering Servant: The Old Testament and the Theology of Liberation," *Tyndale Bulletin* 27 (1976): 104.

Testament did not *add* a spiritual dimension to an otherwise materialistic Old Testament understanding of redemption. It tells the story of how God accomplished that deepest dimension in the climactic work of Christ. Nor is it the *replacement* of the Old by the New, but a recognition of where the Old Testament's insights eventually must lead if the fullness of God's redeeming purpose was to be realized.[17]

Integral interpretation. My plea then is that if we are to regard the exodus as the prototype of God's redemption, as the Bible assuredly does in both Testaments, we must apply the wholeness of its message and meaning to our practice of mission. Reducing our missional mandate to either pole of the whole model will result not only in hermeneutical distortion, but worse, in practical damage and deficiency in the fruit of our mission labors. Walter Brueggemann warns us, rightly in my view, against such reductionism in either direction.

> There is no doubt that the Old Testament witness concerns real socioeconomic and political circumstances, from which Yahweh is said to liberate Israel. There is also no doubt that the rhetoric of the New Testament permits a "spiritualizing" of Exodus language, so that the liberation of the gospel is more readily understood as liberation from sin, in contrast with concrete socioeconomic-political bondage. It is not necessary here to reiterate the arguments concerning the genuine material forms of rescue presented in the New Testament. It is important to recognize, however, that already in the Old Testament, the witnesses to Yahweh understood that real, concrete, material bondage is authorized and enacted by "the powers of death" that actively resist the intention of Yahweh. Thus we must not argue, in my judgment, that deliverance is material rather than spiritual *[in the Old Testament]* or that salvation is spiritual rather than material *[in the New Testament]*. Rather, either side of such dualism distorts true human bondage and misreads Israel's text. . . . The issue of the Bible, in both Testaments, is not one of either/or but of both/and. It will not do to be reductionist in a materialist direction. Conversely it is simply wrong to refuse the material dimension of slavery and freedom in a safer spiritualizing theology, to which much Christian interpretation is tempted.[18]

Social action without evangelism. To think that social action is all there is to mission, while failing to lead people to the knowledge, worship and service of God in Christ, is to condemn those whom we may, in one way or another, "lead

---

[17]"The drift of the New Testament is along the line hinted at by Exodus and developed by Isaiah 40-55. In particular, the motifs of exodus, redemption, and liberation become predominantly spiritual; redemption from sin is the central idea, because man's weakness and wilfulness is his deepest problem, without which his political, social, and economic problems cannot be solved." Ibid., p. 105.

[18]Brueggemann, *Theology of the Old Testament,* p. 180.

out of slavery" to repeat the history of Israel. For the Israelites experienced the political, social and economic effects of God's redemption, but many of them failed to enter into the spiritual requirements of the God who redeemed them. They would not acknowledge him as alone God. They repeatedly went astray in the worship of other gods. They chose to serve other nations in alliances that were spiritually and politically calamitous. They experienced God as Redeemer—the Old Testament affirms that persistently. But they would not submit to God as King and walk in his ways. So in more ways than one, they perished.

The social, political and economic dimensions of God's redeeming work were real and vital, and they still remain as pressing priorities for God—as every prophet testified. But they did not constitute the totality of what God intended by a covenant relationship with this people. Without covenant faith, covenant worship and covenant obedience, Israel stood as much under the severity of God's wrath as any other nation.

Paul and the writer to the Hebrews reflect on this terrible danger when they point out that the generation that experienced the wonders of God's deliverance from slavery in Egypt nevertheless failed to enter into the fullness of God's salvation because of disobedience and unbelief (1 Cor 10:1-5; Heb 3:16-19).

A change of political or economic or geographical landscape, a change of government, a change of social status may all be beneficial in themselves, but they will be of no eternal benefit unless the spiritual goals of exodus are also met. So to change people's social or economic status without leading them to saving faith and obedience to God in Christ leads no further than the wilderness or the exile, both places of death.

Evangelism without social action. But on the other hand, to think that spiritual evangelism is all there is to mission, is to leave people vulnerable in other ways that are also mirrored in Israel. "Spiritual evangelism" means that the gospel is presented only as a means of having your own sins forgiven and having assurance of a future with God in heaven—without either the moral challenge of walking with personal integrity in the world of social, economic and political society around us, or the missional challenge of being actively concerned for issues of justice and compassion for others. The result is a kind of privatized pietism, or one that is cosily shared with like-minded believers but has little cutting edge or prophetic relevance in relation to wider society. One can then be a Christian on the way to heaven, and even make a virtue out of paying little attention to the physical, material, familial, societal, and international needs and crises that abound on every side. These latter things can then be all too easily relegated to such a nonpriority status that they drop below the radar of mission recognition altogether.

Israel fell victim to this temptation too. The prophets saw a people whose appetite for worship was insatiable but whose daily lives were a denial of all the moral standards of the God they claimed to worship. There was plenty of charismatic fervor (Amos 5:21-24), plenty of atonement theology in the blood of multiple sacrifices (Is 1:10-12), plenty of assurance of salvation in the recitation of sound-bite claims for the temple (Jer 7:4-11), plenty of religious observance at great festivals and conventions (Is 1:13-15). But beneath their noses and under their feet, the poor were uncared for at best and trampled on at worst. Spiritual religion flourished amidst social rottenness. And God hated it. God longed for somebody to shut down the whole charade (Mal 1:10), and finally he wiped it out of his sight.

Mission that claims the high spiritual ground of preaching only a gospel of personal forgiveness and salvation without the radical challenge of the full biblical demands of God's justice and compassion, without a hunger and thirst for justice, may well expose those who respond to its partial truths to the same dangerous verdict. The epistle of James seems to say as much to those in his own day who had managed to drive an unbiblical wedge between faith and works, the spiritual and the material. If faith without works is dead, mission without social compassion and justice is biblically deficient.

9

God's Model of Restoration

The Jubilee

Chapter eight on redemption and mission was devoted to thinking about the exodus. And rightly so, since it is such a foundational narrative and dominant influence in the rest of the Bible. It gives initial shape and content to what the Bible means by redemption, and therefore what our mission must take into account. When all is said and done, however, the exodus was a single historical event. And God's concern was that its essential principles should be worked out in Israel's life. There needed to be an ongoing commitment to economic and social justice, freedom from oppression, and due acknowledgement of God through covenant loyalty and worship. For this purpose, the structures, institutions and legislation that we find in Israel's law were given.

God is a realist. It was one thing to rescue people from exploitation and give them a land of their own. It would be another to keep them from exploiting one another. It was one thing to hold before them the ideal that if they lived in obedience to his laws there need be no poor people among them. The reality would be that they would not fully obey and there would always be poor people among them (Deut 15:4, 11). What then could be done to prevent poverty taking hold permanently? How could the relentless downward spiral of misfortune, debt and bondage be broken? These are the questions to which Israel's economic legislation was addressed.

There is in fact a whole raft of such legislation, constituting a systemic address and redress to the factors that lead to impoverishment. They include the duty to lend to the poor. But alongside that duty went several key legislative limits on the power of those who do so: the ban on interest that exploited the needy or the poor, the ban on exorbitant or life-threatening demands for collateral, the sabbatical release of debts and slaves, the provisions for the redemption of mortgaged land and family members who had entered bonded service to pay off debts.[1]

But one institution in particular catches our attention, since it embodies so many of these concerns. And it does so on the foundation of some very clear theological affirmations that lie close to the theology of mission I am seeking to articulate in these pages. That institution was the jubilee, described in Leviticus 25. If the exodus was God's idea of *redemption,* the jubilee was God's idea of *restoration.* Both are equally holistic. That is, the jubilee also is concerned for the whole range of a person's social and economic need, but cannot be understood and could not be practiced without attention to the theological and spiritual principles that are intrinsic to it. We embark, then, on a missional reading of this ancient Israelite institution, moving from its earthy economic details through to its ethical, evangelistic and eschatological implications.

Jubilee in Context

The jubilee *(yōbēl)* came at the end of the cycle of seven sabbatical years. Leviticus 25:8-10 specifies it as the fiftieth year, though some scholars believe it may have been actually the forty-ninth, that is, the seventh sabbatical year. And some suggest it was not a full year but either a single day as an event within the fiftieth year or an intercalary month after the forty-ninth year, with the same calendrical effect as our system of leap years. In this year there was to be a proclamation of liberty to Israelites who had become enslaved for debt and a restoration of land to families who had been compelled to sell it out of economic need sometime during the previous fifty years. Instructions concerning the jubilee and its relation to the procedures of land and slave redemption are found entirely in Leviticus 25. But it is referred to also in Leviticus 26—27. It is an institution that has inspired much curiosity in ancient and modern times, and in recent years it has come to prominence in the writings of those committed to radical Christian social ethics. Our purpose here is to see what it may contribute to a biblical understanding of holistic mission.

The jubilee was in essence an economic institution. It had two main points of concern: the family and the land. It was rooted, therefore, in the *social* structure of Israelite kinship and the *economic* system of land tenure that was based on it. Both of these, however, also had *theological* dimensions in Israel's faith.

---

[1]I have explored Israel's economic system in considerable depth in my *Old Testament Ethics for the People of God* (Leicester, U.K.: Inter-Varsity Press; Downers Grove, Ill.: InterVarsity Press, 2004), chaps. 3, 5.

So we must look briefly at the jubilee from each of these three angles.

The social angle: Israel's kinship system. Israel had a three-tier pattern of kinship, comprising the tribe, the clan, and the household. Gideon's modest reply to his angelic visitor shows us all three: "Look at my clan—it is the weakest in the tribe of Manasseh; and I am the least in my father's house" (Judg 6:15, author's translation). The last two smaller units (household and clan) had greater social and economic importance than the tribe in terms of benefits and responsibilities relating to individual Israelites. The father's house was an extended family that could comprise three or four generations living together, along with servants and hired employees. This was a place of authority, even for married adults like Gideon (Judg 6:27; 8:20). It was also the place of security and protection (Judg 6:30-35). The fathers' houses also played an important role in the judicial and even military functions, and was the place where the individual Israelite found identity, education and religious nurture.[2] *The jubilee was intended primarily for the economic protection of the father's house, or the extended family.*

The economic angle: Israel's system of land tenure. Israel's system of land tenure was based on these kinship units. As Joshua 15—22 makes clear, the territory was allotted to tribes, then "according to their clans," and then within the clans each household had its portion or "heritage." This system had two features that stand in complete contrast to the preceding Canaanite economic structure.

Equitable distribution. In pre-Israelite Canaan the land was owned by kings and their nobles, with the bulk of the population living as tax-paying tenant farmers. In Israel the initial division of the land was explicitly to the clans and households within the tribes, under the general rubric that each should receive land according to size and need. The tribal lists of Numbers 26 (especially note vv. 52-56) and the detailed territorial division of land recorded in Joshua 13—21 are the documentary evidence that the original intention of Israel's land system was that the land should be *distributed throughout the whole kinship system as widely as possible.*

Inalienability. In order to protect this system of kinship distribution, family land was made inalienable. That is, it was not to be bought and sold as a commercial asset but was to remain as far as possible within the extended family,

---

[2] For further information on Israel's kinship system, see, Christopher J. H. Wright, *God's People in God's Land: Family, Land and Property in the Old Testament* (Grand Rapids: Eerdmans, 1990), chap. 2; and Christopher J. H. Wright, "Family," *Anchor Bible Dictionary*, ed. David Noel Freedman (New York: Doubleday, 1992), 2:761-69.

or at least within the circle of families in the clan. It was this principle that lay behind Naboth's refusal to sell his patrimony to Ahab (1 Kings 21), and it is most explicit in the economic regulations of Leviticus 25.

The theological angle: God's land, God's people. "The land must not be sold permanently, because the land is mine and you are but aliens and my tenants" (Lev 25:23). This statement, at the heart of the chapter containing the jubilee, provides the hinge between the social and economic system described above and its theological rationale. It makes two fundamental statements about the land Israel lived on and about the Israelites themselves. These are crucial to understanding the rationale for the jubilee.

God's land. One of the central pillars of the faith of Israel was that the land they inhabited was YHWH's land. It had been his even before Israel entered it (Ex 15:13, 17). This theme of the divine ownership of the land is found often in the prophets and Psalms. Far more often than it is ever called "Israel's land," it is referred to as "YHWH's land." At the same time, although it belonged to YHWH, the land had been promised and then given to Israel in the course of the redemptive history. It was their possession, their inheritance, as Deuteronomy repeatedly describes it.

So the land was in Israel's possession but still under God's ownership. This dual tradition of the land (*divine ownership* and *divine gift*) was associated in some way with every major thread in Israel's theology. The promise of land was an essential part of the patriarchal *election* tradition. The land was the goal of the exodus *redemption* tradition. The maintenance of the *covenant* relationship and the security of life in the land were bound together. Divine *judgment* eventually meant expulsion from the land, until the *restored relationship* was symbolized in the return to the land. The land, then, stood like a fulcrum in the relationship between God and Israel (notice, e.g., its pivotal position in Lev 26:40-45). The land was a monumental, tangible witness both to YHWH's control of history within which the relationship had been established and also to the moral demands on Israel which that relationship entailed.

For the Israelite, living with his family on his allotted share of YHWH's land, the land itself was the proof of his membership of God's people and the focus of his practical response to God's grace. Nothing that concerned the land was free from theological and ethical dimensions—as every harvest reminded him (Deut 26).

God's people. Israel was strangers and sojourners (RSV), aliens and tenants (NIV) with the Lord (Lev 25:23). These terms, (*gērîm wĕtôšābîm*), normally in Old Testament texts describe a class of people who resided among the Israelites in Canaan, but were not ethnic Israelites. They may have been descendants of the dispossessed Canaanites, or immigrants. They had no stake in the tenure of the land, but survived by hiring out their services as residential employees (laborers, craftsmen, etc.) for Israelite land-owning households. Provided an Israelite household itself remained economically viable, then its resident alien employees enjoyed both protection and security. But otherwise, their position could be perilous. Hence these resident aliens are frequently mentioned in Israel's law as the objects of particular concern for justice because of their vulnerability.

The point of Leviticus 25:23 is to say that the Israelites were to regard their own status before God as analogous to that of these residential dependents to themselves. Just as the Israelites had resident guests living on with them in the land they (the Israelites) owned, so the Israelites were resident guests living on the land that YHWH actually owned. Thus the Israelites had no ultimate title to the land—it was owned by God. YHWH was the supreme landlord. Israel was his collective tenant. Nevertheless, the Israelites could enjoy secure benefits of the land under YHWH's protection and in dependence on him. So the terms are not (as they might sound in English) a denial of *rights* but rather an affirmation of a *relationship* of protected dependency.

The practical effect of this model for Israel's relationship with God is seen in Leviticus 25:35, 40, 53. If all Israelites share this same status before God, then the impoverished or indebted brother is to be regarded and treated in the same way as God regards and treats all Israel, that is, with compassion, justice and generosity. So the theology of Israel's land and of Israel's status before God combine to affect this very practical area of social economics.

The practical provisions of the Jubilee. In Leviticus 25 the jubilee provisions are interwoven with other provisions for the practice of redemption of land and slaves. The economic mechanism of redemption is a vital piece of background for understanding the full meaning of God's redemption, as the exodus is called. So it is thus doubly interesting to see how the jubilee was supposed to work alongside redemption in Israel's system. Leviticus 25 is a complex chapter, and I cannot do a thorough exegesis here.[3] It opens with the law of the sabbatical year on the land (vv. 1-7). This is an expansion of the fallow year law of Exodus 23:10-11, which was also further developed in Deuteronomy 15:1-2 into a year in which debts (or more probably the pledges given for loans) were to be released.

The jubilee is then introduced in Leviticus 25:8-12 as the fiftieth year to follow the seventh sabbatical year. Verse 10 presents the twin concepts that are funda-

---

[3]For a detailed exegesis see, Christopher J. H. Wright, "Jubilee, Year Of," *Anchor Bible Dictionary,* ed. D. N. Freedman (New York: Doubleday, 1992), 3:1025-30; and Wright, *Old Testament Ethics,* chap. 6.

mental to the whole jubilee institution, namely, *liberty* and *return*. Liberty from the burden of debt and the bondage it may have entailed; return both to the ancestral property if it had been mortgaged to a creditor and to the family, which may have been split up through debt servitude. It was these two components of the jubilee (freedom and restoration, release and return) that entered into the metaphorical and eschatological use of the jubilee in prophetic and later New Testament thought.

The practical details of redemption and jubilee are outlined from Leviticus 25:25 to the end of the chapter. In these verses three descending stages of poverty are presented, each with a required response. The stages are marked off by the introductory phrase "If your brother becomes poor" (Lev 25:25, 35, 39, 47). The sequence is interrupted by parenthetical sections dealing with houses in cities and Levite properties (Lev 25:29-34) and non-Israelite slaves (Lev 25:44-46), which we need not consider, but the overall legal framework is clear.

Stage 1 (Lev 25: 25-28). Initially, having fallen on hard times (for any reason; none is specified) the Israelite land owner sells, or offers to sell, some of his land. To keep it within the family, in line with the inalienability principle, it was first of all the duty of the nearest kinsman (the *gō'ēl*) either to preempt it (if it was still on offer) or to redeem it (if it had been sold). Second, the seller himself retains the right to redeem it for himself if he later recovers the means to do so. *Third, and in any case, the property, whether sold or redeemed by a kinsman, reverts to the original family in the year of jubilee.*

Stage 2 (Lev 25:35-38). If the poorer brother's plight worsens and he still cannot stay solvent, presumably even after several such sales, it then becomes the duty of the kinsman to maintain him as a dependent laborer, by means of interest-free loans.

Stage 3a (Lev 25:39-43). In the event of a total economic collapse, such that the poorer kinsman has no more land left to sell or pledge for loans, he and his whole family sell themselves to (i.e., enter the bonded service of) the wealthier kinsman. The latter, however, is commanded in strong and repeated terms not to treat the debtor Israelite like a slave but rather as a resident employee. *This undesirable state of affairs is to continue only until the next jubilee, that is, not more than one more generation.* Then the debtor or his children (the original debtor may have died but the next generation was to benefit from the jubilee [vv. 41, 54]), were to recover their original patrimony of land and be enabled to make a fresh start.

Stage 3b (Lev 25:47-55). If a man had entered this debt bondage *outside* the clan, then an obligation lay on the whole clan to prevent this loss of a whole family by exercising their duty to redeem him. The whole clan had the duty of preserving its constituent families and their inherited land. It also had the duty to see that a non-Israelite creditor behaved as an Israelite should toward an Israelite debtor, *and that the jubilee provision was adhered to eventually.*

From this analysis, it can be seen that there were two main differences between the redemption and jubilee provisions: First, *timing.* Redemption (of land or persons) was a duty that could be exercised at any time, locally, as circumstances required, whereas jubilee was intended to be twice a century as a national event. Second, *purpose.* The main aim of redemption was the preservation of the land and persons of the wider *clan,* whereas the main beneficiary of the jubilee was the smaller *household,* or "father's house." The jubilee therefore functioned as a necessary override to the practice of redemption. The regular operation of redemption over a period could result in the whole territory of a clan coming into the hands of a few wealthier families, with the rest of the families in the clan in a kind of debt servitude, living as dependent tenants of the wealthy, that is, precisely the kind of land-tenure system that Israel had overturned. The jubilee was thus a mechanism to prevent this. *The primary purpose of the jubilee was to preserve the socioeconomic fabric of multiple-household land tenure and the comparative equality and independent viability of the smallest family-plus-land units. In other words, the jubilee was intended for the survival and welfare of the families in Israel.*

The inevitable question arises, of course, did it ever historically happen? The fact is that there is no historical narrative recording a jubilee happening. But then, there is no historical record of the Day of Atonement, either. Silence in the narratives proves almost nothing. More divisive is the question whether the jubilee was an early law that fell into disuse or a late piece of utopian idealism from the time of the exile. Many critical scholars affirm the latter, but others, especially those with in-depth knowledge of the ancient Near East, point out that such periodical amnesties for debt and restoration of land were known in Mesopotamia for centuries before the establishment of Israel, though nothing on such a regular fifty year cycle has been found.[4]

My own preference is that it makes sense to see the jubilee as a very ancient

---

[4]For bibliography of earlier works, see Wright, *God's People in God's Land,* pp. 119-27, and Wright, "Jubilee, Year Of." More recent works include Jeffrey A Fager, *Land Tenure and the Biblical Jubilee,* JSOT Supplements 155 (Sheffield, U.K.: JSOT Press, 1993); Hans Ucko, ed., *The Jubilee Challenge: Utopia or Possibility: Jewish and Christian Insights* (Geneva: WCC Publications, 1997), and Moshe Weinfeld, *Social Justice in Ancient Israel and in the Ancient Near East* (Minneapolis: Fortress Press, 1995). A good, recent and balanced survey of all these issues is provided by P. A. Barker, "Sabbath, Sabbatical Year, Jubilee," *Dictionary of the Old Testament: Pentateuch,* ed. David W. Baker and Desmond T. Alexander (Downers Grove, Ill.: InterVarsity Press; Leicester, U.K.: Inter-Varsity Press, 2003), pp. 695-706.

law that fell into neglect during Israel's history in the land. This neglect happened not so much because the jubilee was economically impossible as because it became irrelevant to the scale of social disruption. The jubilee presupposes a situation where a man, though in severe debt, still technically holds the title to his family's land and could be restored to full ownership of it. But from the time of Solomon on this must have become meaningless for growing numbers of families as they fell victim to the acids of debt, slavery, royal intrusion and confiscation, and total dispossession. Many were uprooted and pushed off their ancestral land altogether. After a few generations they had nothing to be restored to in any practicable sense (cf. Is 5:8; Mic 2:2, 9). This would explain why the jubilee is never appealed to by any of the prophets as an economic proposal (though its ideals are reflected metaphorically).

Jubilee, Ethics and Mission

Elsewhere I have argued for a paradigmatic approach to handling the laws of the Old Testament as Christians in order to discern their ethical implications in the contemporary world.[5] This means identifying the coherent body of principles on which an Old Testament law or institution is based and which it embodies or instantiates. To do this, it is helpful once more to move around our three angles and consider how Israel's paradigm, in the particular case of the jubilee institution, speaks to Christian ethics and mission.

The economic angle: Access to resources. The jubilee existed to protect a form of land tenure that was based on an equitable and widespread distribution of the land, and to prevent the accumulation of ownership in the hands of a wealthy few. This echoes the wider creation principle that the whole earth is given by God to all humanity, who act as costewards of its resources. There is a parallel between, on the one hand, the affirmation of Leviticus 25:23, regarding *Israel*, that "the land is mine," and on the other hand, the affirmation of Psalm 24:1, regarding *all humanity*, that "the earth is the LORD's, and everything in it, / the world and all who live in it." The moral principles of the jubilee are therefore universalizable on the basis of the moral consistency of God. What God required of Israel in God's land reflects what in principle he desires for humanity on God's earth—namely, broadly equitable distribution of the resources of the earth, especially land, and a curb on the tendency to accumulation with its inevitable oppression and alienation.

The jubilee thus stands as a critique not only of massive private accumulation

---

[5]Wright, *Old Testament Ethics,* chap. 9.

of land and related wealth but also of large-scale forms of collectivism or nationalization that destroy any meaningful sense of personal or family ownership. It still has a point to make in modern Christian approaches to economics. The jubilee did not, of course, entail a *redistribution* of land, as some popular writings mistakenly suppose. It was not a redistribution but a restoration. It was not a free handout of bread or charity but a restoration to family units of *the opportunity and the resources to provide for themselves* again. In modern application, that calls for some creative thinking as to what forms of opportunity and resources would enable people to do that, and to enjoy the dignity and social involvement that such self-provision entails.[6] The jubilee then is about restoring to people the capacity to participate in the economic life of the community for their own viability and society's benefit. There is both ethical and missional relevance in that.

The social angle: Family viability. The jubilee embodied practical concern for the family unit. In Israel's case, this meant the extended family, the "father's house," which was a sizeable group of related nuclear families descended in the male line from a living progenitor, including up to three or four generations. This was the smallest unit in Israel's kinship structure, and it was the focus of identity, status, responsibility and security for the individual Israelite. It was this social unit, the extended family, that the jubilee aimed to protect and periodically to restore if necessary.

Notably, the jubilee law pursued this objective, not by merely *moral* means, that is, appealing for greater family cohesion or admonishing parents and children to greater exercise of discipline and obedience respectively. Rather, the jubilee approach was immensely practical and fundamentally *socioeconomic*. It established specific structural mechanisms to regulate the economic effects of debt. Family morality was meaningless if families were being split up and dispossessed by economic forces that rendered them powerless (cf. Neh 5:1-5). The jubilee aimed to restore social dignity and participation to families through maintaining or restoring their economic viability.[7]

Debt is a huge cause of social disruption and decay, and tends to breed many

---

[6]Interesting and creative applications of the jubilee and other aspects of Old Testament economics are found in John Mason, "Biblical Teaching and Assisting the Poor," *Transformation* 4, no. 2 (1987): 1-14, and Stephen Charles Mott, "The Contribution of the Bible to Economic Thought," *Transformation* 4, nos. 3-4 (1987): 25-34.

[7]A thorough attempt to apply the relevance of the Old Testament patterns regarding the extended family to contemporary Western society is made by Michael Schluter and Roy Clements, *Reactivating the Extended Family: From Biblical Norms to Public Policy in Britain* (Cambridge: Jubilee Centre, 1986). See further Michael Schluter and John Ashcroft, eds., *Jubilee Manifesto: A Framework, Agenda & Strategy for Christian Social Reform* (Leicester, U.K.: InterVarsity Press, 2005), chap. 9.

other social ills, including crime, poverty, squalor, and violence. Debt happens, and the Old Testament recognizes that fact. But the jubilee was an attempt to limit its otherwise relentless and endless social consequences by limiting its possible duration. The economic collapse of a family in one generation was not to condemn all future generations to the bondage of perpetual indebtedness. Such principles and objectives are certainly not irrelevant to welfare legislation or indeed any legislation with *socioeconomic* implications.

And indeed, taken to a wider level still, the jubilee speaks volumes to the massive issue of international debt. Not for nothing was the worldwide campaign to see an ending of the intolerable and interminable debts of impoverished nations called Jubilee 2000. And many Christians have instinctively felt a moral imperative to support the campaign, not only out of compassion for the poor but out of a biblically rooted sense of justice and what God requires of us.

Another interesting, creative and in my view convincing, paradigmatic handling of the jubilee institution is suggested by Geiko Muller-Fahrenholz in a chapter titled "The Jubilee: Time Ceilings for the Growth of Money."[8] He comments on the powerful theology of time that is implied in the sabbatical cycles of Israel, and its contrast with the commercializing of time in modern debt-and-interest-based economies. Time is a quality that belongs to God, for no created being can make time.

> We enjoy time, we are carried along in the flow of time, everything is embedded in its time, so the very idea of exploiting the flow of time to take interest on money lent seemed preposterous. It does so no more because the sacredness of time has disappeared, even before the sacredness of the land vanished from the memories of our modern societies. Instead capitalist market economies have been elevated to global importance; they are enshrined with the qualities of omnipotence that border on idolatry. So the question arises: does it make sense to attribute to money qualities that no created thing can ever have, namely eternal growth? Every tree must die, every house must one day crumble, every human being must perish. Why should immaterial goods such as capital—and its counterpart, debts—not also have their time? The capital knows no natural barriers to its growth. There is no jubilee to put an end to its accumulative power. And so there is no jubilee to put an end to debts and slavery. Money that feeds on money, with no productive or social obligation, represents a vast flood that threatens even large national economies and drowns small countries. . . . But at the heart of this deregulation is the undisputed concept of the eternal life of money.[9]

---

[8]Geiko Muller-Fahrenholz, "The Jubilee: Time Ceilings for the Growth of Money," in *Jubilee Challenge,* pp. 104-11. There are some other creative interpretations of the jubilee in the same book.
[9]Ibid., p. 109.

The theological angle: A theology for evangelism. The jubilee was based
on several central affirmations of Israel's faith, and the importance of these
should not be overlooked when assessing its relevance to Christian ethics and
mission. As we observed with the exodus, it would be quite wrong to limit the
challenge of the jubilee to the *socioeconomic* realm and ignore its inner spiritual
and theological motivation. From a holistic missiological point of view, each is
as important as the other, for all are fully biblical and all fully reflect the character and will of God. The following points stand out in Leviticus 25.

- Like the rest of the sabbatical provisions, the jubilee proclaimed the *sovereignty of God* over time and nature, and obedience to it would require submission to that sovereignty. That is, you were to keep the jubilee as an act
  of obedience to God. This Godward dimension of the matter is why the year
  is deemed holy, "a sabbath to YHWH," and why it was to be observed out of
  the "fear of YHWH."

- Furthermore, observing the fallow year dimension of the jubilee would also
  require faith in *God's providence* as the one who could command blessing in
  the natural order and thereby provide for your basic needs (Lev 25:18-22).

- Additional motivation for the law is provided by repeated appeals to the
  knowledge of *God's historical act of redemption,* the exodus and all it had
  meant for Israel. The jubilee was a way of working out the implications
  within the community of the fact that all Israelites were simply the former
  slaves of Pharaoh, now the redeemed slaves of YHWH (Lev 25:38, 42-43, 55).

- To this historical dimension was added the cultic and "present" *experience of
  forgiveness* in the fact that the jubilee was to be proclaimed on the Day of
  Atonement (Lev 25:9). To know *yourself* forgiven by God was to issue immediately in practical remission of the debt and bondage of *others.* Some of the
  parables of Jesus spring to mind.

- And the inbuilt future hope of the literal jubilee, blended with an *eschatological hope* of God's final restoration of humanity and nature to his original purpose. There is a strong theological pulse beating in this chapter of Leviticus.

To apply the jubilee model, then, requires that people obey the *sovereignty*
of God, trust the *providence* of God, know the story of the *redeeming action* of
God, experience personally the sacrificial *atonement* provided by God, practice
God's *justice* and put their hope in God's *promise* for the future. Now if we summon people to do these things, what are we engaging in? Surely these are the
very fundamentals of evangelism.

Of course, I am not suggesting that the jubilee was evangelistic in any contemporary sense. What I do mean is that the fundamental theology behind it also lies behind our practice of evangelism. The assumptions are the same. The theological underpinning of the *socioeconomic* legislation of the jubilee is identical to that which undergirds the proclamation of the kingdom of God. It is no wonder that the jubilee itself became a picture of the new age of salvation that the New Testament announces. It is an institution that models in a small corner of ancient Israelite economics the essential contours of God's wider mission for the restoration of humanity and creation.

When appropriately set in the light of the rest of the biblical witness, *the wholeness of the jubilee model embraces the wholeness of the church's evangelistic mission, its personal and social ethics and its future hope.*

Jubilee, Future Hope and Jesus

The future orientation of the jubilee serves additionally as a bridge to seeing how it influenced Jesus, and it helps us answer questions as to whether our insistence on a holistic understanding of mission is sustained in the New Testament.

Looking to the future. Even at a purely economic level in ancient Israel, the jubilee was intended to have a built-in future dimension. Anticipation of the jubilee was supposed to affect all present economic values (including the provisional price of land). It also set a temporal limit on unjust social relations— they would not last forever. The jubilee brought hope for change. It was proclaimed with a blast on the trumpet (the *yôbēl,* from which its name derives), an instrument associated with decisive acts of God (cf. Is 27:13; 1 Cor 15:52). However, as time went by, and even when the jubilee probably fell into disuse in practice, its symbolism remained potent.

The jubilee had two major thrusts: *release/liberty,* and *return/restoration* (Lev 25:10). Both of these were easily transferred from the strictly economic provision of the jubilee itself to a wider metaphorical application. That is, these economic terms became terms of hope and longing for the future, and thus entered into prophetic eschatology.

There are allusive echoes of the jubilee particularly in the later chapters of Isaiah. The mission of the Servant of YHWH has strong elements of the restorative plan of God for his people, aimed specifically at the weak and oppressed (Is 42:1-7). Isaiah 58 is an attack on cultic observance without social justice and calls for liberation of the oppressed (Is 58:6), specifically focussing on one's own kinship obligations (Is 58:7). Most clearly of all, Isaiah 61 uses jubilee images to portray the one anointed as the herald of YHWH to "evangelize" the poor, to proclaim liberty to the captives (using the word *dĕrôr,* which is the explicitly jubilary word for release), and to announce the year of YHWH's favor (almost certainly an allusion to a jubilee year). The hope of *redemption* and *return* for God's people are combined in the future vision of Isaiah 35 and set alongside the equally dramatic hope of a transformation of nature.

Thus, within the Old Testament itself, the jubilee had already attracted an eschatological imagery alongside its ethical application in the present. That is, the jubilee could be used to portray *God's* final intervention for messianic redemption and restoration, but it could still function to justify ethical challenge for *human* justice to the oppressed in the present.

When we see how the jubilee vision and hope inspired prophetic passages such as Isaiah 35 and Isaiah 61, with their beautiful integration of personal, social, physical, economic, political, international and spiritual realms, our own missional and ethical use of the jubilee must preserve a similar balance and integration, preventing us from putting asunder what God will ultimately join together.

Looking to Jesus. How then was the institution of jubilee taken up by Jesus and applied in the New Testament to the age of fulfillment that he inaugurated. How, in other words, did jubilee relate to the wider sense of Old Testament *promise* that Jesus fulfilled? Jesus announced the imminent arrival of the eschatological reign of God. He claimed that his people's hopes for restoration and for messianic reversal were being fulfilled in his own ministry. To explain what he meant, he used imagery from the jubilee circle of ideas (among others, of course).

The "Nazareth manifesto" (Lk 4:16-30) is the clearest programmatic statement of this. It is the closest Jesus comes to a personal mission statement, and it quotes directly from Isaiah 61, which was strongly influenced by jubilee concepts. Most commentators observe this jubilee background to the prophetic text and Jesus' use of it. It certainly builds a holistic dimension into the mission that Jesus sets out for himself by reading this Scripture and claiming to be its embodiment.

> Luke will not allow us to interpret this jubilee language as flowery metaphors or spiritual allegories. . . . Jesus fulfilled the Jubilee that he proclaimed. His radical mission was the very mission of God found in the Old Testament proclamation of Jubilee. It is presented in Luke's Gospel as holistic in four aspects:
>   1. It is both proclaimed and enacted.
>   2. It is both spiritual and physical.
>   3. It is both for Israel and the nations
>   4. It is both present and eschatological.[10]

---

[10]Paul Hertig, "The Jubilee Mission of Jesus in the Gospel of Luke: Reversals of Fortunes," *Missiology* 26 (1998): 176-77.

Other examples of the influence of the jubilee on Jesus' thinking are suggested by Robert Sloan and Sharon Ringe. Sloan observed that Jesus' use of the word for "release," *aphesis,* carries both the sense of *spiritual* forgiveness of sin and also literal and *financial* remission of actual debts. Thus the original jubilee background of economic release has been preserved in Jesus' challenge concerning ethical response to the kingdom of God. If we are to pray the Lord's prayer, "release for us our debts," we must be willing to release others from theirs. It is not a matter of deciding between a spiritual and a material meaning, for both can be included as appropriate.[11]

Ringe traces the interweaving of major jubilee images into various parts of the Gospel narratives and the teaching of Jesus. There are echoes of jubilee in the beatitudes (Mt 5:2-12), in Jesus' response to John the Baptist (Mt 11:2-6), in the parable of the banquet (Lk 14:12-24) and in various episodes of forgiveness, and especially teaching on debts (Mt 18:21-35).[12]

The evidence is broad and conforms to the pattern already observed in the Old Testament. At the level of fairly explicit allusion and implicit influence, the jubilee serves both as a *symbol of future hope* and also as an *ethical demand in the present.*

Looking to the Spirit. The book of Acts shows that the early church had a similar combination of future expectation and present ethical response. The jubilee concept of eschatological restoration is found in the otherwise unique idea of "complete restoration." The unusual word for this, *apokatastasis* occurs in Acts 1:6 and Acts 3:21, where it speaks of God's final restoration of Israel and all things. It seems Peter has taken the core of the jubilee hope (restoration) and applied it not just to the restoration of land to farmers but to the restoration of the whole creation through the coming Messiah (2 Pet 3:10-13).

Significantly, however, the early church responded to this future hope not merely by sitting and waiting for it to happen. Rather, they put into practice some of the jubilee ideals at the level of mutual economic help. Luke almost certainly intends us to understand that in doing so they were fulfilling the sabbatical hopes of Deuteronomy 15. Acts 4:34, with it's simple statement that "there were no needy persons among them," is virtually a quotation of the

---

[11]Robert B. Sloan Jr., *The Favorable Year of the Lord: A Study of Jubilary Theology in the Gospel of Luke* (Austin, Tex.: Schola, 1977).

[12]Sharon H. Ringe, *Jesus, Liberation, and the Biblical Jubilee: Images for Ethics and Christology* (Philadelphia: Fortress Press, 1985). For a concise survey of various interpretations of the way Luke uses Isaiah 61 here, see also Robert Willoughby, "The Concept of Jubilee and Luke 4:18-30," in *Mission and Meaning: Essays Presented to Peter Cotterell,* ed. Anthony Billington, Tony Lane, and Max Turner (Carlisle, U.K.: Paternoster, 1995), pp. 41-55.

Greek Septuagint translation of Deuteronomy 15:4, "there will be no needy person among you." The new community of Christ, now living in the eschatological era of the Spirit, is making the future hope a present reality in economic terms. Or to put it another way, the church by its internal practice was erecting a signpost to the reality of the future. The new age of life in the Messiah and in the Spirit is described in terms that echo the jubilee and its related sabbatical institutions.[13] And the effect was a community in mission marked by an integral combination of verbal proclamation (the evangelistic preaching of the apostles) and visible attraction (the social and economic equality of the believers). Not surprisingly, the church grew in numbers, strength, maturity and mission.

The New Testament and Holistic Mission

A question commonly arises at this point. On occasions when I have presented a biblical foundation for a holistic understanding of Christian mission, pointing to the kind of material we have surveyed in this and the previous chapter (the exodus and the scope of biblical redemption; the jubilee and its social, economic and spiritual dimensions), the question is asked, "But how does this fit with the New Testament? Jesus did not lead an exodus of the Jews from oppression under Rome. In fact he didn't get involved in politics at all. Paul didn't campaign for the liberation of slaves. Isn't it the case that mission in the New Testament is primarily, if not exclusively, to be understood as the task of evangelism?"

A response may be made to this objection at three levels: hermeneutical, historical and theological.

Holistic mission flows from applying the whole Bible. It is of course true that we must read the Old Testament in the light of the New (and vice versa also). And it is true that the New Testament, with its great affirmation of the fulfillment in Jesus Christ of all that God promised through the story of Israel, must govern the way we read the Old. Jesus sums up the whole message and point of the Old Testament as leading to himself, the Messiah, and to the mission of his disciples to the world (Lk 24:44-49). And that mission, in the light of his death and resurrection, was the evangelistic task of preaching repentance and forgiveness in Christ's name to all nations. All this is readily granted and is at the very heart of the whole case I am making in this book.

---

[13]In addition to my own work, already referred to, a full and helpful account of the way Jesus and the rest of the New Testament related to the rich scriptural traditions of the land is David E. Holwerda, *Jesus and Israel: One Covenant or Two?* (Grand Rapids: Eerdmans; Leicester, U.K.: Apollos, 1995), pp. 85-112.

However, it is a distorted and surely false hermeneutic to argue that whatever the New Testament tells us about the mission of the followers of Christ *cancels out* what we already know about the mission of God's people from the Old Testament. Of course the New Testament focuses on the new thing that we now have to proclaim to the nations. Only from the New Testament can we proclaim the good news that

- God has sent his Son into the world.
- God has kept his promise to Israel.
- Jesus has died and is risen and is even now reigning as Lord and King.
- In the name of Jesus Christ we can know forgiveness of sins through repentance and faith in his blood shed on the cross.
- Christ will return in glory.
- The kingdom of God will be fully established in the new creation.

All of these great affirmations, and much more, are the content of the good news that could only be made known in the New Testament, through the historical events of the Gospels and the witness of the apostles. And of course it is our mandate, duty and joy to proclaim these things to the world in the evangelistic task entrusted to us.

But where do we find any justification for imagining that by rightly undertaking what the New Testament commands us to do, we are absolved from doing what the Old Testament commands? Why should we imagine that doing evangelism in obedience to the New Testament excludes doing justice in obedience to the Old? Why have we allowed what we call the *Great Commission* to obscure the twin challenge (endorsed by Jesus himself) of the *Great Commandment?*

It is true that we must take into account the radical newness of the era of salvation history inaugurated in the New Testament. We are not Old Testament Israelites living within a theocratic covenant bound by Old Testament law. So, for example, when we take a theme such as the land of Israel we do need to recognize the typological-prophetic hermeneutic by which the New Testament sees the fulfillment of all it signified for Israel as now fulfilled for Christians by being in Christ. The land of Palestine as territory and turf is no longer theologically (or eschatologically) significant in the New Testament. Nevertheless, as I have argued elsewhere in detail,[14] the paradigmatic force of the *socioeconomic* legislation that governed Israel's life in the land still has ethical and missional

---

[14]See my *Old Testament Ethics for the People of God.*

relevance for Christians—in the church and in society. Just because we no longer live in ancient Israel's society does not mean we have nothing to learn (or to obey) from Israel's social legislation. The divine authority and continuing ethical relevance that Paul asserts for "all Scripture" must apply to the law as much as to any other part of the Bible (2 Tim 3:16-17).

Now there are some things commanded in the Old Testament that we no longer obey, of course, such as the sacrificial system and the clean and unclean regulations. But the reason for this change is clearly given in the New Testament. Jesus has fulfilled all that the sacrificial system pointed to, and in him we have the perfect sacrifice for sin and our perfect high priest (as Hebrews explains in detail). And the distinction between clean and unclean animals and foods was symbolic of the national distinction between Old Testament Israel and the nations, a badge of their holiness. The New Testament tells us that this old distinction is abolished in Christ, in whom there is "neither Jew nor Greek" (Gal 3:28). So we no longer need to observe Old Testament food laws, but this is not because we need not obey the Old Testament per se but because we recognize the provisional nature of those regulations as signposts to a destiny we have now reached in Christ. The rationale for our nonobservance of these matters is explicit: they were always provisional in relation to the circumstances of Israel before the coming of Christ.

But there is no hint at all that the ubiquitous message of the Old Testament about social and economic justice, about personal and political integrity, about practical compassion for the needy are in any sense provisional or dispensable. On the contrary, so central are these matters to God's revealed requirement on his people (in the Law, the Prophets, the Psalms, Wisdom writings and illustrated in so many narratives) that the more ritual regulations are relativized in comparison with them, even within the Old Testament itself.

> He has showed you, O man, what is good.
>   And what does the LORD require of you?
> To act justly and to love mercy
>   and to walk humbly with your God. (Mic 6:8)

Not only are these central demands contrasted with more ritual requirements that Micah envisions he might carry out, they are also addressed in as universal a way as possible. This is no provisional regulation until God gives his people some other priority that overrides it. This is simply "what is good." This is not just for Israel, but for "you, O man." This is what God requires, period. The same fundamental requirement on the people of God, with the same sense of nonnegotiable, nontransient urgency, can be traced through texts such as Isaiah 1:11-

17; 58:5-9; Jeremiah 7:3-11; Amos 5:11-15, 21-24; Hosea 6:6; Zechariah 7:4-12.

And standing in the same prophetic tradition, Jesus himself tells the Pharisees that while their attention to the detail of the law was admirable, they were neglecting its central and weighty concerns—justice, mercy and faithfulness (Mt 23:23-24). Jesus endorsed the moral priorities of the Old Testament and thereby the Scripture-based missional priorities of God's people. Doing these things matters vitally to God. Not doing them was enough to land the rich man in Jesus' parable in hell, because he had lived in blatant disregard for the Law and the Prophets, in dereliction of his covenant obligations, and in defiance of the God whose name was so ironically attached to the beggar he had neglected (Lazarus means, "God is helper").

How then can it be suggested that evangelistic proclamation is the only essential mission of the church? It seems impossible to me to justify such reductionism if we intend to sustain any claim to be taking the whole Bible seriously as our authority for mission and as that which defines the content and scope of our mission. Mission belongs to God—the biblical God. The message of mission is to be drawn from the whole of God's biblical revelation. So we cannot simply relegate the powerful message of events such as the exodus or institutions like the jubilee to a bygone era. They are an integral part of the biblical definition of God's idea of redemption and of God's requirement on his redeemed people. We pay no compliments to the New Testament and the new and urgent mandate of evangelistic mission it entrusts to us in the light of Christ by relegating the Old Testament and the foundations for mission that it had already laid and that Jesus emphatically endorsed. Whole Christian mission is built on the whole Christian Bible.

Jesus and the early church did present a radical political challenge. A second response needs to be directed to the misunderstanding implicit in the question, "How does this Old Testament material fit with the New Testament?" "Jesus did not get involved in politics" is the common assertion, with the implication that neither then should we. So whatever political dimensions we may have discerned in, say, the exodus are all very interesting but no longer anything to do with mission as mandated by Christ. Our concern and our task, like Jesus', must be spiritual and eternal, not earthly and temporal. So runs the argument I have heard so many times in the wake of teaching a biblical holistic understanding of mission. But is it true that Jesus did not get involved in politics? That depends what we mean by *politics*.

Dissolving the sacred-secular assumption. First, we need to get back behind the typically modern dichotomy between politics and religion, the secular-sacred divide. The assumption that Jesus (or any other religious figure of his day) operated in a sacred/spiritual/religious sphere that was quite distinct from the world of political power and action would simply not have made sense to anybody at that time. The whole of life was lived before God, and God was as much involved in affairs of state as affairs of the heart. In fact, more than that, political realities "on the ground" were themselves intricately bound up with spiritual realities in the heavenly realm. Each touched the other and were like the inside and outside of the same piece of cloth. Political activity (whether Jewish or Roman) was suffused with religious meaning and significance at every level. And religious activity had (sometimes life or death) political implications. The God or gods you worshiped did not inhabit some vacuum-sealed spiritual domain.

If you were a Jew, the God you worshiped was supposed to be King over all the earth. So the political realities of the world that seemed to contradict this fundamental conviction were the focus of intense anguish and longing. So if you had commented to any of Jesus contemporaries, who had just listened to him preaching and teaching about the reign of God, that "Jesus doesn't get involved in politics, does he?" you would probably have met a blank stare of incomprehension. The question itself presupposes a radical disjunction of a supposed world of spiritual reality from the empirical world of political reality. That dichotomy is the product of the Enlightenment and not part of the worldview of the Bible (nor, I would want to add, ought it to be part of the worldview of biblical mission).

Nonviolent is not nonpolitical. Second, the allegation that Jesus did not get involved in politics may imply that because Jesus did not lead a political revolution against the injustices of Roman rule, including if necessary violent resistance, he therefore had no political agenda. But a radical political stance is not the same thing as violent politics. Indeed in some situations, proposing nonviolence may be the more radical political agenda. So to say (rightly) that Jesus was neither politically violent nor revolutionary (in the contemporary sense) is not at all the same thing as to say that his claims, teaching and actions were "nonpolitical."

To understand just how radically political Jesus actually was, we only have to ask why he was crucified. Clearly he was seen as such a major threat to the political powers who governed his land (both the Romans and the ruling Jewish establishment) that they saw only one way to deal with the challenge he presented—to remove that challenge by removing him through political execution. The charge against Jesus was manifestly political. He was accused of claiming he would destroy the temple (thereby threatening its monopoly concentration of Jewish power) and claiming to be king of the Jews (thereby threatening Roman power).

It simply will not do at this point to say that the Romans and Jewish leaders misunderstood Jesus. We should not imagine that, somehow, Jesus actually meant it all only in a spiritual sense, as if he were actually talking only about a religious kingdom that had no connection with (and was no threat to) the "real world" of earthly politics. That's all Jesus meant, we might say, but they made the ghastly mistake of taking him far too literally. They should not have felt threatened at all because the message of Jesus was only about God and personal faith, about good behavior and loving everybody and going to heaven in the end.

This will not do because it just is not true. If it had been true, the crucifixion would be an unsolved mystery. The Jewish and Roman authorities may well have misunderstood Jesus in many ways, but they were astute political operators and they knew a threat when they saw one. And they were right to. For the claims of Jesus do indeed subvert all human authority and call it to account to the higher court of God's justice. If God is indeed King, then Caesar is not (in the way the Romans believed him to be). And if Jesus is the messianic King of Israel, then the old order of things in the Jewish establishment, symbolized by the whole temple system, is indeed coming to an end.[15]

"Your kingdom come . . . on earth." Third, we need to overcome the common spiritualizing mode in which we think of the kingdom of God. In popular thinking the phrase is either a synonym for heaven—an other-worldly place into which we one day hope to enter, or an entirely inward and spiritual thing connected only with personal piety.[16] Of course it does have a future dimension, and of course it governs personal behavior, but the kingdom of God as preached by Jesus within the framework of his own people's understanding and expectation was much more than either of these.

Jesus did not invent the term *kingdom of God*. He filled it with fresh significance in relation to himself, but his hearers already knew from their Scriptures about the reign of YHWH. They sang about it most sabbaths in the synagogue from Psalms (like Ps 96—98; 145) that celebrated it. They eagerly anticipated it from the words of prophets who set before the imagination of faith and worship

---

[15]A useful brief summary of the social and political implications of Jesus' claims and teachings is Stephen Mott, *Jesus and Social Ethics,* Grove Booklets on Ethics (Nottingham, U.K.: Grove Books, 1984), first published as Stephen Mott, "The Use of the New Testament in Social Ethics," *Transformation* 1, nos. 2-3 (1984). See also Paul Hertig, "The Subversive Kingship of Jesus and Christian Social Witness," *Missiology* 32 (2004): 475-90.

[16]Matthew's preference for "kingdom of heaven" instead of "kingdom of God" does not imply any distinction, of course. Almost certainly his use of this phrase is out of deference to Jewish reticence in using the name of God and regularly substituting "heaven." The term does not indicates a place somewhere else but the dynamic reign of God here and now, and yet to come.

pictures of what it will be like when God comes to reign. Such pictures were far from merely personalized piety or a realm beyond the sky when you die.

The reign of YHWH, when it would finally come, would mean justice for the oppressed and the overthrow of the wicked. It would bring true peace to the nations and the abolition of war, the means of war, and training for war. It would put an end to poverty, want and need, and provide everyone with economic viability (under the metaphor "under his own vine and fig tree"). It would mean satisfying and fulfilling life for human families, safety for children, and fulfillment for the elderly, without danger from enemies, and all of this within a renewed creation free from harm and threat. It would mean the inversion of the moral values that dominate the current world order, for in the kingdom of God the upside down priorities of the beatitudes operate and the Magnificat is not just wishful thinking.

It was one such Scripture that Jesus used to summarize both the meaning of the coming reign of God and his own role within it—in his famous Nazareth Manifesto in Luke 4:14-30, when he read from Isaiah 61, with its combined echo of both exodus and jubilee.

> The Spirit of the Lord is upon me,
>> because he has anointed me
>> to preach good news to the poor.
> He has sent me to proclaim freedom for the prisoners
>> and recovery of sight for the blind,
> to release the oppressed,
>> to proclaim the year of the Lord's favor. (Lk 4:18-19)

Now if, as Jesus taught, this reign of God was already breaking into human history through his own coming, then even though its complete establishing lay in the future, those who choose to belong to it must live by its standards in the here and now. So followers of Jesus are to be those who "seek first the kingdom of God and his justice" (Mt 6:33, author's translation)—a missional statement if ever there was one, and one that is entirely in line with the burden of argument in this book. For this prioritization of life makes our mission dependent on God's. His is the kingdom and his is the justice. Our mission is to seek both in all we do in our own life and work.

Breaking society's boundary markers. Fourth, the practice of Jesus and the new community he established had more political significance than we often recognize. Jesus was actually more revolutionary than we think. We are aware, of course, that some of what Jesus did was rather shocking to his contemporaries. But this was not just a matter of *social* shock, as if Jesus were merely somewhat embarrassing to conventional good manners. Many outstanding leaders have been embarrassing. It is not a crucifixion thing.

Again, we must remember that Jesus was perceived as a *threat,* and a political threat at that. This was because many of his actions crossed boundaries and broke taboos or cut through established social protocol in a way that subverted the way society was ordered and stratified. And in all societies, political power depends on conventional acceptance of "the way things are and always should be." In first century Jewish society that included a range of assumptions on many matters, such as

- who was clean and who was unclean (which had pervasive social ramifications)
- whom you could touch and whom you made strenuous efforts to avoid
- who belonged among "the righteous" and who did not
- what you could and could not do on the sabbath
- whom you could eat with and whom you never should
- who could dispense forgiveness and in what context, and who thereby had the power to define the social exclusion or inclusion that went with it

Jesus dissolved some of these, abolished some, ignored others and deliberately challenged a few of them.

He turned the clean-unclean distinction inside out. He chose to heal on the sabbath day and to redefine its significance around himself. He reached out to those who were excluded by the taboos of society: women, children, the sick, the unclean, even the dead. He declared forgiveness to people on his own authority, completely bypassing the normal route for such benefit, namely, the official sacrificial cult at the temple. He ate with tax collectors, prostitutes and "sinners" (by official designation). Furthermore, he told stories that gave the "official" story of Israel a very different ending in its damning effect on those in power in society, and they knew he was talking about them. And as he stood on trial before the highest political-religious authority in all Jewish society, he calmly took to himself the identity of the Danielic Son of Man, whose authority would ultimately overthrow the beasts of oppressive and persecuting powers (Dan 7). No wonder the chief priest tore his robes and cried blasphemy. It just won't do when the chief priest is cast in the role of chief beast. Jesus' radical claims and teaching were not just bursting old wineskins; they were enough to burst some political blood vessels.[17]

---

[17]Cf. Colin J. D. Greene, *Christology in Cultural Perspective: Marking out the Horizons* (Grand Rapids: Eerdmans; Carlisle, U.K.: Paternoster, 2003), esp. chap. 7, "Christology and Human Liberation."

The political price of following Jesus. Fifth, the community that Jesus formed, while it was certainly not launched as yet another political party, as a fifth option to the Pharisees, Sadducees, Essenes and Zealots, was a community whose loyalty to Christ had unavoidable social and political implications. Jesus himself warned his followers that their discipleship would involve possible social conflict with their own families and neighbors (as his own obedience to his Father had meant for him). And it would very likely lead them to fall foul of the governing authorities, who would persecute, accuse, arrest, charge, and condemn them. Such would be the price of acknowledging Jesus of Nazareth as Christ and Lord.

Within weeks of the crucifixion of Jesus, exactly this took place, as Peter and John were arraigned before the Sanhedrin. And so the New Testament adds its first case of political disobedience to the noble list in the Old Testament that is headed by Shiphrah and Puah, the Hebrew midwives who disobeyed Pharaoh because they feared the Lord.

And in the wider Roman world the story would be the same. To confess Jesus as Messiah (King) and Lord was effectively to deny that Caesar is Lord. But that latter declaration was the defining creed and political glue of the Roman Empire. Rome did not mind what gods you chose to worship so long as you were willing to give prime allegiance to the gods of Rome, and especially to the emperor. You did that by burning incense before a bust of the emperor in a public place and affirming *"Kyrios Kaisar,"* "Caesar is Lord." But Christians declared there is another King, called Jesus, above whom there is no king, for he is King of the universe. So to confess *"Kyrios Iēsous,* "Jesus is Lord," was to make a statement that is as much political as it is religious, for it relativizes all forms of human authority on earth under the sovereignty of God in Christ. And multitudes of Christians perished paying the political price of refusing to confess the lordship of Caesar with the same lips that confessed the sole lordship of Christ.

But the early Christian community was not marked solely by its affirmation of a claim that subverted the political pretension of the empire. It was also a radically prophetic community, for they sought to live out within the present old order of the world the truths and values of the in-breaking new order of the kingdom of God. This new community, consciously shaped by the eschatological outpouring of God's Spirit, chose to express their spiritual unity through as much economic equality as they could achieve, so that none need be poor within their midst. They were taught by apostles, who insisted that a primary duty of Christians was not just to witness and evangelize but to "do good" (as Paul urges seven times in one tiny letter to Titus) and to be models of practical love in a world full of hatred. They were to be good citizens and pay their taxes, but also to recall that God's mandate to the state authorities (who are "servants of God") was to do justice, punish wickedness and reward goodness (Rom 13:1-7). They accepted that political authorities were there by God's appointment, but they would not have forgotten the words of the prophets, who declared that governments that perverted justice stood under God's ultimate judgment (e.g., Jer 22:1-5). And they were reminded, in true prophetic style, by James not only that faith without practical action of love and justice is dead but also that it was still part of the apostolic duty of the church (as much as the prophetic duty of old) to denounce in no uncertain terms the oppressive practices of unscrupulous employers who feed their obscene luxury on the tears of those they exploit (Jas 2:14-17; 5:1-6). No, the early Christians, with all their unbounded evangelistic energy, were not lacking in awareness of the radical implications of their faith for the political, social and economic world around them. The favorite counterallegation that they did not seek to abolish slavery seems an inadequate basis on which to rest a view that early Christianity had no political or social interest.

The Centrality of the Cross

Any theology of mission that claims to be biblical must have at its core that which is at the very core of biblical faith—the cross of Christ. So if we are to establish that a truly biblical understanding of mission is holistic, integrating all the dimensions we have been surveying hitherto, then we must ask how all of that coheres around the cross.

A mission-centered theology of the cross. I have been arguing throughout this book that the Bible presents to us God's own mission to redeem and renew his whole creation. We have more of that journey still to travel in the chapters to come. However, in the context of this discussion of the meaning of redemption and its relation to mission, a key point must be made at this stage.

God's mission has many dimensions as we trace the theme of his saving purpose through the different strands of Scripture. But every dimension of that mission of God led inexorably to the cross of Christ. *The cross was the unavoidable cost of God's mission.*

Think for a moment of some of the great contours of God's redemptive purpose. The following items (at least) would probably have been included by Paul in what he called "the whole will [or purpose] of God" (Acts 20:27). I list them as minimally as possible. Every point deserves a theological discourse of its own (and has generated many).

It was the purpose or mission of God

- *to deal with the guilt of human sin,* which had to be punished for God's own justice to be vindicated. And at the cross God accomplished this. God took that guilt and punishment upon himself in loving and willing self-substitution through the person of his own Son. For "the LORD has laid on him / the iniquity of us all" (Is 53:6), and Christ "himself bore our sins in his body on the tree" (1 Pet 2:24). The cross is the place of personal pardon, forgiveness and justification for guilty sinners.

- *to defeat the powers of evil* and all the forces (angelic, spiritual, "seen or unseen") that oppress, crush, invade, spoil, and destroy human life, whether directly or by human agency. And at the cross God accomplished this, "having disarmed the powers and authorities, . . . triumphing over them by the cross" (Col 2:15). The cross is the place of defeat for all cosmic evil and seals its ultimate destruction.

- *to destroy death,* the great invader and enemy of human life in God's world. And at the cross God did so, when "by [Christ's] death he might destroy him who holds the power of death—that is, the devil" (Heb 2:14). The cross, paradoxically the most terrible symbol of death in the ancient world, is the fount of life.

- *to remove the barrier of enmity and alienation between Jew and Gentile,* and by implication ultimately all forms of enmity and alienation. And at the cross God did so, "for he himself is our peace, who has made the two one and has destroyed the barrier. . . . His purpose was to create in himself one new man out of the two, thus making peace, and in this one body to reconcile both of them to God through the cross, by which he put to death their hostility" (Eph 2:14-16). The cross is the place of reconciliation, to God and one another.

- *to heal and reconcile his whole creation,* the cosmic mission of God. And at the cross God made this ultimately possible. For it is God's final will "through [Christ] to reconcile all things, whether things on earth or things in heaven, by making peace through his blood, shed on the cross" (Col 1:20; the "all things" here must clearly mean the whole created cosmos, since that is what Paul says has been created by Christ and for Christ (Col 1:15-16), and has now been reconciled by Christ (Col 1:20). The cross is the guarantee of a healed creation to come.

So then, all these huge dimensions of God's redemptive mission are set before us in the Bible. God's mission was that

- sin should be punished and sinners forgiven.
- evil should be defeated and humanity liberated.
- death should be destroyed and life and immortality brought to light.

- enemies should be reconciled to one another and to God.
- creation itself should be restored and reconciled to its Creator.

All of these together constitute the mission of God. And all of these led to the cross of Christ. *The cross was the unavoidable cost of God's total mission*—as Jesus himself accepted, in his agony in Gethsemane: "not my will, but yours, be done."

A full biblical understanding of the atoning work of Christ on the cross goes far beyond (though of course it includes) the matter of personal guilt and individual forgiveness. That Jesus died in my place, bearing the guilt of my sin as my voluntary substitute, is the most gloriously liberating truth to which we cling in glad and grateful worship with tears of wonder. That I should long for others to know this truth and be saved and forgiven by casting their sins on the crucified Savior in repentance and faith is the most energizing motive for evangelism. All of this must be maintained with total commitment and personal conviction.

But there is more in the biblical theology of the cross than individual salvation, and there is more to biblical mission than evangelism. The gospel is good news for the whole creation (to whom, according to the longer ending of Mark, it is to be preached [Mk 16:15; cf. Eph 3:10]). To point out these wider dimensions of God's redemptive mission (and therefore of our committed participation in God's mission) is *not* watering down the gospel of personal salvation (as is sometimes alleged). Rather, we set that most precious personal good news for the individual firmly and affirmatively within its full biblical context of *all* that God has achieved and will finally complete through the cross of Christ.

A cross-centered theology of mission. So the cross was the unavoidable cost of *God's* mission. But it is equally true and biblical to say that *the cross is the unavoidable center of our mission*. All Christian mission flows from the cross—as its source, its power, and as that which defines its scope.

It is vital that we see the cross as central and integral to every aspect of holistic, biblical mission, that is, of all we do in the name of the crucified and risen Jesus. It is a mistake, in my view, to think that while our evangelism must be centered on the cross (as of course it has to be), our social engagement and other forms of practical mission work have some other theological foundation or justification.

Why is the cross just as important across the whole field of mission? Because in all forms of Christian mission in the name of Christ we are confronting the powers of evil and the kingdom of Satan—with all their dismal effects on human life and the wider creation. If we are to proclaim and demonstrate the reality of the reign of God in Christ—that is, if we are to proclaim that Jesus is king, in a world that still likes to chant "we have no king but Caesar" and his many successors, including mammon—then we will be in direct conflict with the usurped reign of the evil one, in all its legion manifestations. The deadly reality of this battle against the powers of evil is the unanimous testimony of those who struggle for justice, for the needs of the poor and oppressed, the sick and the ignorant, and even those who seek to care for and protect God's creation against exploiters and polluters, just as much as it is the experience of those (frequently the same people) who struggle evangelistically to bring people to faith in Christ as Savior and Lord and plant churches. In all such work we confront the reality of sin and Satan. In all such work we are challenging the darkness of the world with the light and good news of Jesus Christ and the reign of God through him.

By what authority can we do so? With what power are we competent to engage the powers of evil? On what basis dare we challenge the chains of Satan, in word and deed, in people's spiritual, moral, physical and social lives? Only though the cross.

- Only in the cross is there forgiveness, justification and cleansing for guilty sinners.
- Only in the cross stands the defeat of evil powers.
- Only in the cross is there release from the fear of death and its ultimate destruction altogether.
- Only in the cross are even the most intractable of enemies reconciled.
- Only in the cross will we finally witness the healing of all creation.

The fact is that sin and evil constitute bad news in every area of life on this planet. The redemptive work of God through the cross of Christ is good news for every area of life on earth that has been touched by sin, which means every area of life. Bluntly, we need a holistic gospel because the world is in a holistic mess. And by God's incredible grace we have a gospel big enough to redeem all that sin and evil has touched. And every dimension of that good news is good news utterly and only because of the blood of Christ on the cross.

Ultimately all that will be there in the new, redeemed creation will be there because of the cross. And conversely, all that will not be there (suffering, tears, sin, Satan, sickness, oppression, corruption, decay and death) will not be there because they will have been defeated and destroyed by the cross. That is the length, breadth, height and depth of God's idea of redemption. It is exceedingly good news. It is the font of all our mission.

So it is my passionate conviction that holistic mission must have a holistic theology of the cross. That includes the conviction that the cross must be as central to our social engagement as it is to our evangelism. There is no other power, no other resource, no other name through which we can offer the whole Gospel to the whole person and the whole world than Jesus Christ crucified and risen.

Practice and Priorities

For the past two chapters we have been considering the biblical case for a holistic understanding of mission. Inevitably, however, a number of questions arise of a more practical nature, which need to be acknowledged in conclusion.

Primacy or ultimacy? Even if we agree that biblical mission is intrinsically holistic and that Christians should be involved in the whole wide range of biblical imperatives—seeking justice, working for the poor and needy, preaching the gospel of Christ, teaching, healing, feeding, educating, and so forth—isn't it still the case that evangelism has primacy in all of this? Evangelism may not be the only thing we should do in mission, but isn't it the most important? Shouldn't it have priority over all else?

There is a strong current of evangelical mission thinking that has argued in this way, and it is not lightly to be challenged, let alone set aside.[18] Advocates of the primacy of evangelism do not deny the holistic nature of biblical mission and the broad scope of all that we should rightly be involved in as we engage in mission for Christ's sake. They see the relationship between evangelism and social action as being totally integral and inseparable—like the two blades of a pair of scissors or the two wings of a bird or airplane. You cannot meaningfully have one without the other, even though they are not identical to each other, nor can the one be substituted for the other. But still, even in a relationship of such integration, evangelism is seen as primary, for the reason that *Christian* social action (as part of mission) requires the existence of socially active *Christians,* and that presupposes the evangelism by which they came to faith in Christ. Evangelism thus has a kind of chronological as well as theological primacy.

There is a strong logic here, and such a position is infinitely preferable to either an extreme affirmation of evangelism as the only rightful owner of the

---

[18]The Lausanne Covenant of 1974 and the extraordinarily productive decade of follow-up conferences and statements on the relationship between evangelism and social action provide the mainstream of such thinking. It can be navigated in the very helpful compendium of all the Lausanne documents up to 1989: John Stott, ed. *Making Christ Known: Historic Mission Documents from the Lausanne Movement 1974-1989* (Carlisle, U.K.: Paternoster, 1996). The thinking in all this material is broadly holistic. Further analysis of the recovery of this understanding of mission can be found in Samuel Escobar, *A Time for Mission: The Challenge for Global Christianity,* Global Christian Library (Leicester, U.K.: Inter-Varsity Press; Downers Grove, Ill.: InterVarsity Press, 2003), chap. 9; and David J. Bosch, *Transforming Mission: Paradigm Shifts in Theology of Mission* (Maryknoll, N.Y.: Orbis, 1991), pp. 400-408.

patent on Christian mission (to the exclusion of all other endeavors from any right to even use the term *mission*) or an extreme liberal and pluralist politicizing of the meaning of mission, such that evangelism is about the only thing you are *not* allowed to do.

However, there are some uncomfortable consequences of such a view when it filters down to the thinking and practice of some individuals, agencies and churches. Consider what follows as a few gentle questions rather than severe critique, since this is a position with which I have considerable sympathy.

First, the language of "priority" implies that all else is "secondary" at best. From the world of sporting clichés, we know that "second is nowhere" (at least that's how my own former sport of rowing would speak of the annual Cambridge-Oxford Boat Race). And indeed, there are churches and mission agencies that have adopted the term *secondary mission* to describe all those who are not directly involved in evangelism and church planting. I have friends serving as medical missionaries in Africa who received a letter from their supporting church informing them that they had now been reclassified as "secondary missionaries." The easily detectable subtext of this kind of language (which is sometimes verbalized exactly thus) is that they are not *real* missionaries at all. In other words, the language of priority and primacy quickly tends to imply singularity and exclusion. Evangelism is the *only* real mission. We are back to so exalting the New Testament evangelistic mandate that we think it absolves us from all other dimensions of God's mission that the rest of the Bible clearly requires of God's people. However, it is one thing to say (rightly) that we *must* engage in evangelism. It is another thing altogether to say (wrongly, as I have tried to argue) that evangelism is the *only* thing that constitutes engaging in mission.

The word *priority* suggests something that has to be your starting point. A priority is whatever is most important or urgent. It is the thing that must get done first before anything else. However, a different way of thinking about mission would be to imagine a whole circle of all the needs and opportunities that God calls (or sends) us to address in the world. This is best done when thinking of a local specific context, of course, rather than attempting it globally. One can construct a spider chart in which presenting problems are traced to deeper causes, and they in turn are related to other underlying problems and factors. Eventually, a complex web of interconnected factors is discerned, constituting the whole range of brokenness and need, of sin and evil, of suffering and loss that may be found in any given human situation, personal or social. The list of contributing factors will doubtless include those that are spiritual, moral, physical, familial, political, environmental, educational, economic, ethnic, cultural, religious and many more.

The question then is posed: What constitutes the good news of the biblical gospel in this whole circle of interlocking presenting needs and underlying causes? What is the mission of God in relation to this whole nexus? How does the power of the cross impinge on each of the evils that are at work here? That should produce a very broad answer—as broad as the scale of the problem, for the gospel addresses all that sin has touched, which is everything.

In an excellent reflection on what constitutes holistic mission (based on a lifetime of personal crosscultural mission in different ministries and locations), Jean-Paul Heldt suggests that we must look at any human problem in the four basic dimensions of our human existence—*physical, mental, spiritual and social.*[19] As we do so, we uncover different underlying causes of presenting problems, and then, of course, we need to apply the power of the gospel to all such causes and their effects. He illustrates his point (and mine) from the prevalent and recurrent problem of night blindness in children, biologically the result of lack of vitamin A. But then he goes on to chart the range of factors that are involved.

> Night blindness has interlocking causes. Night blindness is indeed a symptom of vitamin A deficiency (biological causation). Yet that deficiency is primarily the result of malnutrition, which occurs in a context of poverty (such as inequitable land distribution, unjust labor laws and unfair wage structures). Finally, at the root of social injustice lie greed and selfishness, which are essentially moral and spiritual values. It is then not realistic to expect to cure and prevent night blindness with vitamin A drops unless we also address and confront the issues of malnutrition, poverty, social injustice, and, ultimately, selfishness and greed.[20]

Such a process of analysis and discernment will give us some idea of the scope of a holistic missional response to the situation we are considering. So the next question has to be, Where do we start? The language of the "priority of evangelism" implies that the only proper starting point must always be evangelistic proclamation. *Priority* means it is the most important, most urgent, thing to be done first, and everything else must take second, third or fourth place. But the difficulty with this is that (1) it is not always possible or desirable in the immediate situation, and (2) it does not even reflect the actual practice of Jesus.

Rather, almost any *starting* point can be appropriate, depending possibly on what is the most pressing or obvious need. We can *enter* the circle of missional

---

[19]I have taught the same fourfold dimension of human life for many years, both in expounding Genesis and in teaching biblical foundations for mission. Further reflection on this is offered in chapter 13.

[20]Jean-Paul Heldt, "Revisiting the 'Whole Gospel': Toward a Biblical Model of Holistic Mission in the 21st Century," *Missiology* 32 (2004): 157.

response at any point on the circle of human need. *But ultimately* we must not rest content until we have included within our own missional response the wholeness of *God's* missional response to the human predicament—and that of course includes the good news of Christ, the cross and resurrection, the forgiveness of sin, the gift of eternal life that is offered to men and women through our witness to the gospel and the hope of God's new creation. That is why I speak of ultimacy rather than primacy. Mission may not always *begin* with evangelism. But mission that does not ultimately *include* declaring the Word and the name of Christ, the call to repentance, and faith and obedience has not completed its task. It is defective mission, not holistic mission.

Our study of the exodus in chapter eight illustrates this. God broke into the circle of Israel's need at the level of their economic exploitation and genocidal affliction at the hands of the Egyptians. Having *redeemed* them through the exodus (and that is how the language is first used), God went on to provide for their *physical* needs in the wilderness. Then he entered into a *covenant* relationship with them after revealing his name, his character and his law. All of this, he said, was so that they would truly *know* him as the living God and *worship* him alone. Then he provided the place of his own dwelling where they could *meet* with him, and finally, the system of *sacrifices* by which they could maintain that relationship and deal with sin and uncleanness through the *atonement* God provided. All kinds of elements are involved in this total experience and the narrative that describes it. But *ultimately* the goal was that God's people should know God and love him with wholehearted loyalty, worship and obedience. It is a rich and pregnant model for mission.

Evangelism and social involvement: Chicken or egg? Another way the issue is sometimes framed is this: Surely the best way to achieve social change and all the good objectives we have for society on the basis of what we know God wants (justice, integrity, compassion, care for his creation, etc.) is by vigorous evangelism. The more Christians there are, the better it will be for society. So if you want to change society, do evangelism. Then those who become Christians will do the social action part. I have often heard this as an argument for prioritizing evangelism over social action, and it sounds very plausible, but it has some serious flaws. Again, let me emphasize that what follows is in no way intended to deny that evangelism is utterly vital but rather to deny that it can carry the weight of obedience to the rest of the Bible's commands regarding our social responsibilities in the world.

First (and I think I owe this point to John Stott), there is flawed logic in the assertion that says, If you are a Christian, you should not spend time doing social action. Instead give all your time to evangelism because the best way to change society is to multiply the number of Christians. The logic is flawed because (1) all those new Christians will, following the same advice, give time only to evangelism, so who is going to be engaging in the social engagement side of mission? And (2) you ought to be engaging in social action since you yourself are the product of someone else's evangelism. So by your own logic you should be the one to get involved in the social activity you are so readily transferring to the fruit of your own evangelistic efforts. In other words, the argument becomes an infinite regress in which real social engagement as part of Christian mission in the world is conveniently postponed from one generation of converts to the next, with each one feeling a spurious justification for passing the buck.

Second, this view overlooks the importance of example. We all tend to imitate those who have most influenced us. If someone comes to faith through the effort of a Christian or a church that endorses only the evangelistic mandate and has a negative and nonengaged attitude to all things social, cultural, economic or political, then the likelihood is that the new convert will imbibe, consciously or otherwise, the same dichotomized attitude. We teach as we were taught. We reflect the kind of mission that moved us into faith. Evangelism that offers a safe long-term personal exit strategy from the world rather than a missional engagement with the world is likely to produce Christians and churches that have little cutting edge in the surrounding culture and little incentive as to how or why they ought to have anyway. Evangelism that multiplies Christians who are only interested in more evangelism but who are not wrestling with the challenge of being salt and light in the working world around them may boost church-growth statistics. But we should not pretend that it is an adequate way, let alone the best way, to fulfill the rest of our biblical obligations in society.

Third, and tragically, this view is simply not borne out in the history of Christian mission. Now of course there is such a thing as conversion uplift. That is, the fact that when people become Christians from very poor and deprived backgrounds, they tend to shed some harmful habits (e.g., squandering resources on gambling, alcohol, etc.) and acquire some positive ones (such as a new sense of personal worth and the dignity of work, caring for others, providing for their family, honesty, etc.). The effect can contribute to an upward social drift and can certainly benefit a community if enough people are affected in this way.

However, there are other instances where rapid conversion of whole communities to a pietistic gospel that sings the songs of Zion to come but demands no radical concern for the social, political, ethnic and cultural implications of the whole biblical faith here and now has led to massive and embarrassing dissonance between statistics and reality. Some of the states in northeast India, such as Nagaland, are held up as outstanding examples of the success of late-nineteenth- and early-twentieth-century evangelism. Whole tribes were converted. The state is recorded to be around 90 percent Christian. Yet it has now become one of the most corrupt states in the Indian Union and is riddled with problems of gambling and drugs among the younger generation. Naga students at the Union Biblical Seminary, where I taught in the 1980s, would tell me this as proof of the fact that merely successful evangelism does not always result in lasting social transformation. Others will point with desperate and baffled sadness at the tragic irony of Rwanda—one of the most Christianized nations on earth and birthplace of the East African Revival. And yet whatever form of Christian piety was taken to be the fruit of evangelism there could not stand against the tide of intertribal hatred and violence that engulfed the region in 1994. The blood of tribalism, it was said, was thicker than the water of baptism. Again, successful evangelism, flourishing revivalist spirituality and a majority Christian population did not result in a society where God's biblical values of equality, justice, love and nonviolence had taken root and flourished likewise.

I write as a son of Northern Ireland. That has to be one of the most "evangelized" small patches on the globe. As I grew up, almost anybody I met could have told me the gospel and "how to get saved." Street corner evangelism was a common feature of the urban scene. I took part in it myself on occasions. Yet in my Protestant evangelical culture, the zeal for evangelism was equal only to the suspicion of any form of Christian social concern or conscience about issues of justice. That was the domain of liberals and ecumenicals, and a betrayal of the "pure" gospel. The result was that the de facto politics of Protestantism was actually subsumed under the gospel in such a way that all the political prejudice, partisan patriotism and tribal hatred was sanctified rather than prophetically challenged (except by a very brave few who often paid a heavy price). So the proportionately high number of the evangelizers and the evangelized (in comparison with any other part of the United Kingdom) certainly did not produce a society transformed by the values of the kingdom of God. On the contrary, it was (and sadly still is) possible to hear all the language of evangelistic zeal and all the language of hatred, bigotry, and violence coming from the same mouths. As James would say, "this should not be" (Jas 3:10). But it is. And it is one reason why I beg to dissent from the notion that evangelism by itself will result in social change, unless Christians are also taught the radical demands of discipleship to the Prince of peace, are seeking first the kingdom of God and his justice, and understand the wholeness of what the Bible so emphatically shows to be God's mission for his people.

Holistic mission needs the whole church. A final question that is often raised in the context of teaching holistic mission arises from unavoidable personal limitations. "You are saying that Christian mission involves all these dimensions of God's concern for total human need," someone will say. "But I am finite, with finite time, finite abilities and finite opportunities. Should I not then stick to what seems most important—evangelism—and not try to dissipate myself over such a broad range of otherwise desirable objectives. I can't do everything!"

No, of course you can't. The same thought doubtless occurred to God, which is why he called the church into existence. Here is another reason why our ecclesiology must be rooted in missiology. The mission of God in the world is vast. So he has called and commissioned a people—originally the descendants of Abraham, now a multinational global community in Christ. And it is through the *whole* of that people that God is working his mission purposes out, in all their diversity.

Of course every individual cannot do everything. There are different callings, different giftings, different forms of ministry (remembering that magistrates and other government officials of the state are called "ministers of God" in Rom 13, just as much as apostles and those who organized food aid). Individuals must seek personal guidance from God regarding the particular niche in which they will engage in whatever sphere of mission God has called them to. Some are indeed called to be evangelists. All are certainly called to be witnesses, whatever their context of work. The apostles in Acts recognized their own personal priority had to be the ministry of the Word and prayer. But they did not see that as the only priority for the church as a whole. Caring for the needs of the poor was another essential priority of the community and its evangelistic attractiveness. So they appointed people who would have as *their* priority the practical administration of food distribution to the needy. That did not limit their ministry to such work (as Philip's evangelistic encounter with the Ethiopian shows), but it does show that the overall work of the church requires different people to have different gifts and priorities.

The question is, Is the *church as a whole* reflecting the wholeness of God's redemption? Is the church (thinking here of the local church as the organism effectively and strategically placed for God's mission in any given community) aware of all that God's mission summons them to participate in? Is the church, through the combined engagement of *all* its members, applying the redemptive power of the cross of Christ to *all* the effects of sin and evil in the surrounding lives, society and environment?

The ringing slogan of the Lausanne movement is: "The whole church taking the whole gospel to the whole world." Holistic mission cannot be the responsibility of any one individual. But it is certainly the responsibility of the whole church.

In conclusion, I can do no better than endorse the fine conclusion of Jean-Paul Heldt's article:

> There is no longer a need to qualify mission as "holistic," nor to distinguish between "mission" and "holistic mission." Mission is, by definition, "holistic," and therefore "holistic mission" is, de facto, mission. Proclamation alone, apart from any social concern, may be perceived as a distortion, a truncated version of the true gospel, a parody and travesty of the good news, lacking relevance for the real problems of real people living in the real world. On the other end of the spectrum, exclusive focus on transformation and advocacy may just result in social and humanitarian activism, void of any spiritual dimension. Both approaches are unbiblical; they deny the wholeness of human nature of human beings created in the image of God. Since we are created "whole," and since the Fall affects our total humanity in all its dimensions, then redemption, restoration, and mission can, by definition, only be "holistic."[21]

---

[21]Ibid., p. 166.

10

The Span of God's Missional Covenant

> The whole historical covenant between Yahweh and Israel had from the beginning a universal dimension. The nations are real witnesses. Yahweh's saving actions, the punishments and the restoration that he imposed on Israel were at the same time a preaching to the nations.[1]

With these bold words Walter Vogels opens up for us a missiological approach to the various covenants in the Bible. With the concept of covenant we come to another major plank in Israel's self-identity or worldview. So far we have considered the missiological dimensions of their *election*—their conviction that they were a people uniquely chosen by God, yet for a purpose that reached far beyond themselves (in chaps. 6-7). Then we reflected on the narrative of the exodus as the prime event through which Israel understood the meaning of *redemption* and could speak of themselves as redeemed by God (chap. 8). In both cases we traced the main themes with their missiological dimensions through into the New Testament where they are developed and relaunched as part of the driving force of Christian mission.

Here we come to the next milepost on Israel's journey with God after the exodus—the confirmation of God's *covenant* with them at Sinai. Israel believed themselves to be in a unique relationship with YHWH, a relationship that they likened to the treaty covenants between nations and empires in their wider international world. The covenant at Sinai is a fresh articulation of the original seminal covenant that God made with Abraham, in the light of the new historical reality generated by the exodus. The descendants of Abraham have now

---

[1]Walter Vogels, *God's Universal Covenant: A Biblical Study,* 2nd ed. (Ottawa: University of Ottawa Press, 1986), pp. 67-68.

indeed become a great nation. What will it mean for them to live within the framework of the Abrahamic covenant as a national community? That framework needed a lot of expansion and consolidation to serve as a constitution for the nation's life. The Sinai covenant provides that.

As the nation's life went on, the arrival of monarchy led to another development in the covenant relationship, as God initiated the particular covenant with David and his successors on the throne. The failure of so many of the kings of Israel and Judah, however, called into question the viability of God's whole project in and through Israel. A new vision of the future begins to emerge as several prophets look forward to a new era of covenant relationship in which the old imperfections would be eradicated and God's intentions for Israel and his mission through them would be fulfilled. This hope leads us straight to Jesus, in whom, according to Jesus himself and his first interpreters, that new covenant was inaugurated.

If we have learned anything from a century of Old Testament theology it is that it is futile to isolate any single theme or category as the sole organizing center for the whole discipline. Old Testament theology is not like a wheel with a single theological hub at the center of radiating spokes. Rather, it is like a cable, with several closely entwined wires running along together at the core. So, while it would be rash these days to suggest that covenant is *the* center of the Old Testament faith, it will be granted that the covenant theme may be regarded as one of the core wires. Covenant is one of several major components in Israel's essential theological self-understanding. And the sequence of covenants in the canonical narrative offers us *one* fruitful way of presenting the grand narrative that constitutes the cable.

This grand narrative embodied Israel's coherent worldview, a worldview that included their own sense of election, identity and role in the midst of the nations. The biblical story can be organized and told in many ways (as Jesus demonstrated with his parable of the tenants in the vineyard). But the key point is that it *is* a narrative in which we can look backward to its beginnings in Genesis and forward to its anticipated climax in the new creation. The sequence of covenants is one way to make our way through that historical narrative and also provides a major clue to its significance and eventual outcome.[2] Let's then trace that sequence with our missiological hermeneutic in mind.

The question for us in this chapter, then, in the context of our argument

---

[2]In an earlier book I surveyed the sequence of covenants as one way to understand Jesus in the light of the Old Testament story and promise. See Christopher J. H. Wright, *Knowing Jesus through the Old Testament,* 2nd ed. (Oxford, Monarch, 2005).

throughout the book, is, How we can read the covenant tradition in the biblical texts missiologically? That is, in what ways do the various covenant formulations reveal the mission of God and the derivative mission of God's people in the world?

Noah

The narrative of the covenant that God made with Noah in Genesis 8:15—9:17 is the first explicit reference to covenant-making in the biblical text. Although some theological systems speak of an Adamic covenant, the relationship between God and Adam is not described in that way in the text of Genesis.[3] So our survey of covenant begins with Noah. The Noachic covenant establishes at least two foundational points that are relevant to the rest of the biblical concept of mission.

God's commitment to all life on earth. In the context of God's radical judgment on the comprehensive nature of human sin (repeatedly portrayed as "violence and corruption"), God still commits himself to the created order itself and to the preservation of life on the planet. Although we live on a *cursed* earth, we also live on a *covenanted* earth. There is an unambiguous universality about God's covenantal self-commitment here: His promise is not only with humanity but also with "every living creature on earth" (Gen 9:10). This Noachic covenant provides the platform for the ongoing mission of God throughout the rest of human and natural history, and thereby also, of course, the platform for our own mission in participation with his. Whatever God does, or whatever God calls us to do, there is a basic stability to the context of all our history.

This does not of course mean that God would never again use his natural creation as the agent of his judgment as well as his blessing (as the rest of the Old Testament amply testifies). But it does set limits to such actions *within history*. Apart from the final judgment of God that will bring an end to fallen human history as we presently know and experience it on this sinful planet, the curse will never again be expressed in an act of comprehensive destruction as the flood. This is God's earth, and God is covenantally committed to its survival, just as later revelation will show us that God is also covenantally committed to its ultimate redemption. Even the final judgment will not mean the end of *the earth as God's creation* but the end of the sinful condition that has subjected the whole of cre-

---

[3]However, a strong case for seeing a covenantal pattern in the prefall relationship between God and creation (including humankind), even though the term itself is not used in Genesis 1—2, is argued by Vogels, *God's Universal Covenant,* chap. 1. He draws on other biblical texts as allusions to such an understanding. These include Amos 1:9; Hos 2:20; 6:7; Is 24:5; 54:9-17; Jer 33:20-25; Ezek 34:25; Zech 11:10; Sir 17:12; 44:18.

ation to its present frustration. Our mission then takes place within the framework of God's universal promise to the created order. This is a framework that gives security and scope to all our mission: security because we operate within the parameters of God's commitment to our planet, and scope because there is nothing and no place on earth that lies outside the writ of God's covenant with Noah. The rainbow promise spans whatever horizon we can ever see.

The ecological dimension of mission. The language with which God addresses Noah at the end of the flood clearly echoes Genesis 1. In a sense this is a fresh start for all creation. So Noah and his family are blessed and instructed to fill the earth and (though not with the same phrase) to have dominion over it. The creation mandate is renewed. The human task remains the same—to exercise authority over the rest of the creation, but to do so with care and respect for life, symbolized in the prohibition on eating animal blood (Gen 9:4). So there is a human mission built into our origins in God's creation and God's purpose for creation. To care for creation is in fact the first purposive statement that is made about the human species; it is our primary mission on the planet. The covenant with Noah effectively renews this mission, within the context of God's own commitment to creation. We will look more fully at the ecological dimension of biblical mission in chapter twelve.

Abraham

We have examined the Abrahamic covenant and its missiological implications in depth in chapters six and seven. However, for the sake of completeness in this chapter, it may be helpful to summarize our key findings here also.

From a missiological perspective, the covenant with Abraham is the most significant of all the biblical covenants. It was the origin of God's election of Israel as the means he would use to bless the nations, and it undergirds Paul's theology and practice of mission to the Gentiles in the New Testament. Within the Old Testament context it is theologically proper to see the covenants at Sinai and with David not as wholly distinct covenantal arrangements but as developments of the covenant with Abraham in new circumstances. Richard Bauckham, reflecting on the missiological aspects of these three covenants, sees them all as characteristically moving *from the one to the many,* which he also sees as the dynamic of the key biblical category of election.

God singles out first Abraham, then Israel, then David. The three movements that begin with these three choices by God each has its own distinctive theme, one aspect of God's purpose for the world. We could call these the thematic trajectories of the narrative. The trajectory that moves from Abraham to all the

families of the earth is the trajectory of blessing. The trajectory that moves from
Israel to all the nations is the trajectory of God's revelation of himself to the
world. The trajectory that moves from God's enthronement of David in Zion to
the ends of the earth is the trajectory of rule, of God's kingdom coming in all
creation. Of course, these three movements and themes are closely interrelated.[4]

The canonical context: Genesis 1—11. The Old Testament begins on the
stage of universal history. After the accounts of creation we read the story of God's
dealings with fallen humanity and the problem and challenge of the world of the
nations (Gen 1—11). After the stories of the Fall, Cain and Abel, the flood, and
the tower of Babel, could there be any future for the nations in relation to God?
Or would judgment have to be God's final word? It is against this background of
universal sinfulness and divine judgment that we are introduced to God's determination to "bless." Blessing, of course, had been a key word in the early chapters
of Genesis. Now it becomes God's answer to a broken world.

*The universality of the ultimate goal: "All families/nations of the earth will
find blessing."* The covenant with Abraham is God's answer to the problems
posed by Genesis 1—11. God's declared commitment is that he intends to bring
blessing to the nations: "All the families of the earth will be blessed through you"
(Gen 12:3, author's translation). Repeated six times in Genesis alone, this key
affirmation is the foundation of biblical mission, inasmuch as it presents the mission of God. The Creator God has a purpose, a goal, and it is nothing less than
blessing the nations of humanity. So fundamental is this divine agenda that Paul
defines the Genesis text as declaring "the gospel in advance" (Gal 3:8). And the
concluding vision of the whole Bible signifies the fulfillment of the Abrahamic
promise, as people from every nation, tribe, language and people are gathered
among the redeemed in the new creation (Rev 7:9).

The gospel and mission both begin in Genesis, and both are located in the
redemptive intention of the Creator to bless the nations as the bottom line of
God's covenant with Abraham. Mission is God's address to the problem of fractured humanity. And God's mission is universal in its ultimate goal and scope.

The particularity of the means: "Through you, and your descendants . . ." The
same Genesis texts that affirm the universality of God's mission to bless the nations also and with equal strength affirm the particularity of God's election of
Abraham and his descendants to be the vehicle of that mission.[5] The blessing of

---

[4]Richard Bauckham, *The Bible and Mission: Christian Mission in a Postmodern World* (Carlisle,
U.K.: Paternoster, 2003), p. 27.
[5]On the exegetical questions surrounding the meaning of "through you" and the form of the
verb (whether it is passive or reflexive), see the full discussion on pp. 252-54 in chap 7.

the nations will come about "through you and your seed." The election of Israel is assuredly one of the most fundamental pillars of the biblical worldview and of Israel's historical sense of identity.[6]

It is vital to insist that although the belief in their election was vulnerable to being distorted into a narrow doctrine of national superiority, that move was resisted in Israel's own literature (e.g., Deut 7:7-11). The affirmation is that YHWH, the God who had chosen Israel, was also the Creator, Owner and Lord of the whole world (Deut 10:14-22; cf. Ex 19:4-6). That is, YHWH was not just Israel's God—he was God of all (as Paul insists so emphatically in Rom 4). YHWH had chosen Israel in relation to his purpose for the world, not just for Israel. The election of Israel, therefore, was not tantamount to a rejection of the nations but explicitly for their ultimate benefit. Election is missional in its purpose. If I might paraphrase John, in a way he would probably have accepted, "God so loved the world that he chose Israel."[7]

Sinai

The covenant with Abraham was reconfirmed and given broader substance in the national covenant with Israel, mediated through Moses at Mount Sinai. The volume of relevant textual material would be overwhelming at this point, so for our more limited purpose we will confine ourselves to three texts that bear on the wider missiological dimension of the Sinai covenant.

The first comes from the narrative prologue to the Sinai covenant in Exodus and speaks of Israel's missional role as God's *priesthood*. The second comes from the climax of covenant legislation in Leviticus and highlights the essential *presence* of God as a missional distinctive of God's people. The third comes from the concluding chapters of the whole Torah in Deuteronomy and points us forward to the *prognosis* for Israel's history that eventually lays the foundation for New Testament missional theology and practice.

God's mission and God's priesthood: Exodus 19:4-6

> You yourselves have seen what I have done to Egypt,
> and I carried you on wings of eagles and brought you to myself.

---

[6]The importance of this central core of Israel's worldview for the whole mission of the biblical God through the people of God for the world is made abundantly clear in the works of N. T. Wright, especially *The New Testament and the People of God* (London: SPCK, 1992), and *Jesus and the Victory of God* (London: SPCK, 1996).

[7]Stimulating missiological reflection on the particularity and universality dimensions of the Abraham covenant and of the nature of God himself is found throughout Bauckham, *Bible and Mission*.

> Now then, if you really obey my voice and keep my covenant,
>> you will be for me *[lî]* a special personal possession
>>> among all the peoples;
>>> for to me *[lî]* belongs the whole earth.
>> But you, you will be for me *[lî]* a priestly kingdom and a holy nation.
> (Ex 19:4-6, author's translation)

Exodus 19:4-6 is a key programmatic statement by God, coming, like a hinge in the book of Exodus, in between the exodus narrative (Ex 1—18) and the giving of the law and covenant (Ex 20—24). It defines the identity of Israel and the role God has for them. Further, it sets Israel's identity and role in the historical context of God's past action on behalf of Israel, and in the universal context of God's ownership of the whole earth. It functions as a narrative and theological preamble to the promulgation of the Sinai covenant in the rest of Exodus and Leviticus, so that we must view all the specific details of that covenant from the perspective of this word of orientation. This is a crucial, context-setting orientation to all that follows.

We have already considered one feature of this text in chapter seven (see pp. 255-57). There we observed both the *universality* of its reference to the whole earth and all nations alongside the *particularity* of its description of Israel as YHWH's special personal possession *(sĕgullâ)*. In both respects it has remarkable affinity with the Abrahamic covenant. We will return yet again to the same text in chapter eleven, when we consider the *ethical* implications of Israel's call to be a *holy* nation. Here we are concerned simply with the first part of the double identity that God gives to Israel—to be a *"priestly* kingdom."[8]

To understand what it meant for Israel as a whole to be called God's priesthood in relation to the nations, we have to understand what Israel's priests were in relation to the rest of the people. Priests stood in the middle between God and the rest of the people. In that intermediate position, priests then had a twofold task:

- *Teaching the law* (Lev 10:11; Deut 33:10; Jer 18:18; Mal 2:6-7; Hos 4:1-9). Through the priests God would be known to the people. This was a major duty of Old Testament priests, the neglect of which led to moral and social decay and the prophetic anger reflected in the words of Hosea and Malachi above.

---

[8]It is most likely that this is the correct English word order for the noun and adjective in translating the Hebrew phrase "kingdom of priests." Israel is to be not so much a royal priesthood (whatever that might mean) but a kingdom (in the relatively neutral sense) consisting of priests.

- *Handling the sacrifices* (Lev 1—7). Through the priests and their work of atonement the people could come to God. The priests did the actions with the blood at the altar and made the declaration of atonement to the worshiper.

The priesthood was thus a two-directional representational or mediatory task between God and the rest of the Israelites, bringing the knowledge of God to the people and bringing the sacrifices of the people to God. In addition to these twin tasks, it was of course a prime privilege and responsibility of the priests to *bless the people* in the name of YHWH (Num 6:22-27).

It is thus richly significant that God confers on Israel as a whole people the role of being his priesthood in the midst of the nations. As the people of YHWH they would have the historical task of bringing the knowledge of God to the nations, and bringing the nations to the means of atonement with God. The Abrahamic task of being a means of blessing to the nations also put them in the role of priests in the midst of the nations. Just as it was the role of the priests to bless the Israelites, so it would be the role of Israel as a whole ultimately to be a blessing to the nations.

This dual movement in the priestly role (from God to people and from people to God) is reflected in prophetic visions concerning the nations, which included both centrifugal and centripetal dynamics. There would be a going out from God and a coming in to God. On the one hand, the law or the justice or the light of YHWH would go out to the nations from Israel or from Zion. On the other hand, the nations could be pictured as coming to YHWH or to Israel or to Jerusalem / Zion. (We will explore these themes in chap. 14.)

The priesthood of the people of God is thus a missional function that stands in continuity with their Abrahamic election, and it affects the nations. Just as Israel's priests were called and chosen to be the servants of God and his people, so Israel as a whole is called and chosen to be the servant of God and all peoples.

John Goldingay connects the text with Genesis 12:1-3.

> The fact that Exodus 19:3-8 is a form of reworking of Genesis 12:1-3 reminds us that this designation links with YHWH's lordship over the whole world and works toward the world's inclusion rather than its exclusion. The stretching of the royal priesthood to include other peoples (Rev. 1:6) is in keeping with the Abrahamic vision.[9]

One might add the even more universal extension of the phrase in Revela-

---

[9]John Goldingay, *Old Testament Theology,* vol. 1, *Israel's Gospel* (Downers Grove, Ill.: InterVarsity Press, 2003), p. 374.

tion 5:9-10. Strangely, however, Goldingay says, "Describing Israel as a priest-hood does not attribute to it a priestly role on behalf of the world or between God and the world."[10] But provided we understand this role carefully, in the way that I have suggested, it seems to me that this is precisely what was attrib-uted to Israel.

Alex Motyer is also reluctant to see an intermediary role for Israel among the nations in this text.

> Many interpret the priesthood of Israel as referring to them as a mediating nation, bringing the knowledge of God to the world. . . . This is certainly not the main understanding of priesthood within the Old Testament. . . . The substantial truth . . . of the "priesthood of all believers" in both the Old and New Testament . . . is access into the holy presence.[11]

However, Motyer overlooks the representative dimension of that access into the presence of God, which was (in the case of Israelite priests) on behalf of the rest of the people and (in the case of God's people as a whole) on behalf of the rest of the world (e.g., in prayer). "Israel as a 'kingdom of priests' is Israel committed to the extension throughout the world of the ministry of Yahweh's Presence."[12] Later, Motyer does acknowledge that Israel's priestly status and ac-cess to God constitute "the public testimony of holiness whereby they show themselves to the world in all their distinctiveness."[13] This public distinctiveness, however, is what I argue to be part of Israel's missional identity and role.

Walter Vogels observes:

> The priest was an intermediary and, therefore, had a mission between God and men. If we apply this concept to Israel as a people, it suggests that Israel is also an intermediary between God and the nations. . . .
>
> [Israel] is set apart—distinctive from all other nations—to be consecrated to Yah-weh, to be in his service, a position which ultimately means service towards the nations. Israel's privilege is one of service. Israel was taken from among the nations to be at the service of the nations. Election and covenant are thus not an end in themselves but a means towards something else. This text (Ex. 19:3-8) confirms what we have seen before in the promises to Abraham. He would become a people from whom all the nations would one day receive blessings of salvation.
>
> Israel is mediator. She must bring mankind closer to God, pray to God for man-kind, and intercede for mankind, as Abraham did. Her service to God is in the

---

[10]Ibid.

[11]Alex Motyer, *The Message of Exodus,* The Bible Speaks Today (Leicester, U.K.: Inter-Varsity Press; Downers Grove, Ill.: InterVarsity Press, 2005), p. 199.

[12]Terence E. Fretheim, *Exodus,* Interpretation (Louisville: John Knox Press, 1991), p. 263.

[13]Motyer, *Message of Exodus,* p. 200.

name of others. But Israel has also to bring God closer to men, by bringing them God's revelation, his light and the good news of salvation.[14]

This then conveys something of the broader missional significance of Israel's identity as a priestly people for YHWH in the midst of the nations.

We should remember, however, that this identity and role was dependent on the condition that stood above it: "If you will obey my voice and keep my covenant . . ." (Ex 19:5). Keeping God's covenant was thus not a condition of their redemption. God did not say, "If you obey me and keep my covenant, I will save you and you will be my people." He already had and they already were. No, obedience to the covenant was not a condition of *salvation* but a condition of their *mission*. Only through covenant obedience and community holiness could they claim or fulfill the identity and role here offered to them. The mission of priesthood among the nations is covenantal, and like the covenant itself, its fulfillment and enjoyment is inseparable from ethical obedience. That is why it is immediately followed by "holy nation"—the ethical implications of which we will consider in chapter eleven.

In the New Testament, Peter sees the priestly nature of the church as "declaring the praises" of our exodus God and living in such a way among the nations that they come to glorify God (1 Pet 2:9-12). This is an authentic combination of the missional and ethical reapplication of Exodus 19:4-6. Significantly also, in the only New Testament text to speak of any individual Christian's ministry in priestly terms, Paul describes his *evangelistic* mission as his "priestly duty." Immediately he refers to the same double direction of movement—bringing the gospel to the nations and bringing the nations to God (Rom 15:16). The ethical dimension of the task actually forms an envelope around the whole letter, as Paul twice gives it as his life's work to bring about "the obedience of faith among the nations" (Rom 1:5; 16:26, author's translation).

God's mission and God's presence: Leviticus 26:11-13. "I will put my dwelling place among you, and I will not abhor you. I will walk among you and be your God, and you will be my people" (Lev 26:12).

The presence of God in the midst of his people was one of the most essential and most precious features of the covenant. The covenantal context of this promise here in Leviticus 26 is very clear. It is conditional on Israel's obedience: "If you follow my decrees and are careful to obey my commands" (Lev 26:3). But it is also grounded in the historical redeeming grace of God (Lev 26:13). This double basis is essentially the same as we saw in Exodus 19:4-6. So the

---

[14]Vogels, *God's Universal Covenant,* pp. 48-49.

presence of God, dwelling and walking among his people, is, on the one hand, the goal of God's own act of redemption and, on the other, the fruit of his people's response of obedience. It is God's *covenant* presence.

Eden restored—for all. However, we immediately remind ourselves of the purpose for which this covenant with Israel existed in the first place. It was part of God's long-term mission to bring blessing to all nations and all creation. Indeed, the language of Leviticus 26 up to this point is replete with echoes of the Genesis portrait of creation under God's blessing (especially fruitfulness and increase) or of the rolling back of the curse (in peace and the absence of danger). Even the phrase "I will walk among you" uses a very rare form of the verb *hālak* (the hithpael), which is also used in Genesis 3:8 to describe God's habit of spending the cool of the day just strolling with Adam and Eve in the garden. The covenant presence of God will be a return to the intimacy of Eden. Ultimately, God's presence among his people must point to the blessing of his presence in all the earth. And thereby, what would be true for Israel in covenant blessing—the enjoyment of God's presence—would eventually be true for all who would enter into the same blessing through the outworking of God's covenant with Abraham.

> In the act of fulfilling the covenant, YHWH will bring creation itself to fulfillment: "I will make you fruitful and multiply you." . . . The promise [of Lev 26:9-13] thus brings together creation, exodus, covenant and presence. In the covenant, YHWH is bringing the purpose of creation itself to completion in the experience of blessing and of the very presence of God.[15]

Another connection here is between the *creation* (and especially the Garden of Eden) as the original temple of God (where human beings ruled and served in the capacity of kings and priests) and the *tabernacle* (and later the temple), which was a microcosm of that cosmic temple. The presence of God in Israel's tabernacle and temple looked backward to his presence in Eden, and forward to his ultimate presence among all nations in a renewed creation (Rev 21—22).[16]

God's presence as Israel's distinctiveness. In the meantime, however, it was to be God's covenantal presence in Israel that would mark them out as distinctive from the rest of the nations. This would be the purpose of the tabernacle. After God had given the instructions for every part of it, the purpose of the whole tabernacle was spelled out in this way, stressing once again its covenantal sig-

---

[15]Goldingay, *Old Testament Theology,* 1:371.
[16]On this theme and its rich missiological implications see G. K. Beale, *The Temple and the Church's Mission: A Biblical Theology of the Dwelling Place of God* (Leicester, U.K.: Apollos; Downers Grove, Ill.: InterVarsity Press, 2004).

nificance. The very purpose of redemption was so that God should dwell among his people.

> So I will consecrate the Tent of Meeting and the altar and will consecrate Aaron and his sons to serve me as priests. Then I will dwell among the Israelites and be their God. They will know that I am the LORD their God, who brought them out of Egypt so that I might dwell among them. I am the LORD their God. (Ex 29:44-46)

Even before the tabernacle could be built, however, the presence of God among his people is put in danger by their blatant apostasy. The narrative of Exodus 32—34 records the sin of Israel and Aaron together, while Moses was on Mount Sinai, which threatened to bring the destructive wrath of God instead of his covenant presence. In the protracted negotiated settlement that Moses as intercessor eventually reaches with God, God at one point concedes that he will not destroy the Israelites, but refuses to go any farther with them in person. He offers to send an angel instead. He himself will no longer be with them (Ex 33:1-5).

But that will not do for Moses. Moses knows that without God's presence, the covenant is as good as dead. "Then Moses said to him, 'If your Presence does not go with us, do not send us up from here. How will anyone know that you are pleased with me and with your people unless you go with us?' " (Ex 33:15-16).

But Moses knows more than that. He knows that without the presence of the Lord God, Israel would be no different from the rest of the nations. And *only by Israel being distinct from the nations was there any purpose in being Israel at all,* or any hope for the nations themselves eventually. "*What else* [than the presence of God] will distinguish me and your people from all the other people on the face of the earth?' " (Ex 33:16).

The question is rhetorical, and successfully makes its point in the negotiation. But actually there was rather *a lot else* that was meant to distinguish Israel from the nations, as Moses knew very well.[17] Ethical holiness, for example, and ritual cleanness, to name but two. Indeed, the lack of either or both of these would put the continuing presence of God among his people in severe jeopardy (as Ezekiel saw clearly). So let's look at them both.

God's presence requires ethical holiness. The ethical demands that the Sinai covenant laid upon Israel are well known, filling as they do large sections of Exodus and Deuteronomy. But the purpose for which Israel was summoned to live

---

[17]The extent and pervasiveness of the theme of Israel's self-conscious distinctiveness from the nations is surveyed and analyzed in Peter Machinist, "The Question of Distinctiveness in Ancient Israel," in *Essential Papers on Israel and the Ancient Near East,* ed. F. E. Greenspan (New York: New York University Press, 1991), pp. 420-42.

according to the ways of YHWH—the way of justice, truth, integrity, compassion and so on—was not merely for their own good or even merely to keep God happy. A major part of the motivation underlying Old Testament ethics is the challenge for Israel to be visibly different from the surrounding nations. *Religious* distinctiveness was to be embodied in *ethical* distinctiveness, both of which are included in the rich concept of holiness. And it would be this ethical distinctiveness of Israel that would be a pointer to the presence of the ethical God, YHWH, in their midst. This too is a dimension of meaning of the well-known equation, "You shall be holy: for I the LORD your God am holy" (Lev 19:2 KJV).

That is why Moses can urge Israel to live according to God's law with a motivational eye on the watching nations. They will see the difference, and questions will be asked—questions that, significantly, include the nearness of God in the midst of this people.

> Observe [these laws] carefully, for this will show your wisdom and understanding to the nations, who will hear about all these decrees and say, "Surely this great nation is a wise and understanding people." What other nation is so great as to have their gods near them the way the LORD our God is near us whenever we pray to him? And what other nation is so great as to have such righteous decrees and laws as this body of laws I am setting before you today? (Deut 4:6-8)

This strategically placed piece of covenantal motivation makes a powerful and missiologically significant connection between the presence of God, the ethical obedience of his people, and the observation of the nations. The missional relevance of Old Testament ethics will be explored further in chapter eleven, with a more detailed look at this key text.

God's presence requires ritual cleanness. Ritual cleanness is the burden of much of Leviticus. How is it connected with the covenant promise of the presence of God dwelling among his people, the promise that is so powerfully articulated at the end of the book? And how can it possibly be understood in relation to a missional hermeneutic? The key lies in Israel's conception of life.

In Israel's ritual worldview, everything in life could be divided into two broad categories: the *holy* and the *profane* (or common). God and anything specifically dedicated to God or associated with him was holy. Everything else was just common or ordinary (the proper, neutral meaning of *profane*). But the realm of the common could be further divided in two, between that which was *clean* (the normal state of people and things) and that which was *unclean* (because of pollution or, sometimes, sin). Only that which was clean could come into the presence of God. And God himself could only dwell in the presence of what was clean.

So all of life, then, could be in a state of flux in one of two directions. The effect of sin and pollution was to render the holy profane and the clean unclean. But the blood of sacrifice and other rituals could reverse that process. Sacrificial blood (along with other rituals) would cleanse the unclean and make it clean again (and thereby acceptable to God). And sacrificial blood would be used to sanctify or consecrate the clean to make it holy. The one thing that should *never* happen is that the opposite ends of the spectrum come in contact—the unclean with the holy.[18] God, the ultimate Holy One of Israel, cannot cohabit with uncleanness.

What then, in the light of this worldview, is the overall purpose of the sacrificial system and laws of cleanness in Leviticus? They were to maintain Israel in a fit condition for the holy God, YHWH, to live among. They were to deal with those things that would, if left uncovered and unatoned for, render Israel unfit for divine habitation.

But this then produces a logic that leads us back to the mission of God. In short:

- Holiness and cleanness were the preconditions of the *presence of God.*

- And the presence of God was the mark of *Israel's distinctiveness from the nations.*

- And Israel's distinctiveness from the nations was an essential component of *God's mission* for them in the world.

So we can see that even something so esoterically Israelite as their levitical, ritual and sacrificial system reflects the fundamentally missional orientation of Israel as God's holy and priestly people, embodying the presence of God in the midst of the nations.

In the New Testament, of course, we know that the levitical sacrifices were taken up and fulfilled in the final sacrifice of Christ on the cross. And we know that those laws of clean and unclean foods, which symbolized Israel's distinctiveness from the nations, are now abolished because that which they symbolized no longer obtains in Christ, where Jew and Gentile are now one. Nevertheless, the demand for moral and spiritual cleanliness is still forcefully applied in the context of new covenant loyalty to Christ. Paul quotes our text from Leviticus 26 in 2 Corinthians 6:16, precisely to urge Christians not to compromise their exclusive worship of Christ in temples of other gods, and to maintain their moral

---

[18]For a full explanation of this worldview and how the whole Levitical system fits within it, see, G. J. Wenham, *The Book of Leviticus,* New International Commentary on the Old Testament (Grand Rapids: Eerdmans, 1979), pp. 15-29.

distinctiveness from unbelievers. Only thus would they be a fit dwelling place for their holy God. The old covenant background of the new covenant exhortation is very strong. So while the ritual badge of Israel's separation from the nations (the clean-unclean food laws) has gone, the necessity of spiritual and moral distinctiveness of the people of God certainly has not. It is still an essential part of our missional identity and responsibility.

God's presence lost, restored and extended to the nations. Returning to that old covenant: the trajectory from our passage in Leviticus 26 takes us to Ezekiel, who echoes it several times.

For Ezekiel the worst moment in his life, perhaps other than the death of his wife, was his vision of the glory of God departing from the temple (Ezek 8—10). "The glory," is Ezekiel's favorite term for that tangible presence of YHWH that so filled the temple. But the temple had become a place of such wickedness and idolatry that the Lord could no longer bear to live there. In his vision God showed Ezekiel "the utterly detestable things the house of Israel is doing here, things that will drive me far from my sanctuary" (Ezek 8:6). So God left. Would he ever come back? That was the suspense that was only resolved by the explicit promise of God that, yes, he would. The presence of God would eventually be restored.

The whole section, Ezekiel 34—37, is then a coherent vision of a restored people of God living in covenant protection, covenant loyalty, covenant obedience, covenant unity and—above all—with the covenant dwelling place of God once again in their midst, in the language of Leviticus 26. And, most significantly for our argument here, *this restoration of the presence of God in a cleansed Israel will have its affect on the nations.*

> I will make a covenant of peace with them; it will be an everlasting covenant. I will establish them and increase their numbers, and I will put my sanctuary among them for ever. My dwelling place will be with them. I will be their God, and they will be my people. Then the nations will know that I the LORD make Israel holy, when my sanctuary is among them for ever. (Ezek 37:26-28)

It is a debatable point whether Ezekiel entertained the hope that the nations might actually be *saved* through knowing God in this way. But there can be no doubt at all that Ezekiel had a global frame of reference for what he believed God would do among his own people. The phrase "then they will know" echoes repeatedly like a refrain through these chapters. Whatever the result of such knowledge may be, *the nations will come to know God* when God once more dwells among his people. And that, after all, is the ultimate purpose of the whole final section of Ezekiel's book—the vision of the rebuilt temple and city.

For its significance lies in the name that the final two words of Ezekiel give it: "YHWH *šammâ,* The LORD is there!"—a phrase virtually equivalent to Isaiah's more familiar "*'immānû ēl,* God is with us!" The presence of God is restored to his city and his people (which become identical terms in biblical expectation).

Even if a message of hope for the nations cannot be unequivocally found in Ezekiel, other prophets proclaim it triumphantly. A full exposition must wait until chapter fourteen. Two texts, however, should be noted, in which it is the presence of God among his people (the essence of covenant relationship) that attracts the nations to come and join themselves to those who enjoy such a blessing.

Isaiah 60 pictures the nations coming to Israel as though on pilgrimage. By analogy with the Israelites' own pilgrimages to Jerusalem, in which their priests would receive the offerings of the people presented to God at the temple, so the prophet poetically imagines the nations bringing their offerings to YHWH, with Israel functioning as priests for the nations (the role assigned to them in Ex 19:6; Is 61:6). The Israelites went up to Jerusalem and the temple because the Lord was there. So here, the nations will come to Israel for exactly the same reason. They will come to the worship center of the people of God because that is where they see the presence of God. Although the prophetic rhetoric can portray this in the language of defeat and submission, the primary goal is not to glorify Israel but to worship Israel's God and live in his presence.[19] They will come as those attracted out of darkness into light (Is 60:1-3), but that light will be greater than the sun, for it will be the Lord himself, present among his people (Is 60:19-20, a comparison that inspired the similar vision in Rev 21:22-24).

Zechariah 8 also promises that God will return once more to Zion to dwell with his people (Zech 8:3). The covenant relationship will thus be restored (Zech 8:7-8). The result is that curse will change to blessing. Echoes of the Abrahamic promise surface in verse 13. But the chapter concludes with the picture of the nations urgently encouraging one another to go find the Lord where he may be found—among the people where he dwells. This may be centripetal, but it is certainly also missional. People will clamor to join those who know the living God. God dwelling among his people should be the most attractive force field on earth.

> Many peoples and the inhabitants of many cities will yet come, and the inhabitants of one city will go to another and say, "Let us go at once to entreat the LORD and

---

[19]"The goal to be sought is not the extension of Israel's kingdom, but the extension of God's praise." Craig C. Broyles, *Psalms,* New International Biblical Commentary (Peabody, Mass.: Hendrikson; Carlisle, U.K.: Paternoster, 1999), p. 280, commenting on the universal vision of Ps 67.

seek the LORD Almighty. I myself am going." And many peoples and powerful nations will come to Jerusalem to seek the LORD Almighty and to entreat him.

This is what the LORD Almighty says: "In those days ten men from all languages
and nations will take firm hold of one Jew by the hem of his robe and say, 'Let us
go with you, because we have heard that God is with you.'" (Zech 8:20-23)

*Mission as building God's temple: God's multinational covenant dwelling
place.* Mission then may be compared to building the dwelling place of God and
inviting the nations to come on home. And that is not far from the way Paul
actually portrays it. Ephesians 2:11-22 is packed with covenant imagery, as Paul
reminds his Gentile readers in the churches of Ephesus of the transformation
that has taken place in their status with God. They have indeed come in from
the cold, come home from afar.

The climax of that section of Ephesians, however, makes our point perfectly.
What have the Gentiles, the outsider nations, joined up to in coming to Christ?
Nothing less than being *part of the very temple of God.* They may have been physically excluded from inner parts of the temple in Jerusalem, as Gentiles, but spiritually they now constitute the dwelling place of God in Christ through the Spirit.
The covenant privilege has been universalized through Jesus (cf. Eph 3:6). Such
is the mystery of the mission of the gospel—"Christ among you"—that is, the
Messiah dwelling among you Gentiles, the hope of glory—that is, the reality of
the presence of God in your midst (Col 1:27).[20] For, as Paul has already said, the
fullness of the person and presence of God dwells in Christ (Col 1:19; 2:9). So if
Christ is now among the Gentiles, then the covenant presence of God—the
prime privilege of Israel—has now been extended to the nations through Paul's
missionary work and in fulfillment of the Old Testament promises.

And ultimately, of course, the temple of God will encompass not only his whole
people redeemed from every tribe, nation, people and language but the whole
cosmos, within which we will serve him as kings and priests. That is to say, humanity redeemed through Christ and modeled on Christ's perfect humanity will be
restored to our proper and intended relationship with creation. The temple too,
from the symbolism of Eden, through its earthly particularity in the Old Testament
and its Christ-centered transformation in the New Testament, to its final universality
in Revelation, also functions as a significant missional theme in Scripture.[21]

---

[20]In my view the phrase *Christos en hymin* should be translated as "Christ among you" rather
than simply "in you." Paul's point here is not simply the presence of the indwelling Christ in
the hearts of believers, but (especially in view of the parallel passage of the letter to the Ephesians, where Paul explains what he means by "the mystery" [Eph 3:2-6]), the presence of the
Messiah among the Gentiles through the preaching of the gospel and its acceptance by them.
[21]See especially, Beale, *Temple and Church's Mission.*

God's mission and God's prognosis: Deuteronomy 27—32. We began with the great prologue to the Sinai covenant in Exodus 19. Exodus 19:7-8 records that the people of Israel declared their wholehearted intention to do all that the Lord commanded. They repeat their commitment in Exodus 24:7. But by the time we reach the end of Deuteronomy, they have already on several signal occasions proved their inability to keep this promise (see esp. Ex 32—34; Num 14; and Moses' recollection of these and other rebellions in Deut 9). It is a tragic story in which the dissonance between the people's enthusiastic acceptance of the covenant and their utter failure to keep it had become painfully glaring.

Failure and curse. Worse is to come, for in these closing chapters of Deuteronomy, the Pentateuch ends with the gloomy prediction that this would not be the end of Israel's stiff-necked resistance to God's guiding. Their long future would be as wracked with recalcitrance as their short past.

At its simplest, Deuteronomy's anticipation of the future history of Israel was that, although Israel had been called and given every possible incentive to live in loyalty to their covenant Lord, they would in fact fail to do so. The book of Deuteronomy, for all its magnificent content, paradoxically begins and ends with failure: it opens by looking back to the failure of the generation of the exodus to go and take the land that God set before them, and it ends with the anticipated failure of the generations to come. Israel's endemically stiff-necked nature would lead to rebellion and disobedience.

As a result, the curses that were an integral part of the covenant (Lev 26; Deut 28) would fall, including the terrible threat of scattering among the nations. However, with great amazement and wonderful rhetoric (esp. Deut 30), Moses points beyond that judgment to offer the sure and certain hope of restoration and new life if the people would return and seek God once more. This is the scenario that flows through the great concluding section of the book, chapters 27—32 especially: failure, curse, scattering, return, restoration.

Israel and the nations intertwined in the story. Since Deuteronomy is a record of covenant renewal just prior to entry into the Promised Land, it sets this future anticipation in a thoroughly covenantal framework. And since the covenant with Israel was made in the full awareness that all the earth and all the nations belong to God, we should not be surprised to see that the nations are woven into this future projection in some highly significant ways—ways that are further taken up in the New Testament's understanding of God's mission for the world.

First, the nations *witness* Israel's failure and judgment and are shocked by it. They ask for, and are given, an explanation (Deut 28:37; 29:22-28). Second, the nations are also the human *agents* through whom God executes his judgment in fulfillment of the covenant curses (Deut 28:49-52; 32:21-26). At this point the nations are enemies of Israel but also agents of God. Third, in the amazing inversion and paradox of Deuteronomy 32, God *vindicates* his people in the midst of the nations, in such a way that the nations are finally called on to *praise* YHWH and to rejoice *with* his people (Deut 32:27-43). It is not explained how this mysterious reversal will take place. The different scenes are simply set side by side.

- The nations will be enemies whom God will use to judge Israel.
- Yet God will also finally defend Israel against these very enemies.
- And God will ultimately lead all —Israel and nations together—to the praise and worship of the Lord God.

Thus, the history that will see the judgment and restoration of *Israel* will also see the judgment and blessing of the *nations*. Each sequence will be intertwined with the other. And the total sequence will be the outworking of the covenant in history.

Restoration of Israel and ingathering of the nations. In chapter fourteen, we will look further at the way the prophets handled this covenantal eschatology in relation to the nations. But for the moment we need to recognize that the influence of this Deuteronomic and covenantal theology of anticipated history on the New Testament's understanding of the mission of the church is profound.

It is clear that *Jesus* linked his own mission to the hope of the restoration of Israel and that the Gospel writers had the same interpretation of the significance of his ministry. N. T. Wright, for example, suggests that Matthew has shaped his Gospel not merely in terms of the five books of the Torah (a common scholarly view) but specifically in terms of the sequence of thought in the great final section of Deuteronomy 27—34. In doing so, Matthew brings out the significance of the story of Jesus "as the continuation and climax of the story of Israel, with the implicit understanding that this story is the clue to the story of the whole world."[22] Although Jesus limited his own ministry to the primary objective of the restoration of Israel, he left in his actions and words many hints of an expected ingathering of the nations, and he made that ingathering the explicit mission of his disciples after his resurrection.

It was, however, the apostle Paul who made the most use of Deuteronomy in his theological and missiological reflection. Not only did he see in the continued suffering of Israel a kind of prolongation of the curse of exile (a view shared by many first-century Jews), but he also saw in the death and resurrec-

---

[22]N. T. Wright, *New Testament and the People of God,* pp. 387-90.

tion of Jesus as the Messiah the climax of the judgment and the restoration of Israel respectively. Linking this with his central understanding of the significance of Israel *for the nations* (as the purpose of the Abrahamic covenant), Paul recognized that *the fulfillment of God's purpose for Israel could never be complete without the ingathering of the nations as well.* The failure of many of his contemporary Jews to respond to the message of Messiah Jesus had led to the extension of the good news to the Gentiles (e.g., Acts 13:44-48; Rom 11). But never, in Paul's thinking, did this mean a final rejection or replacement of the Jews.

Rather, in order to portray how he relates this ingathering of the Gentiles to God's ultimate purpose for Israel, Paul picks up a rhetorical pun in Deuteronomy 32:21 and develops it into a theology of history and mission.

> They [the Israelites] made me jealous by a "no god"
> and angered me with their worthless idols.
> So I will make them jealous by a "no people." (author's translation)

Paul argues that the ingathering of the Gentiles (the "no people") through his mission endeavors will arouse jealousy among the Jews, so that ultimately "all Israel," extended and inclusive of believing Jews and Gentiles, will share in salvation (Rom 10:19—11:26). Clearly Paul reflected deeply on Deuteronomy and on the Song of Moses in Deuteronomy 32 especially. (It has been called "Romans in a nutshell.") He quotes its final doxology, calling on the nations to praise God with his people (Deut 32:43), in his exposition of the multinational nature of the gospel and its implications for the need for crosscultural acceptance and sensitivity between Jewish and Gentile Christians (Rom 15:7-10).[23]

The Sinai covenant, then, which provides the backbone for so much of the law and the prophets, has extensive missiological significance. When we seek to read these massive building block texts of the Torah through the lens of a missional hermeneutic, we have to take account of

- the status and role of Israel—as God's covenant priesthood in the midst of the nations

- the central privilege of the presence of God in the midst of his people, constituting their distinctiveness from and their witness to the nations

---

[23]On the full extent of Deuteronomy's influence on Paul's missiology, see J. M. Scott, "Restoration of Israel," in *Dictionary of Paul and His Letters*, ed. G. F. Hawthorne and R. B. Martin (Downers Grove, Ill.: InterVarsity Press; Leicester, U.K.: Inter-Varsity Press, 1993), pp. 796-805.

- the anticipated failure of Israel that in the mysterious providence of God would result in opening the door of grace and salvation to the nations

These international and missional dimensions of Israel's covenant at Sinai eventually influenced and shaped the mission of Jesus and Paul in theology and in practice, and continue to have relevance for the church as the new covenant people of God in Christ.

David

The story of Israel rolled on until the time came when the nation demanded a king. After the failure of Saul, a monarchy was eventually established under David. It was not what God had initiated or asked for. But God was not wrong-footed by human decisions, and so he takes this human initiative within Israel, with all its ambiguities, and turns it into the vehicle of his own purpose.

A king in the purposes of God. Since David was to be king over the covenant people, God entered into a particular covenant with him and his successors. This needs to be seen not as a new covenant unrelated to the Sinai covenant but as a particular outworking of it in the context of monarchy. After all, who was the true king? The Sinai covenant had articulated the conviction that the true king of Israel was YHWH himself. This had been the triumphant declaration made on the back of the exodus—that "the LORD will reign / for ever and ever" (Ex 15:18). And for centuries the conviction that YHWH was the true King of Israel had been enough to resist the whole idea of a human king among the tribes of Israel settled in the land of Canaan. Gideon rejected the kingship when invited (Judg 8:22-23), and Abimelech, who seized it, came to an unenviable end (Judg 9). The reign of Saul had ended up hardly any better.

So when David is anointed as "a man after my own heart,"[24] it must imply that the reign of David is not to be seen as in any way replacing or usurping the reign of YHWH, but rather as an embodiment of it. David as human king of Israel will carry out the purpose of YHWH, their covenant great King. Thus the primary focus of the covenant with the house of David, as recorded in 2 Samuel 7, is on the role of David and his successors in earthing that rule of YHWH in Israel through these new royal arrangements. The king would rule over the people, but only as the representative of the ultimate rule of YHWH—in a more stable way, though no different in principle, than the leadership of the judges in an

---

[24]The phrase does not mean (as it may sound in English) a special favorite of God. Rather since the heart is the seat of the will and intentions in Hebrew, the phrase simply means that David will be the one who will carry out the purposes of God.

earlier era, who had also earthed God's authority among the people.[25]

The Davidic covenant, then, has a primarily Israel focus. There is however an awareness that, just as Israel itself had a more-than-local significance in the mission of God, so did their king. The universalizing aspects of the Davidic covenant, which are relevant for a missional reading of it, can be seen in two ways: on the one hand, the language of praise that links the Davidic kingship to the kingship of YHWH over all the nations, and on the other hand, the building of the temple as the focus of the worship, initially of Israel but ultimately of the nations. To these two missiologically pregnant themes—kingship and temple— we now turn.

A king for all nations. Only when we link the kingship of David and his successors to the kingship of God can we make sense of texts that envision the reign of David over the nations or even over the earth. Some of the Davidic/ Zion psalms also have this note of universality.

Psalm 2:7-9, for example, celebrates the universal rule of the son of David, addressed as the son of God. The language may originally have been coronation hyperbole—that is, an exaggerated affirmation of the worldwide rule of the Davidic king in Jerusalem. But the theological and messianic implications certainly envision the extension of the tiny kingdom of the historical David into the ultimately universal kingdom of "great David's greater Son," and the psalm was already being read in a messianic key well before the time of Jesus.

Psalm 72:8-11, 17 declares a similar expectation of the universal reign of the son of David. There is a very clear echo of the Abrahamic covenant in verse 17: "All nations will be blessed through him, / and they will call him blessed." The Davidic and the Abrahamic covenants are brought into closest connection here. Indeed, it is being affirmed that a king in the line of David will be the means through which God's promise to bless the nations will be fulfilled. Those who stand to be blessed through Abraham here stand to be blessed through the Davidic king.

This strong connection may well have influenced Matthew's joint focus on both of these great ancestors in his genealogy of Jesus in Matthew 1:1. Jesus is the son of David, the son of Abraham. The Messiah who concludes Matthew's Gospel by sending his disciples forth in a mission that would universalize the *Sinai* covenant, opens the Gospel (and the New Testament) as the one who em-

---

[25]John Goldingay observes a link between the warm initial affirmation of David as a man who "did justice and righteousness" (2 Sam 8:15) and led his whole household and nation in that direction, and the intention of God that this was the very purpose of Abraham's election—for the sake of the blessing not only of Israel but of all nations (Gen 18:19). Goldingay, *Old Testament Theology,* 1:555.

bodies the universal blessing of the *Abraham* covenant and the universal kingship of the *Davidic* covenant.

Isaiah 11 pairs up with Isaiah 9:1-7 in promising great things for the people
of God under the reign of a coming son of the house of David. What is immediately striking about this chapter, however, is that the endowment of the Spirit
of YHWH on this future "shoot from the stump of Jesse," that is, a descendant
of David, will empower him for a role that will extend not only to all nations
of the earth but even to all of creation. In the first main song of the chapter,
his rule of justice will encompass the earth (v. 4). And in the commentary that
follows his banner will summon peoples and nations (vv. 10, 12). Not surprisingly, in the song of praise that concludes this whole section of the book of
Isaiah, the good news of such universal importance is indeed to be proclaimed
among the nations and to all the world (Is 12:4-5). The missional mood that
will resonate so strongly later in the book is already anticipated here in the
wake of the prophecies of the worldwide benefits of a future fulfillment of the
Davidic covenant.

In Isaiah 55:3-5 the Lord declares:

> I will make an everlasting covenant with you,
>   my faithful love promised to David.
> See, I have made him a witness to the peoples,
>   a leader and commander of the peoples.
> Surely you will summon nations you know not,
>   and nations that do not know you will hasten to you.

Coming at the climax of a whole section devoted to the encouragement of
the exiles, this word links the future of God's people not only to the hope of
return from exile (including return to God also) but also to the restoration of
the covenant with David. The destruction of Jerusalem and the captivity of the
Davidic king had seemed to put an end to that covenant, as Psalm 89 laments.
Here God not only remembers it, but extends it in two ways. On the one hand,
the promise to David will from now on be a covenant with all the people—"with
you" (plural). And on the other hand, the future rule of the new David will not
be limited to ethnic Israelites but will extend to peoples and nations (plural).
This connects, of course, with the universalizing thrust of these prophecies,
which included the great vision that ultimately "all flesh," that is, *all humanity,*
will see the glory of the Lord (Is 40:5).

A house of prayer for all nations. Alongside the covenant with the house
of David, the same narratives record the building of the temple by David's son,
Solomon. as a "house for the LORD." And with this development comes also the

strong emphasis on Jerusalem as Zion, the city of God. This whole David-temple-Zion nexus of theological traditions is at one level highly centralized and particular. After all, *this* is the place and the sanctuary, where YHWH is to be sought because this is where he has caused his name to dwell. Yet in other respects the temple tradition has a remarkable openness to the rest of the nations and an incipient universality that surfaces in a number of texts.

1 Kings 8:41-43. The prayer of Solomon at the dedication of the temple invites YHWH to pay attention to the prayers not only of Israelites, but also of foreigners (see pp. 228-30). It is an implicit fulfillment of the promise to Abraham that foreigners will be attracted to come and invoke the God of Israel for blessing. The motivation offered to God for answering such prayers of noncovenant people is expressly missional—namely, that "all the peoples of the earth may know your name and fear you, as do your own people Israel" (v. 43). The temple, then, that was so centrally connected to the Davidic covenant in the developing faith of Israel from this point on can be the focus for the fulfillment of the Abrahamic covenant. It should be the place of blessing for representatives of the nations.

Isaiah 56:1-7. This remarkable word offers a reversal of the situation in which foreigners (to different degrees and for different reasons [Deut 23:1-8]) had been excluded from Israel's holiest place. Not only will God himself bring them to his "holy mountain" (the city of Jerusalem), not only will he give them "joy in my house of prayer" (the temple), but their complete inclusion will be proved by the acceptance of their sacrifices "on my altar." This universalizing of the efficacy of the temple to include foreigners is immediately confirmed by the announcement "for my house will be called / a house of prayer for all nations" (v. 7).

This was the text that Jesus knew would be fulfilled in the temple of his own person and those whom he gathered to himself, and quoted as he prophetically enacted the destruction of the temple of his own day (Mk 11:17). It was also the promise that was appropriated (consciously or not) by the Ethiopian eunuch, as he found joy in fulfillment of Isaiah 56:7, not when he visited the temple in Jerusalem but when he was introduced to Jesus by Philip in the desert (Acts 8:39).

Great David's greater son. *Luke 1—2.* Matthew picks up the Davidic descent of Jesus the Messiah and connects it with Abraham. But it is Luke who turns this feature into a symphony of Davidic references and allusions in the first two chapters of his Gospel. As is appropriate, the references to David begin with God's promise specifically to Israel. But it is not long before the horizon widens out to include the nations.

Mary is introduced to us as the fiancée of Joseph, "a descendant of David"

(Lk 1:27). Gabriel's word to her specifies that the child she will bear will be the expected messianic king of Israel: "The Lord God will give him the throne of his father David, and he will reign over the house of Jacob for ever; his kingdom will never end" (Lk 1:32-33). The Song of Zechariah celebrates that God is at last keeping his promises to both Abraham and David, and bringing salvation and deliverance once again to his people (Lk 1:69-73). The choir of angels identify Bethlehem as "the town of David" (Lk 2:11, as if the local shepherds didn't know that) and tell them that the good news they bring is "for all people" (Lk 2:10). *Salvation, glory* and *peace*—key notes in the heavenly harmony of the angels—were all features of the promised new era of the reign of the new David. Finally, Simeon, though he does not mention David, recognizes the full-orbed truth about the infant he holds in his arms. Not only is he "the Lord's Christ" (Lk 2:26), he is (as his name declared) the Lord's salvation, prepared for all people, Gentiles and Israel alike (Lk 2:30-32). So for Luke the universal and missional significance of Jesus the Messiah, and his Abrahamic and Davidic pedigree, belong in the same grammar of divine promise fulfillment.

Acts 15:12-18. In his second volume Luke continues the theme of Davidic fulfillment in two ways. First, in their early preaching both Peter and Paul use Jesus' Davidic descent alongside his resurrection in their argument that he is the promised Messiah (Acts 2:25-36; 13:22-37). Second, at the Council of Jerusalem in Acts 15, called to wrestle theologically and pragmatically with the influx of Gentiles into the church as a result of the successful mission of Paul and others, James chooses a text from Amos that prophesies not only that the nations will come to bear the name of the Lord but also that the "fallen tent" of David will be rebuilt (Amos 9:11-12). The implications of this choice of text are important. It preserves the proper order of the eschatological vision of the Old Testament (which we will study more fully in the chap. 14).

The covenant promises to Israel must be fulfilled. Israel must be redeemed, the Davidic kingdom restored, the Davidic temple rebuilt. Only then could the nations be gathered in. James works the logic backward from the facts on the ground. The nations are clearly being gathered in, and it is manifestly the work of God himself. The only conclusion that could be drawn, therefore, was that in the resurrection of the Messiah, the promised restoration of David's kingdom and rebuilding of the temple had also taken place. But since the Davidic Messiah would be king for all nations, and the Davidic temple would be a house of prayer for all nations, the restoration of these things must now move forward to their appointed purpose—the ingathering of the nations as the subjects of his kingdom and the stones in his temple. The resurrection of Jesus is not just the fulfillment of words of David in the psalms, it is also the restoration of the reign and temple of David, no longer for ethnic Israel only but for all nations.[26]

Romans 1:1-5. Romans is Paul's most sustained exposition of his own missional theology. It presents the scriptural basis on which the gospel declares that the nations can be included in the saving work of God along with Israel, while affirming that God has still remained faithful to his promise to Israel. Indeed, the inclusion of the nations is part of what actually constitutes the fulfillment of God's promise to Israel.

In his opening words of introduction, Paul chooses to include Jesus' human descent from David among the points he makes about the fulfillment of Old Testament Scriptures.

> The gospel of God—the gospel he promised beforehand through his prophets in the Holy Scriptures regarding his Son, who as to his human nature was descendant of David, and who through the Spirit of holiness was declared with power to be the Son of God by his resurrection from the dead: Jesus Christ our Lord. (Rom 1:1-4)

"The gospel he promised beforehand," Paul will go on to show, is utterly universal in its scope, since it was announced first to Abraham and included all nations. That Jesus is the son of David as well as the Son of God must therefore be included in the ingredients of that universality. For it is explicitly in the name of this Jesus, Son of David and Son of God, that Paul has his missionary commission to bring about "the obedience of faith" among the nations in verse 5.

Revelation 5:1-10. A final reference to the Davidic covenant in relation to Jesus comes in John's great vision of the heavenly reality that lies behind or above the present world order in which Christians have to live their lives. Who has the key to the scroll, the meaning of human history in the purposes of God? It is a closed book unless it is unfolded by one with competent authority. "Then one of the elders said to me, 'Do not weep! See, the Lion of the tribe of Judah, *the Root of David* has triumphed. He is able to open the scroll and its seven seals" (Rev 5:5, emphasis added). This figure is then seen as the Lamb who was slain. So the crucified Jesus is the one who is worthy to open the scroll for the cross of Jesus is the key to all God's plan in history. "For with your blood you

---

[26]For a full and rich exposition of the way Luke in Acts clearly identifies the resurrection of Jesus with the eschatological temple, in Peter's speech on the day of Pentecost, in Stephen's speech and in James's speech at the Council of Jerusalem, see Beale, *Temple and Church's Mission,* chap. 6. James quotes Amos 9:11, but his words probably also echo Hosea 3:5 and Jeremiah 12:15-16, with the vision of "Gentiles becoming part of true Israel by means of being built as the true temple. This understanding of Acts 15:14-18 is consistent with several Old Testament prophecies that affirm that Gentiles will come into the divine presence in the temple of the messianic epoch (Ps. 96:7-8; Is. 2:2-3; 25; 56:6-7; Jer. 3:17; Mic. 4:1-2; Zech. 14:16)" (ibid., p. 239).

purchased people for God *from every tribe and language and people and nation*" (Rev 5:9, author's translation).

The Root of David has fulfilled the promise to Abraham. The mission of God is complete.

The New Covenant

The story of Israel rolled on. The history of failure and rebellion that had been anticipated in Deuteronomy became a reality. The people as a whole failed to live by the standards of the Sinai covenant. Successive kings of both Israel and Judah failed to live either by the standards of Sinai or the ideals of Zion. The covenant relationship was strained to breaking point. Indeed some prophetic voices declared that it had indeed been broken, and only an act of God's amazing grace could ever salvage it.

But that was the trademark of YHWH, God of Israel—acts of grace beyond belief and certainly beyond deserving. And so there developed a growing longing for God to act in a new way, to make a fresh start, to inaugurate a renewal of the covenant in such a way that it would not fall prey to the failures of a disobedient people. Only once is this described in the precise terms "a new covenant" (by Jeremiah), but the idea that God's new future would include features of the original covenants, renewed and permanently established, is found across a range of texts.

All of the covenants we have surveyed had dimensions and expectations that looked beyond the boundaries of Israel alone, recognizing that YHWH as the covenant God of Israel was also the sovereign God of all the earth and all nations. It is not surprising, then, that the idea of a new covenant would likewise bring those wider missional hopes into view. Nor is it surprising either that the documents we have received from the earliest Christians came to be collectively called the New Covenant (or Testament). For they read their existing Scriptures in the light of their belief that Jesus was the Messiah and that through him the promised new covenant had been inaugurated, along with mission to the nations as its inescapable corollary.

Prophetic hopes. *Jeremiah.* The one text that explicitly uses the phrase "a new covenant," Jeremiah 31:31-37, gives no clear indication of its universality, that is, that it will involve or include other nations in its scope.[27] The passage comes in a section of Jeremiah known as the Book of Consolation (chaps. 30-33), in which the prophet is absorbed with bringing comfort to the people of Israel

---

[27]I offer a fuller classified analysis of all the New Covenant passages in the prophets in Wright, *Knowing Jesus through the Old Testament.*

through the message of their restoration after exile. This should not be taken, however, to imply that Jeremiah had no interest in or awareness of any promise from God in relation to the nations at large. He was, after all, called to be a "prophet to the nations" (Jer 1:5)—a role he seems to have agonized over with some seriousness. At least two other texts have the nations in view, with a wider offer of God's blessing or salvation.

In a quite remarkable small oracle (Jer 12:14-17), the nations around Israel are offered exactly the same hope of restoration and establishment on exactly the same conditions (repentance and true worship) that Jeremiah elsewhere held out to Israel.

As for Israel itself, if only they would truly repent, then not only would the judgment of God be suspended on Israel but the blessing of God would be released. And in striking allusion to Genesis 12:3, that will mean Abrahamic blessing for the rest of the nations (Jer 4:1-2).

Ezekiel. In chapters 34-37 Ezekiel envisions the future restoration and reestablishment of Israel itself in language that has echoes of all the covenants with Noah, David and at Sinai (e.g., Ezek 34:23-31). The whole flavor of Ezekiel's vision of the future is strongly covenantal.

But did Ezekiel hold out hope for the salvation of *the nations?* Not explicitly, but his silence on the matter should not be used to prove too much. Ezekiel's passion was that the whole earth should come to know the true identity of God as YHWH. An analysis of Ezekiel's use of the phrase "then you [or they] will know that I am YHWH," shows some differentiation between Israel and the nations.

- Israel would come to know YHWH both through judgment and future restoration.

- The nations would come to know YHWH through witnessing God's acts in and for Israel, and through the experience of their own judgment.

Ezekiel never quite says that the nations will come to know YHWH *through their own future salvation.* It could be said that this is at least implied as a possibility, since "knowing YHWH" is such a feature of the covenant between God and Israel, and is strongly connected with his acts of redemption on their behalf. By analogy, if the nations will come to know YHWH, it could include experiencing salvation as Israel did. One must accept, however, that Ezekiel never explicitly says so.

However, it has been pointed out that, standing as he did at the beginning of the exile, Ezekiel's overriding concern was *whether there could be any future at all for Israel.* Unless Israel could be brought to repentance and saving knowledge of God, there was no hope for Israel themselves, let alone for the rest of the world. Any hope for the *nations* depended entirely on *Israel* being put right.

So that is the burning concern of Ezekiel in the first searing onslaught of God's judgment in exile. Nothing mattered more than that Israel should repent, return to God and come to know him again—and that would only happen through the fires of judgment.[28]

Isaiah. The book of Isaiah uses the language of covenant to express future hope in explicitly universalizing ways that include the nations. In Isaiah 42:6 and Isaiah 49:6, the mission of the servant of YHWH is, among other things, to be a "covenant for the people"—a mysterious phrase and something of an exegetical *crux,* but it is surely to be understood through its parallelism with "light for the Gentiles [nations]" (cf. Is 49:6, which further explicates it in terms of YHWH's salvation going "to the ends of the earth").

The language of justice and *torah* in Isaiah 42 is reminiscent of the Sinai covenant, but it is the Davidic covenant that is referred to in Isaiah 55:3-5, and its universalizing tendency is actualized. Even the covenant with Noah is harnessed to the certainty of God's promise of future blessing for his people, in Isaiah 54:7-10.

So we find then that in its Old Testament development, the anticipated new covenant picks up themes from all of the preceding covenants—Noah, Abraham, Sinai and David, and in several places expands them to include the nations within the ultimate scope of God's saving covenantal mission. This eschatological and universalizing development of the covenant trajectory through the Old Testament story is what leads directly to the missionally charged language of fulfillment in the New.

Covenantal "yes" in Christ. "No matter how many promises God has made, they are 'Yes' in Christ," said Paul, in a context in which his own role as a servant of the new covenant is very much in his mind (2 Cor 1:20; cf. chap. 3).

> Jesus Christ, the Son of God made man, the Word of God made flesh like the rest of the human family, has been sent as the "Yes!" to all God's promises. In Jesus of Nazareth God has granted the descendant of Abraham in whom all nations are to be blessed, the prophet like Moses who surpasses Moses in bringing the world "grace and truth," the son of David whose just rule will never end, the Suffering Servant who has become a covenant bringing together in himself the scattered peoples of the world.[29]

---

[28]I have discussed these dimensions of Ezekiel's message in relation to the nations further in *The Message of Ezekiel,* The Bible Speaks Today (Leicester, U.K.: Inter-Varsity Press; Downers Grove, Ill.: InterVarsity Press, 2001), pp. 35-38, and I owe the point being made here to David A. Williams, " 'Then They Will Know That I Am the Lord': The Missiological Significance of Ezekiel's Concern for the Nations as Evident in the Use of the Recognition Formula" (master's diss., All Nations Christian College, 1998).

[29]Christopher J. Baker, *Covenant and Liberation: Giving New Heart to God's Endangered Family* (New York: Peter Lang, 1991), pp. 323-24.

This being so, we might be surprised to find that the New Testament is a bit light on actual covenant vocabulary. It is true that neither Jesus nor Paul mention the word particularly often (though in highly significant ways when they do). But this is simply because they take the covenantal story for granted as the baseline for all their thinking.

I must emphasize again the underlying story that binds all the Old Testament covenant articulations together. Necessarily, we have had to pick our way through a selection of texts in each case. But binding them all together is the grand narrative of God's mission, ever since Abraham, to bring blessing to the nations through this people whom he has called to be his special possession. This is not just any story, it is *the* story, providing Israelites with their fundamental worldview and providing Christians also with theirs. For this is the God whom we worship in Jesus. This is the people to whom we belong through faith in Jesus. And this is the story of which Jesus is the climax and which he will eventually bring to its grand finale. And covenant runs through this story like a core nerve.

So for Jesus and the writers of the New Testament, the covenant was just as crucial to the way they thought of God's purpose for Israel as the certainty that Israel's God was the only living and true God and that Israel was God's elect. So, whether explicitly mentioned or not, we find covenantal realities in all the great fulfillment themes. And especially we find it in the extension of covenant membership to the nations, which was the underlying purpose of the missionary work of the church.

The most memorable (literally) usage of the term "new covenant," of course, is Christ's definitive use of it on the occasion of his final Passover meal with his disciples just before his crucifixion. In that highly charged moment that celebrated the exodus and the subsequent establishing of the covenant with Israel at Sinai, Jesus takes the fourth cup of the meal and declares it to be "the cup of the new covenant in my blood, which is shed for many." The essential words, with minor variations are found in our earliest record, in 1 Corinthians 11:25, and in each of the Synoptic Gospels (Mt 26:28; Mk 14:24; Lk 22:20). The phrase "for many" is usually taken to connect the action in Jesus' mind with Isaiah 53:11 and the vicarious suffering of God's servant on behalf of all who would benefit from his death.

Mission and the extension of the covenant to the nations. Paul sees the gospel story as playing out the covenantal script anticipated in the later chapters of Deuteronomy. Paul was particularly keen to insist that the Gentiles who were coming to Christ were coming into a status of total inclusion within the covenant. Or to put it the other way round, the covenant between God and Israel was being extended in such a way that Israel itself is now redefined to include

Gentiles in Christ. We have already seen how he harangues the Galatians to recognize that if they are *in Christ,* then they are *in Abraham* and heirs of that covenant promise. In fact, it is *only* when Gentiles like them *are* included that the Abrahamic promise is fulfilled at all. God's promise to Abraham remains unfulfilled unless the nations are blessed along with Abraham and Israel.

The supreme exposition of the covenantal inclusion of the Gentiles is Ephesians 2:11-22. In a classic contrast, Paul portrays the status of the nations outside Israel prior to the gospel; it is sheer, bleak, covenant exclusion: "separate from Christ, excluded from citizenship in Israel, foreigners to the covenants of the promise, without hope and without God in the world" (v. 12). Then, following his explanation of the reconciling work of Christ on the cross, Paul piles on the covenantal imagery again, from verse 19. These former covenant outsiders are now no longer foreigners and aliens (technical terms in Old Testament law) but full members of God's *people* and God's *household.* They do not just have access to the presence of God, they actually constitute the *temple,* the very *dwelling place* of God. All of this is top-drawer covenant imagery. And all of it is now the reality for these Gentiles who have been brought in through the instrumentality of Paul's mission.

Mission extends the boundaries of covenant membership wherever the gospel is effectively preached. The Great Commission is the command of the new covenant. It is Matthew, of course, who gives us, as the climax of his Gospel, what has come to be known as the Great Commission. What is not so often noticed is how thoroughly covenantal and indeed Deuteronomic is the form and content of Matthew's record at this point.

> All authority in heaven and on earth has been given to me. Therefore, as you go, disciple all nations, baptizing them into the name of the Father and of the Son and of the Holy Spirit, and teaching them to observe everything I have commanded you. And look, I am with you always, to the end of the age. (Mt 28:18-20, author's translation)

Among the key elements of the Old Testament covenant form were

- the self-introduction of God as the great King with all authority (often shortened simply to "I am YHWH")

- the imperative demands of the covenant relationship—that is, the instructions given by the covenant Lord

- promises of blessing

We can see how all three of these covenantal elements are contained in the words of Jesus.

First, he identifies himself as the one who now possesses all divine authority—he is the covenant Lord.

Second, he gives the disciples (who now, appropriately, are also worshipers [v. 17]) a systematic mandate for their covenant obedience.

Third, he concludes with the promise of his own permanent presence among them—something explicitly promised as the covenantal blessing *par excellence*.[30]

The Great Commission is nothing less than a universalized covenant proclamation. It could even be regarded as the promulgation of the new covenant by the *risen* Jesus, just as his words at the Last Supper were the institution of the new covenant in relation to his *death*.

Even the language of the Great Commission is almost pure Deuteronomy. The people of Israel were told to take to heart that "the LORD is God in heaven above and on the earth below. There is no other" (Deut 4:39). That was the supreme reason for the exclusive covenant loyalty that Israel must give to YHWH alone. The risen Jesus calmly assumes that position of *cosmic identity and authority*. What had been affirmed of YHWH is now claimed by *Jesus*.

And the emphasis on *obedience*, implicit in the command to make disciples, which is Deuteronomic enough in itself, is crystal clear in the phrase "to observe everything that I have commanded you"—the constant refrain of the whole book of Deuteronomy.

And even Christ's *promise* to be with his disciples, is an echo of the promise made to Joshua by both Moses and God himself that he would be with him forever (Deut 31:8, 23; cf. Josh 1:5). The covenant presence of God among his people in the Old Testament becomes the promised presence of Jesus among his disciples as they carry out the mission he lays on them. "The [Old Testament] protection offered by Yahweh to his people or to his messengers in the past is now promised by Jesus, the universal savior, to the new people of this universal covenant."[31]

Mission then, as articulated in the Great Commission, is the reflex of the new covenant. Mission is an unavoidable imperative founded on the *covenantal lordship* of Christ our King. Its task is to produce self-replicating communities of *covenantal obedience* to Christ among the nations. And it is sustained by the *covenantal promise* of the perduring presence of Christ among his followers.

Mission accomplished as the climax of the covenant. But we cannot stop short of the climactic vision of the whole Scripture, the book of Revelation. Revelation is gloriously covenantal and presents the presence of God among his peo-

---

[30]Cf. Vogels, *God's Universal Covenant*, pp. 134-35.
[31]Ibid., p. 139.

ple as the crowning achievement of God's cosmic redemptive mission. Revelation 21—22, indeed, combines imagery from all the covenants of the Scriptures.

Noah is there in the vision of a new creation, a new heavens and a new earth after judgment. Abraham is there in the ingathering and blessing of all nations from every tongue and language. Moses is there in the covenantal assertion that "they will be his people and God himself will be with them and be their God," and "the dwelling of God is with men and he will live with them." David is there in the Holy City, the new Jerusalem, and in the identity of Jesus as the Lion of Judah and Root of David. And the New Covenant is there in the fact that all of this will be accomplished by the blood of the Lamb who was slain.

This is the omega point of the long sweep of covenantal history through the Bible. The covenants proclaim the mission of God as his committed promise to the nations and the whole of creation. The book of Revelation is the covenantal declaration "Mission accomplished."

We may never know for sure what Scriptures Jesus expounded to the two disciples on the road to Emmaus or which passages he may have had particularly in mind when he told the rest of the disciples on the same evening that "this is what is written" (Lk 24:45-48). We can be fairly confident, however, that, having explicitly identified his own death with the new covenant (Lk 22:20), the covenants we have surveyed above would have been at least part of the path he trod through the Scriptures. The covenants thus form an essential part of that Christian reading of the Old Testament Scriptures, which, as Jesus pointed out, must be both *messianic* (because they all lead ultimately to Christ) and *missiological* (because they lead to repentance and forgiveness being preached in the name of Christ to all nations). The mission of God is as integral to the sequence of the covenants as they are to the overarching grand narrative of the whole Bible.

11

The Life of God's Missional People

We have traveled a long way with Israel in the last five chapters. We have traced the story of Israel's God in his actions of election, redemption and covenant on behalf of his people Israel, exploring how each is a dimension of the great mission of the God of the Bible to bring blessing to all nations. In each case we have also explored how these core worldview themes are picked up in the New Testament and form the template for understanding the identity and mission of the church as the people of the same God.

At various points along the way, we have seen hints of the necessity of Israel's *ethical response*. God's mission is to bless all nations through this people whom he has chosen, redeemed and bound to himself in covenant relationship. But that divine purpose calls for human response. All three pillars of Israel's faith and identity (their election, redemption, and covenant) are connected to God's mission. The ethical challenge to God's people is, first, to recognize the mission of God that provides the heartbeat of their very existence and, then, to respond in ways that express and facilitate it rather than deny and hinder it.

In this chapter we will bind together the diverse ethical hints that we have observed so far, consolidating them around certain key texts that give sharp focus to each of the three major themes. Three texts in particular, which are acknowledged as having a programmatic status in their own contexts, will command our attention for the wider light they shed on ethics and mission: Genesis 18, Exodus 19 and Deuteronomy 4.

The common opinion that the Bible is a moral code book for Christians falls far short, of course, of the full reality of what the Bible is and does. The Bible is essentially the story of God, the earth and humanity; it is the story of what has gone wrong, what God has done to put it right, and what the future holds under the sovereign plan of God. Nevertheless, within that grand narrative, moral teaching does have a vital place. The Bible's story is the story of the mission of God. The Bible's demand is for the appropriate response from human beings. God's mission calls for and includes human response. And our mission certainly includes the ethical dimensions of that response.

The people of God in both testaments are called to be a light to the nations. But there can be no light to the nations that is not shining already in transformed lives of a holy people. So what we aim to show in this chapter is that the ethical teaching of the Bible can (indeed should) be read from a missiological angle, that is with the missiological hermeneutic that is the burden of this whole book.

What we will observe beyond doubt, I trust, is that there can be no biblical mission without biblical ethics.

Missional Ethics and Election—Genesis 18

In chapter six we looked in depth at God's election of Abraham, with its "bottom line" promise of blessing to the nations. We observed how the primary purpose of election is contained in the combination of promise and command, "you will be a blessing" (or "be a blessing"). With these words God launched the history of redemptive blessing in the world. But we also saw how Genesis stresses the response of Abraham in faith and obedience. Abraham's own obedience (highlighted as the reason why God will fulfill his promise to bless all nations [Gen 22:16-18]) was to be the model for the continuing education of his descendants from generation to generation. They too must walk in the way of the Lord in righteousness and justice so that God can accomplish the missional purpose of Abraham's election. "The Abrahamic covenant is a moral agenda for God's people as well as a mission statement by God" (see p. 221).

The text that most clearly articulates this connection is Genesis 18:18-19, and to this we now turn.

> Abraham will indeed become a great and mighty nation, and all nations on earth will find blessing through him. For I have known (chosen) him *for the purpose that* he will teach his sons and his household after him so they will keep the way of YHWH by doing righteousness and justice, *for the purpose that* YHWH will bring about for Abraham what he has promised to him. (Gen 18:18-19, author's translation)

This little divine soliloquy comes in the middle of the narrative of God's judgment on Sodom and Gomorrah that comprises Genesis 18—19. So this self-reminder of God's universal promise of blessing is actually nested within the story of one particularly notorious instance of God's historical judgment. We need to pay attention first of all to that surrounding context, since, like the story of the tower of Babel, it both stands in stark contrast to God's words to

Abraham and also shows us the reason why those redemptive words were so necessary.

Sodom: A model of our world. Sodom represents the way of the fallen world. It stands in Scripture as a proverbial prototype of human wickedness and of the judgment of God that ultimately falls upon evildoers. A survey of some texts that refer to Sodom will demonstrate this.

Starting in this chapter, we hear the "outcry" *(zĕʿāqâ)* that comes up to God from Sodom.

> Then the LORD said, "The outcry against Sodom and Gomorrah is so great and their sin is so grievous that I will go down and see if what they have done is as bad as the outcry that has reached me." (Gen 18:20-21)

zĕʿāqâ, or *ṣĕʿāqâ,* is a technical word for the cry of pain or the cry for help from those who are being oppressed or violated.[1] We saw in chapter eight that it is the word used for Israelites crying out under their slavery in Egypt (p. 272). Psalmists use it when appealing to God to hear their cry against unjust treatment (e.g., Ps 34:17). Most graphically of all, it is the scream for help by a woman being raped (Deut 22:24, 27). As early as Genesis 13:13 we were told that "the men of Sodom were wicked and were sinning greatly against the LORD." Here that sin is identified as oppression, for that is what the word "outcry" immediately indicates. Some people in or near Sodom were suffering to such an extent that they were crying out against its oppression and cruelty.

In Genesis 19 we read further of the hostile, perverted and violent sexual immorality that characterized "all the men from every part of the city of Sodom—both young and old" (Gen 19:4).

In Deuteronomy 29:23 the future fate of Israel under God's anger and judgment for their idolatry is compared to that of Sodom and Gomorrah, which suggests that part of the sin of the twin cities was unbridled idolatry, along with their social evils (cf. Lam 4:6).

Isaiah portrays the Jerusalem of his own day in the colors of Sodom and Gomorrah when condemning it for its bloodshed, corruption and injustice (Is 1:9-23). And he further portrays the future judgment of God against Babylon (an-

---

[1]For a full and detailed discussion of this word, including its use in the Psalms and Prophets, see Richard Nelson Boyce, *The Cry to God in the Old Testament* (Atlanta: Scholars Press, 1988). Boyce gives a whole chapter (chap. 3) to the use of this term in the legal setting of the "cry for help" addressed to the authorities by the needy. It certainly sharpens our understanding of Gen 18:20 if what God heard from Sodom was not just "an outcry" but specifically "a cry for help" addressed to himself as the ultimate "Judge of all the earth." In this case, God's intervention to destroy the cities would be seen as breaking their power over the poor and oppressed in the surrounding area—an act of biblical justice.

other prototypical city) for its pride as a replay of God's destruction of Sodom and Gomorrah (Is 13:19-20).

Ezekiel even more caustically compares Judah unfavorably with Sodom, describing Sodom's sin as arrogance, affluence and callousness to the needy. They were overproud, overfed and underconcerned—a very modern sounding list of accusations (Ezek 16:48-50).

So, from the wider Old Testament witness, it is clear that Sodom was used as a paradigm—a model of human society at its worst and of the inevitable and comprehensive judgment of God on such wickedness. It was a place filled with oppression, cruelty, violence, perverted sexuality, idolatry, pride, greedy consumption and void of compassion or care for the needy.

Philip Esler suggests that this catalog of the vice and evil that characterized Sodom shaped the Jewish mind in relation to sin and judgment, and, as such, is reflected in Paul's portrayal of human wickedness in Romans 1:18-32. Though Paul does not name Sodom, his own list of human sin reflects all of the scriptural items in the sin of Sodom. Significantly, Paul begins his list with the statement "the wrath of God is being revealed from heaven against" all such behavior, and ends it with the statement that "those who do such things deserve death." It was indeed from heaven that death rained in fire and brimstone on Sodom and Gomorrah (Gen 19:24).[2] It is a point worth remembering that when Paul spoke of his mission of apostleship to the nations, it was to nations that he saw typified in Sodom. To bring about "the obedience of faith" among a world of humanity that could be soberly described in those terms could be nothing short of the miraculous power of God's grace operating in the gospel. It still is.

Abraham: A model of God's mission. Sodom then stands as a model of the world under judgment. Yet it was also part of the world that was the context of Abraham's calling and residence. Inasmuch as Sodom was in the land to which Abraham was commanded to go, it was, in a sense, the context of his mission. There is a certain irony in the biblical narrative that records Abraham being called out of the land of Babel, not into some heavenly paradise but into the land of Sodom. Whatever else the story of redemption will be, it is not a story of escapism.

So it is in this context of the wickedness of Sodom, the investigation being conducted by God with his two angels and the likelihood of divine judgment upon the cities of the plain, that the conversations of Genesis 18 are set. God's soliloquy in verse 18 is a recapitulation of the original covenant promise. This

---

[2]Philip E. Esler, "The Sodom Tradition in Romans 1:18-32," *Biblical Theology Bulletin* 34 (2004): 4-16.

is the missional goal that sheds light on God's renewed promise to Abraham and Sarah of a son in the first half of the chapter (Gen 18:10, 14). God, on his way to act in judgment on a particular evil society, stops to remind himself of his ultimate purpose of blessing all nations. It is almost as if God cannot do the one (judgment) without setting it in the context of the other (redemption). The immediate particular necessity is investigation and judgment. The ultimate universal goal is (as it always was) blessing.

So then, God stops for a meal with Abraham and Sarah. He need not have done so, any more than, strictly speaking, he needed to "go down" to discover what was going on in Sodom (though the language is identical to his inspection of the tower of Babel). The reason was that God saw in this elderly couple camped on the hills above the cities of the plain the key to his whole missional purpose for history and humanity. The story is a further reminder to us (just as it is presented as a reminder by God to himself [vv. 17-19]) of the centrality of Abraham in the biblical theology of the mission of God.

How Abraham responds to being taken into God's confidence in this way is likewise significant. He turns to intercession (Gen 18:22-33).

This dialogue is sometimes portrayed as a case of Middle Eastern haggling—the dynamics and language being that of the bazaar. The assumption is that God is the harsh judge from whom Abraham eventually extracts, by a process of downward bidding, a greater leniency. Or it has even been taken as Abraham beginning his teaching career (see v. 19) on YHWH himself, by instructing him in a more discriminating way to be judge of all the earth (i.e., by not destroying the righteous with the wicked).[3] Nathan Macdonald however has shown that a "bargaining" interpretation does not fit the conversation at all.[4] Rather, if the image of the bazaar is implied at all, it is subverted. For Abraham discovers YHWH to be far more accommodating than he probably expected.

If one imagines the metaphorical intention is Abraham's attempt to "buy" the salvation of the city for the lowest possible "price" in terms of the numbers of righteous who might be in it, then the "bargaining" goes in the reverse direction to what might be expected. It is Abraham who makes the initial "bid" that the whole city should be spared if fifty righteous people could be found there. Perhaps to his surprise, this is accepted without quibble. Nor is there any counter-proposal. If this actually were a normal bargaining encounter, we should expect a divine reply along the lines of "No, I couldn't do it the sake of just fifty; there

[3]Walter Brueggemann, *Genesis,* Interpretation (Atlanta: John Knox Press, 1982), p. 168.
[4]Nathan MacDonald, "Listening to Abraham—Listening to YHWH: Divine Justice and Mercy in Genesis 18:16-33," *Catholic Biblical Quarterly* 66 (2004): 25-43.

would have to be at least a hundred." There would then be successive rapprochements, leading to some agreed figure in between. On the contrary, however, each *reduction* hesitatingly proposed by Abraham is met with an unhesitating acceptance by God, until the process mysteriously stops at ten. Abraham is learning even as he is interceding. The God he is dealing with, the God who has taken him into his confidence for this very purpose, is prepared to be far more merciful than Abraham probably first hoped for. And this God will certainly not fail to distinguish the righteous from the wicked in his judgment.

In the end the narrative tells us that not even ten righteous people could be found there. As Goldingay comments, "Pity the city that lacks even ten innocent people, as Sodom does: All its men gather at Lot's door—indeed the whole people, to the last person (Gen. 19:4)."[5] So the judgment falls.

Abraham's intercession, however, did not entirely fail. The terms on which God would have spared the whole city had not been met. But Abraham's *first* request, that God should not "sweep away the righteous with the wicked" (Gen 18:23) was indeed granted. Lot and his daughters were rescued from the cataclysm. And, we may presume, those who had cried out against Sodom and Gomorrah (possibly meaning the villages in surrounding lands that were being oppressed by them) were delivered through the destruction of the wicked cities.

Abraham here assumes a role that will later be carried to greater depths by Moses (Ex 32—34; Num 14; Deut 9) and to heaven itself by Christ—that of prophetic and priestly intercessor. Furthermore, it is yet another example of the role of Abraham as an instrument of blessing to the nations—even if in this case the cities in question had sinned themselves beyond the possibility of blessing or reprieve. Astonishing as it may seem, Sodom and Gomorrah had Abraham praying for them and pleading for them to be spared the judgment of God—a very different response to the one displayed by Jonah, or (one has to add) by many Christians as they contemplate the wickedness of the world around them. "If we listen to YHWH, we learn that Abraham's exchange with YHWH teaches the kind of response expected from YHWH's elect so that the divine blessing may be mediated to the nations (12:1-3)."[6] That is to say, we learn the missional significance of intercessory prayer.

"The way of the LORD": A model for God's people. Returning to the key central verse, Genesis 18:19, we find its ethical agenda connected on the one side to Abraham's election and on the other side to God's mission. We need to

---

[5]Goldingay, *Old Testament Theology*, vol. 1, *Israel's Gospel* (Downers Grove, Ill.: InterVarsity Press, 2003), p. 228.
[6]Ibid., p. 43.

examine first the specific ethical content of the phrases "the way of the LORD" and "doing righteousness and justice." Then we will take note of the clear missional logic of the structure and theology of the verse.

The ethical content. Abraham was chosen to be a teacher, specifically a teacher of the way of the LORD and a teacher of righteousness and justice. This ethical pedagogy will start with his children and then pass on to "his household after him," which presumes the transmission of the teaching down through the generations. Already Abraham is anticipating the role of Moses as teacher, just as we have seen that he anticipates Moses as an interceding prophet. Two phrases summarize the content of the Abrahamic family curriculum:

1. "The way of the LORD." The expression "keeping the way of the LORD," or "walking in the way of the LORD," was a favorite metaphor used in the Old Testament to describe a particular aspect of Israel's ethics. A contrast is implied: that is, walking in YHWH's way, as distinct from the ways of other gods or of other nations or one's own way or the way of sinners. Here, the contrast is clearly between the way of YHWH and the way of *Sodom* that immediately follows. As a metaphor, "walking in the way of the LORD" seems to have two possible pictures in mind.

One is that of following someone else on a path, watching their footsteps and following along carefully in the way they are going. In that sense, the metaphor suggests the imitation of God: you observe how God acts and try to follow suit. "O let me see thy footprints and in them plant my own," as the hymn says about following Jesus.[7]

Such imagery implies that Israel was destined to travel on a journey in which God was to lead the way as a guide and example for the people to follow. It also suggests that the moral requirements demanded by God were those that he himself had evinced in an exemplary manner in his dealings with his people. By mirroring the divine activity, the people would become a visible exemplar to the nations as to the nature and character of the God whom they worshiped (Deut 4:5-8).[8]

The other picture is of setting off on a path following the instructions that

---

[7]John F. Bode, "O Jesus, I Have Promised" (1868).

[8]Eryl W. Davies, "Walking in God's Ways: The Concept of Imitatio Dei in the Old Testament," in *True Wisdom,* ed. Edward Ball (Sheffield, U.K.: Sheffield Academic Press, 1999), p. 103. Interestingly, Davies touches here on the same aspect of Israel's missional significance that we are concerned to elucidate. The ethical quality of Israel's life was part of their "witness" to the nations by being a reflection of Yahweh in the midst of the nations. Cf. also, Christopher J. H. Wright, *Deuteronomy,* New International Biblical Commentary (Peabody, Mass.: Hendrikson; Carlisle, U.K.: Paternoster, 1996), pp. 11-14, where this ethical aspect of Israel's mission is discussed, and the section "Missional Ethics and Covenant" in this book (see pp. 375-87).

someone has given you, perhaps a sketch map (if that is not too anachronistic for ancient Israel) or a set of directions to make sure you stay on the right path and do not wander off on wrong paths that may turn out to be dead ends or dangerous. According to Cyril Rodd, this second image fits much better with the use of the metaphor in the Old Testament, since the expression "walking in the way (or ways) of the LORD" is most commonly linked to obeying God's commands, not to imitating God himself. The way of the Lord, according to Rodd, is simply another expression signifying God's law or commands, his instruction kit for life's journey. Rodd is undoubtedly correct in his analysis of the predominant use of the metaphor, but I think he too rigidly rules out the concept of the imitation of God from the expression.[9] The commands of God are not autonomous or arbitrary rules; they are frequently related to the character or values or desires of God. So to obey God's commands is to reflect God in human life. Obedience to the law of God and reflection of the character of God are not mutually exclusive categories: the one is an expression of the other.

One of the clearest examples of this dynamic at work is Deuteronomy 10:12-19. It begins with a rhetorical flourish, rather like Micah 6:8, summarizing the whole law in a single chord of five notes: fear, walk, love, serve and obey.

> And now, O Israel, what does the LORD your God ask of you but to fear the LORD your God, *to walk in all his ways*, to love him, to serve the LORD your God with all your heart and with all your soul, and to observe the LORD's commands and decrees that I am giving you this day for your own good? (Deut 10:12-13, emphasis added)

And what are the ways of YHWH in which Israel is to walk? The answer is given first in broad terms. His was the way of condescending love in choosing Abraham and his descendants to be the special vehicle of his blessing.

> To the LORD your God belong the heavens, even the highest heavens, the earth and everything in it. Yet the LORD set his affection on your forefathers and loved them, and he chose you, their descendants. (Deut 10:14-15)

That required a response of love and humility in return: "Circumcise your hearts, therefore, and do not be stiff-necked any longer" (Deut 10:16). But what *specifically* are the "ways" of YHWH? At last the passage gets down to detail.

---

[9]Cyril Rodd provides a very helpful survey of the usage of the metaphor "walking with, after, or before" Yahweh or other gods in *Glimpses of a Strange Land: Studies in Old Testament Ethics* (Edinburgh: T & T Clark, 2001), pp. 330-33.

[He] shows no partiality and accepts no bribes. He defends the cause of the fatherless and the widow, and loves the alien, giving him food and clothing. *And you are to love those who are aliens,* for you yourselves were aliens in Egypt. (Deut 10:17-19, emphasis added)

To walk in the way of the Lord, then, means (among other things) doing for others what God wishes to have done for them, or more particularly, doing for others what (in Israel's case) God has already done for you (in their experience of his deliverance from alien status in Egypt and provision of food and clothing in the wilderness).

Returning then to our main text, Genesis 18:19, a first-time reader of this whole narrative will hear the phrase "the way of YHWH" as a strong contrast to the ways of the cities, whose wickedness is raising the outcry God plans to investigate. The more experienced reader familiar with the rest of the Old Testament Scriptures will hear the phrase as a summary of the whole rich panorama of Old Testament ethics modeled on the character and action of YHWH.

2. Doing righteousness and justice. *Righteousness* and *justice* would also come in the top five of the Old Testament's ethical vocabulary. Each of them individually, in various verbal, adjectival and noun forms, occurs hundreds of times.

The first is the root *ṣdq,* which is found in two common noun forms, *ṣedeq* and *ṣĕdāqâ.* They are usually translated "righteousness" in English Bibles, but that rather religious-flavored word does not convey the full range of meaning that the words had in Hebrew. The root meaning is probably "straight": something that is fixed and fully what it should be. So it can mean a norm—something by which other things are measured, a standard. It is used literally of actual objects when they are or do what they are supposed to: for example, accurate weights and measures are "measures of *ṣedeq*" (Lev 19:36; Deut 25:15). Safe paths for sheep are "paths of *ṣedeq*" (Ps 23:3). So it comes to mean rightness, that which is at it ought to be, that which matches up to the standard.

When applied to human actions and relationships, it speaks of conformity to what is right or expected—not in some abstract or absolute generic way but according to the demands of the particular relationship or the nature of the specific situation. *Ṣedeq/ṣĕdāqâ* are in fact highly relational words. So much so that Hemchand Gossai includes a whole section on "relationship" as his definition of the term.

In order for an individual to be *ṣaddîq* [righteous], it means that of necessity he or she must exist and live in a manner which allows him or her to respond correctly to the values of the relationship; [which may include relationships of spouse, parent, judge, worker, friend, etc.]. . . . In essence then *ṣdq* is not simply an objective norm which is present within society, and which must be kept, but rather it is a concept which derives its meaning from the relationship in which it finds itself. So we are able to say that right judging, right governing, right worshiping and gracious activity are all covenantal and righteous, despite their diversity.[10]

The second is the root *špṭ,* which has to do with judicial activity at every level. A common verb and noun are derived from it. The verb *šāpaṭ* refers to legal action over a wide range. It can mean to act as a lawgiver, to act as a judge by arbitrating between parties in a dispute, to pronounce judgment by declaring who is guilty and who is innocent respectively, to execute judgment in carrying out the legal consequences of such a verdict. In the widest sense it means "to put things right," to intervene in a situation that is wrong, oppressive or out of control and to fix it.

The derived noun *mišpāṭ* can describe the whole process of litigation (a case) or its end result (the verdict and its execution). It can mean a legal ordinance, usually a case law based on past precedents. Exodus 21—23, known as the Covenant Code, or Book of the Covenant, is called in Hebrew, simply, the *mišpāṭim.* It can also be used in a more personal sense as one's legal right, the cause or case one is bringing as a plaintiff before the elders. The frequent expression "the *mišpāṭ* of the orphan and widow" means their rightful case against those who would exploit them. It is from this last sense in particular that *mišpāṭ* comes to have the wider sense of "justice" in the somewhat active sense, whereas *ṣedeq/ ṣĕdāqâ* has a more static flavor.[11] In the broadest terms (and recognizing that there is a great deal of overlap and interchangeability between the words) *mišpāṭ* is what needs to be done in a given situation if people and circumstances are to be restored to conformity with *ṣedeq/ṣĕdāqâ. Mišpāṭ* is a qualitative set of actions—something you do.[12] *Ṣedeq/ṣĕdāqâ* is a qualitative state of affairs— something you aim to achieve.

Here in Genesis 18:19 the two words are paired, as they frequently are, to form a comprehensive phrase. Found together like this as a couplet (either "righteousness and justice" or "justice and righteousness"), they form what is technically called a "hendiadys"—that is, a single complex idea expressed

---

[10]Hemchand Gossai, *Justice, Righteousness and the Social Critique of the Eighth-Century Prophets,* American University Studies, Series 7, Theology and Religion (New York: Peter Lang, 1993), 141:55-56.

[11]On *mišpāṭ,* see ibid., chap. 3,

[12]"As it is frequently used in biblical texts, justice is a call for action more than it is a principle of evaluation. Justice as an appeal for a response means *taking upon oneself the cause of those who are weak in their own defense* [cf. Is. 58:6 Jb. 29:16; Jer. 21:12]." Stephen Charles Mott, *A Christian Perspective on Political Thought* (Oxford: Oxford University Press, 1993), p. 79.

through the use of two words.[13] Possibly the nearest English expression to the double word phrase would be "social justice." Even that phrase, however, is somewhat too abstract for the dynamic nature of this pair of Hebrew words. For, as John Goldingay points out, the Hebrew words are concrete nouns, unlike the English abstract nouns used to translate them. That is, righteousness and justice are actual things that you do, not concepts you reflect on.[14]

Abraham, then, was to set in motion a process of ethical instruction in the way of the Lord and the doing of righteousness and justice. But how would he himself come to learn what he was supposed to teach? The immediately following narrative is the first lesson. Our tendency is to focus on the end of the story—the fiery judgment on the sinful cities. But actually the very first point that YHWH himself draws to Abraham's attention is his concern about the suffering of the oppressed in the region at the hands of these cities. In the careful account of the conversation, Genesis 18:17-19 are soliloquy, that is, God speaking to himself. At verse 20 God speaks again to Abraham, and the first word in what he says is *zĕʿāqâ*—"cry for help." The trigger for God's investigation and subsequent action is not only the appalling sin of Sodom but the protests and cries of their victims. This is an exact anticipation of what motivated God in the early chapters of Exodus. In fact this incident in Genesis is highly programmatic in the way it defines God's character, actions and requirements. The way of the Lord, which Abraham is about to witness and then to teach is to do righteousness and justice for the oppressed and against the oppressor. In this too Abraham is the forerunner of Moses, who learned the same lesson in the ways of the Lord, turned it into intercession (again like Abraham), and taught it to Israel (Ex 33:13, 19; 34:6-7), who then turned it into worship:

> The LORD works *righteousness*
>   *and justice* for all the oppressed.
> He made known *his ways* to Moses,
>   his deeds to the people of Israel. (Ps 103:6-7, emphasis added)

The missional logic. Returning again to our key text, we must also give attention to its grammatical structure and the logic expressed thereby. It is a compact

---

[13]Other examples of hendiadys in English include "law and order," "health and safety," "board and lodging." Each word in a hendiadys has its own distinct meaning, but when put together in a commonly used phrase, they express a single idea or set of circumstances.

[14]John Goldingay, "Justice and Salvation for Israel and Canaan," in *Reading the Hebrew Bible for a New Millennium: Form, Concept, and Theological Perspective,* ed. Wonil Kim et al. (Harrisburg, Penn.: Trinity Press International, 2000), pp. 169-87.

statement, in which syntax and theology are closely intertwined with powerful ethical and missiological impact.

Genesis 18:19 falls into three clauses, joined by two expressions of purpose. It opens with God's affirmation of the election of Abraham: "I have known him"—which is frequently used for God choosing to bring a person or people into intimate relationship with himself. God then states the ethical purpose of his election: "for the purpose that he will command/teach his children and household after him to keep the way of YHWH by doing righteousness and justice."[15] This in turn is followed by another purpose clause referring to God's mission to bless the nations (which had just been mentioned in v. 18): "for the purpose that YHWH may bring about for Abraham what he has spoken/promised to him."

This one verse thus binds together *election, ethics* and *mission* into a single syntactical and theological sequence located in the will, action and desire of God. It is fundamentally a missional declaration, explaining election and incorporating ethics.

What is most noteworthy in relation to the theme of this section is the way *ethics stands as the mid-term between election and mission,* as the purpose of the former and the basis for the latter. That is, God's election of Abraham is intended to produce a community committed to ethical reflection of God's character. And God's mission of blessing the nations is predicated on such a community actually existing. This is an extension of the link between Abraham's election for blessing others, and Abraham's own *personal* obedience to God. Both Genesis 22:18 and Genesis 26:4-5 make that link, connecting God's intention to bless the nations to Abraham's tested obedience, which the latter text articulates in primary ethical categories. The obedience of Abraham is to be the model for his descendants so that the mission of Abraham can be fulfilled. Now that personal obedience is to be passed on by teaching to his whole community.

One can approach the missional logic of Genesis 18:19 from either end of the verse. Either way, ethics stands in the middle.

- From the end:
  What is God's ultimate mission?
  To bring about the blessing of the nations, as he promised Abraham (mission).

---

[15]The expression of purpose is emphatic since the clauses are not merely joined (as they might easily be in Hebrew) by the ubiquitous conjunction wĕ but by the purposive conjunction lĕmaʿan.

- *How will that be achieved?*
  By the existence in the world of a community that will be taught to live according to the way of the Lord in righteousness and justice (ethics).
  But how will such a community come into existence?
  Because God chose Abraham to be its founding father (election).

- From the beginning:
  Who is Abraham?
  The one whom God has chosen and come to know in personal friendship (election).
  Why did God choose Abraham?
  To initiate a people who would be committed to the way of the Lord and his righteousness and justice, in a world going the way of Sodom (ethics).
  For what purpose should the people of Abraham live according to that high ethical standard?
  So that God can fulfill his mission of bringing blessing to the nations (mission).

This pregnant verse, then, injects another dimension into the link between missiology and ecclesiology. Already we have seen in chapters six and seven how important it is to recognize the missional reason for the very existence of the church as the people of God. We cannot speak biblically of the doctrine of election without insisting that it was never an end in itself but a means to the greater end of the ingathering of the nations. Election must be seen as missiological, not merely soteriological.

Now we see more clearly that this *ecclesiological* link is also an *ethical* one. The community God seeks for the sake of his mission is to be a community shaped by his own ethical character, with specific attention to righteousness and justice in a world filled with oppression and injustice. Only such a community can be a blessing to the nations.

According to Genesis 18:19, *the ethical quality of life of the people of God is the vital link between their calling and their mission.* God's intention to bless the nations is inseparable from God's ethical demand on the people he has created to be the agent of that blessing.

There is no biblical mission without biblical ethics.

Missional Ethics and Redemption—Exodus 19

We turn from one major programmatic text (Gen 18) to another, Exodus 19:4-6.

> You yourselves have seen what I have done to Egypt,
>   and I carried you on wings of eagles and brought you to myself.
>   Now then, if you really obey my voice and keep my covenant,

you will be for me *[li]* a special personal possession
  among all the peoples;
    for to me *[li]* belongs the whole earth
But you, you will be for me *[li]* a priestly kingdom and a holy nation.
(Ex 19:4-6, author's translation)

We have already had occasion to sample the rich content of this text twice. In chapter seven (pp. 224-25) we considered it in relation to the universality and particularity that are both intrinsic to the Abrahamic covenant and the calling of Israel. Then in chapter ten (pp. 329-33) we explored the theme of Israel's priesthood among the nations, with its bidirectional dynamic of bringing the knowledge and law of God to the nations and bringing the nations to God in covenant inclusion and blessing.

Now we need to pick up the other phrase in Israel's God-given identity: "a holy nation." Holiness is intrinsic to priesthood. For Israel to exercise the role of YHWH's priests in the midst of the nations required that they be holy. And holiness was far from merely ritual. It implied a comprehensive ethical agenda. First of all, however, it will be helpful to recall some essential points in the context of the text as a whole. For the context here is crucial for a proper perspective on all biblical ethics and mission. These are things we have noticed before, but they are central enough to bear brief summarizing repetition here.

God's redemptive initiative. "You yourselves have seen what I have done" (Ex 19:4). This reminder points to the preceding eighteen chapters of the book of Exodus, the great narrative of the God's deliverance of the Israelites from slavery in Egypt. It was a matter of historical fact and recent memory. Only three months ago they had been suffering genocidal oppression. Now they were liberated. "And I did it," says God, "and carried you here to myself." Before anything is said about what Israel has to do, God points to what he has already done.

The initiative of God's redeeming grace is the prior reality on which all that follows will be founded—including the giving of the law, the making of the covenant, building of the tabernacle and moving forward to the Promised Land. The life they now live, they live by the grace of God. The life they will be required to live must flow from the same starting point. Of course there is an ethical imperative in these verses—to obey God's voice and keep God's covenant. But it is expressed as a condition, *not of gaining God's redemption* (for that has already happened) *but of fulfilling the mission their identity lays on them*. Identity and obedience flow from grace.

Biblical ethics then must be seen as response to biblical redemption. Any other foundation leads to pride, legalism or despair. And since we have now

seen how closely Israel's ethical agenda is connected to God's missional investment in their existence, we must place biblical mission on the same foundation.
Whatever missional calling we may have flows from the grace of God in our
own lives and the grace of his plans for the future, for us and for the world.
Mission as a dimension of our obedience also flows from grace—the grace of
redemption accomplished and the grace of God's future purposes.

God's universal ownership. "Out of all the nations . . . the whole earth is
mine" (Gen 19:5). With these phrases at its core, our text avoids any narrow exclusivity in God's relationship with or intentions for Israel. On the contrary, it
affirms the universality of God's ownership of the whole earth and interest in
all nations. But in the same breath it affirms the particularity of Israel's unique
identity as YHWH's treasured personal possession, as his priestly kingdom and
holy nation.

The effect of this double affirmation is that Israel is going to live on a very
open stage. There will be nothing cloistered or closeted about Israel's existence
or history. For good or ill (as the narratives and prophets will show), Israel was
visible to the nations, and in that posture they could be either a credit or a disgrace to YHWH their God. Here, however, at the start of that historical journey
in the midst of the nations, God's desire is that they should live consistently with
their status as his treasured possession, in priestly and holy conduct.

Biblical ethics then, from this text, cannot be a matter of cosy esoteric behavior of a cloistered in-group accountable only to itself. The life of God's people
is always turned outward to the watching nations, as priests are always turned
toward their people as well as toward God. Shaping the life of his own particular people in the world is part of the mission of God to the world itself that
universally belongs to him. Once again we observe the connection between ethics and mission. Israel's calling to be holy is not set *over against* the nations and
the whole earth but *in the context of living among them for God.*

Israel's identity and responsibility. "You will be for me a kingdom of
priests and a holy nation" (Gen 19:6). We explored the meaning of Israel's role
as *God's priesthood* in chapter ten (see pp. 330-33). There we saw that this concept of national priesthood has an essentially missional dimension, for it puts Israel in a dual role in relation to God and the nations, and gives them the priestly
function of being the agent of blessing. God confers on Israel as a whole people
the role of being his priesthood in the midst of the nations. As I said earlier

> As the people of YHWH they would have the historical task of bringing the knowl-
> edge of God to the nations, and bringing the nations to the means of atonement
> with God. The Abrahamic task of being a means of blessing to the nations also put

them in the role of priests in the midst of the nations. Just as it was the role of the priests to bless the Israelites, so it would be the role of Israel as a whole ultimately to be a blessing to the nations. (p. 331)

This priestly role, however, required *holiness* of Israel, just as it required holiness of their own priests in the midst of the ordinary people of Israel. If holiness is a condition of priesthood, and if priesthood is a dimension of mission, then clearly we need to understand more fully what the Bible means by holiness. It is unfortunately one of those words (like priesthood also) that have an accretion of connotations in the popular religious mind, not all of which by any means have much connection with its biblical meaning.

Being holy did not mean that the Israelites were to be a specially religious nation. A fundamental part of the meaning of the word is "different or distinctive." Something or someone is holy when set apart for a distinct purpose and kept separate for that purpose. For Israel, it meant being different by reflecting the very different God that YHWH revealed himself to be, compared with other gods. Israel was to be as different from other nations as YHWH was different from other gods.[16]

There were in fact two aspects to Israel's holiness, both of which are extended in their relevance for the church as God's holy people.

Holiness, indicative and imperative. On the one hand *holiness was a given*— a fact of their existence. That is, God had set apart Israel for himself. It was his initiative and choice. "I am the LORD your God, who sanctifies you" (Lev 21:15)—that is, makes you holy, separate, distinct from the nations. Just like the experience of redemption, holiness is a prior gift of God's grace. It was said repeatedly of Israel's own priests that God had set them apart as holy (Lev 21:8, 15, 23). The same thing is also said of the people as a whole in relation to the nations. "You are to be holy to me because I, the LORD, am holy, and *I have set you apart from the nations to be my own*" (Lev 20:26; cf. 22:31-33, emphasis added).

On the other hand, *holiness was a task*. That is, Israel was to live out in daily life the practical implications of their status as God's holy people. "Be what you are" was the message. The following comprehensive instruction indicates the central meaning of this as distinctiveness from the nations:

> You must not do as they do in Egypt, where you used to live, and you must not do as they do in the land of Canaan, where I am bringing you. Do not follow their

---

[16]Cf. the extensive survey of this theme by Peter Machinist, "The Question of Distinctiveness in Ancient Israel," in *Essential Papers on Israel and the Ancient Near East,* ed. F. E. Greenspan (New York: New York University Press, 1991), pp. 420-42.

practices. You must obey my laws and be careful to follow my decrees. I am the
LORD your God. (Lev 18:3-4)

Holiness, symbolic and ethical. This practical task of holiness had two dimensions. It had a *symbolic* dimension, in which Israel gave expression to their distinctiveness from the nations through a complex system of clean and unclean
regulations regarding animals, foods, and other daily eventualities. It is important to recognize this (national distinctiveness from the other nations) as the underlying rationale for the clean-unclean distinction. There are various ways in
which the specific categories and what was included in them may be explained
from an anthropological perspective. But the theological explanation given in
the text for the system as a whole is that it represented the distinction between
Israel and the nations.

> I am the LORD your God, who has made a distinction between you and the nations.
> You must therefore make a distinction between clean and unclean animals and be-
> tween clean and unclean birds. . . You are to be holy to me, because I, the LORD,
> am holy, and I have distinguished you from the nations to be my own.[17] (Lev 20:24-
> 26, author's translation)

Practical holiness also had an *ethical* dimension, for being holy meant living
lives of integrity, justice and compassion in every area—including personal,
family, social, economic, and national life.

The most comprehensive single text that articulates the ethical dimension
of holiness in Israel is Leviticus 19. It is the finest commentary we have on
Exodus 19:6.

Holiness in all of life: Leviticus 19. "Be holy because I, the LORD your God,
am holy" (Lev 19:2). The superscription to the whole chapter expresses YHWH's
fundamental demand. It could be translated more colloquially, "You must be a
distinctive people, because YHWH is a distinctive God." In fact, as we saw in
chapter 3 (pp. 80-81), YHWH is utterly unique and distinct as God. YHWH is not
simply one of the gods of the nations, and not even like them. Holiness, among
other things, includes this total otherness of YHWH as the Holy One of Israel—
the utterly different God. For Israel to be holy then meant that they were to be
a distinctive community among the nations, as Leviticus 18:3-4 had already ex-

---

[17]The language of distinction between is somewhat dissipated by the use of different phrases
in the NIV; it is the same verb in all three instances, showing clearly the connection between
the symbolic clean-unclean distinctions and the fundamental theological distinction between
Israel and the other nations. This is the reason why, when the distinction between Jew and
Gentile was abolished for those in Christ, the regulations regarding clean and unclean food,
which had been symbolic of that distinction, were also abolished.

pressed in summary form. Or to be more precise, Israel was to be YHWH-like rather than like the nations. They were to do as YHWH does, not as the nations do. Holiness for Israel is a practical, down-to-earth reflection of the transcendent holiness of YHWH himself.

So what did this reflective holiness mean for Israel? What would it mean for them, in their earthly, historical and cultural circumstances, to be holy in a way that would reflect the holiness of YHWH? What content might we expect to be suspended under the stark headline of Leviticus 19:2: "Be holy"?

If we are inclined to think of holiness as a matter of private piety (in Christian terms) or as a matter of binding religious rituals (in Old Testament terms), then we might expect either a list of devotional exhortations for our deeper personal sanctity or a manual of obsolete ritual regulations for our relieved abandonment. Actually it contains none of the former and only a few of the latter. The bulk of the Leviticus 19 shows us that the kind of holiness that reflects God's own holiness is thoroughly practical, social and very down-to-earth. Simply listing its contents highlights this dominant note.

Holiness in Leviticus 19 involves

- respect within the family and community (vv. 3, 32)
- exclusive loyalty to YHWH as God; proper treatment of sacrifices (vv. 4, 5-8)
- economic generosity in agriculture (vv. 9-10)
- observing the commandments regarding social relationships (vv. 11-12)
- economic justice in employment rights (v. 13)
- social compassion to the disabled (v. 14)
- judicial integrity in the legal system (vv. 12, 15)
- neighborly attitudes and behavior; loving one's neighbor as oneself (vv. 16-18)
- preserving the symbolic tokens of religious distinctiveness (v. 19)
- sexual integrity (vv. 20-22, 29)
- rejection of practices connected with idolatrous or occult religion (vv. 26-31)
- no ill-treatment of ethnic minorities, but rather racial equality before the law and practical love for the alien as for oneself (vv. 33-34)
- commercial honesty in all trading transactions (vv. 35-36)

And all through the chapter runs the refrain "I am the LORD," as if to say, "*Your* quality of life must reflect *my* character. This is what I require of *you* because this is what reflects *me*. This is what I myself would do."

In all of these ways then—that is, in all the ways of down-to-earth practical social ethics—Israel was to respond to their redemption by reflecting their Redeemer. In doing so they would not only prove their own distinctiveness from the nations but also make visible YHWH's difference from the gods of the nations. And that, as we remind ourselves so often, was their very reason for existence, their mission. If the people of Israel were to be God's priesthood in the midst of the nations, then they had to be different from the nations.

From God's covenant with Abraham we know that the chief agent of God's mission is the people of God.

From Exodus 19 and Leviticus 19, we know that the chief requirement on God's people if they are to fulfill that mission is that they should *be* what they *are*—the holy people of the holy God.

In short, Israel's *identity* (to be a priestly kingdom) declares a *mission,* and Israel's *mission* demands an *ethic* (to be a holy nation).

Missional Ethics and Covenant—Deuteronomy 4

The third great pillar of Israel's faith, their covenant relationship with God as a nation, was set in place in the next phase of their story. The story begins with the *election of Abraham* and the covenant God made with him and his descendants. It then moves to the great narrative of *redemption through the exodus* of the Israelites from Egypt. And it comes to rest, temporarily, at Mount Sinai, where God renews his *covenant* and establishes it with the whole nation. This is done with a view to the next stage of the story, which is the settlement of Israel in the land of Canaan.

We have seen how each of these stages forms part of the ongoing mission of God, which in its long-term perspective is to bring blessing to all the nations of the earth. And we have now seen also, in this chapter, how Israel's ethical response to their election and redemption is woven into that missional identity and role. In the case of the covenant established at Sinai, the ethical response is even more clearly visible. One could hardly miss it. It is embodied in the great collections of laws and guidance for Israel's life in the land, which are embedded in the Sinai narratives of the Torah.

The ethical content of Old Testament law is, of course, a vast edifice that would require another book to elucidate.[18] We must therefore focus our attention in one place, and Deuteronomy as the covenant document *par excellence* seems the most appropriate. The common perception of Deuteronomy, how-

---

[18]Such a book fortunately exists (along with many others in the same field, of course!): Christopher J. H. Wright, *Old Testament Ethics for the People of God* (Leicester, U.K.: Inter-Varsity Press; Downers Grove, Ill.: InterVarsity Press, 2004).

ever, is that it is an exclusively nationalistic document, entirely focused on Israel's relationship with YHWH and uninterested in the wider purposes of God for the nations. In my view this is an unfortunate misconception. We have already observed a number of texts in Deuteronomy and the Deuteronomic History that express the universality of YHWH and of the significance of Israel (see pp. 227-30).

At this point, however, it will be helpful to focus on one chapter—Deuteronomy 4—which makes some remarkable and programmatic affirmations. Furthermore, it is a chapter in which *the nations* make their appearance no less than five times, in very different modes. An overview of the flow of thought in the chapter will be helpful, followed by closer attention to four major thrusts within it.

Deuteronomy 4:1-40: An overview. Like several of the chapters in this part of the book, this section has a chiastic or concentric structure. This means that we find matching points at the outer margins of the text, and then successive matching points at either end, arranged in mirror order around a central thrust. It is not quite so neat as some chapters of Deuteronomy, but the following outline gives an idea of the way these forty verses are carefully built around several key thoughts.

A Live obediently to God's commands so that you may live in the land (vv. 1-2)
   B (Object lesson): following other gods leads to destruction; loyalty to YHWH keeps you safe (vv. 3-4)
      C Is there any people like Israel, the "great nation"? (vv. 5-8)
         D Fire and voice of God (vv. 9-14)
            E Warning and threat against idolatry (vv. 15-28; cf. v. 3)
            E' Promise of mercy for repentance and loyalty (vv. 29-31; cf. v. 4)
         D' Fire and voice of God (vv. 33, 36)
      C' Is there any god like YHWH? "Great nations" will be driven out (vv. 32-38)
   B' YHWH alone is God, so take the lesson to heart (v. 39)
A' Live obediently to God's commands so that you may live long in the land (v. 40)

Working our way through the pattern, then, we see that it begins and ends with exhortations to live obediently to God's laws in the land that he is about to give them, so that they may live there long (vv. 1-2, 40). A prefatory reference to the great apostasy at Baal Peor (vv. 3-4; cf. Num 25) provides a graphic object lesson in the double message of the rest of the chapter: those who reject YHWH as Israel's sole covenant Lord and go after other gods will be destroyed, but those who hold fast to him will be spared. The first point is expanded in verses

15-28, the second in verses 29-31, and the message is repeated just before the end in verse 39.

Verses 5-8 set Israel's obedience to God's law in the land within the context of the nations. The nations will observe and comment on the "greatness" of Israel (a paradox, since they were actually a very small people, as Deut 7:7 more truthfully if less tactfully points out). Reflecting that point, though in a negative way, the nations and the land are again in focus in verse 38, but this time it is the nations who are "greater," but only as a foil to the fact that God would drive them out. Another chiastic element here is that the rhetorical questions in this section (vv. 7-8), which express *the uniqueness of Israel among the nations,* are matched by the rhetorical questions in verses 32-34, which express *the uniqueness of* YHWH *among the gods.*

Verses 9-14 expand the reference to God's law and commandments by reminding Israel of the spectacular events that had accompanied them, and which they must never forget—especially the fire and the voice of God's words (cf. Ex 19). This reference to Sinai is again picked up in verses 33 and 36, with further reminder of the fire and the voice.

The *central section* of the chapter is thus verses 15-31, which falls into two main moods: the *warning* against idolatry with the threat of destruction (vv. 15-28), and the *promise* of restoration if there is repentance and a wholehearted loyalty and obedience to their covenant Lord, YHWH (vv. 29-31).

These two moods are sharply focused on the contrasting double description of YHWH. On the one hand, an idolatrous and disobedient people will confront the Lord God who is "a consuming fire, a jealous God" (v. 24). On the other hand, a repentant and obedient people will run into the arms of the same God, but the one who is also "a merciful God; he will not abandon or destroy you or forget the covenant with your forefathers, which he confirmed to them by oath" (v. 31). Though verses 24 and 31 may seem contradictory when read side by side, the paradox is that both verses express the *consistency* of YHWH. The contradictions lie in his people. God is utterly consistent when he responds to rebels with wrath and to the repentant with mercy.

The whole chapter, then, is a microcosm of Deuteronomy as a whole. It is an urgent call to covenant loyalty through exclusive worship of YHWH alone, based on the unique history of his redeeming and revealing activity through the exodus and at Sinai, and worked out in practical ethical obedience to his laws in the land of promise, with a view to the affect this will have on the nations.

In the midst of this tightly argued articulation of what the covenant between Israel and YHWH was all about, *the nations* feature five times.

- The nations will observe the wisdom and understanding of Israel, providing Israel preserves the presence of God and the practice of justice (vv. 6-8).

- The nations have been assigned the heavenly bodies (for whatever purpose), but Israel is not to engage in any worship of such created things, but to worship only YHWH who delivered them from bondage for that purpose (vv. 19-20).[19]

- The nations will be the location for the scattering of Israel in judgment if Israel abandons YHWH for other gods (v. 27). There is some irony in the language here: In verse 38 God promises to drive the nations out before Israel. But Israel faces the threat, if they turn apostate, of having God drive them out among the nations.

- The nations have never experienced what Israel had recently experienced as the foundation of their unique covenant knowledge of YHWH—namely, his revelation at Sinai and his redemption from Egypt (vv. 32-34).

- The nations will be driven out before Israel in the giving of the land of Canaan, as promised to Abraham (v. 38).

How then, can we combine all this material in relation to our major investigation? In what ways is the covenant between YHWH and Israel, along with the ethical response that is intrinsic to it, related to the mission of God and his action among the nations? Four major points may be made on the basis of Deuteronomy 4.[20]

The visibility of Israel's society (Deut 4:6-8). "Observe [these laws] carefully, for this will show your wisdom and understanding to the nations, who will hear about all these decrees and say, 'Surely this great nation is a wise and understanding people.' What other great nation has their gods near them the way the LORD our God is near us whenever we pray to him? And what other great nation has such righteous decrees and laws as this body of laws I am setting before you today?" (Deut 4:6-8, author's translation).

Obedience to the law was not for Israel's benefit alone. It is a marked feature of the Old Testament that Israel lived on a very public stage. All that happened

---

[19]It is worth noting that Deut 4:19 does not say that God assigned the heavenly bodies to the nations for them to worship. That is a (possibly incorrect) inference from the immediately following words telling Israel not to worship them. The text (which is admittedly difficult) could mean no more than that God created the heavenly bodies for the benefit of the whole human race (according to the account in Gen 1), and if the other nations turn them into objects of worship, that is not something Israel is to imitate.

[20]I have drawn extensively in the following comments on Deut 4 from my own commentary, Christopher J. H Wright, *Deuteronomy,* New International Biblical Commentary (Peabody, Mass.: Hendrickson; Carlisle, U.K.: Paternoster, 1996).

in Israel's history was open to the comment and reaction of the nations at large. Apart from being in any case inevitable, given the fluid international scene of the ancient Near East, this visibility of Israel was part of its theological identity and role as the priesthood of YHWH among the nations. It could be either positive, as here, when the nations are impressed with the wisdom of Israel's law (cf. Deut 28:10), or negative, as when the nations are shocked by the severity of Israel's judgment when they abandon the ways of their God (Deut 28:37; 29:22-28). Either way, faithful or unfaithful, the people of God are an open book to the world, and the world asks questions and draws conclusions.

The nations will notice and take an interest in the phenomenon of Israel as a society, with all the social, economic, legal, political, and religious dimensions of the Torah. And that social system will lead the nations to the conclusion that Israel as a people qualifies as a "great nation," to be applauded as "wise and understanding."[21]

But Moses goes on, with two rhetorical questions, to sharpen the point by emphasizing the foundation of Israel's national greatness as defined. First (v. 7), it is based on the *nearness of Yahweh* to his people. Second (v. 8), it is based on the *righteousness of the Torah.* Israel would have an intimacy with God and a quality of social justice that no other nation could match. These would be the factors that would lie behind the external reputation. As far as the nations could see, the thing that was different about Israel was simply a matter of wisdom and understanding. The inner reality was the presence of God and the justice of God's Torah.

The force of the rhetorical questions is to *invite comparison,* but in the confident expectation that nothing will invalidate the claims being made. The claim for Israel's social uniqueness was being made on a crowded stage, with plenty of other claimants for admirable systems of law. Israel itself knew of the ancient and acclaimed legal traditions of Mesopotamia; as a matter of fact, Israel's own legal traditions intersect with them at many points. Yet this claim for Old Testament law is advanced, quite possibly with deliberate polemical intent, since the law code of Hammurabi, for example, also claimed a divine quality of social righteousness.[22]

---

[21]As my own translation of Deuteronomy 4:6-8 shows (p. 378), the claim of the text is not that there is no other nation greater than Israel, as is implied in the NIV translation ("what other nation is so great as to have . . ."). Rather, the text assumes that Israel is a great nation, but then defines that greatness in surprising terms—not military might or geographical or numerical size, but the nearness of the living God in prayer and the social justice of their constitution and laws.

[22]On the claims of other ancient Near Eastern law codes, see, e.g., Moshe Weinfeld, *Social Justice in Ancient Israel and in the Ancient near East* (Jerusalem: Magnes Press; Minneapolis: Fortress Press, 1995).

Old Testament law explicitly invites, even welcomes, public inspection and comparison. But the expected result of such comparison is that Israel's law will be found superior in wisdom and justice. This is a monumental claim. It grants to the nations and to the readers of this text, including ourselves, the liberty to analyze Old Testament law in comparison with other social systems, ancient and modern, and to evaluate its claim. And indeed, the humaneness and justice of Israel's overall social and legal system have been favorably commented on by many scholars who have done the most meticulous studies of comparative ancient law, and its social relevance can still be profitably mined today.

From our missiological perspective, these verses articulate a motivation for obedience to the law that is easily overlooked but highly significant. The point is that if *Israel* would live as God intended, then *the nations* would notice. But Israel existed in any case for the ultimate purpose of being the vehicle of God's blessing the nations. That was in their "genetic code" from the very loins of Abraham. Here we find that at least one aspect of that blessing of the nations would be by providing such a model of social justice that the nations would observe and ask questions. The missional challenge, therefore, is that the ethical quality of life of the people of God (their obedience to the law, in this context) is a vital factor in the attraction of the nations to the living God—even if only at first out of curiosity.

The motivation for God's people to live by God's law is ultimately to bless the nations. After all, what would the nations actually *see?* The nearness of God is by definition invisible. What, then, would be *visible?* Only the practical evidence of the kind of society that was built on God's righteous laws.[23] There is a vital link between the invisible religious claims of the people of God (that God is near them when they pray) and their very visible practical social ethic. The world will be interested in the first only when it sees the second. Or, conversely, the world will see no reason to pay any attention to our claims about our invisible God, however much we boast of his alleged nearness to us in prayer, if it sees no difference between the lives of those who make such claims and those who don't.

The exclusivity of Israel's worship (Deut 4:9-31). Such a high responsibility—being God's visible model to the nations—needs to be taken seriously.

---

[23]For further reflection on the strongly social ethical aspects of the covenant and their relevance to contemporary issues that are strongly taken up within liberation theology, see Christopher J. Baker, *Covenant and Liberation: Giving New Heart to God's Endangered Family* (New York: Peter Lang, 1991), esp. chap. 13.

Two things could threaten it:

- if the laws of God were simply forgotten (hence the urgent necessity of teaching them [vv. 9-10])

- if God himself were forgotten in the enticement of going after other gods (hence the severe warnings of the central section of the chapter)

Covenant *obedience* (vv. 9-14) and covenant *loyalty* (vv. 15-24), therefore, are here set in the context of covenant *witness* (vv. 6-8). To have any hope of being a witness to the nations of the nearness of God and of the justice of his laws, Israel had to worship YHWH alone and obey his laws. Disobedience to the law would negate the intention of being a just society. Running after other gods would drive YHWH far away, not draw him near in prayer.

So the thrust of this section (vv. 9-31) is well captured in the phrase that is reiterated three times: "Only be careful, and watch yourselves" (vv. 9, 15, 23— the phrase is the same in Hebrew each time, even though translated differently in the NIV). The most fundamental demand of the covenant was exclusive loyalty to YHWH. Correspondingly, the most fundamental way to break the covenant was by worshiping any other god or gods. If this happened, then Israel would lose their primary distinctiveness and indeed be scattered among the very nations from whom they were supposed to be separate and to whom they were supposed to be a model (vv. 25-28).

The negative warnings of this central section of the chapter (vv. 9-31), then, should be seen in the light of and for the sake of the positive missional potential of verses 6-8. That is what is at stake. The exclusivity of Israel's worship of YHWH is integral to the visibility of Israel's society to the nations. The hope of verses 6-8 would never be realized if the people neglect the primary demand of the covenant—to worship and serve the LORD only. Or to put it the other way round, *idolatry is the first and greatest threat to Israel's mission* (and ours).

This point is served even by the strongly repeated emphasis on the fact that YHWH had been heard but not seen at Sinai (vv. 12, 15, 36). Some find here a contrast between the invisible God of Israel and the visible, material, statues of the gods of the nations. But that is not what this text stresses. The contrast in these verses is not between the visible and the invisible but *between the visible and the audible*. Idols do have "form," but do not speak. YHWH has no "form," but he decisively speaks. Idols are visible but dumb. YHWH is invisible but eloquent. YHWH addresses his people unambiguously in words of promise and demand, gift and claim. This introduces a fundamentally moral distinction into the contrast between the aniconic faith of Israel and surrounding visual, iconic polytheism. The issue is not merely one of different gods having different looking idols by which you can tell them apart. What sets YHWH apart is not that *he* looks different from other *gods* but that he calls for a *people* who will look different from other *nations*. *They* are to manifest a visibly different way of life, a different social order and a different dynamic of worship. And in doing so, they will bear witness to the living God, whose form they did not and cannot see, but whose word they have unmistakably heard.

Two further things may be said on verses 16-20.

On the one hand, the list of possible "shapes" that idols might take (the phrase is identical to the words of the second commandment [cf. Deut 5:8]) is given in an order that precisely reverses the order of the creation narrative: human beings, land animals, birds, fish, the heavenly bodies. The point, which this literary tactic is probably deliberately designed to suggest, is that idolatry perverts and turns upside down the whole created order. When the living Creator God is removed from his rightful place of sole and exclusive worship, everything else in creation becomes chaotic.

On the other hand, the text does recognize the double enticement that certain objects in creation would have for Israel: Their awesome majesty seemed to call for worship, and that is exactly what the other nations succumb to. So for Israel to worship them would be once again to fail to preserve their distinctiveness from the rest of the nations and also to subvert the purpose for which God had redeemed them. The emphasis at the beginning and end of verse 20 is on that distinctiveness, a distinctiveness that idolatry would radically compromise.

The mission of God through Israel is nothing less than the redemption of the nations and the restoration of creation. That mission could not be served if Israel indulged in practices that were nothing more than imitation of the nations and the inversion of creation

The uniqueness of Israel's experience (Deut 4:32-35). "Ask now concerning the former days that were before your time, from the day God created humankind on the earth; ask from one end of the heavens to the other. Has there ever happened anything like this great thing, or has anything like it ever been heard? Has any people heard the voice of God speaking from the midst of the fire, as you heard it, and lived? Or did God set out to take for himself any nation from out of the midst of another nation by testings, by signs, by wonders, by war, by a mighty hand and an outstretched arm, by marvelous great deeds, like all that YHWH your God did for you in Egypt before your eyes? You were made to see these things in order to know that YHWH, he is the God; there is no other beside him (Deut 4:32-35, author's translation).[24]

These verses are the climax not just of Deuteronomy 4 but of the whole first discourse of Moses in the book. They are fittingly exalted in content and style. This whole section mirrors verses 5-8 but elevates the theme tremendously. The stylistic device of rhetorical questions that expressed the incomparability of *Israel* in verses 6-8 is employed again here to affirm the incomparability of YHWH, and for a similarly combined ethical and missiological purpose.

The supreme point of this whole speech, then, is a monotheistic acclamation (vv. 35, 39) wreathed in cosmic language, demonstrated in historical experience and demanding ethical response.

A research project of truly cosmic scale is imagined in verse 32, encompassing the whole of human history hitherto and the whole of universal space. Such is Moses' confidence that the questions he is about to pose will find no answer. Moses refers to both the Sinai theophany and the exodus deliverance, but in his opening question they are seen together as a single "great thing." And his claim is that nothing like them has ever happened.[25] What God did in the events of the exodus and Sinai was unprecedented (God had never done such a thing at

---

[24]In vv. 33-34 in the NIV ("The voice of God. . . . Has any god ever tried . . .") mixes up two possible exegetical ways of reading these verses, when it would probably be better to opt for either one or the other in both verses. In Hebrew, *'ĕlōhîm*, without a definite article, can mean God (i.e., assumed to be YHWH) or a god or gods. Contexts usually leave no doubt as to which is intended in each case. If we take the second of the NIV's options (v. 34) first, then Moses' questions are primarily contrasting YHWH with other gods: "Has any people heard the voice of a god [i.e., their own god] speaking out of fire [i.e., in the same way that YHWH spoke to you]? Has any other god ever tried to take a people . . . ?" Taken thus, the emphasis is clearly on the uniqueness of YHWH himself. No other alleged god has done either of these things. But this would leave open the possible question whether or not YHWH himself had done such things for other peoples. No other god had, but YHWH could have.

My view, however, (reflected in my translation) assumes the stronger meaning of *'ĕlōhîm* in both questions. Not only, with the NIV, "Has any other people heard the voice of God [Yahweh]?" (expected answer, no, because God has spoken to no other people in such a way); but also "Has God [i.e., YHWH] ever tried to take for himself one nation out of another? (expected answer, no, because no exodus has been like Israel's as described here). Taken thus, the emphasis is more clearly on the uniqueness of Israel's experience of the work of God, but the first affirmation is still preserved. Only YHWH had made himself known in these ways and only Israel had experienced them. This seems to fit better with the thrust of vv. 35-40. It was precisely because Israel had experienced what no other nation had that they were entrusted with the true knowledge of the one living God and were called to live in the light of such dynamic monotheism.

[25]Once again, the NIV slightly distorts the simplicity of the Hebrew with its phraseology "anything so great as this?" The sentence literally reads, "Has there happened [anything] like this great deed/thing/event *[dābar]* or has there been heard [anything] like it?" The point is not quite that nothing greater had happened but that nothing like it had happened. The emphasis is on the uniqueness of events that were manifestly "a great thing."

any other time) and unparalleled (God had never done such a thing anywhere else for any other nations).

There was a uniqueness about Israel's experience that is being powerfully affirmed here. YHWH spoke to them in a way no other people had experienced (cf. Ps 147:19-20), and YHWH redeemed them in a way that no other people had known (cf. Amos 3:1-2). The people of Israel, then, have had a unique experience of both *revelation* and *redemption,* through which they have come to know the unique God, YHWH.

So what?

Verse 35 (repeated and amplified at verse 39) emphatically declares the purpose of this whole "great thing." All that Israel had so uniquely experienced was so that they would learn something utterly vital—the *identity* of the living God. YHWH, and YHWH alone, is God and there is no other anywhere else in the universe.[26] It is important to take verses 32-34 as seriously as this, and not to dismiss them as mere hyperbole simply because of their rhetorical form, especially in view of what hangs on them in verse 35, namely, the unequivocal affirmation of the uniqueness of YHWH as God. This is the theological freight that the rhetorical rolling stock is carrying. The people of Israel can be confident in their knowledge of God because of the unique experience of God's revealing and redeeming power that was entrusted to them. *You* (the pronoun is emphatic) were shown these things so that *you* might know. In a world of nations that do not know YHWH as God, Israel is now the one nation that has been entrusted with that essential knowledge. They know God as no other nation did because they have experienced God as no other nation had. The question now becomes, What will they do with that knowledge, and how will they respond to the privilege and responsibility of having it?

Before answering that, we might pause for an aside in relation to a major contemporary missiological issue. The emphasis on the uniqueness of Israel and of YHWH speaks to the contemporary question of *the uniqueness of Christ in the context of religious pluralism.*

Far too often, in this latter debate, the uniqueness of Christ is argued over without reference to Jesus' own self-conscious deep roots in the Hebrew Scriptures. Jesus is presented as if he were the founder of a new religion, which assuredly was not his purpose. Jesus came, by his own claims and in the united New Testament witness to him, not to found a new religion but to complete the saving work of YHWH, God of Israel, for the sake of Israel and the world—a work that God had been moving purposively forward for centuries.

---

[26]See p. 77 for broader discussion of the meaning of Old Testament monotheism.

Theologically as well as historically, a line runs from exodus and Sinai in our text to the incarnation and Easter events. What YHWH (and no other god) had redemptively initiated in the history of Israel (and no other people), he brought to completion for the whole world in Jesus of Nazareth (and no other person). The uniqueness of Jesus as the Messiah of Israel, and thereby as Savior of the world, is grounded in the uniqueness of Israel itself and of YHWH as God, for according to the New Testament Jesus embodied the one and incarnated the other. And the central struggle of early Christianity, to which the New Testament bears witness, was to recognize and express this final truth within the parameters of an undiluted commitment to the dynamic monotheism of Israel's own faith as affirmed here.

The missiological urgency of the interfaith debate must be grounded in a fully biblical understanding of the uniqueness of God's saving work in history, which means starting with the affirmation of this and similar Old Testament texts about the one and only living God, and not with a Jesus severed from his scriptural and historical roots. For this same reason, Christians are not at liberty to abandon the Hebrew Scriptures of the Old Testament or to regard the Scriptures of other religions or cultures as equivalent and adequate preparations for Christ. For the thrust of this text is clear: it is *these* events (and no others) that witness to *this* God (and no other). And the thrust of our New Testament is equally clear: It is *this* God (and no other) who became flesh to reconcile the world to himself in *this* man, Jesus of Nazareth (and no other).

The missional responsibility of Israel's obedience. Returning to our text, I must conclude by noting that the final thrust of its rhetoric in verse 40 is once more thoroughly ethical. For unless Israel would go on living in the future in accordance with God's law, what value would there be from their incredible historical and religious experience in the past? The past alone would not guarantee their own continued survival in the land, unaccompanied by responsive obedience. And furthermore, how would the nations come to know of the uniqueness of YHWH as the living God and of his saving action in history unless they are drawn by the ethical distinctiveness of God's people (cf. vv. 6-8)? If God's people abandon their ethical distinctiveness by forgetfulness, idolatry or disobedience, then not only do they jeopardize their own well-being (v. 40), they also frustrate the broader purposes of the God who brought them into existence by his electing love and brought them out of bondage by his redeeming power.

Deuteronomy 4 thus returns at the end (v. 40) to the place where it began (vv. 1-2)—urging Israel to obedience. But now we are able to see two things in much greater depth:

1. the motivation for Israel's obedience (the great things YHWH had done in the past)

2. the goal of Israel's obedience (Israel's well-being in the land in the future as a nation of godliness and social justice, and thereby as a witness to the nations)

The covenantal and missional logic that surges through the chapter runs in a grand loop that we can now summarize as follows:

- Israel is summoned to live in wholehearted obedience to God's covenant law when they take possession of the land (vv. 1-2).

- Failure to do so will lead to the same fate as befell those who were seduced into idolatry and immorality by the Moabites at Beth Peor (vv. 3-4).

- Covenant loyalty and obedience will constitute a witness to the nations whose interest and questions will revolve around the God they worship and the just laws they live by (vv. 5-8).

- This witness, however, would be utterly nullified by Israel going after other gods, and so they must be strenuously warned against that through reminders of their spectacular past and warnings of a horrific future if they ignore the word (vv. 9-31).

- Above all, let them remember that alone among all the nations they have had unique experience of the revelation and redemption of God, on the basis of which they have come to know YHWH as God in all his own transcendent uniqueness (vv. 32-38).

- Let them then demonstrate their acknowledgement of all these things in faithful obedience (vv. 39-40).

- Therein lies their future security as a people, and thereby also hangs their mission as the people chosen by God for the sake of his mission (v. 40).

A very strong echo of the thought of this passage is found in the record of Solomon's prayer of dedication of the temple in 1 Kings 8. The missional hope expressed in the prayer that God would respond even to the prayers of the foreigner, in order that "all the peoples of the earth may know your name and fear you" (1 Kings 8:43), is turned into a missional challenge to the people that they must be as committed to God's law as God is committed to such a worldwide goal. The Deuteronomic historian clearly endorses the ethical and missional logic of his foundational text.

> May [the LORD] uphold the cause of his servant and the cause of his people Israel
> according to each day's need, so that all the peoples of the earth may know that

the LORD is God and that there is no other. But your hearts must be fully committed to the LORD our God, to live by his decrees and obey his commands, as at this time. (1 Kings 8:60-61)

Missional Ethics and the Church

"You," said Peter, writing to scattered groups of Christian believers, almost certainly mixed communities of Jew and Gentiles, "are a chosen people, a royal priesthood, a holy nation, a people belonging to God" (1 Pet 2:9). At one stroke Peter connects his Christian readers with the whole heritage of Old Testament Israel. Indeed, he identifies them as the same people, continuous with those who heard the words he quotes at the foot of Mount Sinai (Ex 19:4-6), heirs of the same purpose of God through the Messiah Jesus. In doing so, Peter is consistent with the rest of the New Testament witness and claim: Those who are in Christ are in Abraham, called for the same purpose, redeemed by the same God, committed to the same response of ethical obedience.

A full-scale presentation of New Testament ethics is out of the question here, of course. My purpose is much more limited. It is to show, on the one hand, that as in the Old Testament, the ethical demand on those who are God's people is a matter of appropriate response to their election, redemption and covenant. That is, Christians also are those who, according to the New Testament, have been called by God, redeemed by God and have been brought into a reciprocal relationship with God. In all these respects, of course, Christian ethics must be seen (again as in the Old Testament) as a response to God's grace, received and anticipated. And on the other hand, my purpose is to draw attention to the way at least some significant texts in the New Testament connect this ethical responsibility to God's wider mission. In other words, there seems to me to be as much value in a missiological hermeneutic in relation to the ethics of the New Testament as of the Old.

Election and ethics. The familiar pattern of several of Paul's letters is to put his teaching about God's calling of his people in the opening sections, followed by the ethical response that should therefore be forthcoming. Even in (probably) his earliest letter, 1 Thessalonians, this theological order is apparent without being clearly structured. "We know, brothers loved by God, that he has chosen you," he says in 1 Thessalonians 1:4, and sees evidence of this in the quality of their life as it has been reported to him. He goes on, in 1 Thessalonians 4, to urge them to continue "to live in order to please God" (v. 1), as a matter of "God's will" (v. 3) and of their calling to holiness (v. 7).

Such transformed living as a response to our election, however, is not merely pleasing to God, it is also a matter of observation by outsiders. Like Israel among the nations, the Thessalonian believers must remember their own visibility to the wider community.

> Make it your ambition to lead a quiet life, to mind your own business and to work with your hands, just as we told you, so that your daily life may win the respect of outsiders and so that you will not be dependent on anybody. (1 Thess 4:11-12)

In Colossians and Ephesians the structure and logic are clearer. God's election and calling of his people is placed right up front and expanded in detail, though its ethical purpose is made clear very quickly also.

> He chose us in him before the creation of the world to be holy and blameless in his sight. (Eph 1:4)

> We have not stopped praying for you and asking God to fill you with the knowledge of his will through all spiritual wisdom and understanding. And we pray this in order that you may live a life worthy of the Lord and please him in every way: bearing fruit in every good work. (Col 1:9-10)

> I urge you to live a life worthy of the calling you have received. (Eph 4:1)

Both epistles, however, place all this within the wider context of God's overall purpose for the whole creation, which is to bring it together in reconciled harmony with God through the cross of Christ (Eph 1:10; Col 1:19-20). The ethical behavior of believers is thus seen as an integral part of that universal mission of God for the healing of creation. It is also seen as that which gives authenticity to the evangelistic preaching of the apostles—another way in which ethics is linked to mission (Eph 6:19-20; Col 4:2-6).

Redemption and ethics. *Paul: Adorn the gospel.* Paul's little letter to Titus is remarkable in that within its forty-six verses it speaks of "what is good" eight times—either loving what is good, teaching what is good, or (most often) doing what is good. The ethical flavor (in contrast to the alleged moral corruption of Crete) is very strong. But it is set in the equally strong context of the language of redemption and salvation. For the phrase "God our Savior" or "Jesus our Savior" occurs with almost equal frequency.

The climax of this combination of God's redemption with human ethical response comes in Paul's instructions to slaves. And notably the missional motivation is that by their behavior Christian slaves can commend the message of God's salvation (Tit 2:9-14). Doubtless what Paul says here to slaves applies in principle to all members of the church. We either adorn the gospel or we are a disgrace to it. Our ethics (or lack of ethics) support (or undermine) our mission.

Peter: Visibly good lives. The closest New Testament text to the one we studied in detail above in relation to ethics in response to redemption, namely, Exodus 19:3-6, is of course 1 Peter 2:9-12. Peter applies to Christian believers terms drawn from this text in Exodus as well as others from Isaiah 43:20-21 and Hosea 2:23. In fact, he combines all three of our key words *(election, redemption* and *covenant)* by speaking of Christians as "chosen" (cf. 1 Pet 1:1-2), as "called . . . out of darkness" (an exodus allusion, but cf. also 1 Pet 1:18-19), and as "a people of God." But having alluded to the priestly identity and holy calling of his readers, Peter goes on to draw out exactly the same ethical and missional implications that we observed in relation to those terms in their Old Testament context. "Live such good lives among the nations that, though they accuse you of doing wrong, they may see your good deeds and glorify God on the day he visits us" (1 Pet 2:12, author's translation).[27]

The flow of logic from verses 9-10 through verses 11-12 (which is sadly sometimes broken up by paragraph divisions), thus runs as follows:

- If this is what you are (your *identity,* through election, redemption and covenant)

- then this is how you must live (your *ethics*)

- and this is what will result among the nations (your *mission*)

The message is plain. Christians are to be as visible to the nations by the quality of their moral lives as Israel had been intended to be (but failed). And the purpose of that ethical visibility is ultimately to bring the nations to glorify God.[28] The same dynamic of ethics and mission is as clear here as in Deuteronomy 4:5-8.

In the same passage Peter connects this nonverbal moral witness before the nations to the more explicitly verbal proclamation of the "praises" or "excellencies" *(aretas)* of God to which Christians are called (v. 9). There is probably an

---

[27]Unfortunately in the place of "nations," many English translations say "pagans" or "heathen," where Peter uses "the nations" *(en tois ethnesin)*—the same Greek word that regularly translates the Hebrew *hāggôyim*—"the Gentile nations." This constitutes a remarkable transformation in the binary opposites: Israel and Gentiles. The difference is no longer being defined as ethnic Jew and ethnic non-Jews. Rather it is being defined in relation to faith in Christ. Just as by claiming that believers in Jesus (Jew and Gentile) are now the inheritors of the identity of Israel, so Peter has transformed the meaning of *Gentile* from "non-Jews" to "non-Christians."

[28]When will the nations "glorify God"? Taken strictly, it might appear that it will only be at the moment of final judgment "on the day of visitation"—and thus without hope of salvation. However, the phrase "glorifying God" normally refers to the worship of those who are God's people (cf. 1 Pet 4:16), "and the use of the term here evidently signals repentance and religious conversion at or before the last day (cf. Rev. 11:13; 14:7; 16:9)." Mark Boyley, "1 Peter—A Mission Document?" *Reformed Theological Review* 63 (2004): 84.

echo in this phrase of Isaiah 42:12, where the nations that have been affected by the mission of the Servant of YHWH are invited to do exactly this.

> Let them give glory to the LORD
>   and proclaim his praise [LXX *aretas*] in the islands.

Thus the nations are now being summoned to join in what was the primary purpose of Israel (Is 43:21). Peter sees the scattered communities of believers, like the exiles of Israel of old, combining the worship and witness of Israel and the nations in their proclamation of God's praiseworthy excellencies.

So the mission of the church, according to Peter, includes both verbal proclamation and ethical living, and the impact of his tight argument is that *both* are utterly essential. Indeed, in one specific case he argues that positively good living can be evangelistically effective even when verbal witness is hindered or inadvisable. Wives of nonbelieving husbands could witness without words through the quality of their lives, so that "if any of them do not believe the word, they may be won over without words by the behavior of their wives, when they see the purity and reverence of your lives" (1 Pet 3:2). Peter is *not,* of course, *prohibiting* wives from using words when the opportunity arose, any more than he is saying that husbands could be saved without eventually coming to believe the Word. But he is reinforcing the message of 1 Peter 2:11-12—that there is great missional and evangelistic power in lives shaped by the standards of biblical holiness and goodness.

> Holy living or good behavior which promotes Christian belief is a particularly strong thrust in this epistle. Rather than defensively withdrawing, Christians are to participate in the created institutions of their society, and precisely there to offer a fearless testimony of good deeds. They do this in imitation of their Lord's response to suffering and with a view to their oppressors being silenced, or perhaps even "won over" to belief in Christ.[29]

Covenant and ethics. *First Peter.* It would seem almost certain that Peter's phraseology in 1 Peter 2:12 is a conscious echo of the teaching he once heard from the lips of Jesus. "You," Jesus had said to his rough band of doubtless astonished disciples, "*are the light of the world.* . . . Let your light shine before men, that they may see your good deeds and praise your Father who is in heaven" (Mt 5:14, 16).

The imagery chosen by Jesus undoubtedly echoes the task given by YHWH to Israel that they were to be "a light to the nations." And in the context of the Sermon on the Mount, Jesus' purpose is to portray the quality of life, character

---

[29]Boyley, "1 Peter," p. 86.

and behavior of those who constitute the new covenant people of God being formed around himself as the messianic Servant King. Just as Israel should have let its light shine as an attraction to the nations (whether the ethical light of Is 58:6-10 or the light of God's presence in their midst [Is 60:1-3]), so the disciples of Jesus must let the light of good works shine in such a way that people will come to glorify the living God. The missional purpose of Jesus' ethical teaching is clear and Peter obviously took it to heart.

Matthew. The famous ending of Matthew's Gospel, the Great Commission (Mt 28:18-20) is equally covenantal in flavor, since it echoes Deuteronomy so strongly (see pp. 354-55). Jesus assumes the position of the Lord God himself, whose authority in heaven and on earth has now been given to him. On that foundation, he commissions his own disciples to go out and replicate themselves by creating communities of obedience among the nations. They are to teach, and the nations are to learn, what it means to "observe all that I have commanded you," a piece of pure Deuteronomy. Thus mission is replicated discipleship, learned through ethical obedience and passed on through teaching.[30]

John. Finally, we should note how John's Gospel sets the obedience of the disciples to the commands of Jesus in the context of the author's explicit missional desire that his readers, whoever they may be, may come to saving faith in Christ (Jn 20:30-31). Again, echoing the covenantal language of Deuteronomy, love is constituted by obedience to the commands of Christ, just as God's Old Testament people were both to love YHWH and to prove it in obeying his commands. The missional implications and motivation of this connection is succinctly captured by Jesus in his further word: "By this all men will know that you are my disciples, if you love one another" (Jn 13:35). The same missional dynamic is operating in Jesus' great prayer for his disciples and their witness in the world in John 17.

The language of covenant is the language of a people in reciprocal relationship with God, initiated by God's grace and responded to in human obedience. We have seen in the Old Testament that this is connected to Israel's identity and mission within the universal mission of God for all nations. Here in the New Testament, the missional nature of the new covenant people of God is seen in these three texts from Peter, Matthew and John. God's new people in Christ are also a people for the sake of the world, and this is to be reflected in their lives.

---

[30]For further discussion of the covenant motif in Matthew, see, Robert L. Brawley, "Reverberations of Abrahamic Covenant Traditions in the Ethics of Matthew," in *Realia Dei,* ed. Prescott H. Williams and Theodore Hiebert (Atlanta: Scholars Press, 1999), pp. 26-46.

In short, as God's covenant people, Christians are meant to be

- a people who are light to the world by their good lives (1 Pet)
- a people who are learning obedience and teaching it to the nations (Mt)
- a people who love one another in order to show who they belong to (Jn)

It would be hard to find a more concise articulation of the integration of Christian ethics and Christian mission.

PART IV   THE ARENA OF MISSION

W e move round finally to the last corner of the triangle that I used in the introduction (p. 28) to describe the structure of the book. We have thought of "The God of Mission" (biblical monotheism and mission) in part two. Then we spent the six chapters of part three in the company of "The People of Mission" (Israel as the people whom God chose, redeemed and called into covenant relationship and ethical distinctiveness for the purpose of his mission to the nations, and the extension of that identity and role to all those in Christ). But the Lord God of Israel is also the God of all the earth and all nations, so now we need to widen our horizons again and consider that grand arena within which the Bible's grand narrative takes place. For the mission of God is as universal as the love of God, and as Psalm 145:13 reminds us:

The LORD is faithful to all his promises
    and loving toward all he has made.

It is helpful to introduce our reflection with the apostle Paul, that great missional interpreter of the Old Testament.

Compare Paul's sermon in the Jewish synagogue in Pisidian Antioch in Acts 13:16-41 with his speech before the Areopagus in Athens in Acts 17:22-31. Both addresses have a common ultimate purpose—to introduce his listeners to Jesus. But the conceptual frameworks are very different. In the first, before a Jewish audience, Paul speaks of "the *God* of the people of *Israel*" and describes how God had overthrown the Canaanites and "gave their *land* to his people as their inheritance" (Acts 13:17, 19, emphasis added). In the second, before a Gentile audience, Paul speaks of "the *God* who made the *world* and everything in it," and describes how this God "made *every nation of men,* that they should inhabit the whole earth" (Acts 17:24, 26, emphasis added).

If you will pardon yet more geometry, we could portray these two frameworks in the form of two interconnected triangles. On the one hand there is the triangle of God, Israel and their land (see fig. II.1).

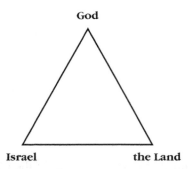

Figure II.1. Conceptual framework of Paul's sermon in Antioch

This is the conceptual framework of Paul's sermon in Antioch, and of course it represents the self-understanding of Old Testament Israel. Their God, YHWH, had chosen and called Israel as a people in covenant relationship with himself, and had redeemed them out of slavery in the land of Egypt, and given them the land of Canaan in which they were to live in covenant obedience to him and thereby under his blessing. This is the framework that underlies the chapters of part three of this book. Insofar as Israel in the Old Testament understood itself as a people with an identity and mission, this was the context of such thinking. The uniqueness of their election, redemption, covenant and ethic was grounded in this triangle of interconnected relationships. The mission of Israel was to live as God's people in God's land for God's glory. And the God in question was YHWH.

But, as I have been stressing throughout, this triangle of relationships did not exist for its own sake. It was part of a wider set of relationships that frame the mission of God for all nations and the whole earth. It is this outer triangle (God, humanity and the earth; see fig. II.2), that Paul has in mind when he speaks to the Gentile audience in Athens—a group of people to whom the inner triangle of God's dealings with Israel in their land would not have made sense as yet. So Paul presents to them what is in effect a scriptural (Old Testament) doctrine of creation, but without directly quoting Old Testament texts.[1]

That outer triangle, however, although it is still the basic platform of all God's

---

[1]I have developed this diagram as a framework for understanding the ethical worldview of Old Testament Israel in Christopher J. H. Wright, *Old Testament Ethics for the People of God* (Leicester, U.K.: Inter-Varsity Press; Downers Grove, Ill.: InterVarsity Press, 2004).

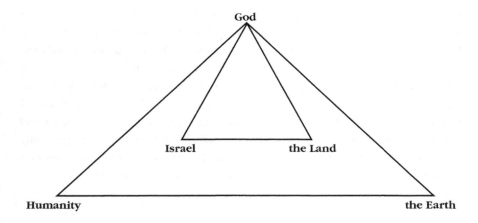

Figure II.2. Conceptual framework of Paul's sermon in Athens

dealings with humanity in history, has been twisted and fractured as a result of human rebellion and sin. All three primary relationships have been affected: human beings no longer love and obey God as they ought, and they live under his wrath; humanity is at odds with the earth; and the earth is subject to God's curse and to the frustration of not being able to glorify God as it ought until humanity is redeemed. Such are the grim realities of our fallen human condition that Paul expounds in Romans. We live as fallen humanity in a cursed earth.

But the outer triangle is also the platform or arena of God's mission. All that God did in, for and through *Israel* (the inner triangle) had as its ultimate goal the blessing of all nations of *humanity* and the final redemption of all *creation* (the outer triangle).

If we were to add into our framework the New Testament fulfillment of the Old Testament vision, we would see another triangle, including the new community of God's people (believing Jews and Gentiles in Christ) and the new creation (the new heavens and new earth in which God will dwell forever with his redeemed humanity).

So we need to pay attention to this wider triangle—the creational platform on which the mission of God traces its path through history. That is the focus of our reflection in part four.

We will look first at *the earth* as the sphere and indeed the object of God's mission activity, and therefore legitimately also the object of the mission to which we are called (chap. 12). Second (in chap. 13), we will look at *humanity* to see how some of the great affirmations of biblical faith about what it means to be human affect our understanding of mission. This must include the dignity of being made in God's image as well as the depravity of our sinful rebellion and the invasion of evil. In that chapter we will also consider that part of the Old Testament Scriptures most closely associated with a creational worldview and an international perspective (but sadly often neglected in mission theology)—the Wisdom Literature—and reflect on its importance in the task of relating mission to different cultural contexts. Finally, we will turn to the world of nations and scan (in chap. 14) the breathtaking eschatological vision that Israel nurtured in relation to God's plan for the nations of humanity that, probably more than any other single theme in the Old Testament, informed and inspired the missionary expansion of the New Testament church (chap. 15).

12

Mission and God's Earth

To the LORD your God belong the heavens, even the highest heavens, the earth and everything in it. (Deut 10:14)

This bold claim that YHWH, the God of Israel, owns the whole universe is echoed in the familiar assertion of Psalm 24:1: "To YHWH belongs the earth and its fullness" (author's translation), and in the less familiar claim that God himself makes to Job in the context of the grand recital of all his works of creation: "Everything under heaven belongs to me" (Job 41:11).[1]

The Earth Is the Lord's

The earth, then, belongs to God because God made it. At the very least this reminds us that if the earth is God's, it is not ours. We do not own this planet, even if our behavior tends to boast that think we do. No, God is the earth's landlord and we are God's tenants. God has given the earth into our resident *possession* (Ps 115:16), but we do not hold the title deed of ultimate ownership. So, as in any landlord-tenant relationship, God holds us accountable to himself for how we treat his property. Several dimensions of this strong creation affirmation of the divine ownership of the earth may be mentioned as having significant ethical and missional implications.

The goodness of creation. That the creation is good is one of the most em-

---

[1]Parts of this section of the chapter are abbreviated from the much fuller account of Old Testament ecological ethics in Christopher J. H. Wright, *Old Testament Ethics for the People of God* (Leicester, U.K.: Inter-Varsity Press; Downers Grove, Ill.: InterVarsity Press, 2004), chap. 4.

phatic points of Genesis 1—2, in view of its repetition.[2] Six times in the narrative God declares his work to be "good." Like a master chef bringing a multicourse banquet before admiring guests, God kisses his fingers with each new delicacy that he brings from his creative workshop, until, after the *piece de resistance,* in a seventh and final verdict on the whole achievement, God declares it all "very good." The whole wonderful meal has been a triumph of the chef's skill and art.[3]

Two things (among many) may be noted here as implications of this resoundingly simple affirmation.

A good creation can only be the work of a good God. This sets the Hebrew account of creation in contrast to other ancient Near Eastern accounts where powers and gods of the natural world are portrayed in various degrees of malevolence, and where some aspects of the natural order are explained as the outcome of that malevolence. In the Old Testament the natural order is fundamentally and in origin good, as the work of the single good God, YHWH. Part of the meaning of the goodness of creation in the Bible is that it testifies to the God who made it, reflecting something of his good character (e.g., Ps 19; 29; 50:6; 65; 104; 148; Job 12:7-9; Acts 14:17; 17:27; Rom 1:20). That being the case, we might suggest an analogy to the text "He who oppresses the poor shows contempt for their Maker" (Prov 14:31; cf. Prov 17:5—because the poor person is also a human being made in the image of his or her Creator) along the lines of "He who destroys or degrades the earth spoils its reflection of its Maker" (because the earth is part of the creation that bears the mark of God's own goodness). Our treatment of the earth reflects our attitude to its Maker and the seriousness (or otherwise) with which we take what he has said about it.

Creation is intrinsically good. The goodness of creation is of the essence of creation itself. It is not contingent on our human presence within it and our ability to observe it. In the creation narratives, the affirmation "It is good" was not made by Adam and Eve but by God himself. So the goodness of creation (which includes its beauty) is theologically and chronologically prior to human observation. It is something that *God* saw and affirmed before humanity was around to see it. So the goodness of creation is not merely a human reflexive response to a pleasant view on a sunny day. Nor is it an instrumental goodness in the

---

[2]Ron Elsdon makes the theme of the goodness of creation the thread running through his survey of biblical material in both Testaments on this issue in his book *Green House Theology: Biblical Perspectives on Caring for Creation* (Tunbridge Wells, U.K.: Monarch, 1992).

[3]I owe the culinary metaphor to Huw Spanner, "Tyrants, Stewards—or Just Kings?" in *Animals on the Agenda: Questions About Animals for Theology and Ethics,* ed. Andrew Linzey and Dorothy Yamamoto (London: SCM Press, 1998), p. 218.

sense that the rest of creation is good simply because it exists for our benefit. Rather, this affirmation of the goodness of creation is the seal of *divine* approval on the whole universe. The declaration "it is good" is made at every phase of creation—from the initial creation of light (Gen 1:4) to the emergence of continents from the oceans (Gen 1:10), the growth of vegetation (Gen 1:13), the function of sun and moon to mark the days and season (Gen 1:18), the emergence of fish and birds (Gen 1:21), and of land animals (Gen 1:25). All of these created orders were present in all their divinely affirmed goodness before humanity arrived on the scene.

So the earth has *intrinsic* value—that is to say, it is valued by God, who is the source of all value. God values the earth because he made it and owns it. It is not enough merely to say that the earth is *valuable to us.* On the contrary, our own value as human beings begins from the fact that *we ourselves are part* of the whole creation that God already values and declares to be good. We will have more to say about human life in a moment, but the starting point is that we take our value from the creation of which we are part, not vice versa. The earth does not derive its value from us but from its Creator. Accordingly, we need to be careful to locate an ecological dimension of mission not primarily in the need-supplying value of the earth to us, but in the glory-giving value of the earth to God.

The Bible is careful to avoid the arrogant human assumption that earth exists solely for our use and enjoyment. On the contrary, Psalm 104 celebrates not only what the earth provides for humanity but all that God has provided within it for all other creatures who also owe their existence, survival and enjoyment of life to God's bountiful Spirit. Walter Harrelson, in a beautiful meditation on this psalm, notes how the poet's celebration goes way beyond the earth's provision for human needs (in vs. 14-15).

> God planted the cedars and other trees and waters them fully. Birds build nests in them. The stork is singled out in particular: God made fir trees for the storks to nest in, and he made storks to nest in the fir trees. He made high, inaccessible mountains for the wild goats to run and jump upon, and he made wild goats to do the jumping and cavorting. He created the vast expanse of rock-covered earth in eastern Jordan for rock badgers to live and play in, and he created rock badgers for the rocks. Storks and goats and badgers do not serve mankind. They do what is appropriate to them, and God provided a place that is itself fulfilling its function when it ministers to the needs of its special creatures. I know of no more direct word in the Bible about the independent significance of things and creatures on which man does not depend for life. The creative and powerful anthropocentrism of biblical religion is here beautifully qualified: God has interest in badgers and

wild goats and storks for their own sakes. He has interest in trees and mountains and rock-cairns that simply serve non-human purposes.

So, adds Harrison, the psalm celebrates the value of human work within creation, but also affirms the value of all that other creatures do, by God's appointment. On verses 21-26 he observes:

> Man's work is significant, but so is lion's work. Ships doing commerce on the high seas are doing significant work, but so also is Leviathan, trailing behind the ships, blowing and cavorting.[4]

The sanctity (but not divinity) of creation. The Bible makes a clear distinction between God the Creator and all things created (see our discussion of this on pp. 142-44). Nothing in creation is in itself divine. This rules out *nature polytheism,* which was prevalent in the cultural and religious environment of Israel. The different forces of nature were regarded as divine beings (or under the control of distinct divine beings), and the function of many religious rituals was to placate or persuade these nature gods or goddesses into agriculturally beneficent action.

In the faith of Israel, however, the great realities of the natural world, whether forces, phenomena or objects, had no inherent *divine* existence. Such power as they had, which was undoubtedly great, was entirely the work of YHWH and under his command. Thus, on the one hand, the fertility cults of Canaan were rejected because Israel was taught that YHWH himself provided the abundance of nature for them (e.g., Hos 2:8-12). On the other hand, the immensely powerful and influential astral deities of Babylon were unmasked as nothing more than created objects under YHWH's authority (Is 40:26). In both cases, fertility and astrology, Israel's distinctive belief about creation brought them into severe cultural and political conflict with surrounding worldviews.

The Hebrew Bible, therefore, while it certainly teaches respect and care for the nonhuman creation, resists and reverses the human tendency to divinize or personalize the natural order, or to imbue it with any power independent of its personal Creator.

It is important to distinguish between *personalizing* and *personifying* nature. The Old Testament frequently personifies nature as a rhetorical device, a figure of speech, for greater effect. Personification is a literary device in which nature is spoken of *as if it were a person.* For example, the heavens and earth are summoned to bear witness to God's address to his people (e.g., Deut 30:19; 32:1; Is

---

[4]Walter Harrelson, "On God's Care for the Earth: Psalm 104," *Currents in Theology and Mission* 2 (1975): 20-21.

1:2; Ps 50:1-6), they declare his glory (Ps 19), they rejoice at his judgment (Ps 96:11-13; 98:7-9). Most vividly, the land itself "vomited out" the previous inhabitants for their wickedness and did the same to the Israelites when they followed suit (Lev 18:25-28). These are all vivid figures of speech.

But the point of this literary and rhetorical personification of nature is either to underline the personal character of the God who created it and who is active in and through it, or to express the personal and moral nature of human beings' relation to God. Such literary usage is not ascribing real personhood or personal capacities to nature or natural forces in themselves. In fact, to personalize nature in that way (that is, to attribute actual personal status to nature itself) results in both depersonalizing God and demoralizing the relationship between humanity and God. To accord to creation the personal status and honor that is due only to God (or derivatively to humans who bear God's image) is a form of idolatry as ancient as the Fall itself (cf. Rom 1:21-25), though now given new characteristically twentieth-first-century dress in the New Age movements.

This countercultural thrust in the Old Testament has strong missional implications, for the gospel today still confronts (as it did in the New Testament) religious traditions that divinize nature, whether in some forms of primal religion, popular Hinduism or recent New Age borrowings from both.

Sometimes this aspect of Israel's faith has been called the "desacralizing" of nature, but that is not the best word to use. To suggest that Israel "descralized nature" implies that they had no sense of the sacredness of the created order and regarded the earth simply as an object to be harnessed for human benefit. This in turn is then claimed as biblical warrant for a scientific, technological and instrumental attitude to the nonhuman creation as a whole. The roots of this misunderstanding go back to the early to mid-twentieth century, when many scholars emphasized the historical nature of Israel's faith. This included the affirmation that Israel "demythologized" the widespread creation myths of the ancient Near East. Israel, it was argued, privileged history over nature; YHWH was the God of *history* in contrast to the surrounding gods of *nature*. However, it is now well-established that other ancient Near Eastern civilizations believed their gods were active to some extent in human history, and not all their gods could be adequately described as merely divinized natural forces. Conversely, YHWH is unquestionably the God of the created order as well as the God of Israel's history.

However, an unfortunate side effect of this common assertion in Old Testament scholarship was the popular view that the Bible "desacralized" nature. This view then rendered the natural order open to human exploration and exploitation, unfettered by religious fears or taboos. The sole purpose of the natural order, on such a view, is to meet our human needs. So whatever we do to it, we need not fear that we are insulting some inherent divine force. Nature is ours to command. Such a secularized view of nature is not at all what is meant here by the dedivinizing of nature.[5]

There is a fundamental difference between treating creation as *sacred* and treating it as *divine* (just as there is a categorical difference between speaking of the sanctity of human life and regarding any human being as divine). The sacredness or sanctity of creation speaks of its essential relatedness to God, not of it being divine in and of itself.

The Old Testament constantly treats creation *in relation to God*. The created order obeys God, submits to God's commands, reveals God's glory, benefits from God's sustaining and providing, and serves God's purposes—including (but not confined to) the purpose of providing for human beings or functioning as the vehicle of God's judgment on them. So there is a sacredness about the nonhuman created order that we are called on to honor, as the laws, worship and prophecy of Israel undoubtedly did. But to *worship* nature in any of its manifestations is to exchange the Creator for the created. And that is a form of idolatry against which Israel was repeatedly warned (e.g., Deut 4:15-20; cf. Job 31:26-28), and which Paul links to the whole tragic litany of humanity's willful rebellion and social evil (Rom 1:25 and the surrounding context).

The radical monotheism of Israel that set itself against all the so-called gods of nature did not rob nature itself of its God-related sacredness and significance.

> From this perspective of radical monotheism in the doctrine of creation, there are no lesser divinities—not the sun and moon (against the worship of which Gen 1:14-18 was a reaction), not golden calves and other "graven images," not sacred groves or ancient trees, not mighty mountains or volcanoes, not fearsome beasts or demons, not caesars or pharaohs or heroes, and not even Gaia or Mother Earth. In this view, polytheism, animism, astrology, totemism and other forms of nature worship are not only idolatry but also, as the prophets regularly suggested, vanity and stupidity (cf. Isa. 40:12-28; 443:9-20; 46:1-11; Acts 14; 15). The Creator alone is worthy of worship. . . . Nevertheless, though only the Creator is worthy of worship, all God's creatures are worthy of moral consideration, as a sign of the worthiness imparted by God and, in fact, as an expression of the worship of God. The monotheistic doctrine of creation does not desacralize nature. Nature is still sacred by virtue of having been created by God, declared to be good, and placed under ultimate divine sovereignty.[6]

---

[5]For a helpful discussion of the effects of this particular distortion in Old Testament theology, see Ronald A. Simkins, *Creator and Creation: Nature in the Worldview of Ancient Israel* (Peabody, Mass.: Hendrickson, 1994), pp. 82-88.

[6]James A. Nash, *Loving Nature: Ecological Integrity and Christian Responsibility* (Nashville: Abingdon, 1991), p. 96.

And if that is the case, are there not compelling ethical and missional implications for us who claim to worship this God as the world's Creator, for us who claim to know him also as the world's Redeemer? If the earth has a sanctity derived from its relation to the Creator, then our treatment of the earth will be a reflex and a measure of our own relationship with the creator.

What ecological and missiological challenges then emerge from the affirmation that the earth belongs to God? Summarizing our study so far, surely there are ecological implications to regarding the created order as good in itself because of the value it has to God. It is not neutral stuff that we can commodify and commercialize, use and abuse for our own ends. Furthermore, as part of the whole creation, we humans exist not only to praise and glorify God ourselves but also to facilitate the rest of creation in doing so. And if the greatest commandment is that we should love God, that surely implies that we should treat what belongs to God with honor, care and respect. This would be true in any human relationship. If you love someone, you care for what belongs to that person.

To love God (even to know God at all, Jeremiah would add [Jer 9:24]) means to value what God values. Conversely, therefore, to contribute to or collude in the abuse, pollution and destruction of the natural order is to trample on the goodness of God reflected in creation. It is to devalue what God values, to mute God's praise and to diminish God's glory.

The whole earth as the field of God's mission and ours. If God owns the universe, there is nowhere that does not belong to him. There is nowhere we can step off his property, either into the property of some other deity or into some autonomous sphere of our own private ownership.

Such claims were made in relation to YHWH in the Old Testament (e.g., in Ps 139, to the writer's great comfort). But in the New Testament the same claims are made in relation to Jesus Christ. Standing on a mountain with his disciples after his resurrection, Jesus paraphrases the affirmations of Deuteronomy about YHWH ("The LORD is God in heaven above and on the earth below. There is no other" [Deut 4:39]. "To the LORD your God belong the heavens, even the highest heavens, the earth and everything in it" [Deut 10:14]. "The LORD your God is God of gods and Lord of lords" [Deut 10:17]), and calmly applies them to himself: "All authority in heaven and earth has been given to me" (Mt 28:18). *The risen Jesus thus claims the same ownership and sovereignty over all creation as the Old Testament affirms for YHWH.*

The whole earth, then, belongs to Jesus. It belongs to him by right of creation, by right of redemption and by right of future inheritance—as Paul affirms in the magnificent cosmic declaration of Colossians 1:15-20. So wherever we go in his name, we are walking on his property. There is not an inch of the planet that does not belong to Christ. Mission then is an authorized activity carried out by tenants on the instructions of the owner of the property.

Suppose you are a tenant resident in your house or apartment and you are challenged about your right to be installing a new kitchen and bathroom. Provided you can point to the written instruction of the owner of the property to attend to the matter on his behalf, your action is authorized. If the one to whom the property belongs entrusts to you his purpose of renovating his property while you live there, then your "mission" is an authorized cooperation with and implementation of his or her "mission." You become the agent of the owner's intentions for the property. You are legitimately carrying out what the owner wants to be done in his or her own property.

So our mission on God's earth is not only authorized by its true owner, it is also protected, nurtured and guaranteed by him. We go in his name. We act on his authority. There is therefore no place for fear, for wherever we tread belongs to him already. There is no place for dualism either. We know of course that the Bible also affirms that the evil one exercises a kind of lordship and power over the earth. But he does not own it. His claim to do so, and to have the right to give it to those who worship him was exposed as fraudulent by Jesus in his wrestling with temptation in the wilderness. Whatever authority Satan exercises is usurped and illegitimate, provisional and subject to the final limits set by the earth's true owner and Lord, the Lamb who reigns from the throne of God (Rev 4—7).

So the simple biblical affirmation "The earth is the LORD's" is a nonnegotiable platform for both ecological ethics and missional confidence.

God's glory as the goal of creation. "What is the chief end of man?" asks the opening question of the Shorter Catechism of the Westminster Confession, inquiring about the meaning and purpose of human existence. It then answers with glorious biblical simplicity: "The chief end of man is to glorify God and enjoy him forever." It would be equally biblical to ask exactly the same question about the whole of creation and to give exactly the same answer. The creation exists for the praise and glory of its Creator God and for mutual enjoyment. We humans, being creatures ourselves, share in that reason for existence—our "chief end" is to bring glory to God, and in doing so to enjoy ourselves because we enjoy God. So that God-focused goal of human life (to glorify and enjoy him) is not something that sets us *apart* from the rest of creation. Rather it is something we *share* with the rest of creation. That is the chief end of all creation. The only difference is that of course we human beings must glorify our Creator in uniquely human ways, as befits our unique status as the one creature that has been made in the image of God. So, as humans we praise God with hearts and hands and voices, with rationality as well as emotion, with language, art, music and craft—with all that reflects the God in whose image we were made.

But all the rest of creation already praises God and can be summoned (repeatedly) to do so (e.g., Ps 145:10, 21; 148; 150:6). There is a response of gratitude that befits not just human beneficiaries of God's generosity but is attributed to the nonhuman creatures as well (e.g., Ps 104:27-28). We may not be able to explain *how* it is that creation praises its Maker—since we know only the reality of our human personhood "from the inside," and what it means for *us* to praise him. But just because we cannot articulate the *how* of creation's inarticulate praise or indeed the *how* of God's receiving of it, we should not therefore deny *that* creation praises God—since it is affirmed throughout the Bible with overwhelming conviction.

> This response of gratitude is a fundamental feature of creaturely being that is shared by all the creatures of the earth, humans and animals, landscapes, seas and mountains, earth, wind, fire and rain. The Psalmist charges all things with the first moral duty of the creation, to worship and praise the creator. . . . In the Hebrew perspective humanity and the cosmos have moral significance, and both are required to make a moral response to the creator, a response to God which reflects his glory and offers the return of gratitude, praise and worship [Ps 150].[7]

Eventually, the whole of creation will join in the joy and thanksgiving that will accompany the Lord when he comes as king to put all things right (i.e., to judge the earth, e.g., Ps 96:10-13; 98:7-9).

Furthermore, as we consider the task of bringing glory to God, it is worth noting that several significant texts link the *glory of God* to the *fullness* of the earth—that is, the magnificently diverse abundance of the whole biosphere—land, sea and sky. The language of fullness is a feature of the creation narrative. From empty void, the story progresses through repeated fillings. So, once the water and the sky have been separated, the fifth day sees the water teeming with fish and the skies with birds, according to God's blessing and command (Gen 1:20-22). Likewise, on the sixth day, after the creation of the rest of the land animals, human beings are blessed and commanded to "fill the earth." Not surprisingly, then, Psalm 104:24 can affirm "the earth is full of your creatures." And Psalm 24:1 can describe this plenitude of creatures as simply "the earth's fullness" (author's translation). So does Psalm 50:12, after an illustrative list in-

---

[7]Michael S. Northcott, *The Environment and Christian Ethics* (Cambridge: Cambridge University Press, 1996), pp. 180-81.

cluding animals of the forest, the cattle on a thousand hills, mountain birds and
creatures in the fields: "to me belongs the world and its fullness" (author's translation). Similarly, the phrase "the earth and its fullness" becomes a characteristic
way of talking about the whole environment—sometimes local, sometimes universal (e.g., Deut 33:16; Ps 89:12; Is 34:1; Jer 47:2; Ezek 30:12; Mic 1:2).

This may give added meaning to the song of the seraphim in Isaiah's temple
vision:

> Holy, holy, holy is Yahweh of hosts.
> The filling (or fullness) of all the earth [is] his glory. (Is 6:3, author's translation)[8]

"The fullness of the earth" is a way of talking about the whole rich abundance of the created order, especially the nonhuman creation (when humans
are in view, they are often added as "and all who live in it" [e.g., Ps 24:1]). So
the seraphim recognize and celebrate the glory of God *in* the fullness of the
earth. That which manifests the glory of God is the teeming abundance of his
creation. The earth is full of God's glory because what fills the earth constitutes
(at least one dimension of) his glory. Similarly, Psalm 104:31 puts God's glory
and God's works of creation in parallel: "May the glory of the LORD endure forever; / may the LORD rejoice in his works."

Of course, we would have to add that the glory of God also transcends the
creation, precedes and surpasses it. As Psalm 8:1 reminds us, God has set his
glory "*above* the heavens." But the creation not only *declares* the glory of God
(Ps 19:1); creation's fullness is also an *essential part* of that glory.

Recognizing the link between the fullness of the earth (i.e., the totality of all
created life on earth) and the glory of God means, as Paul reminds us, that human beings are confronted daily with the reality of God simply by inhabiting
the planet (Rom 1:19-20). Here again we recognize a truth of missional relevance. For all human beings inhabit a glory-filled earth that reveals and declares
something of its Creator and theirs. What we have done with that experience is
another matter, of course. But this truth underlies not only the radical nature of
Paul's exposure of universal sinfulness and idolatry but also the universal applicability and intelligibility of the gospel. Minds that have suppressed and ex-
changed this truth about the Creator can, by God's grace and the illumining

---

[8]I owe this suggested nuance in the meaning of Is 6:3 to a conversation with Hilary Marlowe.
It is also offered as a translation by the NASB and discussed in relation to the concept of the
whole earth constituting the cosmic temple of God in G. K. Beale, *The Temple and the
Church's Mission: A Biblical Theology of the Dwelling Place of God,* New Studies in Biblical
Theology, ed., D. A. Carson (Leicester, U.K.: Apollos; Downers Grove, Ill.: InterVarsity Press,
2004), p. 49.

power of the gospel, be brought from darkness to light, to know their Creator once more as their Redeemer through the message of the cross.

God's redemption of the whole creation. So far we have been considering how important it is to include the Bible's strong doctrine of creation in our thinking about the earth—what we do with it, how we live on it and what it was created for. But looking back to Genesis and affirming its great truths about our world is not enough. You cannot drive a car looking only in the rearview mirror. You have to look ahead toward your destination. Likewise, the Bible teaches us to value the earth, not only because of "where it came from" (or rather, because of who it came from) but also because of its ultimate destiny. We need, in other words, an eschatological as well as a creational foundation to our ecological ethics and mission.

One of the richest places in the Old Testament to find precisely such a foundation is the book of Isaiah, and much of what the New Testament says is simply an exposition of Isaiah's cosmic vision in the light of Jesus Christ. We might begin with the glorious composite vision of Isaiah 11:1-9, in which the just rule of the messianic king will issue in harmony and shalom within the created order. Similarly transforming expectations for the created order attend the return of the redeemed to Zion in Isaiah 35. However, the climax of Old Testament eschatological vision regarding creation is found in Isaiah 65—66. The words "Behold, I will create new heavens and a new earth" (Is 65:17) introduce a wonderful section that has to be read in full.

Behold, I will create
    new heavens and a new earth.
The former things will not be remembered,
    nor will they come to mind.
But be glad and rejoice forever
    in what I will create,
for I will create Jerusalem to be a delight
    and its people a joy.
I will rejoice over Jerusalem
    and take delight in my people;
the sound of weeping and of crying
    will be heard in it no more.
Never again will there be in it
    an infant who lives but a few days,
    or an old man who does not live out his years;
he who dies at a hundred
    will be thought a mere youth;

he who fails to reach a hundred
  will be considered accursed.

They will build houses and dwell in them;
  they will plant vineyards and eat their fruit.
No longer will they build houses and others live in them,
  or plant and others eat.
For as the days of a tree,
  so will be the days of my people;
my chosen ones will long enjoy
  the works of their hands.
They will not toil in vain
  or bear children doomed to misfortune;
for they will be a people blessed by the LORD,
  they and their descendants with them.
Before they call I will answer;
  while they are still speaking I will hear.
The wolf and the lamb will feed together,
  and the lion will eat straw like the ox,
  but dust will be the serpent's food.
They will neither harm nor destroy
  on all my holy mountain,
      says the LORD. (Is 65:17-25)

This inspiring vision portrays God's new creation as a place that will be joyful, free from grief and tears, life-fulfilling, with guaranteed work satisfaction, free from the curses of frustrated labor, and environmentally safe! It is a vision that puts most New Age dreams in the shade.

This and related passages are the scriptural (Old Testament) foundation for the New Testament hope, which, far from rejecting or denying the earth as such or envisioning us floating off to some other place, looks forward likewise to a new, redeemed creation (Rom 8:18-21) in which righteousness will dwell (2 Pet 3:10-13) because God himself will dwell there with his people (Rev 21:1-4).

The burden of this eschatological vision for creation is overwhelmingly positive, and this must affect how we understand the equally biblical portrayal of final and fiery destruction that awaits the present world order. For example, 2 Peter 3:10 says: "The heavens will disappear with a roar; the elements will be destroyed by fire, and the earth and everything in it will be laid bare."

I prefer the textual reading of the final word in this verse that the earth "will be found" (which is adopted by the NIV, "will be laid bare"; NRSV, "will be disclosed"; REB, "will be brought to judgment") to the one reflected in some other

English translations (e.g., KJV and NASB, "will be burned up"). I also find Richard Bauckham's interpretation of this convincing, namely, that the earth and everything in it will be "found out," that is, exposed and laid bare before God's judgment so that the wicked and all their works will no longer be able to hide or find any protection.[9] In other words, the purpose of the conflagration described in these verses is not the *obliteration of the cosmos itself* but rather the *purging of the sinful world order we live in,* through the consuming destruction of all that is evil within creation, so as to establish the new creation. This fits with the previous picture of the judgment of the flood in 2 Peter 3:6-7, used explicitly as an historical precedent for the final judgment. "By these waters also the world of that time was deluged and destroyed. By the same word the present heavens and earth are reserved for fire, being kept for the day of judgment and destruction of ungodly men."

A world of wickedness was wiped out in the flood, but the world as God's creation was preserved. Similarly, by analogy, the world of all evil and wickedness in creation will be wiped out in God's cataclysmic judgment, but the creation itself will be renewed as the dwelling place of God with redeemed humanity.

Paul makes a similar dual assertion when he compares the future of creation to the future of our bodies in Romans 8. There is a comparable continuity and discontinuity for creation as there is between our present bodily life and our future resurrection life—just as there was for Jesus, who in his resurrection body is the firstborn of the whole new creation. This present body of mine may rot in the soil or be burned to ashes. But the resurrection body, which of course is "a new creation" (and in that sense discontinuous) will be truly me, the person God created and redeemed (and in that sense continuous). Similarly, whatever the language of fiery judgment and destruction will actually mean in relation to our physical universe, God's purpose is not the eternal obliteration of the created order but its eternal restoration to his glorious purpose for it.

This gloriously earthy biblical hope adds an important dimension to our ecological ethics. It is not just a matter of looking back to the initial creation but of looking forward to the new creation. This means that our motivation has a double force—a kind of push-pull effect. There is a goal in sight. Granted it lies only in the power of God ultimately to achieve it, but, as is the case with other aspects of biblical eschatology, what we hope for from God affects how we are to live now and what our own objectives should be.

The role of apocalyptic and prophecy in the Bible is not just to predict the

---

[9]Richard J. Bauckham, *2 Peter and Jude,* Word Biblical Commentary 50 (Waco, Tex.: Word, 1983), pp. 316-22.

future but to encourage and to prove change and moral fulfillment in the present. The physical and ecological character of biblical visions of redemption offers hope that the restoration of ecological harmony does lie within the possibilities of a redeemed human history: this does not remove the need for social and moral effort in responding to the ecological crisis but rather affirms that human societies which seek to revere God and to mirror his justice, will also produce the fruits of justice and equity in human moral order and harmony in the natural world. According to Ezekiel, even the driest desert can spring to life again, and the dry bones will rise up again to praise their Creator.[10]

Isaiah and Ezekiel doubtless drew their own inspiring vision of the future in part from the language of Israel's worship—the Psalms. And there in the imagination of faith the whole of creation is not only summoned to praise its Creator but is drawn into a vision of God's future restoration of the whole creation to be the place of reliability, righteousness and rejoicing that he intended for it. The coming reign of YHWH will achieve this goal of justice and liberation for creation as well as for humanity. The theme is particularly seen in the psalms of YHWH's kingship (e.g., Ps 93; 96; 98). The new song that is to fill the mouths of people throughout the whole earth in Psalm 96, for example, also celebrates a new world order for the whole of creation.

> According to Psalm 96 the particular eschatological aspect of God's work that calls for special praise from the side of all creatures is the announcement that he comes to judge in righteousness and in truth (vv. 10, 13). We associate God's judgment with all manner of dread expectations. Yet his judgment does not consist only in calling his opponents to account. It may also be thought of with joyful anticipation, for everything that is now in disarray and disharmony, suffering from injustice and violence, shall be set right. This is the broader aspect of the judgment which Old Testament saints embraced and in which they rejoiced. God does not reign in a tyrannical way or through terror; his reign breathes tenderness and joy.
>
> In a very special way *nature* will rejoice in the restoration of all things, for God's coming will put an end to the violence nature had to suffer. The inauguration of Yahweh's new order manifest itself as much in the realm of nature as in that of history—as is evident in Isaiah 40-42 as well. In a glorious way Psalm 96 and its twin, Psalm 98, remind the believing community that God's purpose with creation is nothing less than a new heaven and a new earth in which justice will be at home.[11]

---

[10]Northcott, *Environment and Christian Ethics,* p. 195.
[11]Jannie Du Preez, "Reading Three 'Enthronement Psalms' from an Ecological Perspective," *Missionalia* 19 (1991): 127.

As Francis Bridger points out, this eschatological orientation protects our ecological concern from becoming centered only on human needs and anxieties, and reminds us that ultimately the earth always has and always will belong to God in Christ. Our efforts therefore have a prophetic value in pointing toward the full cosmic realizing of that truth.

> The primary argument for ecological responsibility lies in the connection between old and new creation. . . . We are called to be stewards of the earth by virtue not simply of our orientation to the Edenic command of the Creator but also because of our orientation to the future. In acting to preserve and enhance the created order we are pointing to the coming rule of God in Christ. . . . Ecological ethics are not, therefore, anthropocentric: they testify to the vindicating acts of God in creation and redemption. . . . Paradoxically, the fact that it is God who will bring about a new order of creation at the End and that we are merely erecting signposts to that future need not act as a disincentive. Rather it frees us from the burden of ethical and technological autonomy and makes it clear that human claims to sovereignty are relative. The knowledge that it is God's world, that our efforts are not directed toward the construction of an ideal utopia but that we are, under God, building bridgeheads of the kingdom serves to humble us and to bring us to the place of ethical obedience.[12]

William Cowper's longing for the future restoration of creation is expressed in these lines from a poem more in the genre of the prophets and psalmists.

> The groans of Nature in this nether world,
> Which Heaven has heard for ages, have an end,
> Foretold by prophets, and by poets sung,
> Whose fire was kindled at the prophets' lamp.
> The time of rest, the promised Sabbath comes!
>
> Rivers of gladness water all the earth,
> And clothe all climes with beauty. The reproach
> Of barrenness is past. The fruitful field
> Laughs with abundance; and the land, once lean
> Or fertile only in its own disgrace,
> Exults to see its thistly curse repeal'd.
> The various seasons woven into one,
> And that one season an eternal spring,
> The garden fears no blight, and needs no fence,

---

[12]Francis Bridger, "Ecology and Eschatology: A Neglected Dimension," *Tyndale Bulletin* 41, no. 2 (1990): 301. This article was a response and addition to an earlier one by Donald A. Hay, "Christians in the Global Greenhouse," *Tyndale Bulletin* 41, no. 1 (1990): 109-27.

For there is none to covet, all are full.
The lion, and the libbard,[13] and the bear,
Graze with the fearless flocks.

> One song employs all nations; and all cry,
> "Worthy the Lamb, for He was slain for us!"
> The dwellers in the vales and on the rocks
> Shout to each other, and the mountain tops
> From distant mountains catch the flying joy;
> Till, nation after nation taught the strain,
> Earth rolls the rapturous Hosanna round.[14]

Care of Creation and Christian Mission

Great would be the multitude, though perhaps not as great yet as it ought to be, of those Christians who care about creation and take their environmental responsibilities seriously. They choose sustainable forms of energy where possible. They switch off unneeded appliances. They buy food, goods and services as far as possible from companies with ethically sound environmental policies. They join conservation societies. They avoid overconsumption and unnecessary waste and recycle as much as possible. May their tribe increase.

Smaller, however, would be the number (and as yet far from any kind of multitude) of those who would include the care of creation within their biblical concept of mission.[15] Smaller still (though cheerfully growing) is the number of those who see active creation care as their own personal and specific mission calling. The explicitly Christian environmental and conservation agency A Rocha, founded in 1983 in Portugal but now at work internationally on every continent, certainly adopts a theology that affirms strongly that their work is not only biblically mandated but also a legitimate and essential dimension of Christian mission.[16]

Speaking personally, I share the conviction with which Jannie du Preez began an article in 1991: "I have, in recent years, increasingly become convinced that justice towards the earth (and for that matter, towards the whole cosmos)

---

[13]Probably meaning the leopard.

[14]William Cowper, "The Task," bk. 6, lines 729-733, 763-774, 791-797, in *The Complete Poetical Works of William Cowper, Esq.,* ed. H. Stebbing (New York: D. Appleton, 1856), pp. 344-45.

[15]Very few theologies of mission include creation care in their agenda. One exception is J. Andrew Kirk, *What Is Mission? Theological Explorations* (London: Darton, Longman & Todd; Minneapolis: Fortress Press, 1999), pp. 164-83.

[16]For details of their vision, their work and the rich biblical theology on which the whole movement is founded, see their website <www.arocha.org>.

forms an integral part of the mission of the church."[17]

But does it? In addition to the detailed biblical theology of the preceding sections of this chapter, I would make just a few more points articulating how and why it seems to me that a biblical theology of mission that flows from the mission of God himself, as I have been seeking to articulate throughout this book, must include the ecological sphere within its scope and see practical environmental action as a legitimate part of Christian mission.

Creation care is an urgent issue in today's world. Does this need to be repeated? Only a willful blindness worse than any proverbial ostrich's head in the sand can ignore the facts of environmental destruction and its accelerating pace. The list is depressingly long:

- the pollution of the air, the sea, rivers, lakes and great aquifers
- the destruction of rainforests and many other habitats, with the terrible effect on dependent life forms
- desertification and soil loss
- the loss of species—animals, plants, birds, insects—and the huge reduction of essential bio-diversity on a planet that depends on it
- the hunting of some species to extinction
- the depletion of the ozone layer
- the increase of "greenhouse gases" and consequent global warming

All this is a vast and interrelated impending catastrophe of loss and destruction, affecting the whole planet and all its human and nonhuman inhabitants. To be unconcerned about it is to be either desperately ignorant or irresponsibly callous.

In the past, Christians have instinctively been concerned about great and urgent issues in every generation, and rightly included them in their overall concept of mission calling and practice. These have included the evils of disease, ignorance, slavery and many other forms of brutality and exploitation. Christians have taken up the cause of widows, orphans, refugees, prisoners, the insane, the hungry—and most recently they have swelled the numbers of those committed to "making poverty history."

Faced now with the horrific facts of the suffering of the earth itself, we must

---

[17]Du Preez, "Reading Three 'Enthronement Psalms,' " p. 122. The same issue of *Missionalia* (19, no. 2 [1991]) included other articles seeking to make an explicit link between mission and ecology: J. A. Loader, "Life, Wonder and Responsibility: Some Thoughts on Ecology and Christian Mission," *Missionalia* 19 (1991): 44-56; and J. J. Kritzinger, "Mission and the Liberation of Creation: A Critical Dialogue with M. L. Daneel," *Missionalia* 20 (1992): 99-115.

surely ask how God himself responds to such abuse of his creation and seek to align our mission objectives to include what matters to him. If, as Jesus tells us, God cares about his creation to the level of knowing when a sparrow falls to earth, what kind of care is required of us by the level of our own knowledge? Granted Jesus made that point in order to compare it with the even greater care God has for his own children. But it would be an utter distortion of Scripture to argue that because God cares for us *more than* for the sparrows, we need not care for sparrows *at all* or that because we are of greater value than they are, they have no value at all.

However, our care for creation should not be merely a negative, prudential or preventive reaction to a growing problem. A much more positive reason for it is that.

Creation care flows from love and obedience to God. "Love the LORD your God" is the first and greatest commandment. In human experience, to love someone means that you care for what belongs to them. Trashing someone else's property is incompatible with any claim to love that other person. We have seen how emphatically the Bible affirms that the earth is God's property, and more specifically that it belongs to Christ, who made it, redeemed it and is heir to it. Taking good care of the earth, for Christ's sake, is surely a fundamental dimension of the calling on all God's people to love him. It seems quite inexplicable to me that there are some Christians who claim to love and worship God, to be disciples of Jesus and yet have no concern for the earth that bears his stamp of ownership. They do not care about the abuse of the earth, and indeed by their wasteful and overconsumptive lifestyles they contribute to it.

"If you love me, keep my commandments" (Jn 14:15), said Jesus, echoing as he so often did the practical ethical devotion of Deuteronomy. And the Lord's commandments begin with the fundamental creation mandate to care for the earth. Obedience to that command is as much a part of our human mission and duty as any of the other duties and responsibilities built into creation—such as the task of filling the earth, engaging in the rhythm of productive work and rest, and marriage.

Being Christian does not release us from being human. Nor does a distinctively Christian mission negate our human mission, for God holds us accountable as much for our humanity as for our Christianity. As *Christian* human beings, therefore, we are doubly bound to see active care for creation as a fundamental part of what it means to love and obey God.

> The creation narrative *appoints* humans as the viceroys of creation with an *assignment* to care for God's property, the sphere with which his love takes shape for

humans, regardless of what they think of him, for all the biotic and abiotic creation, regardless of whether it can think of him. This is much more than an invitation, it is a mission: Go to all of my creation and tend it, since it is the recipient of my love. I suggest that the first missionary commission is the *mandatum dominii terrae* [command to have dominion over the earth] in Genesis 1:28, the assignment to care for the world.[18]

Creation care exercises our priestly and kingly role in relation to the earth. Greg Beale argues persuasively that there are theological connections between the tabernacle/temple in the Old Testament and (1) the picture of Eden in the creation narrative, and (2) the picture of the whole cosmos restored through Christ to be the dwelling place of God. The temple is a microcosm, both of the primal creation reality and of the new creation reality. In both cases we see God dwelling in the earth as his temple, with human beings serving him and it as his appointed priesthood.[19]

The dual account of the mandate God gave to humanity in Genesis 1—2 uses the language of both kingship and priesthood. Humanity is to rule over the rest of creation, and Adam is put in the garden in Eden "to work it and take care of it." Ruling is the function of kingship; serving and keeping were major functions of the priests in relation to the tabernacle and temple.

So humankind is placed in a relationship to the earth that combines the function of king and priest: to rule and to serve. It is a quintessentially biblical combination that we find perfectly modeled in a rich range of meaning in Christ, as our perfect priest and king. But it is also the picture that we see of our restored role in the new creation. Revelation pointedly says that because of the redeeming work of the Lamb of God on the cross, human beings are not only saved but are restored to their kingly and priestly function on earth under God. "You have made them to be a kingdom and priests to serve our God, / and they will reign on the earth" (Rev 5:10).

It follows then, from a creational and eschatological perspective, that ecological care and action is a dimension of our mission inasmuch as it is a dimension of restoring the proper status and responsibility of our humanity. It is to behave as we were originally created to and as we will one day be fully redeemed for. The earth awaits the full revealing of its appointed king and priest—redeemed humanity under the headship of Christ. Our action in the present anticipates and points prophetically toward that final goal.

Creation care tests our motivation for mission. Throughout this book

---

[18]Loader, "Life, Wonder and Responsibility," p. 53.
[19]Beale, *Temple and Church's Mission*.

my argument has been that it will lead to an inadequate view of mission if we start out only from the perspective of what humans do or what humans need. And it will be doubly inadequate if we also end there only. This is not to deny the legitimacy of many different levels of motivation for mission that arise from human need.

One strong motivation is the *evangelistic* response to the reality of human sin. We know people stand under God's judgment, in the alienating darkness and lostness of sin. We are motivated to bring them the good news of what God has done for sinners through Christ, his cross and resurrection. Another strong motivation is the *compassionate* response to the reality of human need—all the physical, mental, emotional and social dimensions of our fractured human condition. So we are motivated to tackle the destructive effects of sin in all those areas too, through medical, social, educational and economic action. I argued in chapters eight and nine for such a holistic understanding of mission and the necessity of seeing the cross of Christ as central to all those dimensions. All of these are valid, biblical and Christ-imitating motivations for mission.

However, it has also been my argument throughout the book that our ultimate starting point and finishing point in our biblical theology of mission must be the mission of God himself. What is "the whole counsel of God"? What is the overarching mission to which God has committed himself and the whole outworking of history? It is not only the salvation of human beings but also the redemption of the whole creation. The eschatological section of this chapter (see pp. 407-12) made this clear. God is in the business of establishing a new creation through the transformation and renewal of creation in a manner analogous to the resurrection of his Son, and as a habitation for the resurrection bodies of his redeemed people.

Holistic mission, then, is not truly holistic if it includes only human beings (even if it includes them holistically!) and excludes the rest of the creation for whose reconciliation Christ shed his blood (Col 1:20). Those Christians who have responded to God's call to serve him through serving his nonhuman creatures in ecological projects are engaged in a specialized form of mission that has its rightful place within the broad framework of all that God's mission has as its goal. Their motivation flows from an awareness of God's own heart for his creation and a desire to respond to that. It is certainly not the case that Christians involved in creation care have no corresponding care for human needs. On the contrary, it often seems to my observation that Christian tenderness toward the nonhuman creation amplifies itself in concern for human needs.

Creation care is a prophetic opportunity for the church. Christians sometimes feel anxious that "the world is setting the agenda," that is, that we simply respond to the flavor of the month in the changing fads of secular concerns. And it is certainly true that environmental concern is very high on the list of anxieties in our world today. Surveys of young people in the West often find that the very survival of planet Earth comes out top of the list of the things they worry about. However, the church surely must respond to the realities the world is facing and struggling with, in any era. The Old Testament prophets addressed the contemporary realities of their own generation. Jesus did the same. That is what made them unpopular—their scorching relevance.

If the church awakens to the urgent need to address the ecological crisis and does so within its biblical framework of resources and vision, then it will engage in missional conflict with at least two other ideologies (and doubtless many more).

1. Destructive global capitalism and the greed that fuels it. There is no doubt that a major contributor to contemporary environmental damage is global capitalism's insatiable demand for "more." It is not only in the private sphere that the biblical truth is relevant that covetousness is idolatry and the love of money is the root of all kinds of evil, including this one. There is greed for

- minerals and oil, at any cost
- land to graze cattle for meat
- exotic animals and birds, to meet obscene human fashions in clothes, toys, ornaments, and aphrodisiacs
- commercial or tourist exploitation of fragile and irreplaceable habitats
- market domination through practices that produce the goods at least cost to the exploiter and maximum cost to the country and people exploited

For the church to get involved with issues of environmental protection it must be prepared to tackle the forces of greed and economic power, to confront vested interests and political machination, to recognize that more is at stake than just being kind to animals and nice to people. It must do the scientific research to make its case credible. It must be willing for the long, hard road that the struggle for justice and compassion in a fallen world demands in this as in all other fields of mission.

2. Pantheistic, neo-pagan and New Age spiritualities. Strangely, we may often find that people for whom such pantheistic, neo-pagan and New Age philosophies have great attraction are passionate about the natural order, but from a very different perspective. The church in its mission must bear witness to the great biblical claim that the earth is the Lord's. The earth is not Gaia or

Mother Earth. It is not a self-sustaining sentient being. It does not have independent potency. It is not to be worshiped, feared or even loved in a way that
usurps the sole deity of the one living and personal Creator God. So our environmental mission is never romantic or mystical. We are not called to "union
with nature" but to care for the earth as an act of love and obedience to its
Creator and Redeemer.

There is, then, surely a cutting-edge prophetic opportunity for the church,
which we seem to be failing to grasp (with a few exceptions such as A Rocha).
Christians are more likely to be *blamed* for the ecological crisis than seen as
bearing any kind of good news in relation to it.

***Creation care embodies a biblical balance of compassion and jus-
tice.*** Creation care embodies *compassion* because to care for God's creation
is essentially an unselfish form of love, exercised for the sake of creatures who
cannot thank or repay us. It is a form of truly biblical and godly altruism. In
this respect it reflects the same quality in the love of God—not only in the
sense that God loves human beings in spite of our unlovable enmity toward
him but also in the wider sense that "the LORD has compassion / is loving toward *all that he has made*" (Ps 145:9, 13, 17, author's translation). Again, Jesus
used God's loving care for birds and adornment of grasses and flowers as a
model for his even greater love for his human children. If God cares with such
minute compassion for his nonhuman creation, how much more should those
who wish to emulate him? I have been particularly moved in witnessing the
compassionate care that is unselfconsciously practiced by A Rocha staff as
they handle every bird in their ringing program. It is a warm, caring and, in
my opinion, genuinely Christlike attitude toward these tiny specimens of
God's creation.

Creation care embodies *justice* because environmental action is a form of defending the weak against the strong, the defenseless against the powerful, the
violated against the attacker, the voiceless against the stridency of the greedy.
And these too are features of the character of God as expressed in his exercise
of justice. Psalm 145 includes God's provision for all his creatures in its definition of his *righteousness* as well as his love (Ps 145:13-17). In fact, it places God's
care for creation in precise parallel with his liberating and vindicating acts of
justice for his people—thus bringing the creational and redemptive traditions of
the Old Testament together in beautiful harmony.

So it is not surprising then that when the Old Testament comes to define the
marks of a righteous *person,* it does not stop at his practical concern for poor and
needy *humans* (though that is of course the dominant note). It is true that "the
righteous care about justice for the poor" (Prov 29:7). But the sage also makes the

warm-hearted observation that "a righteous man cares for the needs of his *animal*" (Prov 12:10). Biblical mission is as holistic as biblical righteousness.

Conclusion

What then, to summarize, establishes ecological concern and specific environmental action as legitimate integral dimensions of biblical mission? I have suggested, with regard to these forms of action, that

- They are responding to an urgent global issue.
- They are expressions of our love and obedience toward God the Creator.
- They restore our proper priestly and kingly role in relation to the earth.
- They expose and expand our motivation for holistic mission.
- They constitute a contemporary prophetic opportunity for the church.
- They embody the core biblical values of compassion and justice.

All of these points are built on the *intrinsic* value of creation to God and the self-standing mandate of God that we should care for it as he does. They do not depend on any other utility or consequence of such action, such as human benefit or evangelistic fruitfulness. We are to care for the earth because it belongs to God and he told us to. That is enough in itself.

Nevertheless, because we are also part of that creation, there is no doubt that what benefits creation ultimately is also good for human beings in the long term (even though short-term human need often clashes with environmental good). Hence, environmental and development issues are often intertwined. And furthermore, since the suffering of creation is bound up with human wickedness, that which is good news for the earth is part of that which is good news for people. The gospel is indeed good news for the whole of creation.

It is not surprising then that those who take seriously, as Christians, our responsibility to embody God's love for creation find that their obedience in that sphere often leads to opportunities to articulate God's love for suffering and lost people also. The story of A Rocha has shown that while the movement's goals and actions in creation care have their own intrinsic biblical validity, God honors such obedience by blessing and building his church as well in the context of such activity.

Truly Christian environmental action is in fact also evangelistically fruitful, not because it is any kind of cover for "real mission" but simply because it declares in word and deed the Creator's limitless love for the whole of his creation (which of course includes his love for his human creatures) and makes no secret of the biblical story of the cost that the Creator paid to redeem both. Such action is a missional embodiment of the biblical truths that the Lord is loving toward all that he has made, and that this same God so loved the world that he gave his only Son not only so that believers should not perish but ultimately so that *all things in heaven and earth* should be reconciled to God through the blood of the cross. For God was in Christ reconciling *the world* to himself.

13

Mission and God's Image

W e turn now from the earth to the human creatures whom God placed within it. What aspects of the Bible's teaching about humanity as a whole are particularly relevant to our exploration of biblical mission?

Humanity in God's Image

Created in God's image. This is not the place to engage in a comprehensive survey of all the attempts that have been made to elucidate the full meaning of the biblical assertion that God created human beings in the image and likeness of God (Gen 1:26-27).

> Much theological ink has been spilled on trying to pin down exactly what it is about human beings that can be identified as the essence of the image of God in us. Is it our rationality, our moral consciousness, our capacity for relationship, our sense of responsibility to God? Even our upright posture and the expressiveness of the human face have been canvassed as the locus of the image of God in humankind. Since the Bible nowhere defines the term, it is probably futile to attempt to do so very precisely. In any case, we should not so much think of the image of God as an independent "thing" that we somehow possess. God did not *give* to human beings the image of God. Rather, it is a dimension of our very creation. The expression "in our image" is adverbial (that is, it describes the way God made us), not adjectival (that is, as if it simply described a quality we possess). The image of God is not so much something we *possess*, as *what we are. To be human is to be the image of God*. It is not an extra feature added on to our species; it is definitive of what it means to be human.[1]

From a missiological perspective the affirmation that human beings have

---

[1]Christopher J. H. Wright, *Old Testament Ethics for the People of God* (Leicester, U.K.: Inter-Varsity Press; Downers Grove, Ill.: InterVarsity Press, 2004), p. 119.

been created in the image of God, along with the immediate context of the narratives of Genesis 1—3, implies at least four further significant truths about humanity, all of which are vital to biblical mission.

1. All human beings are addressable by God. Human beings are the creatures to whom God speaks. In the creation narrative God gives the different orders of subhuman creatures the basic instruction to go and multiply. They seem to need no further encouragement or communication in attending to that task. In the case of the human creature, however, we find God speaking not only words of blessing and fruitfulness but also of instruction, permission and prohibition, followed later by questions, judgments, and promises. The human is the creature who is aware of God through rational communication and address. And the Old Testament goes on to show that this applies to *all* human beings, with no regard for ethnicity or covenant status. God can speak to an Abimelech or a Balaam or a Nebuchadnezzar as easily as to an Abraham, a Moses, or a Daniel. To be human is to have the capacity of being addressed by the living Creator God.

There is therefore a fundamental God-awareness or God-openness that is common to all humanity, in comparison with which all other labels are secondary, including religious ones. Whatever the cultural environment in which a person lives, or whatever the religious worldview through which they see their life in this world, the most fundamental ground of their humanity is that they have been made in God's image. The living Creator God of all flesh needs no permission, no translation, no crosscultural contextualization when he chooses to communicate with any person whom he has made in his own image. To be human is to be addressable by one's Creator. Granted, of course, as Paul says, that in our sin and rebellion we have universally suppressed and perverted this awareness of God. Nevertheless, the word of the gospel has its life-giving potential precisely because even sinners and rebels are people made in God's image and capable of hearing God's voice.

2. All human beings are accountable to God. The other side of the coin of addressability is accountability. The man and woman in the creation narratives are the creatures who must give an answer when God addresses them. Even in hiding from God, they must answer God. This too is a universal phenomenon, independent of culture and religion.

> From heaven the LORD looks down
> and sees all mankind;
> from his dwelling place he watches
> all who live on earth—
> he who forms the hearts of all,
> who considers everything they do. (Ps 33:13-15)

This is an astonishing assertion. Every human being on the planet is known by God, considered and evaluated by God, called to account by God.

Herein lies the basis of universalizable biblical ethics. It is because of this assumption that all human beings are accountable to YHWH that Amos can address God's accusations and punishment to the noncovenant nations around Israel. The nations may not have been taught the laws of YHWH, as Israel had through the great unique revelation at Mount Sinai (Deut 4:32-35; Ps 147:19-20), but they do know the fundamentals of ethical responsibility to God and one another.

So there are common ethical bridges to people of all cultures. There is some universal sense of moral obligation that human beings share, which again is an important missiological foundation.

3. All human beings have dignity and equality. Being made in the image of God is simultaneously that which sets us apart from the rest of the animals and that which we humans all have in common. *No other animal* is created in the image of God, so this forms the basis of the unique dignity and sanctity of human life. *All other humans* are created in the image of God, so this forms the basis of the radical equality of all human beings, regardless of gender, ethnicity, religion or any form of social, economic, or political status.

In these affirmations the faith of Old Testament Israel was quite distinctive from surrounding ancient Near Eastern religions (and enduring religious traditions today, such as Hinduism), in which differences between human beings are not merely cultural or social, but ontological. The old Akkadian proverb "A man is the shadow of a god; and slave is the shadow of a man" found no endorsement in Israel. Israel had functional social gradations, but a slave in Israel did not have to fight for the right to be regarded as human. Speaking of his male and female slaves, Job asserted, fully in line with Israel's creation theology, "Did not he who made me in the womb make them? / Did not the same one form us both within our mothers?" (Job 31:15).

Christian mission must therefore treat all human beings with dignity, equality and respect. When we look at any other person, we do not see the label (Hindu, Buddhist, Muslim, secular atheist, white, black, etc.) but the image of God. We see someone created by God, addressed by God, accountable to God, loved by God, valued and evaluated by God. So while we affirm the validity of reaching out in mission to all people everywhere, we must also think critically about the *methods, attitudes* and *assumptions* with which we do so. The validity of evangelism *in principle* does not legitimize any and every *method* of evangelism *in practice.* Our understanding of the dignity of all persons made in God's image necessitates careful attention to the ethics of mission. Anything that denies other human beings their dignity or fails to show respect, interest and informed understanding for all that they hold precious is actually a failure of love.

To love your neighbor as yourself is not just the second great commandment in the law; it is an essential implication of our common createdness and is as relevant in mission as in any other walk of life. Not that love means accepting everything your neighbor believes or does. Paul did not accept the religiosity of the Athenians, but he did seek to relate to them with polite respect, even while challenging their assumptions. And as we saw in chapter five, even Paul's pagan detractors acknowledged that he had not "blasphemed our goddess" (Acts 19:37). Likewise Peter, while encouraging Christians to be ready to defend their faith in conversation with unbelievers, urges them to "do this with gentleness and respect, keeping a clear conscience" (1 Pet 3:15-16).

4. *The biblical gospel fits all.* The image of God is not, of course, the only thing we human beings universally have in common. We are also all sinners and rebels against our Creator God, as a result of which God's image in us, while not lost (for it is constitutive of our humanity), is spoiled and distorted. God's mission includes the restoration of people to that true image of God, of which his own Son, Jesus, is the perfect model. This means that just as our sin is a universal reality, which underlies the many cultural forms in which it manifests itself, so also the gospel is a universal remedy that addresses human need in any and all cultures.

This is not in any way to ignore the wonderful variety of ethnicity and culture that so enriches the human race. Nor is it to minimize the myriad ways in which the gospel takes root and is lived out in different cultural contexts. On the contrary, the true richness of the biblical gospel will only be fully seen in all its glory when it shines forth, like the many facets of a diamond, in all the redeemed cultures of the new creation. What this point is affirming is that the Bible reveals God's answer to the human problem—an answer and a problem that are both alike universal, not merely culturally relative.

Whatever the appearances or the caricatures have been, Christian mission is not a matter of inviting or compelling people to become Westerners or Koreans or Nigerians. It is inviting people to become more fully *human* through the transforming power of the gospel that fits all because it answers to the most basic need of all and restores the common glory of what it is to be truly human— a man or woman made in the image of God.

This is why the theological struggle that was fought and resolved in the New Testament was so important: conversion of the Gentiles to Christ did not mean conversion to being *Jews*. No, the Gentiles *as Gentiles* were welcomed into God's people on the same basis as the Jews themselves—repentance and faith in the Messiah, Jesus of Nazareth. From that point of view, the gospel Paul proclaimed to Jews in Pisidian Antioch or to Gentiles in sophisticated pagan Athens was the same: "Here is Jesus: the fulfillment of Israel's hopes, the ultimate judge of all the world; trust in him alone for salvation and forgiveness from the living God." Though rooted in the particularity of the history, faith and culture of Old Testament Israel, the gospel of Christ was the power of God for salvation to *all* who believe, Jew or Gentile.

Created for a task. Humanity was put on the earth with a mission—to rule over, to keep and to care for the rest of creation. This enables us to see ecological concern and action as a valid part of biblical Christian mission. Here we look in a little more depth at the meaning of this mandate God gave us.[2]

God instructed the human species not only to fill the earth (an instruction also given to the other creatures) but also to subdue it and to rule over the rest of the creatures. The words *kābaš* and *rādâ* (Gen 1:28) are strong words, implying both exertion and effort, and the imposing of will upon another. However, they are not, as contemporary ecological mythology likes to caricature, terms that imply violence or abuse. The idea that these words could ever imply violent abuse and exploitation, and the implied accusation that Christianity is therefore an intrinsically eco-hostile religion is relatively recent.[3] By far the dominant interpretation of these words in both Jewish and Christian tradition down through the centuries has been that they entail benevolent care for the rest of creation as entrusted into human custodianship.[4]

On one level, the first term, *kābaš,* authorizes humans to do what every other species on earth does, which is to utilize its environment for life and survival. *All* species in some way or another "subdue the earth," to the varying degrees

---

[2] What follows in the rest of this section is largely drawn from Wright, *Old Testament Ethics,* chap. 4.

[3] The source of this widespread idea that Christianity bears major responsibility for our ecological crisis because of its instrumentalist view of nature, allegedly rooted in Genesis 1:28, goes back to the frequently reproduced and much-quoted article by Lynn White, "The Historical Roots of Our Ecologic Crisis," *Science* 155 (1967): 1203-7, in 1967. It has been answered by many others since, and it has been shown to be based on a misunderstanding of the Hebrew text of Genesis. James Barr, e.g., in 1972, showed that "Man's 'dominion' contains no markedly exploitative aspect; it approximates to the well-known Oriental idea of the Shepherd King. . . . The Jewish-Christian doctrine of creation is therefore much less responsible for the ecological crisis than is suggested by arguments such as those of Lynn White. On the contrary, the biblical foundations of that doctrine would tend in the opposite direction, away from a licence to exploit and towards a duty to respect and to protect." James Barr, "Man and Nature—the Ecological Controversy and the Old Testament," *Bulletin of the John Rylands Library of the University of Manchester* 55 (1972): 22, 30.

[4] For a thorough survey of representative expressions of this view down through Christian history, see James A. Nash, "The Ecological Complaint Against Christianity," in *Loving Nature: Ecological Integrity and Christian Responsibility* (Nashville: Abingdon, 1991), pp. 68-92.

necessary for their own prospering. That is the very nature of life on earth. As applied to humans in this verse, it probably implies no more than the task of agriculture. That humans have developed tools and technology to pursue their own distinctive form of subduing the earth for human benefit is no different in principle from what other species do, though clearly vastly different in degree and impact on the total ecosphere.

The latter word, *rādâ,* is more distinctive. It certainly describes a role and function for human beings that is entrusted to no other species—the function of ruling or exercising dominion. It seems clear that what God is doing here is passing on to human hands a delegated form of God's own kingly authority over the whole of his creation. It is commonly pointed out that kings and emperors in ancient times (and even dictators in modern times) would set up an image of themselves in far-flung corners of their domains to signify their sovereignty over that territory and its people. The image represented the authority of the true king. Similarly God installs the human species as the image, within creation, of the authority that finally belongs to God, Creator and Owner of the earth.

Even apart from that analogy, Genesis describes God's work in regal terms, though without using the word *king.* God's creating work exudes wisdom in planning, power in execution and goodness in completion. Wisdom, power and goodness are the very qualities that Psalm 145 exalts in "my God the King," in relation to all his created works. There is a righteousness and benevolence inherent in God's kingly power that is exercised toward all that he has made. "These are, of course, royal qualities; without using the word, the author of Gen 1 celebrates the Creator as *King,* supreme in all the qualities which belong to the ideal of kingship, just as truly as Psalms 93 and 95-100 celebrate the divine King as Creator."[5]

So the natural assumption, then, is that a creature made in the image of this God will reflect these same qualities in carrying out the mandate of delegated dominion. Whatever way this *human* dominion is to be exercised, it must reflect the character and values of *God's* own kingship. "The 'image' is a kingly pattern, and the kind of rule which God entrusted to human kind is that proper to the ideals of kingship. *The ideals,* not the abuses or failures: not tyranny or arbitrary manipulation and exploitation of subjects, but a rule governed by justice, mercy and true concern for the welfare of all."[6]

---

[5]Robert Murray, *The Cosmic Covenant: Biblical Themes of Justice, Peace and the Integrity of Creation* (London: Sheed & Ward, 1992), p. 98.
[6]Ibid.

So, then, human dominion over the rest of creation is to be an exercise of kingship that reflects God's own kingship. The image of God is not a license for abuse based on arrogant supremacy but a pattern that commits us to humble reflection of the character of God.

> This understanding turns our supremacism upside down, for if we resemble God in that we have dominion, we must be called to be "imitators of God" (Eph 5:1) in the way we exercise it. Indeed, far from giving us a free hand on the earth, the *imago Dei* constrains us. We must be kings, not tyrants; if we become the latter we deny and even destroy the image in us. How then does God exercise dominion? Psalm 145 tells us that God is gracious, compassionate, good, faithful, loving, generous and protective, not to humankind only but to "all he has made." God's characteristic act is to bless, and it is God's constant care that ensures that the cattle, the lions, and even the birds are fed and watered (Ps 104; Mt 6:26).[7]

If this is how God acts; then how much more is it incumbent on us, made in his image and commanded to be like him, to exhibit the same solicitous care for the creation he has entrusted to our rule?

Created in relationship. Genesis 1 sets human male-female complementarity closely alongside the image of God.

> So God created man in his own image,
>> in the image of God he created him;
>> male and female he created them. (Gen 1:27)

The implication from the tight parallelism seems clearly to be that there is something about the wholeness of human gender complementarity and the mutual relationship it enables that reflects something true about the very nature of God. Not that God himself is sexually differentiated but that relationship is part of the very being of God, and therefore also part of the very being of humanity, created in his image. Human sexuality reflects within the created order something that is true about God within his divine, noncreated being.

Genesis 2, on the other hand, sets human gender complementarity in the context of the *human task.* The sudden admission of something that is "not good" in God's evaluation of the creation, which has been repeatedly described as "good" and "very good," is startling. What is not good is that the man (the "earth creature") should be alone (Gen 2:18). But in the immediate context, the problem of this aloneness is not merely that he would therefore be *lonely,* in an emotional

---

[7]Huw Spanner, "Tyrants, Stewards—or Just Kings?" in *Animals on the Agenda: Questions About Animals for Theology and Ethics,* ed. Linzey Andrew and Dorothy Yamamoto (London: SCM Press, 1998), p. 222.

sense. God is addressing not merely a psychological problem but a creational one.

The problem is that God has given an immense task to this creature in Genesis 2:15. He has been put in the Garden "to work it and take care of it." When added to the task specified in the earlier creation account—to fill the earth, subdue it and rule over the rest of the animate creation (Gen 1:28)—the human task seems limitless. A man cannot tackle such a challenge alone. That is "not good." He needs help. So it is significant that the term used to describe the project God now embarks on is not to find a *companion* to stop him feeling lonely but to find a *helper* to stand alongside him in this huge task laid upon him as the servant, keeper, filler, subduer and ruler of creation. The man does not just need *company*. He needs *help*. Male and female are necessary not only for mutual relationship in which they will reflect God (though certainly for that) but also for *mutual help* in carrying out the creation mandate entrusted to humanity.[8]

Humanity, then, is created in relationship, for relationship, and for a task that requires relational cooperation—not only at the basic biological level that only a man and a woman can produce children in order to fill the earth but also at the wider societal level that both men and women have their roles of mutual assistance in the great task of ruling the creation on God's behalf.

God's creative intention for human life, right from the start and projected into the new creation, includes social relationship. Loving horizontal relationships between people, starting with marriage but extending to include all other social relationships, are part of God's desire for human life. And since the Fall devastated that relational dimension of human life, it is part of God's mission to restore healthy social relationships where they are broken through sin.

Accordingly, since social relationships, from the basic sexual bond to wider circles of human community, are included in God's own creative and redemptive action, they fall also within the range of our human mission agenda. This is another plank in the biblical foundation for a holistic theology of mission. Our missional objective is not limited to the vital and urgent evangelistic task of helping *individuals* come to a right relationship with God that will secure their individual eternal destiny. We also share God's passion for healthy human relationships here and now—between individuals, in families, in the workplace, throughout society and between nations.[9]

---

[8] I owe this clarification to the fine discussion in Christopher Ash, *Marriage: Sex in the Service of God* (Leicester, U.K.: Inter-Varsity Press, 2003), esp. chap. 7.

[9] The work of the Relationships Foundation has developed this theme, both conceptually and practically, very strongly. The most thorough presentation of their work is Michael Schluter and John Ashcroft, ed., *Jubilee Manifesto: A Framework, Agenda & Strategy for Christian Social Reform* (Leicester, U.K.: Inter-Varsity Press, 2005).

Humanity in Rebellion

Genesis quickly moves on, however, to show that things did not continue as God intended. Sin entered human life through rebellion and disobedience. And just as our theology of mission must embrace a holistic understanding of creation and humanity, so it must work with a radical and comprehensive understanding of sin and evil. The profound simplicity of the narratives of Genesis 1—11 show us at least three things about sin that must be taken into account in biblical mission.

Sin affects every dimension of the human person. The portrait of the human being that we find in the early chapters of Genesis is of an integral, single person, but with different dimensions of life and relationship. Rather than speaking of a human being having "a body" and "a soul" and whatever other "parts" one may wish to add, it seems preferable to speak adjectivally of the human person as living with a fully integrated combination of different dimensions. At least four aspects of human life are seen in these early accounts. Human beings are *physical* (they are creatures in the created physical world), *spiritual* (they have a unique intimacy of relationship with God), *rational* (they have unique powers of communication, language, addressability, consciousness, memory, emotions and will), and *social* (their gender complementarity reflects the relational dimension of God and underlies all human relationships). All of these dimensions—physical, spiritual, rational and social—are combined in the integrated human person described in Genesis 2:7 as a "living being."[10]

What the following narrative in Genesis 3 goes on to show, however, is that every one of these four dimensions was involved in the entry of sin into human life, and every one of them is also affected by the consequences of that choice. The story of the temptation of Eve and the collusion of Adam involves all aspects of human nature.

- *Spiritually,* Eve was led to doubt the truth and goodness of God, thus undermining the prior relationship of trust and obedience.

- *Mentally,* she contemplated the fruit under discussion: her reflection was *rational* (it was good for food), *aesthetic* (it was pleasing to the eye) and *intellectual* (desirable for gaining wisdom). All of these capacities of the human intellect are good in themselves, commended as highly prized gifts of God. There was nothing wrong with Eve using her mind; the problem was she was now using all its powers in a direction that was forbidden by God. The prob-

---

[10]This fourfold perspective on the dimensions of the whole human person is also adopted as a framework for biblical holistic mission by Jean-Paul Heldt, "Revisiting the 'Whole Gospel': Toward a Biblical Model of Holistic Mission in the 21st Century," *Missiology* 32 (2004): 149-72.

lem lay not in rational reflection but in the disobedience being thereby rationalized.

- *Physically*, "she took some and ate it." These are simple verbs describing
  physical action in the physical world.

- *Socially*, she shared the fruit with Adam, "who was with her," and thus he
  acquiesced in the direction that whole conversation, reflection and action
  was taking. And so the sin that was already spiritual, mental and physical also
  became shared—it entered into the core of human relationship, giving birth
  immediately to mutual shame and subsequently to increasingly malevolent
  progeny.

Having thus gained its entry through every dimension of human personality,
sin goes on to permanently corrupt all these same four dimensions in human
life and experience.

- *Spiritually*, we are alienated from God, fearful of his presence, suspicious of
  his truth, hostile to his love.

- *Rationally*, we use our minds, like the first human couple, to rationalize sin,
  blame others and excuse ourselves. We have become darkened in our thinking.

- *Physically*, we are sentenced to death, as God decreed, and suffer its invasion
  through sickness and decay even in life itself, while our whole physical environment likewise groans in futility under God's curse.

- *Socially*, human life is fractured at every level, with anger, jealousy, violence
  and murder even between brothers in the story of Cain and Abel escalating
  into the horrendous social decay that the rest of the biblical narrative graphically portrays.

Romans 1—2 is Paul's incisive commentary on the universal reign of sin in
human life and society. Reading his searing analysis there, we can see all of the
same four dimensions of human personality involved in human sin and rebellion. There is no part of the human person that is unaffected by sin.

Sin affects human society and history. The individual effects of sin are
glaringly apparent in the Genesis narrative. But the Bible goes on to a much
deeper analysis. There is also what might be called the "prophetic perspective"
on sin. In the Old Testament canon the prophets are not merely those whose
books bear their name, from Isaiah to Malachi, but also include those who wrote
the historical books: the former prophets. These history writers were prophetic
because they observed society and history from God's point of view and sought
to interpret both in the light of God's word and purposes. And from that per-

spective they saw that sin was far more than what went on in the hearts and behavior of individuals.

Sin spreads *horizontally within society* and sin propagates itself *vertically between generations*. It thus generates contexts and connections that are laden with collective sin. Sin becomes endemic, structural and embedded in history. Thus the Old Testament historians observe how whole societies become addicted to chaotic evil (as the book of Judges portrays with its slow crescendo of vile behavior). Isaiah attacks those who legalize injustice by passing laws that give structural legitimacy to oppression

> Woe to those who make unjust laws,
>> to those who issue oppressive decrees,
> to deprive the poor of their rights
>> and withhold justice from the oppressed of my people. (Is 10:1-2)

Jeremiah is shocked to discover that the whole of Jerusalem society is rotten from top to bottom (Jer 5). The historians comment that successive kings of Jerusalem (with very few exceptions, such as Hezekiah and Josiah) emulated and then surpassed the wickedness of their predecessors, so that the wickedness of the people accumulated through the generations until the weight of it became simply intolerable to God.

We need to be careful here, of course. Some people are very reluctant to speak of "structural sin," arguing that only *people* can sin. Sin is a personal choice made by free moral persons. Structures cannot sin in that sense. With that I agree. However, no human being is born into or makes his or her moral choices in the context of a clean sheet. We all live within social frameworks that we did not create. They were there before we arrived and will remain after we are gone, even if individually or as a whole generation we may engineer significant change in them. And those frameworks are the result of other people's choices and actions over time—all of them riddled with sin. So although structures may not sin in the personal sense, structures do embody myriad personal choices, many of them sinful, that we have come to accept within our cultural patterns.

By a "societal dimension" to sin, then, I am not personifying structures of society and accusing them of the same kind of personal sin that a human individual commits. But I do think the Bible allows us to speak of sin-laden or sin-generating structures of human community life. It is not that by living within such structures our sin becomes justifiable or inevitable. We are still responsible persons before God. It does mean that sinful ways of life become normalized, rationalized, rendered plausible and acceptable by reference to the structures and conventions we have created.

By a "historical dimension" to sin I mean that we have to look deeper into the causes of sinful behavior, again, not to justify or excuse it but to understand its roots. If a community happens to be riddled with social ills, violence, corruption, fragmented and dysfunctional families, it will be an inadequate missional response merely to preach individual sin and repentance. Pursuing the question "Why?" in relation to the evils we witness in any given situation will inevitably uncover historical roots, sometimes going back a long way. Sometimes helping people to know and understand the historical roots and causes of their current circumstances is a significant (though obviously not adequate) factor in community restoration.

So if our mission is bringing *good news* into every area of human life, then it calls for some research and analysis as to what exactly constitutes the *bad news,* horizontally in the structures of a given society and vertically in its history. Many factors will be uncovered in the process. But only as they are uncovered can the cleansing, healing and reconciling power of the gospel undo their dismal effects.

Sin affects the whole environment of human life. When human beings chose to rebel against their Creator, their disobedience and Fall affected the whole of their physical environment. This is immediately clear from God's words to Adam: "Cursed is the ground because of you" (Gen 3:17). But in view of the connections between human beings and the rest of creation, it could not have been otherwise. Richard Bauckham expresses the inevitable effects well:

> How does the fall affect nature? Is it only in human history that God's creative work is disrupted, necessitating a redemptive work, whereas in the rest of nature creation continues unaffected by the fall? This cannot be the case, because humanity is part of the interdependent whole of nature, so that disruption in human history must disrupt nature, and since humanity is the dominant species on earth human sin is bound to have very widespread effects on nature as a whole. The fall disturbed humanity's harmonious relationship with nature, alienating us from nature, so that we now experience nature as hostile, and introducing elements of struggle and violence into our relationship with nature (Gn. 3:15, 17-19; 9:2).[11]

I do not enter here into the question of whether the Fall of humanity can be said to be responsible for all the phenomena in nature that are threatening to human life (earthquakes, floods, volcanoes, tsunamis, etc.) or morally disturbing to us (the universal fact of predation, that all life forms prey on other life forms,

---

[11]Richard Bauckham, "First Steps to a Theology of Nature," *Evangelical Quarterly* 58 (1986): 240.

but especially as it occurs among animals capable of feeling pain). There are very complex theological and scientific issues in those questions, which are hotly debated among equally Bible-believing Christians.[12] Whatever one's views on them, however, the Bible unequivocally states that the Fall radically distorted and strained our human relationship with the earth itself and also frustrated creation's primary function in relation to God (cf. Rom 8:20). We live in a cursed earth (since Adam) as well as in a covenanted earth (since Noah). Our mission theology needs to take full account of the radical realism of the former and the limitless hope of the latter.

The apparent simplicity then of the narratives of creation and Fall contain enormous depths of truth about the triangle of relationships between God, humanity and the whole created order. It is clear that the Bible offers us a very radical assessment of the effects of our willful rebellion and Fall into disobedience, self-centeredness and sin.

It is not just that every dimension of the human person is affected by sin. It is not just that every human person is a sinner. It is also the case that the totality of our social and economic relationships with each other, horizontally and historically, and of our ecological relationship to the earth itself have all been perverted and twisted.

Clearly, a fully biblical theology and practice of mission must take account of a fully biblical account of sin. Mission strategies that focus exclusively on individual human wrongdoing and applying the remedy of the gospel solely in that realm cannot, of course, be blamed for lack of biblical zeal in that one evangelistic field. However, they do fall short of a full biblical understanding of all that sin is and does, and inevitably therefore fall short likewise of a full biblical understanding of all that the gospel addresses and all that our mission must engage.

A Paradigm Evil? HIV/AIDS and the Church's Mission

Unquestionably the greatest emergency facing the human family today is the HIV/AIDS virus. It is devastating human life on a scale that can scarcely be grasped. Imagine twenty Boeing 747 airliners crashing to earth every day, killing all passengers. At least that many people (approximately 7,000-8,000) die every day from AIDS-related illness. The great majority of these are in sub-Saharan Africa (home to over 70 percent of all HIV/AIDS cases, deaths and new infections).

Scale is a difficult concept in itself. The world was horrified by the attack on

---

[12]A helpful survey of the range of perspectives on "natural" and "moral" evil is concisely offered by Nigel G. Wright, *A Theology of the Dark Side: Putting the Power of Evil in Its Place* (Carlisle, U.K.: Paternoster, 2003).

the Twin Towers of the World Trade Center in New York on September 11, 2001, in which some three thousand people died. *Africa suffers the equivalent of two 9/11s every day.*

The tsunami in the Indian Ocean in December 2004 carried off some 300,000 people in a single day. *HIV/AIDS inflicts the equivalent of a tsunami on Africa every month.*

Globally it is estimated that at least forty-six million people are infected; there are sixteen thousand new infections daily; twenty million have already died of AIDS; and at least sixty-five million will have died by 2020. And whereas past great pandemics in human history, such as outbreaks of plague and Black Death in Europe, tended to carry off mainly the weakest in society, the very young and very old, HIV/AIDS by contrast is most devastating among the young adult population (so that the surviving young and old suffer even more). It carries off the working, childbearing generation, leaving behind precisely the very young and the very old to cope without those who would normally care for them both. HIV/AIDS is hollowing out whole communities in Africa, throwing grandparents and very young children together in a struggle for survival, and creating vast numbers of the most vulnerable of all people, widows and orphans. A new AIDS orphan is created every fourteen seconds. Perhaps three more since you began reading this paragraph.[13]

I have been moved to reflect on the critical nature of HIV/AIDS in relation to mission by two things. One was an article by Kenneth R. Ross, "The HIV/AIDS Pandemic: What Is at Stake for Christian Mission?" in which he argues passionately that there is a redefining moment for the church and mission in this terrible phenomenon, and the stakes are high.[14] The other was the deeply moving gathering of the Mission Leaders Forum at the Overseas Ministry Study Center, New Haven, Connecticut, in December 2004, at which HIV/AIDS was the main topic and presentations were made by people deeply involved at considerable personal cost at the cutting edge of the problem in Africa and China.

It seems to me that HIV/AIDS sucks into its horrific vortex almost every dimension of evil that we face and that the Bible alerts us to and at the same time calls for every dimension of mission that the Bible portrays. But in using HIV/AIDS in this way as a kind of case study or paradigm of evil, *I want to make it*

---

[13]The statistics quoted here, of course, reflect what was available to me at the time of writing. The situation changes (mostly for the worse) constantly.

[14]Kenneth R. Ross, "The HIV/AIDS Pandemic: What Is at Stake for Christian Mission?" *Missiology* 32 (2004): 337-48. The subtitles of his article are "The Church at Stake—New Frontiers for Faith"; "Gender at Stake—Sexual Power and Politics"; "Mission at Stake—The Need to Practice Presence."

absolutely clear that I am not, unequivocally not, suggesting that HIV/AIDS suf-
ferers themselves embody evil or sin in any way that is not common to the rest of
the human race.

Nor do I accept the idea that HIV/AIDS is the specific judgment of God on
its victims. Even if we acknowledge that sexual promiscuity is a major cause of
infection, and so some people reap what they sow, there are just far too many
people (especially women, children and even the unborn) who have become
infected or affected by the disease through no fault or sin of their own for their
suffering to be regarded in any sense as God's direct judgment on them. Indeed
there are many who have become infected by doing what is pleasing to God—
caring for the sick and tending their wounds, both medical workers and family
caregivers. Many young children are tragically infected as a result of the loving
and intimate care they give to dying parents. Sadly, the opinion that the disease
is a direct judgment of God on the sufferer for their own sins, whether exter-
nally inflicted or internally accepted, is itself an added ingredient in their isolation and suffering.

Dimensions of evil present in the context of HIV/AIDS. It is hard to think
of any dimension of evil that is not present in some form in relation to the terrible scourge of HIV/AIDS. Without attempting comprehensive or profound
analysis, my own reading and listening leads me to list at least the following
points where HIV/AIDS is a ghastly mask of evil and mirrors aspects of the Fall.

- It is mysterious, in origin and causation, like evil itself. Why should there be
  such an organism in God's good creation? Why did it make the jump to humans, apparently in 1934? Why is it so resistant to all the efforts of research
  to overcome it? And, like evil, it combines something that is "natural" or external to us, on one hand, with the human agency by which it gains entry
  and spreads, on the other.

- It invades life and delivers inevitable death. Of course, death, the wages of
  sin, awaits every human being since the Fall, but HIV/AIDS brings the sentence forward into the midst of life and destroys life's blessing, abundance
  and fulfillment—the very things that God created us for.

- It induces prolonged physical suffering, anxiety, pain and decay. "Slim" is its
  name in many parts of Africa, for it leaves its victims wasted, as if the very
  life force had been sucked out of them. It attacks and destroys the immune
  system that God built into our human bodies to resist all kinds of other dis-
  eases, rendering the sufferer defenseless against their onslaught. The Bible
  portrays evil also in this "life-sucking" language.

- It spreads in many ways, but a primary one is through human sexuality—

thus exploiting and corrupting the most intimate relationship God has blessed humanity with. More precisely, it thrives on the fallen male sex drive, the rampant masculine tendency toward promiscuous lust. It has been estimated that male sexual behavior underlies 80 percent of the AIDS epidemic. This includes both heterosexual as well as homosexual behavior, but the former is certainly responsible for a far higher proportion of infections.

- It thrives on the gender imbalance between dominant males and exploited females—something that we learn from Genesis 3 is a result of the Fall. In Southern Africa 60 percent of females have their first sexual experience in a context of coercion, and in 40 percent of cases it is with a man in a superior social, employment or familial position.

- It further preys disproportionately on women. In Africa, women and teenage girls are five to six times more likely to become infected than men, mainly because of their low economic and social status and lack of control over sexual practice.

- It is no respecter of innocence. A very high number of infected women have been faithful to their husbands but suffer from infection he has transmitted to them after promiscuity elsewhere. The reverse happens also, of course. Likewise many babies are found to be HIV positive from infection in the womb.

- It creates widows and orphans at a frightening pace. But cultural and economic practices, combined with religious prejudice and fear, often make the plight of these victims even worse. AIDS widows often have their husband's property seized back by his family, and they lose all inheritance rights. Compassion and justice perish too.

- It destroys the future and removes hope from individuals and communities. Young lives, with high expectations, are suddenly handed an imminent death sentence. Even the uninfected find their own life plans thrown into oblivion by the sudden demands of caring for family members who are diagnosed as infected. Whole villages and towns are left with no workers, teachers, doctors, civil servants or even sufficient parents. Fields cannot be cultivated, so hunger and destitution stalk the countryside.

- It generates massive psychological trauma: fear, denial, panic, guilt, self-hatred, anger, violent revenge, despair. And of course, like all evil, it raises acute spiritual questions as well about the goodness and fairness of God.

- It both causes and exploits poverty. "HIV/AIDS reveals the fracture, stresses and strains in society, exploiting disorder, inequality and poverty. The virus seeks the weak, the poor, and the vulnerable. It destroys more quickly where nutrition is low, where health systems are weak and where governments do not govern effectively."[15]

- It also exposes the inequality in the world between rich and poor nations. If you contract HIV/AIDS in a Western country, the availability of antiretroviral drugs (ARVs) at affordable cost will mean that you can expect to live a relatively normal life for many more years, with not much more (according to one expert) than the dangers and inconvenience of a diabetes sufferer. In most Majority World countries, however, such ARVs as are available are priced beyond the dreams, let alone the means, of most sufferers. The battle to get shamefully reluctant pharmaceutical companies to address this injustice is one of the many tragic sagas of the disease. So there is a justice issue also.

- It induces reactions among others (both outside and within the church) that vary from denial to deceit, from condemnation of the victim to false representation of the ways of God.

- It gets locked into the corruption and pride of politics, where concealment, denial and power struggles over resources, foreign funds and so forth compound the problem and delay its remedy.

- It is "a disease that affects every facet of the human condition on earth—*labor, productivity, procreation, pleasure, faith, education, physical health, mental health*. A disease that crushes the very soul of the most innocent among us, leaving them orphaned, without the bare necessities, psychologically traumatized and potentially left to head a household on their own with an elderly grandmother or wander the streets of Kampala, Lusaka and Johannesburg—*children*. A disease that affects every generation of the population—*the unborn, the infant, the child, the youth, adults, grandparents*."[16]

In confronting such a comprehensively devastating phenomenon, it is surely no exaggeration to say that in HIV/AIDS we are looking into the distorted, devouring and diabolical face of an evil that tears at the very heart of human life on God's earth.

---

[15]Quoted from "Holistic Mission," Lausanne Occasional Paper no. 33, ed. Evvy Hay Cambell, 2004, available at <www.lausanne.org>. This short but powerful statement lists the following aspects of the HIV/AIDS crisis. It is, they say, a biological issue, a behavioral issue, a child and youth issue, a gender issue, a poverty issue, a cultural issue, a *socioeconomic* issue, a justice issue, a deception issue, a compassion issue, a world evangelization issue.

[16]Angela M. Wakhweya, "Look After Orphans and Widows in their Distress: A Public Health Professional's Perspective on Mission in an Era of HIV/AIDS," a paper prepared for the Mission Leadership Forum (New Haven, Conn.: Overseas Ministry Study Center, 2004) (quoted with permission).

Dimensions of mission in response to HIV/AIDS. Such holistic evil demands a holistic response. Thankfully many Christians worldwide, both in governments and in nongovernmental organizations, take this matter very seriously indeed, even though one is saddened to hear of churches that ostracize the infected out of a false assumption of God's judgment on their alleged sin. The Lausanne statement on the matter makes the following crucial point:

> HIV/AIDS is a complex and multifaceted pandemic with a wide variety of interacting causes, sustaining factors and impacts. Therefore this pandemic demands a holistic mission response from the churches. We must make our contribution to fighting this disaster by drawing on a Christian worldview that seamlessly unites the material, psychosocial, social, cultural, political and spiritual aspects of life, a worldview that unites evangelism, discipleship, social action and the pursuit of justice.[17]

Such a holistic missional response to HIV/AIDS, it would seem to me, must include at least the following elements:

- Sheer compassionate care for the sick and dying. No disciple of Jesus should need to be persuaded of this.

- More extensive care for those whose lives are devastated in multiple ways by the effects of the disease in their country, whether personally infected or not: generating employment and caring for widows and orphans (one of the most prominent of all biblical commands, from Exodus to the letter of James).

- Education of the infected, the affected, the churches, pastors, local civic leaders and all who have a chance of influencing attitudes and behaviors—especially women.

- Tackling and condemning cultural and religious practices that make the suffering worse—such as stigmatizing and ostracism, gender prejudice and oppression.

- Engaging in the struggle to find the right balance in allocating resources to prevention of infection, on the one hand, and treatment (through ARVs) of the already infected, on the other. There are medical, political, economic, cultural and justice issues in that debate.

- Offering and providing training for psychological and spiritual counselling and support for people at every stage: from a positive test result to the moment of death and the support of the bereaved.

- Engagement in the economic and political dimensions of the issue, for those whose calling is into the political sphere.

---

[17]Cambell, "Holistic Mission," available at <www.lausanne.org>.

- Sensitive evangelistic witness to the new and eternal life that can be ours in Christ, with the forgiveness of sin, the hope of resurrection, and the certainty that death will not have the final word.

From all that has been argued in this book so far, it should be clear that all of these (and doubtless many other) aspects of our missional response are integral parts of the holistic way in which we seek to embody the mission of God in his decisive conflict with evil. No single approach constitutes an adequate missional response in itself. HIV/AIDS, like the evil it embodies, is just too big for one-line answers. If God created and cares for every dimension of human life, then God's mission is the final eradication of everything that attacks every dimension of human life. And since HIV/AIDS attacks everything, it must be confronted on the broadest possible front. Only a holistic missional approach even begins to address the issue.

The ultimacy of evangelism and the nonultimacy of death. And within that biblical holism the necessity of sensitive evangelism is clear and nonnegotiable. I put it as the final item on the list, decidedly not because it is the last thing we need to do but because it is the ultimate thing, the thing that holds all the other imperative responses together within a truly Christian worldview in which death is *not* the ultimate thing.

The most unavoidable fact about AIDS is that it spells *inevitable death*. That is also its most damning fingerprint of evil, for death is *the* great evil, the last enemy to be destroyed. Of course, death faces us all, but AIDS accelerates the process and hurls our last enemy right up in our face. It raises acutely right here and now all the issues that people tend to postpone in life, simply because life is now to be cut tragically short. What is death? What lies beyond death? Is there hope in the face of death?

So while AIDS raises an exhausting list of temporal issues that must be addressed as part of our commitment to God's compassion and justice—medical, social, psychological, sexual, cultural, political, international—it also raises, for the Christian, the ultimacy of evangelism. For however devastating the effects on people's lives here and now, "there is also an eternity question."[18]

"I preach as though ne'er to preach again, *as a dying man to dying men*," said Richard Baxter. Perhaps no sentence captures better the stark reality of the position in which the church finds itself in the midst of communities devastated by HIV/AIDS. This dread and inexplicable disease will rob a precious human being of their expected span of life and will wrench from them the normal bless-

---

[18]Doug McConnell, in an oral expansion of his written response to Wakhweya, "Look After Orphans and Widows in their Distress."

ings meant to be enjoyed on God's earth, all the blessings of productive work, rearing a family, tilling the earth, contributing to society, caring for the elderly. There is no other word for this than the most terrible life-robbing evil.

But when a person puts their faith and hope in the crucified and risen Savior, nothing can rob them of the new creation life of which Christ is the firstborn and first-fruits. Only the gospel offers the finality of that hope and the certainty of that future. Only the gospel offers and proclaims the promise of a new humanity to those whose present humanity has been shattered and shredded by this virus.

I say "only the gospel" with a double intention. First, because this essential gospel promise of eternal life for all who believe, founded on the cross and resurrection of Christ, is nonnegotiable and cannot be substituted for or sublimated into any of the other responses that we must make to HIV/AIDS, all of which have their own equally nonnegotiable validity and Christian imperative. But second, I say only the *Christian* gospel, as distinct from all other religions and their view of death. For actually, it is the stark fact of death that throws up and defines most clearly the chasmic divide between religions and between the myriad views of what *salvation* might mean.

One of the best pieces of writing on this subject I have ever read comes from the pen of Carl Braaten. Having pointed out the general vagueness that exists in interfaith dialogue when people talk about "salvation" without defining what they mean, or when they define it only in terms of a wide range of possible benefits in this life (which the Bible includes also, of course, in its rich vocabulary of salvation), Braaten turns to the distinctively Christian perspective, drawn from the New Testament and focused on the resurrection.

> On a theological level salvation is not whatever you want to call it, the fulfillment of every need or the compensation for every lack. . . . Salvation in the Bible is a promise that God offers the world on the horizon of our expectation of personal and universal death. The gospel is the power of God unto salvation because it promises to break open the vicious cycle of death. Death is the power that draws every living thing into its circle. . . . We can gain the partial salvation we are willing to pay for, but none of these techniques of salvation can succeed in buying off death.
>
> Salvation in the New Testament is what God has done to death in the resurrection of Jesus. Salvation is what happens to you and me and the whole world in spite of death. . . . The gospel is the announcement that in one person's history death is no longer the eschaton, but was only the second to last thing. It has now become past history. Death lies behind Jesus, qualifying him to lead the procession from death unto new life. Since death is what separates persons from God

in the end, only that power which transcends death can liberate humans for eternal life with God. This is the meaning of salvation in the biblical Christian sense. It is eschatological salvation, because the God who raised Jesus from the dead has overcome death as the final eschaton of life. Our final salvation lies in the eschatological future when our own death will be put behind us. This does not mean that there is no salvation in the present, no realized aspect of salvation. It means that the salvation we enjoy now is like borrowing from the future, living now as though our future could already be practiced in the present, because of our union with the risen Christ through faith and hope.

Theologians who speak of salvation in the non-Christian religions should tell us if it is the same salvation which God has promised the world by raising Jesus from the dead. . . . A Christology that is silent about the resurrection of Jesus from the dead is not worthy of the Christian name and should not be called a christology at all.[19]

And, I might add, a missiology that omits the only ultimate answer to death from its range of responses to those in the grip of death has no claim to a Christian name either.

Wisdom and Culture

So far then in chapter twelve and this one, we have scanned the broadest horizons of the great mission field of God—the earth itself and the human race. We have concluded that if our mission is to be true to God's mission, then it must embrace the wholeness of the earth and engage with the wholeness of human existence and need. We turn now to a section of the biblical canon that is often neglected in books about the biblical foundations for mission (as it often has been in books on biblical theology in general also): the Wisdom Literature. For here we find within the Scriptures of ancient Israel a broad tradition of faith and ethics built on a worldview that employs the wide-angle lens of precisely this whole-creation and whole-humanity perspective.

We will observe, first, how Wisdom thinkers and writers in Israel participated in a very international dialogue, with an openness to discern the wisdom of God in cultures other than their own. In this respect it models the kind of bridging dynamic that is part of the missional task of contextualization. Second, we will observe how Wisdom takes its predominant motivation for its ethic from the creation traditions, rather than the historical redemptive story of Israel—thus again setting up a more universalizing tendency. And finally we will listen to the more

---

[19]Carl E. Braaten, "Who Do We Say That He Is? On the Uniqueness and Universality of Jesus Christ," *Missiology* 8 (1980): 25-27.

questioning, struggling voice of Wisdom, which urges us to be honest about the faith we seek to commend to others, for while we may be sure about many things, there are rough edges and mysteries in our world, and many more questions in life than we have answers for.[20]

An international bridge. "The wise" was the term given to a class of people known across the ancient Near Eastern world. These were people renowned for their knowledge, sought out for their advice and guidance. At a popular level, they seem to have been consulted rather like a Citizen's Advice Bureau. At the more elite level, they served in the courts of kings, functioning as administrators and government advisers. A great deal of literature from such groups survives from across the ancient Near East—especially from Egypt and Mesopotamia. There are manuals of instructions for civil servants, handy tips for success in public life, reflections on life in general, dialogues and poems offering a wide variety of practical moral and prudential advice. So the Wisdom Literature that we find in the Bible (mainly the books of Proverbs, Job and Ecclesiastes, along with some Psalms) is part of a class of literature that is common across a wide spectrum of ancient Near Eastern culture, stretching back at least a thousand years before the Israelites even left Egypt and settled in Canaan.

And the Israelites were well aware of this fact. Indeed, they admired the wisdom of other nations, even in the process of praising their own. So, for example, when the historian records that Solomon's wisdom surpassed that of various named wise men of other countries, it only makes sense as a compliment if the latter were justly renowned for their great wisdom. The point was not to vilify the wisdom of other nations but to acknowledge its great reputation in order to exalt Solomon's as even greater.

> Solomon's wisdom was greater than . . . the wisdom of Egypt. He was wiser than any other man, including Ethan the Ezrahite—wiser than Heman, Calcol and Darda, the sons of Mahol. And his fame spread to all the surrounding nations. (1 Kings 4:30-31)

Other nations that are acknowledged in the Old Testament for their class of wise men (both positively and negatively) include Babylon (Is 44:25; 47:10; Jer 50:35; 51:57; Dan 2:12-13), Edom (Jer 49:7; Obad 8), Tyre (Ezek 28; Zech 9:2), Assyria (Is 10:13), and Persia (Esther 1:13; 6:13). Clearly the two most famous were Egypt and Babylon, and this is also reflected in the extrabiblical wisdom texts that survive from those two locations. From Egypt we have texts containing

---

[20]Lucien Legrand includes a chapter on "Wisdom and Cultures" among other biblical reflections in *The Bible on Culture: Belonging or Dissenting* (Maryknoll, N.Y.: Orbis, 2000), pp. 41-60.

the wisdom of Phah-hotep, Merikare, Amenemhet, Ani, Amenemope and Onksheshonqy. From Babylon come the Counsels of Wisdom, Man and his God, Ludlul, the Dialogue of Pessimism, the Babylonian Theodicy and Ahiqar. These texts can be read in translation.[21] And there are several fine and detailed comparisons of their teaching with Old Testament proverbial literature.[22]

When these comparisons are presented, it is clear that there was a lot of contact between Israel's wisdom thinkers and writers and those of surrounding nations.[23] The Wisdom literature is undoubtedly the most overtly international of all the materials in the Bible. This is so in two ways. On the one hand, it deals with many issues that are common in the wisdom texts of other nations. These include basic social and relational skills within society and especially in the corridors of power; concern for moral order and social stability; success, happiness and peace in personal, family and political life; reflections on the problems of divine justice in the world; the absurdities of life and how to cope with them; the challenge of suffering, especially when seemingly undeserved.

On the other hand, it is remarkably clear that Israel was quite prepared to make use of wisdom materials from those other nations, to evaluate and where necessary edit and purge them in the light of Israel's own faith and then calmly incorporate them into their own sacred Scriptures. The most obvious example is the inclusion of the sayings of Agur and of King Lemuel in the book of Proverbs, about whom we know absolutely nothing except that they were clearly not Israelites. And it is now generally accepted that Proverbs 22:17—24:22 has made extensive use of the Egyptian text, the Wisdom of Amenemope. Tremper Longman III, in his concise commentary on Proverbs, systematically lists a wide range of comparisons and similarities between the familiar wisdom contained in Proverbs 22:17—24:22 and texts found many of the ancient Near Eastern wisdom texts.[24]

As we recognize this very sizeable international commonality, however, we

---

[21]See James B. Pritchard, ed., *Ancient Near Eastern Texts* (Princeton, N.J.: Princeton University Press, 1955); D. Winton Thomas, ed., *Documents from Old Testament Times* (New York: Harper Torchbooks, 1958); Miriam Lichtheim, ed., *Ancient Egyptian Literature,* 3 vols. (Berkeley: University of California Press, 1975, 1976, 1980).

[22]E.g., Roland E. Murphy, *Proverbs* (Nashville: Thomas Nelson, 1998); Tremper Longman III, "Proverbs," in *Zondervan Illustrated Bible Backgrounds Commentary* (Grand Rapids: Zondervan, forthcoming).

[23]Just as there were in other aspects of Israel's life, e.g., in the language of worship. It is clear that Israel's psalms have in some places happily taken over Canaanite poetic meter, imagery and even aspects of their mythology and utilized it all in extolling the unique sovereign and providential power of YHWH. See, e.g., Donald Senior and Carroll Stuhlmueller, *The Biblical Foundations for Mission* (London: SCM Press, 1983), chap. 5.

[24]Longman, "Proverbs."

must be equally clear that the Israelite sages did not simply plagiarize the traditions of other nations. The distinctive faith of Israel, especially in those areas we have explored earlier in this book (their monotheistic assertion of the uniqueness of YHWH as God, and their covenantal affirmation of Israel's relationship with him) came into conflict with many of the underlying worldview assumptions to be found in the wisdom texts of other nations. So many things that are common in the latter are entirely absent from the Old Testament Wisdom literature. Most obviously absent are the many gods and goddesses of the polytheistic worldview of surrounding nations.

But it is not only that gods and idols of other nations are absent. There are warnings against them also. It is very likely that the personification of Lady Wisdom and Lady Folly in Proverbs 1—9 represents, respectively, YHWH himself, the source of all true wisdom, and other gods, who may be very seductive but whose ways lead ultimately to death, which is the end of the road of idolatry. The Wisdom literature, by this metaphorical literary method, is warning Israelites against the danger of idolatry as seriously as the law and the prophets.

Along with this absence of other gods, the very common assumption of the validity of all kinds of magical, divinatory and occult practices is also completely missing in the wisdom of Israel. Things forbidden in Israel's law were not advocated by Israel's sages.[25] Among the side effects of a polytheistic worldview are a potential cynicism about morality (it doesn't really matter what you do, some god will get you in the end) and fatalism about life in general (there's really not much you can do but resign yourself to the fact that some circumstances will always be beyond your control).

Both of these attitudes are aired in Ecclesiastes, but without abandoning a strong controlling monotheism ("the fear of the LORD"), on the one hand, and the conviction that however puzzlingly absurd life can get, the values of wisdom, uprightness and godly faith are still axiomatic, on the other. It is this strong monotheistic ethic that is most positively distinctive about Old Testament Wisdom. Its motto, "the fear of YHWH is the beginning of knowledge/wisdom" (Prov 1:7) is the key. "The beginning" does not mean a starting point one leaves behind but a first principle that governs everything else. So although the Wisdom literature makes no explicit reference to the historical traditions of Israel's redemption and covenant, it is that tradition, embodied in the name of YHWH himself, that under-

---

[25]For a very thorough comparison of the accepted religious practices of the surrounding nations and their exclusion from the worship of YHWH, see Glen A. Taylor, "Supernatural Power Ritual and Divination in Ancient Israelite Society: A Social-Scientific, Poetics and Comparative Analysis of Deuteronomy 18" (Ph.D. diss., University of Gloucestershire, 2005).

lies all the reflection, teaching and wrestling that goes on in these pages.

What missiological implications can be drawn from this dual aspect of the international ethos of Old Testament Wisdom literature? At least four suggest themselves.

Common human concerns. First, clearly Israel shared the same kinds of concerns about life—its meaning and how best to live it—that are common to all human cultures. The questions that Israel's wise men and women reflected on, the answers they came up with, the dilemmas they left without final solution, the advice and guidance they offered, all of these resonate with common human experience everywhere. For that reason some missiologists and crosscultural practitioners suggest that the Wisdom literature provides one of the best bridges for biblical faith to establish meaningful contact and engagement with widely different human cultures around the world.[26]

All human cultures are concerned with issues of family life, marriage, parenthood, friendship, working relationships, communication skills and dangers, integrity in the public arena, the control of anger and violence, the use and misuse of money (or its equivalent), the everyday frustrations of life, the tensions between what is and what we think ought to be, the deeper mysteries of sickness, suffering, and death. And all human cultures have traditional wisdom, oral or written, addressing these questions. Indeed it is usually in its collective proverbial wisdom that a whole culture's subconscious worldview can be discerned. So to engage people's own answers to life's questions and then introduce them to how the Bible handles them can be a friendly, nonthreatening way of gaining people's interest in the wider truth of the biblical revelation.[27]

Welcoming the wisdom of the nations. Second, the wise in Israel found it possible to affirm many values and teachings that they found in noncovenant nations. This is an important counterbalance to the more familiar rejection of the gods and religious practices of other nations that we find in the law and the prophets. Wisdom is remarkably open and affirming.

One reason for this must be the strong creational assumption that Israel made about the whole earth and all humanity. The wisdom of the Creator is to be found in all the earth, and all human beings are made in his image. While there

---

[26]See, e.g., Michael Pocock, "Selected Perspectives on World Religions from Wisdom Literature," in *Christianity and the Religions: A Biblical Theology of World Religions,* ed. E. Rommen and H. A. Netland (Pasadena, Calif.: William Carey Library, 1995), pp. 45-55.

[27]An exploration of how this might look in one particular culture is Mark Pietroni, "Wisdom, Islam and Bangladesh: Can the Wisdom Literature Be Used as a Fruitful Starting Point for Communicating the Christian Faith to Muslims? (Master's diss., All Nations Christian College, 1997).

were unique dimensions to Israel's historical experience of God in revelation and redemption, Israel had no monopoly on all things wise and good and true. Neither, of course, have Christians. Nothing is to be gained from denying, and much missional benefit accrues from affirming, those aspects of any human cultural tradition that are compatible with biblical truth and moral standards.

But another reason for Israel's welcoming into its own storehouse the wealth of the wisdom of the nations may lie in the assumption that this was a subtle dimension of the nations offering their tribute and worship to the glory of YHWH. This is a major theme in Israel's theology of the nations, which we will explore in depth in chapter fourteen. But if one dimension of Israel's expectation was that the wealth and splendor of the nations would ultimately contribute to the glory of YHWH, not to the false gods to whom they currently attributed them, then one can see in this drawing in of the nations' wisdom a foretaste of the ingathering of the nations themselves in eschatological fullness. Just as the *wealth of the nations* will ultimately be brought to the temple and offered to YHWH in worship (a picture from Is 60—66 taken up in Rev 21:24-27 as the kingdoms of this world bring all their achievements, purged and redeemed, into the kingdom of God and his Christ), so *the wisdom of the nations* can be brought into the house of the wisdom of Israel, purged of its polytheism, and made to serve the honor and glory of YHWH alone. This is a vast and wonderfully encouraging prospect when one reflects for a moment on the enormous edifice of human cultural wisdom and imagines it, purged of the marks of sin and fingerprints of satan, enriching the life of all redeemed humanity in the new creation.

Critiquing the wisdom of the nations. Third, Israel's welcoming approach to the wisdom of other nations was far from an uncritical acceptance of whatever they found there. On the contrary, not only did they utterly exclude any hint of the involvement of other gods, they also adjusted sayings they adopted to fit into the theological and moral framework of their own faith. They approached the wisdom of other nations with the religious and moral disinfectant provided by Yahwistic monotheism.

Frank Eakin suggests that Israel may even have been conscious of an obligation to do so. God had given a measure of wisdom to all peoples, but he had uniquely given the Torah to Israel (Ps 147:19-20). He notes that Sirach 24:8-24 portrays YHWH as providing Wisdom with a tent to live in, namely, the law of Moses. So he goes on:

> For wisdom thought, what then was Israel's privilege? Like the traditional covenantal view, Israel's privilege was expressed in her unique possession of Torah. . . . Torah was understood as God's special bestowal of wisdom upon Israel. What then

was Israel's responsibility? Since wisdom had both been disseminated upon all men in creation and been given to Israel in special portion, it was Israel's responsibility to evaluate the wisdom expressed by the nations. The Torah gave her the evaluative criterion for judging both the pagan search for and the pagan acquisition of wisdom.[28]

So while a missional approach to other cultures will seek to affirm whatever it can there, it will also discern the marks of sin, selfishness and idolatry that infect all cultures. Such discernment cannot be predetermined but comes from long engagement and profound understanding, otherwise we may reject too quickly and without sympathetic understanding that which is merely strange or exotic to ourselves. A constant missiological task, which is not a modern one but goes back to the Bible itself, is identifying the criteria that determine the fine lines between cultural relevance and theological syncretism. If Israel sought to do this through the revelation contained in the Torah, how much more is it incumbent on us to make use of the whole Bible in this missional task of cultural discernment and critique?

The wisdom bridge is not in itself redemptive. Fourth, while Wisdom may provide a bridge, it does not in itself contain the saving message of the whole biblical gospel. The Wisdom literature of the Old Testament has a built in self-critique that questions its own adequacy to solve the problems it addresses. This is part of the significance of the inclusion of Job and Ecclesiastes alongside Proverbs.

There are, according to Proverbs, general principles that lead to a good and successful life. But it does not always turn out according to these principles. The realities that stem from Genesis 3 are the stark background for the wrestlings of Job and Ecclesiastes: satanic malice, suffering, frustration, meaningless toil, unpredictable consequences, uncertain futures, the twistedness of life and the final mockery of death. Wisdom by itself cannot answer these questions, but it provides the clue that points to where the answer may be found—in the fear of the Lord God himself.

And the Lord, YHWH, of course, is the God whom Israel knew within their historical experience of election, redemption and covenant. That is where the gospel is to be found, the good news of YHWH's indomitable commitment to bless and to save first a nation for himself and then through them a people drawn from all nations. Wisdom then deals with the world of God's creation—

---

[28]Frank E. Eakin, "Wisdom, Creation and Covenant," *Perspectives in Religious Studies* 4 (1977): 237. Though Eaking does not mention it, the fact that "Torah was understood as God's special bestowal of wisdom upon Israel" is consistent with the affirmations of Deut 4:6-8.

both at the level of its magnificent beauty and order and the consistency of its natural processes and moral principles, *and* at the level of its ambiguities, dilemmas, and screaming absurdities. On the one hand, it is God's world because he made it. On the other hand, it is also a fallen world because we spoiled it. So it is a world that needs saving. And wisdom points us to YHWH, the God who is the only hope of that salvation and indirectly therefore to the story of YHWH's revealing and redeeming acts in which the world's salvation is to be found.[29]

A further clue to this perspective is the canonical location of the Wisdom tradition in connection with Solomon and the climax of the Davidic covenant. The texts in 1 Kings that celebrate God's gift of wisdom to Solomon, to the admiration of the nations round about, also include the building of the temple. And we recall that part of Solomon's prayer of dedication that asks God to bless the foreigners who come to pray to him there. So although the Wisdom literature itself does not mention the exodus, the covenant, the gift of the land or the building of the temple, the historical narrative binds Wisdom into that tradition through its association with Solomon. Any wisdom that is associated with Solomon must be connected with the Solomonic tradition that God should bless the nations in their interaction with Israel.

Missional engagement then may well build a bridge with other cultures through the common international quality of biblical Wisdom, but the bridge in itself is not salvific. Eventually something must cross the bridge. And that can only be the message of the biblical gospel, of the identity of YHWH and the full biblical story of his redemption of the world through Jesus Christ.

A creational ethic. When the enemies of Jeremiah quoted what was probably a common saying as an excuse for getting rid of him, they refer to three distinct professional roles within Israelite society:

"The teaching of the law by the *priest* will not be lost, nor will counsel from the *wise*, nor the word from the *prophets*" (Jer 18:18, emphasis added).

The priests were responsible for handling and teaching the Torah. The prophets were expected to bring the directly relevant word of God into given situations or in answer to specific questions. And the wise men and women had a distinct role yet again. So we find quite distinctive approaches and emphases in the Wisdom literature from those of the law and the prophets. This is not to deny the foundational coherence between all three at the level of Israel's faith convictions and moral worldview. But the differences repay careful observation.

For example, whereas the law is more bluntly prescriptive, wisdom is more

---

[29]This point is very helpfully discussed from both angles in John Goldingay, *Theological Diversity and the Authority of the Old Testament* (Grand Rapids: Eerdmans, 1987), chap. 7.

expansively reflective. Compare the laws against adultery with the warnings against the same thing in Proverbs 5—6. The law commands and prohibits on the basis of divine authority. Wisdom advises, warns and persuades on the basis of experience, prudence and unpleasant consequences. In technical ethical terms, the deontological approach of the law is balanced by the consequentialist approach of wisdom. Or again, whereas the prophets tackle political corruption by direct denunciation of specific kings, wisdom states general principles and expectations of good government and points to pitfalls to be avoided.

But the most marked difference between the law and the prophets on the one hand and wisdom on the other lies in the *motivational appeal* that is characteristic of each. The former appeal predominantly to Israel's *redemptive* history, whereas the latter appeals predominantly to Israel's convictions about *creation.*

The best way to illustrate this difference is to take an issue close to the heart of biblical ethics as a whole—the matter of justice and compassion for the poor and needy. Begin by scanning through the following texts from the law and observe the theological and motivational basis that they give for their exhortations on this matter: Exodus 23:9; Leviticus 19:33-36; 25:39-43; Deuteronomy 15:12-15; 24:14-22.

You will notice, no doubt, that the emphasis in all cases is on the history of what God had done for Israel in redeeming them out of Egypt. In the light of and in response to that great demonstration of divine justice and compassion, Israel should do likewise. Redemptive history thus becomes a very powerful motive for practicing social justice. Ethical principles are concretized around emulating the known history of the actions of YHWH. This is part of what it means to "walk in the way of the LORD."

Now read the following Wisdom texts with the same question in mind: Proverbs 14:31; 17:5; 19:17; 22:2; 29:7, 13; Job 31:13-15.

The emphasis here is entirely on our common humanity, common because we all share the one Maker, God. So rich or poor, slave or free, oppressed or oppressor, we are all alike the work of God's hands. What we do to a fellow human being, therefore, we do to his or her Maker, a profound ethical principle that Jesus reconfigured in relation to himself.

What is also clearly absent from these Wisdom texts is any explicit reference to the great historical traditions of Israel's faith (exodus, Sinai, land), such as the prophets often appeal to. It cannot have been because the wise men and women of Israel did not *know* those traditions. They could hardly have lived in Israel and not known them! And of course the prominent use of the covenantal divine name YHWH would imply the story in which that name and character had been revealed. Nevertheless it is a striking fact that while the law and the prophets are so solidly founded on the core history of Israel, the Wisdom literature draws its theology and ethics from a more universal, creation-based moral order.[30]

This too has its missiological implications. In approaching people of other cultures, faiths and worldviews, we nevertheless share a common humanity and (whether they acknowledge the fact or not) a common Creator God. Particularly where our missional engagement operates at a cultural and societal level, addressing issues of ethical, social, economic and political concern, we should not be surprised to find areas of common ground and common cause with people who would not identify with the biblical story of redemption. It is to that story that we hope ultimately to bring them (remembering what I referred to earlier as the "ultimacy of evangelism"), but it need not be the starting point of our engagement with them.

The biblical wisdom tradition shows us that there is a certain universality about biblical ethics simply because we live among people made in the image of God, we inhabit the earth of God's creation, and however distorted these truths become in fallen human cultures, they will yet find an echo in human hearts.[31]

An honest faith. The most challenging difference between Wisdom and the rest of the Old Testament tradition arises when some voices within the former express doubts about or question the universal applicability of some of the mainline affirmations in other parts of the Old Testament. And yet this may be precisely part of the purpose of the presence of this material in the canon of Scripture—to compel us toward an honest faith that is willing to acknowledge the existence of doubts we cannot entirely dismiss and questions we cannot satisfactorily answer within the limits of our experience or even the limits of the revelation God has chosen to give us.

One typical problematic area is the tension between, on the one hand, affirmations (such as abound in Deuteronomy and Psalms) that obedience to God is the road to blessing and success in every area of life whereas the wicked will suffer his anger and punishment, and, on the other hand, the simple observation

---

[30]This is perhaps a more substantial reason for the reticence of the Wisdom writers to invoke the covenantal tradition than the one suggested by Brueggemann, which is that the hiddenness of God in the affairs of everyday life left them with only very modest claims to make about YHWH in contrast with the massive certainties of all the "active verbs" of the great historical tradition. Walter Brueggemann, *Theology of the Old Testament: Testimony, Dispute, Advocacy* (Minneapolis: Fortress Press, 1997), p. 335.

[31]The crosscultural missional significance of this aspect of Old Testament creation faith, as reflected in Wisdom, is used as the basis for some interesting analysis of intercultural ethics by Benno Van Den Toren, "God's Purpose for Creation as the Key to Understanding the Universality and Cultural Variety of Christian Ethics," *Missiology* 30 (2002): 215-33.

that this is often not true in our experience. We may warm to the words of Psalm 146, but things suddenly feel very different when we read Job 24:1-12—in which we see a scorchingly truthful depiction of the real world—and come to verse 12: "But God charges no one with wrongdoing." We then echo the baffled question of the opening verse: "Why does the Almighty not set times for judgment? / Why must those who know him look in vain for such days?" Likewise, we may approve the binary moral logic of Deuteronomy 30:15-20, but do we not also echo the honesty of Ecclesiastes 8:14—9:4 in its complaint about the moral inversion that subverts it?

It is hard to avoid the impression that sometimes the sages of Israel held up core Israelite beliefs ("YHWH loves the weak and the poor"; "the righteous will be blessed and live, while the wicked will be punished and die") and then throw out the challenge "How can this belief be squared with the real world we live in? Life often simply doesn't follow these rules."

And the sages are not the only ones to do this. The language of complaint, protest and baffled questioning is also prominent in the psalms—right at the heart of Israel's worship of YHWH. "How long, O LORD?" (e.g., Ps 6:3; 13:1-2; 62:3; 74:10); "Why . . . ?" (e.g., Ps 10:1; 22:1; 43:2; 44:23-24; 88:14); "Where . . . ?" (e.g., Ps 42:3; 79:10; 89:49).

Walter Brueggemann labels this whole strand of material in the Old Testament "Israel's Counter Testimony," that is, the cross-examination within the Old Testament itself of "Israel's core testimony," their foundational beliefs about God's sovereignty and faithfulness. It is part of the strength and convincing power of the biblical case that it contains *within itself* precisely this degree of internal debate and wrestling with the core affirmations of a worldview that was explicitly founded on God's revelation and redemption.

Furthermore, as Brueggemann adds, this was not merely an internal debate. For among the things Israel knew about itself, as we have repeatedly explored in this book, was that it held its own faith *in trust for the world*. Israel's very existence was for the sake of the nations. Israel's God was God of all the earth. Whatever was true for Israel was true for all. Whatever Israel struggled with would be a problem for all. There is then an implicit missiological dimension to this ruthless honesty in Israel's testimony.

> The core testimony of Israel . . . made a case that Yahweh is competently sovereign and utterly faithful. And on most days that conclusion is adequate. It is a welcome conclusion because it issues in a coherent narrative account of reality. Israel, to be sure, affirms that conclusion of a competent sovereignty and reliable fidelity. But Israel lives in the real world and notices what is going on around it. Israel is candid, refusing to deny what it notices. And so issues of competent sovereignty and reli-

able fidelity will remain in the Old Testament as Israel's belief-ful, candid, unfinished business. We know, moreover, that these two issues are paramount for all those who live in the world, whether they engage in God-talk or not. Thus these two points of cross-examination are not a safe intramural exercise for Israel. They are rather issues with which Israel struggles for the sake of the world.[32]

For the sake of the world, then, we must take this tone of voice in the Wisdom literature seriously, with its awkward questions, its probing observations, its acceptance of the limitations of our finitude. It is part of our missional responsibility to do so. The presence of such texts in our Bible is a challenge to unthinking dogmatism that misapplies undoubted biblical principles in circumstances where they are not relevant (as did the friends of Job). Such biblical texts are also a rebuke to simplistic naivety that draws automatic and reversible direct lines between faith and material rewards or between sin and sickness. Mission that ignores the warnings of Wisdom ends up in the folly and lies of the so-called prosperity gospel, on the one hand, or in the problem-denying triumphalism of the worst kinds of arrogant fundamentalism on the other.

The fact is that the world poses some very hard questions for those who, in line with the whole Bible testimony, believe in one, good, personal, sovereign God. Wisdom provides a license to think, to wrestle, to struggle, to protest and to argue. All it asks is that we do so with the undergirding faith and humble commitment encapsulated in its own core testimony that "the fear of the LORD— that is wisdom, / and to shun evil is understanding" (Job 28:28).

It has been a broad vista indeed that we have surveyed together in this chapter and the last one. But then what else should we expect if we inquire about the arena of the mission of God? For he is the God of all the earth, the God of all who live on the earth, and the God of all wisdom. So we have explored some of the implications of those universal truths.

The whole of creation is God's mission field, and as a result there is an inescapable ecological dimension to the mission to which we are called.

All human beings are made in God's image, and as a result there are many implications for our mission arising from the common humanity that we share with all other inhabitants of our planet. And yet all people are also radically and comprehensively infected and affected by sin and evil. Our missional response must be as radical and comprehensive as the problem we address in the name of Christ and the power of the cross.

All human culture manifests the ambiguity of our humanness. The sages of

---

[32]Brueggemann, *Theology of the Old Testament,* p. 324. See also Walter Brueggemann, "A New Creation—After the Sigh," *Currents in Theology and Mission* 11 (1984): 83-100.

Israel acknowledged that which is good and true in the wisdom of other nations, but also evaluated it according to the revelation of God and rejected all that was idolatrous and morally inadequate. They also acknowledged the limitations of all human wisdom in grappling with the toughest questions and battles of life in this fallen world.

Such biblical wisdom calls loudly to us that our mission endeavor should be marked by

- critical openness to God's world
- respect for God's image in humanity
- humility before him and modesty in the claims and answers we offer to others

14

God and the Nations
in Old Testament Vision

The nations of humanity preoccupy the biblical narrative from beginning to end. When they are not in the foreground, they are there in the background. When they are not the subject of great international events, they are the object of divine inspection or accusation. When they are not the direct focus of God's attention, they remain the surrounding context (for good or ill) of the life of God's people. The obvious reason for this is that the Bible is, of course, preoccupied with the relationship between God and humanity, and humanity exists in nations. And where the Bible focuses especially on the people of God, that people necessarily lives in history in the midst of the nations. "It is clear that 'Israel as a light to the nations' is no peripheral theme within the canonical process. The nations are the matrix of Israel's life, the raison d'être of her very existence."[1]

The nations first appear in the biblical grand narrative in the context of life after the flood—God's catastrophic judgment on human wickedness. By Genesis 11 the nations have been scattered in confusion. The conflict of nations mirrors the brokenness of humanity as a whole. With undoubtedly deliberate intent, the final book of the Bible comes to its climax with the picture of the nations purged of all sin, walking in the light of God, bringing their wealth and splendor into the city of God, contributing their redeemed glory and honor to the glory and honor of the Lamb of God (Rev 21:24-27). The brokenness of hu-

---

[1] Duane L. Christensen, "Nations," in *Anchor Bible Dictionary*, ed. David Noel Freedman et al. (New York: Doubleday, 1992), 4:1037.

manity is healed at the river and tree of life (Rev 22:1-2). And between these two great scenes in Genesis and Revelation—the primal and the ultimate state of the nations—the Bible records the story of how such cosmic transformation will have been accomplished. It is, in short, the mission of God as we have been seeking to elucidate in the preceding chapters. God's mission is what fills the gap between the scattering of the nations in Genesis 11 and the healing of the nations in Revelation 22. It is God's mission in relation to the nations, arguably more than any other single theme, that provides the key that unlocks the biblical grand narrative.

In these final two chapters (14-15) we will survey that great sweep of biblical teaching and expectation, since it lies at the heart of a fully biblical understanding of mission. We will note how the nations were portrayed in the Old Testament as witness of all that God was doing in, for or to Israel. Then we will observe that the expectation of Israel's faith and worship (if not always the outcome of their practice) was that the nations would come to benefit from that history of salvation and give thanks for it. This means that the nations would eventually acknowledge and worship Israel's God, YHWH, with all the concomitant responsibilities and blessings of such worship. More remarkably yet, there were voices and visions within the Old Testament that looked for the day when nations would be included within Israel in such a way that the very word *Israel* would be radically extended and redefined. All of this constituted the horizon of mission to the nations in the New Testament and provided the strong scriptural justification for such mission for those who engaged in it.[2]

Before embarking on the survey just outlined, however, we need to begin by rehearsing some of the basic affirmations that the Old Testament makes about the nations in general in relation to God's creative intention and God's governance of history. For this is the platform or stage on which the historical outworking of God's redemptive mission to the nations takes place.

The Nations in Creation and Providence

Nations are part of created and redeemed humanity. Although we first meet the nations in the context of the fallenness and arrogance of humanity even after the flood, the Bible does not imply that ethnic or national diversity is in itself sinful or the product of the Fall—even if the deleterious effects of strife

---

[2]A helpful survey of some of the themes we will touch on here is provided in Walter Vogels, "The New Universal Covenant," in *God's Universal Covenant: A Biblical Study,* 2nd ed. (Ottawa: University of Ottawa Press, 1986), pp. 111-42.

among nations certainly are.[3] Rather, nations are simply "there" as a given part of the human race as God created it to be. God's rule over the nations, amply affirmed throughout the Old Testament, is simply a function of the fact that he created them in the first place. Speaking as a Jew to Gentiles in an evangelistic context, Paul takes for granted the diversity of nations within the unity of humanity and attributes it to the Creator and to his world-governing providence. "From one man he made every nation of men, that they should inhabit the whole earth; and he determined the times set for them and the exact places where they should live" (Acts 17:26).

Although Paul goes on to quote from Greek writers, his language in this verse is drawn from the Old Testament, from the ancient song of Moses in Deuteronomy 32:

> When the Most High gave the nations their inheritance,
> > when he divided all mankind,
> he set up boundaries for the peoples. (Deut 32:8)

National distinctives, then, are part of the kaleidoscopic diversity of creation at the human level, analogous to the wonderful prodigality of biodiversity at every other level of God's creation.

Furthermore, the eschatological vision of redeemed humanity in the new creation points to the same truth. The inhabitants of the new creation are not portrayed as a homogenized mass or as a single global culture. Rather they will display the continuing glorious diversity of the human race through history: People of every tribe and language and people and nation will bring their wealth and their praises into the city of God (Rev 7:9; 21:24-26). The image we might prefer for the Bible's portrait of the nations is not a melting pot (in which all differences are blended together into a single alloy) but a salad bowl (in which all ingredients preserve their distinctive color, texture and taste). The new creation will preserve the rich diversity of the original creation, but purged of the sin-laden effects of the Fall. Or, the mission of God is not merely the salvation of innumerable souls but specifically the healing of the nations.

The creational given of ethnic diversity and the eschatological vision of all races, languages and cultures being included in redeemed humanity both speak

---

[3]I are using the term *nations* here in a broad sense, as it is used in the Old Testament, not in the more restricted sense of "nation state" that developed in post-Reformation Europe. For a good discussion of ancient Near Eastern and biblical concepts of nationhood in relation to ethnicity, territory, language, kingship and gods, see Daniel I. Block, "Nations/Nationality," in *New International Dictionary of Old Testament Theology and Exegesis,* ed. Willem A. Van-Gemeren (Carlisle, U.K.: Paternoster, 1996), 4:966-72; and Daniel I. Block, *The Gods of the Nations: Studies in Ancient Near Eastern National Theology,* 2nd ed. (Grand Rapids: Baker Academic, 2001).

volumes to the sin and scandal of racism. This is not an issue we can pursue here, but it is certainly a vital task of mission to challenge this particular dimension of our fallenness, for it is clear in the New Testament that the gospel radically undermines any racial or racist assumptions in relation to our standing before God.[4]

All nations stand under God's judgment. For those of us who have absorbed a predominantly individualistic way of thinking about life, faith and our relationship with God, one of the more difficult biblical concepts to get our minds around is the idea that God can and does deal with nations as wholes. Yet the Bible unquestionably affirms it, and not only affirms it but illustrates it in graphic detail over long stretches of history. From the book of Exodus onward, nations play their part in the biblical narrative, and the opening story becomes somewhat paradigmatic. The battle between YHWH and the Pharaoh is not just between God and one recalcitrant individual; the whole nation of Egypt is implicated in the sin of oppression and suffers in the process of God's liberating justice.

The narrative goes on to show how successive nations either set themselves against YHWH and his people out of their own malicious initiative (e.g., the Amalekites, Moabites, Amorites) or have become so incorrigibly wicked that they are to be destroyed in the execution of God's punishment (the Canaanite nations). Thus, while Israel is warned against arrogantly imagining that their victory over the Canaanites will be on account of their own righteousness, God confirms that it *will* be on account of the wickedness of those nations (Deut 9:4-6). God intended to use Israel as the agent of his historical judgment on the wickedness of Canaanite nations.

On this point I find Walter Brueggemann's otherwise excellent treatment of the theme of the nations in the Old Testament very inadequate. He regards the texts that speak of YHWH's judgment on the Canaanites as "a violent insistence that the nations do not count when Yahweh gives gifts to Israel." He speaks of "Israel's preferentiality," of "an exceedingly harsh presentation of the nations in the interests of Israel," which is "ideological," because "the sovereignty of Yahweh is drawn most blatantly and directly into the service of Israel's political agenda. . . . [The destruction of the nations] serves negatively to establish the legitimacy of Israel's claim to the land."[5]

---

[4]A fine, thorough biblical study of the issue is provided by J. Daniel Hays, *From Every People and Nation: A Biblical Theology of Race*, New Studies in Biblical Theology (Leicester, U.K.: Inter-Varsity Press; Downers Grove, Ill.: InterVarsity Press, 2003). An equally perceptive but more practically applied analysis is Dewi Hughes, *Castrating Culture: A Christian Perspective on Ethnic Identity from the Margins* (Carlisle, U.K.: Paternoster, 2001).

[5]Walter Brueggemann, *Theology of the Old Testament: Testimony, Dispute, Advocacy* (Minneapolis: Fortress Press, 1997), pp. 496-97.

But Deuteronomy 9 makes precisely the opposite case: Israel has no legitimate claim to the land at all. She has no greater righteousness than the nations. Indeed, the chapter stresses that if anybody deserved to be destroyed, it was Israel. Israel still existed only by God's forgiving grace. No, the destruction of the Canaanite nations is repeatedly portrayed not in ideological self-serving terms but in moral and theocentric terms. YHWH is acting in his divine justice against the signal and excessive wickedness of these nations. And he will do precisely the same to Israel if they follow the ways of the Canaanites. Far from being ideological and self-serving, these texts actually stand as an explicit counterargument to such assumptions, and are framed as severe warnings that Israel, like all other nations, must recognize their own wickedness that had already aroused the wrath of God and mend their ways before him.

The prophets in their oracles against the nations (though they do have remarkable words of hope and potential restoration) express the overwhelming conviction that the nations in general stand under the imminent judgment of God for a variety of reasons, which are mainly ethical. Isaiah portrays the grim reality in the searing words near the beginning of his so-called "little apocalypse":

> The earth is defiled by its people;
>   they have disobeyed the laws,
> violated the statutes,
>   and broken the everlasting covenant.
> Therefore a curse consumes the earth;
>   its people must bear their guilt.
> Therefore earth's inhabitants are burned up,
>   and very few are left. (Is 24:5-6)

Universal human wickedness faces universal divine judgment. It is abundantly clear throughout the Bible that this is the default position that the human race is in, for nations as much as for individuals. As the story of the exodus is paradigmatic of YHWH acting in salvation, so the story of Sodom and Gomorrah is paradigmatic of God acting in judgment on human wickedness. It seems very likely that Paul endorses this broad tradition, painted in the colours and language of the Sodom episode, in his portrayal of universal human corruption and liability to the wrath of God.[6]

Against such a bleak background, God's mission to bless the nations and the mission of God's people as the vehicle of such blessing constitute very good news indeed.

---

[6]Philip E. Esler, "The Sodom Tradition in Romans 1:18-32," *Biblical Theology Bulletin* 34 (2004): 4-16.

Any nation can be the agent of God's judgment. In the case of Sodom and Gomorrah, God delivered his judgment unmediated. That is why the narrative acquires such proverbial force as a symbol of the naked wrath of God, which reaches its biblical climax, of course, in the book of Revelation. However, in the more normal course of history, God uses one nation or another as the instrument of his sovereign justice. The classic first instance of this in the Bible is the way the conquest of the Canaanites by the tribes of Israel is repeatedly interpreted as the outworking of YHWH's judgment on a society whose "iniquity was full" (a condition they had not yet reached when God predicted it to Abraham in Gen 15:16). The Israelites were severely warned not to interpret their victory over the nations of Canaan as attributable in any way to their own righteousness. But they could certainly infer correctly that it was on account of the nations' wickedness (Deut 9:4-6). In this instance God was using the Israelites as the agent of his judgment on the Canaanites.

The lesson Israel had to learn from this signal part of their own history, however, was far from comforting. The fact was that if God could use Israel as the agent of his judgment on wicked nations, he could readily apply the same principle in reverse to Israel itself. In short, if they adopted the wicked ways of the nations they had driven out, they would suffer the same fate at the hands of other nations. YHWH could use Israel as the agent of judgment on other nations; he could equally use other nations as the agent of judgment on Israel. Warnings to this effect abound in the Torah (e.g., Lev 18:24-28; 26:17; 25, 32-33; Deut 4:25-27; 28:25, 49-52; 29:25-28).

In the long history of Israel in the Old Testament period, it is the latter direction of God's judgment that predominates. Judges 2 describes the pattern set in the early generations after the settlement of the tribes of Israel in the land of Canaan. Time and again YHWH brought other nations as the tools of his anger against Israel's rebellion and apostasy (e.g., Amos 6:14; Hosea 10:10; Is 7:18; 9:11). In the later centuries of the monarchy even the great empires of the world were seen by the prophets as no more than a stick in the hand of YHWH, a rod to punish Israel.

> Woe to the Assyrian, the rod of my anger,
>> in whose hand is the club of my wrath!
> I send him against a godless nation,
>> I dispatch him against a people who anger me [i.e., Israel]. (Is 10:5-6)

Then Babylon becomes God's agent of judgment, not only on Israel but on other smaller states who are urged by Jeremiah to recognize the sovereignty of YHWH, God of Israel, and submit to "his servant" Nebuchadnezzar (Jer 25:9; 27:1-

11). Indeed, the principle that God can use any nation as his agent of judgment on any other nation applies not only to dealings with Israel. God's judgment on Egypt also will be carried out through Nebuchadnezzar, according to Ezekiel 30:10-11. Later, of course, Babylon itself falls under the prophetic word of judgment. Even though God had used it to punish Israel, its excesses put Babylon in turn into the blast path of God's wrath, which will be delivered this time through king Cyrus of the Medes and Persians (Is 13:17-19; 47:6-7).

So the overwhelming message is consistent. All nations are in the hands of YHWH, the living God. Their victories too are not to be attributed to their own gods but rather to the sovereignty of YHWH. And sometimes God may use a nation, any nation, as the agent of historical justice in the arena of international affairs. That in itself does not make the nation so used any more righteous than another (as Israel were categorically told). All it means is that God remains sovereign.

Any nation can be the recipient of God's mercy. The same universality by which all nations stand under the judgment of God for their wickedness and idolatry is also deployed in Old Testament thinking about the mercy of God. "I will have mercy on whom I will have mercy, and I will have compassion on whom I will have compassion," said YHWH, in the course of his remarkable self-revelation to Moses, and in definition of his goodness and his name (Ex 33:19; cf. 34:6-7). This is a principle that operated not only in or on behalf of Israel. Any nation could benefit from it.

The clearest articulation of this impartiality in God's dealings with the nations is given by Jeremiah, after visiting a potter at work. The lesson that Jeremiah draws from his observation of a potter who declared an initial intention but then changed his plans, and therefore the end result because of some "response" in the clay, is that God likewise responds to human response to his declared intentions. The focal point of the potter metaphor in Jeremiah 18 is not so much on the unquestionable sovereignty of the divine potter but on the potential that resides in the clay to cause the potter to change his intention. And that provides an opportunity that God extends, by way of general principle, to any nation at any time. If a nation repents in the face of God's declaration of impending judgment, they will be spared that doom. On the other hand, if a nation does evil in spite of God's declaration of blessing, then they will suffer his judgment (Jer 18:7-10). This point is established as general principle of God's dealings with all nations before it is applied in urgent specificity to Judah.

The book of Jonah could have been written as a case study of Jeremiah 18:7-8. Jonah proclaims the impending doom of Nineveh. From king to beggar, the city repents. So God also "repents" and withholds his judgment. But the amazing twist of the book is that this signal demonstration of the mercy of YHWH as God in dealing with a foreign nation is an embarrassment to Jonah. Jonah knew the exodus character of YHWH perfectly well and quotes the key proof text (Jon 4:1-2; cf. Ex 34:6-7). But what should have been a matter of praise, or even merely grudging admiration (that YHWH should turn out to treat the other nations with the same amazing mercy that he lavished on Israel), becomes a matter of bitter complaint in the mouth of Jonah.

The book of Jonah has always featured in biblical studies of mission, sometimes as almost the only part of the Old Testament deemed to be of any relevance. Here at least is someone who has some semblance of being an actual missionary, sent to another country to preach the word of God. However, for all the fascination of the character and adventures of Jonah, the real missional challenge of the book undoubtedly and intentionally lies in its portrayal of God. If Jonah is intended to represent Israel, as seems likely, then the book issues a strong challenge to Israel regarding *their* attitude to the nations (even enemy nations that prophets placed under God's declared judgment), and regarding their understanding of *God's* attitude to the nations. The concluding open-ended question of the book is an enduring, haunting rebuke to our tendency to foist our own ethnocentric prejudices on to the Almighty.[7]

It is interesting to compare and contrast the response of Jonah to the word of divine judgment on a pagan nation with that of Abraham. Commissioned to proclaim Nineveh's doom, Jonah ran away and jumped in a boat, alleging later that he had done so precisely because he suspected that YHWH would revert to type and show compassion. Informed of God's intention to investigate the outcry from Sodom and Gomorrah, Abraham jumps to intercession and finds YHWH prepared to be even more merciful than he initially bargained for.

Nathan MacDonald finds a thread running through texts such as Genesis 18, Exodus 32—34, Psalm 103:6-10 and Ezekiel 18. "The Judge of all the earth," who will unquestionably do what is right, is also the "gracious and compassionate God" who "takes no pleasure in the death of the wicked but rather that they turn from their ways and live." The character of YHWH is exercised in forgiveness and mercy, extended to all nations, not just to Israel.[8]

Jeremiah himself later held out to the nations around Judah the same offer

---

[7]A fine and perceptive recent missiological reading of Jonah is offered by Howard Peskett and Vinoth Ramachandra, *The Message of Mission,* The Bible Speaks Today (Leicester, U.K.: InterVarsity Press; Downers Grove, Ill.: InterVarsity Press, 2003).

[8]Nathan MacDonald, "Listening to Abraham—Listening to YHWH: Divine Justice and Mercy in Genesis 18:16-33," *Catholic Biblical Quarterly* 66 (2004): 25-43. MacDonald suggests that part of the point of the encounter between God and Abraham in Genesis 18 is to teach the nature of true prophetic intercession and the forgiving nature of God on which it is based. See also the discussion of this passage in chap. 11 (pp. 358-69).

of divine forgiveness and restoration, if only they would turn and learn the ways of YHWH and his people (Jer 12:14-17). It was the same offer, in virtually the same language, as Jeremiah held out to Judah—and probably with as little hope of it being accepted. The point is, however, that there is no favoritism in God's dealings with Israel and the nations. All stand under YHWH's judgment. All can turn to YHWH and find his mercy.

This surely has to be one of the most foundational elements of the Old Testament contribution to our theology of mission.

- *If it were not the case that all nations stand under the impending judgment of God, there would be no need to proclaim the gospel.*

- *But if it were not for the fact that God deals in mercy and forgiveness with all who repent, there would be no gospel to proclaim.*

All nations' histories are under God's control. In previous chapters I have stressed the uniqueness of Israel's relationship with YHWH. Their understanding of election, redemption, covenant and holiness set them apart from the nations at a fundamental level. God had chosen and called Israel and no other nation (Deut 7: 7-11; Amos 3:2). God had redeemed Israel in a way he had done for no other nation (Deut 4:32-39). God had revealed his law to and entered into covenant relationship with Israel and no other nation (Ps 147:19-20). And this nation was called to embody and demonstrate all this uniqueness in practical, ethical distinctiveness from all other nations (Lev 18:1-5). In all these respects the relationship between God and historical Israel of the Old Testament period was unprecedented (he had done nothing like this before) and unparalleled (he had done nothing like this anywhere else).

Furthermore, we have explored the missiological implications of these great unique claims. All of them flow from God's own mission and Israel's identity and role within that mission. God's mission is to bless all the nations of the earth. But for that universal aim he chose the very particular means—the people of Israel. Their uniqueness was for the sake of God's universality. Thus, their unique standing as God's *chosen* people was in order that the rest of the nations would come to be *blessed* through Abraham. Their unique story of *redemption* was the paradigm of what God would ultimately accomplish (through Christ) for the deliverance of all from bondage. Their unique stewardship of God's *revelation* was so that ultimately the law of God could go forth from them to the nations and the ends of the earth. And their unique structure of social, economic and political *ethics* was designed to show what a redeemed community of humanity should (and eventually will) look like under the reign of God.

All these dimensions of Israel's Old Testament uniqueness, then, are central to our biblical understanding of mission, and all of them have their counterparts in the New Testament teaching regarding the uniqueness of Christ and the identity and mission of the church.

However, it would be quite wrong to construe these affirmations of *Israel's* uniqueness as tantamount to an absence of involvement by YHWH in the affairs of *other* nations. On the contrary, it was part of the bold claim of Israel that YHWH, their God, was the supreme mover on the stage of international history. All the nations and their kings, wittingly or unwittingly, wove their stories under the master plan of Israel's God—not their own gods.

This makes the claim to uniqueness actually even more stark. It was not the case that Israel merely claimed that YHWH had uniquely chosen, saved and covenanted with them while remaining ignorant of or indifferent to all the other nations. That in itself would not really have been much different in principle from the way all nations see their own gods as uniquely interested in the nations that worship them. That is what gods are for in the polytheistic worldview. Let each nation have its own god or gods, and let that god look to its own interests and those of its own people.

"Uniqueness" in that reduced, generic, sense is not what Old Testament Israel claimed for YHWH. It was a much more exalted and universal claim—a claim that would be the grossest arrogance if not true. The claim was that YHWH was in fact the sovereign God of all the earth, ruling the histories and destinies of all nations. And in *that* context of universal involvement with *all nations*, YHWH had a unique relationship *with Israel.*[9]

Sometimes this affirmation that YHWH was sovereign over the history of other nations is made in quite unremarkable, almost parenthetical ways. Sometimes it is made in order to draw out implications that were decidedly shocking and unwelcome.

An example of the former comes in the warnings given to Israel in the wilderness not to attempt to take any land from Edom, Moab or Ammon on the grounds that YHWH had already given them their lands after driving out previous inhabitants—in precisely the same way that he was about to do for Israel in relation to Canaan (Deut 2:2-23). The way these affirmations are made, almost in passing, should not obscure their theological significance.

When Deuteronomy's prominent land theology in relation to Israel's possession of Canaan is taken into account, this direct statement that Yahweh had given other

---

[9]For a very informative survey of how the ancient Near Eastern nations viewed their gods and the relationships between gods and nations, and the distinctiveness of some of the claims that Israel made in relation to YHWH, see Block, *Gods of the Nations.*

lands to other peoples, supported by the parenthetical notes that follow, is quite remarkable. Three times this passage says that Yahweh had given land to Edom (Deut 2:5), to Moab (Deut 2:9), and to Ammon (Deut 2:19), using the same vocabulary as is characteristically used of his land gift to Israel. On top of this, the antiquarian footnotes (Deut 2:10-12, 20-23) inform us that the processes of migration and conquest that lay behind the then-current territorial map had also been under the control of YHWH. Not only is the same language used as for Israel's settlement, but the comparison is explicitly drawn: other nations had conquered and settled "just as Israel did in the land the LORD gave them as their possession" (Deut 2:12).

More theology is tucked into these obscure notes than the NIV's understandable use of parentheses might suggest—some of it explicit, some more latent. First, these notes unambiguously assert YHWH's multinational sovereignty. The same God who had declared to Pharaoh that the whole earth belonged to him (Ex 9:14, 16, 29) had been moving other nations around on the chessboard of history long before Israel's historic exodus and settlement. This universal sovereignty over the nations mattered a great deal to Israel in subsequent centuries as they themselves joined the ranks of the attacked and the dispossessed. Later prophetic understanding of Yahweh's "use" of the Assyrians, Babylonians and Persians as agents of Yahweh's purposes in history is in fact consistent with this deeper theme of God's ultimate, universal direction of the destiny of nations (cf. Deut 32:8; Jer 18:1-10; 27:1-7).

Second, these notes relativize Deuteronomy's land gift tradition itself, though not in the sense of questioning or undermining it. The affirmation of Yahweh's gift of land to Israel in fulfillment of his promise to Abraham is one of the fundamental pillars of Deuteronomy's whole worldview. However, it was in principle and at a purely historical level no different from what God had done in other nations. In the immediate context, Israel's defeat and territorial takeover of the lands of Sihon and Og was no different from other nations' earlier migrations and forceful settlements; all are attributed to the sovereign disposition of Yahweh.

> Because God had also given lands to other nations, Israel's uniqueness lay not in having merely received land from Yahweh, but in its covenant relationship with Yahweh. And that covenant was based on God's faithfulness to the promise to Abraham and God's historical act of redemption from Egypt. If that covenant were to be threatened by Israel's neglect, then the mere historical facts of exodus and settlement would count for nothing more in the face of God's judgment than the migrations of other nations.[10]

---

[10]Christopher J. H. Wright, *Deuteronomy,* New International Biblical Commentary (Peabody, Mass.: Hendrikson; Carlisle, U.K.: Paternoster, 1996), p. 36.

And that last sentence is precisely the point that Amos makes, as an example of the more shocking use of this theological conviction. Yes, YHWH's covenantal knowledge of Israel was unique (Amos 3:2), but no, they were not the only nation that YHWH was related to in a wider sense, and certainly not the only nation with a history of exodus, migration and settlement.

> [7a] Is it not the case that, like the sons of Cush,
>   so you [are] to me, sons of Israel? declares YHWH.
> [7b] For is it not also the case that I brought up Israel from Egypt,
>   and the Philistines from Caphtor,
>   the Arameans from Kir? (Amos 9:7, author's translation)[11]

It is clear that Amos is here undermining Israel's false confidence in the mere language of their covenant or the mere historical fact of their exodus. They could not claim "*we* belong to YHWH," as if *no other* nation mattered to God. They could not point to *their* history without observing that other nations had similar histories in which YHWH had been active. Instead of being God's priestly kingdom (Ex 19:6), they have become the sinful kingdom. They might still want to be called YHWH *'s people,* but it was now open to question whether *he* would want to be called *their God.* The uniqueness of their election, far from making them immune from judgment, actually exposes them all the more to God's punishment (Amos 3:2).

Alex Motyer's commentary at this point is helpful:

> There is . . . a sense in which there is no difference between Israel and any other nation . . . the Lord is alike the Agent in every national history, every racial migration. In this regard it is no more a privilege to be an Israelite than to be a Hottentot.

---

[11]The lines of v. 7a are a literal rendering of the Hebrew word order. Most English versions render the construction as meaning "Are you Israelites not the same to me as the Cushites?" This turns the rhetorical question into a simple comparison in which any special status for Israel is undermined: "you are no different/better than even distant nations to me." However, the Hebrew expression "You to me" normally indicates the possessive relationship, i.e., "you belong to me; you are mine." It is the equivalent of one part of the covenant formula "You my people, I your God." Significantly, however, the latter affirmation is omitted, in view of the people's rebellious rejection of YHWH and his covenant (cf. v. 8 where they are described as "the sinful kingdom"). Walter Vogels therefore reads the text with this possessive sense of the phrase "you to me" and so takes the rhetorical question of v. 7a as affirming that other nations belong to YHWH just as much as Israel does: "Are you not mine, sons of Israel, as the Cushites (are mine)?" (Walter Vogels, *God's Universal Covenant,* p. 72). It is doubtful however if the word order of the Hebrew would give this as the primary sense, and the normal English translation is probably correct. However, Vogels is right to highlight the otherwise common covenantal possessive relationship expressed in the two words "you to me." However, Vogels denies that this text implies that the other nations had a covenant relationship with YHWH, for they do not know him as God.

One Lord rules all, appointing the place they shall leave, the distance they shall move and the spot where they shall settle. . . .

The exodus as a historical fact enshrines no more of God than does the coming of the Philistines from Caphtor or the Syrians from Kir and no more brings automatic benefit than do those other divinely engineered events. A historical act of God can by His will become a means of blessing but does not ever of itself convey the blessing. In this sense the Israel of the Exodus is level pegging with the Philistines who came from Caphtor or the Ethiopians who, for all Amos tells us, never went anywhere!

One divine government rules all, and (8a) on moral providence observes all, and judges all. The Lord does not look on people in the light of their historical past but in the light of their moral present. Every nation is equally under this moral scrutiny.[12]

These sharp points, which are quite consistent with all Amos has said hitherto, are clear enough in relation to Israel. The disputed question, however, is, What does Amos 9:7 affirm about the other nations? Is Amos really saying that there is no difference between Israel and the Cushites, the Philistines and the Syrians? By using the language of belonging and the language of exodus, is Amos going so far as to affirm that these other nations stand on equal covenant ground with Israel in relation to YHWH?

Walter Vogels asks whether this text (along with others such as those from Deuteronomy) indicates that there were "parallel divine covenants with different nations."[13] His answer is negative. It is clear that the Old Testament does make some remarkable affirmations which show that

Yahweh's relationship with the nations is very similar to his relationship with Israel. He intervenes directly in their history, and thereby they belong to him and are responsible before him. If the nations refuse to accept Yahweh's relationship, they will experience punishment like that of Israel [as evidenced in Amos 1—2], but there is always hope. But . . . we will notice one important difference: the nations' lack of knowledge of Yahweh's revelation. Therefore, in the strict sense, we can speak only of a covenant with Israel, but not of a covenant with other nations, since a covenant presupposes mutual knowledge.[14]

To put it simply, the covenant demands two sides: Israel belongs to YHWH, and YHWH belongs to Israel ("You my people; I your God"). But in the case of the nations we may say the nations belong to YHWH, but YHWH does not yet belong to the nations. He is not the God they acknowledge, "own" and wor-

---

[12]J. A. Motyer, *The Message of Amos,* The Bible Speaks Today (Leicester, U.K.: Inter-Varsity Press; Downers Grove, Ill.: InterVarsity Press, 1974), pp. 196-97.

[13]Vogels, *God's Universal Covenant,* chap. 3.

[14]Ibid., pp. 71-72.

ship. There is no covenant reciprocity involved.

Nevertheless, though the covenant relationship with Israel is still sustained as unique, we need to give full weight (and perhaps more weight than is usually given) to this tradition in the Old Testament that all the nations of the earth stand in some relation to YHWH God, are held accountable by him and are governed by him in the course of their varied histories. For this is the platform on which God's historical engagement with Israel, as the means of pursuing his redemptive mission, took place.

The God who called Abraham in order to be a blessing to all nations is the God who governs the histories of all nations. The God who called Israel to be his treasured possession and priestly kingdom is the God who can say "the whole earth is mine."[15] We must resist all taming and reductionism by which YHWH is confined to the borders of Israel and give full attention to the universal claims that are made about him in the Old Testament.

If then, on the one hand, all nations on earth are under God's sovereign governance, and if, on the other hand, Israel has a status and a history that are in some ways unique, what is the relationship between the two spheres of God's activity? How do the nations in general "connect" with Israel in particular? The connection may be portrayed in four ways, which build on one another theologically:

- The nations are witnessing observers of what YHWH does in and to Israel.

- The nations can be beneficiaries of the blessing inherent in Israel's covenant.

- The nations will come to know and worship Israel's God.

- The nations will ultimately be included within the identity of Israel as God's people.

To these four perceptions we now give our attention.

The Nations as Witnesses of Israel's History

Israel did not live in vacuum-sealed isolation from the rest of the world. On the contrary, they could not have lived on a more crowded international stage. The land of Canaan, as the land bridge between three continents, was a veritable public concourse of the nations. Israel's presence there was therefore internationally visible. This being the case, the Old Testament envisions several ways

---

[15]See also Bernard Renaud, "Prophetic Criticism of Israel's Attitude to the Nations: A Few Landmarks," in *Truth and its Victims,* Concilium 20, ed. Wim Beuken et al. (Edinburgh: T & T Clark, 1988), pp. 35-43; Paul R. Raabe, "Look to the Holy One of Israel, All You Nations: The Oracles about the Nations Still Speak Today," *Concordia Journal* 30 (2004): 336-49.

in which the story of Israel was supposed to affect the nations. The nations were spectators or, better, witnesses of the great sweep of Old Testament history.

Witnesses of God's mighty acts of redemption.

> The nations will hear and tremble;
> > anguish will grip the people of Philistia.
> The chiefs of Edom will be terrified,
> > the leaders of Moab will be seized with trembling,
> the people of Canaan will melt away;
> > terror and dread will fall upon them.
> By the power of your arm
> > they will be as stone—
> until the people pass by, O LORD,
> > until the people you bought pass by. (Ex 15:14-16)

With these words the Song of Moses envisions the effect on surrounding nations of the great deliverance that had just taken place at the Sea of Reeds. Such a manifest defeat of the most powerful empire in the region, the Pharaoh's Egypt, would doubtless engender fear among the many smaller nations in Israel's pathway. Even a generation later this anticipated effect on the nations proved accurate, as Joshua's spies heard from the mouth of Rahab (Josh 2:9-11).

Even before the crossing of the sea, however, the mighty acts of God in Egypt itself occur "in the eyes of" all the Egyptians. As Vogels points out, the expression "in the eyes of" frequently has the sense of "before witnesses," that is, something done in a publicly witnessed and therefore verifiable way.

> The formula "in the eyes of . . . ", when used in a juridical context, means an action done before legal witnesses [e.g., Jer 32:12]. In some texts those before whom something happens are not merely spectators, but witnesses, who are supposed to take a position as well (Dt. 31:7; Jer. 28:1, 5, 11).
>
> It is often said that Yahweh has bestowed his benefits in favor of Israel in the eyes of the nations. In other words, the nations are witnesses, but at the same time they are invited to take a personal stand.[16]

So the signs given by Moses and Aaron are done "in the eyes of Pharaoh and in the eyes of his servants," and the actual departure from Egypt happened "in the eyes of all the Egyptians," indeed, "in the eyes of the nations" (Ex 7:20; Num 33:3; Lev 26:45, author's translation). Thus the nations are called on to reflect on what they have witnessed and draw conclusions about the uniqueness and power of YHWH—just as Israel is when exactly the same expression is used of

---

[16]Vogels, *God's Universal Covenant*, pp. 65-66.

them as witnesses of all that God did "in the eyes of all Israel" (Deut 34:12; cf. Deut 4:34-35).

Ezekiel holds the same understanding of the great acts of God in Israel's early history. Whereas God would have been fully justified in acting in judgment against Israel, in fact he had withheld his wrath repeatedly and continued instead to preserve and deliver them. And all of this was precisely in order to protect the reputation of his name among the nations, in whose sight he had brought the Israelites out of Egypt. "But for the sake of my name I did what would keep it from being profaned in the eyes of the nations they lived among and in whose sight I had revealed myself to the Israelites by bringing them out of Egypt" (Ezek 20:9; cf. Ezek 14:22).

Ezekiel had the nations in mind even more emphatically when he anticipates God's restoration of Israel after judgment. Then the nations will truly see and know who the true God is.

Witnesses of Israel's covenant obligations. Treaties and covenants in the ancient world, as today, had to have witnesses. In the case of the international treaties contemporary with Israel's Old Testament era, the witnesses were usually the different gods of the parties concerned or the deified natural order (heaven, earth, seas, mountains, etc.). In the case of Israel, of course, no other gods could by definition be called on to witness the covenant between Israel and YHWH, God of heaven and earth beside whom there is no other. So personified nature was summoned to the task. "I call heaven and earth as witnesses against you this day . . ." (Deut 4:26; cf. Deut 30:19; 31:28; 32:1; Is 1:2; Jer 2:12; Mic 6:1-2). But the earth is the habitation of the nations, and so by extension the nations also are portrayed as witnesses to the covenant between YHWH and Israel. Micah calls on both as he embarks on his great covenant lawsuit against Israel:

Hear, O peoples, all of you;
   Listen, O earth and all who are in it,
that the Sovereign LORD may witness against you [i.e., Samaria and Jerusalem
    (v. 1)],
   the Lord from his holy temple. (Mic 1:2)

The same summons to the nations as witnesses of God's covenant with Israel (or its breach) is found in Jeremiah 6:18-19 and Amos 3:9 (where the nations are actually specified as Assyria and Egypt, the two great world powers of the time).

But the nations are not just summoned to witness the making or breaking of the covenant. Ideally, they should be able to observe Israel living by it. In fact, such testimony to the nations of the wisdom of God's ways embodied in the social life of God's people is presented as a major motivation for obedience to God's law. In a passage we have had occasion to notice before for its missiological implications, Deuteronomy 4:6-8 portrays the nations as interested and admiring spectators of Israel, in terms of both the nearness and effectiveness of the God they worship and pray to and of the justice of their social system embodied in the whole constitutional project that is Deuteronomy.

So the nations were in principle invited not only to watch all the wonderful things God did for Israel, they were also supposed to be able to see the responsive righteousness of Israel living within the terms of the covenant. In other words, Israel's visibility to the nations was meant to be not merely historically remarkable but radically and ethically challenging.

God's mission involves God's people living in God's way in the sight of the nations.[17]

Witnesses of God's judgment on Israel. Tragically, it did not turn out that way. Even before they left Sinai, Israel had fallen into the catastrophic rebellion and apostasy of the Golden Calf (Ex 32—34). God's declared intention to destroy them utterly was forestalled only by Moses' intercession. A significant element in that intercession (alongside reminding God of both the Abrahamic covenant and the new relationship established by the exodus) is Moses' warning to God of what the nations (and especially the Egyptians) will think of him if he does so. If YHWH had brought Israel out of Egypt "in the eyes of" all the Egyptians and other nations, let him not imagine that he could now simply wipe them out in the wilderness, as if nobody would notice. What had been so publicly done could not now be secretly undone.

If the nations were expected to draw conclusions from the mighty exodus about YHWH's great redeeming power, what conclusions might they now draw from such an astonishing *volte-face?* Wouldn't they infer that YHWH was either incompetent (he could not complete what he had begun) or even worse, malicious (he raised their hopes of deliverance only to dash them in destruction)? Was that the kind of reputation God wanted to be circulating around the Middle East? (See Ex 32:12; cf. Num14:13-16; Deut 9:28). The clear assumption underlying this bold intercession is that whatever God does to his people in his anger

---

[17]Walter Vogels makes the additional suggestive point that in ancient treaties, it was the witnesses to a treaty (i.e., the gods) who would be called on to execute its penalties on a defaulting partner. Similarly, in Israel's legislation, witnesses also took part in the execution of the one whose conviction their testimony had secured. "The hands of the witnesses must be the first in putting him to death" (Deut 17:7). "All this explains, then, why the nations who were the witnesses of the covenant between Yahweh and Israel are also the instruments in God's hand for the execution of curses and blessings. Israel is judged by the world." Vogels, *God's Universal Covenant,* p. 68.

will be as visible to the nations as all that he did for them in his compassion. And this is a point that echoes on in many places in the Old Testament.

The failure of Israel did not take God by surprise. It is an interesting fact that the book of Deuteronomy begins and ends with failure. Its opening chapter records the failure of the generation of the exodus to go on with God and capture the land of promise. It ends with the anticipated failure of the generations after Moses to stay loyal to the covenant with YHWH. And that future failure will eventually lead to such an outpouring of God's judgment that, yet again, the nations will watch with astonishment.

> All the nations will ask: "Why has the LORD done this to this land? Why this fierce burning anger?"
>
> And the answer will be: "It is because this people abandoned the covenant of the LORD, the God of their fathers." (Deut 29:24-25)

Ezekiel struggles with the public nature of God's dealings with his people, for of course he was of that very generation that experienced the full outpouring of God's wrath at the time of the exile. He recognizes and accepts that the punishment of Israel was a moral necessity and spent his first five years of ministry trying to persuade the first group of exiles of the point. The sin of Israel was so grotesque, scandalous and unremittingly unrepented that they left God no alternative but to fulfill the covenant threats and scatter them among the nations in the curse of exile that had been so prominent among his warning to them from the beginning.

> Son of man, when the people of Israel were living in their own land, they defiled it by their conduct and their actions. Their conduct was like a woman's monthly uncleanness in my sight. So I poured out my wrath on them because they had shed blood in the land and because they had defiled it with their idols. I dispersed them among the nations, and they were scattered through the countries; I judged them according to their conduct and their actions. (Ezek 36:17-19)

But the solution of one problem (God's moral anger against Israel's sin and the necessity of it being punished) led to another. Terrible damage was now being done to God's own reputation, that is, to his personal name, YHWH. It was being mocked among the nations because, clearly (as far as they could see in their interpretation of current events), YHWH was nothing more than one among many defeated gods of the little nations being swallowed up by the Babylonian war machine. This is what is meant by the expression Ezekiel uses to describe the effect of the exile: Israel profaned the name of YHWH. To profane, here, does not mean using bad language. It means treating as common or ordinary something that should be holy. So the name of YHWH, rather than being honored as the name of the only, living God, the Holy One of Israel, was being dragged through the gutters of derision among the very nations whom Israel was supposed to draw into the sphere of YHWH's blessing.

> Wherever they went among the nations they profaned my holy name, for it was said of them, "These are the LORD's people, and yet they had to leave his land." I had concern for [lit. felt pity for] my holy name, which the house of Israel profaned among the nations where they had gone. (Ezek 36:20-21)

Witnesses of God's restoration of Israel. Ezekiel goes on to declare that the resolution of the dilemma God faces will be as much in the sight of the nations as the events that had caused it. That is, by punishing Israel God had vindicated his own moral justice but risked losing his reputation among the nations (as Moses had warned centuries before). So God decides to act in forgiveness and restoration.

But it must be made clear that this will be not merely so that Israel can be rescued from the black hole of exile. God has a wider (though not deeper) passion than his saving love for Israel, and that is the protection of his own name *among the nations,* and the vision of bringing them all ultimately to know and honor him, YHWH, as God. Accordingly, the nations will be witnesses of God's restoration of Israel, just as they were witnesses of the original redemptive act (the exodus). Just as they were witnesses of the covenant judgment (the exile), so also they will be witnesses of God's restorative deliverance (the return).

So the wonderful promises of Ezekiel 36:24-38, including ingathering, cleansing, new heart, new spirit, God's own Spirit, obedience, resettlement and covenant blessing are preceded by the reminder that the primary and ultimate purpose is the glory of God's name among the watching nations.

> It is not for your sake, O house of Israel, that I am doing to do these things, but for the sake of my holy name, which you have profaned among the nations where you have gone. I will show the holiness of my great name, which has been profaned among the nations, the name you have profaned among them. Then the nations will know that I am the LORD, declares the Sovereign LORD, when I show myself holy through you before their eyes. (Ezek 36:22-23)

Before leaving Ezekiel, it is worth noting that his notorious eschatological depiction in chapters 38-39 of the attack on God's people by Gog, prince of Magog, and the host of nations with him, followed by their utter and total destruction, has as its core message that the nations will come to know YHWH as God in all his glory by this signal and ultimate demonstration of his protection of his people from all who seek their destruction. We can become so fascinated with Ezekiel's characteristic penchant for cartoon detail or with contemporary garish and gory amplifications of it in end-times predictions that we overlook the repeated message found in Ezekiel 38:16, 23; 39:6-7, 21-23, 27-29. To the very end, the nations will see and know what God does for his people, and the conclusions to be drawn will finally be irresistible.

What is the relevance of this section (on the nations as witnesses of God's work in Israel) to the missional hermeneutic of Scripture we are seeking to develop throughout this book? I have been insisting throughout that our primary datum in biblical missiology must be the mission of God. And we have seen that the mission of God is strongly connected to God's will to be known by his whole creation. To that end he is at work on the whole stage of human history, not merely among the people he has chosen as the vehicle for his great redemptive agenda for the world. And even when we do focus, with the biblical texts themselves, on the story of God's dealings with his people, we must remember that God always acts among his own people with an eye on the watching nations. The nations are not just part of the incidental scenery of the narrative. They are the intended witnesses of the action. These things happen "before their eyes." A response is therefore expected to what they witness. As Walter Vogels expresses it:

> God has basically the same intention with the nations as he had with Israel because both "will know that I am Yahweh." Far from being pure spectators of something which concerns only Yahweh and Israel, the nations are witnesses, who are directly involved. The whole historical covenant between Yahweh and Israel had from the beginning a universal dimension. The nations are real witnesses. Yahweh's saving actions, the punishment, and the restoration which he imposed upon Israel, were at the same time a preaching to the nations.[18]

In my own discussion of this aspect of the oracles concerning the nations that we find in several of Israel's prophets, including Ezekiel, I have summarized the point in this way:

> The prophets were thus aware of two complementary truths. On the one hand, whatever Yahweh did among the nations was ultimately for the benefit of Israel, his covenant people. Yet on the other hand, what Yahweh did for Israel was ultimately for the benefit of the nations. This double reality is significant for it preserves the universality of God's sovereignty over all nations, while recognizing the particularity of his unique relationship with Israel. God's providential reign over the nations is related to his redemptive purpose for his people; but his redemptive work among his people is related to his missionary purpose among the nations. The two cannot be separated. . . .

---

[18]Ibid., pp. 67-68.

In the same way, assuming that the God of Isaiah and Ezekiel is still our God and is still on the throne of the universe, we need to look at the world of international affairs and seek to discern what God is doing that impinges upon the life and witness of his people, the church. At the same time, we need to be asking whether the church, in its life and witness, is truly engaging in its biblical mission of bringing the blessing of God to the nations. God runs the world for the sake of the church; God calls the church for the sake of the world. We need to fix our theology and our mission to both poles of this biblical dynamic.[19]

The Nations as Beneficiaries of Israel's Blessing

The Old Testament is not content to leave the nations in the passive role of spectators of all that God was doing in Israel. The nations will come to see that God's dealings with Israel were to be, for them, not just a matter of alternating admiration or horror. The whole story was *for their ultimate good.* Or, to pursue the metaphor of spectators, the whole drama was for the benefit of the audience. Two psalms will illustrate this angle of our exploration.

Psalm 47

Clap your hands, all you nations;
    shout to God with cries of joy.
How awesome is the LORD Most High,
    the great King over all the earth! (Ps 47:1-2)

With these words, some psalm writer in ancient Israel invited the nations to join in applause to YHWH, God of Israel. Clapping hands is fairly universally a collective sign of approval. Those who are clapping acknowledge something that has brought them pleasure or benefit. It speaks of appreciation and gratitude. It is a form of physical and audible thanksgiving that supplements or replaces words.

What then does our psalmist invite the nations of the world to give a round of applause to YHWH for? The answer at first sight seems perverse: "He [YHWH] subdued nations under us [Israel], / peoples under our feet" (Ps 47:3).

The nations are being asked to clap for YHWH because he is the God who defeated them through Israel. This is like asking the inhabitants of a defeated country to say thank you to the nation that invaded them. Is the psalm nothing more than imperial cynicism masquerading as worship? The only alternative to reading it in that way is to discern within it a deeper theological conviction about God's deal-

---

[19]Christopher J. H. Wright, *The Message of Ezekiel: A New Heart and a New Spirit,* The Bible Speaks Today (Leicester, U.K.: Inter-Varsity Press; Downers Grove, Ill.: InterVarsity Press, 2001), p. 260. Regarding the statement that "God runs the world for the sake of the church," see Eph 1:21-22, speaking of the cosmic dominion of Christ exercised "for the church."

ings with Israel and the nations in the long sweep of his sovereignty in history.

The nations can be summoned to applaud YHWH because ultimately even the historical defeat of the Canaanites by Israel will be seen to be part of a history for which all of humanity will have ample cause to praise God. While the historical culture of Canaan that confronted the Israelites was degraded to the point of deserving divine judgment, the God who exercised that act of judgment was also the great King over all the earth (the repeated emphasis of the psalm), the justice of whose global reign would one day be acknowledged by all. The nations will be the eventual beneficiaries of that.

Psalm 67. Another Psalmist picks up the most pregnant text in Israel's rich vocabulary and liturgy of blessing, namely, the Aaronic blessing of Numbers 6:24-26. It was the priests' task to pronounce these words and thus "put the Name on the Israelites." It would be YHWH himself who would bless his people.

Blessing, of course, was an integral part of the covenant God had made with Abraham. His descendants would live within a relationship of declared and protected blessing. But they were also to be the medium through whom other nations would come into blessing. Accordingly, the author of Psalm 67 takes the Aaronic blessing, which he probably heard repeatedly in the context of worship at the sanctuary, and does two things.

On the one hand he turns its declarative form into prayer, as if to say, "Yes, may God indeed do what these words say; may God, our God bless us." But on the other hand he turns it inside out and prays that God's blessing may be the focus of praise not only in Israel but among all the peoples to the ends of the earth.

> May God be gracious to us and bless us
>   and make his face to shine upon us,
> that your ways may be known on earth,
>   your salvation among all nations.
> May the peoples praise you, O God;
>   may all the peoples praise you. (Ps 67:1-3)

As in Psalm 47, the particular focus at the center of this psalm (v. 4) is the just rule of God that will be exercised over all nations. However, verse 6 adds a more economic factor to the political one—namely, God's blessing expressed through the harvest of the land.[20] So the final two verses bring the psalm to its climax in a

---

[20]It is characteristic, of course, that the same word,*'eres,* is used for the land of Israel (which is doubtless the location of the harvest referred to in v. 6) and for the earth as a whole in vv. 2, 4, 7). This is a verbal commonplace that nevertheless embodies the theological truth: the land of Israel has a symbolic and eschatological reference point, the whole earth; just as the people of Israel has its significance within God's plan for the whole of humanity.

universality that embraces God, Israel and its land, the nations and the whole earth.

> Then the land will yield its harvest,
>   and God, our God, will bless us.
> God will bless us,
>   and all the ends of the earth will fear him. (Ps 67:6-7)

There are several other texts in which the phrase "the land will yield its harvest" is used, in virtually identical lexical terms to Psalm 67:6 (with minor grammatical differences). They help us grasp the full implications of the words in this psalm. These include Leviticus 25:19 (in the context of God's promise to provide food if Israel observed the jubilee year) and Leviticus 26:4 (as part of the general promise of God's continued blessing if Israel lives in obedience to his law). The psalmist may well have had such Torah promises in mind, given that he anticipates this particular blessing within the realm of God's sovereign rule, which implies an obedient people. Psalm 85:12 similarly locates the promise within the context of a penitent and obedient people. Two prophetic texts, however, also have close parallels.

Ezekiel 34:27 includes agricultural abundance, in these terms, as part of God's promise to Israel in the future restoration after the exile. And in that postexilic period, Zechariah 8:12-13 picks it up again as the sign of that restored covenantal relationship. Indeed Zechariah connects these words of promise to the Abrahamic covenant by saying that Israel will once again become "a blessing" among the nations, instead of an object of cursing.[21] There will be a new beginning for God's people, which Zechariah portrays thus:

> The seed will grow well, the vine will give its fruit, *the earth will give its harvest,* and the heavens will drop their dew. . . . As you have been a curse among the nations, house of Judah and house of Israel, so I will save you, so that you may be a blessing. (Zech 8:12-13, author's translation)[22]

It has been suggested that Psalm 67 and Zechariah 8 may even have been connected to the same historical context, namely, the harvests in the postexilic period that signaled God's fulfillment of his promise to protect and bless his people when they returned to the land. If this is so, it is clear that both texts

---

[21] In this context the meaning of Zechariah's prophecy probably is that whereas nations have used the name of Israel as a curse (in view of its manifest "bad luck"), they will change to using it as a term of blessing (in view of God's manifest restoration of their fortunes).

[22] This translation of the last clause recognizes the common construction, in which one future statement followed by another makes the second the intended purpose of the first. God will save Israel and they will be a blessing. But "being a blessing" was God's intention for Israel from the start, so his new act of salvation will be to enable that intention to be fulfilled.

look well beyond this proof of God's renewed blessing on Israel alone and see in it *the firstfruits of God's wider harvest among all nations on earth*.

> It may well be, therefore, that we have in Psalm 67 an echo of this prophetic word: "The land has yielded its harvest," now may God bless us (cf. Zech. 8:13), and may it be visible to all the nations. . . .
>
> > The land having yielded its harvest,
> >   may God, our God, bless us.
> > May God bless us
> >   so that all ends of the earth may revere him. . . .
>
> A clear analogy to the text of Zechariah 8 is present. The new times, the time of renewal has begun, as is signalled by the fact that a new harvest has been given. May God now continue to bless his people, and may the nations see it and understand what is happening. . . .
>
> It is a sign that God's history goes on not exclusively with his own people. The function of this signally important harvest is to catch the attention of the nations and move them to recognize and praise God. The particular history of God and Israel is meant to become a blessing to all—as the prophecy of Zechariah 8 announces.[23]

Because of the universalizing thrust of Psalm 67 as a whole, Brueggemann thinks that the "us" of its final verse may well be spoken by the nations themselves, not just Israel, who are the clearly the speakers in verse 1. This may or may not be the psalmist's intention, but "either way, the psalm envisions a whole earth and all its peoples now gladly affirming Yahweh's sovereignty and gratefully receiving from Yahweh all the blessings of a rightly governed creation."[24]

Finally, Psalm 67 echoes the priestly prayer of Aaron, and may indeed have been composed by a priest. It distills the missional nature of Israel's own priestly role among the nations. Marvin Tate quotes "a remarkable summary of Ps 67 from I. Abrahams, *Annotations to the Hebrew Prayer Book, Pharisaism and the Gospels*":

> This Psalm is a prayer for salvation in the widest sense, and not for Israel only, but for the whole world. Israel's blessing is to be a blessing for all men. Here, in particular, the Psalmist does more than adopt the Priestly formula (Num 6:22-27); he claims for Israel the sacerdotal dignity. Israel is the world's high priest . . . if Israel has the light of God's face, the world cannot remain in darkness.[25]

---

[23]Eep Talstra and Carl J. Bosma, "Psalm 67: Blessing, Harvest and History," *Calvin Theological Journal* 36 (2001): 308, 309, 313.

[24]Brueggemann, *Old Testament Theology,* p. 501.

[25]Marvin E. Tate, *Psalms 51-100,* Word Biblical Commentary 20 (Dallas: Word, 1990), p. 159.

Thus Israel, who knew themselves to be the recipients of such great and abundant blessings that they could exclaim, "how blessed is the nation whose God is the LORD" (Ps 33:12), knew that the benefits of all God had given and done in their history would eventually be a matter of gratitude among the rest of the nations, for whose ultimate benefit Israel had been called into existence in the loins of Abraham. The nations will be the final (and intended) beneficiaries of the blessing experienced in Israel.

The Nations Will Worship Israel's God

The only proper response to blessings and benefits received at God's hand was worship and obedience. That was another core belief in Israel. But if that was true for them, then it must also be true of all nations because they too came within the sphere of God's blessing. Indeed, Israel's own praises for blessing received had a missional edge, in reaching out in proclamation to the nations.[26] And so there is a range of texts anticipating the praise of the nations, and a few that speak of their obedience as well.[27]

Here we have a theme that carries considerable missiological significance in our survey since the mission of God is to lead the whole creation and all nations to that universal worship that so fills the final vision of the canon of Scripture. *How* the nations will be brought to such worship and obedience to YHWH the God of Israel remains, within the Old Testament era, a mystery (as Paul acknowledged). But *that* the nations will one day bring all their worship to the only true and living God is left in no doubt. The sheer volume of texts that envision it is quite remarkable. Again these are typically a mixture of psalms and prophetic texts.

Psalms. The theme of the worship of the nations being offered to YHWH, God of Israel, occurs from beginning to end of the Psalter. So we can only point out the key texts without much exegetical comment. Some simple classification will help our grasp of the material.

---

[26]Patrick D. Miller, " 'Enthroned on the Praises of Israel': The Praise of God in Old Testament Theology," *Interpretation* 39 (1985): 5-19. See also the quotation from this fine article on page 132.

[27]Scott Hahn argues passionately for what he calls "a liturgical hermeneutic," by which he means an approach to Scripture that sees its primary thrust as leading humanity back to the joyful and fulfilling worship of the Creator God. His lively and illuminating essay fits very effectively with the missiological hermeneutic I have developed in this book, since I have stressed the missional importance of God's will to be known and worshiped by his whole creation. See Scott W. Hahn, "Canon, Cult and Covenant: Towards a Liturgical Hermeneutic," in *Canon and Biblical Interpretation*, Craig Bartholomew et. al. (Carlisle, U.K.: Paternoster; Grand Rapids: Zondervan, forthcoming).

The anticipated *praise of the nations* for YHWH is said to occur

- in response to his mighty acts in general
- in response to the justice of his sovereign cosmic rule in particular
- in response to his restoration of Zion (which will be for the nations' benefit)
- as part of the outpouring of the universal praise of all creation

The mighty acts of God. Quite a number of psalms celebrate the mighty acts of God in the history of Israel in particular or sometimes also in the wider world of creation, and then in that context they call on the nations also to join in praising him. Psalm 66 observes that the power of God will distinguish between his enemies, who will cringe (presumably prior to destruction), and those who willingly praise him.

> Say to God, "How awesome are your deeds!
>> So great is your power
>> that your enemies cringe before you.
> All the earth bows down to you;
>> they sing praise to you,
>> they sing praise to your name." . . .
> Praise our God, O peoples,
>> Let the sound of his praise be heard. (Ps 66:3-4, 8)

Psalm 68, cataloging some of the mighty acts of YHWH, likewise distinguishes between wicked nations to be scattered, and those nations that will submit to God in worship.

> Scatter the nations who delight in war.
> Envoys will come from Egypt;
>> Cush will submit herself to God.
> Sing to God, O kingdoms of the earth,
>> sing praise to the Lord. (Ps 68:30-32)

Psalm 86 sets the worship of the nations in the context of the uniqueness of YHWH as demonstrated in his incomparable mighty acts:

> Among the gods there is none like you O Lord;
>> no deeds can compare with yours.
> All the nations you have made
>> will come and worship before you O Lord;
>> they will bring glory to your name.
> For you alone are great and do marvelous deeds;
>> you alone are God. (Ps 86:8-10)

Psalm 96 and Psalm 98 are very similar. Both celebrate the kingship of YHWH over all creation and call for the great works of God in salvation and creation to be the subject of a new song that will spread throughout the nations. The content of this new song is essentially a remix of the old songs of Israel—the name, the salvation, the glory and the mighty acts of YHWH. What makes it new is *where* it is to be sung (in all the earth) and *who* is going to be doing the singing (all peoples). What was an old song for Israel becomes a new song as it is taken up by new singers in ever expanding circles to the ends of the earth. Psalm 96 in particular recognizes the polemical or confrontational nature of such a universal vision, for it must inevitably transform the religious landscape. Other gods must be recognized for what they are, "nothings" (Ps 96:5), and the nations must instead ascribe all glory to YHWH alone and bring their offerings to him (Ps 96:7-9).

> Sing to the LORD a new song;
> sing to the LORD all the earth.
> Sing to the LORD, praise his name;
>   proclaim his salvation day after day.
> Declare his glory among the nations,
>   his marvelous deeds among all peoples. (Ps 96:1-3)

Psalm 97 and Psalm 99 are also a similar pair, launching their call to praise with the affirmation "The LORD reigns" and summoning the earth and the distant shores to rejoice (Ps 97), and the nations and the earth to tremble and shake (Ps 99). The greatness, justice, holiness and forgiveness of YHWH are the main reasons for anticipating such responses.

Psalm 138 sandwiches a remarkable prayer for the world in the midst of the psalmist's praise and prayer for his own relationship with God. Once again, the longed-for praise of the nations is directly related to great truths that they will perceive about YHWH as God. The praise of the nations is no empty acclamation. It is filled with solid biblical content: the nations will come to praise YHWH in relation to his *words,* his *ways* and his *glory.*

> May all the kings of the earth praise you, O LORD,
>   when they hear the words of your mouth.
> May they sing of the ways of the LORD,
>   for the glory of the LORD is great. (Ps 138:4-5)

God's sovereign rule. The expectation that all nations will come to worship YHWH is further drawn from the theological affirmation that he alone rules over the whole world. The eschatology is fed by the monotheistic thrust we explored in chapter three. The fact that YHWH's reign is one of justice, for which the nations will have cause to bring their praise, has already been noted in relation to Psalm 67 (see pp. 475-76).

Psalm 22 puts the worship of the nations in a very universal frame: it will be offered by the poor and the rich (i.e., every segment of society [Ps 22:26, 29]), and it will be offered by generations who have already died and as yet unborn (Ps 22:29, 31). Whether vertically throughout human society or horizontally throughout human history, the praise of YHWH as sovereign ruler will be universally offered.

> All the ends of the earth
>> will remember and turn to the LORD,
> and all the families of the nations
>> will bow down before him,
> for dominion belongs to the LORD
>> and he rules over the nations. (Ps 22:27-28)

Psalm 2 sees the rule of YHWH as a severe warning to the nations not to continue their rebellion against him but rather to take the wiser course of worshiping him in humility.

> Therefore, you kings, be wise;
>> be warned, you rulers of the earth.
> Serve [worship] the LORD with fear
>> and rejoice with trembling. (Ps 2:10-11)

The nations ought to adopt this stance toward YHWH because he has installed his anointed king on Zion. The reference to the historical Davidic king became increasingly hollow, of course, as the human incumbents of that throne became more rebellious themselves than even the other nations. Far from leading Israel in such a way that the nations would come to acknowledge YHWH, be blessed by him and worship him, it was precisely the kings of Israel whose wickedness precipitated the events that became such a scandal among the nations.[28]

---

[28]It may be that this failure of the Davidic king provides a clue to the organization of the Psalter itself. In this chapter I adopt a primarily thematic approach to the Psalms in garnering their missional relevance. However, the growth of interest in a canonical reading of the book of Psalms as a whole may hold further missional significance. Ever since the seminal work of Gerald H. Wilson, *The Editing of the Hebrew Psalter* (Chicago: Scholars Press, 1985), other scholars have explored the effect of reading the psalms against the narrative background of Old Testament history, and with particular attention to the psalms around the "seams" of the five books into which the Psalter has been edited. (For a survey see Gordon Wenham, "Towards a Canonical Reading of the Psalms," in *Canon and Biblical Interpretation*, ed. Craig Bartholomew et al. (Carlisle, U.K.: Paternoster; Grand Rapids: Zondervan, forthcoming).

God's restoration of Zion. However, after all the lament for those events has been expressed, as it richly is in the later Psalter, the hope of the restoration of Zion emerges there, too, just as it does in the prophets. And this also will be a factor in the anticipated praise of YHWH among the nations. Even before Israel, it will be the nations who will marvel at the wonderful things God has done in restoring Israel from a hopeless situation of captivity (Ps 126:2-3).

Psalm 102 links together very beautifully a restored Zion and worshiping nations, in a text that seems to have had a strong influence on Jewish expectations within which the mission of Jesus himself and his followers emerged. The anticipated scenario was that once Zion was restored, then the nations would be gathered to the worship and praise of God, so that Jerusalem would resonate to the praises of Israel and the nations together. This sequence certainly influenced Paul's understanding of his own times and mission: the restoration of Israel, the ingathering of the nations, the combined rejoicing of both.

> You will arise and have compassion on Zion,
>> for it is time to show favor to her;
>> the appointed time has come. . . .
> The nations will fear the name of the LORD,
>> all the kings of the earth will revere your glory.
> For the LORD will rebuild Zion
>> and appear in his glory. . . .
> So the name of the LORD will be declared in Zion
>> and his praise in Jerusalem

John Wigfield is exploring the links between Psalms and Deuteronomy in the light of Patrick Miller's "Deuteronomy and Psalms: Evoking a Biblical Conversation," *Journal of Biblical Literature* 118/1 (1999) with a view to a missiological reading of the Psalter as a whole. If the model Israelite of Psalm 1 represents the model king of Deuteronomy 17, who should be leading Israel in the ways of obedience to God's law, then, according to Deuteronomy 4:6-8, the nations should observe and be drawn to Israel. The question of Psalm 2 is therefore sharp and surprising: "Why do the nations conspire against the LORD?" Was it because Israel and their king had failed to come anywhere close to the ideals of Psalm 1? In spite of much encouragement to humble and faithful obedience in books 1 and 2, and in spite of the ideals set before the Davidic monarch in Psalm 72 (end of book 2), the reality is that from Solomon on the kings all abandoned God and his law, with the result that the nation ended up in the despairing apparent collapse of the Davidic covenant in Psalm 89 (end of book 3). From then on, the psalms turn more sustained emphasis toward the nations in general and to the kingship of YHWH over both Israel and the nations. The universalizing thrust of the whole collection thus gathers power and volume somewhat similarly to the growing eschatological universality of the prophets.

It is an interesting hypothesis that awaits clarification and demonstration. But it shows another part of the canon on which a missional hermeneutic can open up fresh angles of approach.

> when the peoples and the kingdoms
>> assemble to worship the LORD. (Ps 102:13, 15-16, 21-22)

Universal praise. Finally, some psalms anticipate the praise of the nations for no other reason than that YHWH is worthy of the praise of the whole universe, so no nation can be excluded or excused from that duty. We have noted Psalm 47 in its assumption that YHWH is exalted as the great King (pp. 474-75), so all human kings must naturally join in the shouts of joy and praise. Psalm 100 summons all the earth to shout for joy, while the shortest psalm of all, Psalm 117, invites all nations and peoples to praise YHWH for his great love and enduring faithfulness—qualities known by experience in Israel, eventually to be the subject of universal praise among the nations.

Though the shortest of psalms, Psalm 117 exercised a theological influence on Paul out of all proportion to its length. It provides the vocabulary as well as the thematic content of Romans 15:8-11, emphasizing not only the faithfulness and mercy of God (in what he has accomplished for the nations through Christ) but also the summons to praise that goes forth now to the nations.[29]

The climax of the Psalter, with its outpouring of praise, rises to rhetorical peaks of universality.

Psalm 145 envisages the whole creation praising God, but the human part of it will do so because they have come to know the works and reign of God through the testimony of his people.

> All you have made will praise you, O LORD;
>> your saints will extol you.
> They will tell of the glory of your kingdom
>> and speak of your might,
> so that all men may know of your mighty acts
>> and the glorious splendor of your kingdom. (Ps 145:10-12)

Psalm 148 is also a hymn of praise to YHWH from the whole created order, so not surprisingly it includes "kings of the earth and all nations, / you princes and all rulers on earth" (Ps 148:11).

I have dwelled at length on this material in Psalms on the anticipated praise of YHWH by all the nations because, although it is of such manifest missiological significance, it is easy to overlook. We read the psalms very much as songs of ancient Israel, and we may be inclined to pass over verses such as these as rhetorical flourishes without pausing to marvel at the vast horizons of expectation

---

[29]Jannie du Preez, "The Missionary Significance of Psalm 117 in the Book of Psalms and in the New Testament," *Missionalia* 27 (1999): 369-76.

and imagination contained in them. And we usually read the psalms one at a time, so we miss the opportunity to feel the overwhelming cumulative force of such a pervasive theme in Israel's amazing liturgical discourse.

Yet, within any biblical theology of mission or any missiological reading of Scripture, this is surely material of primary relevance. Their breadth of vision, their universal inclusiveness, their breathtaking eschatological hope—all these features of Psalms are essential components in articulating the scope of the mission of God in Scripture. Creighton Marlowe coins a highly appropriate name for the psalms. He calls them "the music of missions."

> Both Israel and the church have been commissioned or called to reflect and to report the light of revelation, the good news about the true nature of God as Savior, Judge, King, and Lord of the earth and all its inhabitants. The platform upon which God's people of any age earn the opportunity to be heard . . . may and will change dramatically over the centuries or millennia or may be as different as the individuals or institutions seeking to be a witness. But the main object always remains the same: visualizing and verbalizing the revelation of the one, true God . . . before the reachable world of nations. Old Testament psalms are sacred songs (Hebrew poetry set to music) that in part explicitly reinforce this divine purpose for Israel and thus, implicitly for the church. They celebrate the character of cross-cultural outreach. They are the music of missions.[30]

Prophets. The texts we have surveyed in Psalms might well qualify as prophetic, such is their grandeur of vision. However, among the prophets, it is the book of Isaiah that has the most sustained interest in the eschatological vision of the nations offering their worship to YHWH. It is found as early as Isaiah 2 and it forms part of the climax of the whole corpus in Isaiah 66:18-23.

There has been an intensive scholarly debate over the nature of the so-called universalism of Isaiah, especially chapters 40-55. On the one hand, there are those who regard these chapters as the pinnacle of Israel's "missionary" vision—extending the hope of God's salvation to all the nations on earth and generating a vision of centrifugal universalism. On the other hand, there are those who regard these chapters as simply the pinnacle of Israel's exclusivism—all the nations will have to submit to Israel and acknowledge that Israel's God is the only true one. On the latter view, these chapters are imbued more with the spirit of

---

[30]W. Creighton Marlowe, "Music of Missions: Themes of Cross-Cultural Outreach in the Psalms," *Missiology* 26 (1998): 452. George Peters goes rhetorically further, counting "more than 175 references of a universalistic note relating to the nations of the world. Many of them bring hope of salvation to the nations. . . . Indeed, the Psalter is one of the greatest missionary books in the world, though seldom seen from that point of view." George W. Peters, *A Biblical Theology of Missions* (Chicago: Moody Press, 1972), pp. 115-16.

centripetal nationalism than that of universalism.[31]

Excellent and balanced discussions of the debate have been provided by Anthony Gelston and Michael Grisanti. Both argue that to insist on either pole of the above dichotomy would be mistaken. It is worth quoting their conclusions, with which I agree, in full.

> The universalism that I submit is to be found in Second Isaiah consists of three strands. There is first the affirmation that YHWH is the only true God, sovereign over all creation, and therefore over all mankind. There is secondly the expectation that this truth will be recognized by the Gentile nations no less than by Israel, with the corollary that they will submit to him and acknowledge his universal rule. . . . There is a third strand, consisting of the universal offer of the experience of salvation. Nowhere, however, does the prophet affirm that all will avail themselves of this offer. On the contrary, there is a clear implication in 45:25 that some will not . . . to the detriment of those who persist in their idolatry.[32]

> Isaiah 40—55 contains passages that manifest both sides of this tension [between nationalism and universalism]. The customary terms "nationalism" and "universalism" do not sufficiently reveal the constitutive issues in this debate. . . . Assertions that the prophet is the "missionary prophet of the Old Testament" or that he is an ardent nationalist without any concern for the nations frame this debate. Between these two extremes, the prophet Isaiah neither depicts Israel as a nation of world-traversing missionaries, nor does he exclude the nations from participation in divine redemption. . . . [T]he prophet argues that God's special dealings with His chosen people not only benefit Israel, but also carry significance for all nations. Isaiah underscores Israel's role in providing a witness to the nations . . . in the sense of being a people of God whose life shall draw nations to inquire after Yahweh (cf. Isa. 2:1-4; 43:10-11). It is as God's chosen people that Israel can exercise a mediatorial role with regard to the nations. Isaiah's fervent desire for Israel is that they will respond to God's intervention on her behalf and carry out her role as God's servant nation before the world.[33]

---

[31]A selection of the relevant literature in the debate includes Robert Davidson, "Universalism in Second Isaiah," *Scottish Journal of Theology* 16 (1963): 166-85; D. E. Hollenberg, "Nationalism and 'The Nations' in Isaiah XL-LV," *Vetus Testamentum* 19 (1969): 23-36; Harry Orlinsky, "Nationalism-Universalism and Internationalism in Ancient Israel," in *Translating and Understanding the Old Testament: Essays in Honor of Herbert Gordon May,* ed. H. T. Frank and W. L. Reid (Nashville: Abingdon; 1970), pp. 206-36; D. W. Van Winkle, "The Relationship of the Nations to Yahweh and to Israel in Isaiah XL-LV," *Vetus Testamentum* 35 (1985): 446-58; J. Blenkinsopp, "Second Isaiah— Prophet of Universalism," *Journal for the Study of the Old Testament* 41 (1988): 83-103.

[32]Anthony Gelston, "Universalism in Second Isaiah," *Journal of Theological Studies* 43 (1992): 396.

[33]Michael A. Grisanti, "Israel's Mission to the Nations in Isaiah 40-55: An Update," *Master's Seminary Journal* 9 (1998): 61.

Returning then to the theme of the nations bringing their worship to YHWH, Christopher Begg has made an exhaustive study of all the texts in the book of Isaiah that exhibit this theme, dividing the book up into fairly standard sections.[34]

In Isaiah 1—12 the theme puts an envelope around the prophecies concerning Israel. In Isaiah 2:1-5 the eschatological expectation of the obedient, law-seeking, worship of the nations in the future is contrasted sharply with the contemporary rituals of rebellious Israel in chapter 1. This is echoed in chapter 12, where the abating of YHWH's anger against Israel is met by an outpouring of praise that will include the nations and all the world (Is 12:4-5).

In Isaiah 13—27, the section of oracles concerning the nations, the overwhelming burden is, of course, words of judgment against the contemporary nations in the world of the prophet. Nevertheless, "the expectation of some sort of participation by a nation or the nations as a whole in Yahweh's worship keeps being voiced."[35] The most remarkable of these voices is the prophecy concerning Egypt in Isaiah 19:16-25. But in addition to the hope there expressed for Egypt, we find anticipation of worship in the form of gifts and offerings being brought by the Ethiopians (Is 18:7), and by the people of Tyre (Is 23:17-18). The so-called Isaiah Apocalypse (chaps. 24-25) also contains portraits not only of God's judgment on all the earth but of the worship of the nations ultimately being directed to him. After the purging judgment there will be joyful and grateful worship among the survivors (Is 24:14-16). In Isaiah 25 it seems clear that the benefits of God's salvation, including ultimately the destruction of death itself, will be for both Israel and all nations, who will gather on the mountain of Zion for YHWH's rich banquet (v. 6), so that "they" in Isaiah 25:9 includes both:

> In that day they [Israelites and all nations] will say,
> "Surely this is our God;
>   we trusted in him, and he saved us.
> This is the LORD, we trusted in him;
>   let us rejoice and be glad in his salvation.

In Isaiah 40—55 the theme of the worship of the nations returns to even greater prominence. "All flesh" will see the glory of YHWH (Is 40:5), and his justice and law will be delivered to the nations who wait eagerly for them (Is 42:1-

---

[34]Christopher T. Begg, "The Peoples and the Worship of Yahweh in the Book of Isaiah," in *Worship and the Hebrew Bible,* ed. M. P. Graham, R. R. Marrs, and S. L. McKenzie (Sheffield, U.K.: Sheffield Academic Press, 1999).

[35]Ibid., p. 39. See also as a wider study of the theme of the nations in relation to the unity of the book of Isaiah as a whole, G. I. Davies, "The Destiny of the Nations in the Book of Isaiah," in *The Book of Isaiah: Le Livre d'Isaie,* ed. J. Vermeylen (Leuven University Press, 1989), pp. 93-120.

4). Accordingly all nations to the ends of the earth can be summoned to sing his praise (Is 42:10-12) and will indeed eventually do so in the wake of God's new redemptive work (Is 45:6, 14). Summons turns to appeal in the climax of Isaiah 45, as YHWH invites the remnant of the nations (like the remnant of Israel) to turn to him for salvation and thus to convert from their late lamented false worship to the exclusive worship of YHWH (Is 45:22-25). This appeal, mediated through a new David, will assuredly find willing and hasty response among nations hitherto unknown to Israel (Is 55:3-5).

In Isaiah 56—66 the early vision of chapter Isaiah 2:1-5 of the pilgrimage of the nations to Zion is expanded and enhanced in a rich kaleidoscope of anticipation. At an individual level, foreigners previously excluded will find their worship accepted right in the temple itself (Is 56:3-8). Back at the international level Isaiah 60, along with Isaiah 61:5-7, is a glorious evocation for all the senses of the worship of the nations being brought to YHWH, through the mediation of Israel now functioning, as intended, as God's priesthood for the nations. Just as Israelites brought their tithes and offerings to their priests, so the nations will bring their tribute to Israel as the priests of YHWH (Is 61:6). It isn't unlikely that Paul theologically viewed his financial collection from among the Gentile churches for the impoverished Jerusalem church as a token of the eschatological fulfillment of such prophetic visions.[36] Though there is rhetoric of submission to Israel, this is probably no more than figurative of the recognition that it is Israel's God who reigns supreme. "The chapter makes clear that their homage is ultimately meant for Yahweh himself" (cf. Is 60:6, 7, 9, 14, 16).[37]

Walter Brueggemann agrees and goes on to make a further point about the role of the Torah in this eschatological worship of the nations. They will worship as nations who have been taught the ways of YHWH (as Is 2:2-5; 42:4 also envision).

> Two matters are important in this vision. First, the nations come gladly, willingly, and expectantly. They are not coerced or compelled by the political force of the Davidic house, but have come in recognition that this is the only place where the way to peace and justice is available. Second, in the process of coming gladly, it is affirmed that the nations, like Israel, are subject to the Torah of Yahweh. That is, the Torah is as pertinent to the nations as it is to Israel. This makes clear that the nations must deal with Yahweh's sovereignty, but it also makes clear that the Torah, while seated in Jerusalem, is no exclusive Israelite property. It belongs to the nations as much as to Israel.[38]

---

[36]This is argued by C. H. H. Scobie, "Israel and the Nations: An Essay in Biblical Theology," *Tyndale Bulletin* 43, no. 2 (1992): 283-305.

[37]Ibid., p. 50.

[38]Brueggemann, *Old Testament Theology,* pp. 501-2.

Walter Vogels also observes the strong connection between Sinai and Zion in this vision for the nations. "What Israel celebrated at Sinai is celebrated by the nations at Zion. At Sinai, Yahweh gave his law to Israel through Moses. He now gives his revelation to the nations through Israel. At that time Israel was designated as Yahweh's people, but now all the nations are Yahweh's people."[39]

Finally, in Isaiah 66 the nations who have been the object of witness and summons, once they have been gathered to the worship of YHWH, themselves become the agents of witness and proclamation. This is the only unequivocally centrifugal articulation of mission in the Old Testament. Those who have been the recipients of Abrahamic blessing now become the agents of mediating it to others.

> And I, because of their actions and their imaginations, am about to come and gather all nations and tongues, and they will come and see my glory.
>
> I will set a sign among them and I will send some of those who survive to the nations . . . and to the distant islands that have not heard of my fame or seen my glory. They will proclaim my glory among the nations. (Is 66:18-19)

Christopher Begg's conclusion is worth quoting almost in full.

> The theme of the nations' involvement with the worship of Yahweh has indeed emerged as a significant one throughout the book of Isaiah, with increasing attention being devoted to it as one moves from chs. 1-39 to 40-66. To an overwhelming degree the texts speak in positive terms of the nations' relation to Yahweh's worship. . . .
>
> A number of texts as well envisage Israel as exercising a mediatorial role in the worship of the nations for whom it is to make intercession (45:14) or perform the sacrifices for which they supply the victims (60:7; 61:6). . . . [I]t is especially striking to observe how the texts foresee the nations as Yahweh's worshippers, entering fully and equally into the privileges of Israel. Thus titles used elsewhere of Israel ("my people," "the work of my hands," 19:25; "servant[s]," 56:6) will be predicated of them. They will function too as Yahweh's "missionaries" (66:19) and clergy (66:21). Non-Israelites are to have an altar of their own (19:20), will present acceptable sacrifices to the Lord (19:21; 56:7), participate in his feasts (56:6; 66:23) and have a part in his "covenant" (56:6). Yahweh for his part will "teach" the nations (2:3), feed them (25:6), abolish all that causes them grief (25:7-8) and make himself/his "glory" known to them (19:22; 66:18). *In sum, the nations' worship of Yahweh constitutes a key, insistently underscored component of the future hopes that occupy so large a part of the extant book of Isaiah.*[40]

Compared with Isaiah, the theme is much more rare in other prophetic

---

[39] Vogels, *God's Universal Covenant*, p. 122.
[40] Begg, "The Peoples and the Worship of Yahweh," pp. 54-55 (emphasis added).

books, but certainly not entirely lacking. The following list of texts is well worth perusing: Jeremiah 3:17; 17:19-21; Micah 4:1-5; Zephaniah 2:11; 3:9; Zechariah 8:20-22; 14:16; Malachi 1:11.

We can say then, with a broad range of textual support, that a significant part of Israel's eschatological hope in relation to the nations was that *ultimately they would bring their worship to* YHWH, *the one living God of all the earth.* And again we must add that such a vision constitutes a major strand within a biblical theology of mission, for it is the indefatigable mission of God—a mission in which he invites our participation—to bring such universal worship of the nations to joyful reality.

The Nations Will Be Included in Israel's Identity

"It is especially striking to observe," repeating Begg's point, "how the texts foresee the nations as Yahweh's worshippers, *entering fully and equally into the privileges of Israel.*"[41] Striking indeed. And so we must finally turn to this climactic point. For, to revisit my earlier metaphor, the Old Testament is not content merely to portray the nations as the spectators of the great drama being played out between YHWH and Israel, not even as clapping spectators who perceive that the drama is ultimately for their own benefit. The most radical part of the Old Testament vision is yet to come. For the divine director intends eventually to bring the spectators out of the stalls onto the stage, to join the original cast and then to continue the drama with a single, though infinitely enlarged, company. The nations will come to share the very identity of Israel itself. God's people will burst the boundaries of ethnicity and geography. The very name "Israel" will be extended and redefined.

These things were not the ex post facto theological rationalizations of the apostle Paul seeking to justify the inclusion of Gentiles in the church. These things are *unambiguously stated in the Old Testament itself as part of God's mission* in relation to the nations of the earth. As the following survey of texts, drawn again from Psalms and the Prophets, will demonstrate, when God accomplishes his great missional project for history and creation, the nations of the world will be found to have been

- registered in God's city
- blessed with God's salvation
- accepted in God's house
- called by God's name
- joined with God's people

---

[41]Ibid., p. 55.

No more comprehensive inclusion could be imagined.

Registered in God's city. Psalm 47 has already astonished us with its portrayal of the nations as applauding YHWH for what had happened in the history of Israel, even though it included the subjugation of the nations themselves in the history of the conquest. But it goes on to greater surprises. If YHWH is indeed the King of all the earth, then when the great assembly of nations gathers before him, we read:

> The nobles of the nations assemble
> [as] the people of the God of Abraham,
> for the kings of the earth belong to God;
> he is greatly exalted. (Ps 47:9)

As the brackets that I have added indicate, there is no preposition in the phrase in Hebrew. "The nobles of the nations" and "the people of the God of Abraham" are simply set in apposition, the one being identified with the other.[42] That God in this context should be specifically named as the God of Abraham is surely significant, in view of the universality of God's promise to Abraham. So the register of the nations will not set the other nations behind, beneath or even merely alongside Israel, but will actually include them *as* Israel, as part of the people of father Abraham.

> The innumerable princes and peoples are to become one *people,* and they will no longer be outsiders but within the covenant; this is implied in their being called *the people of the God of Abraham*. It is the abundant fulfillment of the promise of Genesis 12:3; it anticipates what Paul expounds of the inclusion of the Gentiles as Abraham's sons (Rom 4:11; Gal 3:7-9).[43]

Psalm 87 actually uses the imagery of a register of the nations (v. 6), and quite astonishingly holds the roll call in Zion itself. Many surrounding nations are listed as having been "born" there, and as being among those who "know me" (v. 4, language normally exclusively used of Israel within the covenant). The expectation clearly is that "Zion" will ultimately come to include not just native-born Israelites but people of other nations who will be adopted and enfranchised as citizens of the city, with as much right as the native born to be registered there by YHWH. Significantly, YHWH is here also named Elyon (v. 5),

---

[42]Commentators speculate if the Hebrew ʿim (with) has dropped out through haplography with the consonantally identical ʿam (people) following. The LXX takes it thus. However, there is no textual evidence for a longer reading, and the Masoretic Text makes sense when taken as above.

[43]Derek Kidner, *Psalms 1-72*, Tyndale Old Testament Commentaries (Leicester: Inter-Varsity Press, 1973), p. 178.

the original name of the God of Jerusalem, with strong connections to Abraham (Gen 14:18-20).

The list of nations to be counted and registered as citizens of Zion even includes the two great historical *enemy* empires, Egypt (Rahab) and Babylon, along with smaller neighboring enemies, the Philistines, trading partners (Tyre), and representatives of the more distant regions (Cush). When the roll is called up yonder, there will be some surprising names on the register.

Blessed with God's salvation. Personally, as I said in chapter seven (p. 236), I find Isaiah 19:16-25 one of the most breathtaking pronouncements of any prophet, and certainly one of the most missiologically significant texts in the Old Testament.

The chapter begins in a way that we have come to expect from the prophetic repertoire—an oracle of doom against Egypt in a sequence of such oracles against Babylon, Moab, Syria and Cush. In Isaiah 19:1-15 Egypt is comprehensively placed under God's coming historical judgment at every level of their religion, agriculture, fisheries, industry and politics. We have heard this kind of thing before.

But then, from verse 15 to verse 22, the more indefinite future ("in that day" is repeated six times) will see an astonishing transformation of Egypt's fortunes, in which they will experience for themselves all that God did for Israel when he rescued them from the Egyptian oppression. The prophet extends to a foreign nation the familiar principle by which predictions of Israel's own future restoration were made in terms drawn from Israel's past (a new exodus, new covenant, new wilderness protection and land entry, etc.). Here Israel's past is used to portray the future blessing promised to a foreign nation that turns to God.[44] They (the Egyptians), who had once refused to acknowledge YHWH, will cry out to him (not to their own gods). He will send them a Savior and Deliverer. They will then know YHWH and worship him (as Israel did through their exodus). They will even speak the language of Canaan (i.e., Hebrew, from an Israelite's perspective; this is in effect to say that the Egyptians will be de facto identified as Israelites). They will be struck by plagues, but YHWH will heal them. All this is Exodus revisited and turned inside out. It is Exodus reloaded, with the characters reversed.

The list of affirmations made about Egypt in this incredible piece of eschatological writing is more detailed than anything said about the nations anywhere else.

---

[44]"The author of Is. 19:16-25 . . . chose images of the experience of his own people to depict the salvation offered to the nations. . . . He dared to apply to other nations what Israel believed to be her privilege." Vogels, *God's Universal Covenant,* p. 96.

Isa. 19.16-25 goes beyond not only the rest of Isaiah, but the entire OT, in foresee-
ing other nations—and traditionally enemy ones at that—coming to participate in
such a range of hitherto distinctively Israelite experiences and prerogatives . . . such
that they will stand on a footing of full equality with Israel.[45]

As if what has been said about Egypt were not surprise enough, the prophet
then brings Assyria into the equation and foretells that these two great nations
would join hands (Is 19:23). Normally, that would have filled Israelite hearts
with dread, for Egypt and Assyria were like giant nutcrackers, squeezing Israel
at either end of their history and from opposite ends of the compass. But historical reality is totally inverted in the prediction that the purpose of their uniting
will be, not that they will join forces to fight against YHWH and his people but
rather that "they will worship together." This goes beyond the promise that *Israelites* who had been scattered in Assyria or Egypt would come together to
worship God again, as in Isaiah 27:12-13. This is not just a prophecy of the ingathering of the exiles of *Israel* but about the ingathering of the *nations* among
whom (and *by* whom in some cases) they had been exiled. The scattering oppressors become the ingathered worshipers. History is inverted in this eschatological transformation. The enemies of God and Israel will be at peace with Israel and with each other.[46]

Doubtless the prophet uses Egypt and Assyria here in this highly eschatological
prophecy in a representational way; that is, they stand for a wider inclusion of
other nations, not just the specifically named nations. In the same way, prophecies concerning Babylon (in both Testaments) move beyond predictions about the
historical fate of the actual city and empire of Babylon into representational visions of the ultimate fate of the enemies of God. Egypt and Assyria never reached
such unity with Israel in Isaiah's time or indeed in ours. But the vision and the
task implied within it (or to put it another way, the mission of God and his people)
embraces more than Middle Eastern geopolitics, ancient or modern.

It therefore invites us to look forward and to pray for the coming of the day when
nations such as Egypt (and we can then add our own nation) revere God, when
its cities (and we can then add our own city) acknowledge Yahweh, when such
nations have a salvation history parallel to Israel's, when the great powers are
united in worship, and when the promise to Abraham indeed comes true.[47]

---

[45]Begg, "The Peoples and the Worship of Yahweh," p. 42.
[46]"The day that Egypt and Assyria are at peace with one another and with Israel will be the day
the whole world is at peace." Barry Webb, *The Message of Isaiah,* The Bible Speaks Today
(Leicester, U.K.: Inter-Varsity Press; Downers Grove, Ill.: InterVarsity Press, 1996), p. 96.
[47]John Goldingay, *Isaiah,* New International Biblical Commentary (Peabody, Mass.: Hendrikson; Carlisle, U.K.: Paternoster, 2001), p. 121.

Then comes the final surprise:

> In that day Israel will be the third, along with Egypt and Assyria, a blessing on the earth. The LORD Almighty will bless them, saying, "Blessed be Egypt my people, Assyria my handiwork, and Israel my inheritance. (Is 19:24-25)

The identity of Israel will be *merged* with that of Egypt and Assyria. In case the implication of verse 24 was not clear enough, the prophet makes it unambiguous (not to mention scandalous) by applying to Egypt and Assyria descriptions that hitherto could only have been said about Israel. In fact, the word order in Hebrew is more emphatic and shocking than the NIV translation. It reads literally: "Blessed be my people, Egypt[!], and the work of my hands, Assyria[!], and my inheritance, Israel." The shock of reading "Egypt" immediately after "my people" (instead of the expected Israel) and of putting Israel third on the list is palpable. Yet there it is. The archenemies of Israel will be absorbed into the identity, titles and privileges of Israel and share in the Abrahamic blessing of the living God, YHWH.

Of course, they will not be absorbed into God's people in this way while they remain enemies. The transformation that is explicit about Egypt must also be assumed about Assyria. It is only as God's enemies cry out to him, acknowledge him, worship him and turn to him (vv. 20-22) that they enjoy rescue, healing, blessing, and inclusion. That was as true for rebellious Israel as for their traditional enemies. But that indeed is what the converting love and power of God will accomplish—for the nations as for Israel. That is God's mission. God is in the business of turning enemies into friends, as Saul of Tarsus knew better than most. It is very possible that his triple expression of the inclusion of the Gentiles within the identity and titles of Israel (as coheirs, a cobody and cosharers with Israel) in Ephesians 3:6 owes something to this verse in Isaiah.

Accepted in God's house. Isaiah 56:3-8 is unusual in being addressed not to nations as wholes but to individual foreigners, along with eunuchs, two groups of people who, in the community to which these words were addressed, feared exclusion from God's people. Their fears were well grounded, for laws such as Deuteronomy 23:1-8 show that castrated males and certain categories of foreigner were indeed denied access to the holy assembly of Israelites at worship.

Among the ancillary reasons for this exclusion may well have been the strong criterion for covenant membership in preexilic Israel of belonging within a landowning household. *Kinship* (belonging to the ethnic tribal structure of Israel) and *land* (sharing in the inheritance of YHWH's land) were key elements in one's

identity and inclusion within Israel.[48] The eunuch could have no family, for, as
he bemoaned, "I am only a dry tree" (Is 56:3). And the foreigner could have no
stake in the land since it was divided up exclusively among the tribes, clans and
households of Israel.

These crippling deficiencies are here directly addressed by God. The eunuch
will have "a memorial and a name" better than any family could give him. The
foreigner will be brought to God's holy mountain—symbolic of having a rightful
share in the land as a whole. They will, in short, fully belong to the citizenry of
Israel.

And on what conditions are such promises made? Precisely the same conditions that applied to Israel's own continued enjoyment of the privilege of being
the people of YHWH, namely, wholehearted covenant *loyalty* to YHWH, exclusive
worship of him, and careful *obedience* to his laws (Is 56:4-6). As has been said,
the definition of Israel here is subtly developing from a *chosen* people to a
choosing people.

> These [foreigners] I will bring to my holy mountain
>   and give them joy in my house of prayer.
> Their burnt offerings and sacrifices
>   will be accepted on my altar;
> for my house of prayer will be called
>   a house of prayer for all nations. (Is 56:7)

It is not difficult to imagine the growing sense of shock and scandal among
the native inhabitants of Jerusalem as the divine invitation draws the foreigner
ever closer to the very heart of Israel's exclusive holiness.

> Foreigners will be brought to the holy mountain.
> That's close enough surely?
> No, God will give them joy right in the temple.
> But in its outer courts, perhaps?
> No, they can bring their sacrifices right up to the altar.

Nothing that was available to *Israelite* worshipers will be denied to *foreigners*
willing to commit themselves to Israel's God. If they accept the terms of covenant
membership, they will be accepted at the heart of the covenant relationship.
They will find joy in the house of the Lord—the joy of identity and inclusion.

Once again, it is very probable that Paul's mind is saturated with the dynamic

---

[48]See further on this whole nexus of theology, economics and ethics: Christopher J. H. Wright,
God's People in God's Land: Family, Land and Property in the Old Testament (Grand Rapids:
Eerdmans, 1990).

of these verses as he wrote these words to the beneficiaries of their fulfillment:

> Remember that at that time you were separate from Christ, excluded from citizenship in Israel and foreigners to the covenants of the promise, without hope and without God in the world. But now in Christ Jesus you who were once far away have been brought near through the blood of Christ. (Eph 2:12-13)

And it is very hard to imagine that Luke did not have this text of Isaiah in mind, with some ironic sense of humor no doubt, when he recorded that the first believer in Jesus from outside the native Jewish community was indeed a *foreigner*, a *eunuch*, and was reading the scroll of Isaiah, just a few column inches from this passage. Luke is careful to point out, however, in line with his understanding of the fulfillment of all such promises in Christ, that the Ethiopian eunuch in Acts 8, though he had indeed been to Jerusalem to worship, found joy, not in the *temple* but when he heard about *Jesus*, trusted and was baptized, and went on his way rejoicing. Jesus is the one through whom people of all nations will be accepted in God's house of prayer for all nations. Mission means bringing the nations to find joy in the house of the Lord by bringing them to the one who embodies that house in his own person and the community of believers.

Called by God's name. Amos 9:11-12 brings the book of Amos to a startling close. After the fires of judgment, destruction and exile that have dominated the whole book so far, the final note is one of hope. Beyond judgment, there lie restoration and renewal in the plans of God. Since other preexilic prophets could combine oracles of judgment and hope, there seems no compelling reason to snip these verses out of Amos's prophecy and assign them elsewhere.

What is striking is that just as Amos began in the international arena, so he ends there. Amos 1—2 portrays the chaotic wickedness of the surrounding nations—of course, Israel is no better—and YHWH's thundering word of coming wrath. These final verses portray the restoration not only of the Davidic kingdom and temple (remembering Amos was from Judah, even though his prophetic ministry took place in the northern kingdom) but also of "the remnant of Edom and all the nations that bear my name."[49]

The great surprise here is the combination of a plural word *nations* with the concept "called by my name." Only one nation, surely, could be legitimately de-

---

[49]Regarding "Edom," the LXX reads "Adam" instead of "Edom" (the Heb. consonants are the same) and thus takes it as "remnant of humankind." This is an understandable and possibly correct reading, and would fit with the universal note of "all the nations." It is certainly the form of the text that is used by James in Acts 15:17.

scribed in that way. The expression "called by the name of" denotes ownership
and intimate relationship. In ordinary use, it expressed the longing of anxious
women to belong to a husband (Is 4:1), or the close, authenticating relationship
of a prophet to his God (Jer 15:16).

But in significant theological usage "being called by YHWH's name" applied
to the central focal points of Israel's unique relationship with YHWH. The ark of
the covenant was called by his name (2 Sam 6:2). So was the temple itself on
the day of its dedication, and Solomon prayed that "all the people of the earth"
would come to know it (1 Kings 8:43). Jerusalem, worthily or not, was the city
that was called by YHWH's name (Jer 25:29). Most significant of all, it was at the
heart of God's covenant blessing on Israel that they would be the people who
were called by his name.

> The LORD will establish you as his holy people, as he promised you on oath, if you
> keep the commands of the LORD your God and walk in his ways. Then all the peo-
> ples on earth will see that you are *called by the name* of the LORD, and they will
> fear you. (Deut 28:9-10, emphasis added)

Indeed, this was precisely one of the distinguishing marks of Israel, for the
foreign nations of Israel's own day could be lumped together simply as those
had *never* been called by YHWH's name (Is 63:19).

So what is Amos saying? Nothing less than that this great privilege, which the
nations were supposed to recognize about the temple and about Israel, would
actually be seen to be true of the nations themselves. This is an eschatological
reversal of status.

As in the other texts we have already observed, this is also the language of
inclusion and identity. To be called by the name of YHWH was the luggage tag
on the ark, the dedication plaque on the temple, the map reference of Jerusalem
and the lapel badge of every Israelite. It was the defining privilege of only one
people on earth—Israel—to be known as "the nation called by the name of
YHWH." Now, declares the prophet, this identity will be available to people of
"all nations." How more included could you get?

The nations who stood under God's judgment with Israel in Amos 1—2 now
stand under God's blessing with Israel in these closing verses. The very concept
of "Israel" has been stretched to include them in the key designation: "called by
my name."

Isaiah 44:1-5 is another unusual text in speaking of individuals rather than
nations as wholes. The context is God's promise to Israel in exile that they will
not wither and die out there. On the contrary, God has plans of future growth
for his people, under the irrigating and fertilizing power of his Spirit. Within that

vision, the prophet describes individual conversions to YHWH.[50]

> One will say, "I belong to the LORD";
>   another will call himself by the name of Jacob;
> still another will write on his hand, "The LORD's,"
>   and will take the name Israel. (Is 44:5)

So the growth of Israel will not just be biological (as the predominant imagery evokes) but also by extension and conversion. Foreigners will join Israel by the double act of identifying themselves with YHWH and with YHWH's people—Israel. There is no belonging to one without the other, but membership is clearly open to those who choose it. Being called by God's name, then, is both an eschatological vision for the *nations* (as in Amos), but it is also a personal choice and action for the *individual.* A biblical theology of mission, of course, comfortably includes both.

Joined with God's people. Zechariah 2:10-11 comes in the midst of a vision of encouragement to the postexilic people of Jerusalem. In contrast to the program initiated by Nehemiah, this prophet says that the city will not need walls, partly because its influx of new inhabitants will be so many and partly because God himself will be a wall of fire around them (Zech 2:3-5). Their enemies who had plundered them will themselves be defeated and plundered (2:8-9). Then the King will come home to dwell once more among his people.

> "Shout and be glad O Daughter of Zion. For look, here I am coming, and I will reside in the midst of you," declares the LORD. "Many nations will join themselves to YHWH in that day. And they will be for me for a people. And I will reside in the midst of you." (Zech 2:10-11, author's translation)

So the prophet's message for the nations was not one of destructive judgment only but also, beyond that, of inclusion in God's people. And the prophet's message for Israel was not one of exclusive favoritism at the hand of God but of an expansion that would include not only their own returning exiles, but also people of "many nations."

The repeated line "I will reside in the midst of you" is important, both in content and position. It is the word *šākan,* strongly associated with God's taking up residence in the tabernacle and then the temple. The related noun is *šěkînâ,* the

---

[50]Some take Is 44:5 as referring not to foreigners but to apostate Israelites returning to the fold in repentance and renewed allegiance. This is possible, but it seems to strain the text. Strictly speaking, no native-born Israelite needed to say what the speakers in this verse affirm. So it makes much more sense, in my view, to regard the words as being spoken by non-Israelites who chose to identify themselves with YHWH and his people through the use of these formulae.

tabernacling presence of God among his people. So the first use of the phrase in Zechariah 2:10 is a word of hope to the postexilic community, in line with the visions of Ezekiel, that God would return to Zion to take up residence once again in the city and temple he had so grievously left. But the second identical use comes after the prediction of the influx of the nations to join themselves to YHWH. And this repetition seals the affirmation of inclusion that has already been signalled in other ways.

First, the nations will join themselves to YHWH—not merely to Israel. In other words, they do not join merely as subordinates of Israel, in some second-class citizenship. They will belong to YHWH just as Israel does (as we saw in Ps 47).

Second, they will enjoy exactly the same covenantal relationship with YHWH that Israel does. The expression "they will be for me for a people" is precisely the language of the covenant, with its roots going back to Sinai, hitherto applied only to Israel. Significantly, although the nations are plural (as is the verb "they will be"), the predicate is singular, *"a people."* This is not "Israel plus the nations" but "the nations as Israel," one people belonging to God.

So, when the phrase "I will reside in the midst" is repeated after the predicted joining of the nations, it significantly does not change the final suffix to "in the midst of *them,*" but retains *"you"*—the second person feminine singular of the original reference to Zion. "You," Zion, remain the dwelling place of God, but "you" are no longer going to be merely a community of returned Jewish exiles. "You," Zion, will become a multinational community of people from many nations, all of whom will belong to YHWH, and therefore they will be rightly counted as belonging to Israel. God himself will dwell in the midst of "you," Zion of the nations (cf. Ps 87). The identity and membership of Israel have thus been radically redrawn by YHWH himself. It is no longer Zion *and* the nations but Zion inclusive of the nations.

Zechariah 9:7 shows the extent to which such a vision could be taken, within the contemporary international political scene of the day. Zechariah 9 begins with a whistle-stop tour of the map of west Asian countries, from north to south, beginning in the heights of Syria and ending in the Gaza strip (Zech 9:1-6). Everything under the flight path of the prophet's vision is placed under the searching eye and imminent judgment of YHWH.

But then, a sudden surprising word of hope intrudes in relation to the Philistines—*the Philistines*, of all people!

> I will take the blood from their mouths, the forbidden food from between their teeth. And the remnant, even it will belong to our God. And it will be like a clan in Judah, and Ekron will be like the Jebusites. (Zech 9:7, author's translation)

Again we find that judgment (in v. 6) is not God's final word for the nations, not even for a nation that had been such an inveterate enemy of Israel from time immemorial. Rather, they can be purged and cleansed of pagan practices. And, just like Israel itself after the purging fires of God's judgment, *a remnant will belong to "our God,"* that is, a remnant of the Philistines will belong to the God of Israel.

So the same hope is held out to the Philistines as to rebellious Israel, the hope of a faithful remnant. To this language of covenant inclusion ("belonging to our God") is added the language of economic inclusion in the land and social structure of Israel (remember the point in Is 56 that land and kinship were essential elements of Israelite identity and covenant inclusion in the Old Testament). The Philistines would become a clan of Judah(!), incorporated in the same way that the Jebusites, the original inhabitants of Canaanite Jerusalem, had been incorporated by David into his new kingdom.

Here is a remarkable word, then, showing the extent to which hope of the general inclusion of the nations within the identity of Israel could be dressed in the very particular garb of contemporary international politics—making it all the more sharply defined. If there is hope for the *Philistines,* there is hope for anybody. If God plans to include Philistines within Israel as part of a people "belonging to our God," who can be excluded?

We need to pause for breath. As we look back over the road we have trodden in this chapter, we must acknowledge the sheer scale of the vistas it has opened up for us. Admittedly, we have collated texts from a wide variety of canonical sources and have not sought to labor their historical, literary or social contexts. However, the scope and volume of the textual witness we have heard is surely impressive. The variety of date and canonical location also makes its own point. From early texts through to the postexilic period we find evidence of a settled conviction in Israel about the relationship between their God and the rest of the nations of the world. Here is an element in the core worldview that shaped the life and thought of this people as firmly embedded, if not as prominently paraded, as the other fundamental aspects of their understanding of themselves, their God and their world.

We have seen that the pillars of Israel's worldview included their *election* by YHWH in Abraham, their *redemption* at the exodus, the *covenant* relationship in which they stood with this God, and the *ethical* response of holiness in life and worship that this relationship demanded. All of these things they believed to be true of themselves in a unique way that did *not* apply to other nations. And yet, they also knew that their Redeemer God was also the Creator of the whole universe, *including* all other nations. So they articulated a theological perspective on those nations that has robust coherence, blending historical realism (the current exclusion of the nations from the experience of Israel) with astonishing eschatological optimism (the ultimate inclusion of the nations in everything that Israel believed about themselves).

According to this broad viewpoint, all nations of the world were created by YHWH, stand under his government in their historical affairs, are accountable to him morally and especially for the doing of justice. Like Israel, however, all nations have fallen short of the glory of God and stand in the same default position: under God's judgment. That judgment will come as surely on the nations as it fell on Israel. But beyond judgment there is hope, for there is always hope with the God of Israel.

So just as the remnant of Israel experienced the miraculous and restorative grace of God in their own historical return from the grave of exile, so ultimately the remnant of the nations will turn to the only saving God, YHWH. Rejecting all false gods, they will join Israel in bringing their worship to YHWH alone. And as they do so, God himself will bind them into covenant relationship, such that the distinction between Israel and the nations will eventually be dissolved in a multinational community belonging to YHWH and living in a relationship of blessing with him, in fulfillment of the great covenantal initiative established through the promise to Abraham. The distinctiveness of Israel from the nations within their Old Testament history was essential to the mission of God. But the mission of God was that the distinction would ultimately be dissolved as the nations flowed into unity and identity with Israel. Only the New Testament gospel would show how that *could* happen. And only New Testament mission would show how it *did* and will continue to happen until their ingathering is complete.

15

God and the Nations
in New Testament Mission

At the end of chapter fourteen I outlined the broad contours of Israel's understanding of the nations within their core worldview convictions about God and the world. This is the sturdy foundation of conviction on which Jesus and his earliest followers built an edifice that has come to be called the mission of the church. For, as they must have reasoned:

1. if the God of Israel is the God of the whole earth

2. if all the nations (including Israel) stood under his wrath and judgment

3. if it is nevertheless God's will that all nations on earth should come to know and worship him

4. if he had chosen Israel to be the means of bringing such blessing to all nations

5. if the Messiah is to be the one who would embody and fulfill that mission of Israel

6. if Jesus of Nazareth, crucified and risen, is that Messiah

7. then it is time for the nations to hear the good news

It was time for the repeated summons of Psalms that the news of YHWH's salvation should be proclaimed and sung among the nations, and for the vision of the prophets that YHWH's salvation should reach the ends of the earth, to move from the imagination of faith into the arena of historical fulfillment.

A Missions Mandate in the Old Testament?

The logic did not all just tumble together quite like that, however; certainly not at first. When the centrifugal dynamic of the early Christian missionary movement finally got under way, it was indeed something remarkably new *in practice if not in concept*. There were precedents, of course, in the Jewish proselyte efforts. But the scale and theological rationale of the mission to the Gentile nations that takes place in the New Testament goes beyond anything achieved in the proselytizing activities of Second Temple Judaism.[1]

We need to step back just one moment and ask whether the logic ought to have generated mission to the nations much earlier, that is, within the history of Old Testament Israel itself. There are those who think that it was indeed God's intention that the Israelites should have engaged in evangelistic centrifugal mission to the nations.

Walter Kaiser builds a strong case for his passionate conviction that Israel had, and knew it had, a duty to take its message of YHWH's salvation to the nations, calling them to trust, as they was supposed to do, in God's promised Seed, the one who would come in fulfillment of God's promises to Adam and Eve, to Abraham, and to David. Kaiser takes the many texts we cataloged in chapter fourteen not merely as a conviction about something God intended to do through Israel but something that Israel had a mandate to do there and then.[2]

However, it seems to me that there is no clear mandate in God's revelation to Israel over the centuries for them to undertake "missions," in our sense of the word, to the nations. If it had been the case that God intended that Israelites should travel to other nations to challenge their worship of other gods, to call them to ethical and religious repentance, to tell the story of all that YHWH had done in and for Israel, and then to lead them to trust in the promised Seed of Abraham for their salvation—if all this had been God's intention for Israel, one might have expected to find certain other lines of evidence. For example, in the Torah, while we have observed the implications of the designation of Israel as God's priesthood among the nations, there is no clear and explicit command that Israelites should *go* to the nations and exercise that priestly function there. There is no shortage of laws for how Israel was to live in their land as YHWH's

---

[1]There is considerable dispute, however, over how much of this Jewish proselytizing activity there actually was. For a positive missiological evaluation of the Jewish diaspora and proselytizing efforts, see Richard R. De Ridder, *Discipling the Nations* (Grand Rapids: Baker, 1975), pp. 58-127. For a wide-ranging discussion of all the sources and secondary literature, see Eckhard J Schnabel, *Early Christian Mission*, vol. 1, *Jesus and the Twelve* (Leicester, U.K.: InterVarsity Press; Downers Grove, Ill.: InterVarsity Press, 2004), pp. 92-172.

[2]Walter C. Kaiser Jr., *Mission in the Old Testament: Israel as a Light to the Nations* (Grand Rapids: Baker, 2000). Kaiser addresses many of the same texts we have surveyed in this book, and at a fundamental level we are in agreement on the strong missional message of the Old Testament. I am not yet convinced, however, of his interpretation of these texts as implying a missionary mandate that ought to have resulted in Israel engaging in centrifugal missions to the nations.

covenant partner in the midst of the nations. So if YHWH's intention had been that they were to organize missions to the nations, instructions to that effect would surely have been framed. But we find none.

And if actual missions to the nations had been a known covenantal obligation (which Israelites were expected to deduce from their narrative traditions of God's promises and the universalizing thrust of their worship songs), we might have expected explicit condemnation in the prophets for Israel's manifest *failure* to undertake such missionary activity, especially if it were such a key and conscious element in Israel's understanding as Kaiser implies. The prophets found no shortage of things to condemn Israel for. Failure to *live* by the standards of their covenant with YHWH among the nations was certainly one of them. But failure to take the message of salvation to the nations by physically *going* to them is not one of them. This suggests that nobody at that point was under the impression that they were supposed to go, including those who stood closest to the mind and revelation of God.

Jonah, of course, is an exception to this principle, but to use him in support of an alleged missionary mandate in the Old Testament begs the hermeneutical question of the book's intention, which is notoriously controverted.[3] The book clearly teaches important lessons about the nature of God and his attitude to outside nations; that is the obvious thrust of the final chapter. It clearly challenges the kind of attitude that Jonah adopts in reaction to God's suspension of judgment on Nineveh. But whether it was written with the additional intention of persuading other Israelites to be foreign missionaries like Jonah, though perhaps with less recalcitrance and sulking anger at the mercies of God, is altogether more questionable.

What we find rather is the clear promise that it is *God's* intention to bring such blessing to the nations, that *God* will summon the nations to himself in the great pilgrimage to Zion. Mission to the nations, from an Old Testament perspective, is an eschatological act of God, not (yet) a missionary sending agenda for God's people. Only in Isaiah 66 is there explicit word of God sending messengers to the nations, and that is as a future expectation contingent on the ingathering of Israel first.

---

[3]Jonah was not, however, the only prophet to go to a foreign nation. Elijah went to the region of Tyre and Sidon to stay with the widow of Zarephath, who subsequently became a believer in YHWH. Elisha, after his encounter with Naaman (who also became a believer after his healing in Israel), went for a while to Damascus, capital of Syria (2 Kings 8:7-15). What he was doing there we are not told, but the text gives no hint of anything resembling evangelism. These accounts certainly show the blessing of God being extended to foreigners (as Solomon had prayed and as Jesus pointedly reminded his audience in Nazareth), but they scarcely take the form of organized missions to them or constitute evidence that such activity was expected of ordinary Israelites. See also, Walter A. Maier III, "The Healing of Naaman in Missiological Perspective," *Concordia Theological Quarterly* 61 (1997): 177-96.

What we also find, however, is that Israel definitely had a sense of mission, not in the sense of *going* somewhere but of *being* something. They were to be the holy people of the living God YHWH. They were to know him for who he is, to preserve the true and exclusive worship YHWH, and to live according to his ways and laws within loyal commitment to their covenant relationship with him. In all these respects they would *be* a light and a witness to the nations.

I agree, therefore, with the views of Eckhard Schnabel and Charles Scobie.

[It is] difficult, if not impossible, to speak of a universal task, or commission of Israel. As I understand the OT, it seems quite clear that the "mission" that YHWH gave to Israel—to worship him and to do his will in thankful and joyous obedience to the covenant stipulations—was a *local* mission, that is a task carried out by the Israelites within the borders of Israel. What is *universal* are the consequences of Israel's obedience—in the future eschaton.[4]

Scobie, having surveyed some of the material we have explored in this chapter, concludes:

Despite this remarkable set of passages the fact remains that there is no real indication of any active missionary outreach on the part of Israel in the Old Testament period. This is so for three important, interlocking reasons.

Firstly, the ingathering of the nations *is an eschatological event*. It is something that will happen "in the latter days." . . . Thus the Gentiles will be fully accepted, but not in the present; this is an event which belongs to God's future.

Secondly, the ingathering of the nations *is not the work of Israel*. Frequently it is the nations themselves who will take the initiative. In a number of significant passages it is God who gathers the nations. . . .

Thirdly, these prophetic passages all envisage *the nations coming to Israel, not Israel going to the nations*. . . . This movement from the periphery to the centre has been appropriately labelled "centripetal."[5]

---

[4]Eckhard J Schnabel, "Israel, the People of God, and the Nations," *Journal of the Evangelical Theological Society* 45 (2002): 40. Cf. also Schnabel's very thorough treatment of the Old Testament material and survey of relevant scholarship on it in the first part of his magisterial study, *Early Christian Mission*, 1:55-91.

[5]Charles H. H. Scobie, "Israel and the Nations: An Essay in Biblical Theology," *Tyndale Bulletin* 43, no. 2 (1992): 291-92. My only quarrel with Schnabel and Scobie in these quotes is that they downplay the element of Israel's conviction about the nations that is (over-)emphasized by Kaiser, namely, the prominent theme in the Psalms of proclamation among the nations of all the works of YHWH. This seems to me to envision more than "local" mission, in terms of the universal significance of the revelation entrusted to Israel, even though I continue to hold that such language belongs to the rhetoric of faith and hope rather than that the psalmists were offering themselves or calling on others to enlist as missionaries who would go and do that proclaiming among the nations.

When we turn the page from Malachi to Matthew, however, we have landed in a totally different world. We find the same understanding of God's ultimate mission to the nations that we have seen breathing so pervasively through the Old Testament. But we now also find that it has been transformed from what Schnabel calls a missionary *idea* into energetic missionary *praxis*.

> In the beginning was Jesus. Without the person of Jesus of Nazareth, the messianic Son of Man, there would be no Christians. Without the ministry of Jesus there would be no Christian missions. Without Christian missions there would have been no Christian Occident. The first Christian missionary was not Paul, but Peter, and Peter would not have preached a "missionary" sermon at Pentecost if he had not been a student of Jesus for three years.[6]

With these bold words Eckhard Schnabel begins his massive study of the mission of the early Christian church. He goes on to trace, in a few stokes, how rapidly the movement spread, from 120 people in A.D. 30 in Jerusalem to a community that was causing a stir in Rome nineteen years later, when the emperor Claudius expelled all Jews from the city, and that within thirty-four years was troublesome enough to attract the persecution of the emperor Nero.

We too, then, must begin with Jesus and the Gospels, then look briefly at Luke's account of the early church in Acts, and finally at the apostle Paul. In each case, our purpose is to see how their scriptural understanding of God and the nations affected the way they conceived their participation in the mission of God. We want to see how the New Testament picks up and brings to fruition all the theology and expectation of the Old Testament in relation to God and the nations.

Jesus and the Evangelists

What were the aims of Jesus?[7] What did he set out to do? How did he understand

---

[6]Schnabel, *Early Christian Mission,* 1:3. By "Christian Occident," of course, Schnabel is referring to the historical reality of the broad conversion of Europe over the post-New Testament centuries, not to present global realities. The phenomenal growth of the church around the world in the past century has turned the (inappropriately so-called) Christian West into a marginal minority of global Christianity. More than 75 percent of all the world's Christians now live in the global south—or the Majority World of Africa, Latin America and some parts of Asia.

[7]What follows is very summary and focuses on themes we have followed hitherto in this book, especially in chap. 14. More detailed accounts of the distinctive missional message of each of the Gospels can be found in chap. 2, "Matthew: Mission as Disciple-Making," and chap. 3, "Luke-Acts: Practicing Forgiveness and Solidarity with the Poor," David J. Bosch, *Transforming Mission: Paradigm Shifts in Theology of Mission* (Maryknoll, N.Y.: Orbis, 1991); chaps. 9, 10, 11, 12, on Mark, Matthew, Luke-Acts and the Johannine literature, respectively, in D. Senior and C. Stuhlmueller, *The Biblical Foundations for Mission* (London: SCM Press, 1983); Andreas J. Koestenberger and Peter T. O'Brien, *Salvation to the Ends of the Earth: A Biblical Theology of Mission* (Leicester, U.K.: Apollos, 2001); chaps. 4, 5, 6, 8, on Mark, Matthew, Luke-Acts and

his own personal mission, and what did he envision happening after his death? These are massive questions on which oceans of scholarly ink have been spilled. Fortunately there are some very helpful surveys of the relevant scholarship, and we need not rehearse here what is abundantly available elsewhere.[8]

One of the simplest ways in framing a reasonably coherent answer to the questions above is to observe what immediately preceded and what immediately followed Jesus' earthly ministry.

All the records agree that the ministry of Jesus began out of the ministry of John the Baptist, and that John's ministry was aimed at calling Israel to repentance in preparation for the coming of the Lord himself. That is, it was fundamentally a prophetic ministry seeking the restoration of Israel. Jesus identified himself with John's message and used it as the foundation of his own.

Then, very soon after Jesus' death and resurrection, we find his first followers crossing the boundaries of Jewish separateness from the Gentiles in order to share the good news about Jesus, supported and authenticated in doing so by manifestations of the Holy Spirit. Within a few short years, those who named Jesus as Lord and Savior had grown beyond the original group of convinced Jewish believers to include Hellenized Jews, then Samaritans, then Greeks, then people of many ethnic groups in Asia Minor and eventually had taken root in the cosmopolitan city of Rome itself.

In other words, Jesus' earthly ministry was launched by a movement that aimed at the restoration of *Israel*. But he himself launched a movement that aimed at the ingathering of the *nations* to the new messianic people of God. The *initial impetus* for his ministry was to call Israel back to their God. The *subsequent impact* of his ministry was a new community that called the nations to faith in the God of Israel.

This double dimension of the mission of Jesus needs to be kept in mind as we read the New Testament. It is consistent not only with the Old Testament passages we have surveyed, in which the eschatological scenario often included this sequence: Israel would be restored and then the nations would be gathered. Or, as in Zechariah 2 and Zechariah 9, the King (i.e., YHWH) would return to Zion (thus restoring his kingdom in their midst), and then the nations would be

---

John, respectively, in Andreas J. Koestenberger, *The Missions of Jesus and the Disciples According to the Fourth Gospel: With Implications for the Fourth Gospel's Purpose and the Mission of the Contemporary Church* (Grand Rapids: Eerdmans, 1998).

[8]In addition to the magisterial works of N. T. Wright, see also R. T. France, *Jesus and the Old Testament: His Application of Old Testament Passages to Himself and His Mission* (London: Tyndale, 1971); Ben F. Meyer, *The Aims of Jesus* (London: SCM Press, 1979); Eckhard Schnabel, *Early Christian Mission,* vol. 1; Ben Witherington III, *The Christolology of Jesus* (Minneapolis: Fortress Press, 1990).

joined to his people. It also reflects what is known of Jewish hopes in the inter-testamental period. Among the huge variety of eschatological scenarios found in the post-Old Testament literature, the dominant note is that of the redemption/restoration of Israel, but a subordinate note is also that, after the purging fires of judgment on the enemies of God, the way would be open for the in-gathering of the nations as foreseen in the great canonical prophets.

Jesus and Gentiles. The Gospels record that Jesus deliberately limited his itinerant ministry and that of his disciples for the most part to "the lost sheep of Israel" (Mt 10:6; 15:24). But they also show some significant engagements with Gentiles and an awareness that the arrival of the kingdom of God through Jesus must affect the Gentiles also. When the following incidents and sayings are compiled, they show that it is simply false to say that Jesus had no interest in the world beyond his own Jewish people.[9]

The Roman centurion's servant (Mt 8:5-13; Lk 7:1-10). Jesus responds with astonishment to the determined faith of the centurion, commenting that it is greater than anything he has found within Israel. It may be that what was significant about the centurion's faith was not merely that Jesus could work miracles of healing. Rather it was precisely that he, a Gentile, believed that the compassion and healing of Jesus could reach across the divide between Jew and Gentile and touch a Gentile's servant. This was something that Jesus' own townsfolk at Nazareth had found too much to stomach. Jesus therefore uses his Gentile faith as an opportunity to point to the eschatological hope of the ingathering of the nations to the messianic banquet in the kingdom of God. Jesus is

---

[9]A particularly fine and detailed discussion of the relationship between the way Jesus confined his own and his disciples' ministry to the boundaries of Israel in his lifetime, and then released them into mission to the nations after his death and resurrection, showing the scriptural roots for precisely such a "split" mission, is provided by Joachim Jeremias, *Jesus' Promise to the Nations,* Studies in Biblical Theology (London: SCM Press, 1958; Philadelphia: Fortress, 1982).

A shorter, but thought-provoking article on the same subject is T. W. Manson, *Jesus and the Non-Jews* (London: Athlone Press, 1955). Manson rejects the idea of liberal Christianity that the mission of Jesus was merely the promulgation of religious ideals to Jews and Gentiles, but rather the creation of a new community altogether, and this was the concern of the early church also. "It was the incorporation of Gentiles into the Christian body, not the inculcation of Christian ideas into Gentile minds, that was the live issue in the middle of the first century" (ibid., p. 6). "[Jesus' aim was] building up within Israel a body of men and women who were set free from chauvinistic nationalism from the ambition to impose Israelite ideals of faith and conduct on the rest of the world by force of arms; men and women set free from spiritual pride with its condescending readiness to instruct lesser breeds in the elements of true religion and sound morality; men and women who had learned in apprenticeship to Jesus how to accept the rule of God for themselves, and how to extend it to their neighbors at home and abroad by serving them in love. I think that Jesus saw the immediate task as that of creating such a community within Israel, in the faith that it would transform the life of his own people, and that a transformed Israel would transform the world" (ibid., p. 18).

probably combining here texts that spoke of the return of the diaspora Jews from all points of the compass (cf. Ps 107:3; Is 49:12), with the theme of the pilgrimage and worship of the nations (cf. Is 59:19; Mal 1:11). Certainly it shows that while Jesus limited his earthly mission predominantly to Jewish people, the ultimate horizon of his vision was much wider.

The Gadarene demoniac and the deaf-mute in Decapolis (Mt 8:28-34; Mk 5:1-20; Lk 8:26-39; Mk 7:31-35). The decision to cross over the Sea of Galilee came from Jesus himself, though he knew well that the other side of the lake was Gentile territory. The situation that confronts him there reeks of triple uncleanness. A large herd of unclean pigs is nearby; the man he meets lives in the unclean world of the dead; and the man is possessed by a legion of unclean spirits. But Jesus, far from being personally contaminated himself through his contact with such Gentile pollution, transforms it by his presence and word.

Jesus then takes the very unusual step of telling the healed man to spread the word about the mighty deeds and mercy of the Lord—which he proceeded to do with enthusiasm. He is in fact the first Gentile missionary to Gentiles, commissioned by Christ himself. Clearly his testimony bore fruit in the region, for on Jesus' next visit to the Decapolis (from which, remember, he had been begged to depart), people brought the man who was both deaf and dumb for healing, and it is highly probable, from its position in the narrative, that the feeding of the crowd of four thousand also took place on the Decapolis side of the lake—thus mirroring for the benefit of the Gentiles one of the most significant miracles through which Jesus demonstrated his identity to the Jews.

The Syro-Phoenician woman (Mt 15:21-28; Mk 7:24-31). Like the Roman centurion, the Syro-Phoenician woman is another Gentile who astonishes Jesus with the tenacity of her faith, even in the face of Jesus' reminder of the gulf that separated Jews from Gentiles. The positioning of the story is also richly significant. Both Matthew and Mark record the event in the wake of the dispute between Jesus and the Pharisees, and teachers of the law regarding clean and unclean food. In a radical reinterpretation, Jesus declares that the distinction between clean and unclean must be understood now in moral terms, not in terms of food; in terms of what comes out of the heart, not what goes into the mouth. "In saying this," comments Mark, "Jesus declared all foods 'clean' " (Mk 7:19).

But the clean-unclean distinction in Israel was fundamentally symbolic of the distinction between Israel and the nations. Accordingly, if Jesus abolished the distinction in relation to food (the symbol), then he simultaneously abolished the distinction in relation to Jews and Gentiles (the reality that the symbol pointed to). This makes it all the more significant that both Matthew and Mark follow the dispute with two miracles for Gentiles (the woman of Tyre and the man in Decapolis) and probably a third (if the feeding of the four thousand took place on the Decapolis side of the lake). By word and action Jesus is pointing to the nations as the wider horizon of the saving power of God.

The prophetic sign in the temple (Mt 21:12-13; Mk 11:15-17; Lk 19:45-46). It is now widely agreed that Jesus' action in the temple was much more than a "cleansing." Rather it was a prophetic sign that predicted the imminent destruction of the temple itself.[10] This was certainly the primary charge on which the Jewish authorities sought his execution.

However, Jesus linked his action to two Scriptures that clarified his action and spoke of its wider significance. His quotation from Jeremiah 7:11 about the temple as a "den of robbers" comes from the famous sermon of Jeremiah in the first temple, predicting its destruction by YHWH himself because of the unrepentant wickedness of those who still claimed to worship God there. His other quotation from Isaiah 56:7 about God's intention that his temple should be "a house of prayer for all nations" shows that what was in Jesus' mind was not merely judgment on the present temple system but also that wider prophetic vision of "the universal significance of the presence of Yahweh in Israel."[11] His action was "the announcement of the 'hour of judgment' of the temple and its leaders, and the announcement of 'the hour of salvation for the nations' who henceforth independently of the temple, will worship the God of Israel."[12]

The parable of the tenants of the vineyard (Mt 21:33-46; Mk 12:1-12; Lk 20:9-19). All three synoptic Gospels record the parable of the tenants as a climactic parable of Jesus, with such a pointed ending and such a clear target (the current leaders of the Jewish people) that it precipitated the plans to arrest and charge him. It is clearly the story of Israel (seen as YHWH's vine or vineyard, a well-known Old Testament metaphor [cf. Is 5:1-7; Ps 80:8-19]). But the twist in the tale was that whereas the story would usually have been told in such a way as to have God eventually vindicate Israel and destroy all those external enemies who threatened his vineyard (as in Ps 80), Jesus tells it so that the real enemies of God, the owner of the vineyard, are those he has entrusted to look after it, namely, the Jewish leaders themselves. And worse, he predicts that the owner will take the vineyard out of the hands of those original stewards and entrust it instead to "a people who will produce its fruit" (Mt 21:43).

---

[10]For this understanding, see especially, N. T. Wright, *Jesus and the Victory of God* (London: SPCK, 1996), pp. 405-28.

[11]Schnabel, *Early Christian Mission,* 1:341.

[12]Ibid., p. 342.

Two points are important here. On the one hand, Jesus clearly points to an ending of the monopoly of the Jewish people on God's vineyard; others will be called in to serve God in his kingdom. On the other hand, there is only one vineyard, and God's purpose is for it to bear fruit. That was the mission of Israel. God seeks a people who will bear the fruit of lives lived before him in reflection of his own character of justice, integrity and compassion. That was the fruit Israel had failed to bear (cf. Is 5:7), which God will now seek from a wider company of "tenants." So these "other tenants," pointing toward the Gentiles whom God will call, are not installed in some other vineyard of their own to the abandonment of the original vineyard per se. No, God's plan is for his one and only vineyard—his own people. What is happening is the *extension* of its stewardship beyond the original Jewish "tenants" to the wider world of Gentiles, who will achieve for God his original purpose—the fruit of the vineyard.

The parable of the wedding banquet (Mt 22:1-10; Lk 14:15-24). The figure changes from Israel as a vineyard to Israel as the covenant partner with YHWH in the great banquet. But because the original invitees refuse to come, the invitation goes out to all and sundry to come to the wedding feast, so that it should be filled. The contours of the Gentile mission are already being sketched in.

The parable of Jesus refers to the great eschatological banquet that would include Jews and Gentiles. But in the meantime, actual meals here on earth became significant symbols of that unified fellowship. The question of who would eat with whom in "table fellowship" was of huge importance in the ancient world. (It has not lost its potency in many modern societies as well.) For Jews there was the matter of clean and unclean food laws. For both Jews and Gentiles, social and class networks were built around inclusion or exclusion from the table. Thus, for the early Christians the importance of eating together as a sign of unity in Christ was highly visible and very significant. Such table fellowship within the early church cut right across both the Jew-Gentile divide and also the social divide of economic status. A fascinating study of this theme in Luke-Acts by Hisao Kayama links it to Luke's concept of mission in both volumes. He concludes:

> The meal motif appears very frequently and conveys an important theological message in Luke-Acts. It is our understanding that it integrally relates to Luke's universalism, i.e. his global missionary program beginning in Jerusalem and extending to the ends of the earth (Acts 1:8). Luke finds himself in this global Christianity in which the Gentile Christians are also invited to the table as Gentiles. . . . The readers of Luke-Acts are reminded that Jesus ate with tax collectors and sinners (Lk. 5:27-32; 7:34; 15:2). Jesus' table fellowship with sinners provides for Luke and his community a theological basis for a Christian table fellowship of Jews and Gentiles.

. . . Christianity as a form of table fellowship was to reach out beyond Rome, further into Asia, even to the Far East, and unto the ends of the earth, challenging and liberating people from indigenous and cultural taboos.[13]

Good news to be preached to the nations (Mt 24:14; Mk 13:10). In his warnings to his disciples about the trials that lay ahead and his cautions about what could truly be regarded as a sign of the end, Jesus portrays the whole period as "birth pangs." That is to say, events such as he describes are not in themselves the end, but like the onset of labor they point to an inevitable outcome—a new birth of a new age. In the meantime, says Jesus, the messengers of Jesus will face all kinds of opposition and suffering. In spite of all that, the task must be accomplished. The "gospel must first be preached to all nations" (Mk 13:10).

The "must" in Jesus' prophecy here refers to the great scriptural drive, the inexorable mission of God to make his salvation known to all nations. Jesus is not setting a timetable; he is simply stating an order of events that lies within the prophesied plan of God.

> The time before the end, with its tribulations, is the time of missionary activity among the Gentiles and thus the time of the fulfillment of the old prophecies that anticipated the conversion of the nations. The term δεῖ (*dei,* "must") refers to God's plan for salvation history, to God's purposes of the time of the "last days": the assignment of the disciples is and remains, as an assignment given by Jesus, the universal proclamation of the gospel, even in precarious times and in dangerous situations.[14]

James W. Thompson takes a similar view, comparing Mark's use of the expression *prōton dei* ("must first [happen]") in Mark 13:10, on the one hand with the same words in Mark 9:11 regarding the necessity of the coming of Elijah before the messianic age, and on the other hand with Paul's clear conviction that "the fullness of the Gentiles" must come in before the end. Mission is thus an eschatological necessity, not only for Paul but for Jesus and the earliest community of disciples also.

> This community, believing that the end time had begun through the work of Christ, understood the universal mission as an eschatological necessity. Mark 13:10 is thus not a peripheral text to the New Testament understanding of mission. When this text is compared to the understanding of mission in other New Testament texts, notably in Paul, it is to be observed that the world mission was understood com-

---

[13]Hisao Kayama, "Christianity as Table Fellowship: Meals as a Symbol of the Universalism in Luke-Acts," in *From East to West: Essays in Honor of Donald G. Bloesch,* ed. Daniel J. Adams (Lanham, Md.: University Press of America, 1997), p. 62.

[14]Schnabel, *Early Christian Mission,* 1:346.

monly in the New Testament as an eschatological necessity and a precondition for
the end.[15]

*The postresurrection commission to the disciples (Mt 28:18-20; Lk 24:46-49;
Jn 20:21).* In the wake of all these indications in the body of the Gospels, it is
not surprising to find the risen Jesus making fully explicit the universal implications of his identity as Messiah and his mission to Israel and the nations.

The language of the Great Commission (especially in Matthew) is steeped in
Old Testament covenant vocabulary and concepts.[16] Jesus adopts the posture of
the cosmic Lord, YHWH, himself; he sets down the stipulations of his new covenant partners, discipling, baptizing and teaching the nations; and then he concludes with the great covenant promise—his personal presence to the very end.

The limitations of Jesus' earthly ministry and the early mission trips of the disciples to the borders of Israel are now utterly removed. The Messiah is risen; the
nations must hear and be drawn into covenant faith and obedience (Matthew),
through repentance and forgiveness (Luke).

The evangelists and the Gentiles. To these events and sayings within the
ministry of Jesus, we should add some of the hints that the evangelists themselves give of their understanding of the universal significance of Jesus for the
nations, not just for the Jews.

The Gentiles in Jesus' genealogy. Both Matthew and Luke record genealogies
for Jesus (the reconciliation of which is not my concern here). Luke indicates
the universality of the significance of Jesus by tracing him back to "Adam, the
son of God." Matthew does the same through tracing Jesus back to Abraham,
the one through whom God promised blessing for all nations.

Matthew goes further by including within his list of fathers only four mothers
(Mt 1:3, 5, 6). But each of those four mothers is a Gentile—Tamar (Canaanite),
Rahab (Canaanite), Ruth (Moabite) and Bathsheba (Hittite). Jesus, the Messiah
of Israel had Gentile blood in his veins also.

The international aspects of Jesus' infancy. Matthew portrays the international significance of Jesus by recording first how Magi came from the east to
worship him, and then how Joseph took Mary and Jesus west, to Egypt. Luke

---

[15]James M. Thompson, "The Gentile Mission as an Eschatological Necessity," *Restoration Quarterly* 14 (1971): 27.

[16]For a very comprehensive study of the universal and missional thrust of Matthew's Gospel as
a whole and its consistency with both Pauline and Old Testament theology, see James
LaGrand, *The Earliest Christian Mission to "All Nations" in the Light of Matthew's Gospel*
(Grand Rapids: Eerdmans, 1995). A more popular but usefully comprehensive survey of the
same thing can be found in Martin Goldsmith, *Matthew and Mission: The Gospel Through Jewish Eyes* (Carlisle, U.K.: Paternoster, 2001).

sets the birth of Jesus within the context of the decree of Augustus that "all the world" *(oikoumenē)* should be censused (Lk 2:1 KJV). He emphasizes the promise to Abraham with its implicit universal thrust (Lk 1:55, 73) and puts the words of universality into the mouth of Simeon, who recognizes in Jesus, not only the "glory" of Israel but also the "light" to enlighten the Gentiles (Lk 2:30-32). Simeon also observes that the work of salvation now beginning through the infant in his arms will take place "in the sight of all people"—an Old Testament term for the witness of the nations. So when Luke moves on in his second volume to the story of the Gentile mission, "the mission to the nations in Acts is thus the continuation and fulfillment of Jesus' own divinely appointed destiny."[17]

The editorial summaries of the international extent of Jesus' influence. Though we might be tempted to dismiss these short notes by the Gospel writers as merely local color, it is more likely that they are intentional signals of the wider impact of Jesus. His ministry was not actually confined to the borders of Israel, even if that was what he primarily wanted. For his fame spread far and wide, and representatives of the nations came to know and to benefit from his ministry. These notes are found in Matthew 4:24-25, Mark 3:7-8 and Luke 6:17-18. The geographical spread of the regions listed is substantial.

The confession of the centurion at the cross (Mt 27:54; Mk 15:39). Finally, both Matthew and Mark probably intend some irony in their crucifixion accounts at the point where, as the leaders of the Jews refuse to recognize the identity of Jesus and are intent on doing away with him, a representative of the Gentiles exclaims that "this man was the Son of God." While we cannot of course read into his statement a sudden burst of trinitarian illumination, and while he probably meant the words in the same way as he would have described the emperor Caesar as "a son of a god," it is still significant that a Roman soldier who owed allegiance to Caesar should actually speak such words of the one he had just nailed to a cross a few hours earlier. A Gentile recognizes the truth about the crucified one while Jewish leaders reject it. John probably intends the same irony in his account of Pontius Pilate's interchange with Jesus and the words Pilate eventually wrote on the inscription above Jesus' head. Even in sarcasm, Gentiles affirmed what his crucifiers denied.

The quotation of Gentile-focused Scriptures. Matthew's use of scriptural quotation in relation to Jesus is pervasive. Two in particular, not surprisingly drawn from Isaiah, link Jesus to prophecies of the inclusion of the Gentile na-

---

[17]James M. Scott, "Acts 2:9-11 as an Anticipation of the Mission to the Nations," in *The Mission of the Early Church to Jews and Gentiles,* ed. J. Adna and H. Kvalbein (Tübingen: Mohr Siebeck, 2000), p. 88.

tions in the redemptive purpose of God now being fulfilled through the Messiah. Thus Matthew 4:15-16 quotes Isaiah 9:1-2 in relation to Jesus going to live in "Galilee of the Gentiles." While Matthew 12:18-21 quotes Isaiah 42:1-4 in relation the ministry of God's Servant, which would extend to the nations.

The Early Church in Acts

At the very beginning of this book we observed how Luke, at the end of his Gospel, portrays the risen Jesus insisting that his disciples must now read their Scriptures (the Old Testament), both *messianically* and *missiologically*. The same Scriptures that point inexorably to the Messiah also point to the good news going to the nations. Luke continues this angle in his second volume, again and again showing how the Gentile mission is nothing more nor less than a fulfillment of the Scriptures, and especially of the prophecies of Isaiah.[18]

Even the overall structure of Luke's two-volume work expresses this underlying theology. It begins in Jerusalem and ends in Rome; from the heart of the faith of Israel (the temple) to the heart of the world of all the nations. That is the great arch that constitutes both the geographical progress and the theological dynamic of Luke's account of "the things that have been fulfilled among us." And it reflects the whole scriptural understanding that I have been elucidating in the preceding sections. The things that happen in Luke's story, from John the Baptist to Paul, are not just an exciting narrative. They are "things that have been fulfilled." They bring the whole Old Testament story of Israel to its climax and destination, as the purpose for which God created Israel in the first place—the blessing of all nations—now becomes a reality through the mission of the church.[19]

It would require much more space than we can take here to elucidate all the texts in which Luke's perspective on the nations is expressed or implied.[20] Some highlights are all I can present.

Peter and Philip. *Pentecost and after.* The early preaching of Peter, even before his encounter with Cornelius, indicates an awareness of the wider significance of the events of Easter and Pentecost. Even the list of peoples whom he addressed on the day of Pentecost probably has universalizing intention. James

---

[18]Thomas Moore considers that Luke's mind was saturated with Isaiah, and that he drew his whole conception of salvation history, including his understanding of what had happened in Jesus and was now happening in the mission of the church, from that prophet: " 'To the End of the Earth': The Geographical and Ethnic Universalism of Acts 1:8 in Light of Isaianic Influence on Luke," *Journal of the Evangelical Theological Society* 40 (1997): 389-99.

[19]Cf. Ben F. Meyer, *The Early Christians: Their World Mission and Self-Discovery* (Wilmington, Del.: Michael Glazier, 1986).

[20]Unquestionably, in my view, the most exhaustive and satisfying account is provided in Eckhard Schnabel's monumental study *Early Christian Mission.*

Scott links it, along with the allusions to Babel in Acts 2:2-4, to the Table of Nations in Genesis 10, and argues that "the Diaspora Jews who gathered in Jerusalem represent 'every nation under heaven' (Acts 2:5) and point to the universalistic thrust of the Book of Acts."[21] Accordingly, Peter's appeal to the crowd for repentance and baptism affirms that the promise of forgiveness is for "all who are far off—for all whom the Lord our God will call" (which has echoes of Is 44:3 and Joel 2:32).

Similarly, in his preaching after the healing of the cripple at the temple gate, Peter proclaims the fulfillment of the words of the prophets, not just in bringing messianic blessing to Israel itself (which the healing in the name of Jesus demonstrated) but also in fulfilling the promise to Abraham, specifically that all peoples on earth will be blessed (Acts 3:25). Thus for Peter (and Luke) the *universality and particularity* of the Abrahamic covenant are now both embodied in Jesus of Nazareth. For he is the one through whom salvation is now available to *all* nations; but he is the *only* one to fill that role—not just for Israel but for all, for "salvation is found in no one else, for there is no other name under heaven given to men by which we must be saved" (Acts 4:12). The phrase *under heaven* echoes the roll call of nations at Pentecost and indicates the universal claim that is being made.

Cornelius. It took angels and visions, however, to move Peter beyond theological conviction to practical action. A worldview shaped by a lifetime lived within the rules of Jewish food laws and the paradigm of segregation they symbolized was not easily set aside. The story of Cornelius, the god-fearing Roman centurion, in Acts 10—11 has often been described as the conversion of Peter as much as of Cornelius. Cornelius, as a "god-fearer" was already, in a sense, converted to the God of Israel, but he did not yet know of Jesus and the fulfillment of Israel's hopes in him. Peter had long ago confessed Jesus as "the Christ, the Son of the living God" and understood something of the universal significance of that. But it was only through the encounter with Cornelius and his testimony that he was converted to the recognition that "God does not show favoritism but accepts people from every nation" (Acts 10:34-35).

The mere fact that Luke devotes two chapters to tell the story and then to repeat it indicates how pivotal it was in his narrative. The astonished comments, first of Peter's companions and then of the Jerusalem church, make clear the significance of the moment: "the gift of the Holy Spirit has been poured out even on the Gentiles"; "God has granted even the Gentiles repentance unto life" (Acts 10:45; 11:18). The outpouring of the Spirit and granting of repentance and for-

---

[21]Scott, "Acts 2:9-11," p. 122.

giveness were among the key signs of the eschatological reign of God in the messianic age. If God were now granting these things to the nations, then that era must have dawned, with all its universal implications for the nations.

The Ethiopian eunuch. Even before Peter, however, Philip had engaged in evangelism beyond the boundaries of the strictly Jewish community—first in the remarkable mass movement in Samaria, and then in individual witness to the Ethiopian eunuch, in Acts 8.

We cannot be certain whether the Ethiopian court official was simply a god-fearing Gentile, through contact with Jews in Ethiopia who had gone to Jerusalem to worship (perhaps in addition to diplomatic duties), or whether he was actually a full proselyte. It depends on whether the description "eunuch" is intended literally as a castrated male (certain royal servants underwent this procedure; e.g., those place in charge of the royal harem) or is simply a synonym for a court official (as it sometimes was). If he were physically a eunuch, then according to the exclusion rule of Deuteronomy 23:1, he probably could not have been a circumcised proselyte. If on the other hand he were merely a royal servant with that official title, then he may well have been a proselyte and therefore no longer truly a Gentile (from an official Jewish point of view). It may be, then, that Luke indicates the steady progression of the gospel, from Jerusalem Jews to Samaritans to a *proselyte* Gentile (the Ethiopian), then to a *god-fearer* Gentile (Cornelius) and finally to the real Gentile world of Greeks and other nationalities (Antioch).

Whatever the true status of the Ethiopian, Philip wastes no time in pointing him through the words of Isaiah to their fulfillment in the crucified and risen Jesus of Nazareth. Luke undoubtedly saw in this event a fulfillment of the promise of God to eunuchs and foreigners in Isaiah 56. And he probably also records the event for the significance of the fact that, with this man's conversion, the gospel reaches south into Africa, the land of Ham. It was already reaching the lands of Shem. And soon, under Paul, it would go north and west to the lands of Japheth.[22]

James and the Jerusalem Council. The combination of Peter's mission to Cornelius and the success of the mission of the Antioch church in Asia Minor and Cyprus, through Paul and Barnabas, created a major theological problem. The first council of Jerusalem was summoned in A.D. 48 to resolve the issue and the ac-

---

[22]The interesting suggestion has been made that Luke deliberately portrays the spread of the gospel across the "map of the world" implicit in the Jerusalem-centered Jewish division of the nations into the sons of Noah—Ham, Shem and Japheth. See James M. Scott, "Luke's Geographical Horizon," in *The Book of Acts in Its Graeco-Roman Setting*, ed. David W. J. Gill and Conrad Gempf (Exeter, U.K.: Paternoster, 1994), pp. 483-544.

count of this crucial event in the early Christian mission is to be found in Acts 15.

The first thing that has to be said is that the issue in dispute was not the *legitimacy* of the Gentile mission per se. The question was not *whether* it was right to take the gospel to the Gentiles but *on what conditions and criteria* converting Gentiles could be admitted into the new fellowship of God's people. It is important to stress this because there are those who argue against the authenticity of the Gospel records of the Great Commission on the grounds that it appears to be unknown at this council of Jerusalem.

That is, according to this view, if Jesus had in fact ever spoken the words attributed to him at the end of Matthew and Luke (namely, an explicit command to go to the Gentiles), then that would have been a clinching argument for James, Peter or Paul to appeal to against the more conservative Jewish Christians and their scruples.[23]

However, this misunderstands the situation in Acts 15. The news of the conversion of Gentiles was received with *joy* (v. 3), while the missionary apostles were also *welcomed* in Jerusalem (v. 4). The issue was not the legitimacy of seeking to bring the Gentiles to faith and conversion; it was whether converting Gentiles could be accepted into the church without circumcision and observance of the law (i.e., without becoming proper proselytes to Judaism). The conservative Jewish believers wanted to insist that this must be the case. The apostles (including Peter and James along with Paul) argued that the new reality inaugurated by the Messiah rendered proselyte requirements unnecessary.

This issue (the terms of conversion) would not have been resolved merely by an appeal to the command of Jesus to go to the Gentiles. Both sides in the debate would have accepted and agreed on that: the good news must go to the Gentiles and they must be brought into obedient discipleship. The question was, What did such discipleship entail, and what were the entry requirements? Did the Gentiles have to become Jews as well as believe in Jesus?

> We would surely be wrong if we blamed the Jewish Christians who demanded circumcision for Gentile believers for disregarding the promises to the Gentiles in the Holy Scriptures. They definitely acknowledged these promises, but . . . interpreted them as a call to become circumcised, Law-obeying proselytes.[24]

---

[23]This is the line taken by Alan Le Grys, *Preaching to the Nations: The Origin of Mission in the Early Church* (London: SPCK, 1998). The negative skepticism and historically dubious reading of the New Testament offered in this book needs to be countered by the massive analysis of Schnabel, *Early Christian Mission*.

[24]Jostein Adna, "James' Position at the Summit Meeting of the Apostles and Elders in Jerusalem (Acts 15)," in *The Mission of the Early Church to Jews and Gentiles,* ed. Jostein Adna and Hans Kvalbein (Tübingen: Mohr Siebeck, 2000), p. 148.

The second major point to note in this account is how carefully James puts together several prophetic texts in an exegetical argument of considerable skill and subtlety. The major text, of course, is Amos 9:11-12, but around this are echoes also of Hosea 3:5 ("after these things," referring to the eschatological return to the Lord and restoration of Davidic rule), Jeremiah 12:15 (the promise that other nations can be built in to live in the midst of God's people), and Isaiah 45:21 (that God had declared long ago his intention to bring in the Gentile nations). Within this framework James quotes Amos 9:11-12, which looks forward on the one hand to the restoration of the "David's fallen tent" (which almost certainly was understood to refer to the eschatological temple, namely, the messianic people of God), and on the other hand to the inclusion of Gentiles as those who now "bear [the LORD's] name"—that is, who are counted as belonging within Israel simply as Gentiles, not as having become proselyte Jews.

The fullest and most satisfying study of this complex text has been made by Richard Bauckham. His conclusions are clear and convincing. The early Christian community regarded itself as the eschatological temple that Jesus had said he would build. Unlike the physical temple, Gentiles could be admitted into this new messianic temple without the requirements of proselytism, and Scriptures could be adduced to prove the legitimacy, the antiquity even, of this interpretation.

> Acts 15:16-18 is not the only text that associates the inclusion of the Gentiles in the eschatological people of God with an interpretation of the eschatological Temple as the eschatological people of God. Eph. 2:11-22 and 1 Pet. 2:4-10 do the same. . . . It must have been a critically important association of ideas. The Temple was the heart of Israel. It was where God's people had access to God's presence, whereas Gentiles, allowed only into the outer court of the Second Temple, were banned, on pain of death, from the sacred precincts themselves. A people of God defined by and centred on this Temple as the place of God's dwelling with them could not include Gentiles unless they became Jews. But numerous prophecies portrayed the Temple of the messianic age as a place where the Gentiles would come into God's presence (Ps. 96:7-8; Isa. 2:2-3; 25:6; 56:6-7; 66:23; Jer. 3:17; Mic. 4:1-2; Zech. 14:16; 1 Enoch 90:33). If these were understood to refer to Gentiles *as Gentiles,* rather than to Gentiles as proselytes, the early church's self-understanding as itself the eschatological Temple, the place of God's presence, could accommodate the inclusion of Gentiles in the church, without their becoming Jews by circumcision and full observance of the Mosaic law. It is therefore entirely plausible that Amos 9:11-12, interpreted as a prophecy that God would build the eschatological Temple (the Christian community) so that Gentiles might seek his presence there, should have played a decisive role in the Jerusalem church's debate and decision about the status of Gentile Christians. . . .
>
> The significance of Amos 9:12, especially in the LXX, is very close to Zech. 2:11

(Heb. 2:15): "Many nations shall join themselves . . . to YHWH on that day, and shall be my [LXX his] people." But whereas this verse might more readily be understood to mean that the Gentiles will join the people of God as proselytes, Amos 9:12 says that the nations *qua* Gentile nations belong to YHWH. It is not implied that they become Jews, but that precisely as "all the nations" they are included in the covenant relationship. It is doubtful whether any other Old Testament text could have been used to make this point so clearly.[25]

Paul's adoption of the Servant mission. That Paul saw himself as God's eschatological apostle, commissioned to be the one to bring about the ingathering of the nations as portrayed in so many Old Testament Scriptures, needs no argument. The evidence is abundant. But in the book of Acts, Luke recounts a significant moment in Paul's early missionary journeys, when Paul presents a particularly rich scriptural justification for the direction of his mission strategy. Consistent with his policy of "to the Jew first," Paul normally went first to Jewish synagogues of the Diaspora when he arrived in a new city. Luke records what happened when he did so in Pisidian Antioch (Acts 13:14-48).

On the first sabbath, Paul gives a long scriptural sermon that leads up to Jesus. The message, Paul says, is both for the children of Abraham and god-fearing Gentiles. And the message is that in the resurrection of Jesus, God has fulfilled what he promised the fathers (Acts 13:32) and through him offers forgiveness of sins. A mixture of Jews and proselytes accept the word and become believers (Acts 13:43). But the next sabbath some of the Jews cause trouble and turn against Paul. This draws from Paul and Barnabas the following decisive answer:

> We had to speak the word of God to you first. Since you reject it and do not consider yourselves worthy of eternal life, we now turn to the Gentiles. For this is what the Lord has commanded us:
>
> > "I have made you a light for the Gentiles,
> > that you may bring salvation to the ends of the earth." (Acts 13:46-47)

Paul here is quoting from Isaiah 49:6, words originally spoken by God to his Servant in the second of the so-called Servant Songs. And he is taking these words as a personal mandate for himself in his missionary task. It is a bold hermeneutical step.

---

[25]Richard Bauckham, "James and the Gentiles (Acts 15:13-21)," in *History, Literature, and Society in the Book of Acts,* ed. Ben Witherington III (Cambridge: Cambridge University Press, 1996), pp. 167, 169. Cf. also Adna, "James' Position at the Summit Meeting." For a discussion of the exegesis and interpretation of this text in connection with contemporary debate over dispensational and Reformed understandings of Jews and Gentiles, see also, Walter C. Kaiser Jr., "The Davidic Promise and the Inclusion of the Gentiles (Amos 9:9-15 and Acts 15:13-18)," *Journal of the Evangelical Theological Society* 20 (1977): 97-111.

The Servant in Isaiah. The Servant passages in Isaiah 40—55 are exceedingly rich and beyond full exposition here. As a merest sketch of the flow of thought I might summarize the theme as follows.

Israel was called to be the Servant of YHWH, as a dimension of their election in Abraham (Is 41:8-10). However, the historical reality was that in exile Israel was a failed servant, blind and deaf to the works and words of God, and effectively paralyzed in relation to their mission for God (Is 42:18-25).

In a mysterious unveiling, God introduces his own Servant, whose identity seems to oscillate between a corporate embodiment *of* Israel and its mission, on the one hand, and an individual figure who has a mission *to* Israel and beyond, on the other. This figure will have as his primary mission the establishment of God's justice among the nations by means of a ministry of compassion, enlightenment and liberation (Is 42:1-9). He will be both a covenant for the people (which probably implies Israel) and a light for the nations (v. 6).

This double mission is made even more explicit in Isaiah 49:1-6, where, in response to the Servant's complaint that his mission to Israel is getting nowhere, the Servant receives from God the explicit commission to be a light to the Gentiles to bring God's salvation to the ends of the earth. So his mission to the nations does not *replace* his mission to Israel but is an *extension* of it.

Later Servant passages show how the Servant will suffer rejection and contempt (Is 50:4-11), and eventually this will culminate in a violent and unjust execution (Is 53). However, it will then be recognized that his suffering and death were actually on behalf of those who rejected him. God will vindicate him through resurrection, and he will finally be exalted and glorified and recognized by the nations.

Jesus as the Servant. Now it is clear from the Gospels that Jesus strongly identified himself with the Isaianic Servant, both in having his primary mission directed to Israel and in his willingness to lay down his life as an offering and ransom (using the language of Is 53). And it is equally clear that the early church in Acts also made that identification.

What Paul has perceived is that the dual mission of the Servant has, in a sense, been split chronologically. Jesus, Paul affirms, was indeed the "servant of the Jews." But the purpose was "to confirm the promises made to the patriarchs so that the Gentiles may glorify God for his mercy" (Rom 15:8-9). In other words, the mission of the Servant Jesus was indeed primarily aimed at the restoration of Israel—and that was what he accomplished in anticipation through the resurrection. But the extended mission of the Servant to the nations "to the ends of the earth" had obviously not been accomplished by Jesus in his earthly lifetime. It was, rather, a task that he had now entrusted to his servant church.

Paul and the Servant mission. So, in a leap of hermeneutical logic, Paul can take words from Isaiah, spoken by God to his *Servant,* which he knew ultimately applied to *Christ,* and read them as addressed to *himself* as the embodiment at that moment of the mission of the *church* to the nations. He interprets his own mission firmly within the framework of biblical salvation history and prophecy. The Servant had come, had died and had risen again. In that sense the primary mission of the Servant has been accomplished once and for all. But yet the remaining mission of the Servant—to bring God's salvation to the ends of the earth—goes on.

In the book of Acts, then, Luke presents some of the key apostles of the early Christian movement: Peter, James and Paul. And he shows them united in these great biblical and missiological convictions. All that the Old Testament Scriptures had envisioned of God's plans for the future of the nations in the eschatological age of salvation must be fulfilled. Since Jesus, through his cross and resurrection, is to be proclaimed and worshiped as Lord and Christ, that new age has now dawned. The redemption of Israel has begun, though it is not yet complete. The kingdom of God is here, though not yet in its final fullness. The eschatological temple is being rebuilt in the new community of God's people. And the nations are being gathered in to that new community through the preaching of the gospel and power of the outpoured Spirit of God.[26]

For Luke, all of this flowed from his understanding of the history of Israel. In a sense Luke was not writing the early history of the church. He was writing the climax of the history of Israel. The past, as recounted in the Scriptures, already held the promise of the future, a future which was now Luke's present. And in that history alone lay the salvation not only of Israel but of the world. That is why Luke includes two detailed accounts of the story of Israel (chaps. 7, 13), in both cases showing how only their destination in Christ could make sense of the story. And from the Scriptures, Luke shows that the new centrifugal phenomenon of *mission to the nations,* to the ends of the earth, was not some unheard of innovation but simply (in the words of Jesus) "what is written" (Lk 24:46-47) and (in the words of Paul) "nothing beyond what the prophets and Moses said would happen" (Acts 26:22).[27]

---

[26]Even the role of the outpoured Spirit has missiological significance for Luke in relation to the fulfillment of Old Testament promises about the restoration of Israel. See John Michael Penny, *The Missionary Emphasis of Lukan Pneumatology,* Journal of Pentecostal Theology Supplements 12 (Sheffield, U.K.: Sheffield Acadamic, 1997).

[27]Cf. Jacob Jervell, "The Future of the Past: Luke's Vision of Salvation History and Its Bearing on His Writing of History," in *History, Literature and Society in the Book of Acts,* ed. Ben Witherington III (Cambridge: Cambridge University Press, 1996), pp. 104-26. Also Thomas J. Lane, *Luke and the Gentile Mission: Gospel Anticipates Acts* (New York: Peter Lang, 1996).

The Apostle Paul

There is no need to rehearse the pervasive evidence of Paul's sense of identity and calling as the apostle to the Gentiles. His theology is replete with his understanding of how the climactic work of God in the Messiah Jesus has now opened the way for people of all nations to come to "the obedience of faith" and into covenant righteousness before God.[28]

It would be interesting to observe how some of what Paul has to say about the nations/Gentiles matches the outline that we traced in chapter fourteen regarding Old Testament expectations for the nations. This is not to suggest that Paul had any such framework consciously in mind as he formulated his reflections. Rather it is simply to say that the whole pattern of Paul's thinking was so shaped by the pattern of the Scriptures that almost any scheme we might devise to map those Scriptures would be seen to be reflected in Paul.

The nations are seeing what God has done. The witness of the nations to all that God did in Israel was a significant Old Testament theme. Paul (like Peter before the Sanhedrin) makes much of the fact that the events of the life, death and resurrection of Jesus were not "done in a corner" but were a matter of public record and witness, even among the Roman community. This is a feature of his various testimonies and defenses in the second half of Acts (e.g., Acts 26:26).

When commending new churches for their faith and zeal, Paul sometimes comments on the way they have become very visible to the outside world (1 Thess 1:8). At times this becomes a kind of geographical hyperbole, in which Paul can claim that the gospel has been preached "all over the world" (Col 1:6) "to every creature under heaven" (Col 1:23). Doubtless Paul was aware that this was not literally true, but it expresses for him the same kind of universal visibility of the acts of God among his people that one finds in the Old Testament also.[29]

And just as the Israelites were called to live lives of distinctive ethical holiness

---

[28]On Paul's theology and practice of mission in general, see W. Paul Bowers, "Mission," in *Dictionary of Paul and His Letters,* ed. Gerald F. Hawthorne et al. (Downers Grove, Ill.: InterVarsity Press, 1993), pp. 608-19; David Bosch, *Transforming Mission,* chap. 4; the superb collection of essays in Peter Bolt and Mark Thompson, ed., *The Gospel to the Nations: Perspectives on Paul's Mission* (Downers Grove, Ill.: InterVarsity Press; Leicester, U.K.: Apollos, 2000); Koestenberger, *Ends of the Earth,* chap. 7; Peter T. O'Brien, *Gospel and Mission in the Writings of Paul: An Exegetical and Theological Analysis* (Grand Rapids: Baker, 1993; Carlisle, U.K.: Paternoster, 1995); and the magisterial Eckhard J. Schnabel, *Early Christian Mission,* vol. 2, *Paul and the Early Church* (Leicester, U.K.: Inter-Varsity Press; Downers Grove, Ill.: InterVarsity Press, 2004).

[29]For a helpful discussion of the missiological significance of Paul's rhetorical hyperbole in these texts, see Richard Bauckham, *The Bible and Mission: Christian Mission in a Postmodern World* (Carlisle, U.K.: Paternoster, 2003), pp. 21-26.

in the sight of the nations, so Paul urges Christians to remember that they are being watched and need to behave in ways that commend the gospel (Phil 2:15; Col 4:5-6; 1 Thess 4:11-12; Tit 2:9-10; cf. 1 Pet 2:12).

The nations are benefiting from what God has done. When the Gentiles heard Paul's words in Acts 13:48 that God was directing his good news to them, "they were glad and honored the word of the Lord." The blessing that God had brought to Israel is now spilling over to the nations. This, of course, was always the mission of God in any case, as we have seen since the call of Abraham (Gen 12:1-3). Accordingly, Paul particularly links the fulfillment of the promise to Abraham in Christ with the benefits that have now come to the Gentiles. "He redeemed us in order that the blessing given to Abraham might come to the Gentiles through Christ Jesus, so that by faith we might receive the promise of the Spirit" (Gal 3:14).

The richest passage listing the benefits that have accrued to the nations through the work of God in Christ is undoubtedly Ephesians 2:11-22. From the picture of utter alienation from all that Israel possessed (v. 12), the passage goes on to show how the Gentiles have been become citizens of God's country (no longer foreigners and aliens), members of God's family (the house of Israel), and the place of God's dwelling (being built into his temple). All the rich benefits of Israel now belong to the nations, through Christ. God's missional purpose in blessing Israel is now bearing fruit in the blessing of the nations.

The nations are bringing their worship to God. Centripetal or centrifugal? It is often said that the major difference between the Old Testament and the New Testament in their concepts of mission is that the Old Testament is basically centripetal (the nations will come to Israel/Zion/YHWH), whereas the New Testament is basically centrifugal (the disciples of Jesus are to go out to the nations). There is an obvious level of truth in this broad assertion, but it is not entirely adequate.

On the one hand, there are centrifugal elements in the Old Testament vision also. While the nations are portrayed gathering in to the center, there are things that also go out to the nations: the law goes forth to the islands who wait for it; the Servant will bring justice to the nations; God's salvation is to go to the ends of the earth; God will send emissaries to the nations to proclaim God's glory.

And in the New Testament, on the other hand, while it is certainly true that the centrifugal commission of Jesus to go to the nations is a radical new departure, consistent with the dawning of the new age of salvation, the purpose of that *going out* is so that the nations might be *gathered into* God's kingdom, in fulfillment of the scriptural vision.

The central affirmation of the New Testament . . . is that with the Christ Event the New Order has already dawned. The Old Testament promises are in process of being fulfilled. Christians are living in an interim period which already belongs to the end, and yet still forms part of "this present age." If the final victory still lies in the future, nevertheless God's reign has already been inaugurated. *Thus the time for the ingathering of the Gentiles is now,* even though this may only be fully accomplished at the final consummation.[30]

So the centrifugal mission of the New Testament church had its centripetal theology also: the nations were indeed being gathered in—not to Jerusalem or to the physical temple or to national Israel—but *to Christ* as the center and *to the new temple* of God that he was building through Christ as a dwelling place for God by the Spirit. Thus Paul can use the language of distance and nearness in his classic description of the transformation that faith in Christ has made to the location of the Gentiles. From being far away, on the periphery, alienated from all that God had done and promised in Israel, the Gentiles have now been "brought near" through the blood of Christ (Eph 2:11-22). So as the gospel goes out to the nations (centrifugal), the nations are gathered in to Christ (centripetal).

The offering of the nations. It is very probable that Paul saw in the collection he organized among his Gentile churches to take to the poverty-stricken believers in Jerusalem (1 Cor 16:1-4; 2 Cor 8—9; Rom 15:23-29; Acts 24:17) a token or symbol of the tribute of the nations as prophesied in the Old Testament. He invested a lot of energy, both theologically and logistically, in this act, which doubtless had straightforward charitable objectives as its primary motivation.

Certainly Paul saw it as a potent sign of the unity between Gentile and Jewish believers that he so staunchly affirmed. It would, he believed, result in thanksgiving among the Jerusalem Christians that these Gentile believers were manifesting such a tangible proof of their obedience to the gospel (2 Cor 9:12-13), which was precisely what the Old Testament had foreseen: the nations responding in obedience to the living God manifested through bringing offerings to his people.

> As the various groups of Gentiles gathered money and made their way to Jerusalem Paul must have seen this at least in part as a symbolic enactment of the eschatological tribute of the nations. . . . Old Testament prophecy is once again given a new twist for while the tribute of the Gentiles is brought to Jerusalem, it is not brought to the Temple, but rather to "the saints," to the community which now constitutes the eschatological temple.[31]

---

[30]C. H. H. Scobie, "Israel and the Nations: An Essay in Biblical Theology," *Tyndale Bulletin* 43, no. 2 (1992): 297 (emphasis added).

[31]Ibid., p. 303.

Another strand in Paul's thinking on this matter, however, may have been to regard the *nations themselves,* with the worship they now bring, as an offering to God. In Romans 15 he celebrates with a profusion of scriptural quotations the fulfillment of God's promise to Abraham, now being realized in the way the nations are coming to glorify and worship God. He quotes from Psalm 18:49, Deuteronomy 32:43, Psalm 117 and Isaiah 11:10. All of these texts speak of the role of the nations in praising and worshiping the God of Israel. Isaiah 11:10 portrays the coming messianic son of David raising a banner to which the nations will rally—another centripetal image here picked up by Paul.

Paul's priestly ministry of evangelism. But Paul then goes on to reflect on his own role in this process using priestly imagery. He speaks of the grace God gave him

> to be a "temple servant" *[leitourgos]* of Christ Jesus to the nations, offering the gospel of God like a priestly sacrifice *[hierourgounta],* so that the offering of the nations *[prosphora tōn ethnōn]* might be acceptable, having been sanctified by the Holy Spirit. (Rom 15:16, author's translation)

This is a remarkable statement since it is the only place in the New Testament where anyone speaks of their own ministry in priestly terms.[32] Priesthood is either affirmed of Jesus, our great high priest, or of the whole Christian community collectively (1 Pet 2:9). Priestly imagery is never used of ministry *within* the church, but Paul here uses it of his *evangelistic* ministry to the nations.

It is hard to know exactly what Scriptures lie behind Paul's imagery, but it is not impossible that he sees himself, in his role of mediating God to the nations and bringing the nations to God, as embodying the priestly ministry of Israel itself, whom God had called to be a "kingdom of priests" in the midst of the nations, in Exodus 19:3-6.

Or it may be equally likely that he is influenced here by the vision of Isaiah 66:18-21. For there God promises that the emissaries to the nations will bring in both Jews and Gentiles as an offering to the Lord, and the language used is that

---

[32]It is in fact a crucially important statement by Paul in relation to his whole understanding of his ministry and the theology that undergirded it. Daniel Chae takes Romans 15:14-21 as "an interpretative key for the letter" and goes on to argue that Paul's understanding of his own apostleship to the Gentiles is bound up with his insistence on the equality of Jew and Gentile in sinfulness, in justification, in their new status in Christ, and in the plan of God as a whole. See Daniel Jong-Sang Chae, *Paul as Apostle to the Gentiles: His Apostolic Self-Awareness and Its Influence on the Soteriological Argument in Romans* (Carlisle, U.K.: Paternoster, 1997). A shorter version of his argument is available in "Paul's Apostolic Self-Awareness and the Occasion and Purpose of Romans," in *Mission and Meaning: Essays Presented to Peter Cotterell,* ed. Anthony Billington, Tony Lane and Max Turner (Carlisle, U.K.: Paternoster, 1995), pp. 116-37.

of priesthood and sacrifice. This would fit with Paul's probable echo of Isaiah 66 later in Romans 15 when he describes his own missionary intentions as going in a great arc from Jerusalem, through Asia Minor, via Macedonia and Illyricum, and onward to the farthest west. And it would also tie in closely with his immediately following reference to his collection among the Gentiles for the church in Jerusalem (Acts 15:25-35) and confirm the interpretation of it in the last paragraph. "This monetary collection for the earthly Jerusalem could also be understood as a material concretion of the fact that the apostle was bringing the Gentiles into the eschatological Jerusalem as an offering of the end time (Is 66:20)."[33]

It is also somewhat ambiguous whether his phrase "the offering of the nations" should be taken as a subjective or objective genitive. That is, is Paul thinking of "the offering made *by* the nations," the eschatological tribute of the nations in the form of the worship and praise that these Gentile believers now give to the living God instead of to their previous idols? Or does he mean "the offering *that consists of* the nations," seeing the nations themselves as the offering that *Paul* is making to God as the fruit of his evangelistic/priestly ministry? Whichever is the exact meaning, it is clear that Paul sees the whole Gentile mission as the fulfillment of Old Testament prophecies regarding the ingathering of the nations and the worship that will ascend to the God of Israel from the nations in the process.[34]

The obedience of the nations. The great visions of the Old Testament, however, envisioned the nations of the world not merely bringing their *worship and offerings* to YHWH, God of Israel, but also learning *obedience* to him. The nations too must come to understand and accept his covenant law, walk in his ways and do his justice (Is 2:3). The Old Testament hope is strongly ethical, as ethical as the whole election-redemption-covenant story on which its hope is founded.

And this too we find to be a powerful element in Paul's understanding of his mission. His task was not merely to bring the nations to worship the right God and find salvation through faith in the gospel of Jesus Christ. He aimed at ethical

---

[33]Cf. Rainer Riesner, *Paul's Early Period: Chronology, Mission Strategy, Theology* (Grand Rapids: Eerdmans, 1998), p. 250.

[34]For additional missional aspects of Rom 15 and Paul's extensive use of the Old Testament in it, see Steve Strauss, "Missions Theology in Romans 15:14-33," *Bibliotheca Sacra* 160 (2003): 457-74 (with perceptive further comments on the relevance of this passage for contemporary mission strategy). For further reflections on the geographical directions of the Pauline and Petrine missions, see Lucien Legrand, "Gal 2:9 and the Missionary Strategy of the Early Church," in *Bible, Hermeneutics, Mission: A Contribution to the Contextual Study of Holy Scripture,* ed. Tord Fornberg (Uppsala: Swedish Institute for Missionary Research, 1995), pp. 21-83; John Knox, "Romans 15:14-33 and Paul's Conception of His Apostolic Mission," *Journal of Biblical Literature* 83 (1964): 1-11; and for a discussion of the issue and further bibliography, Schnabel, *Early Christian Mission,* 2:1294-1300.

transformation as well—a massive challenge in the degraded world of Greco-Roman culture, as his epistles bear witness.

So it is significant that he begins and ends his great missionary exposition of the gospel (which he hopes to take to Spain and invites the church at Rome to support him in doing so) with a summary of his life's work as being aimed at achieving *"the obedience of faith among all the nations."* He uses this phrase in the significant sections of Romans 1:5 and Romans 16:26, and again at Romans 15:18. And when it occurs in the climax of the letter, it is rooted in the Old Testament Scriptures ("through the prophetic writings") and in the mission of God ("through the command of the eternal God").

Paul then clearly saw his own mission in the light of the mission of God and the Scriptures, and summarized it as bringing all nations to believing knowledge of and ethical obedience to the one living God whose glory is now revealed in Jesus Christ.

The nations are sharing the identity of Israel. The most breathtaking visions concerning the nations that we saw in the Old Testament are those that envision them eventually becoming one with Israel. Various prophets and psalms speak of the nations being registered as part of Zion, coming to be accepted by God at his altar, sharing the names and titles of Israel, being joined to the Lord, being called by his name, having him dwell in their midst—all the language of identification with Israel. The vision is not, ultimately, simply Israel *and* the nations but the nations *as* Israel.

The curse of Babel in the division of the nations (which preceded the existence and call of Israel) will be ended, so that people of all nations will do what Israel did—"call on the name of the LORD."

> Then I will purify the lips of the peoples,
>> that all of them may call on the name of the LORD
>> and serve him shoulder to shoulder. (Zeph 3:9)

The *Shema,* the great privilege of Israel's monotheistic confession, will be universalized throughout the whole earth. "The LORD will be king over the whole earth. On that day there will be one LORD, and his name the only name (Zech 14:9), and, by implication, there will be one people, from "the whole earth," worshiping that name.

Paul was captivated by this vision. Along with the other apostles at the council of Jerusalem he rejected any interpretation of such Scriptures that perpetuated the old system of the Jerusalem temple and all the requirements of proselytism. It was not that all the nations would become part of God's people merely by becoming Jews within the old covenant, as if the Messiah had not come and inaugurated the new age of eschatological fulfillment. Rather, all must now be incorporated *into Christ* through faith—whether Jew or Gentile. There is no difference between Jews and Gentiles in their sin and rebellion; neither is there any difference between them in the way they will find salvation and inclusion in God's people. But once they are "in Christ," whether Jew or Gentile, they become "all one in Christ Jesus" (Gal 3:28), and thereby all one as Abraham's spiritual seed.

The classic exposition of this is Ephesians 2—3. By piling up all the metaphors drawn from the Old Testament, Paul emphasizes again and again the unity that now exists between Jew and Gentile in Christ as "one new humanity." Again, I have to emphasize that Paul's picture is decidedly not Jews *plus* Gentiles, remaining forever distinct with separate means of covenant membership and access to God, but rather that through the cross God has destroyed the barrier between the two and created a new entity, so that both together and both alike have access to God through the same Spirit. So Paul packs in the language of citizenship and family (Eph 2:19) and of the temple (Eph 2:21-22) to emphasize the total inclusion of Gentiles within the identity of the Israel of God. Then he goes further and even coins words to express this unity. "Through the gospel, the Gentiles are heirs together with Israel, members together of one body, and sharers together in the promise in Christ Jesus" (Eph 3:6).

In Romans 9—11 Paul labors with massive scriptural argumentation to demonstrate that the inclusion of the Gentiles, far from being a *denial* of the Scriptures or an *abandonment* by God of his promise to Israel is rather a *fulfillment* of both. It is precisely through the ingathering of the nations that God is keeping his promise to Israel.

There remains one olive tree. Nations are being grafted in, and Paul's expectation is that in the astonishing plan of God, the ingathering of the Gentiles will cause such jealousy among the currently unbelieving branches that even they will come to repentance, faith, and regrafting. "And so all Israel will be saved," adds Paul—not so much indicating a *time* frame as pointing out the *method* that God has chosen to reach that ultimate goal (Rom 11:25-26). The implication of the whole metaphor and its exposition is clear. There is ultimately only one people of God, and the only way to belong to it now, for Jews as much as for Gentiles, is through faith in the Messiah, Jesus of Nazareth. The regrafting of Israel that Paul envisions cannot be on some other criterion, for he explicitly says "if they do not persist in unbelief, they will be grafted in" (Rom 11:23). Paul does not hold out any other way for Jews to be part of eschatological Israel other than the same way that Gentiles are now joining that community—only through faith in Jesus of Nazareth, the Messiah.

For this reason, as I have strongly affirmed in other writings, I can see no biblical justification either for the so-called "two covenant" theory, which claims that Jews still have a valid covenantal relationship with God independently of Jesus, while Gentiles have their covenantal relationship through Jesus, or for its dismal result: that evangelism among Jewish people is unnecessary and offensive.

Paul is utterly adamant that

- the only proper fulfillment of the Old Testament Scriptures is to be found in the new messianic community of disciples of Jesus.

- this constitutes Israel, redefined and extended as the Old Testament foretold.

- there is one and only one new people of God, created as a new humanity in Christ, consisting of both Jews and Gentiles who trust in him.

- the gospel must therefore of necessity be preached to both Jews and Gentiles—indeed, "to the Jew first," for all have sinned and fallen short of the glory of God—Jew and Gentile alike. So all have urgent need of the good news of the cross and resurrection of the Messiah.

We need to remember that the word *Christian* was in origin a mere nickname, possibly even a term of abuse. So in calling Jewish people to faith in Jesus as Messiah, we are not pressing them to convert to Christianity (however much that is the popular misrepresentation of the facts and the motives in Jewish evangelism). Rather we are, like Paul and Jesus and John the Baptist before them, inviting Jews to enter the community of redeemed and restored Israel, constituted by Jesus, purchased through the blood of his perfect Passover, and launched in the new age of God's kingdom through his resurrection.

The idea that Christian mission from its earliest days was an abandonment of the Jews is demonstrably false. The Great Commission directs the disciples to "all the nations."

> It is as impossible to exclude the Jews from the order to make disciples of all nations as it is impossible to limit the power of the resurrected Lord to the whole world except Israel. The expansion of his mission to all nations cannot imply any exclusion of the Jews if we take his declaration of universal and unlimited royal power seriously.[35]

Such, then, is the gloriously comprehensive missional theology of the nations that Paul had quarried from profound engagement with the Scriptures. It is most unlikely that Paul lived to ever have had the opportunity to read the final great

---

[35]Hans Kvalbein, "Has Matthew Abandoned the Jews?" in *The Mission of the Early Church to Jews and Gentiles,* ed. Jostein Adna and Hans Kvalbein (Tübingen: Mohr Siebeck, 2000), pp. 45-62.

prophetic book of the biblical canon, the Revelation, but if he had it would have warmed his heart and had his full agreement. For it too is saturated with Old Testament images, visions and quotations, not least in the way it envisions the completion of God's mission for the nations and the fulfillment of all his covenant promises.

As we saw at the end of chapter ten (pp. 355-56), all the great covenantal figureheads are there.

Noah is there in the vision of a new creation, a new heavens and a new earth after judgment (Rev 21:1). Abraham is there in the ingathering and blessing of all nations from every tongue and language (Rev 7:9). Moses is there in the covenantal assertions that "they will be his people, and God himself will be with them and be their God," and "the dwelling of God is with men, and he will live with them" (Rev 21:3). David is there in the holy city, the new Jerusalem, and the expansion of the temple to include the whole of creation (Rev 21), and in the identity of Jesus as the Lion of Judah and Root of David (Rev 5:5). And the new covenant is there in the fact that all of this will be accomplished by the blood of the Lamb who was slain (Rev 5:12).

Purged by judgment and the destruction of all wickedness and evil, human and satanic, the nations of the world will join in the praise of God for his salvation (Rev 7: 9-10). They will bring all the wealth of their historical achievements into the city of God, as Isaiah had said they would (Rev 21:24, 26), the city that now embraces the full extent of the whole new creation. And the river and tree of life, from which humanity had been barred in the earliest chapters of the Bible's grand narrative, will, in its final chapter, provide the healing of the nations which the narrative has longed for ever since the scattering of Babel (Rev 22:2). The curse will be gone from the whole of creation (Rev 22:3). The earth will be filled with the glory of God and all the nations of humanity will walk in his light (Rev 21:24).

Such is the glorious climax of the Bible's grand narrative. Such is the triumph of the mission of God.

Epilogue

So what was the question?

In the introduction I said that the roots of this book go a long way back in my own thinking, but the trigger that launched the direction it has taken was the challenging question addressed to me by Anthony Billington after a lecture I gave in 1998. It was a question about the validity of using a missiological framework as a hermeneutical approach to reading the Bible. Is it possible, is it legitimate, is it helpful for Christians to read the whole Bible from the angle of mission? And what happens if they do?

The immediate challenge that bounced back in our attempt to answer that radical question was: it all depends on whose mission you mean. If by "mission" we are thinking of "missions," and the great and laudable efforts of crosscultural missionaries, then we would be struggling to defend an affirmative answer to the first question. While our human missionary endeavor can find ample justification and explicit textual imperative in the Bible, it would be a distorted and exaggerated hermeneutic, in my view, that tried to argue that the whole Bible was "about" mission in the narrowly defined sense of human missionary activities.

However, not merely because of that tactical consideration, but rather out of a profound theological conviction, I have argued that it is in any case misleading to take our missiological starting point and paradigm only from the human activities of mission—however necessary, biblically-mandated and Spirit-directed they may be. Rather, just as "salvation belongs to our God" (Rev 7:10), so does mission. The Bible renders and reveals to us the God whose creative and redemptive work is permeated from beginning to end with God's own great mission, his purposeful, sovereign intentionality. All mission or missions which we initiate, or into which we invest our own vocation, gifts and energies, flow from the prior and larger reality of the mission of God. *God* is on mission, and we, in that wonderful phrase of Paul, are "co-workers with God" (1 Cor 3:9).

Having made that reorienting paradigm shift in our concept of the fundamental meaning of biblical mission, then indeed the whole Bible can (and I would argue, should), be read in the light of this overarching, governing perspective. The whole Bible delivers to us "the whole counsel of God"—the plan, purpose and mission of God for the whole creation, that it will be reconciled to God through Christ by the cross (Col 1:20).

From this launch pad, we then proceeded through the book to explore the trajectory of the mission of God as it unfolds in the great tapestry of the Scriptures (if one can pardon such mixed metaphors).

- In Part 2, we saw the driving will of the one true living God to be known throughout his whole creation for who he truly is, the LORD God, YHWH, the Holy One of Israel, incarnate in Jesus of Nazareth, crucified, risen, ascended and returning. And in contrast to this dynamic missional monotheism we saw the exposure, rejection and ultimate destruction of all false gods, whatever their origin, identity or power.

- In Part 3, we marvelled at the indefatigable self-commitment of God to bless all nations of humanity through the creation of a people as the vehicle of his goal of redemption. Through both testaments we travelled: taking in the paradox of the election of this particular people with their universal mission; grasping the comprehensive scope of the redemptive work of God in their history; hearing the accumulating assurances of the covenant relationship to which he called them; being challenged by the ethical demands the new life which they are to live in the sight of the nations for the sake of the nations. This is the people to whom we belong. This is the story of which we are part. This is the mission in which we are called to participate.

- In Part 4, we broadened our gaze further still as we contemplated God's involvement with his whole creation, with the earth itself, with humans made in his image, and with all cultures and nations. And we finished, as the Bible itself does, overwhelmed with the vision of God's ultimate eschatological goal that one day people of every tribe, people, nation and language will sing his praises in the new creation.

This, I have tried to argue, is something like what it means to engage in a missiological reading of the whole canon of Scripture.

But what happens when we read it in this way? This was our second question. Our first was whether the mission of God provides a valid hermeneutical framework, or a trustworthy map for the journey of biblical understanding, and I have presented a case which, I believe, justifies the conclusion that Christians can and should read their whole Bibles within such an overarching framework. But what happens when they do?

I began the book with some reminiscence of personal experiences that influenced me long before writing this book. Perhaps I may conclude with reflection on some transformations of personal perspective that have accompanied the writing of it. For this book has indeed been a journey of discovery for its author. I genuinely took up the challenge of Anthony Billington's question not quite knowing where it might lead me.

When we grasp that the whole Bible constitutes the coherent revelation of the mission of God, when we see this as the key that unlocks the driving purposefulness of the whole grand narrative (to cite our subtitle), then we find our whole worldview impacted by this vision. As has been well documented, every human worldview is an outworking of *some* narrative. We live out of the story or stories we believe to be true, the story or stories that "tell it like it is," we think. So what does it mean to live out of *this* story? Here is *The Story*, the grand universal narrative that stretches from creation to new creation, and accounts for everything in between. This is The Story that tells us where we have come from, how we got to be here, who we are, why the world is in the mess it is, how it can be (and has been) changed, and where we are ultimately going. And the whole story is predicated on the reality of this God and the mission of this God. He is the originator of the story, the teller of the story, the prime actor in the story, the planner and guide of the story's plot, the meaning of the story and its ultimate completion. He is its beginning, end and center. It is the story of the mission of God, of this God and no other.

Now such an understanding of the mission of God as the very heartbeat of all reality, all creation, all history and all that yet lies ahead of us generates a distinctive worldview that is radically and transformingly God-centered. And my experience in wrestling with the massive contours of this Bible-sculpted, God-centered, mission-driven vision of reality, has been to find that it turns inside out and upside down some of the common ways in which we are accustomed to thinking about the Christian life and the kinds of questions we are inclined to ask. This worldview, constituted by putting the mission of God at the very center of all existence, is disturbingly subversive and it uncomfortably relativizes one's own place in the great scheme of things. It is certainly a very healthy corrective to the egocentric obsession of much Western culture —including, sadly, even Western Christian culture. It constantly forces us to open our eyes to the big picture, rather than shelter in the cosy narcissism of our own small worlds.

- We ask, "Where does God fit into the story of my life?" when the real question is where does my little life fit into this great story of God's mission.

- We want to be driven by a purpose that has been tailored just right for our own individual lives (which is of course infinitely preferable to living aimlessly), when we should be seeing the purpose of all life, including our own, wrapped up in the great mission of God for the whole of creation.

- We talk about the problems of "applying the Bible to our lives," which often means modifying the Bible somewhat adjectivally to fit into the assumed "reality" of the life we live "in the real world." What would it mean to apply our lives to the Bible instead, assuming *the Bible* to be the reality—the real story —to which *we* are called to conform ourselves?

- We wrestle with the question of how we can "make the gospel relevant to the world" (again, at least that is clearly preferable to treating it as irrelevant). But in *this* Story, God is about the business of transforming the world to fit the shape of the gospel.

- We wonder whether and how the care of creation, for example, might fit into *our* concept and practice of mission, when *this* Story challenges us to ask whether our lives, lived on God's earth and under God's gaze, are aligned with, or horrendously misaligned with, God's mission that stretches from creation to cosmic transformation and the arrival of a new heaven and new earth.

- We argue about what can legitimately be included in the mission God expects from the church, when we should ask what kind of church God expects for his mission in all its comprehensive fullness.

- I may wonder what kind of mission God has for *me*, when I should ask what kind of me God wants for *his* mission.

The only concept of mission into which God fits is the one of which he is the beginning, the center and the end (to paraphrase what Lesslie Newbigin once said about the resurrection).[1] And the only access that we have to that mission of God is given to us in the Bible. This is the grand narrative that is unlocked when we turn the hermeneutical key of reading all the Scriptures in the light of the mission of God.

It was the risen Jesus, to return to where we began in the introduction to Part 1, who opened the eyes of the disciples to understand the Scriptures, by reading them in the double light of his own identity as the Messiah and of their ongoing

---

[1]"Indeed, the simple truth is that the resurrection cannot be accommodated in any way of understanding the world except one of which it is the starting point"; in *Truth to Tell: the Gospel as Public Truth* (London: SPCK 1991), p. 11.

mission to all nations in the power of the Spirit. "This is what is written, . . . and you will be my witnesses . . . to the ends of the earth," he said, in that richly missional account which spans the ending of Luke's Gospel and the beginning of Acts.

It is the risen Jesus who alone is worthy to open the scroll, signifying the meaning of all history. And his worthiness and authority to do so rests on the cross, which is redemptive, universal and victorious (Rev 5:9-10). Christ crucified and risen is the key to all history, for he is the one who accomplished the mission of God for all creation.

If, then, it is in Christ crucified and risen that we find the focal point of the whole Bible's grand narrative, and therein also the focal point of the whole mission of God, our response is surely clear. Before we set about the essential task of working out what it means in practice that Jesus said to his disciples, "As the Father has sent me, I am sending you" (Jn 20:21), in terms of our personal participation in God's mission in our own context and generation, we first of all need to kneel with Thomas before Christ and confess, "My Lord and my God" (Jn 20:28).

Bibliography

Adna, Jostein. "James' Position at the Summit Meeting of the Apostles and Elders in Jerusalem (Acts 15)." In *The Mission of the Early Church to Jews and Gentiles,* edited by Adna Jostein and Hans Kvalbein, pp. 125-61. Tübingen: Mohr Siebeck, 2000.

Adna, Jostein, and Hans Kvalbein, ed. *The Mission of the Early Church to Jews and Gentiles.* Tübingen: Mohr Siebeck, 2000.

Albrektson, Bertil. *History and the Gods: An Essay on the Idea of Historical Events as Divine Manifestations in the Ancient Near East and in Israel.* Lund: Gleerup, 1967.

Allis, O. T., "The Blessing of Abraham." *Princeton Theological Review* 25 (1927): 263-98.

Anderson, Bernard W. "Unity and Diversity in God's Creation: A Study of the Babel Story." *Currents in Theology and Mission* 5 (1978): 69-81.

Anderson, Gerald H., ed. *The Theology of Christian Missions.* New York: McGraw Hill; London: SCM Press, 1961.

Arnold, Clinton. *Powers of Darkness: A Thoughtful, Biblical Look at an Urgent Challenge Facing the Church.* Leicester, U.K.: Inter-Varsity Press; Downers Grove, Ill.: InterVarsity Press, 1992.

Ash, Christopher. *Marriage: Sex in the Service of God.* Leicester: Inter-Varsity Press, 2003.

Ashley, Timothy. *The Book of Numbers.* New International Commentary on the Old Testament. Grand Rapids: Eerdmans, 1993.

Bailley Wells, Jo. *God's Holy People: A Theme in Biblical Theology.* JSOT Supplement Series 305. Sheffield, U.K.: Sheffield Academic Press, 2000.

Baker, Christopher J. *Covenant and Liberation: Giving New Heart to God's En-*

dangered Family. Frankfurt: Peter Lang; New York: Peter Lang, 1991.

Barker, P. A. "Sabbath, Sabbatical Year, Jubilee." In *Dictionary of the Old Testament: Pentateuch,* edited by David W. Baker and Alexander T. Desmond, pp. 695-706. Downers Grove, Ill.: InterVarsity Press; Leicester, U.K.: Inter-Varsity Press, 2003.

Barr, James, "Man and Nature—The Ecological Controversy and the Old Testament." *Bulletin of the John Rylands Library of the University of Manchester* 55 (1972): 9-32.

Bartholomew, Craig et al., ed. *Canon and Biblical Interpretation.* Carlisle, U.K.: Paternoster; Grand Rapids: Zondervan, forthcoming.

Bartholomew, Craig, and Michael W. Goheen. "Story and Biblical Theology." In *Out of Egypt: Biblical Theology and Biblical Interpretation,* edited by Craig Bartholomew et al., pp. 144-71. Carlisle, U.K.: Paternoster; Grand Rapids: Zondervan, 2004.

Bartholomew, Craig, and Thorsten Moritz, ed. *Christ and Consumerism: A Critical Analysis of the Spirit of the Age.* Carlisle, U.K.: Paternoster, 2000.

Bartholomew, Craig, et al., ed. *Out of Egypt: Biblical Theology and Biblical Interpretation.* Scripture and Hermeneutics Series. Carlisle, U.K.: Paternoster; Grand Rapids: Zondervan, 2004.

Barton, John. " 'The Work of Human Hands' (Ps 115:4): Idolatry in the Old Testament." *Ex Auditu* 15 (1999): 63-72.

Bauckham, Richard. *2 Peter, Jude.* Word Biblical Commentary 50. Waco, Tex.: Word, 1983.

———. "First Steps to a Theology of Nature." *Evangelical Quarterly* 58 (1986): 229-44.

———. "James and the Gentiles (Acts 15:13-21)." In *History, Literature, and Society in the Book of Acts,* edited by Ben Witherington III, pp. 154-84. Cambridge: Cambridge University Press, 1996.

———. *God Crucified: Monotheism and Christology in the New Testament.* Carlisle, U.K.: Paternoster, 1998.

———. *The Bible and Mission: Christian Mission in a Postmodern World.* Carlisle, U.K.: Paternoster, 2003.

———. "Biblical Theology and the Problems of Monotheism." In *Out of Egypt: Biblical Theology and Biblical Interpretation,* edited by Craig Bartholomew et al., pp. 187-232. Carlisle, U.K.: Paternoster; Grand Rapids: Zondervan, 2004.

Beale, G. K. *The Temple and the Church's Mission: A Biblical Theology of the Dwelling Place of God.* New Studies in Biblical Theology, edited by D. A. Carson. Downers Grove, Ill.: InterVarsity Press; Leicester, U.K.: Apollos, 2004.

Begg, Christopher T. "The Peoples and the Worship of Yahweh in the Book of

Isaiah." In *Worship and the Hebrew Bible,* edited by M. P. Graham, R. R. Marrs and S. L. McKenzie, pp. 35-55. Sheffield, U.K.: Sheffield Academic Press, 1999.

Billington, Antony, Tony Lane and Max Turner, ed. *Mission and Meaning: Essays Presented to Peter Cotterell.* Carlisle, U.K.: Paternoster, 1995.

Blauw, Johannes. *The Missionary Nature of the Church.* New York: McGraw Hill, 1962.

Blenkinsopp, J. "Second Isaiah—Prophet of Universalism." *Journal for the Study of the Old Testament* 41 (1988): 83-103.

Block, Daniel I. "Nations/Nationality." In *New International Dictionary of Old Testament Theology and Exegesis,* edited by Willem A. VanGemeren, 4:966-72. Carlisle, U.K.: Paternoster, 1996.

———. *The Gods of the Nations: Studies in Ancient Near Eastern National Theology.* 2nd ed. Grand Rapids: Baker; Leicester, U.K.: Apollos, 2000.

Bluedorn, Wolfgang. *Yahweh Versus Baalism: A Theological Reading of the Gideon-Abimelech Narrative.* JSOT Supplements 329. Sheffield, U.K.: Sheffield Academic, 2001.

Bockmuehl, Klaus. *Evangelicals and Social Ethics.* Downers Grove, Ill.: InterVarsity Press; Exeter, U.K.: Paternoster, 1975.

Bolt, Peter, and Mark Thompson, ed. *The Gospel to the Nations: Perspectives on Paul's Mission.* Downers Grove, Ill.: InterVarsity Press; Leicester, U.K.: Apollos, 2000.

Bosch, David J. *Witness to the World: The Christian Mission in Theological Perspective.* London: Marshall, Morgan & Scott, 1980.

———. *Transforming Mission: Paradigm Shifts in Theology of Mission.* Maryknoll, N.Y.: Orbis, 1991.

———. "Hermeneutical Principles in the Biblical Foundation for Mission." *Evangelical Review of Theology* 17 (1993): 437-51.

Bowers, W. Paul. "Fulfilling the Gospel: The Scope of the Pauline Mission." *Journal of the Evangelical Theological Society* 30 (1987): 185-98.

———. "Mission." In *Dictionary of Paul and His Letters,* edited by Gerald F. Hawthorne et al., pp. 608-19. Downers Grove, Ill.: InterVarsity Press; Leicester, U.K.: Inter-Varsity Press, 1993.

Boyce, Richard Nelson. *The Cry to God in the Old Testament.* Atlanta: Scholars Press, 1988.

Boyley, Mark. "1 Peter—A Mission Document?" *Reformed Theological Review* 63 (2004): 72-86.

Braaten, Carl E. "Who Do We Say That He Is? On the Uniqueness and Universality of Jesus Christ." *Missiology* 8 (1980): 13-30.

————. "The Mission of the Gospel to the Nations." *Dialog* 30 (1991): 124-31.

Brawley, Robert L. "For Blessing All Families of the Earth: Covenant Traditions in Luke-Acts." *Currents in Theology and Mission* 22 (1995): 18-26.

————. "Reverberations of Abrahamic Covenant Traditions in the Ethics of Matthew." In *Realia Dei,* edited by Prescott H. Williams and Theodore Hiebert, pp. 26-46. Atlanta: Scholars Press, 1999.

Brett, Mark G. "Nationalism and the Hebrew Bible." In *The Bible in Ethics,* edited by John W. Rogerson, Margaret Davies and M. Daniel Carroll R., pp. 136-63. Sheffield: Sheffield Academic, 1995.

Bridger, Francis. "Ecology and Eschatology: A Neglected Dimension." *Tyndale Bulletin* 41, no. 2 (1990): 290-301.

Briggs, Richard S. "The Uses of Speech-Act Theory in Biblical Interpretation." *Currents in Theology and Mission* 9 (2001): 229-76.

Bronner, Leah. *The Stories of Elijah and Elisha: As Polemics Against Baal Worship.* Leiden: E. J. Brill, 1968.

Brownson, James V., "Speaking the Truth in Love: Elements of a Missional Hermeneutic." In *The Church Between Gospel and Culture,* edited by George R. Hunsberger and Craig Van Gelder, pp. 228-59. Grand Rapids: Eerdmans, 1996.

————. *Speaking the Truth in Love: New Testament Resources for a Missional Hermeneutic.* Harrisburg, Penn.: Trinity Press International, 1998.

Broyles, Craig C. *Psalms.* New International Biblical Commentary. Peabody, Mass.: Hendrikson; Carlisle, U.K.: Paternoster, 1999.

Bruce, F. F. *This Is That: The New Testament Development of Some Old Testament Themes.* Exeter, U.K.: Paternoster; Grand Rapids: Eerdmans, 1968.

Bruckner, James K. *Implied Law in the Abraham Narrative: A Literary and Theological Analysis.* JSOT Supplements 335. Sheffield, U.K.: Sheffield Academic Press, 2001.

Brueggemann, Walter. *Genesis.* Interpretation. Atlanta: John Knox Press, 1982.

————. "A New Creation—After the Sigh." *Currents in Theology and Mission* 11 (1984): 83-100.

————. *To Pluck up, To Tear Down: A Commentary on the Book of Jeremiah 1-25.* International Theological Commentary. Grand Rapids: Eerdmans; Edinburgh: Handsel Press, 1988.

————. *First and Second Samuel.* Interpretation. Louisville: John Knox Press, 1990.

————. *A Social Reading of the Old Testament: Prophetic Approaches to Israel's Communal Life,* edited by Patrick D. Miller. Minneapolis: Fortress, 1994.

————. *Theology of the Old Testament: Testimony, Dispute, Advocacy.* Minneapolis: Fortress, 1997.

Burnett, David. *God's Mission, Healing the Nations.* Revised ed. Carlisle, U.K.: Paternoster, 1996.

Calvin, John. *Genesis.* Crossway Classic Commentaries, edited by Alister McGrath and J. I. Packer. Wheaton, Ill.: Crossway Books, 2001.

Capes, David B. *Old Testament Yahweh Texts in Paul's Christology.* Tübingen: Mohr Siebeck, 1992.

Carrick, Ian. " 'The Earth God Has Given to Human Beings' (Ps 115:16): Unwrapping the Gift and Its Consequences." *Missionalia* 19 (1991): 33-43.

Carroll R., M. Daniel. "Blessing the Nations: Toward a Biblical Theology of Mission from Genesis." *Bulletin for Biblical Research* 10 (2000): 17-34.

Chae, Daniel Jong-Sang. "Paul's Apostolic Self-Awareness and the Occasion and Purpose of Romans." In *Mission and Meaning: Essays Presented to Peter Cotterell,* edited by Anthony Billington, Tony Lane and Max Turner, pp. 116-37. Carlisle, U.K.: Paternoster, 1995.

Chae, Daniel Jong-Sang. *Paul as Apostle to the Gentiles: His Apostolic Self-Awareness and Its Influence on the Soteriological Argument in Romans.* Carlisle, U.K.: Paternoster, 1997.

Chisholm, Robert B. "The Polemic Against Baalism in Israel's Early History and Literature." *Bibliotheca Sacra* 150 (1994): 267-83.

———. " 'To Whom Shall You Compare Me?' Yahweh's Polemic Against Baal and the Babylonian Idol-Gods in Prophetic Literature." In *Christianity and the Religions: A Biblical Theology of World Religions,* edited by E. Rommen and H. A. Netland, pp. 56-71. Pasadena: William Carey Library, 1995.

Christensen, Duane L. "Nations." In *Anchor Bible Dictionary,* edited by David Noel Freedman et al., 4:1037-49. New York: Doubleday, 1992.

Clements, Ronald E. "Worship and Ethics: A Re-examination of Psalm 15." In *Worship and the Hebrew Bible,* edited by M. P. Graham, R. R. Marrs and S. L. McKenzie, p. 284. Sheffield, U.K.: Sheffield Academic Press, 1999.

Clements, Ronald E. "Monotheism and the Canonical Process." *Theology* 87 (1984): 336-44.

Clifford, Richard J. "The Function of the Idol Passages in Second Isaiah." *Catholic Biblical Quarterly* 42 (1980): 450-64.

Comfort, P. W. "Idolatry." In *Dictionary of Paul and His Letters,* edited by Gerald F. Hawthorne et al., pp. 424-26. Downers Grove, Ill.: InterVarsity Press; Leicester, U.K.: Inter-Varsity Press, 1993.

Cotterell, Peter. *Mission and Meaninglessness: The Good News in a World of Suffering and Disorder.* London: SPCK, 1990.

Craigie, Peter C. *Psalms 1-50.* Word Bible Commentary 19. Waco, Tex.: Word, 1983.

Crawley, Winston. *Biblical Light for the Global Task: The Bible and Mission Strategy.* Nashville: Convention Press, 1989.

Daneel, M. L. "The Liberation of Creation: African Traditional Religious and Independent Church Perspectives." *Missionalia* 19 (1991): 99-121.

Davidson, Robert. "Universalism in Second Isaiah." *Scottish Journal of Theology* 16 (1963): 166-85.

Davies, Eryl W. "Walking in God's Ways: The Concept of *Imitatio Dei* in the Old Testament." In *True Wisdom,* edited by Edward Ball, pp. 99-115. Sheffield, U.K.: Sheffield Academic Press, 1999.

Davies, G. I. "The Destiny of the Nations in the Book of Isaiah." In *The Book of Isaiah,* edited by Jacques Vermeylen, pp. 93-120. Leuven: Leuven University Press, 1989.

Davies, Graham. "The Theology of Exodus." In *In Search of True Wisdom: Essays in Old Testament Interpretation in Honor of Ronald E. Clements,* edited by Edward Ball, pp. 137-52. Sheffield, U.K.: Sheffield Academic Press, 1999.

Day, John. "Asherah," "Baal (Deity)," and "Canaan, Religion Of." In *Anchor Bible Dictionary,* edited by David Noel Freedman, 1:483-87, 545-49, 831-37. New York: Doubleday, 1992.

De Ridder, Richard R. *Discipling the Nations.* Kampen: J. H. Kok, 1971; Grand Rapids: Baker, 1975.

Deist, Ferdinand. "The Exodus Motif in the Old Testament and the Theology of Liberation." *Missionalia* 5 (1977): 58-69.

Dever, William G. *Did God Have a Wife? Archaeology and Folk Religion in Ancient Israel.* Grand Rapids: Eerdmans, 2005.

DeVries, Simon J. *1 Kings.* Word Biblical Commentary. Waco, Tex.: Word, 1985.

Donaldson, Terence L., " 'The Gospel That I Proclaim among the Gentiles' (Gal. 2.2): Universalistic or Israel-Centred?" In *Gospel in Paul: Studies on Corinthians, Galatians and Romans for Richard N. Longenecker,* edited by Peter Richardson and L. Ann Jervis, pp. 166-93. Sheffield, U.K.: Sheffield Academic Press, 1994.

Du Preez, J. "Reading Three 'Enthronement Psalms' from an Ecological Perspective." *Missionalia* 19 (1991): 122-30.

———. "The Missionary Significance of Psalm 117 in the Book of Psalms and in the New Testament." *Missionalia* 27 (1999): 369-76.

DuBois, Francis M. Edited by *Classics of Christian Missions.* Nashville: Broadman, 1979.

Duchrow, Ulrich. " 'It Is Not So Among You': On the Mission of the People of God Among the Nations." *Reformed World* 43 (1993): 112-24.

Durham, John I. *Exodus.* Word Biblical Commentary 3. Waco, Tex.: Word, 1987.

Eakin, Frank E. "Wisdom, Creation and Covenant." *Perspectives in Religious Studies* 4 (1977): 226-39.

Ellul, Jacques. *The New Demons*. London: Mowbrays, 1976.

Elsdon, Ron. *Green House Theology: Biblical Perspectives on Caring for Creation*. Tunbridge Wells, U.K.: Monarch, 1992.

Engle, Richard W. "Contextualization in Missions: A Biblical and Theological Appraisal." *Grace Theological Journal* 4 (1983): 85-107.

Escobar, Samuel. *A Time for Mission: The Challenge for Global Christianity*. Global Christian Library. Leicester, U.K.: Inter-Varsity Press; Downers Grove, Ill.: InterVarsity Press, 2003.

Esler, Philip E. "The Sodom Tradition in Romans 1:18-32." *Biblical Theology Bulletin* 34 (2004): 4-16.

Fager, Jeffrey A. *Land Tenure and the Biblical Jubilee*. JSOT Supplements 155. Sheffield, U.K.: JSOT Press, 1993.

Fee, Gordon D. *The First Epistle to the Corinthians*. New International Commentary on the New Testament. Grand Rapids: Eerdmans, 1987.

Fensham, F. C. "A Few Observations on the Polarisation between Yahweh and Baal in 1 Kings 17-19." *Zeitschrift für die alttestamentliche Wissenschaft* 92 (1980): 227-36.

Filbeck, David. *Yes, God of the Gentiles Too: The Missionary Message of the Old Testament*. Wheaton, Ill.: Billy Graham Center, 1994.

France, R. T. *Jesus and the Old Testament: His Application of Old Testament Passages to Himself and His Mission*. London: Tyndale, 1971.

Franks, Martha. "Election, Pluralism, and the Missiology of Scripture in a Postmodern Age." *Missiology* 26 (1998): 329-43.

Fretheim, Terence E. *Exodus*. Interpretation. Louisville: John Knox Press, 1991.

Gelston, Anthony. "The Missionary Message of Second Isaiah." *Scottish Journal of Theology* 18 (1965): 308-18.

———. "Universalism in Second Isaiah." *Journal of Theological Studies* 43 (1992): 377-98.

Glasser, Arthur. "Help from an Unexpected Quarter, Or the Old Testament and Contextualization." *Missiology* 7 (1979): 403-10.

Gnanakan, Ken. *Kingdom Concerns: A Biblical Theology of Mission Today*. Bangalore: Theological Book Trust, 1989; Leicester, U.K.: Inter-Varsity Press, 1993.

Gnuse, Robert Karl. *No Other Gods: Emergent Monotheism in Israel*. JSOT Supplement Series 241. Sheffield, U.K.: Sheffield Academic Press, 1997.

Goerner, Henry C. *Thus It Is Written*. Nashville: Broadman Press, 1971.

———. *All Nations in God's Purpose: What the Bible Teaches About Missions*. Nashville: Broadman, 1979.

Goldenberg, Robert. *The Nations That Know Thee Not: Ancient Jewish Attitudes Towards Other Religions*. Sheffield, U.K.: Sheffield Academic Press, 1997.

Goldingay, John. "The Man of War and the Suffering Servant: The Old Testament and the Theology of Liberation." *Tyndale Bulletin* 27 (1976): 79-113.

———. *Theological Diversity and the Authority of the Old Testament*. Grand Rapids: Eerdmans, 1987.

———. "Justice and Salvation for Israel and Canaan." In *Reading the Hebrew Bible for a New Millennium: Form, Concept, and Theological Perspective*, edited by Wonil Kim et al., pp. 169-87. Harrisburg, Penn.: Trinity Press International, 2000.

———. *Isaiah*. New International Biblical Commentary. Peabody, Mass.: Hendrikson; Carlisle, U.K.: Paternoster, 2001.

———. *Old Testament Theology*. 2 vols. Downers Grove, Ill.: InterVarsity Press, 2003.

Goldingay, John, and Christopher Wright. " 'Yahweh Our God Yahweh One': The Oneness of God in the Old Testament." In *One God, One Lord: Christianity in a World of Religious Pluralism*, edited by Andrew D. Clarke and Bruce Winter, pp. 43-62. Carlisle, U.K.: Paternoster, Grand Rapids: Baker, 1992.

Goldsmith, Martin. *Matthew and Mission: The Gospel through Jewish Eyes*. Carlisle, U.K.: Paternoster, 2001.

Goldsworthy, Graeme L. "The Great Indicative: An Aspect of a Biblical Theology of Mission." *Reformed Theological Review* 55 (1996): 2-13.

Gossai, Hemchand. *Justice, Righteousness and the Social Critique of the Eighth-Century Prophets*. American University Studies Series 7: Theology and Religion 141. New York: Peter Lang, 1993.

Gottwald, Norman K. *The Tribes of Yahweh: A Sociology of the Religion of Liberated Israel 1250-1050 BCE*. Maryknoll, N.Y.: Orbis; London: SCM Press, 1979.

Goudzwaard, Bob. *Idols of Our Time*. Downers Grove, Ill.: InterVarsity Press, 1984.

Granberg-Michaelson, Wesley. "Redeeming the Earth: A Theology for This World." *Covenant Quarterly* 42 (1984): 17-29.

Greenberg, Moshe. "Mankind, Israel and the Nations in the Hebraic Heritage." In *No Man Is Alien: Essays on the Unity of Mankind*, edited by J. Robert Nelson, pp. 15-40. Leiden: E. J. Brill, 1971.

Greene, Colin J. D. *Christology in Cultural Perspective: Marking out the Horizons*. Grand Rapids: Eerdmans; Carlisle, U.K.: Paternoster, 2003.

Greenslade, Philip. *A Passion for God's Story*. Carlisle, U.K.: Paternoster, 2002.

Grisanti, Michael A. "Israel's Mission to the Nations in Isaiah 40-55: An Update." *Master's Seminary Journal* 9 (1998): 39-61.

Groot, A. de. "One Bible and Many Interpretive Contexts: Hermeneutics in Missiology." In *Missiology: An Ecumenical Introduction,* edited by A. Camps, L. A. Hoedemaker and M. R. Spindler. Grand Rapids: Eerdmans, 1995.

Grueneberg, Keith N. *Abraham, Blessing and the Nation: A Philological and Exegetical Study of Genesis 12:3 in Its Narrative Context.* Beihefte zur Zeitschrift für die alttestamentliche Wissenschaft. Berlin: Walter de Gruyter; New York: Walter de Gruyter, 2003.

Guenther, Titus F. "Missionary Vision and Practice in the Old Testament." In *Reclaiming the Old Testament: Essays in Honor of Waldemar Janzen,* edited by Gordon Zerbe, pp. 146-64. Winnepeg: CMBC Publications, 2001.

Hahn, Scott W. "Canon, Cult and Covenant: Towards a Liturgical Hermeneutic." In *Canon and Biblical Interpretation,* edited by Craig Bartholomew et al. Grand Rapids: Zondervan; Carlisle, U.K.: Paternoster, forthcoming.

Hanke, Howard A. *From Eden to Eternity: A Survey of Christology and Ecclesiology I the Old Testament and Their Redemptive Relationship to Man from Adam to the End of Time.* Grand Rapids: Eerdmans, 1960.

Harrelson, Walter. "On God's Care for the Earth: Psalm 104." *Currents in Theology and Mission* 2 (1975): 19-22.

Harris, Murray J. *Jesus as God: The New Testament Use of Theos in Reference to Jesus.* Grand Rapids: Baker, 1992.

Hartley, John E. *Leviticus.* Word Biblical Commentary 4. Dallas: Word, 1992.

Hay, Donald A. "Christians in the Global Greenhouse." *Tyndale Bulletin* 41, no. 1 (1990): 109-27.

Hays, J. Daniel. *From Every People and Nation: A Biblical Theology of Race.* New Studies in Biblical Theology. Leicester, U.K.: Inter-Varsity Press; Downers Grove: InterVarsity Press, 2003.

Hedlund, Roger, *The Mission of the Church in the World: A Biblical Theology.* Grand Rapids: Baker, 1991.

Heldt, Jean-Paul. "Revisiting the 'Whole Gospel': Toward a Biblical Model of Holistic Mission in the 21st Century." *Missiology* 32 (2004): 149-72.

Hertig, Paul. "The Jubilee Mission of Jesus in the Gospel of Luke: Reversals of Fortunes." *Missiology* 26 (1998): 167-79.

———. "The Subversive Kingship of Jesus and Christian Social Witness." *Missiology* 32 (2004): 475-90.

Hesselgrave, David J. "A Missionary Hermeneutic: Understanding Scripture in the Light of World Mission." *International Journal of Frontier Missions* 10 (1993): 17-20.

Hoedemaker, L. A. "The People of God and the Ends of the Earth." In *Missiology: An Ecumenical Introduction,* edited by A. Camps, L. A. Hoedemaker and M. R. Spindler. Grand Rapids: Eerdmans, 1995.

Hoffman, Yair. "The Concept of 'Other Gods' in the Deuteronomistic Litera-
ture." In *Politics and Theopolitics,* edited by Henning Graf Reventlow, Yair
Hoffman and Benjamin Uffenheimer, pp. 66-84. Sheffield, U.K.: JSOT
Press, 1994.

Holert, M. Louise. "Extrinsic Evil Powers in the Old Testament." Master's thesis,
Fuller Theological Seminary, 1985.

Hollenberg, C. E. "Nationalism and the Nations in Isaiah XL-LV." *Vetus Testamentum* 19 (1969): 23-36.

Holwerda, David E. *Jesus and Israel: One Covenant or Two?* Grand Rapids: Eerdmans; Leicester, U.K.: Apollos, 1995.

Honig, A. G. *What Is Mission? The Meaning of the Rootedness of the Church in
Israel for a Correct Conception of Mission.* Kampen: Uitgeversmaatschappij
J. H. Kok, 1982.

Houston, Walter. *Purity and Monotheism: Clean and Unclean Animals in Biblical Law.* JSOT Supplement Series. Sheffield, U.K.: Sheffield Academic, 1993.

Hubbard, Robert L. *"yāša‘".* In *New International Dictionary of Old Testament
Theology and Exegesis,* edited by Willem A. VanGemeren, 2:556-62. Grand
Rapids: Zondervan, 1997.

Hughes, Dewi. *Castrating Culture: A Christian Perspective on Ethnic Identity
from the Margins.* Carlisle, U.K.: Paternoster, 2001.

Hurtado, Larry W. *One God, One Lord: Early Christian Devotion and Ancient
Jewish Monotheism.* Edinburgh: T & T Clark, 1998.

———. *Lord Jesus Christ: Devotion to Jesus in Earliest Christianity.* Grand Rapids: Eerdmans, 2003.

———. *How on Earth Did Jesus Become a God? Historical Questions About Earliest Devotion to Jesus.* Grand Rapids: Eerdmans, 2006.

Jenkins, Philip. *The Next Christendom: The Coming of Global Christianity.* Oxford: Oxford University Press, 2002.

Jeremias, Joachim. *Jesus' Promise to the Nations.* Studies in Biblical Theology.
London: SCM Press, 1958; Philadelphia: Fortress, 1982.

Jervell, Jacob. "The Future of the Past: Luke's Vision of Salvation History and Its
Bearing on His Writing of History." In *History, Literature and Society in the
Book of Acts,* edited by Ben Witherington III, pp. 104-26. Cambridge: Cam-
bridge University Press, 1996.

Jonge, Marinus de. *God's Final Envoy: Early Christology and Jesus' View of His
Mission.* Grand Rapids: Eerdmans, 1998.

Kaiser, Walter C., Jr. "The Davidic Promise and the Inclusion of the Gentiles
(Amos 9:9-15 and Acts 15:13-18)." *Journal of the Evangelical Theological Society* 20 (1977): 97-111.

————. *Mission in the Old Testament: Israel as a Light to the Nations*. Grand Rapids: Baker, 2000.

Kayama, Hisao. "Christianity as Table Fellowship: Meals as a Symbol of the Universalism in Luke-Acts." In *From East to West: Essays in Honor of Donald G. Bloesch,* edited by Daniel J. Adams, pp. 51-62. Lanham, Md., and Oxford: University Press of America, 1997.

Keck, Leander E. *Who Is Jesus? History in Perfect Tense*. Columbia: University of South Carolina Press, 2000.

Kim, Seyoon, *The Origin of Paul's Gospel*. 2nd ed. Grand Rapids: Eerdmans, 1984.

Kirk, J. Andrew. *What Is Mission? Theological Explorations*. London: Darton, Longman & Todd; Minneapolis: Fortress Press, 1999.

Kirk, J. Andrew, and Kevin J. Vanhoozer, ed. *To Stake a Claim: Mission and the Western Crisis of Knowledge*. Maryknoll, N.Y.: Orbis, 1999.

Klein, Ralph W. "Liberated Leadership. Masters and 'Lords' in Biblical Perspective." *Currents in Theology and Mission* 9 (1982): 282-90.

Knox, John. "Romans 15:14-33 and Paul's Conception of His Apostolic Mission." *Journal of Biblical Literature* 83 (1964): 1-11.

Koestenberger, A. J., and P. T. O'Brien, *Salvation to the Ends of the Earth: A Biblical Theology of Mission*. Leicester, U.K.: Apollos, 2001.

Koestenberger, Andreas J. "The Challenge of a Systematized Biblical Theology of Mission: Missiological Insights from the Gospel of John." *Missiology* 23 (1995): 445-64.

————. *The Missions of Jesus and the Disciples According to the Fourth Gospel: With Implications for the Fourth Gospel's Purpose and the Mission of the Contemporary Church*. Grand Rapids: Eerdmans, 1998.

————. "The Place of Mission in New Testament Theology: An Attempt to Determine the Significance of Mission Within the Scope of the New Testament's Message as a Whole." *Missiology* 27 (1999): 347-62.

Kritzinger, J. J. "Mission, Development, and Ecology." *Missionalia* 19 (1991): 4-19.

————. "Mission and the Liberation of Creation: A Critical Dialogue with M. L. Daneel." *Missionalia* 20 (1992): 99-115.

Kruse, Heinz. "Exodus 19:5 and the Mission of Israel." *Northeast Asia Journal of Theology* 24-25 (1980): 129-35.

Kvalbein, Hans. "Has Matthew Abandoned the Jews?" in *The Mission of the Early Church to Jews and Gentiles,* edited by Jostein Adna and Hans Kvalbein, pp. 45-62. Tübingen: Mohr Siebeck, 2000.

LaGrand, James. *The Earliest Christian Mission to "All Nations" in the Light of Matthew's Gospel*. Grand Rapids: Eerdmans, 1995.

Lane, Thomas J. *Luke and the Gentile Mission: Gospel Anticipates Acts*. Frankfurt and New York: Peter Lang, 1996.

Lang, Bernard. *The Hebrew God: Portrait of an Ancient Deity*. New Haven, Conn., and London: Yale University Press, 2002.

Larkin, William J., and Joel F. Williams, eds. *Mission in the New Testament: An Evangelical Approach*. Maryknoll, N.Y.: Orbis, 1998.

Le Grys, Alan. *Preaching to the Nations: The Origin of Mission in the Early Church*. London: SPCK, 1998.

Legrand, Lucien. *Unity and Plurality: Mission in the Bible*. Maryknoll, N.Y.: Orbis, 1990.

———. "Gal 2:9 and the Missionary Strategy of the Early Church." In *Bible, Hermeneutics, Mission: A Contribution to the Contextual Study of Holy Scripture,* edited by Tord Fornberg, pp. 21-83. Uppsala: Swedish Institute for Missionary Research, 1995.

———. *The Bible on Culture: Belonging or Dissenting.* Maryknoll, N.Y.: Orbis, 2000.

Lichtheim, Miriam, ed. *Ancient Egyptian Literature*. 3 vols. Berkeley: University of California Press, 1975, 1976, 1980.

Lind, Millard C., "Refocusing Theological Education to Mission: The Old Testament and Contextualization." *Missiology* 10 (1982): 141-60.

———. "Monotheism, Power and Justice: A Study in Isaiah 40-55." *Catholic Biblical Quarterly* 46 (1984): 432-46.

Loader, J. A. "Life, Wonder and Responsibility: Some Thoughts on Ecology and Christian Mission." *Missionalia* 19 (1991): 44-56.

Lohfink, Norbert, and Erich Zenger. *God of Israel and the Nations: Studies in Isaiah and the Psalms*. Collegeville, Minn.: Liturgical Press, 2000.

Longman, Tremper, III. "Proverbs." In *Zondervan Illustrated Bible Backgrounds Commentary*. Grand Rapids: Zondervan, forthcoming,

Lubeck, R. J. "Prophetic Sabotage: A Look at Jonah 3:2-4." *Trinity Journal* 9 (1988): 37-46.

MacDonald, Nathan. *Deuteronomy and the Meaning of "Monotheism."* Tübingen: Mohr Siebeck, 2003.

———. "Listening to Abraham—Listening to YHWH: Divine Justice and Mercy in Genesis 18:16-33." *Catholic Biblical Quarterly* 66 (2004): 25-43.

———. "Whose Monotheism? Which Rationality?" In *The Old Testament in Its World,* edited by R. P. Gordon and Johannes C. de Moor, pp. 45-67. Leiden: Brill, 2005.

Machinist, Peter. "The Question of Distinctiveness in Ancient Israel." In *Essential Papers on Israel and the Ancient near East,* edited by F. E. Greenspan, pp. 420-42. New York and London: New York University Press, 1991.

Maier, Walter A., III. "The Healing of Naaman in Missiological Perspective." *Concordia Theological Quarterly* 61 (1997): 177-96.

Manson, T. W. *Jesus and the Non-Jews*. London: Athlone Press, 1955.

Marak, Krickwin C., and Atul Y. Aghamkar, ed. *Ecological Challenge and Christian Mission*. Delhi: ISPCK, 1998.

Marlowe, W. Creighton. "Music of Missions: Themes of Cross-Cultural Outreach in the Psalms." *Missiology* 26 (1998): 445-56.

Marshall, I. Howard, *New Testament Theology: Many Witnesses, One Gospel*. Leicester, U.K.: Inter-Varsity Press; Downers Grove: InterVarsity Press, 2004.

Martens, Elmer A. *God's Design: A Focus on Old Testament Theology*. 2nd ed. Grand Rapids: Baker; Leicester, U.K.: Apollos, 1994.

Martin-Achard, Robert. *A Light to the Nations: A Study of the Old Testament Conception of Israel's Mission to the World,* translated by John Penney Smith. Edinburgh and London: Oliver & Boyd, 1962.

Mason, John. "Biblical Teaching and Assisting the Poor." *Transformation* 4, no. 2 (1987): 1-14.

Matlack, Hugh. "The Play of Wisdom." *Currents in Theology and Mission* 15 (1988): 425-30.

Matthew, C. V., ed. *Integral Mission: The Way Forward: Essays in Honour of Dr. Saphir P. Athyal*. Tiruvalla, India: Christava Sahitya Samithi, 2006.

May, Herbert G. "Theological Universalism in the Old Testament." *Journal of Bible and Religion* 15 (1947): 100-107.

————. "Aspects of the Imagery of World Dominion and World State in the Old Testament." In *Essays in Old Testament Ethics,* edited by John T. Willis and James L. Crenshaw, pp. 57-76. New York: KTAV, 1974.

McConville, J. G. *Deuteronomy*. Apollos Old Testament Commentary. Leicester, U.K.: Apollos; Downers Grove, Ill.: InterVarsity Press, 2002.

Meyer, Ben F. *The Aims of Jesus*. London: SCM Press, 1979.

————. *The Early Christians: Their World Mission and Self-Discovery*. Wilmington, Del.: Michael Glazier, 1986.

Middleton, J. Richard, and Brian J. Walsh. *Truth Is Stranger Than It Used to Be: Biblical Faith in a Postmodern Age*. Downers Grove, Ill.: InterVarsity Press; London: SPCK, 1995.

Miller, Patrick D., Jr. "Syntax and Theology in Genesis XII 3a." *Vetus Testamentum* 34 (1984): 472-75.

————. "Deuteronomy and Psalms: Evoking a Biblical Conversation." *Journal of Biblical Literature* 118 (1999): 3-18.

————. " 'Enthroned on the Praises of Israel': The Praise of God in Old Testament Theology." *Interpretation* 39 (1985): 5-19.

————. "Cosmology and World Order in the Old Testament: The Divine Council as Cosmic-Political Symbol." *Horizons in Biblical Theology* 9 (1987): 53-78.

————. "God's Other Stories: On the Margins of Deuteronomic Theology." In *Realia Dei,* edited by P. H. Williams and T. Hiebert, pp. 185-94. Atlanta: Scholars Press, 1999.

Moberly, R. W. L. "Christ as the Key to Scripture: Genesis 22 Reconsidered." In *He Swore an Oath: Biblical Themes from Genesis 12-50.* Edited by R. S. Hess et al. Carlisle, U.K.: Paternoster; Grand Rapids: Baker, 1994.

Mohol, Eliya. "The Covenantal Rationale for Membership in the Zion Community Envisaged in Isaiah 56-66." Ph.D. diss., All Nations Christian College, 1998.

Moore, Peter C. *Disarming the Secular Gods.* Downers Grove, Ill.: InterVarsity Press; Leicester, U.K.: Inter-Varsity Press, 1989.

Moore, Thomas S. " 'To the End of the Earth': The Geographical and Ethnic Universalism of Acts 1:8 in Light of Isaianic Influence on Luke." *Journal of the Evangelical Theological Society* 40 (1997): 389-99.

Mott, Stephen Charles. *Jesus and Social Ethics.* Grove Booklets on Ethics. Nottingham, U.K.: Grove Books, 1984.

————. "The Use of the New Testament in Social Ethics." *Transformation* 1, nos. 2-3 (1984): 21-26, 19-25.

————. "The Contribution of the Bible to Economic Thought." *Transformation* 4, nos. 3-4 (1987): 25-34.

————. *A Christian Perspective on Political Thought.* Oxford: Oxford University Press, 1993.

Motyer, Alex. *The Message of Exodus.* The Bible Speaks Today. Leicester, U.K.: Inter-Varsity Press; Downers Grove, Ill.: InterVarsity Press, 2005.

Motyer, J. A., *The Message of Amos.* The Bible Speaks Today. Leicester, U.K.: Inter-Varsity Press; Downers Grove, Ill.: InterVarsity Press, 1974.

————. *The Prophecy of Isaiah.* Leicester, U.K.: Inter-Varsity Press; Downers Grove, Ill.: InterVarsity Press, 1993.

Mouw, Richard J. *When the Kings Come Marching In.* Revised ed. Grand Rapids and Cambridge: Eerdmans, 2000.

Muilenburg, James. "Abraham and the Nations: Blessing and World History." *Interpretation* 19 (1965): 387-98.

Murphy, Roland E. *Proverbs.* Nashville: Thomas Nelson, 1998.

Murray, Robert. *The Cosmic Covenant: Biblical Themes of Justice, Peace and the Integrity of Creation.* London: Sheed & Ward, 1992.

Nash, James A. *Loving Nature: Ecological Integrity and Christian Responsibility.* Nashville: Abingdon, 1991.

Newbigin, Lesslie. *Trinitarian Doctrine for Today's Mission*. Carlisle, U.K.: Paternoster, 1998.

Newton, Thurber L. "Care for the Creation as Mission Responsibility." *International Review of Mission* 79 (1990): 143-49.

Northcott, Michael S. *The Environment and Christian Ethics*. Cambridge: Cambridge University Press, 1996.

O'Brien, P. T. *Gospel and Mission in the Writings of Paul: An Exegetical and Theological Analysis*. Grand Rapids: Baker, 1993: Carlisle, U.K.: Paternoster, 1995.

O'Donovan, Oliver. *Resurrection and Moral Order: An Outline for Evangelical Ethics*. Leicester, U.K.: Inter-Varsity Press, 1986.

Orlinsky, Harry M. "Nationalism-Universalism and Internationalism in Ancient Israel." In *Translating and Understanding the Old Testament: Essays in Honor of Herbert Gordon May,* edited by Harry Thomas Frank and William L. Reed. Nashville: Abingdon, 1970.

Pao, David. *Acts and the Isaianic New Exodus*. Grand Rapids: Baker, 2000.

Pate, C. Marvin, et al. *The Story of Israel: A Biblical Theology*. Downers Grove, Ill.: InterVarsity Press; Leicester, U.K.: Inter-Varsity Press, 2004.

Paterson, John. "From Nationalism to Universalism in the Old Testament." In *Christian World Mission,* edited by William K. Anderson. Nashville: Parthenon, 1946.

Patrick, Dale. *The Rendering of God in the Old Testament*. Overtures to Biblical Theology. Philadelphia: Fortress, 1981.

Patterson, Richard D., and Michael Travers. "Contours of the Exodus Motif in Jesus' Earthly Ministry." *Westminster Theological Journal* 66 (2004): 25-47.

Penny, John Michael. *The Missionary Emphasis of Lukan Pneumatology*. Journal of Pentecostal Theology Supplements 12. Sheffield, U.K.: Sheffield Academic, 1997.

Peskett, Howard, and Vinoth Ramachandra. *The Message of Mission*. The Bible Speaks Today. Leicester, U.K.: Inter-Varsity Press; Downers Grove, Ill.: Inter-Varsity Press, 2003.

Peters, George W. *A Biblical Theology of Missions*. Chicago: Moody Press, 1972.

Pietroni, Mark. "Wisdom, Islam and Bangladesh: Can the Wisdom Literature Be Used as a Fruitful Starting Point for Communicating the Christian Faith to Muslims?" Master's thesis, All Nations Christian College, 1997.

Piper, John. *Let the Nations Be Glad! The Supremacy of God in Missions*. 2nd ed. Grand Rapids: Baker Academic, 1993; Leicester, U.K.: Inter-Varsity Press, 2003.

Plant, Raymond. *Politics, Theology and History*. Cambridge: Cambridge University Press, 2001.

Pleins, J. David. *The Social Visions of the Hebrew Bible: A Theological Introduction*. Louisville: Westminster John Knox, 2001.

Pocock, Michael. "Selected Perspectives on World Religions from Wisdom Literature." In *Christianity and the Religions: A Biblical Theology of World Religions*, edited by E. Rommen and Harold A. Netland, pp. 45-55. Pasadena: William Carey Library, 1995.

Poston, Larry. "Christian Reconstructionism and the Christian World Mission." *Missiology* 23 (1995): 467-75.

Priebe, Duane. "A Holy God, an Idolatrous People, and Religious Pluralism: Hosea 1-3." *Currents in Theology and Mission* 23 (1996): 126-33.

Pritchard, James B., ed. *Ancient Near Eastern Texts*. Princeton, N.J.: Princeton University Press, 1955.

Raabe, Paul R. "Look to the Holy One of Israel, All You Nations: The Oracles About the Nations Still Speak Today." *Concordia Journal* 30 (2004): 336-49.

Rabinowitz, Jacob. *The Faces of God: Canaanite Mythology as Hebrew Theology*. Woodstock, Conn.: Spring Publications, 1998.

Rad, Gerhard von. *Genesis: A Commentary*. 2nd ed. London: SCM Press, 1963.

Ramachandra, Vinoth. *Gods That Fail: Modern Idolatry and Christian Mission*. Carlisle, U.K.: Paternoster; Downers Grove, Ill.: InterVarsity Press, 1996.

————. *The Recovery of Mission*. Carlisle, U.K.: Paternoster, 1996.

Renaud, Bernard. "Prophetic Criticism of Israel's Attitude to the Nations: A Few Landmarks." *Concilium* 20 (1988): 35-43.

Retif, A., and P. Lamarche. *The Salvation of the Gentiles and the Prophets*. Living Word Series 4. Edited by Gerard S. Sloyan. Baltimore and Dublin: Helicon Press, 1966.

Reventlow, Henning Graf, Yair Hoffman and Benjamin Uffenheimer. *Politics and Theopolitics in the Bible and Postbiblical Literature*. JSOT Supplement Series 171. Edited by David J. A. Clines and Philip R. Davies. Sheffield, U.K.: JSOT Press, 1994.

Ridder, Richard R. de. *Discipling the Nations*. Grand Rapids: Baker, 1975.

Riesner, Rainer. *Paul's Early Period: Chronology, Mission Strategy, Theology*. Grand Rapids and Cambridge: Eerdmans, 1998.

Ringe, S. H. *Jesus, Liberation, and the Biblical Jubilee: Images for Ethics and Christology*. Philadelphia: Fortress, 1985.

Rodd, Cyril. *Glimpses of a Strange Land: Studies in Old Testament Ethics*. Edinburgh: T & T Clark, 2001.

Ross, Kenneth R. "The HIV/Aids Pandemic: What Is at Stake for Christian Mission?" *Missiology* 32 (2004): 337-48.

Rowe, Jonathan Y. "Holy to the Lord: Universality in the Deuteronomic History and Its Relationship to the Authors' Theology of History." Master's thesis, All Nations Christian College, 1997.

Rowley, H. H. *Israel's Mission to the World*. London: SCM Press, 1939.

———. *The Missionary Message of the Old Testament*. London: Carey Press, 1944.

Samuel, Vinay, and Chris Sugden, ed. *Sharing Jesus in the Two-thirds World: Evangelical Christologies from the Contexts of Poverty, Powerlessness and Religious Pluralism*. Grand Rapids: Eerdmans, 1983.

Scheurer, Erich. *Altes Testament und Mission: Zur Begruendung des Missionsauftrages*. Basel: Brunnen, 1996.

Schluter, Michael, and Roy Clements. *Reactivating the Extended Family: From Biblical Norms to Public Policy in Britain*. Cambridge: Jubilee Centre, 1986.

Schluter, Michael, and John Ashcroft, eds. *Jubilee Manifesto: A Framework, Agenda & Strategy for Christian Social Reform*. Leicester, U.K.: Inter-Varsity Press, 2005.

Schmidt, Werner H. *The Faith of the Old Testament: A History*, translated by John Sturdy. Philadelphia: Westminster Press; Oxford: Blackwell, 1983.

Schnabel, Eckhard J. "Jesus and the Beginnings of the Mission to the Gentiles." In *Jesus of Nazareth: Lord and Christ*, edited by Joel B. Green and Max Turner, pp. 37-58. Carlisle, U.K.: Paternoster; Grand Rapids: Eerdmans, 1994.

———. "Israel, the People of God, and the Nations." *Journal of the Evangelical Theological Society* 45 (2002): 35-57.

———. "John and the Future of the Nations." *Bulletin for Biblical Research* 12 (2002): 243-71.

———. *Early Christian Mission*. Vol. 1, *Jesus and the Twelve*. Downers Grove, Ill.: InterVarsity Press; Leicester, U.K.: Inter-Varsity Press, 2004.

———. *Early Christian Mission*. Vol. 2, *Paul and the Early Church*. Downers Grove, Ill.: InterVarsity Press; Leicester, U.K.: Inter-Varsity Press, 2004.

Scobie, C. H. H. "Israel and the Nations: An Essay in Biblical Theology." *Tyndale Bulletin* 43, no. 2 (1992): 283-305.

Scott, James M. "Restoration of Israel." In *Dictionary of Paul and His Letters,* edited by Gerald F. Hawthorne and Ralph. P. Martin, pp. 796-805. Downers Grove, Ill.: InterVarsity Press; Leicester, U.K.: Inter-Varsity Press, 1993.

———. "Luke's Geographical Horizon." In *The Book of Acts in Its Graeco-Roman Setting*, edited by David W. J. Gill and Conrad Gempf, pp. 483-544. Exeter, U.K.: Paternoster, 1994.

———. *Paul and the Nations: The Old Testament and Jewish Background of Paul's Mission to the Nations with Special Reference to the Destination of Galatians*. Tübingen: Mohr Siebeck, 1995.

————. "Acts 2:9-11 as an Anticipation of the Mission to the Nations." In *The Mission of the Early Church to Jews and Gentiles,* edited by Jostein Adna and Hans Kvalbein, pp. 87-123. Tübingen: Mohr Siebeck, 2000.

Seitz, Christopher. *Word Without End.* Grand Rapids: Eerdmans, 1998.

————. *Figured Out: Typology and Providence in Christian Scripture.* Louisville: Westminster John Knox, 2001.

Senior, Donald. "Correlating Images of Church and Images of Mission in the New Testament." *Missiology* 23 (1995): 3-16.

Senior, Donald, and Stuhlmueller, C. *The Biblical Foundations for Mission.* London: SCM Press, 1983.

Sherwin, Simon. " 'I Am against You': Yahweh's Judgment on the Nations and Its Ancient Near Eastern Context." *Tyndale Bulletin* 54 (2003): 149-60.

Simkins, Ronald A. *Creator and Creation: Nature in the Worldview of Ancient Israel.* Peabody, Mass.: Hendrickson, 1994.

Sloan, R. B., Jr. *The Favorable Year of the Lord: A Study of Jubilary Theology in the Gospel of Luke.* Austin, Tex.: Schola, 1977.

Smith, Morton. "The Common Theology of the Ancient Near East." In *Essential Papers on Israel and the Ancient Near East,* edited by F. E. Greenspan, pp. 49-65. New York and London: New York University Press, 1991.

Smith, W. Cantwell. "Idolatry in Comparative Perspective." In *The Myth of Christian Uniqueness,* edited by J. Hick and P. F. Knitter, pp. 53-68. Maryknoll, N.Y.: Orbis; London: SCM Press, 1987.

Soards, Marion L. "Key Issues in Biblical Studies and Their Bearing on Mission Studies." *Missiology* 24 (1996): 93-109.

Spanner, Huw. "Tyrants, Stewards—or Just Kings?" in *Animals on the Agenda: Questions About Animals for Theology and Ethics,* edited by Linzey Andrew and Dorothy Yamamoto. London: SCM Press, 1998.

Spindler, M. R. *La Mission: Combat Pour Le Salut Du Monde.* Neuchatel, Switzerland: Delachaux & Niestle, 1967.

————. "The Biblical Grounding and Orientation of Mission." In *Missiology: An Ecumenical Introduction,* edited by A. Camps, L. A. Hoedemaker and M. R. Spindler, pp. 123-43. Grand Rapids: Eerdmans, 1995.

Squires, John T. *The Plan of God in Luke-Acts.* SNTS Monographs 76. Cambridge: Cambridge University Press, 1993.

Stott, John R. W. *Christian Mission in the Modern World.* London: Falcon, 1975.

Stott, John R. W., ed. *Making Christ Known: Historic Mission Documents from the Lausanne Movement 1974-1989.* Carlisle, U.K.: Paternoster, 1996.

Strauss, Steve. "Missions Theology in Romans 15:14-33." *Bibliotheca Sacra* 160 (2003): 457-74.

Taber, Charles R. "Missiology and the Bible." *Missiology* 11 (1983): 229-45.

———. "Mission and Ideologies: Confronting the Idols." *Mission Studies* 10 (1993): 179-81.

Talstra, Eep, and Carl J. Bosma. "Psalm 67: Blessing, Harvest and History: A Proposal for Exegetical Methodology." *Calvin Theological Journal* 36 (2001): 290-313.

Tate, Marvin E. *Psalms 51-100*. Word Biblical Commentary 20. Dallas: Word, 1990.

Taylor, Glen A. "Supernatural Power Ritual and Divination in Ancient Israelite Society: A Social-Scientific, Poetics and Comparative Analysis of Deuteronomy 18." Ph.D. diss., University of Gloucester, 2005.

Taylor, William D., ed. *Global Missiology for the 21st Century: The Iguassu Dialogue*. Grand Rapids: Baker, 2000.

Thomas, D. Winton, ed. *Documents from Old Testament Times*. New York: Harper Torchbooks, 1958.

Thompson, J. A. *The Book of Jeremiah*. New International Commentary on the Old Testament. Grand Rapids: Eerdmans, 1980.

Thompson, James M. "The Gentile Mission as an Eschatological Necessity." *Restoration Quarterly* 14 (1971): 18-27.

Ucko, Hans, ed. *The Jubilee Challenge: Utopia or Possibility: Jewish and Christian Insights*. Geneva: World Council of Churches Publications, 1997.

Van Den Toren, Benno. "God's Purpose for Creation as the Key to Understanding the Universality and Cultural Variety of Christian Ethics." *Missiology* 30 (2002): 215-33.

Van Engen, Charles. "The Relation of Bible and Mission in Mission Theology." In *The Good News of the Kingdom*, edited by Charles Van Engen, Dean S. Gilliland and Paul Pierson, pp. 27-36. Maryknoll, N.Y.: Orbis, 1993.

———. *Mission on the Way: Issues in Mission Theology*. Grand Rapids: Baker, 1996.

Van Winkle, D. W. "The Relationship of the Nations to Yahweh and to Israel in Isaiah XL-LV." *Vetus Testamentum* 35 (1985): 446-58.

Verkuyl, J. *Contemporary Missiology: An Introduction*. Grand Rapids: Eerdmans, 1978.

Vicedom, Georg F. *The Mission of God: An Introduction to a Theology of Mission*. Trans. Gilbert A. Thiele and Dennis Hilgendorf. St. Louis: Concordia, 1965.

Voegelin, E. *Israel and Revelation*. Baton Rouge: Louisiana State University, 1956.

Vogels, Walter. "Covenant and Universalism: A Guide for a Missionary Reading of the Old Testament." *Zeitschrift für Missionswissenschaft und Religionswissenschaft* 57 (1973): 25-32.

————. *God's Universal Covenant: A Biblical Study.* 2nd ed. Ottawa: University of Ottawa Press, 1986.

Walls, Andrew F. *The Missionary Movement in Christian History: Studies in the Transmission of Faith.* Maryknoll, N.Y.: Orbis; Edinburgh: T & T Clark, 1996.

Walter, J. A. *A Long Way from Home: A Sociological Exploration of Contemporary Idolatry.* Carlisle, U.K.: Paternoster, 1979.

Walzer, Michael. *Exodus and Revolution.* New York: Basic Books, 1985.

Warren, Max. *I Believe in the Great Commission.* London: Hodder & Stoughton; Grand Rapids: Eerdmans, 1976.

Watts, Rikki. *Isaiah's New Exodus in Mark.* Grand Rapids: Baker, 1997.

Webb, Barry. *The Message of Isaiah.* The Bible Speaks Today. Leicester, U.K.: Inter-Varsity Press; Downers Grove, Ill.: InterVarsity Press, 1996.

Weinfeld, Moshe. *Social Justice in Ancient Israel and in the Ancient Near East.* Minneapolis: Fortress Press, 1995.

Wells, Jo Bailey. *God's Holy People: A Theme in Biblical Theology.* JSOT Supplements 305. Sheffield, U.K.: Sheffield Academic, 2000.

Wengst, Klaus. "Babylon the Great and the New Jerusalem: The Visionary View of Political Reality in the Revelation of John." In *Politics and Theopolitics,* edited by Henning Graf Reventlow, Yair Hoffman and Benjamin Uffenheimer, pp. 189-202. Sheffield, U.K.: JSOT Press, 1994.

Wenham, Gordon J. *The Book of Leviticus.* New International Commentary on the Old Testament. Grand Rapids: Eerdmans, 1979.

————. "Towards a Canonical Reading of the Psalms." In *Canon and Biblical Interpretation,* edited by Craig Bartholomew et al. Grand Rapids: Zondervan; Carlisle, U.K.: Paternoster, forthcoming.

————. *Genesis 1-15.* Word Biblical Commentary 1. Dallas: Word, 1987.

————. *Genesis 16-50.* Word Biblical Commentary 2. Dallas: Word, 1994.

Wente, Edward F. "Egyptian Religion." In *Anchor Bible Dictionary,* edited by David Noel Freedman, 2:408-12. New York: Doubleday, 1992.

Westermann, Claus. *Isaiah 40-66: A Commentary,* translated by David Stalker. London: SCM Press, 1969.

————. *Genesis 12-36: A Commentary,* translated by John J. Scullion. Minneapolis: Augsburg Press; London: SPCK, 1985.

White, Lynn. "The Historical Roots of Our Ecologic Crisis." *Science* 155 (1967): 1203-07.

Williams, David A. " 'Then They Will Know That I Am the Lord': The Missiological Significance of Ezekiel's Concern for the Nations as Evident in the Use of the Recognition Formula." Master's thesis, All Nations Christian College, 1998.

Willoughby, Robert. "The Concept of Jubilee and Luke 4:18-30." In *Mission and*

Meaning: Essays Presented to Peter Cotterell, edited by Anthony Billington, Tony Lane and Max Turner, pp. 41-55. Carlisle, U.K.: Paternoster, 1995.

Wilson, Gerald H. *The Editing of the Hebrew Psalter.* Chicago: Scholars Press, 1985.

Wilson, Stephen G. *The Gentiles and the Gentile Mission in Luke-Acts.* SNTS Monograph 23. Cambridge: Cambridge University Press, 1973.

Wink, Walter. *Naming the Powers: The Language of Power in the New Testament.* Philadelphia: Fortress Press, 1984.

———. *Unmasking the Powers: The Invisible Forces That Determine Human Existence.* Philadelphia: Fortress Press, 1986.

———. *Engaging the Powers: Discernment and Resistance in a World of Domination.* Minneapolis: Fortress Press, 1992.

Winter, Bruce. "On Introducing Gods to Athens: An Alternative Reading of Acts 17:18-20." *Tyndale Bulletin* 47 (1996): 71-90.

Wintle, Brian. "A Biblical Perspective on Idolatry." In *The Indian Church in Context: Her Emergence, Growth and Mission,* edited by Mark T. B. Laing, pp. 55-77. Delhi: ISPCK, 2003.

Witherington, Ben, III. *The Christolology of Jesus.* Minneapolis: Fortress Press, 1990.

———. *Paul's Narrative Thought World: The Tapestry of Tragedy and Triumph.* Louisville: Westminster/John Knox, 1994.

Wright, Christopher J. H. *The Uniqueness of Jesus.* London and Grand Rapids: Monarch, 1997.

———. *God's People in God's Land: Family, Land and Property in the Old Testament.* Grand Rapids: Eerdmans; Carlisle, U.K.: Paternoster, 1990.

———. "Family." In *Anchor Bible Dictionary,* edited by David Noel Freedman, 2:761-69. New York: Doubleday, 1992.

———. "Jubilee, Year Of." In *Anchor Bible Dictionary,* edited by D. N. Freedman, 3:1025-30. New York: Doubleday, 1992.

———. *Knowing Jesus through the Old Testament.* London: Marshall Pickering; Downers Grove, Ill.: InterVarsity Press, 1992.

———. *Deuteronomy.* New International Biblical Commentary. Peabody, Mass.: Hendrikson; Carlisle, U.K.: Paternoster, 1996.

———. "Christ and the Mosaic of Pluralisms: Challenges to Evangelical Missiology in the 21st Century." In *Global Missiology for the 21st Century: The Iguassu Dialogue,* edited by William D. Taylor. Grand Rapids: Baker, 2000.

———. *The Message of Ezekiel: A New Heart and a New Spirit.* The Bible Speaks Today. Leicester, U.K.: Inter-Varsity Press; Downers Grove, Ill.: InterVarsity Press, 2001.

————. "Future Trends in Mission." In *The Futures of Evangelicalism: Issues and Prospects,* edited by Craig Bartholomew, Robin Parry and Andrew West, pp. 149-63. Leicester, U.K.: Inter-Varsity Press, 2003.

————. "Implications of Conversion in the Old Testament and the New." *International Bulletin of Missionary Research* 28 (2004): 14-19.

————. "Mission as a Matrix for Hermeneutics and Biblical Theology." In *Out of Egypt: Biblical Theology and Biblical Interpretation,* edited by Craig Bartholomew et al., pp. 102-43. Carlisle, U.K.: Paternoster; Grand Rapids: Zondervan, 2004.

————. *Old Testament Ethics for the People of God.* Leicester, U.K.: Inter-Varsity Press; Downers Grove, Ill.: InterVarsity Press, 2004.

Wright, G. E. "The Old Testament Basis for the Christian Mission." In *The Theology of Christian Missions,* edited by Gerald H. Anderson. New York: McGraw Hill; London: SCM Press, 1961.

Wright, N. T. "Monotheism, Christology and Ethics: 1 Corinthians 8." In *The Climax of the Covenant: Christ and the Law in Pauline Theology,* pp. 120-36. Edinburgh: T & T Clark, 1991.

————. *The New Testament and the People of God.* London: SPCK, 1992.

————. "Gospel and Theology in Galatians." In *Gospel in Paul: Studies on Corinthians, Galatians and Romans for Richard N. Longenecker,* edited by L. Ann Jervis and Peter Richardson, p. 108. Sheffield, U.K.: Sheffield Academic, 1994.

————. *Jesus and the Victory of God.* London: SPCK, 1996.

Wright, Nigel G. *A Theology of the Dark Side: Putting the Power of Evil in Its Place.* Carlisle, U.K.: Paternoster, 2003.

Wyatt, N. *Religious Texts from Ugarit.* Sheffield, U.K.: Sheffield Academic Press, 1998.

Name Index

Scripture Index

Langham Literature

All the royalties from this book have been irrevocably assigned to Langham Literature (formerly the Evangelical Literature Trust).

Langham Literature is a program of the Langham Partnership International, founded by John Stott. Chris Wright is the International Ministries Director.

Langham Literature distributes evangelical books to pastors, theological students and seminary libraries in the Majority World, and fosters the writing and publishing of Christian literature in many regional languages.

For further information on Langham Literature, and the other program of LPI, visit the website at www.langhampartnership.org.

In the USA, the national member of the Langham Partnership International is John Stott Ministries. Visit the JSM website at www.johnstott.org.